DISCOVERING THE
GLOBAL PAST

Volume II: Since 1400

DISCOVERING THE GLOBAL PAST

A LOOK AT THE EVIDENCE

THIRD EDITION

Merry E. Wiesner
University of Wisconsin—Milwaukee

William Bruce Wheeler
University of Tennessee

Franklin M. Doeringer
Lawrence University

Kenneth R. Curtis
California State University Long Beach

HOUGHTON MIFFLIN COMPANY   Boston   New York

Sponsoring Editor: Nancy Blaine
Development Editor: Julie Swasey
Project Editor: Andrea Dodge
Editorial Assistant: Carrie Parker
Production/Design Coordinator: Gary Crespo
Senior Manufacturing Coordinator: Priscilla Manchester
Cover Design Manager: Anne S. Katzeff
Senior Marketing Manager: Sandra McGuire

Cover image: Tsinan, Shantung Province, China (about 386 miles southeast of Peking): a huge poster of the late actor, Charlie Chaplin, advertising his film, *Modern Times,* is on display on a wall along the main street. © Bettmann/Corbis.

Printed in the U.S.A.

Library of Congress Catalog Card Number: 2006925534

ISBN 10: 0-618-52638-2
ISBN 13: 978-0-618-52638-3

2 3 4 5 6 7 8 9-MV-10 09 08 07

CONTENTS

CHAPTER FIFTEEN
Religious Fundamentalism in the Modern World: Faith, Identity, and Contemporary Politics (1970s–present)   460

PREFACE

Almost from the founding of the United States itself, those who chose to call themselves "Americans" maintained a deep and abiding curiosity about and interest in other lands and their peoples. Indeed, although they often were characterized as provincial, narrow, and even rustic, Americans read all they could find about faraway peoples, flocked to lectures and lyceums offered by world travelers in the early nineteenth century, packed into nineteenth- and twentieth-century expositions and world's fairs to see "exotic" peoples, and even more recently became a "nation of tourists."

In order to convert this widespread curiosity into a deeper knowledge, schools began to offer classes in World History. In 1821 the first high school–level World History course was offered, at the Boston English High School, and a World History textbook (by Samuel G. Goodrich) appeared in 1828 to serve the growing teacher and student interest. Colleges and universities followed suit quickly thereafter, and in 1885 historian Mary D. Sheldon of Wellesley College first introduced the examination and analysis of primary sources into her World History (it was called "General History") course.[1]

The advent of professionally trained historians in the late nineteenth and early twentieth centuries, however, nearly spelled the end of the World History course. Essentially, these new professors charged that by trying to teach everything, the result was to teach nothing—or at least nothing in depth. By 1915 fewer than 5 percent of the high schools surveyed by the U.S. commissioner of education still taught a World History course. And after the introduction of the Western Civilization course (at Columbia University in 1919), colleges and universities too abandoned the single course in World History.[2]

And yet the curiosity that prompted the first World History courses in the early nineteenth century never abated. Indeed, with the recent emergence of the "global village," interest grew significantly. In 1982 the World History Association was founded, in part to encourage the reintroduction of World History courses and in part to assist people eager to teach such a course. As William H. McNeill, one of the founders of the modern movement to reintroduce World

---

1. Gilbert Allardyce, "Toward World History: American Historians and the Coming of the World History Course," in *Journal of World History*, vol. I (Spring 1990), pp. 23–76, esp. 45 and 47.

2. Ibid., pp. 30, 47.

History courses, put it, "Surely it takes only a little common sense to see that some sort of world history is the *only* way a college can do justice to students who live in a world where events in Asia, Africa, and Latin America are as likely to involve the United States in critical action as anything happening in Europe or North America."[3]

The response to the First Edition of *Discovering the Global Past* has been a gratifying one. It means that Mary D. Sheldon at Wellesley College over a century ago understood how to tap the already high level of student curiosity about far-away people. In our opinion, it also means that William H. McNeill had it right: that students understand not only the satisfaction of studying world history, but, in today's world, its *necessity*. This book honors both of these historians, as well as the countless numbers of curious and challenging students and their equally challenging teachers.

The primary goal of *Discovering the Global Past: A Look at the Evidence* is to allow students enrolled in world history courses to *do* history in the same way that we as historians do—to examine a group of original sources to answer questions about the past. The unique structure of this book clusters primary sources around a set of historical questions that students are asked to "solve." Unlike a source reader, this book prompts students to actually *analyze* a wide variety of authentic primary source material, to make inferences, and to draw conclusions in much the same way that historians do.

The evidence in this book is more varied than that in most source collections. We have included such visual evidence as coins, paintings, statues, literary illustrations, historical photographs, maps, cartoons, advertisements, and political posters. In choosing written evidence we again have tried to offer a broad sample—eulogies, wills, court records, oral testimonies, and statistical data all supplement letters, newspaper articles, speeches, memoirs, and other more traditional sources.

In order for students to learn history the way we as historians do, they must not only be confronted with the evidence but must also learn how to use that evidence to arrive at a conclusion. In other words, they must learn historical methodology. Too often methodology (or even the notion that historians *have* a methodology) is reserved for upper-level majors or graduate students; beginning students are simply presented with historical facts and interpretations without being shown how these were unearthed or formulated. Students may learn that historians hold different interpretations of the significance of an event or individual or different ideas about causation, but they are not informed of how historians come to such conclusions.

Thus, along with evidence, we have provided explicit suggestions about how one might analyze that evidence, guiding students as they reach their own conclusions. As they work through the various chapters, students will discover

3. Ibid., p. 72. Italics added.

both that the sources of historical information are wide-ranging and that the methodologies appropriate to understanding and using them are equally diverse. By doing history themselves, students will learn how intellectual historians handle philosophical treatises, economic historians quantitative data, social historians court records, and political and diplomatic historians theoretical treatises and memoirs. They will also be asked to consider the limitations of their evidence, to explore what historical questions it cannot answer as well as those it can. Instead of remaining passive observers, students become active participants.

Each chapter is divided into six parts: The Problem, Background, The Method, The Evidence, Questions to Consider, and Epilogue. Each of the parts relates to or builds upon the others, creating a uniquely integrated chapter structure that helps guide the reader through the analytical process. "The Problem" section begins with a brief discussion of the central issues of the chapter and then states the questions students will explore. A "Background" section follows, designed to help students understand the historical context of the problem. The section called "The Method" gives students suggestions for studying and analyzing the evidence. "The Evidence" section is the heart of the chapter, providing a variety of primary source material on the particular historical event or issue described in the chapter's "Problem" section. The section called "Questions to Consider" focuses students' attention on specific evidence and on linkages among different evidence material. The "Epilogue" section gives the aftermath or the historical outcome of the evidence—what happened to the people involved, the results of a debate, and so on.

Within this framework, we have tried to present a series of historical issues and events of significance to the instructor as well as of interest to the student. We have also aimed to provide a balance among political, social, diplomatic, intellectual, and cultural history. In other words, we have attempted to create a kind of historical sampler that we believe will help students learn the methods and skills used by historians. Not only will these skills—analyzing arguments, developing hypotheses, comparing evidence, testing conclusions, and reevaluating material—enable students to master historical content; they will also provide the necessary foundation for critical thinking in other college courses and after college as well.

Because the amount of material in global history is so vast, we had to pick certain topics and geographic areas to highlight, though here too we have aimed at a balance. Some chapters are narrow in focus, providing students with an opportunity to delve deeply into a single case study, while others ask students to make comparisons among individuals, events, or developments in different cultures. We have included cultural comparisons that are frequently discussed in World History courses, such as classical Rome and Han China, as well as more unusual ones, such as peasant family life in early modern central Europe and Southeast Asia.

Discovering the Global Past is designed to accommodate any format of the World History course, from the small lecture/discussion class at a liberal arts or community college to the large lecture with discussions led by teaching assistants at a sizable university. The chapters may be used for individual assignments, team projects, class discussions, papers, and exams. Each is self-contained, so that any combination may be assigned. The book is not intended to replace a standard textbook, and it was written to accompany any World History text the instructor chooses. The Instructor's Resource Manual, written by the authors of the text, offers further suggestions for class discussion, as well as a variety of ways in which students' learning may be evaluated and annotated lists of recommendations for further reading.

A note on spellings: Many of the sources presented in this book were originally written in a language other than English, and often in an alphabet other than the Western (Roman) one. Over the centuries, translators have devised various means of representing the sounds of other languages, and these conventions of translation have also changed over time. In general, we have used the most current spelling and orthographic conventions in our discussions and have left spellings as they appeared in the original translation in the sources. This means, for example, that Indian, Arabic, and Japanese words often have diacritical marks in the sources but not in our own material. For Chinese, in our own text we have used the pinyin system developed by the Chinese in the 1950s, with pinyin spellings indicated in brackets in the sources, most of which use the older Wade-Giles system.

New to the Third Edition

Volume I includes two entirely new chapters: the Mongol impact (Chapter 9) and the education of students in China, Paris, and Timbuktu (Chapter 12). Volume II includes three new chapters: land and property in rural societies (Chapter 3); a discussion of motherhood, nationalism, and women's rights in Brazil, Egypt, and Japan (Chapter 10); and an examination of religious fundamentalism in Islam, Christianity, Hinduism, and Judaism (Chapter 15).

In addition to the five new chapters, each volume has been carefully revised throughout. To bolster the book's comparative approach to global history, we have expanded the geographic coverage in several chapters. In Volume I, Chapter 2 now includes the Mayan creation myth of the *Popol Vuh*; new first-hand accounts of the Crusades and the sack of Constantinople now appear in Chapters 7 and 10, respectively; and the discussion of pilgrimages in Chapter 11 has been expanded to include a new Chinese account. In Volume II, Chapter 4 now includes African accounts of plantation life and the despair of enslavement; Chapter 6 adds Simón Bolívar, the leader of the Latin American wars of independence, to the list of "liberator-heros"; a new account by Jawaharlal Nehru in Chapter 7 adds another non-Western voice to the discussion of modernity; the discussion of department stores in Chapter 11 has been broadened to include examples from Turkey and China; and the discussion of World Wars I and II in Chapter 13 now features an article on the Nanking Massacre.

Lastly, to preserve the chronological organization of both volumes, we have rearranged the order of some chapters in this edition. For instance, the chapter "First Encounters: The Creation of Cultural Stereotypes (1450–1650)" is now the final chapter in Volume I and also the opening chapter of Volume II.

Acknowledgments

We would like to thank the many students and instructors who have helped us in our efforts. We extend our gratitude to the following professors who have helped us and criticized the manuscript through its development:

Abel Alves, *Ball State University*

Martin J. Blackwell, *Indiana University—Purdue University Indianapolis*

Gayle K. Brunelle, *California State University, Fullerton*

Jürgen Buchenau, *University of North Carolina, Charlotte*

Andrew F. Clark, *University of North Carolina, Wilmington*

Anna Dronzek, *Rhodes College*

Andrew Frank, *Florida Atlantic University*

Mark Hampton, *Wesleyan College*

JIANG Yonglin, *Oklahoma State University*

Margot Lovett, *Saddleback College*

Margaret Eleanor Menninger, *Texas State University, San Marcos*

Kenneth J. Orosz, *University of Maine, Farmington*

Alice K. Pate, *Columbus State University*

Donna Amelia Vinson, *Salem State University*

In addition to our colleagues across the United States, we would like to thank especially our colleagues at the University of Wisconsin—Milwaukee; the University of Tennessee, Knoxville; Lawrence University; and California State University Long Beach. Merry E. Wiesner wishes especially to thank Darlene Abreu-Ferreira, Barbara Andaya, Judith Bennett, Susan Besse, Philip C. Brown, Martha Carlin, Jean Fleet, Charlotte Furth, Faye Getz, Anne Good, Michael Gordon, Abbas Hamdani, Anne Hansen, Jean Johnson, Teresa Meade, Jeffrey Merrick, Barbara Molony, Sheilagh Ogilvie, Jean Quataert, Irene Silverblatt, Andrea Stone, Hitomi Tonomura, Jane Waldbaum, and Charlotte Weber. Bruce Wheeler would like to thank Robert Bast, Palmira Brummett, Thomas Burman,

J. P. Dessel, Hilde DeWeerdt, Todd Diacon, Catherine Higgs, and Lu Liu. Franklin M. Doeringer wishes to thank all of his colleagues in the Lawrence University Department of History for their support and interest in this project. J. Michael Hittle and Edmund M. Kern deserve particular mention for reading over portions of manuscript and offering helpful comments. He also expresses his gratitude to Jane Parish Tany and Kui-ming Sung in the Department of East Asian Languages and Cultures for their suggestiongs on material pertaining to China and East Asia. Finally, he extends special thanks to Peter J. Gilbert of the Lawrence library for his unflagging help in tracking down elusive sources and obscure references. Kenneth R. Curtis would especially like to thank Christos Bartsocas, Francine Curtis, Steve Curtis, Ross Dunn, Tim Keirn, Lezlie Knox, Emilie Savage-Smith, Donald Schwartz, and his coauthors.

Finally we would like to thank Julie Swasey, Andrea Dodge, and the rest of the staff at Houghton Mifflin for their support.

M.E.W.
W.B.W
F.M.D.
K.R.C.

DISCOVERING THE
GLOBAL PAST

CHAPTER ONE

FIRST ENCOUNTERS: THE CREATION

OF CULTURAL STEREOTYPES (1450–1650)

One of the most important aspects of world history involves the interactions of various peoples with one another. Centuries before what Europeans call their Age of Discovery, groups of people were aware that there were other human beings—some of them like themselves and others quite different—who inhabited other places; some made their homes in nearby valleys or plains or mountains, and others were unimaginably far away.

How these groups of people chose to deal with "the others"—in harmony or hostility, in trade, warfare, intermarriage, and so on—depended to a great extent on how these peoples perceived one another. For it was often these perceptions, far more than realities, that tempered and even determined the types of relations they had.

Thus, as European explorers, traders, missionaries, and colonizers began to expand their horizons and influence beyond the Mediterranean in the fifteenth and sixteenth centuries and embarked for what were for them the strange new lands of Africa, Asia, and the Americas, they inevitably carried with them a set of intellectual and cultural lenses through which they viewed the peoples they encountered. Moreover, they spread their own perceptions throughout Europe in the forms of published letters, journals, memoirs, and observations, many of which were immensely popular. Indeed, it seemed as if Europe could not get enough of these marvelous accounts of "new people" and "new worlds." For example, the great Dutch painter Rembrandt van Rijn was fascinated by non-Europeans who were brought, sometimes forcibly, to the Netherlands and painted portraits of many of them.[1]

1. On the popularity of explorers' accounts, Amerigo Vespucci's published letters were reprinted in sixty editions, Christopher Columbus's

Chapter 1

First Encounters:

The Creation

of Cultural

Stereotypes

(1450–1650)

Similarly, Africans, Americans, and Asians possessed their own cultures and saw Europeans through their own lenses. Ultimately, these perceptions—the Europeans' of non-Europeans and non-Europeans' of them—had an impact on how these different peoples treated and dealt with one another. Sometimes, the results were beneficial. Often, they were tragic.

In this chapter, you will be analyzing selected written accounts of first encounters between Europeans and sub-Saharan Africans, Native Americans, and Japanese. Your task in the chapter is twofold. First, by examining these accounts, determine the initial impressions that each side formed of the other. Then, use your historical imagination to reach some conclusions about how those impressions (whether accurate or inaccurate) might have influenced how these peoples chose to deal with one another.

Before you begin, we want to emphasize the fact that these intellectual and cultural filters often prevented each side from understanding what the other was really like. The evidence presented in this chapter consists of *perceptions,* but not necessarily *realities.* And yet, as you might imagine, perceptions often are extremely powerful in influencing thought and actions. For example, Europeans dealt with non-Europeans not according to what those people were *really* like, but rather according to what Europeans *perceived* them to be like. The same is true of non-Europeans' dealings with European explorers, traders, missionaries, and colonizers. This chapter addresses these perceptions (or misperceptions) and their consequences.

Of course, Europeans were not the *only* peoples who were traveling beyond their own borders. Indeed, beginning in the fifth century Chinese and Japanese Buddhist pilgrims were spreading their doctrines throughout India, Southeast Asia, and Tibet. Somewhat later, around the seventh century, Arab merchants began to establish what ultimately became well-traveled trade routes from Japan to Baghdad, throughout North Africa, and (aided by the domestication of the camel) across the Sahara Desert to trade with the kingdoms of Mali and Songhay, among others. In the Americas, both the Incas and Aztecs had well-developed commercial connections in South and Central America.

In the fifteenth century, Admiral Zheng He of China's Ming dynasty commanded seven huge ocean armadas, one of which some believe actually reached the Western Hemisphere in 1421. Moroccan Ibn Battuta (1304–1368) traveled through much of the Muslim world, by his own reckoning journeying 73,000 miles without taking the same route twice. In 1324, the year before Ibn Battuta began his travels, King Mansa Musa of Mali made a pilgrimage to Mecca, as did Persian poet Naser-e Khosraw (in 1046) and Spanish Moor Ibn Jubayr (who also traveled through Egypt, Jerusalem, and Sicily between 1183 and 1185). Thus Europeans were by no means the only ones

journal in twenty-two editions, and Hernando Cortés's in eighteen editions. See Fredi Chiappelli, et al., eds., *First Images of America: The Impact of the New World on the Old,* 2 vols. (Berkeley: University of California Press, 1976), vol. 2, p. 538.

who were "on the move" or who were aware of other lands and other peoples.[2]

In this chapter, however, we have decided to concentrate on the perceptions of European missionaries, traders, conquistadors, and travelers and on non-Europeans' perceptions of them, for three principal reasons. To begin with, Europeans were the only peoples who traveled to all the other habitable

2. Excellent primary and secondary sources are available on non-European travelers. Perhaps the best primary sources are the accounts written by Muslim traders and pilgrims, such as Ibn Battuta, Naser-e Khosraw, and Ibn Jubayr. Perhaps the most controversial recent secondary source has to do with Zheng He: Gavin Menzies's *1421: The Year China Discovered America* (New York: HarperCollins, 2003).

continents—to engage in commerce, conversion, conquest, and finally colonization. Second, it was these Europeans who laid the groundwork for what later would be the first epoch of Western imperialism. Finally, in large part because of the printing press, Europeans were able to disseminate their observations and (not unimportantly) leave published evidence that later would be invaluable to historians. Therefore, while many people were "on the move" from the seventh to the sixteenth centuries and after, we have confined our evidence in this chapter to European perceptions of the non-Europeans they encountered and the perceptions that non-Europeans had of them.

BACKGROUND

By the 1400s, Europeans were dramatically different from their ancestors of but a few centuries earlier—so different, in fact, that they were now prepared economically, scientifically, intellectually, and politically to embark upon their Age of Discovery (1450–1650).

Economically, the limited commerce of the era of the Crusades (1100s–1200s) had given way to burgeoning trade. The growth of trade had been made possible by increasing concentrations of wealth, which not only stimulated demand but also made possible new methods of investing and borrowing needed capital. The development of maritime insurance, first seen in Italian seaport cities but soon commonplace throughout Europe, made investors

more willing to take risks. Finally, with the horrors of the Black Death behind them, Europe's population slowly began to recover, thus generating increasing demand for goods and making possible the production of surpluses.

Intellectually and technologically, Europe was also prepared to undertake explorations. The Age of Discovery in Europe was also the age of Renaissance humanism, as Christopher Columbus, Amerigo Vespucci, Bartolomeu Dias, Leonardo da Vinci, Michelangelo, Erasmus, and William Shakespeare were roughly contemporaries. To such visionaries and others, old answers were pathetically insufficient, and a hunger for new knowledge prompted investigation and advances in astronomy, mathematics, geography, and physics as well as in literature, art, philosophy, and political theory. To improve

Chapter 1

First Encounters:

The Creation

of Cultural

Stereotypes

(1450–1650)

navigation, Europeans were prepared to borrow from others: the magnetic compass from China via Muslims and the astrolabe (used to locate latitude) and the triangular ship's sail from the Arabs, among other innovations.

At the same time that Europe was becoming economically, intellectually, and technologically ready to expand its sway, the political institution of the nation-state was beginning to emerge, at first in Portugal and Spain and later in France, the Low Countries, and England. The monarchs of these evolving states groped toward a more permanent and stable government than mere dynastic rule. Such permanence and stability, these "enlightened" monarchs reasoned, could be achieved in part through the accumulation of great wealth by the central government. Looking to Italian port cities and Arab merchants as models, European monarchs saw that this wealth could be produced through trade.

But with Italian traders dominant in the Mediterranean and with the Turks' capture of Constantinople in 1453 sealing off land trade routes to the East, European monarchs and state-encouraged private merchants were forced into the Atlantic to find new trade routes. The European monarch who traditionally has been given credit for this vision is the Portuguese Infante Dom Henrique, better known to us as Prince Henry the Navigator. Under Henry's sponsorship, Portuguese seamen inched down the western coast of Africa in attempts to find new sea routes to India and the Far East. Although Henry did not live to see his dream achieved (he died in 1460), his

vision was taken up by his successors. In 1487, Bartolomeu Dias rounded the southern tip of Africa (Cape Agulhas),[3] and in May 1498 Vasco da Gama at last reached India.[4] By 1542, Portuguese explorers and traders had sailed to Japan.

With Portugal in control of the African sea routes to the East, rival monarchs of other emerging nations were forced to seek other trade lanes. Spain sponsored the voyages of Christopher Columbus, who convinced the Spanish throne that he could reach the riches of the East by sailing due west into the uncharted Atlantic. France, the Netherlands, and England, although slower starters in the frantic competition for trade routes because political unity and stability were achieved later in those nation-states, also sponsored voyages. Indeed, in spite of the fact that explorers found two continents that had the potential to produce enormous wealth, the dream of finding a sea route to the East remained so strong that as late as 1638 French fur trader Jean Nicolet, encountering the Winnebago tribe of Native Americans on the western shore of Lake Michigan, donned a Chinese robe in anticipation of meeting the ruler of China.

The period in which Portuguese explorers and traders first began to probe the coastal areas of West Africa coincidentally was one of considerable

3. Cape Agulhas, not the Cape of Good Hope, is actually the southernmost point of Africa. Dias originally called the Cape of Good Hope the Cape of Storms, but the name was changed by King John II of Portugal.

4. Da Gama had the help of Indian navigator Ahmed ibn Majid, who came on board da Gama's ship at Malindi, a port on the east coast of Africa, in present-day Kenya, founded by the Portuguese in 1498.

instability in that region. Earlier, North African Berber and Arab traders had found organized kingdoms in West Africa and had carried on a brisk commerce in gold, silk and cotton cloth, dates, ivory, salt, and slaves.[5] By the year 1100, camel caravans regularly crossed the Sahara to reach the bustling trading centers of Timbuktu and Gao, bringing trade goods from the East as well as the Islamic religion. Politically, the Kingdom of Ghana, a highly centralized military state, had been the dominant force in the region, but by 1200 it had declined, giving way to the Kingdom of Mali. North of Mali, the state of Songhai (also spelled Songhay and Songhi) had by 1400 declared its independence from Mali. At the time of the Portuguese encounters, population increases and invasions of Senegambia and Guinea in order to secure more gold for foreign trade had left West Africa politically and economically weakened and vulnerable to outside intrusion. By the 1500s, these political rivalries between West African states increased the number of slaves captured in battle, slaves that Europeans were only too willing to purchase to work their new colonies in America.

By the time Europeans first encountered the various peoples they mistakenly but insistently called Indians, Native Americans had inhabited the Western Hemisphere for approximately 20,000 to 40,000 years. Although there is considerable disagreement about when these people first appeared in the Americas, it is virtually certain that they were not native to the Western Hemisphere, since no subhuman remains have ever been found. Probably they migrated from Asia sometime in the middle of the Pleistocene Age (75,000 to 8,000 B.C.E.). During that period, huge glaciers covered a large portion of North America, the ice cap extending southward to approximately the present United States–Canadian border. These glaciers, nearly 2 miles thick in some places, interrupted the water cycle because moisture falling as rain or snow was caught by the glaciers and frozen and thus was prevented from draining back into the seas or evaporating into the atmosphere. This process lowered ocean levels 250 to 300 feet, exposing a natural land bridge spanning the Bering Strait (between present-day Alaska and Russia)[6] across which people from Asia could easily migrate, probably in search of game. It is almost certain that various peoples from Asia did exactly that and then followed an ice-free corridor along the base of the Rocky Mountains southward into the more temperate areas of the American Southwest (which, because of the glaciers, were wetter and cooler than now and contained large lakes and forests) and then either eastward into other areas of North America or even farther southward into Central and South America. These migrations took thousands of years, and some peoples were still moving when European sails appeared on the horizon.

5. The Arabs called West Africa *Bilad al-Sudan*, or "Land of the Blacks."

6. Today the Bering Strait is only 180 feet deep; thus a lowering of ocean levels 250–300 feet would have exposed a considerable land bridge between Asia and North America.

Chapter 1

First Encounters:

The Creation

of Cultural

Stereotypes

(1450–1650)

About 8000 B.C.E., the glacial cap began to retreat fairly rapidly, raising ocean levels to approximately their present-day levels, cutting off further migration from Asia and isolating America's first human inhabitants from other peoples for thousands of years (although some canoe travel was still possible). This isolation was almost surely the cause of the inhabitants' extraordinarily high susceptibility to the diseases that Europeans later brought with them, such as measles, tuberculosis, and smallpox, to which the populations of other continents had built up natural resistance. The glacial retreat also caused stretches of the American Southwest to become hot and arid, thus scattering Indian peoples in almost all directions. Nevertheless, for thousands of years a strong oral tradition enabled Native Americans to preserve stories of their origins and subsequent isolation. Almost all Native American peoples retained accounts of a long migration from the west and a flood.

The original inhabitants of the Western Hemisphere obtained their food principally by hunting and gathering, killing mammoths, huge bison, deer, elk, antelope, camels, horses, and other game with stone weapons and picking wild fruits and grasses. Beginning about 5000 B.C.E., however, people in present-day Mexico began practicing agriculture. By the time Europeans arrived, most Native Americans were domesticating plants and raising crops, although their levels of agricultural sophistication varied widely.

The development of agriculture (which occurred about the same time in Europe and the Americas) profoundly affected Native American life. Those peoples who adopted agriculture abandoned their nomadic ways and lived in settled villages (some of the Central American communities became magnificent cities). This more sedentary life permitted them to erect permanent housing, create and preserve pottery and art, and establish more complex political and social institutions. Agriculture also led to a gender-based division of labor, with women planting, raising, and harvesting crops and men hunting to supplement their villages' diets with game. With better food, and that in abundance, most likely Native American populations grew rapidly, thus prompting the onset of more complex political and social structures. The development of agriculture also affected these peoples' religious beliefs and ceremonies, increasing the homage to sun and rain gods who were thought to bring forth fruitful harvests. Contact with other Native American peoples led to trading, a practice with which Native Americans were quite familiar by the time of European intrusion.

Those Native American cultures that made the transition from food gathering to food producing often attained an impressive degree of economic, political, social, and technological sophistication. In Central America, the Mayas of present-day Mexico and Guatemala built great cities, fashioned elaborate gold and silver jewelry, devised a form of writing, were proficient in mathematics and astronomy, and constructed a calendar that could predict solar eclipses and was more accurate than any system in use in Europe at the time. The conquerors of the Mayas, the Aztecs, built on the achievements of their predecessors, extending their political and economic power chiefly by subjugating other Native American peoples.[7] By the time Cortés and his army of four hundred men, sixteen horses, and a few cannon landed at Vera Cruz in 1519, the Aztecs had constructed the magnificent city of Tenochtitlán (the site of present-day Mexico City), which rivaled European cities in both size (approximately 300,000 people) and splendor.

Tenochtitlán contained monumental pyramids and public buildings, a fresh water supply brought to the city by complex engineering, causeways that connected the island city to other islands and the mainland, numerous skilled craftsmen, and even a compulsory education system for all male children. Raw materials and treasure flowed into Tenochtitlán as tribute from peoples under Aztec dominance, which stretched from the Pacific Ocean to the Gulf of Mexico and from central Mexico to present-day Guatemala. Little wonder that the conquistadors with Hernando Cortés were awed and enchanted when they saw it.

In the late thirteenth century, Kubilai Khan had attempted an invasion of Japan, thwarted when his fleet was destroyed by a typhoon, which the Japanese called *kamikaze* ("divine winds"). But, like the states of West Africa, Japan was suffering through an era of political instability when Portuguese explorers, traders, and missionaries first landed

in the early 1540s. With the country wracked by almost constant civil war, the authority of the central government had been reduced to near-impotence. Similar to the feudal societies in Western Europe in the tenth and eleventh centuries, Japan in the 1400s and 1500s was controlled by approximately 250 *daimyos* ("lords"), who kept the islands in utter turmoil with their rivalries. Portuguese and, later, Dutch traders quickly moved in, as did Christian missionaries. In 1549, the Jesuit missionary Francis Xavier (later raised to sainthood) landed at Kagoshima. By 1600, approximately 300,000 Japanese people had been baptized Christians.

Beginning in 1568, Japan began a period of national consolidation. Under Oda Nobunaga, a samurai warrior, the daimyos gradually were brought under central authority. Despite Nobunaga's assassination in 1582, the work of political centralization was continued under Nobunaga's principal general and successor Toyotomi Hideyoshi and was essentially complete by 1598.

The centralization of authority did not bode well for Europeans. Suspicious of Japanese Christians' conflicting loyalties and fearing that contact with European merchants was diluting the glories of Japanese culture, the Japanese government in 1635 began expelling Europeans, banning all things European (except firearms), and persecuting Japanese Christians (many of whom were crucified). Yet Dutch traders were allowed to remain on the tiny island of Deshima (in Nagasaki harbor) and Japanese people continued to be fascinated by western things. Many continued to engage in *rangaku* ("foreign studies").

---

7. The Aztecs actually called themselves Mexica. Nor did Cortés ever use the word *Aztec*. The name "Aztec" was made popular in the eighteenth century by Jesuit scholar Francisco Javier Calavijero. Like the erroneous name "Indian," the name "Aztec" has persisted.

Chapter 1

First Encounters:

The Creation

of Cultural

Stereotypes

(1450–1650)

To repeat, your task in this chapter is twofold. First, by examining several accounts of "first encounters," determine the initial impressions that each side created of the other. Once you have completed that analysis, then use your historical ingenuity to reach some conclusions about how these initial impressions might have influenced the ways Europeans and non-Europeans chose to deal with one another.

THE METHOD

To begin with, all of the accounts you will read, both by Europeans and by non-Europeans, pose some problems for historians. For one thing, each author is describing people of another culture through the lens of his own culture and experiences. Therefore, each observer may not have fully grasped what he actually was seeing. (For example, if you were to invite a person from another culture to accompany you to a college football game and then ask that person what he or she observed, you would expect the result to be a far cry from your daily sports page rundown.) In addition, each of the authors clearly hoped that his account would be read by other people. This invisible audience too may have affected what and how he wrote. Nevertheless, because we are dealing with *perceptions* that various cultures had of one another at first contact, the accounts are not so flawed as they might at first appear. Moreover, nearly all the authors represented here actually were eyewitnesses to the events they describe; thus, for our purposes their evidence serves quite well.

As you read each account, pay special attention to reports of the following features (the fifth often will require you to indulge in historical speculation):

1. Physical appearance (bodies, hair, clothing, jewelry, and so on). Such descriptions can provide important clues about the authors' attitudes toward the peoples they are describing. Two particularly good examples are Columbus's description of the Arawaks (Source 4) and the anonymous Japanese author's description of the European (Source 13).

2. Nature or character (childlike, bellicose, honest, lazy, greedy, and so on). Be willing to read between the lines. For example, King Nzinga Mbemba of Kongo does not refer directly to Europeans and, in fact, on the surface seems to be more critical of his own people (Source 3). Is the king, however, implying something else?

3. Political, social, and religious traditions and practices (behavior of women, ceremonies, eating habits, government, sexual practices, and so on). These descriptions provide you with excellent material, as Europeans were often shocked by some of the practices of the peoples they encountered (Sources 2, 5, 11, and 12, for examples), as were non-Europeans of European practices (Sources 6, 13, 14, and 15 for examples).

Remember that each narrator is looking through the lens of his own culture.

4. Overall impressions. Although these are rarely stated explicitly, each author certainly intended to give his readers a collective image of the peoples he encountered. Often you will have to infer that overall impression yourself from the bits of evidence in the accounts.

5. Advice. How should the people being described be dealt with? Here again, you may have to deduce this from each account. Just as often, however, you will have to be especially sensitive to what each author is *really* saying. For example, several European accounts reported that the peoples being described could be easily converted to Christianity (Sources 1 and 4, to name but two). Is the author implying that these peoples *should* be converted? Also, in Source 2 the anonymous reporter describes a brisk trade in West Africa in gold and slaves. Might one assume that this Portuguese seaman believes his country *should* engage in that profitable commerce? In the Native American account of Europeans, you will have to infer how they believed Europeans should be dealt with, since the account does not explicitly deal with that question. The African and Japanese accounts are somewhat more direct.

Be willing to read between the lines. Sometimes, for example, the author may tell a story about the people he is describing. What meaning is that story intended to convey? Also be sensitive to how the author's own culture has affected his perceptions (as, for example, when Mexia attempts to describe Japanese music in Source 12).

Finally, use the collective images you have found to predict how those views—often pervasive—might have affected the way these peoples chose to treat one another. That is, what behavior resulted from these attitudes?

Source 1 is an account of a 1593 shipwreck that took place off the coast of Africa. The author, not himself an eyewitness in this case, took the journal of the ship's pilot and interviewed several of the survivors before writing his account of the wreck of the *Santo Alberto* in 1597. Source 2 is a first-person account of encounters with Africans in Benin (in West Africa). The account was written sometime after 1535 and a popular Italian translation was published in 1550.

Nzinga Mbemba (Source 3) was the King of Kongo, the largest state in central West Africa. He came to the throne around 1506, succeeding his father, and in 1526 wrote three insistent letters to the king of Portugal. The Portuguese knew Nzinga Mbemba by his Christian name, Alfonso I.

Christopher Columbus kept a journal of his first voyage, which he presented to his patrons Ferdinand and Isabella upon his return. Both the journal and a duplicate copy have been lost forever. What we have in Source 4 is a reworked version of the original, done by Bartolome de las Casas in the 1530s. That document too was lost for approximately 250 years but was recovered in 1790 and now is preserved in the National Library in Madrid. Amerigo Vespucci's account (Source 5) of his 1497–1498 voyage was the most popular explorer account in Europe (can you guess why?), part of the reason why the New World became his namesake.

Chapter 1

First Encounters:

The Creation

of Cultural

Stereotypes

(1450–1650)

The Native American account of Cortés's invasion (Source 6) was rescued from destruction by Spanish priests and survived the *conquistadors'* ("conquerors") attempts to obliterate all Native American records of what they had done. The account was preserved for centuries in Roman Catholic monasteries and now resides in national museums or libraries both in Europe and in Mexico.

Girón (Source 7) was a merchant who traded in Japan. Torres, Xavier, Rodrigues, Valignano, and Mexia (Sources 8 through 12) all were Jesuit missionaries who spent years in Japan, China, and Macao attempting to convert the locals to Christianity. Indeed, all of these missionaries died in the East—Torres in Japan, Xavier and Mexia in China, and Rodrigues and Valignano in Macao.

Source 13, written by an anonymous author in 1639, is the initial chapter of a popular book entitled *Kirishitan [Christian] monogatari*. Suzuki Shosan wrote his attack on Christianity (Source 14) in Japan in 1642. He was an advocate of "ferocious Zen," a rather aggressive version of that philosophy. Tokugawa Iemitsu, author of the 1635 edict ordering the closing of Japan (Source 15), was *Shogun* ("supreme military leader") from 1623 to 1651. The edict was written to the two *bugyo* ("commissioners") of Nagasaki, a center of Japanese Christianity.

Before you begin examining the evidence, let us offer a note of caution. Some of these accounts include strong ethnocentric, even racist, language and images. We included these accounts not to either shock or offend readers, but rather to accurately represent the kinds of descriptions individuals wrote after their "first encounters" with strangers.

THE EVIDENCE

AFRICA

European Accounts

Source 1 from C. R. Boxer, ed., The Tragic History of the Sea, 1589–1622: Narratives of the Shipwrecks of the Portuguese East Indiamen *(Cambridge: The Hakluyt Society, 1959), pp. 119–123.*

1. Joao Baptista Lavanha, 1597

It being now late, the chief of that region, who had heard from some of his Kaffirs that our people were there, came with about sixty Negroes to visit the Captain-major. When he drew near, Nuno Velho got up and went a few steps to receive him, and the Negro, after welcoming him by saying 'Nanhatá, Nanhatá,' as a sign of peace and friendship laid his hand on the Captain-major's beard and after stroking it kissed his own hand. All the other barbarians performed the same courtesy to our people, and ours to them. This Negro was called Luspance. He was fairly tall, well made, of a cheerful countenance, not very black, with a short beard, long moustaches, and appeared to be about forty-five years old. . . .

The dress of these Kaffirs was a mantle of calf-skins, with the hair on the outside, which they rub with grease to make soft. They are shod with two or three soles of raw hide fastened together in a round shape, secured to the foot with thongs and with this they run with great speed. They carry in their hand a thin stick to which is fastened the tail of an ape or of a fox, with which they clean themselves and shade their eyes when observing. This dress is used by nearly all the Negroes of this Kaffraria, and the kings and chiefs wear hanging from their left ear a little copper bell, without a clapper, which they make after their fashion.

These and all the other Kaffirs are herdsmen and husbandmen, by which means they subsist. Their husbandry is millet, which is white, about the size of a peppercorn, and forms the ear of a plant which resembles a reed in shape and size. From this millet, ground between two stones or in wooden mortars, they make flour, and of this they make cakes, which they bake under the embers. Of the same grain they make wine, mixing it with a lot of water, which after being fermented in a clay jar, cooled off, and turned sour, they drink with great gusto.

Their cattle are numerous, fat, tender, tasty, and large, the pastures being very fertile. Most of them are polled cows,[8] in whose number and abundance their wealth consists. They also subsist on their milk and on the butter which they make from it.

They live together in small villages, in huts made of reed mats, which do not keep out the rain. These huts are round and low, and if any person dies in one of them, all the other huts and the whole village are pulled down, and they make others from the same material in another place, believing that in the village where their neighbour or relation died, everything will turn out unluckily. And thus, to save themselves this trouble, when anyone falls ill they carry him into the bush, so that if he dies it may be outside their huts. They surround their huts with a fence, within which they keep their cattle.

They sleep in skins of animals, on the earth, in a narrow pit measuring six or seven spans long and one or two deep. They use vessels of clay dried in the sun, and also of wood carved with some iron hatchets, which resemble a wedge set in a piece of wood, and they also use these for clearing the bush. In war they make use of assegais [slender spears]; and they have gelded whelps[9] about the shape and size of our large curs.

They are very brutish and worship nothing, and thus they would receive our holy Christian faith very easily. They believe that the sky is another world like this one in which we live, inhabited by another kind of people, who cause the thunder by running and the rain by urinating. Most of the inhabitants of this

8. **polled cows:** cows that have no horns.
9. **gelded whelps:** castrated young dogs.

Chapter 1

First Encounters:

The Creation

of Cultural

Stereotypes

(1450–1650)

land from latitude 29° southwards are circumcised. They are very sensual, and have as many wives as they can maintain, of whom they are jealous. They obey chiefs whom they call Ancosses.

The language is almost the same in the whole of Kaffraria, the difference between them resembling that between the languages of Italy, or between the ordinary ones of Spain. They seldom go far away from their villages, and thus they know and hear nothing except what concerns their neighbours. They are very covetous, and so long as they have not received payment they will serve, but if payment is made in advance no service is to be expected of them, for when they have received it they make off with it.

They value the most essential metals, such as iron and copper, and thus for very small pieces of either of these they will barter cattle, which is what they most prize, and with cattle they drive their trade and commerce, and cattle forms their treasure. Gold and silver have no value among them, nor does there appear to be either of these two metals in the country, for our people saw no signs of them in the regions through which they passed.

The above is all they noticed of the dress, customs, ceremonies, and laws of these Kaffirs, nor can there be more to take note of among so barbarous a people. . . .

Source 2 from John William Blake, ed. and trans., Europeans in West Africa, 1450–1560 *(London: The Hakluyt Society, 1942), vol. 1, pp. 145–153.*

2. Anonymous Portuguese Pilot, ca. 1535

To understand the Negro traffic, one must know that over all the African coast facing west there are various countries and provinces, such as Guinea, the coast of Melegete, the kingdom of Benin, the kingdom of Kongo, six degrees from the equator and towards the south pole. There are many tribes and Negro kings here, and also communities which are partly Muslim and partly heathen. These are constantly making war among themselves. The kings are worshiped by their subjects, who believe that they come from heaven, and speak of them always with great reverence, at a distance and on bended knees. Great ceremony surrounds them, and many of these kings never allow themselves to be seen eating, so as not to destroy the belief of their subjects that they can live without food. They worship the sun, and believe that spirits are immortal, and that after death they go to the sun. Among others, there is in the kingdom of Benin an ancient custom, observed to the present day, that when the king dies, the people all assemble in a large field, in the center of which is a very deep well, wider at the bottom than at the mouth. They cast the body of the dead king into this well, and all his friends and servants gather round, and those who are judged to have been most dear to and favored by the king (this includes not a few, as all are anxious for the honor) voluntarily go down to keep him company. When they have done so, the people place a great stone over the mouth of the well, and remain by it day and night. On the second day, a few deputies remove the stone, and ask those below what they know, and if any of them have already gone to serve the king; and the reply is, No. On the third day, the same question is asked; and someone then replies that so-and-so, mentioning a name, has been the first to go, and so-and-so the second. It is considered highly praiseworthy to be the first, and he is spoken of with the greatest admiration by all the people, and considered happy and blessed. After four or five days all these unfortunate people die. When this is apparent to those above, since none reply to their questions, they inform their new king; who causes a great fire to be lit near the well, where numerous animals are roasted. These are given to the people to eat, and he with great ceremony is declared to be the true king, and takes the oath to govern well.

The Negroes of Guinea and Benin are very haphazard in their habits of eating. They have no set times for meals, and eat and drink four or five times a day, drinking water, or a wine which they distill from palms. They have no hair except for a few bristly strands on top of the head, and none grows; and the rest of the bodies are completely hairless. They live for the best part of 100 years, and are always vigorous, except at certain times of the year when they become very weak, as if they had fever. They are then bled, and recover, having a great deal of blood in their system. Some of the Negroes in this country are so superstitious that they worship the first object they see on the day of recovery. A kind of plant called melegete, very like the sorgum of Italy, but in flavor like pepper, grows on this coast. . . .

African Account

Source 3 from Basil Davidson, trans., The African Past *(London: Curtis Brown, 1964), pp. 191–194.*

3. Nzinga Mbemba, 1526

Sir, Your Highness [King of Portugal] should know how our Kingdom is being lost in so many ways that it is convenient to provide for the necessary remedy, since this is caused by the excessive freedom given by your agents and officials to the men and merchants who are allowed to come to this Kingdom to set up shops with goods and many things which have been prohibited by us, and which they spread throughout our Kingdoms and Domains in such an abundance that many of our vassals, whom we had in obedience, do not comply because they have the things in greater abundance than we ourselves; and it was with these things that we had them content and subjected under our vassalage

Chapter 1

First Encounters:

The Creation

of Cultural

Stereotypes

(1450–1650)

and jurisdiction, so it is doing a great harm not only to the service of God, but the security and peace of our Kingdoms and State as well.

And we cannot reckon how great the damage is, since the mentioned merchants are taking every day our natives, sons of the land and the sons of our noblemen and vassals and our relatives, because the thieves and men of bad conscience grab them wishing to have the things and wares of this Kingdom which they are ambitious of; they grab them and get them to be sold; and so great, Sir, is the corruption and licentiousness that our country is being completely depopulated, and Your Highness should not agree with this nor accept it as in your service. And to avoid it we need from those (your) Kingdoms no more than some priests and a few people to teach in schools, and no other goods except wine and flour for the holy sacrament. That is why we beg of Your Highness to help and assist us in this matter, commanding your factors that they should not send here either merchants or wares, because it is *our will that in these Kingdoms there should not be any trade of slaves nor outlet for them.* Concerning what is referred [to] above, again we beg of Your Highness to agree with it, since otherwise we cannot remedy such an obvious damage. Pray Our Lord in His mercy to have Your Highness under His guard and let you do forever the things of His service. . . .

Moreover, Sir, in our Kingdoms there is another great inconvenience which is of little service to God, and this is that many of our people, keenly desirous as they are of the wares and things of your Kingdoms, which are brought here by your people, and in order to satisfy their voracious appetite, seize many of our people, freed and exempt men, and very often it happens that they kidnap even noblemen and the sons of noblemen, and our relatives, and take them to be sold to the white men who are in our Kingdoms; and for this purpose they have concealed them; and others are brought during the night so that they might not be recognized.

And as soon as they are taken by the white men they are immediately ironed and branded with fire, and when they are carried to be embarked, if they are caught by our guards' men the whites allege that they have bought them but they cannot say from whom, so that it is our duty to do justice and to restore to the freemen their freedom, but it cannot be done if your subjects feel offended, as they claim to be.

And to avoid such a great evil we passed a law so that any white man living in our Kingdoms and wanting to purchase goods in any way should first inform three of our noblemen and officials of our court whom we rely upon in this matter, and these are Dom Pedro Manipanza and Dom Manuel Manissaba, our chief usher, and Gonçalo Pires our chief freighter, who should investigate if the mentioned goods are captives or free men, and if cleared by them there will be no further doubt nor embargo for them to be taken and embarked. But if the white men do not comply with it they will lose the aforementioned goods. And if we do them this favor and concession it is for the part Your Highness has in it, since we know that it is in your service too that these goods are taken from our Kingdom, otherwise we should not consent to this. . . .

AMERICA

European Accounts

Source 4 from Journal of the First Voyage to America, by Christopher Columbus *(New York: Albert Boni and Charles Boni, 1924), pp. 24–29.*

4. Christopher Columbus,
1530s

As I saw that they were very friendly to us, and perceived that they could be much more easily converted to our holy faith by gentle means than by force, I presented them with some red caps, and strings of beads to wear upon the neck, and many other trifles of small value, wherewith they were much delighted, and became wonderfully attached to us. Afterwards they came swimming to the boats, bringing parrots, balls of cotton thread, javelins and many other things which they exchanged for articles we gave them, such as glass beads, and hawk's bells; which trade was carried on with the utmost good will. But they seemed on the whole to me, to be a very poor people. They all go completely naked, even the women, though I saw but one girl. All whom I saw were young, not above thirty years of age, well made, with fine shapes and faces; their hair short, and coarse like that of a horse's tail, combed toward the forehead, except a small portion which they suffer to hang down behind, and never cut. Some paint themselves with black, which makes them appear like those of the Canaries, neither black nor white; others with white, others with red, and others with such colours as they can find. Some paint the face, and some the whole body; others only the eyes, and others the nose. Weapons they have none, nor are acquainted with them, for I showed them swords which they grasped by the blades, and cut themselves through ignorance. They have no iron, their javelins being without it, and nothing more than sticks, though some have fish-bones or other things at the ends. They are all of a good size and stature, and handsomely formed. I saw some with scars of wounds upon their bodies, and demanded by signs the cause of them; they answered me in the same way, that there came people from other islands in the neighbourhood who endeavoured to make prisoners of them, and they defended themselves. I thought then, and still believe, that these were from the continent. It appears to me, that the people are ingenious, and would be good servants; and I am of opinion that they would very readily become Christians, as they appear to have no religion. They very quickly learn such words as are spoken to them. If it please our Lord, I intend at my return

[15]

Chapter 1

First Encounters:

The Creation

of Cultural

Stereotypes

(1450–1650)

to carry home six of them to your Highnesses [Spain's monarchs, Ferdinand and Isabella] that they may learn our language. . . .

At daybreak great multitudes of men came to the shore, all young and of fine shapes, very handsome; their hair not curled but straight and coarse like horse-hair, and all with foreheads and heads much broader than any people I had hitherto seen; their eyes were large and very beautiful. . . .

They were straight-limbed without exception, and not with prominent bellies but handsomely shaped. They came to the ship in canoes, made of a single trunk of a tree, wrought in a wonderful manner considering the country; some of them large enough to contain forty or forty-five men, others of different sizes down to those fitted to hold but a single person. They rowed with an oar like a baker's peel,[10] and wonderfully swift. . . .

Seeing some of them with little bits of this metal hanging at their noses, I gathered from them by signs that by going southward or steering round the island in that direction, there would be found a king who possessed large vessels of gold, and in great quantities. I endeavoured to procure them to lead the way thither, but found they were unacquainted with the route. . . .

The natives are an inoffensive people, and so desirous to possess any thing they saw with us, that they kept swimming off to the ships with whatever they could find, and readily bartered for any article we saw fit to give them in return, even such as broken platters and fragments of glass. . . .

I do not . . . see the necessity of fortifying the place, as the people here are simple in war-like matters, as your Highnesses will see by those seven which I have ordered to be taken and carried to Spain in order to learn our language and return, unless your Highnesses should choose to have them all transported to Castile, or held captive in the island. I could conquer the whole of them with fifty men, and govern them as I pleased. . . .

Source 5 from The Letters of Amerigo Vespucci, *trans. Clements R. Markham (London: The Hakluyt Society, 1894), pp. 6–21.*

5. Amerigo Vespucci, 1497–1498

What we knew of their life and customs was that they all go naked, as well the men as the women, without covering anything, no otherwise than as they come out of their mothers' wombs. They are of medium stature, and very well proportioned. The colour of their skins inclines to red, like the skin of a lion, and I believe that, if they were properly clothed, they would be white like ourselves.

---

10. **baker's peel:** a long-handled shovellike tool used by bakers to move bread into and out of the oven.

They have no hair whatever on their bodies, but they have very long black hair, especially the women, which beautifies them. They have not very beautiful faces, because they have long eyelids, which make them look like Tartars. They do not allow any hairs to grow on their eyebrows, nor eyelashes, nor in any other part except on the head, where it is rough and dishevelled. They are very agile in their persons, both in walking and running, as well the men as the women; and think nothing of running a league or two, as we often witnessed; and in this they have a very great advantage over us Christians. They swim wonderfully well, and the women better than the men; for we have found and seen them many times two leagues at sea, without any help whatever in swimming.

Their arms are bows and arrows, well made, except that they have no iron, nor any other kind of hard metal. Instead of iron they use teeth of animals or of fish, or a bit of wood well burnt at the point. They are sure shots, and where they aim they hit. In some places the women use these bows. They have other weapons like lances, hardened by fire, and clubs with the knobs very well carved. They wage war among themselves with people who do not speak their language, carrying it on with great cruelty, giving no quarter, if not inflicting greater punishment. . . .

They have no leader, nor do they march in any order, no one being captain. The cause of their wars is not the desire of rule nor to extend the limits of their dominions, but owing to some ancient feud that has arisen among them in former times. When asked why they made war, they have no other answer than that it is to avenge the death of their ancestors and their fathers. They have neither king nor lord, nor do they obey anyone, but live in freedom. Having moved themselves to wage war, when the enemy have killed or captured any of them, the oldest relation arises and goes preaching through the streets and calling upon his countrymen to come with him to avenge the death of his relation, and thus he moves them by compassion. They do not bring men to justice, nor punish a criminal. Neither the mother nor the father chastise their children, and it is wonderful that we never saw a quarrel among them. They show themselves simple in their talk, and are very sharp and cunning in securing their ends. They speak little, and in a low voice. . . .

Their mode of life is very barbarous, for they have no regular time for their meals, but they eat at any time that they have the wish, as often at night as in the day—indeed, they eat at all hours. They take their food on the ground, without napkin or any other cloth, eating out of earthen pots which they make, or out of half calabashes.[11] They sleep in certain very large nets made of cotton, and suspended in the air. . . .

They are a people of cleanly habits as regards their bodies, and are constantly washing themselves. When they empty the stomach they do everything so as not to be seen, and in this they are clean and decent; but in making water they

---

11. **calabash:** a hand-shelled gourd.

Chapter 1

First Encounters:

The Creation

of Cultural

Stereotypes

(1450–1650)

are dirty and without shame, for while talking with us they do such things without turning round, and without any shame. They do not practise matrimony among them, each man taking as many women as he likes, and when he is tired of a woman he repudiates her without either injury to himself or shame to the woman, for in this matter the woman has the same liberty as the man. They are not very jealous, but lascivious beyond measure, the women much more so than the men. I do not further refer to their contrivances for satisfying their inordinate desires, so that I may not offend against modesty. They are very prolific in bearing children, and in their pregnancy they are not excused any work whatever. The parturition[12] is so easy, and accompanied by so little pain, that they are up and about the next day. They go to some river to wash, and presently are quite well, appearing on the water like fish. If they are angry with their husbands they easily cause abortion with certain poisonous herbs or roots, and destroy the child. Many infants perish in this way. . . .

They eat little flesh, unless it be human flesh, and your Magnificence must know that they are so inhuman as to transgress regarding this most bestial custom. For they eat all their enemies that they kill or take, as well females as males, with so much barbarity that it is a brutal thing to mention, how much more to see it, as has happened to me an infinite number of times. They were astonished at us when we told them that we did not eat our enemies. . . .

At a distance of three leagues from the beach we came to a village of few houses and many inhabitants, there not being more than nine habitations. Here we were received with so many barbarous ceremonies that the pen will not suffice to write them down. There were songs, dances, tears mingled with rejoicings, and plenty of food. We remained here for the night. Here they offered their wives to us, and we were unable to defend ourselves from them. We remained all night and half the next day. . . .

Next day we saw a great number of the people on shore, still with signs of war, sounding horns and various other instruments used by them for defiance, and all plumed and painted, so that it was a very strange thing to behold them. All the ships, therefore, consulted together, and it was concluded that these people desired hostility with us. It was then decided that we should do all in our power to make friends with them, and if they rejected our friendship we should treat them as enemies, and that we should make slaves of as many as we could take. Being armed as well as our means admitted, we returned to the shore. They did not oppose our landing, I believe from fear of the guns. Forty of our men landed in four detachments, each with a captain, and attacked them. After a long battle, many of them being killed, the rest were put to flight. We followed in pursuit until we came to a village, having taken nearly 250 prisoners. We burnt the village and returned to the ships with these 250 prisoners, leaving many killed and wounded. On our side no more than *one was killed, and twenty-two were wounded,* who all recovered. God be thanked! . . .

12. **parturition:** the act of childbirth.

Native American Account

Source 6 from Miguel Leon-Portilla, ed., The Broken Spears: The Aztec Account of the Conquest of Mexico, *trans. Lysander Kemp (Boston: Beacon Press, 1962), pp. viii–ix, 30, 92–93, 128–144.*

6. Native American Account of Cortés's Conquest, ca. 1530

The envoys made sacrifices in front of the Captain.[13] At this, he grew very angry. When they offered him blood in an "eagle dish," he shouted at the man who offered it and struck him with his sword. The envoys departed at once. . . .

When the sacrifice was finished, the messengers reported to the king. They told him how they had made the journey, and what they had seen, and what food the strangers ate. Motecuhzoma[14] was astonished and terrified by their report, and the description of the strangers' food astonished him above all else.

He was also terrified to learn how the cannon roared, how its noise resounded, how it caused one to faint and grow deaf. The messengers told him: "A thing like a ball of stone comes out of its entrails: it comes out shooting sparks and raining fire. The smoke that comes out with it has a pestilent odor, like that of rotten mud. This odor penetrates even to the brain and causes the greatest discomfort. If the cannon is aimed against a mountain, the mountain splits and cracks open. If it is aimed against a tree, it shatters the tree into splinters. This is a most unnatural sight, as if the tree had exploded from within."

The messengers also said: "Their trappings and arms are all made of iron. They dress in iron and wear iron casques on their heads. Their swords are iron; their bows are iron; their shields are iron; their spears are iron. Their deer[15] carry them on their backs wherever they wish to go. These deer, our lord, are as tall as the roof of a house.

"The strangers' bodies are completely covered, so that only their faces can be seen. Their skin is white, as if it were made of lime. They have yellow hair, though some of them have black. Their beards are long and yellow, and their moustaches are also yellow. Their hair is curly, with very fine strands.

"As for their food, it is like human food. It is large and white, and not heavy.[16] It is something like straw, but with the taste of a cornstalk, of the pith of a cornstalk. It is a little sweet, as if it were flavored with honey; it tastes of honey, it is sweet-tasting food.

13. **the Captain:** Cortés.
14. **Motecuhzoma:** Montezuma.
15. **deer:** horses.
16. **their food:** probably some form of pasta.

Chapter 1

First Encounters:

The Creation

of Cultural

Stereotypes

(1450–1650)

"Their dogs are enormous, with flat ears and long, dangling tongues. The color of their eyes is a burning yellow; their eyes flash fire and shoot off sparks. Their bellies are hollow, their flanks long and narrow. They are tireless and very powerful. They bound here and there, panting, with their tongues hanging out. And they are spotted like an ocelot."

When Motecuhzoma heard this report, he was filled with terror. It was as if his heart had fainted, as if it had shriveled. It was as if he were conquered by despair. . . .

Then the Captain marched to Tenochtitlan. He arrived here during the month called Bird, under the sign of the day 8-Wind. When he entered the city, we gave him chickens, eggs, corn, tortillas and drink. We also gave him firewood, and fodder for his deer. Some of these gifts were sent by the lord of Tenochtitlan, the rest by the lord of Tlatelolco.

Later the Captain marched back to the coast, leaving Don Pedro de Alvarado— The Sun—in command.

During this time, the people asked Motecuhzoma how they should celebrate their god's fiesta. He said: "Dress him in all his finery, in all his sacred ornaments." . . . They left their posts and went to dress him in his sacred finery: his ornaments and his paper clothing.

When this had been done, the celebrants began to sing their songs. That is how they celebrated the first day of the fiesta. On the second day they began to sing again, but without warning they were all put to death. . . . They [the Spanish soldiers] ran in among the dancers, forcing their way to the place where the drums were played. They attacked the man who was drumming and cut off his arms. Then they cut off his head, and it rolled across the floor.

They attacked the celebrants, stabbing them, spearing them, striking them with their swords. They attacked some of them from behind, and these fell instantly to the ground with their entrails hanging out. Others they beheaded: they cut off their heads, or split their heads to pieces.

They struck others in the shoulders, and their arms were torn from their bodies. They wounded some in the thigh and some in the calf. They slashed others in the abdomen, and their entrails all spilled to the ground. Some attempted to run away, but their intestines dragged as they ran; they seemed to tangle their feet in their own entrails. No matter how they tried to save themselves, they could find no escape. . . .

The Sun treacherously murdered our people on the twentieth day after the Captain left for the coast. We allowed the Captain to return to the city in peace. But on the following day we attacked him with all our might, and that was the beginning of the war. . . .

JAPAN

European Accounts

Sources 7 through 12 from Michael Cooper, ed., They Came to Japan: An Anthology of European Reports on Japan, 1543–1640 *(Berkeley: University of California Press, 1965), pp. 39–41; p. 45; p. 46; p. 47; pp. 64–65; pp. 256–257.*

7. Bernardino de Avila Girón,
1590s

The women are white and usually of goodly appearance; many, indeed, are extremely comely and graceful. All the married women have their teeth stained black with the bark of a tree; maidens and widows do not stain their teeth in this way. None of them has fair hair or blue eyes, nor do they esteem such features. The women use neither perfume nor oil on their faces, neither do they use those filthy things which the women of our country are wont to employ. For indeed there are women who possess more bottles, phials and jugs of cosmetics than any apothecary, yet for all that do not have a better complexion than the Japanese woman who merely washes her face with water from any pond. But it is true that as a mark of honour married women are accustomed to putting on a little powder dissolved in water (although it is not really necessary) and a touch of colour on their lips to hide the dye which comes off on their lips when they stain their teeth. These days worldly women and those married to Chinese whiten their faces exceedingly.

They are of excellent character and as pious as their menfolk are cruel; they are very polite and have less defects than any other persons I have met. The most infamous woman of all Japan will, at the very worst, be immodest; and for the most part this happens when they are widows and very rich, or when they have been weakened by poverty since childhood, or when their father, either because he was poor or because he was a knave, sold them, or when they allowed themselves to be abused, as happens amongst us at every hour. The worst possible woman is the one who drinks, but this happens only amongst the lowest women. Withal the women drink very little, although their menfolk are like Frenchmen. Once the women are married, they may be trusted completely for they are the most upright and faithful women in the whole world. And she who errs in this matter pays for it with her head.

8. Cosme de Torres,
1550s–1560s

These Japanese are better disposed to embrace our holy Faith than any other people in the world. They are as prudent as could be desired and are governed by reason just as much as, or even more than, Spaniards; they are more inquisitive than any other people I have met. No men in the wide world more like to hear

Chapter 1

First Encounters:

The Creation

of Cultural

Stereotypes

(1450–1650)

sermons on how to serve their Creator and save their souls. Their conversation is so polite that they all seem to have been brought up in the palaces of great nobles; in fact, the compliments they pay each other are beyond description. They grumble but little about their neighbours and envy nobody. They do not gamble; just as theft is punished by death, so also gambling. As a pastime they practise with their weapons, at which they are extremely adept, or write couplets, just as the Romans composed poetry, and most of the gentry occupy themselves in this way. They are very brave and put much faith in their weapons; boys over the age of thirteen carry a sword and dagger, and never take them off. They have every kind of weapon, both offensive and defensive, and some are of great value; you may even find swords worth 1,500 *cruzados*. They do not have any kind of guns because they declare that they are for cowards alone. They are the best archers I have seen in this world. They look down on all other nations. . . .

9. Francis Xavier, 1549–1551

The Japanese have a high opinion of themselves because they think that no other nation can compare with them as regards weapons and valour, and so they look down on all foreigners. They greatly prize and value their arms, and prefer to have good weapons, decorated with gold and silver, more than anything else in the world. They carry a sword and dagger both inside and outside the house and lay them at their pillows when they sleep. Never in my life have I met people who rely so much on their arms. They are excellent archers and fight on foot, although there are horses in the country. They are very courteous to each other, but they do not show this courtesy to foreigners, whom they despise. They spend all their money on dress, weapons and servants, and do not possess any treasure. They are very warlike and are always involved in wars, and thus the ablest man becomes the greatest lord. They have but one king, although they have not obeyed him for more than 150 years, and for this reason these internal wars continue.

10. Joao Rodrigues, ca. 1620

[The Japanese] are so crafty in their hearts that nobody can understand them. Whence it is said that they have three hearts: a false one in their mouths for all the world to see, another within their breasts only for their friends, and the third in the depths of their hearts, reserved for themselves alone and never manifested to anybody. As a result all order decays here for everyone acts merely according to the present moment and speaks according to the circumstances and occasion. But they do not use this double dealing to cheat people in business matters, as do the Chinese in their transactions and thieving, for in this respect the Japanese are most exact; but they reserve their treachery for affairs of diplomacy and war in order not to be deceived themselves. And in particular when they wish to kill a person by treachery (a strategem often employed to avoid many deaths), they put on a great pretence by entertaining him with every sign of love and joy—and then in the middle of it all, off comes his head.

11. Alessandro Valignano, ca. 1583

[The] first bad quality [of the Japanese] is that they are much addicted to sensual vices and sins, a thing which has always been true of pagans. The men do not pay much attention to what their wives do in this respect because they trust them exceedingly, but both husbands and relatives may kill an adulterous wife and her partner at will. But even worse is their great dissipation in the sin that does not bear mentioning. This is regarded so lightly that both the boys and the men who consort with them brag and talk about it openly without trying to cover the matter up. This is because the bonzes[17] teach that not only is it not a sin but that it is even something quite natural and virtuous and as such the bonzes to a certain extent reserve this practice for themselves. They are forbidden under grave penalties by ancient laws and customs to have the use of women and so they find a remedy for their disorderly appetites by preaching this pernicious doctrine to the blind pagans. They are certainly past masters in this teaching and so they are worse and more openly involved in it than other people. But their great influence over the people, coupled with the customs handed down by their forefathers, completely blinds the Japanese, who consequently do not realise how abominable and wicked is this sin, as reason itself plainly shows. . . .

They also have rites and ceremonies so different from those of all the other nations that it seems they deliberately try to be unlike any other people. The things which they do in this respect are beyond imagining and it may truly be said that Japan is a world the reverse of Europe; everything is so different and opposite that they are like us in practically nothing. So great is the difference in their food, clothing, honours, ceremonies, language, management of the household, in their way of negotiating, sitting, building, curing the wounded and sick, teaching and bringing up children, and in everything else, that it can be neither described nor understood. . . .

12. Lourenço Mexia, 1590s

Although [the Japanese] make use of pitch, neither going up nor down, their natural and artificial music is so dissonant and harsh to our ears that it is quite a trial to listen to it for a quarter of an hour; but to please the Japanese we are obliged to listen to it for many hours. They themselves like it so much that they do not think there is anything to equal it in the wide world, and although our music is melodious, it is regarded by them with repugnance. They put on many

17. **bonze:** a Mahayana Buddhist monk.

Chapter 1

First Encounters:

The Creation

of Cultural

Stereotypes

(1450–1650)

plays and dramas about various wholesome and joyful things during their festivals, but they are always accompanied by this music.

Japanese Accounts

Sources 13 and 14 from George Elison, Deus Destroyed: The Image of Christianity in Early Modern Japan *(Cambridge: Harvard University Press, 1973), pp. 321–324; 377–378.*

13. Anonymous, *Kirishitan monogatari*, 1639

In the reign of Mikado Go-Nara no In, the hundred and eighth Emperor since the days of Jimmu, some time about the Kōji Period, a Southern Barbarian trading vessel came to our shores. From this ship for the first time emerged an unnamable creature, somewhat similar in shape to a human being, but looking rather more like a long-nosed goblin or the giant demon Mikoshi Nyūdō. Upon close interrogation it was discovered that this was a being called Bateren.

The length of his nose was the first thing which attracted attention: it was like a conch shell (though without its surface warts) attached by suction to his face. His eyes were as large as spectacles, and their insides were yellow. His head was small. On his hands and feet he had long claws. His height exceeded seven feet, and he was black all over; only his nose was red. His teeth were longer than the teeth of a horse. His hair was mouse-grey in color, and over his brow was a shaved spot in the outline of a winebowl turned over. What he said could not be understood at all: his voice was like the screech of an owl. One and all rushed to see him, crowding all the roads in total lack of restraint. And all were agreed that this apparition was even more dreadful than the fiercest of goblins could ever be. His name was Urugan Bateren. Though at heart he planned to spread the Kirishitan [Christian] religion, he seemed intent first to survey the wisdom of the Japanese people. He brought with him all sort and manner of curious things from South Barbary.

In the Province of Tsu there lived at that time Takayama Lord Hida and his son Ukon Daibu. They extended reverence to this Bateren and became followers of his religion. Introducing him to the likes of Miyoshi Shūri no Daibu and Matsunaga Sōtai, they enabled him to remain in Japan. . . .

14. Suzuki Shosan, 1642

According to the Kirishitan teachings, the Great Buddha named Deus is the Lord of Heaven and Earth and is the One Buddha, self-sufficient in all things. He is the Creator of Heaven and Earth and of the myriad phenomena. This Buddha made his entry into the world one thousand six hundred years ago in South Barbary, saving all sentient beings. His name is Jesus Christus. That other lands do not know him, worshipping instead the worthless Amida and Shaka, is the depth of stupidity. Thus they claim, as I have heard.

To counter, I reply: If Deus is the Lord of Heaven and Earth, and if he created the terrestrial domain and the myriad phenomena, then why has this Deus until now left abandoned a boundless number of countries without making an appearance? Ever since heaven and earth were opened up, the Buddhas of the Three Worlds in alternating appearance have endeavored to save all sentient beings, for how many thousands and tens of thousands of years! But meanwhile, in the end Deus has not appeared in countries other than South Barbary; and what proof is there that he did make an appearance of late, in South Barbary alone? If Deus were truly the Lord of Heaven and Earth, then it has been great inattention on his part to permit mere attendant Buddhas to take over country upon country which he personally created, and allow them to spread their Law and endeavor to save all sentient beings, from the opening up of heaven and earth down to the present day. In truth, this Deus is a foolscap Buddha!

And then there is the story that Jesus Christus upon making his appearance was suspended upon a cross by unenlightened fools of this lower world. Is one to call this the Lord of Heaven and Earth? Is anything more bereft of reason? This Kirishitan sect will not recognize the existence of the One Buddha of Original Illumination and Thusness. They have falsely misappropriated one Buddha to venerate, and have come to this country to spread perniciousness and deviltry. They shall not escape Heaven's punishment for this offence! But many are the unenlightened who fail to see through their clumsy claims, who revere their teachings and even cast away their lives for them. Is this not a disgrace upon our country? Notorious even in foreign lands, lamentable indeed!

Source 15 from David J. Lu, Japan: A Documentary History *(Armonk, N.Y.: M. E. Sharpe, 1997), p. 221.*

15. Tokugawa Iemitsu, Edict of 1635 Ordering Closing of Japan

1. Japanese ships are strictly forbidden to leave for foreign countries.

2. No Japanese is permitted to go abroad. If there is anyone who attempts to do so secretly, he must be executed. The ship so involved must be impounded and its owner arrested, and the matter must be reported to the higher authority.

3. If any Japanese returns from overseas after residing there, he must be put to death.

4. If there is any place where the teachings of padres[18] is practiced, the two of you must order a thorough investigation.

18. **padres:** fathers, or Roman Catholic priests.

Chapter 1

First Encounters:

The Creation

of Cultural

Stereotypes

(1450–1650)

5. Any informer revealing the whereabouts of the followers of padres must be rewarded accordingly. If anyone reveals the whereabouts of a high ranking padre, he must be given one hundred pieces of silver. For those of lower ranks, depending on the deed, the reward must be set accordingly.

6. If a foreign ship has an objection [to the measures adopted] and it becomes necessary to report the matter to Edo,[19] you may ask the Ōmura[20] domain to provide ships to guard the foreign ship. . . .

7. If there are any Southern Barbarians[21] who propagate the teachings of padres, or otherwise commit crimes, they may be incarcerated in the prison. . . .

8. All incoming ships must be carefully searched for the followers of padres. . . .

19. **Edo:** Tokyo.
20. **Ōmura:** the area around Nagasaki.
21. **Southern Barbarians:** Europeans.

QUESTIONS TO CONSIDER

Now that you have read each account, paying special attention to the five items listed in the Method section of this chapter, you are ready to draw some inferences and conclusions from the evidence.

To begin, review each account and think of some adjectives (beautiful, ugly, honest, dishonest, and the like) that people reading the account at the time might have used to describe or characterize the people who are portrayed. List these adjectives for each account, arranging them according to the categories mentioned earlier: physical appearance, nature or character, traditions and practices, overall impressions, and advice on dealings. After you have done this for each account, use the adjectives to shape a collective image of the people being described. Do the same for the combined European accounts of Africans (or Native Americans or Japanese), and vice versa. Remember to be willing to "read between the lines."

The non-European accounts will require considerably more inference and guesswork on your part. In part this is because three of the five non-European accounts (Sources 3, 6, and 15) were not written specifically to describe Europeans (Source 6 does this somewhat). Only the anonymous *Kirishitan monogatari* (Source 13) and Shosan's attack on Christianity (Source 14) can be said to have been intended to discuss Europeans. Even so, close examination and analysis of all of these sources, as well as a good deal of historical imagination, will reap surprisingly good results. Again, think of adjectives.

EPILOGUE

In his introduction to an anthology of European accounts of Japan written between 1543 and 1640, historian Michael Cooper observes, "The Europeans had generally adopted the role of representatives of a superior race. . . . They had taken for granted that Europe was synonymous with the civilized world."[22] By viewing themselves as a superior people and consequently placing a badge of inferiority on every non-European they encountered, most Europeans could justify the sometimes shameful ways in which they dealt with non-European peoples. In Africa, the warring West African states offered Europeans slaves for the guns they were desperate to own. By 1730, approximately 180,000 guns annually were being brought to West Africa by European traders, a figure that increased to over 300,000 before 1800. In exchange, slave ships carried off an estimated 7.3 million people between 1600 and 1810, an average between 1700 and 1810 of approximately 54,500 per year. The destinations for most slaves were Brazil (which first instituted the plantation system in its most complete form), the sugar islands of the West Indies, and the British colonies of North America.

Yet Europeans generally avoided massive intrusion into West Africa until the late nineteenth century. Ironically, what gave Africans this respite was their native diseases. Would-be European colonizers fell prey to diseases like malaria, which had a 75 percent mortality rate at first contact among nonimmune people. Not until the late 1800s, when medical advances gave them protection, could Europeans penetrate Africa to swallow up that continent. Having failed to use the respite for unification and preparation, the African states, still in disarray, fell quickly if violently.

The same factor that gave West Africans some breathing room against European incursion nearly wiped out Native Americans: disease. Millions of Native Americans succumbed to the numerous diseases that Europeans unwittingly brought with them, especially smallpox and measles. Whole villages were wiped out, whole nations decimated, as (in the words of one Roman Catholic priest who traveled with Cortés) "they died in heaps." When the superiority of European military technology and the Native Americans' inability to unite against the invaders are added to the equation, their terrible vulnerability to European conquest is easy to understand.

Those Native Americans not subdued by disease, European force of arms, or lack of unity often undercut their own positions. As Native Americans came to desire the products of European mills and factories, they increasingly engaged in wholesale hunting and trapping of animals bearing the skins and furs prized in Europe, exchanging pelts for manufactured goods. Before the arrival of Europeans, Native Americans saw themselves as part of a complete ecosystem that could sustain all life as long as it was kept in

---

22. Michael Cooper, ed., *They Came to Japan* (Berkeley: University of California Press, 1965), pp. xi–xii.

Chapter 1

First Encounters:

The Creation

of Cultural

Stereotypes

(1450–1650)

balance. In contrast, Europeans saw the environment as a collection of commodities to be extracted and exploited, a perception that Native Americans who coveted European goods were forced to adopt. Thus not only did Native Americans lose their economic and cultural independence, but they also nearly annihilated certain animal species that had sustained them until then. Just as warring West African states became dependent on European firearms and traded human beings in order to secure them, many Native Americans bartered their ecosystem for ironware, weapons, and whiskey.

Japan's expulsion of most Europeans and European ideas (including Christianity) in 1635 and 1639 may have saved Japan from the fates that befell Africans and Native Americans. In 1720, when those prohibitions finally were relaxed, Japan was ready to embark on the ambitious task of economic modernization while at the same time attempting to preserve what they saw as a culture vastly superior to that of the European "barbarians." In 1854, the opening through which trade and ideas passed grew wider. By the late nineteenth century, Japan was the great economic power of Asia, a position it has continued to hold.

As the earth's peoples gradually began to encounter one another, they set in motion a biological "event" that would change many of their lives forever. This process involved the transplantation, sometimes accidentally, of various plants (sugar cane, rice, wheat, bananas, and so forth), animals (horses, pigs, cattle, sheep, cats), and diseases (smallpox, syphilis, and, in our own

time, AIDS). Indeed, almost five centuries later, that phenomenon is a universal fact of life. An Asian variety of gypsy moth is chewing its way through the forests of the Pacific Northwest. The zebra mussel, released by accident into the Great Lakes in ballast water from Eastern European ships, has spread into Illinois, Mississippi, Ohio, and Tennessee. In the Great Smoky Mountains of North Carolina and Tennessee, wild boars (imported from Germany for sportsmen in the nineteenth century) threaten the plants, grasses, and small animals of the region. A recent survey in Olympia National Park has identified 169 species of plants and animals not indigenous to the Western Hemisphere. In the southern United States, the kudzu vine (imported from Japan to combat erosion) was dubbed by the *Los Angeles Times* (July 21, 1992) "the national plant of Dixie" and is almost out of control in some areas. Whether purposeful or accidental, whether beneficial or detrimental, the environmental exchange continues.

Most of the Europeans who first encountered other peoples were celebrated as heroes in their native lands. Jesuit missionary to Japan Francis Xavier was elevated to sainthood in the Roman Catholic Church. Bartolomeu Dias and Vasco da Gama were honored in Portugal, as were Columbus, Cortés, and a host of conquistadors in Spain. Yet for some, fame was fleeting. Cortés returned to Spain in 1528 a fabulously wealthy man but over time lost most of his fortune in ill-fated expeditions and died in modest circumstances in 1547. In his will, he recognized the four children he had fathered by Native

American women (Cortés was married at the time) and worried about the morality of what he had done. In 1562, his body was taken to Mexico to be reburied. In 1794, his remains were moved again, this time to the chapel of a Mexican hospital that he had endowed. In 1823, Cortés's remains disappeared for good, perhaps hidden to protect them from politically motivated grave robbers after Mexico declared its independence from Spain. (Rumors abound that the remains were secretly carried back across the Atlantic.) The ultimate, invincible conquistador has vanished, but his legacy lives on.

CHAPTER TWO

VILLAGES IN AN ERA OF

CENTRALIZING STATES

(1450–1650)

Political history is often told as the story of military conquests and the growth, consolidation, and fall of large-scale political units such as empires, kingdoms, and nations. According to these accounts, the era around 1500 was a time of significant developments in many parts of the world. In England, the years 1455 to 1471 saw bitter conflict between competing claimants to the throne—the Wars of the Roses— and then unification under a new dynasty, the Tudors. In the Andes, the people who came to be known as the Incas first slowly and then more quickly expanded their authority over other peoples, creating by the end of the fifteenth century the largest empire ever built in South America. In Japan, the period between 1467 and 1568— known as the age of the Warring States (*Sengoku*)—was one of nearly constant warfare between local military leaders,

followed by a period of regional consolidation and ultimately the establishment of peace after 1590 under a series of military leaders, including Toyotomi Hideyoshi and Tokugawa Ieyasu.

All large-scale governments—what political historians usually refer to as "states"—depend on extracting revenues from their populations that enable them to carry out their aims, whether these are conquest, further centralization, or simply the maintenance of power. This may take the form of monetary taxation, as it does in most of the modern world, or of taxes paid in the form of goods and services, as it did in most of the pre-modern world. Governments may also require and demand labor services for a variety of purposes, of which military conscription has been the longest lasting. States can collect these taxes and obligations directly, as the United States government does today through the Internal Revenue Service, or they can depend on intermediaries. In England and Japan, these intermediary authorities were often members of the hereditary aristocracy who also had jurisdiction over certain aspects of life and collected their own taxes and payments. In the Andes, the Incas relied on both leaders of the conquered people and officials sent out from their capital at Cuzco to enforce their demands for payments. Better exploitation of surpluses from largely agricultural populations was a major part of political developments in all three of these areas in the period around 1500.

Central and regional governments and members of the nobility were not the only political authorities that had an impact on people's lives in this era, however. In many parts of the world, including England, the Andes, and Japan, most people lived in villages, supporting themselves and providing the required taxes and payments by growing agricultural products of various types. In many places these villages developed political structures of their own, institutions of self-governance that regulated what went on and conducted relations with national or regional authorities. These institutions changed over time depending on a variety of factors; the impositions of authorities beyond the village was one of these,

but new agricultural techniques, epidemic diseases, climate change, and cultural developments such as the introduction of new belief systems also influenced village self-government and political life. As historians have studied village life more closely over the last thirty years as part of their growing interest in the lives of ordinary people, they have discovered that although villages are often portrayed as passive and timeless, they can be quite dynamic. Thus, to be comprehensive, political history must include not only the story of large-scale governments, but also that of local structures of power.

Your task in this chapter is to use sources from three widely divergent areas, England, the Andes, and Japan, to explore some of the ways in which villages and states interacted and the ways different levels of political authority sought to shape people's actions in the period from 1450 to 1650. How did the state seek to control villages and their resources? How did villages respond to these efforts and themselves seek to regulate the lives of their inhabitants? What similarities and differences can you see across these three cultures, and how might the life of villagers in them have been different or similar as a result?

BACKGROUND

Scholars of village life often spend their entire career exploring a single village in great depth, investigating family relationships, land ownership and settlement patterns, legal developments,

and other issues. They point out that every village is distinct, and that there are often great differences between villages that are quite close together. Some of them might be horrified at the type of analysis and comparison we are doing in this chapter, but their intensive local research is what has allowed us to gain the knowledge we have of individual villages, and makes such comparisons possible. In order to understand village–state interactions in these three areas, we must rely first on the work of local historians to learn something about the organization of villages in each area, then on the work of political historians to learn about the larger political structures within which these villages were enmeshed.

In England, most of the villages were nucleated; that is, the houses were clumped together, with the fields stretching beyond this compact center. In many parts of England, the fields of the village were farmed in what is termed open-field agriculture, a pattern that differs sharply from modern farming practices. In open-field agriculture, the village as a whole—or actually the adult male heads of household— decided what crops would be planted in each field, rotating the crops according to tradition and need. Some fields would be planted in crops such as wheat and rye for human consumption, some would be planted in oats or other crops for both animals and humans, and some would be left unworked, or fallow, to allow the soil to rejuvenate. Most families were also allowed to run some animals, such as pigs, cattle, and sheep, in the woods or meadows outside the cultivated fields.

The open-field system and many other local issues were largely handled by the village itself, but much of the economic and political life of the village fell under the jurisdiction of lords, members of the nobility or gentry who might live in a large house in the village but often lived elsewhere. The territory controlled by a lord, generally termed a *manor,* might consist of one village, a number of villages, or even only part of a village. Within each manor, the lord established the duties each villager owed, which generally included labor obligations and payments of taxes in cash or goods such as wheat or animals. Lords generally appointed officials termed *bailiffs* or *reeves* from outside the village to oversee the legal and business operations of their manors, and additional officials were chosen by the village residents themselves from among the adult men to supervise the harvest, watch over the use of the mill, or perform similar tasks.

Several times a year in most English villages, the villagers, or at least some of them, gathered for court proceedings during which the legal and financial affairs of both the lord and the village were dealt with; these courts handled matters such as land transfers or inheritance disputes. The courts often went beyond what we would recognize as judicial activities and issued new ordinances—which historians now term *by-laws*—in the name of the lord and the village to regulate activities in the village or its fields and forests. In the thirteenth century, manorial courts began keeping formal records written on pieces of parchment that were stitched end to end and then rolled up; they were generally made while the court was in session, not written up afterward. Such court rolls are the most important type of documents surviving for exploring English villages during this period.

Along with laws passed by the manorial courts, England had national laws and ordinances that were issued by the king, sometimes in conjunction with Parliament. These were generally sent out as written documents to the sheriffs in every county, who would then be the main agents of enforcement. So that people could know the law, the sheriff would often order it to be read out loud at places where people gathered, such as marketplaces and churches. Once a national law became known, those who broke it could be tried at higher-level courts, or at manorial courts if the amount set as the fine for breaking the law was not too great. Protests against national and manorial laws generally took the form of evasion rather than outright disobedience, although opposition to a royal poll tax levied in 1378 to pay for war with France led to a nationwide rebellion in 1381.

In the Andes, the main staple crops were various types of potatoes in highland areas and maize in more low-lying areas. Villagers often built terraces, separated by stone retaining walls, on the steeper slopes to plant their crops, and irrigation channels and ditches to bring water to the fields. At the time of the Inca conquest, families in most Andean cultures were organized into *ayllus,* groups of related kin that cooperated in farming and ritual activities. Each ayllu was located in a specific territory and organized the agricultural work for that area, such as clearing fields, planting and harvesting crops, and building irrigation channels, but the boundaries between the areas were not always clearly delineated. The ayllus were economically independent, but most villages

were actually made up of more than one ayllu. Land was owned by the ayllu, not by individuals, with parallel lines of descent; women achieved access to resources such as land, water, and herds through their mothers, and men through their fathers.

Along with the ayllus, several other forms of social organization were important in Andean culture. One of these was a division of society into two parts, termed *moieties,* which were related to other categories that were regarded as binary, such as light and dark or right and left. The moiety system divided society into an upper moiety called the *hanansaya* and a lower moiety called the *hurinsaya;* within each village, ayllus were grouped into one of these two moieties, with the larger and more prominent ayllus having a higher rank within that moiety. The two moieties together made up a whole, with both of them viewed as necessary for social stability, but the hanansaya were also regarded as superior to the hurinsaya, and the leader of the hanansaya in any village was viewed as the village's leader. After the Inca conquest, this division between upper and lower also came to be associated with the Incas and those they had conquered, with the Incas and those who had dealings with them being regarded as having more social prestige than others. Luis Capoche, a Spanish official, described this social division in 1585 in this way: "And the *hanansaya,* which means the group from above, held the first rank of nobility and they rallied as military people to the calls for war made by the Inca; and the *hurinsaya* are understood to be the people from below and the class of the common and simple people, who carried the provisions and necessities of the warriors."[1]

The word *Inca* originally meant a single person, the Inca king, who picked his successor from among his sons. Though most Incas were monogamous, the king had many wives and children, and his ayllu could be very large; on his death, that group continued to live off his wealth, and the new king formed a new ayllu. By the 1530s, the time of European conquest, there were eleven royal ayllus, corresponding to the first eleven kings. Each of them had to extract a surplus from villagers somewhere in order to provide food and other necessary goods; this system may have been one of the reasons for the Inca wars of conquest.

The Inca system for collecting taxes was quite different from that in England. Instead of paying in a combination of goods, cash, and labor, conquered peoples within the Inca empire paid their tribute solely in labor. The food produced on conquered land was divided into three parts, with one part supporting the Inca bureaucracy, one part the religious personnel of the Inca empire, and the third the people who actually worked the land. (These parts were not always equal, and appear to have been adjusted if Inca officials decided that a family or ayllu did not have enough land to feed itself.) Along with this agricultural labor, all heads of household were also required to send a person (or them-

selves) to work a certain number of days per year at other tasks, including road building and military service. This labor tax, called the *m'ita*, was rotated among households throughout the year, with some labor required of each household every year.

The Incas did not develop a system of writing before the arrival of the Spanish, but Inca officials recorded statistical information, including tax data, on *quipus*, which were collections of knotted cords of various colors and lengths, all suspended from one thicker cord. The ability to read quipus has been lost; however, early Spanish officials sometimes recorded the words of people who were reading these quipus and a few native or mixed-race individuals wrote chronicles based in part on quipus, so that the information they contained has not been completely lost. These records were, of course, written in Spanish or Latin, not Quecha (the language of the Incas), and there were certainly some misunderstandings, but they are still very valuable. They were also generally written from the perspective of the conquering Incas rather than that of other Andean peoples; for other peoples' perspectives, we must rely on archaeological evidence.

In Japan, the major crop was rice, grown either on dry fields or on flooded, enclosed paddies, which produced significantly more than the dry fields. Villages were different in size and structure, but in the fourteenth and fifteenth centuries many of them, especially those near the capital of Kyoto, formed themselves into semi-autonomous communities (*so*) made up of one or more villages, with economic, social, religious, and political

1. Luis Capoche, "Relación general de la villa imperial de Potosí..." [1585], translated and quoted in Brian S. Bauer, *The Development of the Inca State* (Austin: University of Texas Press, 1992), p. 126.

functions. The so developed means of handling disputes among villagers, issued and enforced ordinances, owned some property in common, controlled irrigation and common lands collectively, and assumed collective responsibility for tax payments. The so as a whole decided how much each family farmed and paid in taxes, and redistributed land if it seemed that certain families were not able to support themselves. So signed agreements with authorities beyond the village and often existed as permanent institutions for centuries. Disputes with higher authorities were often expressed in the form of collectively written petitions of grievances or litigation, and sometimes led to revolt.

During the Warring States period, the central government of the shogun was very weak, and the main agents of political authority were the *daimyo*, local military leaders who began to develop into territorial rulers in control of all aspects of life. Daimyo sometimes granted land to military retainers, who administered their own holdings somewhat independently, handling legal issues and collecting taxes. The daimyo and their retainers relied on shares of the rice and soybean harvest along with payments of cloth for their income, so they encouraged more intensified farming; greater yields would also make more rice or other grains available for sale at local markets, whose transactions also yielded revenue to them. By 1550 many of the more powerful daimyo sought to restrict the independent authority of their military retainers while still keeping them loyal, and to assess land values and land holdings more accurately in

order to maximize both rice production and the resultant income. Thus, as in England, village–state interactions really involved three actors—the ruling daimyo, lower-level military retainers, and the villagers acting through their communal so—each of which could work with one of the others against the third. In some cases, villages also joined together in leagues (*ikki*) to defend their interests against the actions of overlords.

During the sixteenth century, a series of powerful military leaders began to create a national political structure based on a coalition of daimyo, from whom they demanded strict obedience. As part of his efforts at centralization, one of these generals, Toyotomi Hideyoshi (r. 1590–1598), created models for tax collection and encouraged surveys of all land that would classify land according to its level of productivity. These surveys were supposed to encourage peasant landownership and create uniformity in landholding, but in many areas drastic reorganization never occurred. In addition, Hideyoshi did not undermine the importance of the so in villages that were organized in this way, but instead used the so to ensure order at the local level. Hideyoshi's successor, Tokugawa Ieyasu, also allowed so to continue issuing ordinances, handling disputes, and carrying out religious observances, though his government also appointed new types of officials on lands he directly controlled to represent the village and oversee tax collection and household registration. These centralizing rulers (Tokugawa Ieyasu took on the old title of *shogun*, a title that had earlier been given to the supreme military commander over all Japan) thus became a fourth force in village–state interactions. Scholars have paid great attention to the daimyo and to centralizing rulers, and there are many sources that represent their point of view. Individual so maintained records regarding laws and administration that stretch over many centuries as well, however, and through these

we can have some insight into the villagers' own view of their situation. These records are generally made from paper made of the bark of mulberry trees, stitched together into book form. Access to them is still sometimes controlled by village officials or the families of former village leaders, with the collections including thousands or even tens of thousands of documents.

THE METHOD

As with many other aspects of life in the early modern world, we have much more information about the way village–state interactions were *supposed* to be than about the way they were. Many of our sources are clearly prescriptive, such as laws and ordinances issued by the villages themselves or by higher governmental authorities. Others are idealizations; they may look like descriptions of reality, but they are strongly influenced by the opinions of the author about proper political relations. Historians have sometimes been misled into thinking that such sources describe the actual operations of political authority, which has led them to overemphasize the power of large-scale governments. The first two questions for this chapter have been posed carefully to avoid such misunderstandings, for they ask you to examine ways in which states *sought* to control villages and ways in which villages *sought* to respond to these measures and to control their own residents. These questions can be answered using both prescriptive and idealizing sources, and your

method in interpreting the written sources for this chapter should be one of careful reading and analysis. As you read each source, note the actions and the aims of the village structures of power and those of the higher-level state authorities; making a list of these would be very helpful. The first two questions require you to put together information from the sources for each culture, and the third question asks you to compare the three cultures and make some inferences based on these comparisons. You will thus need to develop your answers to the first two questions before moving on to the third.

Along with written evidence, the chapter includes a visual source from each of the three cultures that portrays some aspect of the enforcement of political power. We may think of visual depictions as descriptive, as portraying an actual scene; this is sometimes true, but they may just as often be intended to describe an ideal or to make a point that the artist wished to stress. This does not limit our use of them in this chapter, but, as with law codes, we must be careful not to assume that they are simply representations of reality.

Sources 1 through 4 come from England. Source 1 is a series of by-laws from the village of Great Horwood in central England, which you should read carefully. What types of activities did these laws seek to prohibit? What punishments were set for those who broke these regulations? Who is described as issuing these laws? In which situations do the villagers enforce their own laws, and in which is the lord involved? Source 2 is the record of a manorial court held in the village of Teynton in central England in 1541; it is the only document in this chapter that describes the actual operations of a court and the enforcement of laws. What types of taxes and fees do the villagers pay to the king? How else does he exert his authority? What by-laws do villagers appear to have broken, and how are these infractions punished? Source 3 is a Statute of the Realm, issued by Henry VIII in 1511, which to a great degree repeats a statute issued by Edward III in 1363 during the Hundred Years' War. What does Henry order villagers to do? What does he forbid them to do? What justifications does he give for these measures? How is this law to be enforced? Source 4 is an illumination from the Smithfield Decretals, a manuscript from a slightly earlier period that depicts many scenes of English life, especially in its small marginal paintings. This one shows the king dispatching a messenger. How does the artist convey the speed of the messenger? In what form is the message he takes?

Sources 5 through 8 come from the Andes. Source 5 is from the report of a Spanish inspector dating from 1549; the area concerned, the Huallaga Valley, had put up strong resistance to Spanish rule and had been conquered only in 1542. Spanish authorities wished to know about the obligations imposed by the Incas on the Chupaychu, the main ethnic group in this area, whom the Incas deemed to have consisted of 4000 households. The record was written in Spanish by a European scribe, based on an Andean's reading of a quipu. According to this report, what types of labor had the villagers been required to do? If all of these labor obligations were actually met (which we have no way of knowing), how many villagers were engaged in labor for the Incas, and how many in basic food production or care of animals? Sources 6 and 7 are chronicles written in Spanish that also describe the taxation system of the Incas. Source 6 is from the chronicles of Pedro de Cieza de León (1520–1554), a Spanish soldier and writer who compiled a history of Peru during his seventeen years there. Source 7 is from the chronicles of Garcilosa de la Vega (1539–1616), the son of a Spanish conquistador and an Inca princess, who grew up in Peru but left there as a young man and spent the rest of his life in Spain. Both of these authors are generally favorable to the Incas, viewing them as benign conquerors, which may have influenced their reporting on Inca demands. According to these authors, what types of labor are required of the villagers? How are the laws requiring tribute enforced? Who was liable to pay labor tribute? How do these authors assess the level of labor service required? How does their assessment fit with the information recorded in Source 5?

Source 8 is from another chronicle, this one by the Andean noble author Felipe Guaman Poma de Ayala; his very long chronicle, written between 1584 and 1615 and addressed to the Spanish king, includes hundreds of illustrations that have been an important source for many aspects of Peruvian life, including gender relations and agricultural techniques. In this illustration, an Inca official labeled "governor of the royal roads" is talking with a runner, whom Guaman Poma describes as having "the speed of sparrow-hawks." Along the road are special huts, which the Incas built every mile or so; runners carried oral messages and perhaps quipus to the runner in the next hut, a system that allowed news to travel about 150 miles a day. In the written sources, you have already read about demands for labor tribute for road building, and roads were an essential part of the Inca empire. How would these runners further enhance the strength of the empire? Why might the Inca have selected "the most nimble" from their subject peoples and trained them for this task, rather than training their own young men as runners?

Sources 9 through 13 are from Japan. Source 9 is a series of regulations from several *so* in the region around Kyoto. What actions on the part of villagers are required? What is prohibited? Who is responsible for enforcing these regulations? Source 10 is an extract from a petition from a group of villagers to their overlord. What are they requesting? What obligations do they wish to have lessened, and what reasons do they give? Source 11 includes two decrees, the first dating from 1587 and the second from the following year, from

two different sides in the battle for centralized state power. The first decree comes from Hojo Ujimasa, one of the last major opponents of Hideyoshi, who was being pressed militarily, and the second from Hideyoshi himself. What does each of them order? What does each set for punishments if the order is not followed? How does Hojo Ujimasa justify the need for military conscription? How does Hideyoshi justify the need to *prevent* villagers from having weapons? What are they to do instead of fighting? (Hideyoshi's method was ultimately more successful, and the conscripted army of Hojo Ujimasa was no match for Hideyoshi's professional army, though commoners were involved in battles into the seventeenth century.)

Source 12 is a series of regulations for villagers, issued by the shogunate in 1643. What are villagers prohibited from doing? Why are certain crops and foods to be encouraged and others prohibited? Source 13 is a detail from one of the screens painted by Kusumi Morikage (ca. 1620–1690), one of the few Japanese artists from this period who depicts rural life in a sympathetic manner. In this scene, people are engaged in agricultural activities and a tax collector is visiting the village. Which of the *so*'s own regulations and of those imposed by the shogunate are being followed? What else do you notice about rural life in this painting?

You have now developed three lists of some of the ways in which state authorities impinged on villagers' lives and, for England and Japan, some of the ways in which villagers responded and regulated themselves. (No records comparable to English by-laws or Japanese *so* regulations exist for the Andes, though scholars are now using archaeological evidence to discover many details about village life. Large-scale agriculture and irrigation projects indicate that villages and ayllus certainly imposed some type of regulations, passed down through oral tradition and perhaps recorded on quipus.) These lists will provide you with numerous examples with which to answer the first two questions in the chapter. Before starting your comparisons in answer to the third question, we recommend turning to the Questions to Consider section, which offers some suggestions for lines of comparison.

THE EVIDENCE

Source 1 from Warren O. Ault, Open-Field Farming in Medieval England: A Study of Village By-Laws *(London: George Allen and Unwin, 1972), pp. 125, 132, 134, 136, 138, 141.*

1. Village By-laws from Great Horwood

1433

Plebiscite. It is ordered by all the tenants that no one shall have his beasts on the green of the town by night until the end of autumn next to come under pain each one of 4d.[2] And there were chosen as wardens John Hayes and Robert Baynard.

Plebiscite. And that every tenant be at Nether forde next Monday about Vespers with tools to clean the watercourse under pain of 1d. for default and John Baynard of Nether Ende is chosen warden.

1465

It is ordered by the consent of all the tenants there that no one henceforth shall wilfully allow his foals openly to go into the fields of grain after they are three weeks old unless tethered to their mothers under pain of each one doing the contrary paying 12d. namely for each foal every time.

1480

The township of Great Horwood is ordered to make anew part of the butts[3] this side the Feast of the Nativity of St John the Baptist[4] under pain for each one in default of 8d., 4d. of which to the parish church there pay 4d.

2. **d.** = denarius, or penny; 12 pennies made a shilling, abbreviated s.
3. **butt:** a mound of earth on which a target is set.
4. **Feast of St. John the Baptist:** June 24.

And if any one shoots with arrows at the metes[5] and does not close the bars after him he shall forfeit to the lord as often as he does it 4d.

1503

It is ordered by common consent and assent that all tenants having hedges on the eastern part of the town aforesaid shall cause them well and sufficiently to be repaired, namely from Colles Lane to the eastern end of the aforesaid town leading toward Little Horwood, under pain for each of them failing in default of 12d.

And under the aforesaid pain that each of them who puts his cattle on their land adjacent to their closes next to sown land shall keep them safely and securely under guard.

And that henceforth each of them who has land next to his close shall plough it and bring it into cultivation under the aforesaid pain.

1516

It is ordained that all the tenants and inhabitants shall tether their foals and mares in the sown fields and not allow them to go at large in the grain of the tenants under pain for each delinquent of 40d.

And that none of the inhabitants shall cut or carry furze[6] from the common called the Priourswode except by order of the bailiff under pain each delinquent of 20d.

And that no one shall take fish in the common fishing stream called 'le brok' flowing within the aforesaid town unless it be on his own ground under pain for each delinquent of 40d.

1531

It is ordered that they shall not allow their beasts to go at large before the end of autumn under pain of 40d.

It is ordered that no tenant by copy of court [roll] shall have several . . . subtenants in one house without the lord's leave, under pain of 40s.

It is ordained that no one shall pasture any beast except oxen in the wheat field before the Feast of Pentecost[7] under pain of 40d.

1534

It is ordered that no one shall harbour or entertain any woman or women of ill fame more than one night under pain for each delinquent, of 6s. 8d.

5. **mete:** boundary.

6. **furze:** a spiny evergreen shrub.

7. **Feast of Pentecost:** The seventh Sunday after Easter; in 1531, this was May 28.

[40]

Source 2 from Nathaniel J. Hone, The Manor and Manorial Records *(Port Washington, N.Y.: Kennikat Press, 1971), pp. 177–178.*

2. Court Roll of Teynton, 1541

Court of the manor of the lord King held there 13th Dec. 32 Hen. viij.

Essoins[8]—none.

The homage[9] there to wit Robert Frebury, William Burchall, Robert Baker, William Bedell, Thomas Mychell, Ralph Tayllor, Robert Stokes, John Agas, Thomas Frebury, Robert Shelffocke, William Ansley, Clement Michell, Thomas Hill, and John Hychene, being sworn and charged by the Steward present, upon their oath that the lands and tenements[10] [of the] late George Lord Cobham's remain in the hands of the lord King by reason of an exchange for other lands.

And that Robert Lambard, John Edwards, Robert Payne, John Ward, and Robert Stokes are free tenants and owe suit of Court and have appeared.

And that Laurence Pemerton, who held of the lord King according to the custom of the manor, three messuages[11] whereof one is called Hornes Barne another Stayarhows and a third late in the tenure of William Welles, and before him of Richard Michell, and three virgates[12] of land by a rent for the whole per ann. is dead since the last court; whereupon there falls to the lord of heriot[13] for the two messuages one young ox and a cow valued both at 18[d] delivered to Ralph Norwood esq. the King's farmer there, and for the third messuage no heriot as yet. And let there be an inquiry thereof before the next court, because the homage present the said messuage is not heriotable. And the first proclamation is made. And no one comes.

To this court comes Robert Lamberd, son and heir of Thomas Lamberd, deceased, and does fealty to the lord for a messuage and virgate of land with appurtenance late of Thomas his father, and gives for relief 6[s] 8[d].

And Robert Tayllor, since the last court, has cut down an elm, to wit a timber tree worth 6[d], without licence of any of the lord King's officers; but the said Robert used the same tree for repair of his tenement; therefore let him have a talk thereupon with the King's officer before next court.

And the aforesaid Laurence Pemerton, in his life time, substituted Walter Milleward as his subtenant in the said messuage called the Stayarhows, contrary to the custom of the manor, without licence; therefore let him have a talk thereon with the King's officer before the next court.

---

8. **essoins:** people's excuses for not appearing in court, brought in by others.
9. **homage:** free male residents of the town required to swear an oath to their lord.
10. **tenement:** building.
11. **messuage:** land surrounding a house.
12. **virgate:** roughly 25 to 30 acres of land.
13. **heriot:** fee due to the lord on the death of a tenant, usually the best animal owned by the family.

And that William Bedell, Robert Baker, John Agas, Thomas Frebury, Robert Stokes, and Clement Michell have forfeited to the lord King each of them 40^d because they have not repaired the defects of their tenements before the feast of All Saints last past as they had in precept at the last Court. But they are bound till the next court, because no one was assigned to deliver them timber for the said repairs.

And Robert Huchyns, the miller there, has not restored his encroachment of the land by the mill, as he had in precept at the last Court, under pain of forfeiture to the lord King 40^d but said pain in respite till next Court, upon view thereof to be had.

It is ordained that no keeper shall place his penning sheep on the wheat field after the feast of St Martin in future, under pain for each offence of forfeiture to the King 6^s 8^d.

Sum of Court 24s 8d.

Source 3 from Statutes of the Realm, 3rd. Henry VIII, c. 3, p. 25. *Spelling and orthography modernized.*

3. Statute of Henry VIII Regarding the Shooting of Longbows, 1511

The King our sovereign lord, calling to his most noble and gracious remembrance, that by the feat and exercise of the subjects of this his realm in shooting of longbows there hath continually grown and been within the same great number and multitude of good archers which hath not only defended this realm and the subjects thereof against the cruel malice and danger of their outward enemies in time heretofore passed . . . and albeit that diverse good and profitable statutes in the time of his noble progenitors and predecessors kings of this land for the maintenance of archery and longbows heretofore have been made, amongst which the right famous king of noble memory Henry VII, father to our said sovereign lord by authority of diverse parliaments caused good and noble acts and statutes to be established and made . . . yet nevertheless archery and shooting in longbows is right little used but daily diminishes, decays, and abates more and more. . . . And also by means and occasion of customable usage of tennis-play, bowles [lawn-bowling], classhe [skittles], and other unlawful games, prohibited by many good and beneficial estates by authority of parliament in that behalf provided and made, great impoverishment hath ensued. And many heinous murders, robberies, and felonies be committed and done. And also the divine [service] by such misdoers on holy and festival days not heard or solemnized to the high displeasure of the Almighty God.

Wherefor the King . . . hath ordained, enacted, and established that the Statute of Winchester for archers be put in due execution. And moreover that every man being the King's subject not lame, decrepit, or maimed, nor having any other lawful or reasonable cause or impediment, being within 60 years, (except those men, spiritual men, justices of one bench or of the other, justices of the assize and barons of the exchequer) do use and exercise shooting in longbows, and also to have a bow and arrows ready continually in his house to use himself, and do use himself in shooting. And also that the father, governors, and rulers of such as be of tender age do teach and bring upon them the knowledge of the same shooting. And that every man having a man child or men children in his house shall provide, ordain, and have in his house for every man child being of the age of seven years and above till he shall come to the age of seventeen years, a bow and two shafts to induce and learn them and bring them up in shooting and shall deliver all the same bow and arrows to the same young men to use and occupy. And if the same young men be servants that then their masters shall abate the money that they shall pay for the same bows and arrows of their wages. And after all such young men shall come to the age of seventeen years every of them shall provide and have a bow and four arrows continually for himself at his proper costs and charges, or else of the gift and provision of his friends, and use and occupy the same in shooting as is afore rehearsed. . . . And every person that shall be found by inquiry or examination in default or not providing and having bows, arrows, and shafts ready by the space of one month shall forfeit and pay for every such default 12d. . . .

And that all statutes heretofore made against them that use unlawful games be duly put in execution, and punishment had according to the penalties of the same, as well against the offenders and occupiers of such unlawful games as against them that be owners or keepers of houses or other places where any such unlawful games be used. . . . And furthermore that all justices of the peace, bailiffs, sheriffs, constables, and all other head officers, and every of them finding or knowing any mans person or persons using or exercising any unlawful games contrary to the said estate, shall have full power and authority to commit every such offender to ward [jail], there to remain without bail to such time he or they so offending be bound by obligation to the king's use in such sum of money as by the discretion of the said justices, mayors, bailiffs, or other head officers shall be thought reasonable that they nor any of them shall not from thence forth use any unlawful games. And that every bower [bow-maker] within this realm always make for every bow of ewe that he maketh to sell at least two bows of elm or other wood of mean [moderate] price.

Source 4: British Library, Royal MS 10. E. IV, fo. 302V.

4. King and Messenger, from the Smithfield Decretals, ca. 1340

Source 5 from John V. Murra, "The Mit'a Obligations of Ethnic Groups to the Inka State," in The Inca and Aztec States 1400–1800: Anthropology and History, *ed. George A. Collier, Renato Rosaldo, and John D. Wirth (New York: Academic Press, 1982), pp. 240–243.*

5. Report from the General Inspection of the Chupaychu, 1549

[Cord 1] They were asked what services did [the Chupaychu] give to the Inca in Cuzco *a la continua*[14]

and they said that 400 Indian men and women remained in Cuzco *a la continua* to build walls and if one died they gave another.

[Cord 2] They also gave 400 Indians to plant the fields in Cuzco so people could eat

[Cord 3] They also gave 150 Indians *a la continua* as *yana*[15] of Guayna Capac.[16]

[Cord 4] 150 more to guard the body of Topa Ynga Yupanqui[17] after he died, *a la continua*

[Cord 5] 10 *yana* more to guard his weapons

[Cord 6] 200 Indians more to guard the Chachapoya[18]

[Cord 7] 200 Indians more to guard Quito[19]

[Cord 8] 20 Indians more for the guard of the body of Guana Cava[20] after his death

[Cord 9] 120 Indians more to make feathers

[Cord 10] 60 more to extract honey

[Cord 11] 400 Indians to weave fine cloth

[Cord 12] 40 Indians to make more dyes and colors

[Cord 13] 240 Indians to guard the sheep [camelids]

[Cord 14] 40 Indians to guard the fields which they had throughout this valley; the maize grown was mostly taken to Cuzco and the rest to the warehouses [at Huanuco Pampa].

[Cord 15] 40 additional Indians to plant hot peppers which were taken to Cuzco

[Cord 16] and they also gave 60 Indians and sometimes 45 to make salt

14. *a la continua:* full time.
15. *yana:* personal attendant to the nobility.
16. **Guayna (or Huayna) Capac:** the Inca king who ruled from 1493 to 1527.
17. **Topa Ynga Yupanqui:** the Inca king who ruled from 1471 to 1493.
18. **Chachapoya:** a region of the Inca empire on the edge of the jungle, now northeastern Peru.
19. **Quito:** a city in the Andes, now in Ecuador.
20. **Guana Cava:** Guayna Capac.

[Cord 17] 60 Indians to make [raise] the coca leaf which they took to Cuzco and to the warehouses of Huanuco [Pampa] and sometimes they hauled 200 sacks and at others 40

[Cord 18] 40 Indians to accompany the Inca in person to hunt deer

[Cord 19] and 40 Indians more to make soles and they took them to Cuzco and to the storehouses

[Cord 20] 40 more carpenters [woodworkers] to make plates and bowls and other things for the Inca and they took them to Cuzco

[Cord 21] 40 more potters to make pots and they took them to Huanuco [Pampa]

[Cord 22] and 68 more Indians to guard the *tampu*[21] at Huanuco

[Cord 23] 80 more to carry loads from the *tampu* to Pumpu [some five to six days' march] and from Sutun Cancha to Tambo [one day's, coming back]

[Cord 24] 40 more Indians to guard the women of the Inca

[Cord 25] 500 to go with the person of the Inca to war, to carry him to hammocks, and they went to Quito and to other places

[Cord 26] 500 more Indians, to plant and [do] other things without leaving their territory

Source 6 from Pedro de Ciez de León, The Incas, *trans. Harriet de Onis (Norman: University of Oklahoma Press, 1959), pp. 161, 163–165.*

6. Pedro de Cieza de León, *Crónicas*, 1553

As in the previous chapter I described the way in which the Incas carried out their conquests, in this it would be well to tell how the different nations were taxed, and how the returns of this taxation were handled in Cuzco. For as is well known to all, not a single village of the highlands or the plains failed to pay the tribute levied on it by those who were in charge of these matters. There were even provinces where, when the natives alleged that they were unable to pay their tribute, the Inca ordered that each inhabitant should be obliged to turn in every four months a large quill full of live lice, which was the Inca's way of teaching and accustoming them to pay tribute. We know that for a time they paid their tax in lice until, after they had been given flocks and had raised them, and made clothing, they were able to pay tribute henceforth.

On these visits of the envoys of the Incas to the provinces, as soon as they arrived they could tell from the quipus the number of people, men and women,

21. *tampu:* a small way station along the Inca highways; this one is located two days' walk west of the Huallaga Valley where the Chupaychu live.

old folks and children, and gold or silver miners, and they ordered that so many thousand Indians be put to work in the mines, to dig the amount of those metals that had been set to be turned over to the inspectors assigned for that purpose. And as during the time the Indians appointed to work the mines were doing this they could not cultivate their fields, the Incas ordered those from other provinces to come and plant the crops at the proper season in lieu of tribute, so that they [the fields] would not lie fallow. If the province was a large one, it furnished Indians both to mine the metals and to sow and work the land. If one of the Indians working in the mines got sick, he was allowed to return home at once, and another came to take his place; but none was assigned to the mines unless he was married so that his wives could look after his food and drink, and, aside from this, it was seen to it that they were supplied with food in abundance. With this way of doing things, none of them considered it hard work even if they spent their whole life in the mines, and none of them died from overwork. Besides, they were permitted to stop work several days in the month for their feasts and recreation; and the same Indians were not continuously in the mines, but every so often they were sent away and others came in their place.

So well had the Incas organized this that the amount of gold and silver mined throughout the kingdom was so great that there must have been years when they took out over fifty thousand arrobas[22] of silver, and over fifteen thousand of gold, and all this metal was for their use. These metals were brought to the capital of each province, and the same system of mining and delivering them prevailed throughout the kingdom. If in certain regions there were no metals to be mined, so that all should contribute their share, they set tribute of small things, and of women and children who left their villages without any sorrow, for if a man had only one son or daughter, they did not take the child, but if he had three or four, they took one in payment of his service.

Other regions paid as many thousand loads of corn as there were houses in it, which was done at every harvest, and was credited to the province. In other areas they similarly supplied as many loads of *chuño*[23] as the others of corn, and others *quinoa*,[24] and others tubers. Some places gave as many blankets as there were married Indians in it, and others as many shirts as there were people. Others were obliged to supply so many thousand loads of lances, and others, slings and *ayllos;*[25] and the other arms they use. Certain provinces were ordered to contribute so many thousand Indians to go to Cuzco to work on the public

22. **arroba:** a measure of weight, about 25 pounds.
23. *chuño:* freeze-dried potatoes.
24. *quinoa:* a grain grown at mid-altitude.
25. *ayllo:* a sling with stones attached used to entangle the feet of warriors or animals. Now called a *bola,* it is still used in Argentina.

buildings of the city and those of the Incas, supplying them with the necessary food. Others contributed cables to haul stones; others, coca. In this way all the provinces and regions of Peru, from the smallest to the most important, paid tribute to the Incas, and all this was accomplished in such orderly fashion that neither did the natives fail to pay what they owed and were assessed, nor did those who collected these tributes venture to take one grain of corn in excess. And all the food and articles necessary for making war which were contributed were expended on the soldiers or the regular garrisons that were established in different parts of the kingdom for its defense. When there was no war, most of this was eaten and consumed by the poor, for when the Incas were in Cuzco they had their *hatun-conas*, which is the name for a bondsman, and in such number that they sufficed to work their lands and care for their houses and sow the necessary food supplies, aside from that which was always brought for their table from the different regions, many lambs and fowls and fish, and corn, coca, tubers, and all the fruits they raise. And there was such order in these tributes which the natives paid and the Incas were so powerful that they never had a war break out again.

To know how and in what way the tributes were paid and the other taxes collected, each *huata*, which is the word for year, they sent out certain *Orejones* as supervisory magistrates, for they had no authority beyond visiting the provinces and notifying the inhabitants that if any of them had a complaint, he should state it, so that the one who had done him a wrong could be punished. And when the complaints were heard, if there were any, or it was learned that somewhere a debt was pending, they returned to Cuzco, from which another set out with authority to punish the culprits. In addition to this, there was another important provision, which was that from time to time the headmen of the provinces appeared on the day appointed for each nation to speak to bring to the knowledge of the Inca the state of the province and the shortage or abundance that existed in it, and whether the tribute was too large or too small, and whether they could pay it or not. After which they were sent away satisfied, for the Inca rulers were certain they were not lying but telling the truth. For if there was any attempt at deceit, stern punishment followed and the tribute was increased. Of the women given by the provinces, some of them were brought to Cuzco to become the possession of the Lord-Incas, and some of them were sent to the temple of the sun.[26]

26. Girls were selected from conquered peoples to be Chosen Women (*acllyas*), and were dedicated to the Sun or other gods, or married to the Inca king or other prominent men.

Source 7 from Garcilosa de la Vega, Royal Commentaries of the Incas and General History of Peru, *trans. Harold V. Livermore, vol. 1 (Austin: University of Texas Press, 1966), pp. 272–274.*

7. Extract from Garcilosa de la Vega

Coming to the subject of the tribute levied and collected by the Inca kings of Peru from their vassals, this was so moderate that when one realizes what it consisted of and how much it was, it can truthfully be affirmed that none of the kings of the ancients, nor the great Caesars who were called Augustus and Pius can be compared with the Inca kings in this respect. For properly speaking it seems that they did not receive taxes and tributes from their subjects, but rather that they paid their subjects or merely imposed taxes for their benefit, such was their liberality toward their vassals. Considered in relation to the general circumstances of those times, the daily pay of laborers, and the value of commodities, and the expenses of the Incas, the tribute was so small in quantity that many Indians barely paid the value of four reals of the current time. Although there could not fail to be some inconvenience attached to the payment of the tribute or the service of the king or the *curacas*,[27] it was borne cheerfully and contentedly owing to the smallness of the tribute, the perquisites the Indians received, and the numerous advantages that arose from the performance of the tasks. The rights of the tribute payer and the laws in his favor were inviolably preserved so that neither the judges nor the governors, nor the captain generals, nor the Inca himself could pervert them to the disadvantage of the vassals. They were as follows: the first and most important was that no one who was exempt from tribute could be obliged to pay it at any time or for any reason. All those of royal blood were exempt, as were all captain generals and other captains, even the centurions and their children and grandchildren, and all the *curacas* and their kinsmen. Royal officials who were commoners and held minor posts were exempted from paying tribute during their term of office, as were soldiers on active service and youths of under twenty-five since they were required to serve their parents until that age. Old men of fifty and upwards were exempt from tribute, and so were all women, whether married or maidens, spinsters or widows. The sick were exempt until they were completely recovered, and all the disabled, such as the blind, lame, limbless, and others who were deprived of the use of their limbs, though the deaf and dumb were allotted tasks for which they did not need to hear or speak.

The second law was that all the rest apart from these were obliged to pay tribute unless they were priests or officials in the temples of the Sun or of the chosen virgins. The third law was that no Indian was ever obliged for any reason to pay anything instead of tribute, but only to pay in labor, with his skill or

---

27. **curaca:** an official with jurisdiction over a certain number of households.

with the time he devoted to the service of the king and the state. To this extent rich and poor were equal, for none paid more or less than others. The word rich was applied to anyone who had children or family to help him in his work and so to finish his share of the tributary labor sooner: anyone who had no children or family, though he might be well off in other respects, was accounted poor. The fourth law was that no one could compel anyone to perform or undertake any craft but his own, unless it was the tilling of the soil or military service, two duties to which all were liable in general. The fifth law was that each should pay his tribute in whatever goods were found in his own province, without being forced to go abroad in search of things that did not occur where he lived: it seemed to the Inca a great injustice to ask his subjects to deliver fruits their own earth did not produce. The sixth law required that each of the craftsmen who worked in the service of the Inca or his chiefs should be supplied with everything necessary for his work: thus the smith was given gold, silver, or copper, the weaver wool or cotton, the painter colors, and all the other requirements of their respective callings. Each craftsman was therefore only obliged to supply his labor and the time needed for the work, which was two months, or at most three. This done, he was not obliged to work any more. However, if there was any work left unfinished, and he wished to go on working of his own free will and see it through, what he did was discounted from the tribute he owed for the following year, and the amount was so recorded by means of their knots and beads. The seventh law required that all craftsmen of whatever occupation should be supplied if they fell ill with all they required for food, clothes, comforts, and medicine, instead of having to pay tribute: if the Indian concerned was working alone, he alone was helped, but if he had brought his wife and children so as to finish the work sooner, they too were fed.

In the allocation of such tasks, the question of time was not taken into consideration, but only the completion of the job. Thus if a man could take advantage of the help of his family and friends to complete two months' work in a week, he was regarded as having fully satisfied his obligation for the year, and no other tribute could be pressed upon him. This alone is sufficient to refute the contention of those who say that formerly tribute was paid by sons, daughters, and mothers, whoever they were. This is false, for although these all worked, it was not because the obligation to pay tribute was imposed upon them, but because they helped their fathers, husbands, or masters: if the man did not wish his dependents to share in his work, but preferred to work alone, his wife and children remained free to busy themselves about the house, and the judges and decurions were unable to bring any compulsion to bear on them, as long as they were not idle. It was for this reason that in the days of the Incas those who had many children and large families were accounted rich: those who had not were often taken ill owing to the length of time they had to devote to their work until their tribute was settled. In order to remedy this there was a law that those who were rich by reason of their families and the rest who had finished their tasks should help them for a day or two. This was agreeable to all the Indians.

Source 8 from Guaman Poma de Ayala, El Primer Nueva Corónica y Buen Gobierno *(Caracas: Ayacucho, 1980). Photo: Det Kongelige Bibliotek.*

8. Illustration from Guaman Poma de Ayala, *El Primer Nueva Corónica y Buen Gobierno*

Source 9 from Hitomi Tonomura, Community and Commerce in Late Medieval Japan: The
Corporate Villages of Tokuchin-ho (Stanford: Stanford University Press), pp. 199, 203, and
206; and David John Lu, Sources of Japanese History, Vol. I (New York: McGraw-Hill, 1973),
p. 157.

9. *So* Regulations

1448

1. Those who do not come to the meeting after two beats of the drum shall
be fined 50 *mon*.[28]

2. A penalty of 500 *mon* shall be imposed for cutting down forest trees and
seedlings.

3. A penalty of 100 *mon* shall be imposed for taking firewood [or leaves] and
mulberry leaves.

1489

Regulations commonly agreed to by the people of the village of Imahori, dated
first year of Entoku . . . , eleventh month, 4th day.

1. Anyone who receives his right to residence from the *sō* (village self-
governing association) will not be permitted to board anyone from outside of
this village.

2. No one from other villages will be permitted to reside in this village, unless
someone from this village serves as his guarantor.

3. If there is any boundary dispute between privately-owned land and land
owned by the *sō*, the matter must be settled with the payment of money.

4. No one will be permitted to keep dogs.

5. From the common fund of the *sō*, an amount of one *kan* will be paid each
year for the performance of *sarugaku*[29] to be held on the sixth day of the second
month.

6. Anyone who sells his house must pay to the *sō* three *mon* out of one hundred *mon,* and thirty *mon* out of one *kan* realized from the sale. Anyone who dis-
obeys this rule shall be expelled from the *za* (in this instance, *za* signifies a
worshipper's group of the village shrine).

7. Anyone who conceals the amount of the sale price of his house shall be
punished.

8. No house shall be built to the east of the moat.

28. **mon:** a unit of money; 1000 *mon* equaled one *kan*.

29. **sarugaku:** a form of popular theatrical entertainment.

1583

1. Those listed on the register shall have the right to discuss [matters concerning the survey].

2. Do not cover other people's land. Once the owner is agreed upon, do not make different claims.

3. Should there be troublesome people among the landholding peasants [*hyakushō*], dissociate from them as the regulations stipulate.

[Signed] Imabori *sōchū*

1626

Items stipulated:

1. For harvesting grass in someone else's paddy, 1 *koku*[30] of rice shall be charged as a penalty.

2. Breaking off branches and leaves by hand shall also invoke a penalty of 1 *koku*.

3. Breaking off branches and leaves in the *sō* forest will invoke the same penalty. Anyone violating these rules shall be driven out [of the village] by the *sō*.
    Thus commanded.

[Signed] *sōchū*

Source 10 from David J. Lu, Japan: A Documentary History *(Armonk, N.Y.: M. E. Sharpe, 1997), pp. 162–163.*

10. From Joint Petition by Villagers, 1407

We beg your indulgence in the following matters:

1. We request that the rice offered to the temple which is earmarked for festivals be distributed to the farmers. . . .

3. We wish to report that the flood damage has resulted in a reduction of eight *koku* and four *to*[31] in rice production, and there is an additional damage of three *koku* and one *to* of rice.

4. On account of poor crops or abandonment of land, you previously ordered us to pay one half of the rent due from Nishidai (part of Oyama *shō*),[32] which amounts to twenty-four *koku*, eight *to* and three *shō*. However, cultivators of

---

30. *koku:* a unit of dry measure for grain, about five bushels.

31. *to* **and** *sho:* units of dry measure for grain; 100 *sho* = 1 *to*, 100 *to* = 1 *koku*.

32. **Oyama** *shō:* the estate (*shō*) on which these villagers lived.

these fields come from other distant *shō,* and we cannot force them to work. Therefore, this year please count this as a complete loss. . . .

8. After having paid our annual rent, we wish to report that those farmers who absconded have now returned.

9. The illegal acts of the deputy (*daikan*) were the root cause of the absconding of the farmers in the way they did, after exhausting all available means [to fight against such illegal acts]. Relying on the help you are granting us, they have returned. However, if the deputy continues to occupy his position, then their return will be in vain. We venture to speak out in this manner, because the sinful and illegal deeds of the deputy are many. If [a new] deputy can be dispatched from the temple, it will benefit the farmers greatly. We have heard that the *ryōshu*[33] of Ōyama *shō* is consulting with the *shugo*[34] to summon the farmers [for additional duties]. We are very much surprised. This makes us to have no other recourse but to think of [moving to] other provinces.

May we submit our humble thoughts?

With trepidation, respectfully

Farmers from Kazuidani

To the Chief of the Administrative Department (*bugyōshu*) [of Tōji].

Source 11 from David J. Lu, Japan: A Documentary History *(Armonk, N.Y.: M. E. Sharpe, 1997), p. 186.*

11. Decrees Regarding Military Service of Villagers

DECREE OF HŌJŌ UJIMASA, 1587

1. All men, without distinction as to being of the samurai class or of common people, in this county (*gō*) are ordered to come and register for the service of this province in an emergency. Of these, eight [are to be drafted].

2. They are to bring with them any of the following three weapons: an arrow, spear, or gun. However, a spear, whether its shaft is made of bamboo or wood, is useless if it is shorter than two *ken* [about twelve feet]. Even if one claims to be an official of the higher authorities, and does not follow the above injunctions, he must still be treated the same as merchants or petty artisans. The registration applies to all men from fifteen to seventy years of age.

3. Those who respond to the call must prepare their daggers and military emblems in such a way as to make them look like worthy warriors.

33. ***ryoshu:*** lord of the estate.
34. ***shugo:*** military governor of a province or several provinces.

4. If an able-bodied man is deliberately left behind, he and the one who has ordered him to remain will be beheaded immediately by the Minor Deputy (*shō-daikan*) of the county upon hearing of it.

5. Anyone who abides by the provisions of this circular diligently, whether he be of the samurai class or of common men, can expect to receive rewards.

The above provisions describe the need in time of emergency. Everyone is directed to complete preparation of their implements of war by the end of the eighth month. The names of those who register must be submitted by a responsible party by the twentieth day of the next month. The above provisions must be widely circulated within the county.

Fifteenth year of Tenshō [1587], last day of the seventh month.
To the Minor Deputy and People of the Iwase Village.

DECREE OF TOYOTOMI HIDEYOSHI, 1588

(a) The Edict:

1. The farmers of all provinces are strictly forbidden to have in their possession any swords, short swords, bows, spears, firearms or other types of weapons. If unnecessary implements of war are kept, the collection of annual rent (*nengu*) may become more difficult, and without provocation uprisings can be fomented. Therefore those who perpetrate improper acts against samurai who receive a grant of land (*kyūnin*) must be brought to trial and punished. However, in that event, their wet and dry fields will remain unattended, and the samurai will lose their rights (*chigyō*) to the yields from the fields. Therefore, the heads of provinces, samurai who receive a grant of land, and deputies must collect all the weapons described above and submit them to Hideyoshi's government.

2. The swords and short swords collected in the above manner will not be wasted. They will be used as nails and bolts in the construction of the Great Image of Buddha. In this way, the farmers will benefit not only in this life but also in the lives to come.

3. If farmers possess only agricultural implements and devote themselves exclusively to cultivating the fields, they and their descendants will prosper. This compassionate concern for the well-being of the farmers is the reason for the issuance of this edict, and such a concern is the foundation for the peace and security of the country and the joy and happiness of all the people. In China, in olden days, the sage ruler Yao pacified the country and converted precious swords and sharp knives into agricultural implements. But there is no precedent for such an act in this country. Thus, all the people must abide by the provisions of this edict and understand its intent, and farmers must work diligently in agriculture and sericulture.[35]

35. **sericulture:** the raising of mulberry trees as food for silkworms.

All the implements cited above shall be collected and submitted forthwith.

Vermilion seal of Hideyoshi

Sixteenth year of Tenshō [1588], seventh month, 8th day.

Source 12 from David J. Lu, Japan: A Documentary History *(Armonk, N.Y.: M. E. Sharpe, 1997), pp. 213–215.*

12. Regulations for Villagers Issued by the Tokugawa Shogunate, 1643

1. Hereafter, both the village headman (*shōya*) and higher village officials (*sōbyakushō*) may not build houses which are not consistent with their stations in life. However, town houses (*machiya*) may be built under the direction of the fief holder (*jitō*) or magistrate (*daikan*).

2. Concerning farmer's clothing, in accordance with the previous *bakufu*[36] edict, the village headman and his family may wear silk, pongee, linen, and cotton; lower village officials (*wakibyakushō*) may wear only linen or cotton. Other materials may not be used to make the neckband (*eri*) or waist sash (*obi*).

3. Neither the village headman nor the higher village officials may dye their clothing purple or crimson. Other colors may be used to dye clothing for wear but no design is permitted.

4. Farmers must be told that their normal meals must consist of grains other than rice and wheat. Rice especially must not be consumed indiscriminately.

5. In villages, hot noodles, thin noodles, buckwheat noodles, bean-jam buns, bean curds and the like may not be traded. This is to prevent wasteful use of the five grains.

6. *Sake* (rice wine) must not be brewed in villages. Nor can it be bought from elsewhere to be sold locally.

7. Do not go to market towns to drink freely.

8. Farmers must be told that they must take good care of their wet and dry fields, and weed them attentively and conscientiously. If there are insolent farmers who are negligent, the matter will be investigated and the offenders duly punished.

9. If a single farmer is unmistakably overburdened, and cannot carry on his share of farm work, not only his five-man group (*goningumi*)[37] but also the entire village must [in the spirit of] mutual help, assist in his rice planting, and otherwise enable him to pay his annual taxes (*nengu*).

---

36. *bakufu:* shogunate.

37. *goningumi* **or five-man group:** neighborhood groups that higher authorities sought to establish, responsible for mutual surveillance of each other and paying taxes.

10. From this year on, planting of tobacco on either old fields or new fields is strictly forbidden, because its cultivation wastes the lands that can be used to grow the five grains.

11. The village elders (*nanushi*) and higher village officials, both men and women are forbidden to use any kind of conveyance.[38]

12. Farmers must be told that no shelter can be given in the district to anyone who comes from another village and does not cultivate the fields, and is not reliable. If any farmer gives shelter to such a person, the gravity of his offense is to be investigated, and he becomes subject to arrest and imprisonment.

13. Wet and dry fields may not be sold in perpetuity.

14. Farmers may not, on account of disputes involving annual taxes and other matters, desert their places and take refuge with those who have absconded. Anyone who violates this, after an investigation may be considered as committing a culpable offense.

15. If the *jitō*[39] or *daikan*[40] administers the area so poorly that the farmers find it impossible to endure it any longer, they may first pay up all the annual taxes, and leave the village. They may even establish their residence in a neighboring county. If there is no tax overdue, the *jitō* or *daikan* cannot punish them with banishment (*kamae*).

16. Even in the matters of Buddhist ceremonies and religious festivals, overindulgence beyond one's own status must be avoided.

17. Within the city limits of Edo, no one is to ride on top of a horse loaded with wood, hay, goods in straw sacks and the like.

The above articles must be made known to all the villages, to secure immediate observance of their intent. Care must be taken continuously to conform to these injunctions.

Twentieth year of Kanei [1643], third month, 11th day.

---

38. **conveyance:** here, a sedan chair or other item carried or pulled by people.

39. *jito:* vassal of the shogun or a *daimyo* who had the right to collect his own taxes.

40. *daikan:* an official in charge of collecting taxes for a *daimyo* or the shogun.

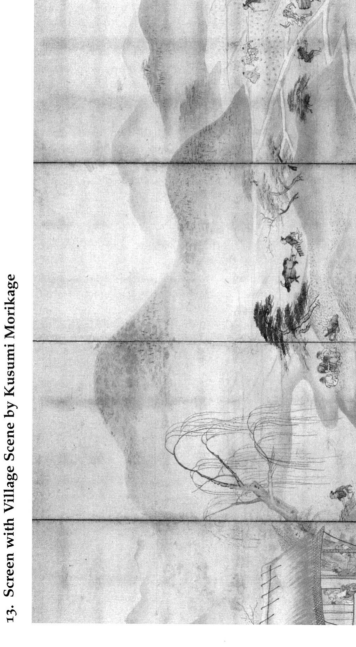

Source 13: Rice Cultivation in the Four Seasons *(detail). Photo: Kyoto National Museum.*

13. Screen with Village Scene by Kusumi Morikage

QUESTIONS TO CONSIDER

As you look over your lists, some points of comparison among all three cultures or at least two of them will be immediately obvious. One of these is military conscription, training, and supplies. Who provides the weapons in Henry VIII's and Hojo Ujimasa's decrees (Sources 3 and 11)? What is the age range of the men who are expected to be prepared to fight? Is anyone exempt from these provisions? According to Cieza de León (Source 6), who makes the weapons for the Incas? According to the general inspection of the Chupaychu (Source 5), how much of the labor demanded of conquered villages is for military purposes? Why do you think Cieza de León and de la Vega make so little reference to military service in their discussions of labor tribute?

The village by-laws and court roll from England (Sources 1 and 2) and the *so* and Tokugawa regulations from Japan (Sources 9 and 12) offer many points of comparison. Why do you think the villagers and their overlords in both places were concerned about the cutting down of trees and the harvesting of grass and shrubs? Why might they have been concerned that strangers not be allowed to board or to become subtenants? The English by-laws frequently mention animals roaming around at large and getting into sown land, while this is not mentioned in the Japanese regulations. What might account for this difference? Does Morikage's painting (Source 13) support your speculations about this? The Japanese regulations refer often to religious ceremonies and obligations, whereas these are mentioned only once in the English by-laws or court roll. Given that most English villages had a church in them, and that everyone in England during this period was baptized as a Christian, why do you think religious matters are not mentioned more often in these sources? What other concerns are particular to one of these areas but not the other?

Sources 2 and 10 both provide examples of villagers disobeying laws or carrying out prohibited activities. In Source 2, what are Robert Tayllor, Laurence Pemerton, Robert Huchyns, and the group of people beginning with William Bedell accused of doing? How do they justify their actions? What are the consequences of their actions? In Source 10, how is the absconding of farmers explained by the petitioners? What have they heard that the consequences of this will be, and how do they respond to this? How do the consequences of illegal actions in both of these cases fit with the general tone regarding penalties in many of the sources in this chapter? Would you expect that the death penalty set for not enlisting in the military in Hojo Ujimasa's decree (Source 11) or the requirement that taxes be paid in live lice described in Cieza de León's chronicle (Source 6) was actually enforced? If not, why would the rulers have prescribed such penalties?

Both Cieza de León's chronicle (Source 6) and the petition by the Japanese villagers (Source 10) refer to requirements of labor or produce that have been set too high. How do the villagers in each case seek to have these lessened? De la Vega's chronicle

(Source 7) and the Tokugawa regulations (Source 12) both discuss some form of communal responsibility if obligations are not met. In each case, who is to assist those who cannot carry out the required work?

Look at the two pictures of messengers (Sources 4 and 8). How do the artists indicate that the king in Source 4 and the governor of the roads in Source 8 are figures of authority? What differences between the two pictures do you see? Why might Guaman Poma have chosen to place his figures in a background showing the system of roads and huts?

A point of comparison that may not emerge immediately is the way in which historical examples are used to justify the actions of contemporary rulers. Read the opening section of Garcilosa de la Vega (Source 7). To whom does he compare the Inca rulers? Now read the decree of Toyotomi Hideyoshi carefully (Source 11). Who is set up as an example of a former ruler who beat swords into plowshares (to use the phrase in the Book of Isaiah in Hebrew Scripture), an image found in many cultures? Why might these authors include references such as these? To whom does Henry VIII refer when he orders the shooting of longbows? Why might he use this type of example, rather than one from the distant past?

You are now ready to use your information about the specific cultures and your comparative analyses to answer the questions for this chapter. Though these states are widely separated geographically, are there some concerns that appear to be common to all rulers and authorities as they seek to extract surpluses from their populations? How do these concerns differ from those of the villages themselves?

EPILOGUE

The interactions you have traced here—between states and villages, between higher-level officials and individuals, between individuals and village authorities—actually began much earlier than 1450. Since the agricultural revolution, people have lived in villages planting crops and raising animals, and devising ways to best do this given the climate and terrain in their area. Almost everywhere this has involved communal activities, which means that some method of local decision-making had to be devised and some means of punishing those who did not abide by these decisions developed. Since the first growth of large-scale states in Mesopotamia, China, and elsewhere, leaders and officials have extracted revenues from those villages, and the villages and their residents have responded to these demands in various ways. In the millennia before 1450, however, very few records of those responses and other aspects of village life were left, so that what we can learn about local political structures or other issues is often quite limited. This chapter begins at the point where such sources start to emerge for a few parts of the world, allowing us for the first time to get a glimpse of the structures that had shaped people's lives for so long.

Along with starting long before 1450, the processes and issues you have traced in this chapter continued long after 1650. By that date, two of the areas discussed, England and Japan, had developed into the form of government most common in the modern world: the nation-state. (In 1650 England was embroiled in a civil war over the limits of royal authority within that state, and the king had just been executed; however, the civil war ultimately led to increased consolidation under national institutions of government.) The Incas' creation of a centralized state was cut off by the Spanish conquest, but Spanish authorities built on Inca foundations when they assessed taxes and work duties owed by indigenous communities. (This was the main reason they were so interested in finding out exactly what the Inca system had been, and why they sent out officials and scribes such as those who produced Source 5.) The Andean area remained part of the Spanish Empire until the early nineteenth century, when a series of Spanish-American wars of independence led to the creation of several nation-sates in what had been the Inca Empire. Since then, nations have been established in the rest of the world, through the revolts against European colonization in the period after World War II, as well as after the breakup of the Soviet Union and Yugoslavia in the late twentieth century.

The consolidation of centralized state power, early examples of which you have traced in this chapter, might now seem to be complete. The whole world is understood to be divided into nations, each of which sends a representative to the United Nations, a body whose title reinforces this conceptualization of world politics. Various ethnic groups around the world today are carrying out bitter military campaigns against their national governments, but their aim is also to establish new independent nations. Thus recent political history might seem to be even more a matter of large-scale governments than in the era covered in this chapter, and the concerns you have read about here—about cutting down trees, tethering animals, or providing bows and arrows for boys—are part of a quaint "traditional" world that is long gone.

Viewing the issues we have discussed here as part of a "world we have lost" (the title of a well-known book on English village life) might be misleading, however. Not only could you easily find local regulations about cutting trees (or grass), tethering animals (at least dogs and cats), or providing weapons to children in the most highly developed American cities and suburbs today, but those local regulations continue to have repercussions on the larger political realm. As the American presidential election of 2000 made eminently clear, telling political history as if it were only the story of large-scale governments can miss the point. Speaker of the U.S. House of Representatives Tip O'Neill famously said that "all politics is local"; the fact that the choice of the leader of the world's most powerful country may have ultimately been determined by the shape of the ballots in one county only reinforces O'Neill's point.

[61]

CHAPTER THREE

LABOR AND PROPERTY

IN RURAL SOCIETIES

(1500–1800)

Since the development of agriculture and the domestication of animals, most of the world's population have been farmers or herders, living in family units in villages or small settlements. Despite their great numbers, however, rural men and women left little historical record until the twentieth century. They were largely illiterate, and the groups that were literate in their societies—priests, scribes, government officials, chroniclers—were not interested in the day-to-day life of rural people as long as they supplied the necessary food and other products for city residents and provided soldiers and military support for the needs of rulers. Literate people often looked down on rural residents, dismissing them as hicks or hoi polloi, an expression that comes from the Greek words for "the many." Only during times of crisis, such as famines, natural disasters, or war, might their lives be worthy of

comment, and then often only as numbers of dead or complaints about crops that were not being harvested or animals that were not being tended.

Today we are often much more interested in the lives of ordinary rural people. There are now thousands of book-length studies from around the world on this subject, as well as specialized journals such as *Peasant Studies* and *Agricultural History*. Other historical periodicals, such as the *Journal of Social History* or the *Journal of Women's History*, frequently include articles about rural people. The problem of sources has not gone away, but historians are using many different types of evidence to explore the lives of people who themselves left neither writing nor an extensive visual record.

This research has made it clear that rural farmers and pastoralists were not the uniform group of downtrodden yokels that sophisticated urban dwellers often thought they were. There was wide variety in their experiences across cultures and across time, and also within one place and one historical era. Life certainly revolved around hard physical work, but exactly what work people did varied, with divisions of labor based on a number of different factors. Many families and individuals also owned or controlled some property, including land and the tools to work it in agricultural societies, and animals among both farmers and herders. How this property was to be passed between family members and on to the next generation was thus a common concern of many rural residents, not simply wealthier members of the elite. Hard work (along with good luck) might lead to an increase in property, so labor and property were to some degree related, though drought, war, disease among people, crops, or animals, and any number of other difficulties often disrupted this relationship.

Your task in this chapter is to investigate these two topics—labor and property—among rural people in three parts of the world during the period 1500–1800, an era usually called "post-classical" or "early modern." These three areas—central Europe, Southeast Asia, and southwestern Africa—are widely separated geographically, though they were increasingly linked by trade connections during this era, as you will discover when exploring the impact of sugar in Chapter 4. This chapter does not focus on those connections, however, but asks you to compare these three areas in terms of labor and property. What similarities and differences do you see in the division of labor and the ownership and inheritance of property in these three areas? What might account for the patterns that you find?

BACKGROUND

To understand our sources, we need to know something about the rural economy and family structure in each of these areas. Southeast Asia and central Europe were both agricultural economies that revolved around grain growing, with rice the predominant crop in the lowland areas of Southeast Asia and wheat and rye the main crops in central Europe. In both areas grain production was organized in a variety of ways: some agricultural work was subsistence (for the use of one's own family), some was for wages, and some was for paying off labor or tax obligations to one's landlord or lender. People also raised other sorts of fruit and vegetable crops, maintained livestock, and gathered natural products. Houses were built quite close together in villages (termed a nucleated settlement pattern), with garden plots close by and grain fields more distant. In Southeast Asia, mild climate and frequent monsoons meant houses were built primarily of palm and bamboo; they were easily destroyed but quickly rebuilt. In central Europe, houses were also built of perishable materials such as wood and mud and had thatch roofs, but they had much thicker walls to withstand snow, sleet, and cold winds. In neither area could most peasants afford many furnishings, though these were particularly sparse in Southeast Asia, where eating was done on the floor and mats were often used in place of beds.

In southwestern Africa, the largest group of indigenous residents, who called themselves Khoikhoi, were pastoralists rather than farmers, with herds and flocks of cattle, sheep, and sometimes goats. (Dutch traders founded a permanent colony at the Cape of Good Hope in 1652, but our focus in this chapter is on the indigenous pastoralists.) They and their animals had probably migrated into this area from what is now northern Botswana around 200–400 C.E. Khoikhoi herders lived in clan-based village settlements—called *kraals* by the Dutch—of dome-shaped houses that could be dismantled and transported when the group drove the herds to better pasture, which generally happened every few months. Like the villagers in central Europe and Southeast Asia, Khoikhoi ate gathered products as well as those from their domestic animals; in contrast to Bantu-speaking farmers further north in Africa, they did not plant crops, except perhaps for dagga, a type of hemp.

In all three of these areas, family units and households were generally small, made up of a nuclear family and perhaps a few other relatives, and sometimes some nonrelated individuals such as servants in central Europe or southwestern Africa and debt-slaves in Southeast Asia.[1] Marriage in central Europe and southwestern Africa was monogamous, though the death of a spouse was a frequent occurrence, so that second marriages were quite common and families often included half-siblings and step-parents. Remarriage was acceptable within the Christian religious tradition of central Europe, though this practice sometimes created complications in terms of inheritance. Remarriage was viewed as more problematic among the Khoikhoi, so that spouses in a second marriage went through extra rituals designed to guard and protect them. Polygamy was tolerated in Southeast Asia, but most men could only afford one wife.

1. Debt-slavery or debt-bondage was a system in which one could exchange one's own labor or that of family members in order to repay debts or meet obligations. Sons-in-law could make themselves debt-bondsmen of their fathers-in-law in order to gain a wife, fathers could sell their children into bondage if their crops failed, individuals could sell themselves into bondage if business deals went bad. All members of a peasant family might become debt-bondsmen, though they continued to live together and worked some days of the week for themselves; debt-slaves did not necessarily live in the house of their master.

THE METHOD

We will be using three basic types of sources for this chapter: law codes, travelers' reports, and visual depictions of rural life. Each of these must be approached slightly differently.

Law codes are one of the earliest types of records from many of the world's societies. They have the benefit of being produced by a member of the society involved, so they are generally viewed as reflecting local ideas and values, but what we mean by "local" can get quite complicated. Law codes in postclassical Southeast Asia and central Europe were drawn up by educated men, men whose grandfathers may have been rural villagers but who were no longer part of this group themselves.[2] They thus discuss aspects of rural life such as land ownership and labor obligations, but they do not necessarily reflect rural views or values. It is also important to remember that all law codes are prescriptive; that is, they are a description of how things *ought* to be, not necessarily what was actually going on.

Travelers' reports are in some ways the opposite of law codes. They were produced by outsiders, not insiders, and purported to be descriptions of what the author actually saw. These three geographic areas were of great interest to outsiders during this period, who often commented on rural life. The Portuguese and the Spanish traded and conquered in Southeast Asia beginning in the sixteenth century, and later the Dutch, British, and French took over parts of this area in their colonial empires. Missionaries, merchants, and government officials from all of these countries reported on their experiences. Beginning with Bartholomeu Dias in 1488, Portuguese, Dutch, French, and British ships landed in southwestern Africa on their way to and from the Indian Ocean, trading with the Khoikhoi for cattle and sheep. Travelers frequently noted what they had seen or heard about Khoikhoi society, and after the founding of the Dutch colony

in 1652, governors and other officials sent dispatches and wrote reports.

Though central Europe was not colonized by outsiders, it, too, was often regarded as "exotic" by travelers of a different sort, especially young men and their tutors who were on what came to be known as the "Grand Tour." Beginning in the eighteenth century, wealthy young men from western Europe, especially from England, began to view an extended tour of all of the countries of Europe as essential to their education. The more inspired among them decided to describe their travels, often in multivolume works. Much of this travel literature only discusses cities, since the young men found the accommodations and entertainments there much more to their liking than those in small villages, but some of it also discusses rural life.

Especially before the nineteenth century, travelers' reports sometimes provide the only written evidence we have about certain cultures, but they must be used carefully. The authors may have been describing what they saw, but they saw things through the lens of their own culture and may have misunderstood the meaning of what was going on. Authors also had expectations about what they would find in the culture they were visiting, which shaped the way they saw things. Authors usually reported only what seemed unusual or different, so that things that were similar to their own culture went unnoted. Every author also had a specific purpose in writing: colonists and government officials to convince a ruler to extend further support, merchants to explain and justify to their superiors any difficulties they

2. There were no written law codes among the Khoikhoi, so this type of source is not available for the indigenous societies of southwestern Africa.

were having, young men on tour to highlight their own exploits. These reservations do not mean we should simply discount such reports as fiction, but we should keep the background and intents of the authors in mind when we use them.

Our third type of source—artistic depictions of rural life—might seem to be more objective, but here some of the same cautions apply. Most visual portrayals of rural life have not been done by villagers but by trained artists, some of whom came from outside the culture they were depicting. Thus, as with written sources, we need to pay attention to the artist's point of view.

You may at this point be thinking that the sources we will be using in this chapter are so limited by interpretive cautions that they can't be useful. Here it is important to ask yourself, as you should about any historical source, "Why would my sources lie?" It is easy to see why colonists' reports of indigenous religious beliefs or the sections in law codes issued by kings describing how the nobles had "willingly" given up their power might not be accurate. It is harder to see why an author or artist would not tell the truth about what work rural people performed, or why drafters of law codes would misrepresent the way families were supposed to pass down property, when laying out inheritance systems was exactly their intent. Thus on the topics we are exploring in this chapter, our sources are more likely to be reliable than they might be on other issues. Using a range of sources, as we do in this chapter, also helps us assess the validity of any one document.

Our methods in this chapter will be quite simple: careful reading and observation to gather information, then assembly of that information to note similarities and differences, and finally analysis of the patterns discovered. The sources are arranged roughly in chronological order within each of the three geographic areas we are examining. Some of them refer to labor, some to property and inheritance, and some to both, so that it will be useful for you to keep notes on these two issues as you work through the sources.

The first six sources come from Southeast Asia, of which the first two are law codes. Source 1 is a selection from the Lê Code from Vietnam, a law code put together during the Lê dynasty that ruled Vietnam from 1428 to 1788. The oldest originals of the Lê Code are on woodblock prints. The founder of the Lê dynasty expelled the Ming Chinese from Vietnam, where they had been ruling for twenty years, and many historians see a strong Chinese influence in this code; among other things, they comment that Vietnam was more influenced by China than the rest of Southeast Asia in attitudes toward the family, so that we should be careful not to generalize from the Vietnamese situation to all of Southeast Asia. They also note, however, that in some situations the Lê Code departed from more restrictive Chinese legal practices. Source 2 is an extract from the Agama Law Code from Java in the mid-sixteenth century. Read each of these and the explanatory notes that accompany them carefully. In the Lê Code, distinctions are made among heirs in terms of inheritance and duties; what are these distinctions based on? How is the ancestor worship of sons and daughters differently valued? That of older children and younger children? What distinctions are made between children of the principal wife and those of secondary wives? In the Agama Law Code, what sort of property transfer occurs at marriage? Does marriage immediately create an economic unit in terms of the property of husband and wife?

Sources 3 through 5 come from European officials and missionaries in Southeast Asia. Source 3 is from a history of the Philippines written by Antonio de Morga, a Spanish lawyer and royal official, in 1609. Source 4 is an illustration of Filipinos working in the field from a 1734 map of the Philippines by the Spanish Jesuit priest Pedro Murillo Velarde. Source 5 is from a history of Sumatra first published in 1783 and written by William Marsden, an English government official who had lived in Sumatra for eight years. How do these three sources describe or portray the division of labor in rural areas? According to de Morga and Marsden, what sort of property transfer occurs with marriage? How is inheritance divided among children, according to de Morga?

With Sources 6 through 9 we turn to southwestern Africa. Sources 6 and 7 are descriptions of the Khoikhoi from Dutch and German travelers in southwestern Africa. Source 6 comes from a description of the Cape of Good Hope colony published in Latin in 1686 and written by William ten Rhyne, a physician and official working for the Dutch East India Company. Ten Rhyne had visited southwestern Africa in 1673, and he based his account on personal observations, discussions with European residents, and conversations with Khoikhoi who had learned to speak Dutch. Source 7 is an extract from the 1731 English translation of a book by the German astronomer and mathematician Peter Kolb. Kolb lived in the Cape Colony from 1705 to 1713, originally traveling there to make scientific observations and later serving as a secretary to the Dutch East India Company; his book was first published in German in 1719. Both of these men describe many Khoikhoi customs as backward and "savage," but their language about patterns of labor and transfer of stock within families is quite measured, much less demeaning than their descriptions of Khoikhoi religious beliefs or outward appearance. Read these sources carefully. What tasks are women's tasks, and what are men's? What does Kolb appear to think about this division of labor? What sort of property transfer occurs at marriage? How, according to Kolb, is livestock handed down from one generation to the next?

Sources 8 and 9 are pen and ink drawings made by an unknown Dutch artist in about 1700; they were accidentally discovered in 1986, and the date they were sketched can only be estimated by analyzing the watermarks on the paper. Source 8 shows a Khoikhoi family traveling with livestock, perhaps to trade them; had they been moving to new pasture, the family would have been transporting its houses and possessions as well. Source 9 shows women milking. How do these visual sources fit with the written descriptions of work in Khoikhoi culture?

Sources 10 through 15 come from central Europe; the first three of these are law codes. Source 10 includes several articles from the law code of the territory of Salzburg, Austria, in 1526; Source 11 is an ordinance for vineyard workers from the south German duchy of Württemberg in 1550; Source 12 is part of the land register from the Silesian village of Zedlitz in 1790 describing the obligations of village residents toward their landlord. (Silesia is now part of Poland and the Czech Republic.) In the Salzburg law code, what sorts of property transfers occur on marriage? Does marriage immediately create an economic unit in terms of the property of husband and wife? What are the limitations on husbands and wives in terms of handling property? How is inheritance divided among children? All three sources set out a division of labor in jobs for servants and agricultural workers. On what is this division of labor based? How are different tasks rewarded? Source 13 is from a description of the island of Rügen, off the coast of eastern Germany in the Baltic Sea, by Johann Jacob Grümbke, a tutor and law student on a "Grand Tour," published in 1805. What does Grümbke observe about work during harvest-time?

Source 14 is a woodcut of German peasants harvesting hay, produced in 1532 by an anonymous artist known as the Petrarch Master; Source 15 is an illustration and description of a woman dairy farmer, published in the German city of Nuremberg in 1766. Look carefully at each of these pictures. What additional evidence do they provide about the division of labor that you have found in the written sources?

You now have notes about the topics for this chapter for each of the three geographic areas, and you can begin to make some comparisons. Starting with labor: What work is done by men and by women in each area? By children and by adults? Is labor divided along other lines as well? Do these divisions of labor change with the season of the year, or are they always the same? How is the rhythm of the workday different for different groups within each area? Do the tasks that they perform appear to be valued differently? Who controls the products of agricultural or pastoral labor?

Then look at property ownership and inheritance. How is property transferred with marriage in each of these areas? Does marriage create a community of property in the same way in each place? Who makes decisions about family property? What differences and similarities do you see in systems of inheritance?

Once you have made your comparisons and answered the first question, you will need to step back and analyze the patterns that you have found to answer the second. What do the various divisions of labor appear to be based on? Do they differ in the two agricultural societies as compared to the Khoikhoi pastoralists? If there is an explicit statement given as to why these divisions exist, does this appear to be valid, or might other factors also be important? Similarly in terms of property and inheritance: Why might various members of the family have different access to property? Do statements about the reasons for these differences seem legitimate, or might other factors also be at work? How might family relations be shaped by the fact that property goes from the groom's family to the bride's in Southeast Asia and south-western Africa, but from the bride's family to the groom's in central Europe? Why do you think these two very different patterns developed? Your answer to the second main question in this chapter will involve more guess-work than your answer to the first, but speculation as to causation is an important part of historical analysis.

THE EVIDENCE

Source 1 from The Lê Code: Law in Traditional Vietnam, *Nguyen Ngoc Huy and Ta Van Tai with the cooperation of Tran Van Liem (Athens: University of Ohio Press, 1987), pp. 110, 111.*

1. From the Lê Code, Vietnam, 16th–17th century

When a father and a mother have died intestate [leaving no will] and left land, the brothers and sisters who divide the property among themselves shall reserve one-twentieth of this property to constitute the *hương hỏa* [incense and fire] property[3] which shall be entrusted to the eldest brother. The remainder of the property shall be divided among them. Children of secondary wives or female serfs shall receive smaller parts [than children of the principal wife].

In the case in which the father and mother have left an oral will or a testament, the relevant regulations [concerning wills] shall apply. Heirs who violate this provision shall be deprived of their parts.

Whether in the families of high dignitaries, public servants, or ordinary people, old age or youth, or high or low social rank shall not be taken into account when choosing descendants to perform ancestor worship: the normal rule is to entrust this task to the principal son; or, if this son has died, to the eldest grandson; or, there being no eldest grandson, to a younger son of the principal wife; or, the principal wife having no child, to the most virtuous among the children of the secondary wives.

In the case of the eldest son or eldest grandson being disabled or unworthy and thereby unable to assume responsibilities for ancestor worship, the family concerned shall inform the local authorities and select another descendant for the task. . . .

The management of the *hương hỏa* property shall be entrusted to the eldest son or, failing that, to the eldest daughter. Such property shall be one-twentieth of the total of the real property in the estate. . . .

---

3. *hương hỏa* **property:** a portion of the family property reserved to cover the expenses for sacrifices to the ancestors and for the maintenance of their tombs. The words *hương hỏa* actually mean incense and fire, which were kept burning on the ancestors' altar.

[69]

If a son, although born of a man's former principal wife and already entrusted with the management of the *hương hỏa* property, has only a daughter, while another son, although born of a secondary wife or a serf of such a man or even chronically incapacitated, has a male offspring, the management of the *hương hỏa* property shall be entrusted to this grandson. This is to illustrate the principle that a family's name should never be left extinct [for lack of male worship heir]. . . .

When the eldest of two brothers in a family has only daughters while the younger has one son who has been already entrusted with the management of the *hương hỏa* property, if this son in turn has only daughters, such property shall be returned to the granddaughter of the eldest brother.

Source 2 from M. C. Hoadley and M. B. Hooker, An Introduction to Javanese Law: A Translation of and Commentary on the Agama *(Tucson: University of Arizona Press, 1981), pp. 192–193. Notes by Barbara Watson Andaya.*

2. From the Agama Law Code, Java, 16th century

Concerning a person giving goods to children-in-law on the occasion of marriage; if then the new wife dies her possessions go to the husband, if the husband dies his possessions go to the wife. It is not permitted for the giver to take back the goods if there has occurred the "mixing of goods." The minimum time for this "mixing of goods" is twelve years.

Concerning a maiden given goods by her father out of love for her and later she marries but not long thereafter the girl dies; all the goods brought by her to the marriage are returned to the girl's father and mother because there has not yet occurred the "mixing of goods." In a like manner, all the goods of the husband if he dies shortly after the marriage are returned to his father.

If a person takes a dislike to his son-in-law, then the marriage of his daughter is dissolved; the bride price paid by the husband is repaid two-fold. In addition, the bridal gifts and all that given earlier, such as clothing, male sash, kain,[4] all of those things which were given, must be returned to the disliked former son-in-law.

Concerning a newly married maiden who has not yet lain with her husband because she will not have him; the girl's bride price is returned two-fold. This is termed "scorned coitus."

---

4. **kain:** a sarong; cloth was always an important part of wedding gifts, representing the "female" side in contrast to money, knives, and other metal objects, which were considered "masculine."

Source 3 from Antonio de Morga, History of the Philippine Islands, *ed. and trans. E. H. Blair and J. A. Robertson (Cleveland: Arthur H. Clark, 1907), vol. 2, pp. 79, 125–126.*

3. From Antonio de Morga, *History of the Philippine Islands,* 1609

The women have needlework as their employment and occupation, and they are very clever at it, and at all kinds of sewing. They weave cloth and spin cotton, and serve in the houses of their husbands and fathers. They pound the rice for eating, and prepare the other food. They raise fowls and swine, and keep the houses, while the men are engaged in the labors of the field, and in their fishing, navigation, and trading. . . .

The dowry was furnished by the man, being given by his parents. The wife furnished nothing for the marriage, until she had inherited it from her parents. The solemnity of the marriage consisted in nothing more than the agreement between the parents and relatives of the contracting parties, the payment of the dowry agreed upon to the father of the bride, and the assembling at the wife's parents' house of all the relatives to eat and drink until they would fall down. . . .

In inheritances all the legitimate children inherited equally from their parents whatever property they had acquired. If there were any movable or landed property which they had received from their parents, such went to the nearest relatives and the collateral side of that stock, if there were no legitimate children. . . .

Source 4 from Anthony Reid, Southeast Asia in the Age of Commerce, *vol. 1:* The Lands Below the Winds *(New Haven: Yale University Press, 1988), p. 23. Reproduced courtesy of the Harvard-Yenching Library.*

4. Illustration from a Map of the Philippines, 1734

Source 5 *from William Marsden,* The History of Sumatra, *reprint of the 3rd ed. (Kuala Lumpur: Oxford University Press, 1966), pp. 71, 137, 382.*

5. From William Marsden, *The History of Sumatra,* 1783

When the periodical rains begin to fall, which takes place gradually about October, the planter assembles his neighbours (whom he assists in turn), and with the aid of his whole family proceeds to sow his ground, endeavouring to complete the task in the course of one day. In order to ensure success, he fixes, by the priest's assistance, on a lucky day, and vows the sacrifice of a kid, if his crop should prove favourable; the performance of which is sacredly observed, and is the occasion of a feast in every family after harvest. The manner of sowing is this. Two or three men enter the plantation, as it is usual to call the *padi*-field, holding in each hand sticks about five feet long and two inches diameter, bluntly pointed, with which, striking them into the ground as they advance, they make small, shallow holes, at the distance of about five inches from each other. These are followed by the women and elder children with small baskets containing the seed-grain (saved with care from the choicest of the preceding crop) of which they drop four or five grains into every hole, and passing on, are followed by the younger children, who with their feet (in the use of which the natives are nearly as expert as with their hands) cover them lightly from the adjacent earth, that the seed may not be too much exposed to the birds, which, as might be expected, often prove destructive foes. . . .

[On pepper-harvesting.] As soon as any of the berries or corns redden, the bunch is reckoned fit for gathering, the remainder being then generally full-grown, although green; nor would it answer to wait for the whole to change colour, as the most mature would drop off. It is collected in small baskets slung over the shoulder, and with the assistance of the women and children conveyed to a smooth, level spot of clean, hard ground, near the garden or the village, where it is spread, sometimes upon mats, to dry in the sun; but exposed at the same time to the vicissitudes of the weather, which are not much regarded, nor thought to injure it. In this situation it becomes black and shrivelled, as we see it in Europe, and as it dries is hand-rubbed occasionally to separate the grains from the stalk. . . .

[On marriage.] The parents of the girl always receive a valuable consideration (in buffaloes or horses) from the person to whom she is given in marriage; which is returned when a divorce takes place against the man's inclination. The daughters, as elsewhere, are looked upon as the riches of the fathers.

Source 6 from William ten Rhyne, A Short Account of the Cape of Good Hope, *in Isaac Schapera, ed. and trans.,* The Early Cape Hottentots *(Westport, Conn.: Negro Universities Press, 1970), pp. 119, 129, 145.*

6. William ten Rhyne, *A Short Account of the Cape of Good Hope,* 1686

Apart from their huts they have no houses, nor shelter, nor dwelling-place, for they are always engaged in pasturing their herds and flocks, and are accustomed to wander through uncultivated wildernesses. Their little cabins have but one opening, and their roof and gable and walls consist of the leaves and stalks of the African gladiolus, the bulbs of which they eat instead of bread (our country-men call it Hottentot's bread). They are so closely built that they protect the dwellers from rain and other inclemencies of the weather. Poles, gutters, and shingles are made from small branches of trees. The porch is arched and wind-ing. Each husband digs out a hollow on the floor, in which, as on a bed, he spreads a sheep-skin; he then wraps himself up in another sheep-skin so cosily that neither head, nor foot, nor hand can be seen, assuming the posture naturally taken by the child in the womb. The wife sleeps higher up on the edge of the man's hollow bed. This little cabin holds fifteen, sometimes more, lodgers. They place the huts on hill or plain, or among trees on the banks of rivers, and lay them out in a circle at a distance of five or six paces from one another. In this way they protect the cattle, which are enclosed within these bounds, from the attack rather of wild beasts than of an enemy. But when the chiefs give the signal to move to a new place, they warn their subjects by kindling huge fires. Then the women alone collect all the stock, and all the gear which at other times is cast into leathern bags and carried on their own shoulders, and place them together with the hut on pack-oxen, while the men drive away the forces of the enemy. . . .

. . . They have no variety of food; from marshes and mounds they root up sword-lilies; with the leaves of this plant they roof their huts, the bulbs they use for bread. These are dug up by the women, for it is the women who provide food for the men; the men look after the huts and the herds, or else are occupied in war. The only interruption to this diet is in the event of a marriage or a birth, when they slaughter an ox, or at least a sheep, to provide a feast for their friends, unless some wild animal should happen to be taken. They also eat the leaves of many kinds of sedum.[5] They drink the milk of cows and sheep. The women do the milking at fixed times of dawn and dusk, and they make it into butter by an elegant process. They skin a bird, and turn the skin inside out so that the

---

5. **sedum:** a wild plant.

feathers are inside; they tie this to a hollow stick and shake it so that the milk is separated into butter and whey. . . .

When they wish to embark on marriage they approach their parents, who then approach the chief, so that they may have full permission to marry a maiden. But they never do this unless they possess at least one draft-ox for removing the hut with its furniture, one or two milch cows, and ten or twelve sheep to celebrate the betrothal or the bringing home of the bride, etc.

Source 7 from Peter Kolb, The Present State of the Cape of Good-Hope, *trans. G. Medley (London: W. Innys, 1731), pp. 156–157, 158–160, 161, 168–169. Orthography modernized.*

7. Extract from Peter Kolb, *The Present State of the Cape of Good-Hope,* 1719

With regards to the portions on both sides of the Hottentot[6] marriages, the eldest son inherits all the estate the father dies possessed of. But if an eldest son marries while his father is still living, he stands no better a chance for a fortune in hand than his younger brothers, who are all in this matter at the courtesy of the father, if they marry in his life-time. And a father seldom gives a son for his marriage portion (though he gives him such a feast) above a couple of cows, and a couple of sheep, with which he must shift in the world as well as he can. The father dying, the younger sons unmarried are, for their fortunes, at the courtesy of the eldest, who rarely does anything better for them than what has been said of the father.

The daughters have rarely any portion at all. If they have, it is not above a cow and a couple of sheep; and these, or the like, must be returned to the family she came of, in case she dies before she has a child.

The men look not for fortunes or great alliances by marriage. All they have their eyes upon in the choice of their wives is wit, beauty, or agreeableness. So that it sometimes happens the daughter of a poor obscure fellow is married to the captain of a *kraal,* or the chief of a nation. . . .

A Hottentot never has a hut of his own till he marries; nor does he think of erecting it till after his marriage feast. From his first nuptial day to the time he shall have built him a hut, which is ordinarily about eight days, he and his bride are entertained and accommodated at the hut of a relation or friend. His bride assists him, not only in erecting the hut, but in getting up the materials, every one

---

6. Kolb and other Europeans referred to Khoikhoi as "Hottentots," a word of uncertain origin that is regarded as insulting in contemporary South Africa.

of which are quite new. His bride assists him likewise in providing the furniture, which is all new.

The hut finished, and he and his bride settled in it, he troubles his head no more about the house or household matters. He abandons to her the care and toil of seeking and dressing provisions for both. . . .

A Hottentot has some care for his cattle. He does go from time to time to look after them; but he makes his wife, notwithstanding all her domestic fatigues, go as often. Rarely will he abate her anything of the time and trouble he bestows on them himself. Only she never meddles in the sale of them. Oh, no! That's his grand prerogative; he glories in it and woe be to her that invades it.

If he has a son, he bestows more care on the preservation and increase of his cattle, that he may leave him well in the world. And if he is the master of any handicraft he teaches it to him.

For the wife . . . has all the care and drudgery within doors, and a share of the fatigue in tending the cattle. Every morning, excepting when her husband goes hunting or fishing, which happens not very often, she goes out to gather certain roots, and milk the cows, for the sustenance of the family. These roots, which abound in Hottentot country, and which are easily known by the leafage they produce, she digs up with a stick of iron or olive-wood, pointed. She washes them in fair water, and boils or broils them. And either way they made a pretty good sort of food. She cuts and brings home all the wood for fires. . . .

They neither of them [husband and wife] meddle in the province of the other, excepting the tending of their cattle, which is common to both. . . .

The cattle of a *kraal* run all together, the great in one herd, the small in another. The poorest inhabitant, who has but a single sheep, has the privilege of turning it into the flock, where it is tended and taken as much care of, though he is not present, as the sheep of the richest and most powerful of the *kraal*. They have no particular herdsmen or shepherds for driving their cattle to pasture and tending and guarding them from wild beasts. They take those offices upon them by turns, three or four or more together, according to the number of the men of the *kraal*, and the proportion of the herds. They drive them to pasture between 6 and 7 in the morning, and back to the *kraal* between 5 and 6 in the evening. And morning and evening the women milk the cows.

8. Pen and Ink Drawing of Khoikhoi Family and Stock, Unknown Artist, ca. 1700

9. Pen and Ink Drawing of Khoikhoi Woman Milking, Unknown Artist, ca. 1700

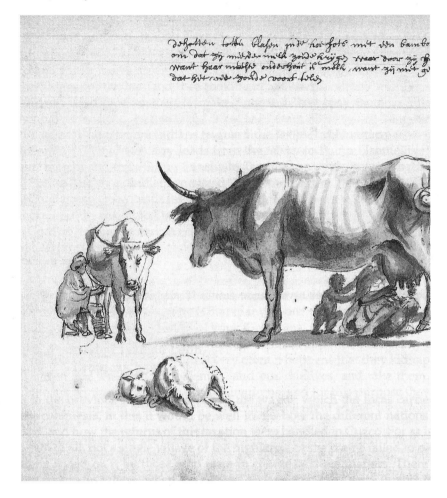

Source 10 from Franz V. Spechtler and Rudolf Uminsky, eds., Die Salzburger Landesordnung
von 1526, *Göppinger Arbeiten zur Germanistik, Nr. 305 (Göppingen, Kümmerle, 1981), pp. 119,
154, 197, 248–249. Translations by Merry E. Wiesner.*

10. From the Law Code
of the Territory of Salzburg,
Austria, 1526

It is to be accepted that both spouses have married themselves together from
the time of the consummation of their marriage, body to body and goods to
goods. . . .

The husband shall not spend away the dowry[7] or other goods of his wife unnecessarily with gambling or other useless frivolous pastimes, wasting and
squandering it. Whoever does this is guilty of sending his wife into poverty. His
wife, in order to secure her legacy and other goods she has brought to the marriage, may get an order requiring him to pledge and hold in trust for her some
of his property. . . . [But] without his knowledge and agreement she is not to do
business [with any household goods] except those which she has brought to the
marriage; if she does it will not be legally binding. . . .

The first and foremost heirs are the children who inherit from their parents. If
a father and mother leave behind legitimate children out of their bodies, one or
more sons or daughters, then these children inherit all paternal and maternal
goods, landed property and movables, equally with each other. . . .

Women who do not have husbands, whether they are young or old, shall
have a guardian and advisor in all matters of consequence and property, such as
the selling of or other legal matters regarding landed property. Otherwise these
transactions are not binding. In matters which do not involve court actions and
in other matters of little account they are not to be burdened with guardians
against their will. . . .

Regarding wages for servants in the territory: Every builder's assistant who is
skillful and capable should be given no more than 6 or 7 gulden per year and 5
pair of shoes. . . . A skillful and capable herdsman is to be given 3 gulden per
year, one pair of cloth pants and 4 pair of shoes. A grown male servant or strong
boy who is capable of doing a man's work is to be given 2 or 3 gulden and 4 pair
of shoes and one pair of cloth pants. A female cook who can cook especially well
and who has lots to cook in the houses of great lords or inns should be given 5
gulden and three pairs of shoes. A normal female cook who doesn't have to cook
so much is to be given 3 or at the most 4 gulden and three pair of shoes. A strong

---

7. **dowry:** an amount of goods, cash, and/or property that was brought by a wife to her husband
on marriage; the husband could do with the dowry whatever he wished within the course of
the marriage, though legally it continued to belong to his wife.

adult dairy- or house-maid who is capable of doing all types of work is not to be given more than 2 gulden and 4 pair of shoes. A children's maid who is not capable of doing heavy work is not to be given more than 1 gulden as wages.

Source 11 from Stuttgart, Württembergisches Hauptstaatsarchiv, Generalreskripta, A38, Bü. 2, 1550. Translation by Merry E. Wiesner.

11. Regulations for Vineyard Workers in the Duchy of Württemberg, 1550

Men who work in the vineyards, doing work that is skilled, are to be paid 16 pence per day; in addition, they are to receive soup and wine to eat in the morning, at midday beer, vegetables, and meat, and in the evening soup, vegetables, and wine. Young boys are to be paid 10 pence per day. Women who work as haymakers are to be given 6 pence a day. If the employer wants to have them doing other work, he may make an agreement with them to pay them 7 or 8 pence. He may also give them soup and vegetables to eat in the morning—but no wine—milk and bread at midday, but nothing in the evening.

Source 12 from August Meitzen, Urkunden schlesicher Dörfer *(Breslau, 1863), pp. 334–335. Translation by Merry E. Wiesner.*

12. From the Land Register in the Silesian Village of Zedlitz, 1790

The eighteen households . . . are obliged to send as workers every day two people, that is the husband and also the wife, or instead of the latter, a qualified maid, to do whatever work is necessary. For the harvest they must bring a third person with them. The fieldworkers begin harvest work at sunrise, stop from 6:30 to 7 for a half-hour breakfast, work again until 10, when they eat for an hour in the fields, and then work from 11 until 2. They eat an evening meal from 2 to 3, and then they work again without stopping until sunset. The wives of the fieldworkers begin work once they have taken care of the herds, work with the men and maids until 6:30, and then go from the fields back to the house to prepare the meal, which they bring to the men and maids in the fields at 10:00. They eat until 11, and then stay working in the fields until evening, although they do the same things between 2 and 3 with the evening meal. If a fieldworker's wife has a baby during the harvest season, she is free from service for six weeks, but the maid must still come to work regardless of this. If she has a baby when it is not harvest-time, the maid is also free from service for fourteen days [and can help her].

Source 13 from Johann Jacob Grümbke, Streifzüge durch das Rügenland, *ed. Albert Burckhardt (Leipzig: F. A. Brockhaus, 1805), p. 182.*

13. Johann Jacob Grümbke's Description of Harvesting Grain in Rügen, 1805

The harvest begins around the middle of August and is ended in the first half of September, although it is often extended because of bad thunderstorms. With rye one uses only a scythe, which the landowner's officials on large estates own and for which they receive a certain payment. Sickles are not at all common, for on large fields their use is too tiresome and time-consuming. It is an entertaining view when one sees a row of 12, 16, or 20 strong men swinging scythes according to the beat that the front reaper sets. . . . The cut grain normally lays for a short time in rows, before it is put in sheaves, though care is taken to bind the rye as quickly as possible after it has been cut with the scythe. The sheaves are piled against one another in heaps, and each heap is about six or seven rows apart. The number of sheaves in each pile is arbitrary. Binding, piling into heaps, and loading the grain is normally done by women, who appear throughout the fields in white clothing.

Source 14 from W. Scheidig, Die Holzschnitte des Petrarca-Meisters *(Berlin, 1955), p. 255.*

14. Hay-making in Germany, 1532

Source 15 from Deutliche Vorstellung der Nürnbergischen Trachten *(Nürnberg, 1766). Translation by Merry E. Wiesner.*

15. A Female Dairy Farmer in Nuremberg, Germany, 1766

Beneath her picture in this book of costumes was a description:

She comes every day from the country to the city, or she stays several days during the week, and sells the products of her animals and things that she has made. She belongs to the people who shout [in the streets], of which there are many in Nuremberg. Here is her call: "Good milk, you housewives! Eggs and lard! Good butter! Good buttermilk!" Connected with these cries are a certain Nuremberg peasant dialect and a certain tone, that one can recognize immediately once one has heard it. Sometimes she also calls out: "Sauerkraut! White cabbage! Cream!" and other things. Some of these women do not call out, but go silently through the streets and have their own houses where they always unload their wares and where people wait for them, or at least wait for their milk and butter for their morning coffee. The cleaner each dairy-farmer is, the more customers and buyers she has. There are also those who arrange themselves and their baskets, cloths, and copper jugs in such an attractive way that their wares easily meet with approval.

QUESTIONS TO CONSIDER

The Method section for this chapter gives you a number of questions that relate to specific sources and ways in which you can compare information gained from these sources. Before you prepare your answers to the central questions in this chapter, it might be good to reflect on some of the interpretive issues noted in that section.

All of our sources are by educated men, and you may have found some surprising similarities among them in terms of their attitudes toward rural men and women. For example, several of the travelers' reports describe the women as busy and industrious, but the men as less so. Why do you think this was a common observation? The same thing is repeated in many other reports by explorers, missionaries, and travelers from throughout the world. Why might it become a stereotype for travelers reporting on cultures they regarded as inferior or backward? What other comments in the travelers' reports appear to rise more from preconceptions than observations? How would you compare the written record in this regard with the visual one; that is, do preconceptions also appear to shape the pictorial sources?

As you have discovered, the stereotype that women worked harder than men did not affect the wages of men and women, for men were invariably paid more for work at a similar skill level than women. What attitudes might account for this difference? From reading Source 11, you know that male and female agricultural workers were sometimes given different amounts and types of food. How might this in turn affect their ability to do various agricultural tasks?

Wage differentials provide evidence that preconceived ideas shape not only reports by outsiders but also law codes, regulations, and other official statements. Looking again at the Lê Code in Source 1, what ideas or cultural values appear to underlie the way that inheritance and the tasks of heirs are divided? Vietnam is often viewed as the part of Southeast Asia most influenced by China; do you find evidence of that influence in this source? How might Chinese influence explain the difference in inheritance systems in Vietnam (Source 1) and the Philippines (Source 3)?

One of the basic differences you have probably discovered is that on marriage property goes from the groom's family to the bride's in Southeast Asia and southwestern Africa, but from the bride's family to the groom's in central Europe. This pattern of property transfer in early modern central Europe, termed "giving a dowry," was common throughout most of the continent, and centuries old. When Europeans encountered the opposite pattern, they were often horrified, viewing it as husbands buying wives—they called it "bride-price"—and thus not much different from slavery. Critics of the dowry system within Europe, such as the novelist Jane Austen, also sometimes called it "buying a husband," but this was never official terminology. Why do you think most Europeans were not able to view these two property transfer systems in the same way?

Though the sources we have used do reflect cultural biases, we have also gained enough information from them to answer the central questions for this chapter: What similarities and differences do you see in the division of labor and the ownership and inheritance of property in Southeast Asia, central Europe, and among the Khoikhoi in southwestern Africa? What might account for the patterns that you find?

EPILOGUE

The issues you have explored in this chapter are not limited to rural groups in these three areas in the early modern period; they may be found in nearly all human societies across time. Every culture, including modern postindustrial culture, has a division of labor in which the work of different types of people is valued differently. Every culture has an inheritance system and a system for regulating control of property within families. The division of labor and inheritance systems change over time and are often vehemently contested, both within families and within society as a whole. (An example is the current debate over limiting or ending inheritance taxes in the United States.) As you have discovered in this chapter, these debates occur because they reflect key cultural values more than we at first suspect.

Through using new technologies, research into rural life in the past is revealing additional areas in which there are continuities with the present. Oral historians and anthropologists are finding out more about the ideas and sentiments of peasant women and men themselves by interviewing contemporary village residents and then extrapolating backwards. These anthropological accounts are used to flesh out historical studies, resulting in a much livelier story. Physical evidence can yield further information. In South Africa, surviving rock paintings showing various breeds of cattle tell more than European travelers' accounts about the type of animals herded. Marriage chests decorated with paintings or carvings have survived for centuries from both Southeast Asia and central Europe; these were not usually made by trained artists but by villagers themselves, and they can sometimes provide clues about their ideas about what men and women were supposed to do.

Statistical studies begun in the twentieth century provide additional evidence. In one of these, government observers in East Java in the 1920s who recorded the number of working hours for men, women, and children in rice production discovered that two-thirds of the time spent on the production of rice was spent by women.[8] The women were observed doing the same tasks in rice production that early modern women did: planting, weeding, and

8. Elsbeth Locher-Scholten, "Female Labour in Twentieth Century Java," in *Indonesian Women in Focus: Past and Present Notions*, ed. Elsbeth Locher-Scholten and Anke Niehof (Dordrecht, Holland: Foris Publications, 1987), pp. 82–83.

harvesting. We must always use such evidence with caution, for economic changes such as the availability of work outside the village may have dramatically altered the gender and age balance of the work force, but it can be helpful as support for conclusions gained from historical evidence.

The search for sources goes on, and many of the questions we can now answer with some certainty regarding rural men and women in many parts of the world were considered unanswerable just a short time ago. There will continue to be many questions whose answers elude us, but now that rural farmers and herders have clearly joined more elite groups as people with a history, their stories may disappear at a slower rate.

CHAPTER FOUR

SWEET NEXUS: SUGAR AND THE

ORIGINS OF THE MODERN WORLD

(1600–1800)

It will be no exaggeration to put the tale and toll of the Slave Trade as twenty million Africans, of which two-thirds are to be charged against sugar.

—*Noel Deerr*[1]

I pity them greatly, but I must be mum,
For how could we do without sugar
    and rum?
Especially sugar, so needful we see.
What, give up our desserts, our coffee
    and tea?

—*William Cowper, (1731–1800),*
"Poor Africans"

We live in a world of commodities. Virtually every tool we use, everything we eat, every piece of material we use to clothe or house ourselves has been produced for us by people we will never know, often by people who are very distant from us geographically and culturally. There is no more concrete way to understand our intimate connection to the global market than by following back to its point of origin every component of every item we touch or consume each day: soap, clothing, gasoline, a banana, a candy bar, a compact disk, the book you are holding in your hand. That we do not stop to think about and wonder at the processes that make this global nexus of commodities possible shows how thoroughly integrated we are in a profit-based international market in which people produce what they do not consume, and consume what they do not produce. Even in the poorest parts of the world, where hundreds of millions of people continue to supply their own basic daily needs, the global market is ever present.

1. Noel Deerr, *The History of Sugar* (London: Chapman & Hall, 1949), quoted in L. A. G. Strong, *The Story of Sugar* (London: Weidenfeld & Nicolson, 1954), p. 102.

Chapter 4

Sweet Nexus:

Sugar and the

Origins of the

Modern World

(1600–1800)

The exchange of commodities through long-distance trade is an ancient part of the human experience. But in most times and places, the goods that passed along these routes were so valuable that they could be consumed only rarely; usually their use was restricted to the elites of hierarchical societies. Only in the nineteenth and twentieth centuries, beginning in the industrialized parts of the world, did mass consumption of commodities produced for a global market become commonplace. But the international political and economic structures that guided that development had their origins somewhat earlier, in the mercantilist economic systems of the seventeenth and eighteenth centuries. Historians have therefore focused on the early modern period as a key to understanding the development of the commodity-based capitalist world economy.

Some historians of the early modern "world system" have focused on the division between areas of accumulation and areas of exploitation. Those national economies that managed to combine commercial capitalism with military expansion and colonial conquest (e.g., England, France, and Holland) accumulated capital by exploiting the land, labor, and natural resources of other societies. In this view, northwestern Europe became the "core" of a modern world economy, building its accumulation of wealth at the expense of the "periphery" in Africa, Asia, and the Americas.

If we use the entire world system as our unit of analysis, however, we tend to lose sight of the role of individuals in this story and of the social and cultural changes that accompanied the economic transformation. Some historians have found that following the story of a single commodity is a way to keep the larger economic picture in view while also involving a broader range of historical factors. Particular attention has been paid to what Kenneth Pomeranz and Steven Topik refer to as "the economic culture of drugs":

> The fact is that historically, goods considered drugs, that is, products ingested, smoked, sniffed or drunk to produce an altered state of being, have been central to exchange and production.... In the seventeenth century affluent people all over the world began to drink, smoke and eat exotic plants that came from long distances. Coffee, tea, cocoa, tobacco and sugar all became popular at roughly the same time.... Before long, most of the drug foods were being produced in new, distant parts of the world that Europeans had colonized.... Colonial empires were built on the foundation of drug trades.[2]

Today we would not classify a candy bar or a cup of sweetened coffee as a "drug" product, but the point is still a good one: A growing taste for rare and stimulating commodities had a transformative effect on the world and its people.

In this chapter we focus on the role of sugar in the development of the modern world economy, with an emphasis on Great Britain in the seventeenth and

2. Kenneth Pomeranz and Steven Topik, *The World That Trade Created: Society, Culture, and the World Economy, 1400 to the Present* (London: M. E. Sharpe, 1999), pp. 77–78.

eighteenth centuries. Your task will be to use the documents provided to follow the "trail" of sugar backward from the consumer, through stages of trade and manufacture, to the growing of the cane itself, and finally to the original supply of labor on which the great sugar enterprises of this era were built.

In the process, you will learn something about how and why European capital, American land, and African labor came to be combined in a single international economic enterprise meant to satisfy what is still in today's world a seemingly insatiable demand for sweets.

BACKGROUND

The story of sugar takes us from South Asia to the Caribbean. Greek conquerors encountered sugar in northwestern India in the fourth century B.C.E., but it remained little more than a vague rumor to ancient Europeans, who called it "honey from reeds." Sugar was better known in China, but it was only with the Muslim expansion after the seventh century that its global importance began. With the rise and expansion of Islam came the closer integration of the trade worlds of the Indian Ocean and the Mediterranean. Sugar was one of the luxury goods introduced to the markets of western Asia and Europe in the later Middle Ages; plantations were established near the Persian Gulf and on Mediterranean islands such as Cyprus and Sicily.

Even at this early stage, we can identify four aspects of cane sugar production that would be of enduring importance. First, sugar cane grows best in hot, moist areas. Second, sugar production is exceptionally labor-intensive, requiring labor to be available year round. Third, sugar is commercially viable only when it is produced on a relatively large scale. Fourth, production of sugar for the market requires an initial stage of processing, making it, at least partially, an industrial enterprise.

For all of these reasons, the plantation was the characteristic form of sugar production even before it spread to the New World. Large-scale organization, the massed use of coerced labor, and significant capital investment set sugar production apart in a world where most agricultural goods were produced on a relatively small scale by peasant farmers. Finally, since sugar can in no way establish itself as a central source of carbohydrates in the human diet, it is a crop with very limited potential for local consumption. Sugar by its nature requires export outlets if it is to flourish.

Before the Crusades, sugar was virtually unknown in Europe, except perhaps as a very rare medical substance. Increasing contact with the eastern Mediterranean made sugar, while still very exotic, a bit more familiar. The Venetians established themselves as the principal intermediaries in the sugar trade between areas of production in and around the Mediterranean and consumers elsewhere in Europe. Christian conquests in the Mediterranean in

Chapter 4

Sweet Nexus:

Sugar and the

Origins of the

Modern World

(1600–1800)

the late medieval period both stimulated demand for sugar and for the first time put Europeans in control of production. By the fifteenth century, sugar was being grown in southern Spain and in Portugal. European mariners were therefore quite familiar with the crop as they began the ocean voyages that would ultimately lead to the circumnavigation of Africa and, of course, the creation of a transoceanic connection with the Americas.

The beginnings of Atlantic sugar production were modest. Columbus had brought sugar cane to Hispaniola on his second voyage, but because of a shortage of manual labor to work the crop, little was produced at first. The most important initiatives in the Atlantic sugar complex were taken by the Portuguese, who brought the sugar plantation economy from the Mediterranean to the Atlantic, to islands like São Tomé. There they used enslaved African labor, in which they had begun to trade in the late 1400s, to work the crop. Black labor, white sugar: that connection had now been made. From the Atlantic islands, the slave-based sugar complex made its way to Brazil, the dominant producer of the sixteenth century, and then to the islands of the Caribbean. As the Dutch, British, and French displaced the Spanish and Portuguese as the dominant economic actors in the late sixteenth and seventeenth centuries, they came to control what had now become an integrated sugar production system, drawing together the resources of three continents in a single Atlantic economy. The world economy, and the Western diet, would never be the same.

The fantastic growth of sugar production in the New World in the sixteenth through eighteenth centuries, the fortunes that were made and the misery that was endured, would not have been possible without the seemingly infinite demand for sugar (and associated products like molasses and rum) that developed in Europe. At first, limited supplies meant that only the elite could have their demand for sugar from the New World satisfied. Queen Elizabeth I of England was notoriously fond of sweet foods, and the tooth decay she suffered as a result was an early sign that sugar could be in some ways unhealthy. But even royal consumption was very limited by later standards, and sugar was still thought of primarily as a medicine or a spice, to be used in very small quantities. It was not until the Restoration of the Stuart line in England in 1660, coinciding with a rise in Caribbean production, that the use of sugar spread more widely among the aristocracy and the emerging middle class of merchants, shopkeepers, and artisans.

In the eighteenth century, when sugar consumption spread to the lower classes and the use of sugar as a sweetener of newly popular beverages (coffee, cocoa, tea) became common, the transition from elite luxury to mass commodity was completed. The trend began in the coffeehouses frequented by middle-class Londoners in the late 1600s, but it was the introduction of tea from Asia and its association with sugar that put England at the forefront of world consumption. The East India Company became a powerful vested interest in British society, and tea was the key to its success. By the late eighteenth century, sweetened tea was essential to the diet of all classes of British society.

The implications were immense. Though some social commentators scorned the poor for wasting their money on sugared tea, it seems that the poor were making a logical choice given the economic circumstances of the time. While a switch from an afternoon refreshment of beer to one of sweetened tea might seem healthy, the fact is that the traditional beer was much more nutritious. Sugar provides quick calories, but nothing else. Sweetened tea provided the illusion of a hot meal when there was no time or money to fix a proper one, and this made a diet of plain bread seem more palatable. In what was becoming one of the most powerful nations in the world, dominant in global commerce and experiencing the first stirrings of the industrial revolution, the growth of tea and sugar consumption among the average citizens showed not their wealth but their poverty and lack of adequate nourishment.

In the period when the sugar trade rose to predominance, the British and the French, increasingly combative, saw trade as a zero-sum game in which economics mirrored political and military competition. The establishment of colonies and trade monopolies backed by military force was therefore characteristic of the so-called triangular trade. In fact, there were really two different but related "triangles" involved in the Atlantic trade. The first sent African slaves to New World plantations, tropical commodities such as sugar and tobacco from the Americas to Europe, and finished goods like iron and cloth from Europe to Africa. The second triangle, frowned upon by British authorities, sent rum from New England to Africa, slaves to the West Indies, and molasses back to New England (from which more rum could be manufactured.) Because rum distillers in Boston were getting their sugar duty free, the British government attempted to use the Navigation Acts to restrain unauthorized commerce between the North American colonies and the West Indies, creating one of the tensions that would lead to the American Revolution. Powerful vested interests became associated with sugar, as planters, traders, and manufacturers (as well as the politicians they patronized) tried to protect their economic interests.

The plantations themselves, as both consumers of labor and providers of commodities, were the focal point of this system. There was some variation in how plantations were organized; the British, for example, preferred to feed their slaves, whereas the Portuguese more commonly had the slaves provide their own sustenance from small plots given them for that purpose. Nevertheless, the organization of sugar plantations, and the technology on which they ran, was very consistent throughout this period. On a typical Caribbean plantation, a "great house" was occupied by the owner and his family, or stood empty waiting for their occasional arrival. On the other end of the social scale, African slaves planted, weeded, and harvested the cane. It was nasty and brutal work. As difficult as it is to cut sugar by

Chapter 4

Sweet Nexus:

Sugar and the

Origins of the

Modern World

(1600–1800)

hand, involving as it does the risk of having your limbs cut by the tough and fibrous cane, the most difficult tasks were probably planting the cane and weeding the fields, an endless stooping drudgery.

These two extremes of the social and economic life of the plantation, master and field slave, were common to all commodity-producing slave economies of the period. What set sugar apart was its character as an *agro-industrial* enterprise. Agriculture, however the labor system is organized, usually follows a seasonal pattern that allows for at least some "down time." The commercial production of sugar, however, was organized more like a modern factory, where profitable operation requires that the assembly line is always rolling and raw materials are constantly at hand. The reason was that cane sugar was much too bulky to be a profitable export. The initial stages of processing had to take place on or very near the plantation. Sugar cane had to be planted year round, so that it could be harvested year round, so that the complex machinery that crushed the juice from the cane and began the initial processing could be constantly employed. In this way, early modern sugar production anticipated later industrial patterns.

Sugar was also at the cutting edge of an emerging global economic system. While the initial processing of cane into sugar took place in Brazil or the West Indies, the final stage of manufacture, in which the most value was added to the product, was completed in Europe or North America. This pattern brings to mind "core-periphery" economic relationships, in which the production of raw materials or of commodities that had been partially processed to a stage where they could be profitably transported (e.g., rough brown sugar or molasses) was characteristic of the economic periphery. The most profitable stages in the commodity cycle, such as the refining of pure white sugar, packaging, and retailing, took place in the more developed core. In spite of the early appearance of factory production in the West Indies, therefore, the profits from sugar were highly concentrated not there but in Europe.

THE METHOD

The sources in this chapter approach the topic of sugar from a variety of different angles. Your ultimate goal is to better understand the "commodity chain" that connects consumers, merchants, manufacturers, organizers of production, and laborers into a single social and economic system. Each source can be thought of as describing one or more links in this chain. Another important set of questions has to do with how the participants in this nexus of sugar *themselves* regarded the economic, social, and political implications of the system. Keep the following questions in mind as you read:

- If the author of the source mentions sugar in a positive way, what does he consider to be the benefits of sugar consumption, exchange, or production? Make note of all the *positive* elements of sugar mentioned in these documents.

- Are any *negative* aspects of sugar consumption, exchange, or production mentioned? How do the authors of these pieces include (or exclude) information about slavery in their observations? What are the different effects of sugar on England, the West Indies, and Africa?

- If the subject of slavery is mentioned, is it treated more as an economic or as a moral issue? If the author thinks it necessary to justify slavery, how does he do so? If the source indicates opposition to slavery, what are the grounds for that opposition?

- Taken together, how do these sources represent the economic, social, and political consequences of sugar in a trans-Atlantic context?

In the following paragraphs, some background is given for each source. You will want to refer back to this section when reading the evidence.

Source 1, *A Vindication of Sugars against the charge of Dr. Willis, other physicians, and common prejudices, dedicated to the ladies,* was written in 1715 by Dr. Frederick Slare, a prominent member of the College of Physicians. While Slare had a very positive attitude toward the increasing consumption of sugar in England, not everyone did. The Dr. Willis to whom the title refers had published a well-regarded medical encyclopedia in 1685. In that book, Willis connected increasing sugar consumption with declining health. He wrote:

> I so much disapprove things preserved, or very much seasoned with sugar, that I judge the invention of it and its immoderate use to have very much contributed to the vast increase of the scurvy in this late age. . . . A certain famous author had laid the cause of the English consumption [tuberculosis] on the immoderate use of sugar amongst our countrymen.[3]

In the thirty years between Willis's warnings and Slare's response, sugar consumption in England had increased dramatically. Slare's *Vindication* goes beyond the medical debate to show the importance that sugar had attained in the daily life of the English.

The drawing by E. T. Parris reproduced as Source 2 shows the end of that process in the mid-nineteenth century, when the English were the great sugar consumers of the world. His drawing of a near-empty sugar barrel in front of a grocer's shop has much to tell us about English attitudes toward sugar consumption by that time.

Another difference between 1685 and 1715 was that by the latter date sugar had created additional powerful vested interests in British society and politics. Source 3 is a letter to a member of Parliament in 1745 from an individual who was lobbying politicians on behalf of sugar interests. The question had to do with how much the

3. Dr. Thomas Willis, *The London Practice of Physick: Or the whole practical part of Physick contained in the work of Dr. Willis* (London: Thomas Basset and William Crooke, 1685).

Chapter 4

Sweet Nexus:

Sugar and the

Origins of the

Modern World

(1600–1800)

British government should tax sugar at the point of its arrival in England, i.e., how high the "duties" should be. The huge profits that were generated by the sugar industry made a tempting target for a government that was trying to raise revenue to fight its increasingly expensive wars with France. This author warns that raising the tax would do more harm than good, and in the course of his argument shows that sugar had become closely tied up with economic, political, and military policies by the mid-eighteenth century.

Source 4 gives a visual sense of how a late-eighteenth-century Englishman conceptualized the economic relationship between three continents. "Europe Supported by Africa and America," published in 1796 by the great poet and graphic artist William Blake, can perhaps best be read in conjunction with this short passage taken from a description of the French sugar islands from approximately the same period:

> I do not know if coffee and sugar are essential to the happiness of Europe, but I know well that these two products have accounted for the unhappiness of two great regions of the world: America has been depopulated so as to have land on which to plant them; Africa has been depopulated so as to have the people to cultivate them.[4]

William Blake saw himself as a prophet using his art to restore ancient moral virtues to Britain, an attitude that informs this engraving.

Source 5 moves us away from English consumption patterns and trade policies and focuses our attention on where and how this commodity was produced. These statistics show the total number of slaves imported into the British West Indies (Barbados, Jamaica, and the Leeward Islands) between 1640 and 1700, as well as the total black population of each of these areas in 1670, 1680, and 1713. You should consider what these statistics tell us about the demographics of slavery. When interpreting these numbers, remember this simple statement about African slaves in the Caribbean from historian Patrick Manning: "Most of the slaves died early and without progeny."[5]

Source 6 gives us an African perspective on plantation life in the West Indies. The extracts come from an autobiography originally published in 1793, *The Life of Olaudah Equiano, or Gustavus Vassa, the African.* Equiano's book, intended to support the cause of those fighting to abolish the Atlantic slave trade, is best known for its description of his capture as a child in West Africa and his experience of the terrible "Middle Passage" across the Atlantic.[6] Equiano became the slave of a British

4. J. H. Bernardin de Saint Pierre, *Voyage to the Isle de France, the Isle de Bourbon, the Cape of Good Hope, with New Observations on Nature and Mankind by an Officer of the King* (1773), cited in Sidney Mintz, *Sweetness and Power: The Place of Sugar in Modern History* (New York: Penguin, 1985), frontispiece.

5. Patrick Manning, "Migrations of Africans to the Americas: The Impact on Africans, Africa and the World," *The History Teacher,* 26 (May 1993), p. 295.

6. However, some historians now believe that Equiano may have been born in the Americas and created the story of kidnap and transportation using the stories of other Africans who experienced them firsthand.

naval officer, and after fighting in many battles against the French during the Seven Years War (1756–1763), he thought he had earned his freedom. The extract begins with his despondency in learning that his master has sold him to an American merchant, for whom he then becomes a trusted clerk. In the course of doing his master's business, Equiano observes and comments on the effects of plantation slavery in the Caribbean. Not included in these extracts is the story of how Equiano later won his own freedom and became an important figure in the British abolitionist movement.

Source 7 gives us quite a different view of plantation life in the West Indies. Richard Ligon's *True and Exact History of the Island of Barbadoes* (1673) is a fascinating account of all aspects of sugar production on Barbados in the late seventeenth century, when that island was just establishing itself as a principal supplier of the expanding British market. Ligon was himself a sugar planter, and his book shows us both the early establishment of sugar in the British West Indies and its development into one of the great sources of wealth for the British Empire. Ligon gives us a close-up look at the complex, time-sensitive organization of labor and machinery required to produce sugar for profit, as well as a view of the "Masters, Servants, and Slaves" who made up plantation society.

The two pictures that make up Source 8 are taken from William Clark's *Ten Views of Antigua* (1823). While these representations were made more than a century and a half after Ligon described the process of sugar production on Barbados, we can still correlate the two sources, since no fundamental changes had taken place in that time. These pictures both illustrate the world that Ligon describes and give us a chance to see how English artists presented that reality to their audiences.

Source 9 is also a visual one, but it takes us in a different direction. In the late eighteenth century there was a growing abolitionist movement in England. We can see the connection that some abolitionists made with sugar when they organized themselves into an Anti-Saccharite Society. Here we see an advertisement appealing to that market from a maker of sugar bowls for the English table.

Finally, Source 10 gives us an African account of the despair of enslavement, the horrors of transport across the Atlantic, and the difficult adjustment to slave status in the Americas. *The Biography of Mahommah Gardo Baquaqua* tells the tale of a young African man who was captured by his African enemies, taken to the coast, across the Atlantic, and finally to Brazil. While slavery had been abolished in the British Empire by this time, its use continued in Brazil and Cuba until 1888, creating a continuing demand in Africa. Baquaqua soon escaped from Brazil to New York. There he attended college and told his story to a Christian minister, an abolitionist who revised and edited Baquaqua's story for publication. Though Baquaqua was raised as a Muslim, he had by this time converted to Christianity.

Chapter 4

Sweet Nexus:

Sugar and the

Origins of the

Modern World

(1600–1800)

THE EVIDENCE

Source 1 from Frederick Slare, A Vindication of Sugars against the charge of Dr. Willis, other physicians, and common prejudices, dedicated to the ladies *(London: Timothy Goodwin, 1715).*

1. Frederick Slare Defends Sugar, 1715

The making an apology for **SUGAR** might seem either needless or impertinent, especially in England, where the general use of it does so much commend and justify its goodness. But having met with great opponents to so useful a blessing, and finding not only the mouths of many opened to defame and cry down, but their pens also employed to blacken and calumniate the noble subject of this discourse, even at the same time they are eating and drinking it; this makes it require and justly deserve a vindication.

To you, Ladies, on several accounts I address this, my appeal, in vindication of injured and defamed **SUGAR.** Nature, who has given you more accurate and refined palates, had made you more competent judges of taste; as not being debauched by sour or uncouth wines, or drams, or offensive smoke, or the more sordid juice of the Indian . . . tobacco; or vitiated by salt and sour pickles, too much to the delight of our coarser sex. . . .

I have frequently commended the ladies' well chosen morning repasts, called breakfasts, as consisting of good materials; namely, bread, butter, milk, water and sugar; chocolate and tea are also endowed with uncommon virtues, when warily and discretely used. Nor do I decry and condemn coffee . . . especially where they join with it a quantity of fine sugar.

Out of respect to the fair sex, especially those that love their beauty, or fine proportions, as well, if not better than their lives, I shall suggest one caveat, or caution, to those that are inclining to be too fat: namely, that sugar being so very high a nourisher may dispose them to be fatter than they desire to be, who are afraid of their fine shapes; but then it makes them amends by supplying a very wholesome and goodly countenance, and sweeten peevish and cross humors, where they unhappily prevail.

The West Indian merchant, who loads his ships with this sweet treasure, will certainly be pleased with this defense made in the behalf of sweet Indian Cane. By this commodity have numbers of persons, of inconsiderable estates, raised plantations, and from thence have gained such wealth as to return to their native country very rich, and have purchased, and do daily purchase great estates.

The grocer, who retails what the merchant furnishes by wholesale, is also concerned for the credit and good name of his defamed and scandalized goods, out of which he has also made his fortune, his family rich and wealthy. In short, there is no family throughout the kingdom but would make use of it, if they can get it, and would look on it as a matter of great complaint and a grievance to be debarred the use of it. . . .

There has been a great and popular outcry against sugar, as if it contained in it a secret acid, or some dangerous sharpness which causes scurveys, consumptions, and other dreaded distempers.

The design of this discourse is to vindicate sugar from such an undeserved and unjust censure. . . .

I have heard many ladies of the better rank, who read books of some learned persons, condemn sugar, and have denied their poor babes very injuriously. . . . But I have a strong . . . argument to recommend the use of sugar to infants, of which to defraud them is a very cruel thing, if not a crying sin. The argument I bring from nature's first . . . intended food for children so soon as they are born, which is that fine juice or liquor prepared in the mother's breasts . . . of a fine, delicate sweet taste. This sweet is somewhat analogous, or a taste agreeable to sugar. . . . Is it not therefore reasonable to conclude that this excellent and pleasant sweet, which imitates our first and most natural food and nutriment, should be with praises embraced and used?

If we but examine the preserving quality of sugar, how it prevents many corruptible and perishing fruits and juices for months, such as will not keep 24 hours from turning sour . . . this both shows the great use, as well as the healthy and salubrious quality of sugar. . . .

I have also inquired of such as have lived in the Indies and have seen sugar made in their own work house, to inform myself what property the sugar had in its primitive juice, which they told me was pleasant and wholesome; and that the worst of the scum and sediment would fatten hogs, and that the scum or sediment of the second boiling was given the slaves for food. . . .

I will set down an experiment I had from a friend. He was a little lean man who used to drink much wine in the company of strong drinkers. I asked him how he was able to bear it? He told me that he received much damage in his health, and was apt to be fuddled before he used to dissolve sugar in his wine, from that time he was never sick, nor inflamed, nor fuddled with wine.

I do declare that I cannot charge sugar with one ail or injury that it ever brought upon me. . . . I am, God be praised, free from any disease, have no symptoms of scurvy or consumption, and though near sixty-seven yet few will allow of it by my countenance or activity that I present that age; notwithstanding my having indulged myself in such quantities of sugar. I have lived to bury above fourscore fellows of the College of Physicians that were my seniors since my first admission, and a vast number that were my juniors; many of this number were bitter enemies to that most delicious and curious preparation, fine sugar. . . . I may justly attribute a great deal of the healthful constitution which I now enjoy to the nourishing virtue of sugar.

Chapter 4

Sweet Nexus:

Sugar and the

Origins of the

Modern World

(1600–1800)

Source 2 from L. A. G. Strong, The Story of Sugar *(London: Weidenfeld & Nicolson, 1954). Photo: Centre for the Study of Cartoons and Caricature, University of Kent, Canterbury.*

2. E. T. Parris Cartoon Showing English Attitudes Toward Sugar Consumption

Source 3 from A Letter to a Member of Parliament, Concerning the Importance of our Sugar-Colonies to Great Britain, by a Gentleman, who resided many Years in the Island of Jamaica *(London: J. Taylor, 1745).*

3. A Letter to a Member of Parliament, 1745

Sir, You will remember, that when I had the pleasure of your company, One evening last week, the subject of our conversation was chiefly about the laying on an Additional Duty upon SUGAR, which I told you would be a great hardship on the sugar planter in the West Indies, and very little if any benefit to the revenue, whilst you were of a different opinion . . . you desired me to commit my arguments to writing. I come now to answer your request, and for the sake of method, will lay out the reasons and arguments that I have to advance on the subject, under three principal heads:

First, In the first place, I will endeavour to convince you, that whatever additional duty shall be laid on sugar, it will be at the cost of the sugar planter, at least for some years.

Secondly, I shall show, that such an additional duty will be an oppression and discouragement and an unequal load upon our sugar colonies at this juncture especially, and will render abortive the very scheme itself which is intended by it, of advancing the revenue. And

Thirdly, I shall set forth the great advantages that this nation receives from the sugar colonies, and especially from the island of Jamaica, and the great advantages that it will continue to receive, if due encouragement be given to the sugar planter.

The principal of our home manufactures which are taxed are leather, soap, candles, salt, malt, beer, ale and spirits. . . . The commodities are such as people can't live without . . . and every family in the parish is an immediate purchaser from the manufacturer.

Now the case of the sugar planter is, that he is at a prodigious distance from the market, does not know what the consumption may be, nor what quantity of sugar may be sent from the other islands, and being already in debt, as the greatest number of the sugar planters are, and having already established his sugar works . . . he must be ruined if those are not kept employed, and he can have no other way to employ them but in making sugar, and makes as much as he can, and sends it to market, upon distant hopes it will fetch a price in proportion to the expense and trouble he hath been at, and when it is at market he must sell it for what the sugar baker and grocer will please to give him.

After that he hath been at the charge of making it, and at the expense of the extraordinary high freight and insurance, and the duty, and many contingent charges . . . and it being a heavy wasting perishable commodity, and the owner in debt, the factor [agent] must sell it, he can't keep it long by him; and instead

Chapter 4
Sweet Nexus:
Sugar and the
Origins of the
Modern World
(1600–1800)

of having every consumer for his purchaser, as I mentioned before to be the case of our home manufactures, he has but two purchasers, that is, the sugar baker and the grocer. . . .

I hope, Sir, that from the premises you will easily conclude, that unless the price of sugar here at market do advance very considerably, the sugar planter can't go on, but will be ruined. . . . If the planter, to all his other advanced charges, hath a further duty laid upon his commodity, he will be disabled from purchasing every year a fresh supply of Negroes, mules, and cattle; and as his present stock drops off, he will be disabled from making the quantity of sugar he does at present . . . by which means the scheme for raising more money upon that commodity, by advancing the duty, will be rendered abortive. . . .

The principal charge which the sugar planter is at, to raise and carry on his work, is Negroes; and those are purchased in Africa by the English merchants, chiefly with the produce and manufactures of this nation, such as woolen goods. . . . At the same time that they are purchasing the Negroes on the coast of Africa, with those cargoes of British manufactures, they purchase also a great deal of gold, elephants teeth, and some very valuable dying woods.

And after that these Negroes are thus purchased, and carried to the West Indies for a market, the sugar planter having furnished himself, the surplus are disposed of on the Spanish coast for gold and silver; and, together with the Negroes, are also introduced into the Spanish settlements, a good quantity of our British manufactures; so much, that for these many years past we have seldom received less, by the trade from Jamaica to the Spanish coast, than two hundred thousand pounds a year, in gold and silver; which has been transmitted from Jamaica to England.

For strength to carry on his sugar work, next to the Negroes, the planter must be furnished with mules, cattle, horses, etc. . . . Add to this, the great quantity of nails, locks, hinges, bolts, and other sorts of iron ware; and lead that he must have for his buildings. And for his field work he must have great quantities of bills, hoes, axes, iron chains; also gear for his mill and his cattle . . . and all this of *English* manufacture. . . .

Besides this extraordinary expense . . . he must have a house to live in, and furniture, and clothes, and other necessaries for himself and family, servants and slaves. To build his house he must have materials from England . . . and his furniture and clothing entirely from England. And as the climate is excessively hot, for the convenience of their wives and children, those who can afford it have coaches, chariots, chaises and other such conveniences to accommodate themselves; and all from England.

And for their food, they have a great deal, as cheese, bacon, pickles, some flour and biscuits, when cheap, and beer, ale and cider, in great quantities from England; salted beef and butter from Ireland; and salted fish, flour, biscuits and sundry other kinds of provisions for their Negroes from North America.

There are in the island of Jamaica only, a hundred thousand Negroes, a few more or less; every one of these . . . do make use of the value of twenty shillings a year, in goods from England. In clothing they make use of a vast quantity of Manchester goods . . . and many other implements, all of *British* manufacture. I believe . . . it amounts to a hundred thousand pounds a year in British manufactures, consumed by the Negroes in Jamaica only.

And now, Sir, if you'll be pleased to take a view of the whole process of the sugar manufacture, from the beginning to the time of delivering the commodity into the hands of the consumer; that is to say, from purchasing the Negroes on the coast of Africa, and transporting them to the West Indies . . . I am sure that you will be amazed to consider, what a prodigious number of ships, of sailors, of merchants, of tradesmen, manufacturers, mechanics, and labourers, are continually employed, and reap a profit thereby. . . .

And should the sugar colonies be so much discouraged, by the laying on of an additional duty, or by any other ways or means whatever, which may disable them from carrying on their works, and making the quantity of sugar which they do at present, or have done for some years past, you see plainly how very much our trade and navigation, and how many of our manufactures would be affected by it, and that would not be the worst of it neither, because . . . in proportion as our sugar colonies should decline, those of our neighbors, our enemies and rivals in trade and navigation would advance.

Chapter 4

Sweet Nexus:

Sugar and the

Origins of the

Modern World

(1600–1800)

Source 4 from J. G. Steadman, Narrative of a five years' expedition, against the Revolted Negroes of Surinam *(London: J. Johnson and J. Edwards, 1796); reprinted in Sidney Mintz,* Sweetness and Power: The Place of Sugar in Modern History *(New York: Viking Press, 1995). Photo: Courtesy of the James Ford Bell Library, University of Minnesota.*

4. William Blake, "Europe Supported by Africa and America," 1796

Source 5 from Richard Dunn, Sugar and Slaves: The Rise of the Planter Class in the English West Indies, 1624–1713 (New York: Norton, 1972), pp. 230, 312.

5. Importation and Population Statistics for the British West Indies in the 18th Century

Year	Barbados: Slave Imports	Barbados: Total Black Population	Jamaica: Slave Imports	Jamaica: Total Black Population	Leeward Islands: Slave Imports	Leeward Islands: Total Black Population
1640–1650	18,700		?		2,000	
1670		30,000		7,000		3,000
1651–1675	51,100		8,000		10,100	
1680		50,000		15,000		9,000
1676–1700	64,700		77,100		32,000	
1713		45,000		55,000		30,000

Note: The British Leeward Islands consisted of Antigua, Barbuda, Anguilla, the British Virgin Islands, Montserrat, and St. Kitts–Nevis.

Chapter 4

Sweet Nexus:

Sugar and the

Origins of the

Modern World

(1600–1800)

Source 6 from Olaudah Equiano, The Life of Olaudah Equiano, or Gustavus Vassa, the African *(Mineola: N.Y.: Dover, 1999; originally published by James Nicholls, Leeds, 1814), pp. 69–81.*

6. From Olaudah Equiano,
The Life of Olaudah Equiano,
1814

On the 13th of February 1763, from the mast-head, we descried our destined island, Montserrat, and soon after I beheld those

Regions of sorrow, doleful shades, where peace
And rest can rarely dwell. Hope never comes
That comes to all, but torture without end
Still urges.

At the sight of this land of bondage, a fresh horror ran through all my frame, and chilled me to the heart. My former slavery now rose in dreadful review to my mind, and displayed nothing but misery, stripes, and chains; and in the first paroxysm of my grief, I called upon God's thunder, and his avenging power, to direct the stroke of death to me, rather than . . . to be sold from lord to lord.

In this state of my mind our ship came to an anchor, and soon after discharged her cargo. I now knew what it was to work hard; I was made to help to unload the ship. And to comfort me in my distress, at that time two of the sailors robbed me of all my money, and ran away from the ship. I had been so long used to an European climate, that at first I felt the scorching West-India sun very painful, while the dashing surf would toss the boat and the people in it, frequently above high-watermark. Sometimes our limbs were broken with this, or even attended with instant death, and I was day by day mangled and torn.

About the middle of May, when the ship was got ready to sail for England, . . . Captain Doran sent for me on shore one morning; and I was told by the messenger that my fate was determined. With trembling steps and a fluttering heart I came to the captain, and found with him one Mr. Robert King, a Quaker, and the first merchant in the place. . . . Captain Doran said . . . if he were to stay in the West-Indies he would be glad to keep me himself; but he could not venture to take me to London, for he was very sure that when I came there, I would leave him. I at that instant burst out a crying, and begged much of him to take me with him to England, but all to no purpose. He told me he had got me the very best master in the whole island, with whom I should be as happy as if I were in England, and for that reason he chose to let him have me, though he could sell me to his own brother-in-law for a great deal more money than what he got from that gentleman. My new master, Mr. King, then made a reply, and said the reason he had bought me was on account of my good character; and, as he had not the least doubt of my good behaviour, I should be very well off with him. He also told me he did not live in the West-Indies, but at Philadelphia, where he was soon going. . . .

. . . Mr. King soon asked me what I could do, and at the same time said he did not mean to treat me as a common slave. I told him I knew something of seamanship, and could shave and dress hair pretty well; I could refine wines, which I had learned on shipboard, where I had often done it; and that I could write, and understood arithmetic tolerably well as far as the Rule of Three. . . .

Mr. King dealt in all manner of merchandize. . . . He had . . . many vessels . . . of different sizes, which used to go about the island . . . to collect rum, sugar, and other goods. I understood pulling and managing those boats very well; and this hard work, which was the first that he set me to, in the sugar seasons used to be my constant employment. I have rowed the boat and slaved at the oars, from one hour to sixteen in the twenty-four; during which I had fifteen pence sterling per day to live on, though sometimes only ten pence. However, this was much more than was allowed to other slaves that used to work often with me, and belonged to other gentlemen on the island. . . . For it is a common practice in the West-Indies for men to purchase slaves, though they have not plantations themselves, in order to let them out to planters and merchants, at so much a piece by the day, and they give what they choose, out of this produce of their daily work; to their slaves for subsistence. This allowance is often very scanty. . . .

. . . In many of the estates, on the different islands where I used to be sent for rum or sugar, . . . I had all the opportunity I could wish for to see the dreadful usage of the poor men—usage that reconciled me to my situation, and made me bless God for the hands into which I had fallen. . . .

. . . I was often a witness to cruelties of every kind, which were exercised on my unhappy fellow slaves. I used frequently to have different cargoes of new negroes in my care for sale; and it was almost a constant practice with our clerks, and other whites, to commit violent depredations on the chastity of the female slaves; and to these atrocities I was, though with reluctance, obliged to submit at all times, being unable to help them. When we have had some of these slaves on board my master's vessels to carry them to other islands, or to America, I have known our mates commit these acts most shamefully, to the disgrace not of christians only, but of men. I have even known them gratify their brutal passion with females not ten years old; and these abominations some of them practised to such a scandalous excess, that one of our captains discharged the mate and others on that account. And yet in Montserrat I have seen a negro-man staked to the ground, and cut most shockingly, and then his ears cut off, bit by bit, because he had been connected with a white woman, who was a common prostitute! As if it were no crime in the whites to rob an innocent African girl of her virtue; but most heinous in a black man only to gratify a passion of nature, where the temptation was offered by one of a different color, though the most abandoned woman of her species.

One Mr. D——, told me he had sold 41,000 negroes, and he once cut off a negro-man's leg for running away. I asked him if the man had died in the operation,

Chapter 4

Sweet Nexus:

Sugar and the

Origins of the

Modern World

(1600–1800)

how he, as a christian, could answer, for the horrid act, before God. And he told me, answering was a thing of another world; what he thought and did were policy. I told him that the christian doctrine taught us "to do unto others as we would that others should do unto us." He then said that his scheme had the desired effect—it cured that man and some others of running away.

Another negro-man was half hanged, and then burnt, for attempting to poison a cruel overseer. Thus, by repeated cruelties, are the wretched first urged to despair, and then murdered, because they still retain so much of human nature about them as to wish to put an end to their misery, and to retaliate on their tyrants! These overseers are, indeed, for the most part, persons of the worst character of any denomination of men in the West-Indies. Unfortunately, many humane gentlemen, by not residing on their estates, are obliged to leave the management of them in the hands of these human butchers, who cut and mangle the slaves in a shocking manner, on the most trivial occasions, and altogether treat them, in every respect, like brutes. They pay no regard to the situation of pregnant women, nor the least attention to the lodging of the field negroes. Their huts, which ought to be well covered, and the place dry where they take their short repose, are often open sheds, built in damp places; so that, when the poor creatures return tired from the toils of the field, they contract many disorders, from being exposed to the damp air in this uncomfortable state. . . .

The neglect certainly conspires with many others to cause a decrease in the births, as well as in the lives of the grown negroes. I can quote many instances of gentlemen who reside on their own estates in the West-Indies, and then the scene is quite changed; the negroes are treated with lenity and proper care, by which their lives are prolonged, and their masters profited. To the honour of humanity, I know several gentlemen who managed their estates in this manner, and found that benevolence was their true interest. And, among many I could mention in Montserrat, whose slaves looked remarkably well, and never needed any fresh supplies of negroes . . . , I have the honour of knowing a most worthy and humane gentleman, who is a native of Barbadoes, and has estates there. This gentleman has written a treatise on the usage of his own slaves. He allows them two hours for refreshment at mid-day, and many other indulgences and comforts, . . . so that by these attentions he saves the lives of his negroes, and keeps them healthy, and as happy as the condition of slavery can admit. I myself, as shall appear in the sequel, managed an estate, where, by such attentions, the negroes were uncommonly cheerful and healthy, and did more work by half than by the common mode of treatment they usually do. For want, therefore, of such care and attention to the poor negroes, and otherwise oppressed as they are, it is no wonder that the decrease should require 20,000 new negroes annually to fill up the vacant places of the dead.

Even in Barbadoes, notwithstanding those humane exceptions which I have mentioned and others with which I am acquainted that justly make it quoted as a place where slaves meet with the best treatment, and need fewest recruits of any in the West-Indies; yet this island requires 1,000 negroes annually to keep up the original stock, which is only 80,000. So that the whole term of a negro's life may be said to be there, but sixteen years! And yet the climate here is in every respect the same as that from which they are taken, except in being more wholesome. . . .

It was very common in several of the islands, particularly in St. Kitt's, for the slaves to be branded with the initial letters of their master's name, and a load of heavy iron hooks hung about their necks. Indeed on the most trivial occasions they were loaded with chains, and often instruments of torture were added. The iron muzzle, thumb-screws, &c. are so well known as not to need a description, and were sometimes applied for the slightest faults. I have seen a negro beaten till some of his bones were broken, for only letting a pot boil over. It is not uncommon, after a flogging, to make slaves go on their knees and thank their owners, and pray, or rather say, "God bless you." I have often asked many of the men slaves (who used to go several miles to their wives, and late in the night, after having been wearied with a hard day's labour) why they went so far for wives, and did not take them of their own master's negro-women, and particularly those who lived together as household slaves. Their answers have ever been— "Because when the master or mistress choose to punish the women, they make the husbands flog their own wives, and that we could not bear to do." Is it surprising such usage should drive the poor creatures to despair, and make them seek a refuge in death, from those evils which render their lives intolerable[?]

This they frequently do. A negro-man, on board a vessel of my master's, while I belonged to her, having been put in irons for some trifling misdemeanour, and kept in that state some days, being weary of life, took an opportunity of jumping over-board into the sea; however he was picked up without being drowned. Another, whose life was also a burden to him, resolved to starve himself to death, and refused to eat any victuals: this procured him a severe flogging; and he also on the first occasion that offered, jumped overboard at Charles Town, but was saved.

Nor is there any greater reward shewn to the little property than there is to the persons and lives of the negroes. . . . The wretched field-slaves, after toiling all the day for an unfeeling owner, who gives them but little victuals, steal sometimes a few moments from rest or refreshment to gather some small portion of grass, according as their time will admit. This they commonly tie up in a parcel; either a bits worth (sixpence) or half a bit's worth, and bring it to town, or to the market to sell. Nothing is more common than for the white people, on this occasion, to take the grass from them without paying for it; and not only so, but too often also, to my knowledge, our clerks and many others, at the same time have committed acts of violence on the poor, wretched, and helpless females; whom I have seen for hours stand crying to no purpose, and get no redress or pay of any kind. Is not this one common and crying sin enough to bring down God's judgment on the islands? He tells us the oppressor and the oppressed are

Chapter 4

Sweet Nexus:

Sugar and the

Origins of the

Modern World

(1600–1800)

both in his hands; and if these are not the poor, the broken-hearted, the blind, the captive, the bruised, of which our Saviour speaks, who are they? . . .

. . . Mr. James Tobin, a zealous labourer in the vineyard of slavery, gives an account of a French planter, of his acquaintance, in the island of Martinico, who shewed him many mulattoes working in the fields like beasts of burden; and he told Mr. Tobin these *were all the produce of his own loins*! And I myself have known similar instances. Pray, reader, are these sons and daughters of the French planter less his children by being begotten on black women? And what must be the virtue of those legislators, and the feelings of those fathers, who estimate the lives of their sons, however begotten, at no more than fifteen pounds, though they should be murdered, as the act says, *out of wantonness and bloody-mindedness*? But is not the slave-trade entirely a war with the heart of man? And surely that which is begun by breaking down the barriers of virtue, involves in its continuance destruction to every principle, and buries all sentiments in ruin!

I have often seen slaves, particularly those who were meager, in different islands, put into scales and weighed; and then sold from three-pence to six-pence or nine-pence a pound. . . . And at or after a sale, even those negroes born in the islands it is not uncommon to see taken from their wives, wives from their husbands, and children from their parents, and sent off to other islands, and wherever else their merciless lords choose; and, probably, never more, during life, see each other! Oftentimes my heart has bled at these partings; when the friends of the departed have been at the water-side, and, with sighs and tears, have kept their eyes fixed on the vessel till it went out of sight. . . .

Nor was such usage as this confined to particular places or individuals; for, in all the different islands in which I have been (and I have visited no less than fifteen) the treatment of the slaves was nearly the same; so nearly, indeed, that the history of an island, or even a plantation, with a few such exceptions as I have mentioned, might serve for a history of the whole. Such a tendency has the slave-trade to debauch men's minds, and harden them to every feeling of humanity! For I will not suppose that the dealers in slaves are born worse than other men. No; it is the fatality of this mistaken avarice, that it corrupts the milk of human kindness and turns it into gall. And, had the pursuits of those men been different, they might have been as generous, as tender-hearted, and just, as they are unfeeling, rapacious and cruel. Surely this traffic cannot be good, which spreads like a pestilence, and taints what it touches! Which violates that first natural right of mankind, equality, and independency; and gives one man a dominion over his fellows which God could never intend! For it raises the owner to a state as far above man as it depresses the slave below it; and, with the presumption of human pride, sets distinction between them, immeasurable in extent, and endless in duration! Yet how mistaken is the avarice even of the planters. Are slaves more useful by being thus humbled to the condition of brutes, than they would be if suffered to enjoy the privileges of men? The freedom which diffuses health and prosperity throughout Britain answers you— "No." When you make men slaves, you deprive them of half their virtue, you set them, in your own conduct, an example of fraud, rapine, and cruelty, and compel them to live with you in a state of war; and yet you complain that they are not honest or faithful! You stupefy them with stripes, and think it necessary to keep them in a state of ignorance; and yet you assert that they are incapable of learning; that their minds are such a barren soil or moor that culture would be lost on them; and that they came from a climate, where nature, though prodigal of her bounties in a degree unknown to yourselves, has left man alone scant and unfinished, and incapable of enjoying the treasures she has poured out for him!—An assertion at once impious and absurd. Why do you use those instruments of torture? Are they fit to be applied by one rational being to another? And are ye not struck with shame and mortification, to see the partakers of your nature reduced so low? But, above all, are there no dangers attending this mode of treatment? Are you not hourly in dread of an insurrection?

Source 7 from Richard Ligon, A True & Exact History of the Island of Barbadoes *(London: Parker & Guy, 1673).*

7. From Richard Ligon, *A True & Exact History of the Island of Barbadoes,* 1673

The island [of Barbados] is divided into three sorts of men, *viz.* Masters, [indentured] Servants, and Slaves. The slaves and their posterity, being subject to their masters forever, are kept and preserved with greater care than the servants, who are theirs but for five years, according to the law of the island. So that for the time, the servants have the worser lives, for they are put to very hard labour, ill lodging, and their diet very slight. When we first came on the island some planters themselves did not eat bone meat above twice a week. . . . But the servants no bone meat at all, unless an ox died and then they were feasted as long as that lasted. And till they had planted good store of plantains, the Negroes were fed with . . . food . . . which gave them much discontent. But when they had plantains enough to serve them they were heard no more to complain; for tis a food they take great delight in, and their manner of dressing and eating it is this: 'tis gathered for them . . . upon Saturday, by the keeper of the plantain grove; who is an able Negro and knows well the number who are to be fed with this fruit; and as he gathers, lays them all together, till they fetch them away, which is about five a clock in the afternoon, for that day they break off work sooner by an hour, partly for this purpose and partly for the fire in the furnaces to be put out, and the Ingenio [machinery] and the rooms made clean; besides they are to wash, shave and trim themselves against Sunday. But 'tis a lovely sight to see a hundred handsome Negroes, men and women, with every one a grass-green bunch of these fruits on their heads. . . . Having brought this fruit

Chapter 4

Sweet Nexus:

Sugar and the

Origins of the

Modern World

(1600–1800)

home to their own houses, and pulling off the skin of so much as they will use, they boil it in water, making it into balls, and so they eat it. One bunch a week is a Negroe's allowance. To this, no bread nor drink, but water. Their lodging at night a board, with nothing under, nor anything a top of them. They are happy people, whom so little contents. Very good servants, if they be not spoiled by the English. . . .

As for the usage of the servants, it is much as the master is, merciful or cruel. Those that are merciful treat their servants well, both in their meat, drink and lodging, and give them work such as is not unfit for a Christian to do. But if the masters be cruel, the servants have very wearisome and miserable lives. . . . I have seen an overseer beat a servant with a cane about the head, till the blood has followed, for a fault that is not worth the speaking of; and yet he must have patience or worse will follow. Truly, I have seen such cruelty there done to servants as I did not think one Christian could have done to another. But as more discrete and better natured men have come to rule there, the servants' lives have been much bettered; for now, most of the servants lie in hammocks, and in warm rooms, and when they come in wet have shift of shirts and drawers, which are all the clothes they wear, and are fed with bone meat twice or thrice a week. . . .

It has been accounted a strange thing, that the Negroes, being more than double the number of Christians that are there, and they accounted a bloody people . . . that they should not commit some horrid massacre upon the Christians thereby to enfranchise themselves and become masters of the island. But there are three reasons that take away this wonder: the one is, they are not suffered to touch or handle any weapons; the other, that they are held in such awe and slavery as they are fearful to appear in any daring act; and seeing the mustering of our men and hearing their gun shot (which nothing is more terrible to them) their spirits are subjugated to follow a condition, as they dare not look up to any bold attempt. Besides these, there is a third reason, which stops all designs of that kind, and that is they are fetched from several parts of Africa who speak several languages, and by that means one of them understands not another. For some of them are fetched from Guinea and Bonny . . . some from Angola, and some from the river of Gambia. And in some of these places where petty kingdoms are, they sell their subjects, as such as they take in battle, whom they make slaves; and some mean men sell their servants, their children, or sometimes their wives; and think all good traffic for such commodities as our merchants feed them.

When they are brought to us, the planters buy them out of the ship, where they find them stark naked, and therefore cannot be deceived in any outward infirmity. They choose them as they do horses in a market; the strongest, youngest, and most beautiful yield the greatest prices. . . . And we buy them so the sexes may be equal; for if they have more men than women the men who are unmarried will come to their masters and complain, that they cannot live without wives. And he tells them that the next ship that comes he will buy them wives, which satisfies them for the present; and so they expect the good time: which the master performing with them, the bravest fellow is to choose first, and so in order, as they are in place, and every one of them knows his better and gives him precedence, as cows do one another in passing through a narrow gate; for the most of them are as near beasts as may be, setting their souls aside. . . .

At the time the wife is to [give birth], her husband removes his board (which is his bed) to another room (for many several divisions they have, in their little houses, and none above six foot square) and leaves his wife to God, and her good fortune, in the room, and upon the board alone, and calls a neighbour to come to her, who gives little help to her delivery, but when the child is born (which she calls her Pickininny) she helps to make a little fire near her feet. . . . In a fortnight this woman is at work with her Pickininny at her back, as merry a soul as any there is. If the overseer be discreet, she is suffered to rest herself a little more than ordinary; but if not, she is compelled to do as others do. Times they have of suckling their children in the fields, and refreshing themselves; and good reason, for they carry burdens on their backs, and yet work too. . . . The work which the women do is most of it weeding, a stooping and painful work; at noon and night they are called home by the ring of a bell, where they have two hours time for their repast at noon; and at night, they rest from six till six a clock the next morning.

On Sunday they rest, and have the whole day at their pleasure; and the most of them use it as a day of rest and pleasure; but some of them who will make benefit of that day's liberty go where the mangrove trees grow and gather the bark, of which they make ropes, which they truck away for other commodities, as shirts and drawers. . . .

What their other opinions are in the matter of religion, I know not . . . they believe a resurrection, and that they shall go into their own country again, and have their youth renewed. And lodging this opinion in their hearts they make it an ordinary practice, upon any great fright, or threatening of their masters, to hang themselves. But Colonel Walrond having lost three or four of his best Negroes this way, and in a very little time, caused one of their heads to be cut off and set upon a pole a dozen foot high; and having done that caused all his Negroes to come forth and march around this head, and bid them look on it, whether this were not the head of such a one that hanged himself. Which they acknowledging he then told them that they were in a main error in thinking they went into their own countries after they were dead; for this man's head was here, as they all were witness of; and how was it possible, the body could go without a head. Being convinced by this sad yet lively spectacle they changed their opinions; and after that, no more hanged themselves. . . .

Though there be a mark set upon these people which will hardly ever be wiped off, as of their cruelties when they have advantages, and of their fearfulness and falseness; but no general rule but hath his exception: for I believe, and I have strong motives to cause me to be of that persuasion, that there are as honest,

[111]

Chapter 4

Sweet Nexus:

Sugar and the

Origins of the

Modern World

(1600–1800)

faithful, and conscionable people amongst them as amongst those of Europe, or any other part of the world. . . . And this is all I can remember concerning the Negroes, except of their games, which I could never learn because they lacked the language to teach me. . . .

Now for the masters, I have said but little, nor am able to say half of what they deserve. They are men of great abilities and parts, otherwise they could not go through with such great works as they undertake; the managing of one of their plantations being a work of such a latitude as will require a very good headpiece, to put in order and continue it so.

I can name a planter there, that feeds daily two hundred mouths, and keeps them in such order as there are no mutinies amongst them; and yet of several nations. All these are to be employed in their several abilities so as no one be idle. . . . After weeding comes planting . . . canes are to be planted at all times, that they may come in, one field after another; otherwise the work will stand still. . . . This work of planting and weeding the master himself is to see done; unless he have a very trusty and able overseer; and without such a one he will have too much to do. The next thing he is to consider, is the Ingenio [factory] . . . which is the *primum mobile* of the whole work. . . . If anything in the rollers . . . be at fault, the whole work stands still; or in the boiling house if the frames which hold the coppers . . . from the violence of the heat from the furnaces . . . crack or break, there is a stop in the work till that be mended. Or if any of the coppers have a mischance, and be burnt, and a new one must presently be had, there is a stay in the work . . . for all these depend upon one another, as wheels in a clock. . . . But the main impediment and stop of all is the loss of our cattle, and amongst them there are such diseases, as I have known that in one plantation thirty that have died in two days. . . . So that if any of these stops continue long, or the cattle cannot be recruited in a reasonable time, the work is at a stand; and by that means the canes grow over ripe and will in a very short time have their juice dried up, and will not be worth the grinding.

Now to recruit these cattle and horses . . . who are all liable to these mischances and decays, merchants must be consulted, ships provided, and a competent cargo of goods adventured, to make new voyages to foreign parts to supply those losses; and when that is done the casualties at sea are to be considered, and those happen several ways, either by shipwreck, piracy, or fire. A master of a ship, and a man accounted both able, stout, and honest, having transported goods of several kinds from England to a part of Africa, the river of Gambia, and had there exchanged his commodities for Negroes, which was that he intended to make his voyage of . . . did not, as the manner is, shackle one to another . . . but having an opinion of their honesty and faithfulness to him, as they had promised; and he being a credulous man, and himself good natured and merciful, suffered them to go loose, and they being double the number of those in the ship found their advantages, got weapons in their hands, and fell upon the sailors, knocking them on the heads, and cutting their throats so fast as the master found they were all lost . . . and so went down into the hold and blew all up with himself; and this was before they got out of the river. These, and several other ways there will happen that extremely retard the work of sugar making.

Now let us consider how many things there are to be thought on, that go to the actuating of this great work, and how many cares to prevent the mischances . . . and you will find them wise and provident men that go on and prosper in a work that depends upon so many contingents. . . .

The next thing is of their natures and dispositions, which I found compliable in a high degree to all virtues that those of the best sort of gentlemen call excellent. . . . So frank, so loving, and so good natured were these gentlemen one to another . . . that I perceived nothing wanting, that might make up a firm and lasting friendship amongst them. . . .

Colonel Thomas Modiford has often told me that he had taken a resolution to himself not to set his face for England till he had made his voyage and employment there worth him a hundred thousand pounds sterling; and all by this sugar plant. . . . Now if such estates as these may be raised by the well ordering of this plant, by industrious . . . men, why may not such estates, by careful keeping and moderate expending, be preserved in their posterity to the tenth generation, and by all the sweet negotiation of sugar?

Chapter 4

Sweet Nexus:

Sugar and the

Origins of the

Modern World

(1600–1800)

Source 8 from L. A. G. Strong, The Story of Sugar *(London: Weidenfeld & Nicolson, 1954). Photos: The British Library.*

8. From W. Clark, "Ten Views of Antigua," 1823

Source 9 from W. R. Aykroyd, The Story of Sugar *(Chicago: Quadrangle Books, 1967), plate 9.*

9. Advertisement for East India Sugar Basins

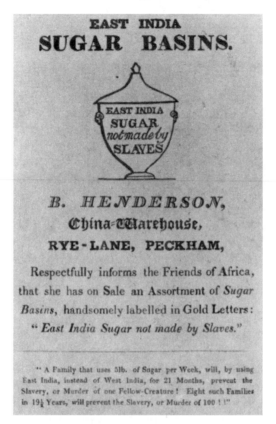

Source 10 from Robin Law and Paul E. Lovejoy, eds., The Biography of Mahommah Gardo Baquaqua: His Passage from Slavery to Freedom in Africa and America *(Princeton: Markus Wiener Publishers, 2001), pp. 136–161.*

10. Selection from *The Biography of Mahommah Gardo Baquaqua, 1854*

We will now, at once, turn to . . . Mahommah's history, which treats of his capture in Africa and subsequent slavery. We will give the matter in nearly his own words.

It has already been stated, that when any person gives evidence of gaining an eminent position in the country, he is immediately envied, and means are taken

Chapter 4

Sweet Nexus:

Sugar and the

Origins of the

Modern World

(1600–1800)

to put him out of the way; thus when it was seen that my situation was one of trust and confidence with the king, I was of course soon singled out as a fit object of vengeance by an envious class of my countrymen, decoyed away and sold into slavery. I went to the city one day to see my mother, when I was followed by music (the drum) and called to by name, the drum beating to the measure of a song which had been composed apparently in honor of me, on account of, as I supposed, my elevated position with the king. This pleased me mightily, and I felt highly flattered, and was very liberal, and gave the people money and wine, they singing and gesturing the time. About a mile from my mother's house, where a strong drink called Bah-gee, was made out of the grain Har-nee; thither we repaired; and when I had drank plentifully of Bah-gee, I was quite intoxicated, and they persuaded me to go with them to Zar-ach-o, about one mile from Zoogoo, to visit a strange king that I had never seen before. When we arrived there, the king made much of us all, and a great feast was prepared, and plenty of drink was given to me, indeed all appeared to drink very freely.

In the morning when I arose, I found that I was a prisoner, and my companions were all gone. Oh, horror! I then discovered that I had been betrayed into the hands of my enemies, and sold for a slave. Never shall I forget my feelings on that occasion; the thoughts of my poor mother harrassed me very much, and the loss of my liberty and honorable position with the king, grieved me very sorely. I lamented bitterly my folly in being so easily deceived, and was led to drown all caution in the bowl. Had it not been that my senses had been taken from me, the chance was that I should have escaped their snares, at least for that time.

The man, in whose company I found myself left by my cruel companions, was one, whose employment was to rid the country of all such as myself. The way he secured me, was after the following manner:—He took a limb of a tree that had two prongs, and shaped it so that it would cross the back of my neck, it was then fastened in front with an iron bolt; the stick was about six feet long.

Confined thus, I was marched forward towards the coast, to a place called Ar-oo-zo, which was a large village; there I found some friends, who felt very much about my position, but had no means of helping me. We only stayed there one night, as my master wanted to hurry on, as I had told him I would get away from him and go home. He then took me to a place called Chir-a-chur-ee, there I also had friends, but could not see them, as he kept very close watch over me, and he always stayed at places prepared for the purpose of keeping the slaves in security; there were holes in the walls in which my feet were placed, (a kind of stocks.) He then took me on to a place called Cham-mah, (after passing through many strange places, the names of which I do not recollect) where he sold me. We had then been about four days from home and had traveled very rapidly. I remained only one day, when I was again sold to a woman, who took me to E-fau; she had along with her some young men, into whose charge I was given, but she journeyed with us; we were several days going there; I suffered very much traveling through the woods, and never saw a human being all the journey. There was no regular road, but we had to make our passage as well as we could.

. . . After passing through the woods, we came to a small place, where the woman who had purchased me, had some friends; here I was treated very well, indeed, during the day, but at night I was closely confined, as they were afraid I would make my escape; I could not sleep all night, I was so tightly kept. . . .

. . . At length we arrived at Efau, where I was again sold; the woman seemed sorry to part with me, and gave me a small present on my leaving them. Efau is quite a large place, the houses were of different construction to those in Zoogoo, and had not so good an appearance.

The man to whom I was again sold, was very rich, and had a great number of wives and slaves. I was placed in charge of an old slave; whilst there a great dance was held and I was fearful they were going to kill me, as I had heard they did so in some places, and I fancied the dance was only a preliminary part of the ceremony; at any rate I did not feel at all comfortable about the matter. I was at Efau several weeks and was very well treated during that time; but as I did not like the work assigned me, they saw that I was uneasy, and as they were fearful of losing me, I was locked up every night. . . .

After leaving Efau, we had no stopping place until we reached Dohama [Dahomey]; we remained in the woods by night and traveled during the day, as there were wild beasts in great abundance, and we were compelled to build up large fires at night to keep away the ferocious animals, which otherwise would have fallen upon us and torn us to pieces, we could hear them howling round about during the night. . . .

Dohama is about three days journey from Efau, and is quite a large city; the houses being built differently to any I had previously seen. The surrounding country is level and the roads are good; it is more thickly settled than any other part I had passed through, though not so well as Zoogoo, the manners of the people too, were altogether different to anything I had ever before seen.

I was being conducted through the city, and as we passed along, we were met by a woman, and my keeper who was with me immediately took to his heels and ran back as hard as he could. I stood stock still, not knowing the meaning of it; he saw I did not attempt to follow him, or to move one way or another, and he called me in the Efau language to follow him, which I did, he then told me, after we rested, that the woman we had met was the king's wife, and it is a mark of respect to run whenever she is in sight of any of her subjects. There were gates to this city, and a toll was demanded on passing through. I remained there for but a short time, but I learned that it was a great place for whisky, and the people were very fond of dancing. At this place I saw oranges for the first time in my life. I was told, whilst there, that the king's house was ornamented on the outside with the human skulls, but did not see it. When we arrived here I began to give up all hopes of ever getting back to my home

Chapter 4

Sweet Nexus:

Sugar and the

Origins of the

Modern World

(1600–1800)

again, but had entertained hopes until this time of being able to make my escape, and by some means or other of once more seeing my native place, but at last, hope gave way; the last ray seemed fading away, and my heart felt sad and weary within me, as I thought of my home, my mother! whom I loved most tenderly, and the thought of never more beholding her, added very much to my perplexities. I felt sad and lonely, wherever I did roam, and my heart sank within me, when I thought of the "old folks at home." Some persons suppose that the African has none of the finer feelings of humanity within his breast, and that the milk of human kindness runs not through his composition; this is an error, an error of the grossest kind; the feelings which animated the whole human race, lives [sic] within the sable creatures of the torrid zone, as well as the inhabitants of the temperate and frigid; the same impulses drive them to action, the same feeling[s] of love move within their bosom, the same maternal and paternal affections are there, the same hopes and fears, griefs and joys, indeed all is there as in the rest of mankind; the only difference is their color, and that has been arranged by him who made the world and all that therein is, the heavens, and the waters of the mighty deep, the moon, the sun and stars, the firmament and all that has been made from the beginning until now, therefore why should any despise the works of his hands which has been [sic] made and fashioned according to his Almighty power, in the plentitude of his goodness and mercy.

O ye despisers of his works, look ye to yourselves, and take heed; let him who thinks he stands, take heed lest he fall. We then proceeded to Gra-fe, about a day and half's journey; the land we passed was pretty thickly settled and generally well cultivated. . . . At Gra-fe, I saw the first white man, which you may be sure took my attention very much; the windows in the houses also looked strange, as this was the first time in my life that I had ever seen houses having windows. They took me to a white man's house, where we remained until the morning, when my breakfast was brought in to me, and judge my astonishment to find that the person who brought in my breakfast was an old acquaintance, who came from the same place. He did not exactly know me at first, but when he asked me if my name was Gardo, and I told him it was, the poor fellow was overjoyed and took me by the hands and shook me violently he was so glad to see me; his name was Woo-roo, and had come from Zoogoo, having been enslaved about two years; his friends could never tell what had become of him. He inquired after his friends at Zoogoo, asked me if I had lately come from there, looked at my head and observed that I had the same shave that I had when we were in Zoogoo together; I told him that I had. It may be as well to remark in this place, that in Africa, the nations of the different parts of the country have their different modes of shaving the head and are known from that mark to what part of the country they belong. In Zoogoo, the hair is shaven off each side of the head, and on the top of the head from the forehead to the back part, it is left to grow in three round spots, which is allowed to grow quite long; the spaces between being shaven very close; there is no difficulty to a person acquainted with the different shaves, to know what part any man belongs to.

Woo-roo seemed very anxious that I should remain at Gra-fe, but I was destined for other parts; this town is situated on a large river. After breakfast I was taken down to the river and placed on board a boat; the river was very large and branched off in two different directions, previous to emptying itself into the sea. The boat in which the slaves were placed was large and propelled by oars, although it had sails as well, but the wind not being strong enough, oars were used as well. We were two nights and one day on this river, when we came to a very beautiful place; the name of which I do not remember; we did not remain here very long, but as soon as the slaves were all collected together, and the ship ready to sail, we lost no time in putting to sea. Whilst at this place, the slaves were all put into a pen, and placed with our backs to the fire, and ordered not to look about us, and to insure obedience, a man was placed in front with a whip in his hand ready to strike the first who should dare to disobey orders; another man then went round with a hot iron, and branded us the same as they would the heads or barrels or any other inanimate goods or merchandize.

When all were ready to go aboard, we were chained together, and tied with ropes round about our necks, and were thus drawn down to the sea shore. The ship was lying some distance off. I had never seen a ship before, and my idea of it was, that it was some object of worship of the white man. I imagined that we were all to be slaughtered, and were being led there for that purpose. I felt alarmed for my safety, and despondency had almost taken sole possession of me.

A kind of feast was made ashore that day, and those who rowed the boats were plentifully regaled with whiskey, and the slaves were given rice and other good things in abundance. I was not aware that it was to be my last feast in Africa. I did not know my destiny. Happy for me, that I did not. All I knew was, that I was a slave, chained by the neck, and that I must readily and willingly submit, come what would, which I considered was as much as I had any right to know.

At length, when we reached the beach, and stood on the sand, oh! how I wished that the sand would open and swallow me up. My wretchedness I cannot describe. It was beyond description. The reader may imagine, but anything like an outline of my feelings would fall very short of the mark, indeed. There were slaves brought hither from all parts of the country, and taken on board the ship. The first boat had reached the vessel in safety, notwithstanding the high wind and rough sea; but the last boat that ventured was upset, and all in her but one man were drowned. The number who were lost was about thirty. The man that was saved was very stout, and stood at the head of the boat with a chain in his hand, which he grasped very tightly in order to steady the boat; and when the boat turned over, he was thrown with the rest into the sea, but on rising, by some means under the boat, managed to turn it over, and thus saved himself by springing into her, when she was righted. This required great strength, and being a powerful man, gave him the advantage over the rest. The next boat that

Chapter 4
Sweet Nexus:
Sugar and the
Origins of the
Modern World
(1600–1800)

was put to sea, I was placed in; but God saw fit to spare me, perhaps for some good purpose. I was then placed in that most horrible of all places.

THE SLAVE SHIP.

Its horrors, ah! who can describe? None can so truly depict its horrors as the poor unfortunate, miserable wretch that has been confined within its portals. Oh! friends of humanity, pity the poor African, who has been trepanned [entrapped] and sold away from friends and home, and consigned to the hold of a slave ship, to await even more horrors and miseries in a distant land. . . . We were thrust into the hold of the vessel in a state of nudity, the males being crammed on one side and the females on the other; the hold was so low that we could not stand up, but were obliged to crouch upon the floor or sit down; day and night were the same to us, sleep being denied us from the confined position of our bodies, and we became desperate through suffering and fatigue.

Oh! the loathsomeness and filth of that horrible place will never be effaced from my memory; nay, as long as memory holds her seat in this distracted brain, will I remember that. My heart even at this day, sickens at the thought of it. Let those *humane individuals,* who are in favor of slavery, only allow themselves to take the slave's position in the noisome hold of a slave ship, just for one trip from Africa to America, and without going into the horrors of slavery further than this, if they do not come out thorough-going abolitionists, then I have no more to say in favor of abolition. But I think their views and feelings regarding slavery will be changed in some degree, however; if not, let them continue in the course of slavery, and work out their term in a cotton or rice field, or [sugar] plantation, and then if they do not say hold, enough! I think they must be of iron frames, possessing neither hearts nor souls. I imagine there can be but one place more horrible in all creation than the hold of a slave ship, and that place is where slaveholders and their myrmidons [subordinates] are the most likely to find themselves some day, when alas, 'twill be late, too late, alas!

The only food we had during the voyage was corn soaked and boiled. I cannot tell how long we were thus confined, but it seemed a very long while. We suffered very much for want of water, but was [sic] denied all we needed. A pint a day was all that was allowed, and no more; and a great many slaves died upon the passage. There was one poor fellow became so very desperate for want of water, that he attempted to snatch a knife from the white man who brought in the water, when he was taken up on deck and I never knew what became of him. I supposed he was thrown overboard.

When any one of us became refractory, his flesh was cut with a knife, and pepper or vinegar was rubbed in to make him peaceable(!) I suffered, and so did the rest of us, very much from sea sickness at first, but that did not cause our brutal owners any trouble. Our sufferings were our own, we had no one to share our troubles, none to care for us, or even to speak a word of comfort to us. Some were thrown overboard before breath was out of their bodies; when it was thought any would not live, they were got rid of in that way. Only twice during the voyage were we allowed to go on deck to wash ourselves—once whilst at sea, and again just before going into port.

We arrived at Pernambuco, South America, early in the morning, and the vessel played about during the day, without coming to anchor. All that day we neither ate or drank anything, and we were given to understand that we were to remain perfectly silent, and not make any out-cry, otherwise our lives were in danger. But when "night threw her sable mantle on the earth and sea," the anchor dropped, and we were permitted to go on deck to be viewed and handled by our future masters, who had come aboard from the city. We landed a few miles from the city, at a farmer's house, which was used as a kind of slave market. The farmer had a great many slaves, and I had not been there very long before I saw him use the lash pretty freely on a boy, which made a deep impression on my mind, as of course I imagined that would be my fate ere long, and oh! too soon, alas! were my fears realized.

When I reached the shore, I felt thankful to Providence that I was once more permitted to breathe pure air, the thought of which almost absorbed every other. I cared but little then that I was a slave, having escaped the ship was all I thought about. Some of the slaves on board could talk Portuguese. They had been living on the coast with Portuguese families, and they used to interpret to us. They were not placed in the hold with the rest of us, but come [sic] down occasionally to tell us something or other.

These slaves never knew they were to be sent away, until they were placed on board the ship. I remained in this slave market but a day or two, before I was again sold to a slave dealer in the city, who again sold me to a man in the country. . . .

When a slaver comes in, the news spreads like wild-fire, and down come all those that are interested in the arrival of the vessel with its cargo of living merchandize, who select from the stock those most suited to their different purposes, and purchase the slaves precisely in the same way that oxen or horses would be purchased in a market; but if there are not the kind of slaves in the one cargo, suited to the wants and wishes of the slave buyers, an order is given to the Captain for the particular sorts required, which are furnished to order the next time the ship comes into port. Great numbers make quite a business of this buying and selling human flesh, and do nothing else for a living, depending entirely upon this kind of traffic.

I had contrived whilst on my passage in the slave ship, to gather up a little knowledge of the Portuguese language, from the men before spoken of, and as my master was a Portuguese I could comprehend what he wanted very well, and gave him to understand that I would do all he needed as well as I was able, upon which he appeared quite satisfied.

His family consisted of himself, wife, two children and a woman who was related to them. He had four other slaves as well as myself. He was a Roman Catholic, and had family worship regularly twice a day, which was something after the following: He had a large clock standing in the entry of the house in

Chapter 4

Sweet Nexus:

Sugar and the

Origins of the

Modern World

(1600–1800)

which were some images made of clay, which were used in worship. We all had to kneel before them; the family in front, and the slaves behind. We were taught to chant some words which we did not know the meaning of. We also had to make the sign of the cross several times. Whilst worshipping, my master held a whip in his hand, and those who showed signs of inattention or drowsiness, were immediately brought to consciousness by a smart application of the whip. This mostly fell to the lot of the female slave, who would often fall asleep in spite of the images, crossings, and other like pieces of amusement.

I was soon placed at hard labor, such as none but slaves and horses are put to. At the time of this man's purchasing me, he was building a house, and had to fetch building stone from across the river, a considerable distance, and I was compelled to carry them that were so heavy it took three men to raise them upon my head, which burden I was obliged to bear for a quarter of a mile at least, down to where the boat lay. Sometimes the stone would press so hard upon my head that I was obliged to throw it down upon the ground, and then my master would be very angry indeed, and would say the cassoori (dog) had thrown down the stone, when I thought in my heart that he was the worst dog; but it was only a thought, as I dared not give utterance in words. . . .

My companions in slavery were not quite so steady as I was, being much given to drink, so that they were not so profitable to my master. I took advantage of this, to raise myself in his opinion, by being very attentive and obedient; but it was all the same, do what I would, I found I had a tyrant to serve, nothing seemed to satisfy him, so I took to drinking likewise, then we were all of a sort, bad master, bad slaves.

Things went on worse and worse, and I was very anxious to change masters, so I tried running away, but was soon caught, tied and carried back. . . . I was beaten very severely. I told him he must not whip me any more, and got quite angry, for the thought came into my head that I would kill him, and afterwards destroy myself. I at last made up my mind to drown myself; I would rather die than live to be a slave. I then ran down to the river and threw myself in, but being seen by some persons who were in a boat, I was rescued from drowning. The tide was low at the time, or their efforts would most likely have been unavailing, and notwithstanding my predetermination, I thanked God that my life had been preserved, and that so wicked a deed had not been consummated. It led me seriously to reflect that "God moves in a mysterious way," and that all his acts are acts of kindness and mercy.

I was then but a poor heathen, almost as ignorant as a Hottentot, and had not learned the true God, nor any of his divine commandments. Yet ignorant and slave as I was, slavery I loathed, principally as I suppose, because I was its victim. After this sad attempt upon my life, I was taken to my master's house, who tied my hands behind me, and placed my feet together and whipped me most unmercifully, and beat me about the head and face with a heavy stick, then shook me by the neck, and struck my head against the door posts, which cut and bruised me about the temples, the scars from which savage treatment are visible at this time, and will remain so as long as I live.

. . . I have not related a tithe of the cruel suffering which I endured whilst in the service of [this] wretch in human form. . . . I could tell more than would be pleasant for "ears polite," . . . I could relate occurrences which would "freeze thy young blood, harrow up thy soul, and make each particular hair to stand on end like quills upon the fretful porcupine;" and yet it would be but a repetition of the thousand and one oft told tales of the horrors of the cruel system of slavery.

QUESTIONS TO CONSIDER

Now that you have read the evidence, the challenge is to put together the pieces of the sugar puzzle, to figure out how these different perspectives can fit together to give us a more complete understanding of the economic, social, and political ramifications of the plantation system and the Atlantic economy of the seventeenth and eighteenth centuries.

First of all, what were the main benefits of this system, and who were the main beneficiaries? Imagine a conversation between William Blake and Olaudah Equiano. How might they discuss this question, given the attitudes displayed in their writings and engravings? How might they discuss the benefits of sugar production from a global, national, individual, or moral point of view? What was the overall importance of sugar to Britain in this period?

From the standpoint of sugar consumption, how might an advocate of sugar like Dr. Frederick Slare respond to Source 9? Do you think it was fair in the eighteenth century to hold consumers responsible for the conditions

under which commodities like sugar were produced? What message does the advertisement for the sugar bowl convey in these terms? Do you think Equiano, as an abolitionist, would have approved of that advertising campaign, or thought it sufficient to address the problem of slavery?

What connections might we find when we look at sugar from the standpoint of capital? Drawing from Ligon and other sources, what self-image did the sugar planters seem to have? How do the advocates of planters and merchants present their activities as valuable not just to individuals, but to a wider community? What special pressures did the sugar planters face, and what were the consequences for their workers?

How does the same world look from the standpoint of labor? Drawing from Ligon, Equiano, and other sources, what seem to have been the main characteristics of sugar production in terms of who did what work and how that work was organized? What do the statistics in Source 5 tell us about slave mortality? What conditions led to that outcome?

How do these descriptions reinforce or challenge views of slave labor you

Chapter 4

Sweet Nexus:

Sugar and the

Origins of the

Modern World

(1600–1800)

might have had before reading these selections? What does Equiano's description of how labor was acquired for the plantations tell us about the effects of this system not just on the enslaved Africans, but on African societies themselves? How do the traditional forms of slavery he describes in Africa differ from those of the New World plantations?

EPILOGUE

The connection between slavery and sugar was broken in the nineteenth century. The Haitian Revolution led by Touissant Louverture in the 1790s led to a steep decline of production on what had been the most important French sugar island in the West Indies. The abolition by the British of the slave trade (1808) and of slavery itself (1834) in the British Empire ended the connection between slaves and sugar in places like Jamaica and Barbados. As in Haiti, the freed slaves left the plantations as soon as they had a chance to do so. Slave-based sugar production continued in Cuba and Brazil, the last two places in the Americas to abolish slavery, but by the middle of the nineteenth century new means had been found to supply the still-increasing demand for sugar in world markets.

First, the sugar beet was developed within Europe itself as an alternative source of sugar. Second, new areas of plantation production of cane sugar were opened up in such places as Hawaii, Fiji, and South Africa. Indentured labor, which had largely disappeared from the Caribbean by the eighteenth century, made a comeback as part of this new sugar plantation complex in the late nineteenth century. Millions of workers from Japan, China, and India agreed to contracts that moved them across the seas to toil for low wages on sugar estates in Asia, Africa, and the Pacific.

Sugar production has since been mechanized, and alternative sources of sucrose have been developed. Satisfaction of the world's sweet tooth no longer depends on as harsh a form of exploitation as it did in the days of slaves and indentured workers. That does not mean, however, that the exercise you have undertaken in this chapter does not have contemporary applications. Just a few miles from where this chapter is being written, at the port of Long Beach in southern California, giant container ships arrive to unload commodities from around the world for the American market. Like sugar, those commodities arriving at the port can be traced back to the origins of the materials from which they were made and the labor that produced them. What different attitudes might we have toward the goods we buy if we knew the full story about how they were produced? Even more than in the days of the old sugar trade, humanity is united by the global market, not just economically, but socially, politically, and culturally as well.

CHAPTER FIVE

THE CONFUCIAN FAMILY

(1600–1800)

In a novel called *Family,* Ba Jin, one of China's foremost modern writers, portrays the frustrations of Westernized youth in early twentieth-century China through the story of a single, well-to-do household. Stifled by familial conventions and the authority of their elders, the young people in this family crave the individual freedom associated with modern life. The boldest of them, goaded to the point of rebellion, finally cries out, "What a cursed life . . . ," and berates his brothers for their docility. "How much abuse can you take? You talk a lot about opposing the patriarchal family system, but actually you support it. Your ideas are new but your conduct is old. You're all spineless! You're full of contradictions!"[1]

1. This passage comes from the Sidney Shapiro translation of *Family* (New York: Doubleday Anchor Books, 1972), pp. 94–95, a version originally published in China (Beijing: Foreign Languages Press, 1958).

To the generation of Ba Jin in the 1920s, the old-style family depicted in this novel represented what was wrong with China and needed changing. They saw it as both a symbol and a source of China's backwardness because it embodied an outmoded Confucian doctrine of familialism known as *xiao* that hindered the growth of individualism. Often translated as "filiality" or "filial piety," this doctrine presumed that households, not individuals, formed the basis of society and that social health and stability depended on the vitality of a particular kind of patriarchal family. Consequently, it called upon people to seek esteem and identity through their family rather than through individual accomplishments and to set aside personal interests in deference to household leaders. Such values, twentieth-century reformers felt, stood in sharp contrast to those of the modern West, where the individual was recognized as the basic unit of society and accorded legal rights and freedoms.

They argued that this familialism and the traditional family patterned upon it had to be destroyed before China could hope to adopt other modern Western institutions and values. Opposition to the Confucian family thus played a major role in Chinese reform movements from the first Cultural Revolution of 1916 down to the Great Proletarian Cultural Revolution of the 1960s. As a result, the Confucian family often served as a symbol of all the antiquated social and cultural values that reformers wished to change, continuing in a strange new way the old belief that society and family were intimately related. Rebellion against one clearly implied rebellion against the other.

Westernized reformers, however, were not the first Chinese to view the old family system with a critical eye. Already in the seventeenth and eighteenth centuries, a number of social observers had begun to show concern for what they viewed as its shortcomings, and a literary movement sprang up to expose some of its worst abuses. Unlike Westernized reformers of a later date, these premodern critics did not reject the Confucian family outright nor advocate a new set of social values. They accepted the idea that a healthy society depended on solid, traditional families. But they strongly objected to some of the practices that occurred within it, particularly the mistreatment of women and children. In their view, too many men took undue advantage of the household authority that the Confucian family system vested in them to victimize weaker members. Using novels and short stories to portray the most outrageous of these offenses, writers tried to bring about a more humane family—and society—by discrediting such abuse.

In doing so, in fact, these traditional critics reaffirmed what originally attracted Confucian thinkers to family life: the tendency of families to temper authority with compassion. Beginning with Confucius himself, who lived at the turn of the fifth century B.C.E., Confucians called for an ethical society in which people put principle above selfish desires. And because they felt that submission to authority helped people curb selfishness, they advocated hierarchical rather than equal social relations. Recognizing the problems created by overly rigid or overbearing authority, however, they cautioned people in positions of power to be humane as well as principled. No other institution, in their view, demonstrated how to balance these two qualities better than the patriarchal family, a seemingly "natural" group in which the affectionate authority of fathers elicited the loving respect of spouses and children. As they saw it, this family, with its unique combination of compassion and power, provided a model for society as a whole. For its patterns of leadership and deference assured humane rulers on one hand and respectful subjects on the other. For over two millennia, therefore, they argued that a just and stable society in China depended on the vitality of the Confucian family.

The strong and often conflicting opinions of the family held by these Chinese observers reflects a dilemma contemporary historians face in studying such institutions, particularly those that come out of non-Western traditions. They must consciously choose the cultural and ethical standpoint from which to approach their subjects. Such decisions are hard enough for those who want to view the past through non-Eurocentric eyes but remain culturally indebted to the West. But current ethical concerns complicate the matter further. Should contemporary historians, for example, try to set aside all current Western values and view the patriarchal family strictly from a traditional Confucian point of view? Or should they deal with it from an openly feminist stance, say, or perhaps as advocates of traditional Western family standards? A globally minded historian, of course, must always be concerned with such perspectives. But dealing with an emotionally laden subject of this sort requires extra care in deciding how to treat the subject.

It should come as no surprise, then, that your task here is to decide how to approach the Confucian family. Should we, for example, treat it as a backward and oppressive institution that needs to be discredited—in order to foster a more individualistic, Western society in China, perhaps, or to counter abuses to women everywhere? Or should we present it as an important cultural legacy that may bring some balance to a contemporary world that has become supremely individualistic? Or yet again, in a related vein, maybe we should feature it as an institution with validity for East Asian societies, but not necessarily for the contemporary West. Other possibilities, too, will no doubt come to mind. But the question remains, how would *you* decide to approach an institution of this sort?

BACKGROUND

The family model envisioned by Confucian thinkers was always more of a social ideal than a widespread reality. In actual practice, the family, or *jia*, proved a rather flexible institution throughout Chinese history, assuming different forms and sizes to accommodate changing needs. By custom as well as imperial law, residential households, or *hu*, remained the basic family unit, but such households could and did vary a great deal in their composition as well as in their interaction with more distant kin. In some situations, related

households operated quite independently of each other, whereas in others they actively cooperated as branches of a common lineage. Variations frequently resulted from the different roles households played in traditional society.

Although primarily a social unit, providing companionship, nurture, and group support to its members, the household often also functioned as an economic institution. Farms, workshops, and businesses, for example, were often run as family enterprises in premodern China, so that traditional households not only consumed goods in common but usually produced them in common as well. The family also served as a framework through which members could pool funds in order to undertake projects too expensive for individual members to afford and to provide social services for the young, the aged, and the needy. Households were religious units, too, and members regularly joined together in veneration of household gods and ancestral spirits. Belief in the continuing presence of deceased members who needed tending, of course, gave the living a unique sense of the family. As caretakers of past as well as future generations, they tended to regard the household patrimony as not so much their own property but a shared legacy that belonged as much to their forebears and progeny as to themselves.

By late traditional times, that is from the sixteenth through the nineteenth centuries, the most prevalent type of family found in China was the small *conjugal family* in which a married couple lived alone with their unwed children. This two-generational family well suited most of the population, who were farmers engaged in labor-intensive, subsistence agriculture, a form of farming in which people grew crops to feed their own households rather than for sale in a market. Because average farm holdings tended to be small, they could not support large numbers of dependents. Estimates vary, but probably something like two-thirds of all families in late traditional times were of this type and typically included no more than three to six members. Most Chinese of the time thus grew up and lived out their lives in small households. Because farm families typically lived together in villages rather than on separate home sites scattered across the countryside, however, people regularly interacted in a larger social context.

Despite the fact that it was commonplace, the small, conjugal household was not the family that Confucians venerated. Their attention focused instead upon a less common version known as the *joint family*. In the joint family, male children remained with their parents after getting married, creating a large, multigenerational household whose adult members shared a common income along with domestic tasks. In its basic form, the joint family consisted of at least three generations: an original set of parents, their married sons and their wives, and all the grandchildren. But tradition held that up to five generations should remain together. Inasmuch as men could legally take more than one consort, even households with only the minimal number of generations could become very large indeed. And because most also employed large numbers of live-in porters, maids, cooks, and other domestic help, joint households often included dozens of people, and some became enormous establishments with a hundred or more residents.

A large income was generally necessary to support such large households, and so such joint families tended to be found only among wealthy strata of society. Affluent merchants and successful farmers who accumulated large acreage favored it, as did members of the official Mandarin elite, who by virtue of their success in the imperial examination system received special legal privileges and employment opportunities, including a near monopoly of government posts. Although elite households often maintained homes in the cities, most invested in farmland that could be rented out to increase their income. The need to supervise these investments as well as a tradition of genteel country living induced many to keep rural residences, too. And the ideal, if not always the reality, of upper-class life was a spacious, well-run country house overflowing with children and servants and surrounded by gardens and cultivated fields.

Even the wealthiest of the elite, however, found it difficult to maintain a large, multigenerational household over long periods of time. To do so, couples in each generation had to produce numerous sons who survived into adulthood to bear their offspring in turn. Moreover, the family had to avoid a break-up whenever the head of the household died. Because imperial law did not recognize primogeniture (inheritance by the eldest son), the death of the patriarch created a vulnerable situation for joint families. All sons could legally claim an equal portion of the estate, and any one of them might thus take his share of the family assets and move away, leaving the others that much poorer. This system of *partible* or equal inheritance tended to diminish a joint family's wealth and property over time and could ultimately deprive remaining members of the resources necessary to sustain even a moderate household. It did, however, force new heads of the family to be considerate of siblings in order to attempt to forestall future splits.

To help offset this tendency toward fragmentation and to strengthen familialism, members of the elite, particularly in south China, often formed common

descent groups called *zu*, or lineages. These were associations of families believed to have descended on the male side from a common ancestor. Viewing themselves as natural kinsmen, they promoted a corporate sense of identity by compiling genealogies and conducting family affairs in common. One of their most important functions was to assist with important family events like funerals and weddings and to conduct annual ancestral rites. But they also frequently ran schools for the children of members, loaned out capital within the group, and dispensed charity to needier branches. To finance these services, most invested funds collected from their membership in land or other revenue-producing property. Such activities helped participating families survive difficult times and avoid their own disintegration.

Nonetheless, really large joint families remained relatively rare. Far more common was a smaller variant known as the *stem family*. In this version, only one married son, usually the eldest, remained at home with his parents. Since family descent was traced in a patrilinear fashion, with the line from eldest son to eldest son viewed as its core, this combination of father and eldest son represented the main "stem" or trunk of the immediate family tree. Often the stem family resulted from the fragmentation of a bigger household or from the first efforts of a more prosperous couple to establish a joint family. It offered parents an important benefit: A live-in son and his wife could provide them with care in their old age. And because by custom such caretakers could enjoy full use of family property, it proved attractive to the younger generation, too, providing some protection from the claims of other siblings on the family patrimony.

Life in any of these elite households was far from casual. A strict hierarchy prevailed in all affairs, regulating who could do what and when. Status and authority depended upon the sex, age, and proximity of household members to the head of the family, who was usually the oldest adult male. Tradition firmly fixed the principles behind this hierarchy: Females took second place to males, the young deferred to the old, and all obeyed the patriarch without question. Differences of age and relationship to the patriarch created distinctions within generations as well as between them. Although cousins, who usually grew up together within such families, were deemed a close-knit group and often given a common element in their names to emphasize their connection, they did not enjoy equal status. Boys, of course, outranked girls. But even among male children, those descended from the patriarch's principal wife rated higher than others, and the firstborn sons of all couples enjoyed greater favor than their siblings. These distinctions reflected a belief in patrilinear descent. Family lineage was reckoned only in terms of the male side and primarily through a main stem or family line engendered by the eldest son in every generation.

From this vantage point, women seemed to be only temporary adjuncts to the family rather than essential members—despite the fact that they were biologically as significant as the men to its continuity. Daughters, who would leave the paternal home to join other households at marriage and bear children elsewhere, seemed particularly superfluous. Though the birth of a girl as a firstborn child might occasionally be celebrated because it proved the fertility of the mother, female births were usually received with disappointment. The birth of a boy, however, was invariably a source of joy, representing renewal and continuity for the family and security for the mother. Only by producing a son could she really establish her position as a valuable member of her husband's family. Until she did so, in fact, she tended to be viewed as an outsider who could be sent away or replaced by another consort. A wife's sense of family, therefore, was probably very different from a husband's, since she had no acknowledged ties to ancestors nor any feeling of closeness to her spouse's relatives. Her immediate children, especially her sons, and their eventual male children were the only relatives to whom she was securely bound. For that reason, a woman who failed to bear a son faced a life of great anxiety.

Because of their lower rank in the family, daughters were usually raised differently from sons. Elite families had no need to resort to female infanticide, as poor families sometimes did, but they generally lavished far more attention and affection upon sons, who would remain in the household after they grew up, than upon daughters, who would be married off into other families. Both might enjoy considerable indulgence until about the age of six, when serious training for later life usually began. Boys then began studying with male tutors who taught them to read and write so that they could go on to higher study outside the home. Girls, however, seldom received this kind of education. Instead, other women in the household taught them how to do needlework and perform household tasks.

Even more debilitating than denying girls education was the practice of tightly binding their feet. This painful custom was performed to keep their feet tiny, since the resulting "golden lotuses" were deemed highly erotic and an important allure in securing a husband. First adopted by professional entertainers in the fashionable quarters of commercial cities that sprang up in the Sung dynasty during the eleventh and twelfth centuries, this practice gradually gained popularity among the Mandarin elite. By the start of the Ming dynasty in the fourteenth century, it had become a prevalent status symbol for all who aspired to the upper reaches of the social world. Although the practice posed problems for all women who had their feet bound, it proved particularly difficult for those who were not wealthy enough to afford many servants: It left them near-cripples with limited mobility and restricted them even more than their lack of education to a domestic life within the confines of the home.

Patrilineal considerations dominated marriage rites as much as child-rearing practices. Seen as a family rather than an individual matter, marriage was understood as a means of securing heirs to perpetuate the male line of descent. Romantic feelings, therefore, seldom received much consideration in marriages. Indeed, tradition held that the bride and groom should not be too emotionally involved at the start of a marriage because closeness might encourage them to side against the rest of the family. Ideally, both would be teenagers who met face to face only on their wedding night. For obvious reasons, then, marriages had to be arranged by older members of the family, who relied on professional brokers, or "go-betweens," to find suitable partners for their offspring. A groom's family worried primarily about the health and character of a prospective bride, whereas a girl's family had to think about the status and security she would enjoy in the new home—and both weighed any advantages the alliance would bring their household.

Even after marriage, a couple seldom spent a lot of time together. Men had little to do with the day-to-day running of the household and were frequently out of the home. New brides, therefore, were left largely to the company of their mothers-in-law and other female relatives, with whom they had to work closely in performing household tasks. The relationship between daughter-in-law and mother-in-law often proved more critical to the happiness of a family than the bond between husband and wife. A daughter-in-law, of course, posed a potential rival to a mother-in-law, because both depended on the same man to secure their status in the family. Tension between these two "outsiders" was proverbial. In the case of conflict, however, a daughter-in-law generally fared worse, because she was a newcomer and lower in generational status. Pleasing her mother-in-law thus became a bride's highest priority, but she also had to worry about pleasing her husband, if only to ensure that he fathered children who would enhance her value in the family.

[131]

Here, too, she was often at a disadvantage, for the standard of fidelity differed for men and women. Women were expected to remain absolutely faithful to their husbands, ostensibly to preserve their honor as well as to avoid bearing sons whose legitimacy might be questioned. Upper-class morals thus dictated that women stay within their homes as much as possible and keep to particular areas of the household where they would not encounter men other than their husbands and sons. Men, however, were under no such constraints. Although enjoined not to live dissolute lives, they were free to engage in occasional, discreet affairs with household maids or professional entertainers. They could also bring women into the household as concubines. Though not formal wives, concubines enjoyed a legal status in the family, particularly if they bore a son. In theory a man took a concubine only when his wife proved unable to bear an heir, and thus the practice could be justified as a means of perpetuating the family. But men of means often acquired concubines to gratify their own pleasure as much as to secure heirs. Generally purchased from poor families and thus considered a form of property, concubines had a more tenuous role in the patriarchal family than wives. Both wives and mothers-in-law had reason to resent concubines, and jealousy between these women was a frequent source of domestic strife in big, wealthy households.

However unpleasant life might become in a traditional household, wives seldom sought a divorce. Although legally available, it did not offer a very satisfactory solution, because "respectable" women had almost nowhere to turn once they left the marriage home. The stigma of divorce made second marriages difficult to arrange, and upper-class women could find almost no opportunities for acceptable employment outside the home. Moreover, the belief that daughters did not belong with their natal family made parents reluctant to welcome back a divorcee. As a result, unhappy wives usually remained with their husbands' families, trying to find solace in children, if they had any. In extreme cases, they escaped hopeless situations through suicide, finding in death a way to punish uncaring relatives with dishonor as well as to end their own suffering.

Difficult as the Confucian family may have proved for some of its individual members, it clearly did train people to think in group rather than personal terms. Children grew up not only with multiple siblings but often with many cousins. And from an early age, they became accustomed to recognizing and accommodating a vast array of older relatives. Precise names, most without any Western equivalent, thus existed for all possible kinship relationships, and family members routinely defined themselves in terms of a complex household that instilled in them a keen sense of gender and age hierarchy. Peaks of authority regularly alternated with valleys of submission, forcing almost everyone to explore the nuances of group dynamics. Such experiences no doubt explain why group solidarity and harmony came to be so prized in the Confucian family.

THE METHOD

If you think about it, the question of how to view the Confucian family really has several facets. There is, of course, the matter of what the Confucian family may have been like in practice. This may seem a straightforward problem in social history, but a moment's reflection will remind you that what we today see of the past depends in no small part on what the people of the past have handed down to us. Thus it is important to know how the Chinese themselves have regarded the institution—both in traditional and in modern terms—for their viewpoints have helped to determine how the institution has been remembered and represented. And underlying this consideration lurks still another: How do our contemporary attitudes affect what we choose to emphasize or show about a problematic institution of this sort?

In one way or another, therefore, you will have to come to grips with each of these questions as you try to decide what position to take with regard to this institution. Doing so may not only give you some insight into how to regard the Confucian family in its historical context. We hope it will also make you aware of the problem all historians face in defining their relationship to a subject. That is, how does one approach something from another time or place? What is the proper degree of distance or involvement to take? In whose perspective, or in what context, should it be presented? These questions have no easy

answers, particularly today, when new fields of history and new viewpoints are challenging long-standing assumptions almost daily.

Sources that bear directly on two of the considerations raised above appear in the Evidence section that follows. The first five represent documents that afford us some evidence of actual life in the Confucian family in late traditional times in China before the advent of modern Western ways. Source 1, a conventional elite family portrait from the sixteenth century, and Source 3, a painting of a typical upper-class rural compound from the same period, offer visual glimpses of such families and their homes. You can glean a more detailed sense of elite family life, however, from Source 2, part of a manual or set of practical instructions compiled in the late sixteenth century by one of the elders of the Miu lineage to help kinsmen run their member households. Gui Youguang's sixteenth-century essay entitled "A Sketch of My Mother," which appears as Source 4, reveals the personal side of such life in very moving and positive terms. On the other hand, Source 5, taken from a sixteenth-century village handbook, suggests a harsher side of family life, presenting sample contracts that detailed the legal terms for the sale of women and children.

The other five sources, though they do provide some additional information about family life, primarily illustrate different Chinese perspectives on the Confucian family. Sources 6 and 7 give orthodox Confucian views. Both come from texts written much earlier than the sixteenth century, but these two works, the *Classic of Filiality* of about the second century B.C.E. and Zhu Xi's (Chu Hsi's) twelfth-century *Family Rituals,* remained standard references on ideal family behavior throughout the late traditional period. Indeed, references to both appear in the first batch of documents. Sources 8 and 9 by way of contrast point out the abuses in the family system that began to trouble literary writers of the seventeenth and eighteenth centuries. Source 8, taken from Pu Suling's novel *The Bonds of Matrimony,* focuses on issues stemming from concubinage and divorce, while Source 9, a poem by Zheng Xie (Cheng Hsieh), deals with the problematic relationship between brides and their mothers-in-law. Finally, Source 10, part of a famous essay by the first head of the Chinese Communist Party and one of twentieth-century China's leading intellectuals, Chen Duxiu (Ch'en Tu-hsiu), expresses the disparaging view of the Confucian family adopted by westernizing reformers at the end of the traditional period.

A review of this documentary material should help to answer the first two questions posed at the start of this section—that is, what was the Confucian family like, and how have the Chinese regarded it? But in dealing with the third problem, the way in which a current Westerner may see the Confucian family, you will have to think on your own about contemporary values and how they intrude to shape our perspective on the past. To help you in this process, you might take a moment at the start to jot down some key aspects of family life like romance, fidelity, divorce, child-rearing, gender, generational roles, and so on. Then as you go through the sources, take notes on how early Confucians, later critics, and eventual reformers viewed each of these. And finally, ask yourself how *you* view these same aspects. Do your views accord with any of the others? Why might that be so? Which views overall do you think should determine how we look back at the Confucian family? Why?

THE EVIDENCE

Source 1: Metropolitan Museum of Art. Anonymous gift, 1942 (42.190.1).

1. Ming Family Portrait, late 16th century

Source 2 from Patricia Buckley Ebrey, Chinese Civilization and Society: A Sourcebook *(New York: The Free Press, 1981), pp. 161–166.*

2. Family Instructions for the Miu Lineage, late 16th century

OBSERVE THE RITUALS AND PROPRIETIES

1. Capping and wedding ceremonies should be carried out according to one's means. Funerals and burials, being important matters, should be more elaborate, but one should still be mindful of financial considerations. Any other petty formalities not found in the *Book of Rites* should be abolished.

2. Marriage arrangements should not be made final by the presenting of betrothal gifts until the boy and girl have both reached thirteen; otherwise, time might bring about changes which cause regrets.

3. For the seasonal sacrifices, the ancestral temple should be prepared in advance and the ceremonies performed at dawn in accordance with [Chu Hsi's] *Family Rituals* and our own ancestral temple regulations. . . .

5. Sacrifices at the graves should be made on Tomb-Sweeping Day and at the Autumn Festival. Because the distances to different mountains vary, it is difficult to reach every grave on those days. Therefore, all branch families should be notified in advance of the order of priority: first, the founding father of our lineage; then ancestors earlier than great-great-grandfather; next, ancestors down to each person's grandfather. Established customs should be followed in deciding how much wine and meat should be used, how many different kinds of sacrificial offerings should be presented, and how much of the yearly budget should be spent on the sacrifices. All of these should be recorded in a special "sacrifice book" in order to set standards.

6. Not celebrating one's birthday has since ancient times been regarded as an exemplary virtue. An exception is the birthdays of those who are beyond their sixty-first year, which should be celebrated by their sons and grandsons drinking to their health. But under no circumstances should birthdays become pretexts for heavy drinking. If either of one's parents has died, it is an especially unfilial act to forget him or her and indulge in drinking and feasting. Furthermore, to drink until dead-drunk not only affects one's mind but also harms one's health. The numbers of people who have been ruined by drinking should serve as a warning.

7. On reaching five, a boy should be taught to recite the primers and not be allowed to show arrogance or laziness. On reaching six, a girl should be taught *Admonitions for Women* and not be allowed to venture out of her chamber. If children are frequently given snacks and playfully entertained, their nature will be

spoiled and they will grow up to be unruly and bad. This can be prevented if caught at an early age.

EXERCISE RESTRAINT

1. Our young people should know their place and observe correct manners. They are not permitted to gamble, to fight, to engage in lawsuits, or to deal in salt privately. Such unlawful acts will only lead to their own downfall.

2. If land or property is not obtained by righteous means, descendants will not be able to enjoy it. When the ancients invented characters, they put gold next to two spears to mean "money," indicating that the danger of plunder or robbery is associated with it. If money is not accumulated by good means, it will disperse like overflowing water; how could it be put to any good? The result is misfortune for oneself as well as for one's posterity. This is the meaning of the saying: "The way of Heaven detests fullness, and only the humble gain." Therefore, accumulation of great wealth inevitably leads to great loss. How true are the words of Lao Tzu!

A person's fortune and rank are predestined. One can only do one's best according to propriety and one's own ability; the rest is up to Heaven. If one is easily contented, then a diet of vegetables and soups provides a lifetime of joy. If one does not know one's limitations and tries to accumulate wealth by immoral and dishonest means, how can one avoid disaster? To be able to support oneself through life and not leave one's sons and grandsons in hunger and cold is enough; why should one toil so much?

3. Pride is a dangerous trait. Those who pride themselves on wealth, rank, or learning are inviting evil consequences. Even if one's accomplishments are indeed unique, there is no need to press them on anyone else. "The way of Heaven detests fullness, and only the humble gain." I have seen the truth of this saying many times.

4. Taking concubines in order to beget heirs should be a last resort, for the sons of the legal wife and the sons of the concubine are never of one mind, causing innumerable conflicts between half brothers. If the parents are in the least partial, problems will multiply, creating misfortune in later generations. Since families have been ruined because of this, it should not be taken lightly.

5. Just as diseases are caused by what goes into one's mouth, misfortunes are caused by what comes out of one's mouth. Those who are immoderate in eating and unrestrained in speaking have no one else to blame for their own ruin.

6. Most men lack resolve and listen to what their women say. As a result, blood relatives become estranged and competitiveness, suspicion, and distance arise between them. Therefore, when a wife first comes into a family, it should be made clear to her that such things are prohibited. "Start teaching one's son

when he is a baby, start teaching one's daughter-in-law when she first arrives." That is to say, preventive measures should be taken early.

7. "A family's fortune can be foretold from whether its members are early risers" is a maxim of our ancient sages. Everyone, male and female, should rise before dawn and should not go to bed until after the first drum. Never should they indulge themselves in a false sense of security and leisure, for such behavior will eventually lead them to poverty.

8. Young family members who deliberately violate family regulations should be taken to the family temple, have their offenses reported to the ancestors, and be severely punished. They should then be taught to improve themselves. Those who do not accept punishment or persist in their wrongdoings will bring harm to themselves.

9. As a preventive measure against the unpredictable, the gates should be closed at dusk, and no one should be allowed to go out. Even when there are visitors, dinner parties should end early, so that there will be no need for lighting lamps and candles. On very hot or very cold days, one should be especially considerate of the kitchen servants.

10. For generations this family has dwelt in the country, and everyone has had a set profession; therefore, our descendants should not be allowed to change their place of residence. After living in the city for three years, a person forgets everything about farming; after ten years, he does not even know his lineage. Extravagance and leisure transform people, and it is hard for anyone to remain unaffected. I once remarked that country living has all the advantages, and that the only legitimate excuse to live in a city temporarily is to flee from bandits.

11. The inner and outer rooms, halls, doorways, and furniture should be swept and dusted every morning at dawn. Dirty doorways and courtyards and haphazardly placed furniture are sure signs of a declining family. Therefore, a schedule should be followed for cleaning them, with no excuses allowed.

12. Those in charge of cooking and kitchen work should make sure that breakfast is served before nine o'clock in the morning and dinner before five o'clock in the afternoon. Every evening the iron wok and other utensils should be washed and put away, so that the next morning, after rising at dawn, one can expect tea and breakfast to be prepared immediately and served on time. In the kitchen no lamps are allowed in the morning or at night. This is not only to save the expense, but also to avoid harmful contamination of food. Although this is a small matter, it has a great effect on health. Furthermore, since all members of the family have their regular work to do, letting them toil all day without giving them meals at regular hours is no way to provide comfort and relief for them. If these rules are deliberately violated, the person in charge will be punished as an example to the rest.

13. On the tenth and twenty-fifth days of every month, all the members of this branch, from the honored aged members to the youngsters, should gather at dusk for a meeting. Each will give an account of what he has learned, by either calling attention to examples of good and evil, or encouraging diligence, or expounding his obligations, or pointing out tasks to be completed. Each member will take turns presenting his own opinions and listening attentively to others. He should examine himself in the matters being discussed and make efforts to improve himself. The purpose of these meetings is to encourage one another in virtue and to correct each other's mistakes.

14. Women from lower-class families who stop at our houses tend to gossip, create conflicts, peek into the kitchens, or induce our women to believe in prayer and fortune-telling, thereby cheating them out of their money and possessions. Consequently, one should question these women often and punish those who come for no reason, so as to put a stop to the traffic.

15. Blood relatives are as close as the branches of a tree, yet their relationships can still be differentiated according to importance and priority: parents should be considered before brothers, and brothers should be considered before wives and children. Each person should fulfill his own duties and share with others profit and loss, joy and sorrow, life and death. In this way, the family will get along well and be blessed by Heaven. Should family members fight over property or end up treating each other like enemies, then when death or misfortune strikes they will be of even less use than strangers. If our ancestors have consciousness, they will not tolerate these unprincipled descendants who are but animals in man's clothing. Heaven responds to human vices with punishments as surely as an echo follows a sound. I hope my sons and grandsons take my words seriously.

16. To get along with patrilineal relatives, fellow villagers, and relatives through marriage, one should be gentle in speech and mild in manners. When one is opposed by others, one may remonstrate with them; but when others fall short because of their limitations, one should be tolerant. If one's youngsters or servants get into fights with others, one should look into oneself to find the blame. It is better to be wronged than to wrong others. Those who take affront and become enraged, who conceal their own shortcomings and seek to defeat others, are courting immediate misfortune. Even if the other party is unbearably unreasonable, one should contemplate the fact that the ancient sages had to endure much more. If one remains tolerant and forgiving, one will be able to curb the other party's violence.

PRESERVE THE FAMILY PROPERTY

1. The houses, fields, and ponds that have been accumulated by the family should not be divided or sold. Violators of this rule will be severely admonished and barred from the ancestral temple.

2. Maps of the family graves should be printed. The graves are to be well taken care of and frequently repaired. The custodians of the graves should be treated well.

3. Books constitute the lifeline of a family. A record should be kept of their titles. They should be aired out at regular intervals, stored in a high chamber, and kept from being dispersed. In this way we can keep intact our ancestors' writings.

4. Paintings, maps, books, scrolls, and utensils should be stored in separate wooden cabinets. There should be a notebook in which all these are registered. Whenever an item is loaned to someone, a slip of paper with the description of the item should be temporarily pasted on the shelf. When the item is returned, it should be replaced in its original position.

5. There are many thieves in the country; therefore, one should be careful not to leave clothing and other objects about. Doors should be locked and carefully guarded. Be prepared! On noticing anything suspicious, look into it immediately and take preventive action, in order to achieve maximum security.

6. In order to cultivate the moral character of the young, one must severely punish those who are so unruly that they have no sense of righteousness or who so indulge their desires that they destroy their own health. One should also correct those who have improper hobbies, such as making too many friends and avoiding work, indulging in playing musical instruments and the game of Go, collecting art and valuables, composing music, singing, or dancing. All these hobbies destroy a person's ambition. Those who indulge in them may consider themselves free spirits; yet little do they know that these hobbies are their most harmful enemies.

7. If among patrilineal and affinal [by marriage] relatives and fellow villagers there are people who give importance to propriety and are respected for their learning and ability, one should frequently visit them to request advice and offer one's respects. Then, in case of emergencies in the family, one will be able to obtain help from them. Besides, receiving frequent advice is good in itself. By contrast, to make friends with the wrong sort of people and join them in evil deeds is to set a trap for oneself. If one is jealous of upright gentlemen and avoids upright discourse, misfortune will strike, the family will be ruined, lives may even be lost. Then it will be too late for regrets.

8. Scholars, farmers, artisans, and merchants all hold respectable occupations. Scholarship ranks the highest; farming is next; and then craft and business. However, it should be up to the individual to measure his ability against his aspirations as well as to find the most suitable occupation for himself. In these family instructions, I have given first place to the profession of scholarship, but have also devoted a great deal of attention to the work of farmers, artisans, and merchants. These family instructions attempt to show the correct procedures to

be followed in everyday life. If one truly understands them and fulfills the duties appropriate to his way of life; if one upholds public and private obligations; if one can in good conscience invite Heaven's favor, then misfortune will stay away and bliss will enter without conscious effort on one's part. In this way, a person can face his ancestors without shame and instruct his posterity; there are no other secrets to having good and capable descendants.

Source 3 from James Cahill, The Painter's Practice: How Artists Lived and Worked in Traditional China *(New York: Columbia University Press), p. 79. Reproduced by permission of the Shanghai Museum.*

3. Yüan Chiang, Section of "The East Garden" Handscroll, late 17th century

Source 4 from Poetry and Prose of the Ming and Qing *(Beijing: Chinese Literature, Panda Books, 1986), pp. 40–42.*

4. Gui Youguang, "A Sketch of My Mother," late 16th century

My mother, a daughter of the Zhou family, was born on the eleventh day of the second month of the first year of the Hong Zhi period [1488]. She came to our family at the age of sixteen and the next year gave birth to Shujing, my elder sister. The year after that I was born. The following year she had a girl who died at birth and a miscarriage a year later. The next year after a twelve-month pregnancy she was delivered of another son, Youshang. Shushun and Yougong were born in the two years following. Her health was better after Yougong's birth than when nursing the rest of us; but her mind was troubled and she confided to her maids that she felt such a brood of little ones a great burden. Then one old servant gave her two snails in a cup of water, saying, "Drink this, and you will have no more children." My mother drank the potion and subsequently lost her voice. On the twenty-third day of the fifth month of the eighth year of the Zheng De period [1513], she died. When we children saw our elders weep, we wept too, although we thought—poor fools!—that our mother was only sleeping. Then a portrait-painter was summoned to paint her portrait, and the family led out two of us, telling him: "For the upper half of the face, take Youguang as model; for the lower half, his elder sister." For we were the two who most re-sembled our mother.

My mother's own name was Gui. Her grandfather's name was Ming, her fa-ther's Xing, and he was a student of the Imperial College. Her mother's maiden name was He. Her family had lived for generations in Wujiaqiao, thirty *li* to the southeast of the county town. South of Qiandunpu, all the inhabitants from Zhiqiao to east of Xiaogang belong to the Zhou clan. Her father and three uncles were big merchants, but they were honest, simple folk, chatty as villagers and immensely attached to all their nephews and nieces. When my mother went back to Wujiaqiao she would work in the cotton fields, while during visits to town she would often weave by lamplight late into the night. Her father used to send men with gifts for us almost every other day; but though she had no worry about rice or salt, she worked as hard as if her next meal depended on it. In winter she got the maids to knead coal dust into coal-balls for the stove and lay them to dry by the steps. In her rooms was no waste, no idle hands in her house. While the bigger boys and girls clung to her clothes and the small-est sucked at her breast, her hands were still busy with sewing. Our home was spotless, the servants so kindly treated that even when she punished them they never complained. Every year when gifts of fish, crabs and sweetmeats came from her home, she would see that everybody had his share, and so the whole household rejoiced at the sight of messengers from Wujiaqiao. At seven I went to school with my cousin Yujia, and if the weather was bad, windy or drizzling, he stayed at home; but this was never allowed me, much as I longed for it. When my mother woke up in the night she made me recite whole passages from the *Book of Filial Piety*, pleased whenever I rattled them off without hesitating over a single word.

After my mother's death her own mother died. Indeed, an epidemic carried off thirty members of the Zhou family including her brother's wife and her fourth sister, who had married a man named Gu. Only her father and second brother survived. Eleven years after my mother's death, my eldest sister married Wang Sanjie—a match arranged by my mother. The year after that I started attending the prefectural school and four years later I married—another match she had arranged. In due course we had a daughter whom I loved dearly, for the little girl reminded us of my mother. In the middle of the night my wife and I would shed tears, because I could remember one or two trifles as if they had happened only yesterday, while all the rest was forgotten. Ah, Heaven have pity on those who have lost their mothers!

Source 5 from Patricia Buckley Ebrey, Chinese Civilization and Society: A Sourcebook *(New York: The Free Press, 1981), p. 139.*

5. Sample Contracts for Purchasing a Concubine and Selling a Son, 16th century

SAMPLE CONTRACT FOR THE PURCHASE OF A CONCUBINE

The undersigned, _____ , from _____ village, has agreed to give in marriage his own daughter _____ , aged _____ years, to the second party, _____ , as a concubine, through the mediator, _____.

On this date the undersigned has received _____ amount as betrothal payment. He agrees to give his daughter away on the date selected by the second party. He will not dare to cause any difficulties or to extort more money from the second party. He also guarantees that the girl has not been previously betrothed, and that there is no question as to her origin. Should such questions arise, or should the girl run away, he will be held responsible. Should the girl die of unexpected circumstances, it is her fate, and not the responsibility of the second party.

This contract is drawn up as evidence of the agreement.

SAMPLE CONTRACT FOR THE SELLING OF A SON FOR ADOPTION

The undersigned, _____ , from _____ county, _____ village, is unable to raise his own son _____ , aged _____ years, because of poverty. After consulting his wife and relatives (uncle/brother _____ and

[143]

_____ , etc.), he has decided to sell the child, through a mediator, to _____ as an adopted son.

On this date the undersigned received _____ amount of money from the second party, and the transaction was completed. The second party agrees to raise the child, who will be at his disposal for marriage, will be as obedient to him as a servant, and will not avoid labor or run away. This contract is signed out of the free will of both parties, there being no prior sales, and no questions as to the origin of the child; nor is the seller forced by a creditor to sell the child as payment for debts. From now on the child belongs to his new owner; alive, he shall never return to his original family; dead, he shall not be buried in the graveyard of his original family. Should he run away or be kidnapped, only the seller and the mediator are responsible; should the child die of unexpected circumstances, it is his fate, and not the responsibility of his owner.

This contract, stamped with the palm prints of the child, is to be held by the owner as evidence of the transaction.

Source 6 from The Humanist Way in Ancient China: Essential Works of Confucianism, *ed. and trans. Ch'u Chai and Winberg Chai (New York: Bantam Books, 1965), pp. 326–334.*

6. From *Classic of Filiality,* or *Xiao Jing (Hsiao Ching),* ca. 2nd century B.C.E.

CHAPTER I: THE GENERAL THEME

The Master said: "Filial piety is the basis of virtue and the source of culture. Sit down again, and I will explain it to you. The body and the limbs, the hair and the skin, are given to one by one's parents, and to them no injury should come; this is where filial piety begins. To establish oneself and practice the *Tao* is to immortalize one's name and thereby to glorify one's parents; this is where filial piety ends. Thus, filial piety commences with service to parents; it proceeds with service to the sovereign; it is completed by the establishment of one's own personality.

"In the *Shih* it is said:

May you think of your ancestors,
And so cultivate their virtues!"

CHAPTER II: THE SON OF HEAVEN

The Master said: "One who loves one's parents does not dare to hate others. One who reveres one's parents does not dare to spurn others. When love and reverence are thus cherished in the service of one's parents, one's moral influence

[144]

transforms the people, and one becomes a pattern to all within the four seas. This is the filial piety of the Son of Heaven.

"In the *Fu Code*, it is said:

When the One Man has blessings,
The millions of people rely on him."

CHAPTER VIII: GOVERNMENT BY FILIAL PIETY

The Master said: "Formerly the enlightened kings governed the world by filial piety. They did not dare to neglect the ministers of small states—to say nothing of the dukes, marquises, earls, viscounts, and barons! They thereby gained the good will of all the states to serve their early kings.

"Those who governed the states did not dare to ignore the widows and widowers—to say nothing of scholars and the people! They thereby gained the good will of all the subjects to serve their former princes.

"Those who regulated their families did not dare to mistreat their servants and concubines—to say nothing of their wives and children! They thereby gained the good will of others who served their parents.

CHAPTER XIV: ILLUSTRATION OF PERPETUATING THE NAME

The Master said: "The *chün-tzu* [gentleman] serves his parents with filial piety; thus his loyalty can be transferred to his sovereign. He serves his elder brother with brotherly deference; thus his respect can be transferred to his superiors. He orders his family well; thus his good order can be transferred to his public administration.

"Therefore, when one cultivates one's conduct within oneself, one's name will be perpetuated for future generations."

Source 7 from Chu Hsi's Family Rituals, trans. Patricia Ebrey (Princeton: Princeton University Press, 1991), pp. 28–32.

7. From Zhu Xi (Chu Hsi), *Family Rituals*, 12th century

In ancient times even prenatal instruction was practiced, not to mention postnatal education. From the time of a child's birth, even before he can understand, we familiarize him with the proprieties. How, then, can we ignore proper behavior when he is old enough to understand it? Confucius said that what is formed in childhood is like part of one's nature, what has been learned through practice becomes like instinct. The *Family Instructions of Mr. Yen* says, "Teach a bride when she first arrives; teach a child while it is still a baby." Therefore, from the time children begin to understand, they must be made to learn the distinctions of etiquette based on age and generation. In cases where they insult their parents or hit their elder brothers and sisters, if their parents laugh and praise them instead of scolding or punishing them, the children, not knowing right from wrong, will think such behavior is natural. By the time they are grown, their habits have been formed. Their parents now become angry and forbid them to do such things, but they find themselves unable to control them. As a result, the father will hate his son, and the son will resent his father. Cruelty and defiance of any sort can then occur, and all because the parents were short-sighted and failed to prevent the evil from the beginning; in other words, bad character is nourished by indulgence.

Source 8 from The Bonds of Matrimony/Hsing-shih Yin-yüan Chuan *(volume one), A Seventeenth Century Chinese Novel,* trans. Eve Alison Nyren (Lewiston, New York: The Edwin Mellen Press, 1995), pp. 117–120.

8. From Pu Suling (P'u Su-ling), *The Bonds of Matrimony*, 17th century

Two types of people bring downfall to home and state
The home falls to concubines and favorites
The state crumbles before eunuchs
New friends divide old with their wiles
Strangers break up homes with a few little words
False tales might as well be true
When duty, goodness, flesh and blood
all turn to dust
Done to death and no regrets
Let the bystanders laugh until their jaws crack

Mrs. Kao talked Ms. Chi back into the house and with sweet words and sharp talked her out of her tantrum.

Ch'ao Yüan knew in his heart that there had been no priest. He knew that Chen ko had been conjuring up fake spectres and catching at the air. However, he didn't dare say anything that would put Chen ko in the wrong, and, also, now he had Ms. Chi where he wanted her he could divorce her on this pretext. With Ms. Chi out of the house, one of the goads to Chen ko's temper would be gone. That would make Chen ko happy, and then he could raise her to the position of his wife. He hadn't counted on old Chi and Chi Pa-la coming so fluently to Ms. Chi's defense.

Ms. Chi had a temper and couldn't be expected to stand for this injustice. Ch'ao Yüan had made the mistake of trying to split a rock with an iron spear and had ended up with his spear broken in two. Even though it looked as if he'd failed in his attempt to discredit her, was Ms. Chi content to be generous and let bygones be bygones? No, she was plotting how to peel off Chen ko's hide and reduce Chen ko to a bloody pulp. She was willing to pit her life against his in her quarrel with her husband.

However, she thought, "How could a mere weak woman like me kill him? Even if I did succeed in it, it isn't any good for a woman to kill her husband, and if I did kill him but then failed in killing myself—I couldn't bear how people would treat me! But how else can I clear my name of his accusations that I keep priests?"

She thought it over and over and finally concluded, "I'm no match for him in a fight to the death. Why bother to go on like this? Even if I wait for my mother-in-law to come back, I don't suppose she'll protect me from the storm! No, after all, I'd be better off dead."

She was ninety-nine and then some percent decided when Old Mr. Chi and Chi Pa-la came to see her.

When they arrived at the front gate, Old Chi first sent in a message to Ch'ao Yüan asking, "Did you write that declaration of divorce? I'm here to take my innocent girl home."

Ch'ao Yüan evasively claimed to be sick in bed from all the stress of the quarrel and said he'd talk to them when he felt better.

Old Chi said, "We'd better get it over with. It won't stop with priests—next you'll be claiming she keeps actors." With that he went back to see Ms. Chi.

Ms. Chi asked her father, "Dad, is it true what Mrs. Kao told me, that you and Pa-la were across the street with Yü Mingwu when I came out screaming?"

Old Chi said, "Wasn't I just standing there talking about all this when out you came."

Ms. Chi asked, "What did Yü Ming-wu have to say?"

Old Chi replied, "Just after they left you, Hai-hui and the Nun Kuo ran into Yü Ming-wu, who was seeing some guests off. He asked them 'aren't you afraid of drying up under this wicked sun?' and he invited them to rest inside where it was cool. When you came out and stirred up such a fracas, those two were inside his house eating lunch."

Ms. Chi brought out a small package from an inside room.

"Here are fifty taels, two gold taels, and two pearls. My mother-in-law gave them all to me. Dad, you take these home and keep them for me until I come back home myself. These thirty taels of broken silver are what I've saved in the past few years, and this here is some jewelry I never wear—two bracelets, two pearl tiaras, and two gold hair ornaments—brother, you take these home for me. Take this length of blue satin and have a tailor sew it up quickly into a long sleeved robe for me, and have a half-coat made of this pink gauze. Have my sister-in-law make me some underthings with this floss, and keep the catty of floss that will be left over. Tomorrow, as soon as the clothes are made up, send them to me so I can go home dressed properly."

Old Chi asked, "Why do you want winter clothes like that now in the middle of the summer?"

"What's it to you?" she asked. "Don't ask such irritating questions. If you're going to hang around here telling me what to do, instead of getting those clothes made up for me, I guess I would be better off taking my case to court! I'm going to put a few other things of mine in a chest. Send a servant tomorrow to take the chest home. It's important to get those clothes made—I won't keep you to dinner."

She sent off her father and brother, and put everything in her room in order, just as if she really were planning to go home. She also took out a lot of clothes and gave them one by one to her maids and women.

One woman said, "Ma'am, it's silly to divide up all of your things like this. When the master said he was going to divorce you, he was just letting his mouth run away with him! You're his lawful wife, and he married you in a proper ceremony in front of his parents. How can he divorce you while his parents are absent? Ma'am, you shouldn't go home."

Ms. Chi said, "So according to you, I should wait until he drives me away with a stick?"

"Who would dare do that?" the woman said.

Ms. Chi also had them take some loose change from her bed and distribute it among the servants.

She said, "This is for you to remember me by."

Her maids said, "If you do go home for a while, you'd better lock up this room and take us with you to serve you there. It isn't as if there would be anything left for us to do here."

Ms. Chi said, "Of course you'll go, too, even if you don't come with me."

By now it was about eight in the morning, and nobody had sent them firewood for breakfast. With her own hands, Ms. Chi broke a couple of panels off her new sedan chair, heated up a pot and made breakfast.

One of the servants said, "What a shame! Wouldn't it be better to burn the old sedan chair and use the new one to travel in?"

Ms. Chi told her, "I'm going to be divorced and I won't be a member of the Ch'ao family any more. How can I use their sedan chair then?"

Ch'ao Yüan had found out that Ms. Chi was all packed up and ready to go home to her father. That fit in with his plans, but he didn't know when she would leave. In the morning of the eighth day of the sixth month, old Chi and Chi Pa-la had the clothes ready, and they took the clothes to Ms. Chi, in a package. They also had a few men go to pick up her trunk. Ms. Chi had only a cloth bundle left.

She said, "I decided this old furniture isn't worth more than a few cash and if I take it people will accuse me of being a thief, so who wants their things anyway."

"You're absolutely right," said Old Chi.

Ms. Chi said, "I haven't finished packing up, so I guess I'd better go back tomorrow, but you two don't have to come. The weather is hot, so I'll want to get into the house quickly. We can talk afterwards. If you have any use for the things I gave you yesterday, go ahead and use them. Don't sell them to give me money."

Old Chi said, "Listen to her talk! Aren't you being a little short-sighted? You'd better reconsider. Never mind that I'm no match for him, with his wealth and position. Even if I were, it isn't as if you could make him pay with his life. Listen to what I'm telling you."

For a while he tried to argue her out of her resolve to go through with the divorce.

They used wood from the new sedan chair to cook lunch.

Close to evening, Ms. Chi took a bath, lit some incense, and bound her hair up tight. She put many hair ornaments in her hair, and rings on her fingers. She wrapped her footbindings neatly. She put on new cinnabar-pink silk trousers with a moon-white damask under-garment next to her skin, then a sky blue short jacket with a cinnabar-pink pongee jacket over it, a moon-white great robe and over it all her new blue satin wide-sleeved robe. Then she used a needle and thread to sew together all the layers of her clothes, so there wasn't the tiniest opening anywhere. She placed one gold and one silver piece in her mouth. Then she took a peach-red phoenix sash. Very quietly, she opened her door, walked out to the door of Ch'ao Yüan's rooms and hung herself on his door frame.

It all took less time than two cups of hot tea.

Ethereal steps on air, the shade of a girl on a swing.

Source 9 from The Columbia Book of Later Chinese Poetry: Yüan, Ming, and Ch'ing Dynasties (1279–1911), *trans. and ed. Jonathan Chaves (New York: Columbia University Press, 1986), pp. 437–439.*

9. Zheng Xie (Cheng Hsieh), "Mother-in-law Is Cruel," 18th century

An old poem says, "'Mother-in-law is cruel?' 'Mother-in-law is cruel?' No, it's not that she's cruel, just that my fate is bad!" This can be said to be the height of loyalty, and it captures the traditional purport of the Three Hundred Poems. But the mothers-in-law do not appear to repent of their ways, so I have written this poem to describe in detail what the daughter-in-law's life is like, in the hope that it will act as an exhortation.

A young girl, only eleven,
leaves home to serve her in-laws.
How could she know how it feels to be a wife?
It's like calling her elder brother, "Husband."

The two young people feel bashful with each other;
they try to speak, but can only mumble.
Father-in-law sends her to the women's quarters
to embroider some new ornaments.
Mother-in-law gives her all kinds of awful jobs,
and sends her to the kitchen, knife in hand.
She tries dicing meat, but can't cut perfect cubes:
instead, she serves up ugly chunks on the tray.
She tries making soup, but gets the spicing wrong,
failing to distinguish "sour" and "hot."
Cutting firewood, she tears her soft hands;
tending the fires, the skin on her fingers wrinkles and dries.
Father-in-law says, "She's still young—
we must be patient in teaching her."
Mother-in-law says, "If she can't be taught when young,
who'll be able to handle her when she's grown up?
Haughty and proud, she'll take advantage of us when we're old and decrepit.
Arrogant and lewd, she'll drive our son to his knees!"
So today, she curses and scolds her,
and the next day has her whipped and beaten.
After five days of this, the girl has no untorn clothes to wear;
after ten days, even her skin is completely torn.
Facing the wall, she moans and weeps,
with sounds of sobbing and bitter sighs.
Mother-in-law says, "You're casting spells!
Bring the stick! Bring the knife and saw!
Your flesh can still be cut—
you're pretty chubby, not too skinny at all!
You still have hair on your head—
we'll pull it all out so your head looks like a gourd!
I can't live in the same life as you,
if you live, then my life is done!"
The old witch glares in anger
as if she's about to slaughter her.
And the husband?—He watches a while,
then joins in and shouts, "Have you no shame?"
Father-in-law tries to calm down his wife,
and gets yelled at himself: "You stupid old slave!"
The neighbors try to find out what's going on,
and they're yelled at too: "None of your business!"
Oh, this poor, poor girl from an impoverished family:
why doesn't she just jump into the river?
She can become a meal for the fish and turtles,
and escape this terrible suffering.

[150]

Oh, how cruel of heaven to allow this evil!
and to hear nothing of her cries.
A girl who becomes a young wife in this world
will suffer pain and unjust accusation.
Better to be a cow, a sheep or a pig:
you eat your fill—then one cut of the knife ends it all.
When her parents visit,
she wipes her tears and pretends that she is happy.
When her brothers visit,
she bears the pain, and says, "Mother-in-law is exhausted."
Her scars she covers with tattered clothes,
her bald head she explains as illness.
If she said a single word against mother-in-law
her life would end in a minute.

Source 10 from Sources of Chinese Tradition, *compiled by Wm. Theodore de Bary et al. (New York: Columbia University Press, 1960), pp. 815–818.*

10. From Chen Duxiu (Ch'en Tu-hsiu), "The Ways of Confucius and Modern Life," 1916

The pulse of modern life is economic and the fundamental principle of economic production is individual independence. Its effect has penetrated ethics. Consequently the independence of the individual in the ethical field and the independence of property in the economic field bear witness to each other, thus reaffirming the theory [of such interaction]. Because of this [interaction], social mores and material culture have taken a great step forward.

In China, the Confucianists have based their teachings on their ethical norms. Sons and wives possess neither personal individuality nor personal property. Fathers and elder brothers bring up their sons and younger brothers and are in turn supported by them. It is said in chapter thirty of the *Book of Rites* that "While parents are living, the son dares not regard his person or property as his own." [27:14] This is absolutely not the way to personal independence. . . .

In all modern constitutional states, whether monarchies or republics, there are political parties. Those who engage in party activities all express their spirit of independent conviction. They go their own way and need not agree with their fathers or husbands. When people are bound by the Confucian teachings of filial piety and obedience to the point of the son not deviating from the father's way even three years after his death and the woman obeying not only her father and husband but also her son, how can they form their own political party and make their own choice? The movement of women's participation in politics is

[151]

also an aspect of women's life in modern civilization. When they are bound by the Confucian teaching that "To be a woman means to submit," that "The wife's words should not travel beyond her own apartment," and that "A woman does not discuss affairs outside the home," would it not be unusual if they participated in politics?

In the West some widows choose to remain single because they are strongly attached to their late husbands and sometimes because they prefer a single life; they have nothing to do with what is called the chastity of widowhood. Widows who remarry are not despised by society at all. On the other hand, in the Chinese teaching of decorum, there is the doctrine of "no remarriage after the husband's death." It is considered to be extremely shameful and unchaste for a woman to serve two husbands or a man to serve two rulers. The *Book of Rites* also prohibits widows from wailing at night [27:21] and people from being friends with sons of widows. [9:21] For the sake of their family reputation, people have forced their daughters-in-law to remain widows. These women have had no freedom and have endured a most miserable life. Year after year these many promising young women have lived a physically and spiritually abnormal life. All this is the result of Confucian teachings of decorum [or rites].

In today's civilized society, social intercourse between men and women is a common practice. Some even say that because women have a tender nature and can temper the crudeness of man, they are necessary in public or private gatherings. It is not considered improper even for strangers to sit or dance together once they have been introduced by the host. In the way of Confucian teaching, however, "Men and women do not sit on the same mat," "Brothers- and sisters-in-law do not exchange inquiries about each other," "Married sisters do not sit on the same mat with brothers or eat from the same dish," "Men and women do not know each other's name except through a matchmaker and should have no social relations or show affection until after marriage presents have been exchanged," "Women must cover their faces when they go out," "Boys and girls seven years or older do not sit or eat together," "Men and women have no social relations except through a matchmaker and do not meet until after marriage presents have been exchanged," and "Except in religious sacrifices, men and women do not exchange wine cups." Such rules of decorum are not only inconsistent with the mode of life in Western society; they cannot even be observed in today's China.

Western women make their own living in various professions such as that of lawyer, physician, and store employee. But in the Confucian way, "In giving or receiving anything, a man or woman should not touch the other's hand," "A man does not talk about affairs inside [the household] and a woman does not talk about affairs outside [the household]," and "They do not exchange cups except in sacrificial rites and funerals." "A married woman is to obey" and the husband is the standard of the wife. Thus the wife is naturally supported by the husband and needs no independent livelihood.

A married woman is at first a stranger to her parents-in-law. She has only affection but no obligation toward them. In the West parents and children usually do not live together, and daughters-in-law, particularly, have no obligation to serve parents-in-law. But in the way of Confucius, a woman is to "revere and respect them and never to disobey day or night," "A woman obeys, that is, obeys her parents-in-law," "A woman serves her parent-in-law as she serves her own parents," she "never should disobey or be lazy in carrying out the orders of parents and parents-in-law." "If a man is very fond of his wife, but his parents do not like her, she should be divorced." (In ancient times there were many such cases, like that of Lu Yü [1125–1210].) "Unless told to retire to her own apartment, a woman does not do so, and if she has an errand to do, she must get permission from her parents-in-law." This is the reason why the tragedy of cruelty to daughters-in-law has never ceased in Chinese society.

According to Western customs, fathers do not discipline grown-up sons but leave them to the law of the country and the control of society. But in the way of Confucius, "When one's parents are angry and not pleased and beat him until he bleeds, he does not complain but instead arouses in himself the feelings of reverence and filial piety." This is the reason why in China there is the saying, "One has to die if his father wants him to, and the minister has to perish if his ruler wants him to.". . .

QUESTIONS TO CONSIDER

Breaking a complex problem down into smaller parts often helps to make it more manageable. Instead of addressing the larger issue of how to view the Confucian family all at once, therefore, try asking some more limited, specific questions about each of the sources in turn. As noted in the Method section, the first five offer glimpses into different aspects of family life in late traditional times. Collectively they provide a logical place to look for answers to the first question: What was the Confucian family like?

Source 1, the family portrait, provides a relatively realistic picture of an elite family toward the end of the Ming dynasty (1368–1644), in some ways a counterpart to the snapshots in our own family albums. But keep in mind that ordinary people could not afford to commission such paintings in Ming China, and so such portraiture, far from seeking to reveal a casual moment in family life, served to call attention to the importance of the household in a very public and formal way. Note the posed, symmetrical arrangement of family members. What does the placement of different individuals suggest about relationships between members and their relative importance? Do some seem to stand out more than others? Why do you suppose no young children are shown? Compare this view with photographs you may have of your family. Would you want your family to be remembered this way?

The formality of the portrait reflects a great concern for careful, deliberate behavior that shows up in other documents as well. Source 2, the Miu family instructions, for example, painstakingly

[153]

explains "the correct procedures to be followed in everyday life" as well as the particulars for formal family rituals. It repeatedly urges members to "exercise restraint" in all household affairs and observe a strict sense of propriety that rules out spontaneity and casual behavior. In this connection, look carefully at the final passage in the text, which purports to disclose the "secrets" of a successful family life. Would people today regard fulfillment of "duty" a measure of such success? What standard would you use to judge family success?

The need to reduce conflict in a large household may explain some of this concern for rules and restraint. What kinds of friction and fighting does Source 2 anticipate? The guide seems to attribute most such problems to unruly individual behavior. But the text singles out certain family members as most likely to be troublemakers. Who are they? What does this suggest about prevailing attitudes with regard to gender, age, and social level? How would you react to the "preventive measures" the texts prescribe as cure for such problems—particularly the seclusion of women or the household meetings called "to encourage one another in virtue and to correct each other's mistakes"? As you can see in this instance, family rules emphasized collective responsibility and group harmony. Individuality, however, was not totally ignored. For the text advises members to follow their own aspirations for occupations. Would this encouragement apply equally to all members?

The distaste of cities expressed in Source 2 reflects a deep-seated Confucian bias toward rural life. Upper-class Confucians believed that the simplicity and frugality of country living promoted a level of virtue difficult to sustain in urban environments. The text thus praises farming as second only to elite scholarship as an occupation and warns that the family's rural "houses, fields, and ponds" should never be divided or sold. As Source 3 shows, however, the country houses of the elite were hardly rustic cottages. Like urban residences, they were walled compounds with many interior halls and courtyards that could be assigned to different conjugal families and the many servants needed to maintain such an expansive household. Because the front halls served as public reception rooms and men's studies, women generally kept to the back parts. Outside its immediate walls spread park-like gardens, and farther beyond stretched farmland that was usually rented out to less fortunate families. Compare this kind of residence with contemporary suburban homes. What does architecture and setting in each case tell about the residents' interests and values?

Sources 4 and 5 offer two different glimpses into the lives of women and children in such big households. Source 4, "A Sketch of My Mother," shows the tender personal affections that often developed between men and women despite all the formality and ceremony that characterized life in the Confucian family. Notice which women in his family the author, Gui Youguang mentions—and whom he seems to have loved most. Because his father occupied a government post that kept him away from home for long periods, Gui's mother supervised his education and saw to his marriage on her own. Although she may have been as strict with him as any Confucian patriarch, he clearly felt close to her. Perhaps his regard for her explains his similar affection for his wife and daughter, and the fact that he makes nothing of his lack of a son. As Source 5, sample contracts for purchasing concubines and adoptive sons, indicates, many men in his situation did not accept an absence of male heirs so nonchalantly and resorted to these solutions. What do these documents tell you about the social and legal rights of women and children? Who seems to be in a position to determine their fate? How do you react to the idea that some people could own others?

Confucians, who accepted adoption and concubinage, did so only as expedients to assure the continuity of the family. Here, as in most situations, they justified the sacrifice of individual satisfaction in the name of family benefit. The familialism underlying this attitude served as the subject of a much-quoted Confucian work known as the *Xiao Jing,* or *Classic of Filiality,* portions of which appear as Source 6. Notice how this work finds a larger social and political meaning in the subordination of individual needs to family benefit. To what higher purposes than family success does it say "filiality" leads? Do you think that such ends justify restraints on individualism? The importance of the home as the basic site for socialization and moral training continued to be a cherished Confucian idea, as you can see in Source 7. Taken from a work compiled by Zhu Xi, often ranked as the "Second Master" after Confucius, this

passage affirms the Confucian belief that social order ultimately depends on family values and behavior. Note whom this text, too, identifies as most needing correction. Do you agree with its claim that in such cases "bad character is nourished by indulgence"?

Sources 8 and 9 provide sympathetic views of those who bore the brunt of punishment and sacrifice within the Confucian family. Source 8, taken from a seventeenth-century novel called *The Bonds of Matrimony* attributed to Pu Suling, presents the tragic end of an unhappy marriage. In his youth, the ambitious husband, Chao Yuan (Ch'ao Yüan), agreed to marry the homely Ms. Qi (Chi) because of her family's prestige. Never very fond or considerate of her, he used her childlessness as an excuse to bring a concubine into the household. And when conflicts flared between the women, he threatened to divorce his wife on the pretext that she had had an affair with a Buddhist priest who had come to counsel her. In the excerpt given here, she brings their marital crisis to a dramatic close. Why does she take this course? What do her reasons suggest about the options for unhappy women in the Confucian family?

The poem called "Mother-in-law Is Cruel," Source 9, looks at another kind of family crisis, the conflict between a new wife and her husband's mother. As you may have observed in some of the other sources, girls married at a young age in China, often at about thirteen, or at the onset of puberty. In this poem, the wife is even younger. Would such a marriage be legal, or even socially acceptable, in present-day Western society? Why not? Here again problems seem to stem from a conflict between two "women," although one is but a child. What explains the friction here? Inasmuch as a matriarch seems to be the source of misery in this case, could the author be implying that the nature of the Confucian family—rather than male domination—invites such abuse? For whom does he thus intend this exhortation?

In Source 10 Chen Duxiu offers a modern Western rationale for eliminating this Chinese institution altogether. For the most part he bases his argument on an appeal for greater individual freedom and equality. This argument, which typifies the modernizing trends that began to rock the world in the twentieth century, seemed extremely radical in China back in 1916. Would all Westerners have accepted it in 1916? For that matter, do you find all of it acceptable today? What do you think a staunch Confucian would have said in rebuttal to some of Chen's specific points, such as his claim that "the law of country and the control of society" should fully replace family authority? Would everyone in the West agree with that proposition now? Despite his scorn of tradition, Chen curiously perpetuates (in an inverted way) the Confucian insistence on an important link between family life and the state of society. For he says that open, conjugal families of the Western sort promote not only individualistic societies but economic development. In other words, national prosperity, as well as social health, depends on what goes on in the home. How reasonable does this claim seem to you? Would an erosion of family influence over individuals help or hinder a nation?

Having spent some time considering these separate questions, you should now be in a better position to deal with the larger issue posed as the central problem in this chapter. That is, what standpoint would *you* take in developing a history of the Confucian family? Before you give your final answer, think back over your replies to the various issues raised about individual sources in this section. Do you detect any clear pattern to your responses? What do they show about your own perspective on this institution? Is this a perspective you would consciously choose to adopt? Would you expect others to do the same? How would you defend or critique such a choice? What might be lost or gained by taking this approach?

EPILOGUE

Western reformers like Chen Duxiu eventually carried the day in China, following the initial turmoil unleashed by the collapse of the imperial monarchy in 1911 and decades of civil strife and foreign invasion. By 1949, the Chinese Communist Party, which Chen helped to found in 1921, took control over China and began a radical reform of the country. During the 1950s new reforms swept away the legal basis of the old patriarchal tradition, granting women and children full equality and protection under the law, while land redistribution and political modernization destroyed the elites with whom it had flourished. At the height of the Great Proletarian Cultural Revolution of the 1960s, Communist Party leader Mao Zedong lent his support to even more radical efforts, calling for the abolition of all family life in favor of collective living in giant communes. Although this extreme step failed, the last quarter of the twentieth century seemed to mark the end of the old Chinese tradition of familialism as well as of the patriarchal Confucian family.

Strangely enough, however, interest in this tradition began to revive during the 1980s, not in China but in the wealthier parts of East Asia where successful modernization had occurred. Indeed, some observers credit much of the success of countries like Japan, South Korea, Taiwan, and China in industrial growth to the survival of Confucian culture and family values that promote group interests over individual demands. They contend that the willingness of people in these areas to defer personal gains, obey authority, and uphold rules creates a stable and orderly society necessary for economic growth. Leaders in some East Asian countries have even begun to praise these traditional values and the Confucian family ethos as superior to once-coveted Western modernism. They point to sluggish economic growth and mounting social tensions in the West as symptoms of a social decline set in motion by excessive individualism and disregard for authority. It should come as no surprise, then, that attitudes toward the Confucian family may again change in East Asia and even in China, where economic growth is accelerating. How might this eventuality affect the way future historians view the institution? Would it change the way you have decided to view the Confucian family?

CHAPTER SIX

THE LIBERATOR-HERO AND

WESTERN REVOLUTIONS (1770s–1810s)

THE PROBLEM

During the late eighteenth and early nineteenth centuries, successful revolts, failed uprisings, and both real and imagined revolutionary plots swept across much of Europe and the Americas. While visiting her native city of Liège in 1791, Théroinge de Méricourt, a woman who sympathized with and participated in the early stages of the French Revolution, was arrested and imprisoned by the Austrians. Believing she was a spy, the Austrians interrogated her, without success, and then sent for the prison doctor, who diagnosed her as suffering from "revolutionary fever."[1]

In the eyes of many, Méricourt was not the only person struck down with "revolutionary fever." Indeed, according to historian R. R. Palmer, English conservative Edmund Burke "was so afraid of invasion and revolution . . . that he gave orders for his remains to be secretly buried, lest triumphant democrats dig them up for desecration."[2]

Whatever their differences, the Western revolutionaries of the late eighteenth and early nineteenth centuries were an extremely self-conscious lot. Convinced that they were altering history, not only for their own people but for all the world, these revolutionists wanted to justify their revolts as the

1. Théroinge de Méricourt, real name Anne-Joseph Méricourt (1762–1817), was one of the many fascinating participants in the French Revolution. See Simon Schama, *Citizens: A Chronicle of the French Revolution* (New York: Alfred A. Knopf, 1989), pp. 462–463, 530, 605, 611, 873–875.

2. R. R. Palmer, *The Age of the Democratic Revolution: A Political History of Europe and America, 1760–1800,* 2 vols. (Princeton: Princeton University Press, 1959), vol. I, p. 5. According to Palmer, revolutions, threats of revolutions, or plots took place in what was to become the United States as well as in France, Ireland, the Netherlands, Switzerland, Milan, Rome, Naples, Poland, Hungary, Greece, Ecuador, Brazil, what would become Haiti, and some of the German states.

fulfillment of a higher purpose (rather than a mere grab for power), as well as to pass on to future generations what they considered to be the true essence or meaning of their respective revolutions.

One way they were able to accomplish both objectives was through the creation of a *national hero* who would justify the revolution, explain its causes and its successes, and tell how life was better after the revolution than it had been before it. Through the use of speeches, eulogies, memorials, songs, pageants, paintings and statuary, and (later) national holidays, commemorative postage stamps and coins, etc., the Western revolutionaries could bind their contemporaries to the revolution as well as communicate to later generations its nature or essence.

Revolutionaries often embodied their national mythology in a *liberator-hero,* a person who could symbolize the revolution. In such a liberator-hero, the character of the revolution could be imbued, and people could use the liberator-hero as an object of veneration as well as a personification of the revolution itself.

In this chapter you will examine the creation of four liberator-heroes: George Washington of the American Revolution, Jean-Paul Marat of the French Revolution, Toussaint Louverture of the Haitian Revolution, and Simón Bolívar of the Latin American revolutions. Using eulogies and contemporary portraits, you will be asked to analyze how the participants in each revolution attempted to fashion a liberator-hero who symbolized the character, goals, and nature of the revolution as the participants themselves understood it *and* as they wanted others to see it. How was George Washington used by his contemporaries as a symbol of the American Revolution? Jean-Paul Marat of the French Revolution? Toussaint Louverture of the Haitian Revolution? Simón Bolívar of the Latin American revolutions? Although these revolutions had much in common and in many ways were intertwined, the American, French, Haitian, and Latin American revolutions were profoundly different, as were their respective liberator-heroes.

BACKGROUND

In Britain's North American colonies, a struggle for home rule evolved into a war for separation. In the 1760s and early 1770s an increasing number of people in Britain's North American colonies began to oppose taxation by the mother country, as well as what they feared was an erosion of their political rights. In 1775 these protests erupted into open warfare, and in the

next year the colonies declared their independence from Great Britain and their intention to form a new nation. Independence and nationhood, however, were not actually achieved until the British gave up the armed struggle in 1781 and grudgingly recognized the former colonies' independence in 1783. For their part, the colonial elites who had led the fight for independence (New England and Middle Colonies merchants and lawyers and southern planters) did not want the war to be

Chapter 6

The Liberator-

Hero and

Western

Revolutions

(1770s–1810s)

accompanied by democratic reforms, and were able to prevent such an upsurge by forming a new government that favored rule by the elite, property qualifications for voting, and other conservative measures.

After the opening battles of what would become the American Revolution (at Lexington and Concord on April 19, 1775, later referred to by Ralph Waldo Emerson as "the shot heard 'round the world"), revolutionary leaders in Britain's North American colonies[3] realized they needed a military leader who could organize the ragtag militia besieging the British forces in Boston into what would become the Continental Army. Reasoning that a man from the southern colonies would give the rebellion the unity it needed, Congress named forty-three-year-old George Washington of Virginia. Washington was born on February 11, 1732,[4] into Virginia's minor gentry. Trained as a surveyor, as a young man his goal was a commission in the regular British army. The intercession of a friend secured Washington an officership in the Virginia militia and the potentially dangerous assignment (at the age of only twenty-one) of delivering to the French, poised along the western frontier, an ultima-

tum to leave what Virginians believed was British territory. The following year (1754), Washington, now a colonel in the militia, returned to the frontier to challenge the French, but he was forced to surrender a fort he had constructed (Fort Necessity, in present-day western Pennsylvania) and to return to eastern Virginia.

In 1755 Washington became an aide to General Edward Braddock, who led a force of 1,400 British regulars and 450 colonial militiamen on an expedition to capture Fort Duquesne (present-day Pittsburgh) in western Pennsylvania. About eight miles below the fort, the army was attacked and defeated by a combined force of Frenchmen and Native Americans. Braddock was mortally wounded, and Washington led the remnant of the force to safety, an accomplishment that earned him an international reputation. But in 1758, frustrated by his inability to secure a commission in the British army as well as by insufficient support for the Virginia militia's campaign in the West, he resigned his militia post and retired to his home, Mount Vernon.

Although not in the forefront of colonial leaders who urged resistance to the mother country, Washington was so well known that he was elected to most of the major colonial congresses that met to protest British policies and, as noted above, was a popular choice to command the American army formed after the outbreak of hostilities at Lexington and Concord.

George Washington's principal accomplishments were organizing what became the United States Army (called the Continental Line and never numbering more than 18,000 troops); preventing desertions from decimating that

3. Canada was invited to join Britain's thirteen other North American colonies in the rebellion, but refused. See Justin H. Smith, *Our Struggle for the Fourteenth Colony: Canada and the American Revolution*, 2 vols. (New York: G. P. Putnam's Sons, 1907). See also George A. Rawlyk, *Revolution Rejected, 1775–1776* (Scarborough, Ont.: Prentice-Hall, 1968).

4. When the English changed from the Julian to the Gregorian calendar in 1752, eleven days were added to the calendar to realign it with the sun and stars. Therefore, Washington's birthday became February 22.

force (he once wrote, "We shall have to detach half of the army to look for the other half"); and keeping that force in the field for six years of skirmishes and battles, many of which were lost. The British, however, faced with the defeat of General Cornwallis at Yorktown in 1781 and mounting opposition to the war at home, were forced to give up the struggle. After once again retiring to Mount Vernon, Washington was called back to service as the Constitutional government's first president (the article of the Constitution dealing with the executive branch was written with Washington in mind, in the hope that he would accept the position). Having retired yet again in 1797, he died on December 14, 1799. By then, he was generally being referred to as the "father of his country," and was enshrined as the liberator-hero of the United States, the symbol of the successful American Revolution.

The French Revolution was the result of the convergence of several problems that overtook the French monarchy in the 1780s. The most critical of these problems was the government's fiscal bankruptcy. As a consequence of the costly wars of the eighteenth century and a system of taxation that virtually exempted the nobility and the clergy from fiscal obligations, the French monarchy was deeply in debt by 1787.[5] Several finance ministers struggled with the crown's debts (which by 1788 had reached 4 billion livres and took 51 percent of the government's

total revenues just to make the interest payments), but eventually all of them arrived at the same conclusion: Bankruptcy could be avoided only through fundamental reforms that would tax the Church and nobility and not just the commoners.

In proposing such changes, however, the finance ministers encountered opposition from the noble judges of the great law courts (the *parlements*), who had to approve any new royal laws before they could be enforced. Such basic changes in taxation policy, these judges alleged, had to be approved by a nationwide representative body, and their objections forced the king to call for a meeting in 1789 of the Estates General, an elected assembly that had not met since 1614.

The election of 1789 was held in a country suffering from enormous economic problems. Since 1705 France's population had increased by 24.5 percent, with no corresponding increase in the food supply. Poor harvests in 1788 and 1789 and a commercial depression in 1789 only made matters worse. Inflation of prices had increased the cost of living for the working person by 62 percent over the eighteenth century, while wages for construction workers had risen only 24 percent and agricultural workers' wages a meager 16 percent. Nearly 40 percent of France's population in 1789 was destitute, living by squatting on land they did not own, begging, charity, or crime.

The result of France's economic and political problems was the election of an Estates General that was prepared to seek far more than tax reform. When Louis XVI refused to approve voting rules for the Estates General that would have assured the representatives of the

---

5. France's successful intervention in the American Revolution had cost the French government 2 billion livres, a figure that was four times the government's tax receipts in 1788.

Chapter 6

The Liberator-

Hero and

Western

Revolutions

(1770s–1810s)

commoners (known as the Third Estate) a chance at enacting tax reform and of realizing some degree of political equality with the clergy and the nobility (the First and Second Estates), the king encountered the first act of revolution. Declaring themselves a National Assembly and the rightful representatives of all the French people, the representatives of the Third Estate pledged to draft a written constitution that would clearly limit royal authority—in essence making Louis XVI a constitutional monarch. When the king countered by ordering troops to disperse the National Assembly, the people of Paris took up arms and seized the Bastille, a strategically important fort and prison, on July 14, 1789. In the countryside, peasants attacked the castles and manor houses of their noble lords and broke into grain storage facilities.

Faced with mounting opposition and rising violence, Louis XVI ostensibly agreed to live within a new constitutional order. Taking the king at his word, the National Assembly began work on a constitution that would have made France a constitutional monarchy. But Louis never really accepted the new constitutional order, and in 1791 he attempted to flee to eastern France to assume leadership of counterrevolutionary forces. Captured and forcibly returned to Paris, where he was virtually made a prisoner in his own country, Louis's situation was hopeless. In September 1792, the republic was proclaimed, Louis XVI was tried for treason and condemned in December 1792, and the monarch went to the guillotine on January 16, 1793. His wife Marie Antoinette (who probably never said, "Let them eat cake") followed soon thereafter, and their son, next in line to the now nonexistent throne, died in prison in 1795.

Jean-Paul Marat was among the Jacobin radicals who were supported by the shopkeepers and craftsmen of Paris, known as *sans-culottes*,[6] in their regicide[7] and their search for other enemies of the revolution. Marat was born on May 24, 1743, the oldest of six children in a lower-middle-class family (the family's original name had been Mara, but Jean-Paul changed his name to appear more French). Later admitting that his dominant passion was a love of glory (*amour de la gloire*), Marat became a prosperous physician who treated the wealthy and published his research on the medical properties of electricity. His friends called him a brilliant doctor-scientist-philosopher, while his detractors dubbed him a desperate charlatan. Drifting toward radicalism (driven, perhaps, by the rejection of his bid for admission to the Academy of Sciences), in February 1789 Marat published an attack on the government, calling for a constitutional monarchy with full political rights to the people. In September 1789, he began to publish his newspaper *L'Ami du Peuple* (*The Friend of the People*).

6. *sans-culottes* (**without breeches**): the shopkeepers and craftsmen of Paris, so named because they wore clothing characteristic of their social group. Their garb included pants that extended to their shoe tops, not the elegant knee breeches of aristocrats. This group was unified by more than just a common mode of dress, however. It espoused a political ideology of direct democracy and an economic policy of government regulation of wages and prices to protect its economic security.

7. **regicide:** the killing of a king.

From the first, *L'Ami du Peuple* echoed Marat's fears of plots against the Revolution by its enemies, and his responses to such plots became increasingly radical. As early as October 1789 he called for a revolutionary dictatorship that would preserve the Revolution's gains. One month earlier, Marat had declared that "five or six hundred heads cut off would have assured you peace, liberty and happiness." But by May 27, 1791, he had raised that number: "Today fifty thousand would be necessary" to protect the Revolution. Seen by his opponents as a dangerous radical and blamed by the police for instigating an October 1789 march on the royal palace at Versailles, Marat was forced into hiding and fled briefly to England, but he soon returned to France. Continuing to publish his newspaper, Marat gained more power when he was elected to the National Convention in 1792.

Marat supported *sans-culottes* ideals of direct democracy, aid to the economically disadvantaged funded by a progressive income tax, state-sponsored vocational schools, and shorter terms of military service. These positions won him the support of the Parisian *sans-culottes* and the enmity of the more moderate Girondin faction in the Convention. Indeed, the Girondins secured Marat's indictment on charges of inciting insurrection, but he was acquitted of these capital charges and gained his revenge by playing a major role in the Parisian insurrection that purged the Convention of its Girondin members on June 2, 1793.

After June 2, 1793, Marat was much less active politically. He was dying from skin and lung diseases, and was forced to spend long hours in medicinal baths in his Paris apartment. It was there that he was visited by a young woman named Charlotte Corday on July 13, 1793. Corday was a Girondist sympathizer who had become convinced that radicals like Marat were destroying the Revolution. Gaining admission to Marat's bathroom by claiming to have information on counterrevolutionary plots, she stabbed the revolutionary leader to death. Apprehended immediately, the twenty-five-year-old Corday was guillotined on July 17. A magnificent funeral and numerous eulogies turned Jean-Paul Marat into a revolutionary martyr and a liberator-hero. The ceremonies would have lasted longer, but, in the hot Paris summer, Marat's body began to decompose. His embalmed heart was hung from the ceiling of the Cordeliers Club, but the remainder of Marat was quickly buried in the club's garden.

The search for enemies of the revolution led to the Reign of Terror of 1793–1794, in which perhaps as many as 40,000 citizens lost their lives. And their search for a secular state in which the Church would have no influence led the radicals to scrap the traditional calendar based on the Christian year in favor of a new revolutionary calendar that began counting years from 1791, when the new constitution came into force.

True stability, however, continued to elude France. Recurrent coups marked the rest of the decade until Napoleon Bonaparte's seizure of power in 1799 restored some measure of political stability.

Christopher Columbus had landed on the island he named Hispaniola (Little

Chapter 6

The Liberator-

Hero and

Western

Revolutions

(1770s–1810s)

Spain) on December 6, 1492, and he claimed it for Spain.[8] French settlers began moving into the western part of the island in the late 1600s, and the Treaty of Ryswick (1697) officially divided the island between the two European nations, the French calling their portion Saint-Domingue and the Spanish calling theirs Santo Domingo. Gradually the French developed a plantation system with approximately 3,000 plantations that raised sugar, coffee, cotton, and indigo. The Native American population, not immune to European diseases, was virtually wiped out. The French planters, therefore, relied on slave labor from Africa, importing over 800,000 Africans between 1680 and 1776. By 1787, the population of Saint-Domingue was composed of around 24,000 whites, 408,000 black slaves (approximately two-thirds of whom were African born, largely from the Congo and Angola), and 20,000 *gens de couleur* (mulattos and free blacks).

The death toll among the slave population was enormous; thus planters had to import Africans continuously to keep up the labor pool. Largely because a significant majority of the slave population had been born in freedom in Africa, slave resistance was a regular feature of life in the French colony. A large revolt took place in 1522, and four other armed conspiracies occurred between 1679 and 1704. Runaway slaves hid in the mountains, where, according to one European observer in 1705,

8. The origin of the name *Haiti* is somewhat unclear. Many scholars believe that the Native American Arawaks who were living on the island when Columbus arrived called the island Haiti. But other scholars of the region disagree.

"[t]hey gather together in the woods and live there exempt from service to their masters without any other leader but one elected among them." African culture among the slaves and runaways remained both vital and durable, including the practice of voodoo, an African form of worship that the French tried in vain to eradicate but that formed an important bond among the blacks—even those who had nominally been converted to the Catholic faith. In 1757 another widespread rebellion, the Makandal conspiracy, broke out. Involving mostly African-born slaves, it sought to overthrow the white masters and win political independence. Crushed by the white planters, the conspirators were burned at the stake.

The French Revolution provided the opportunity for another revolt. Aware of revolutionary events in France, in 1791 mulattos sent a delegation to the National Assembly in Paris to secure the rights enumerated in France's Declaration of the Rights of Man and Citizen (1789). Being refused, mulattos rebelled against the white planters but were quickly overcome, as they had been in an earlier revolt in October 1790. Leaders of the uprising were executed and then decapitated, their heads placed on poles which were left standing for around three years as a warning to other would-be revolutionaries.

Once again, however, the French Revolution intruded on life in Saint-Domingue. Later in 1791, the National Assembly granted rights to all mulattos and all blacks born of free parents. When news of the National Assembly's actions reached the Caribbean colony (on June 30, 1791), whites were enraged.

Civil war once again broke out between mulattos and whites.

In August 1791, the situation was made even more complex—and bloody—by an uprising of the slaves. Many whites fled to U.S. seaports like Savannah, Charleston, and Baltimore, terrifying American plantation owners with reports of burning plantations, widespread killing, and atrocities. By 1793, slaves had built up an army of between 4,000 and 5,000 troops who were fierce, courageous, and tactically brilliant fighters. Led by Toussaint Louverture, this army beat back an attempted British invasion, a Spanish intrusion from Santo Domingo, and another uprising of mulattos in 1799.

François-Dominique Toussaint à Bréda was born on May 20, 1743, on the Bréda plantation in Saint-Domingue. The oldest of eight children, Toussaint's father had been born in Africa, captured in a war, and sold into slavery in the New World. Taught to read and write by a Roman Catholic priest, Toussaint was given more and more responsibility on the plantation until he was made coachman and livestock steward; the plantation's overseer (the owner lived in Paris) gave him forty acres and thirteen slaves to manage. Permitted to marry (a rarity for slaves in Saint-Domingue), Toussaint wed Suzanne Simone Baptiste, and the union produced two sons. Therefore, although Toussaint was technically a slave and no manumission papers ever were drawn up, essentially he was looked upon and treated as a free man (*affranchi*).

When the slave rebellion first broke out in August 1791, Toussaint played only a minor role and was believed to be conservative in his thinking (he had helped his plantation's white factor, or agent, escape from a mob of ex-slaves). Gradually his powerful and articulate speeches to the troops (Toussaint spoke both the Creole patois and his father's African tribal language, in addition to French) and his charisma, tactical genius, and emphasis on training and discipline lifted him to the position of commander of the rebellion.

Seeing an opportunity to drive the French from Saint-Domingue, Toussaint briefly sided with the Spanish. It was at this time that he wrote a letter to blacks and signed it Toussaint Louverture, which means *the opening*. "I thought it was a good name for bravery," Toussaint reflected. But when he learned that the National Convention in Paris had abolished slavery (in February 1794), he switched sides and led his army against the Spanish and the British invaders, both of whom gave up the fight. In 1796 Toussaint was named lieutenant governor of Saint-Domingue, in 1800 he put down an uprising of the mulattos, and in 1801 he issued a constitution for the republic.

And yet Toussaint believed that Haiti's economic future was tied to that of France. In 1802, Napoleon Bonaparte revived French ambitions for an empire in the Western Hemisphere. Intending to reap enormous profits from the sugar and coffee trade and determined to restore slavery in order to do it, Napoleon sent a French invading army to the island in 1802. When the French army invaded the island in 1802, Toussaint, foolishly, was prepared to welcome it. His two sons were being educated in France (they were received by the Empress Josephine) and he had

Chapter 6
The Liberator-
Hero and
Western
Revolutions
(1770s–1810s)

tried to convince the ex-slaves to adopt French ways (he criticized the low necklines of Haitian women's dresses).

Tricked into surrendering, Toussaint was hustled off to a prison in France (Fort de Joux), where he died on April 7, 1803. His entreaties to meet with Napoleon had gone unheeded. Yet the Haitians ultimately won their independence from the French, and Toussaint Louverture became the symbol of the revolution, the liberator-hero.

The French army, decimated by yellow fever, was forced to withdraw from Haiti, ending Napoleon's dreams of an American empire. It was at that point that he offered to sell the Louisiana Territory to the United States. The Republic of Haiti (so named in 1804) had secured its independence, but the instability and terror of the revolution did not cease for decades.

In Spain's other Latin American[9] colonies, the struggles for independence, like those of Britain's North American colonies,[10] were led not from the bottom of the socioeconomic ladder but from the top. In the late eighteenth century, Spain's monarch Charles III attempted to assert more direct control over the colonies, in part by filling the colonial bureaucracies with *peninsulares*, people who had been born in Spain and were sent out to enforce royal proclamations, streamline tax collection, and reassert direct royal authority over Spain's American possessions. This angered the *creoles*, whites of European descent who had been born in America and who believed that they, not the *peninsulares*, should be awarded those high administrative posts. Yet their complaints were ignored in Madrid: of the 107 viceroys appointed by the Crown during the colonial era, only four were *creoles*.[11]

Although the *creoles* and others had been restive for some time, the 1807–1808 invasion of Spain by Napoleon Bonaparte and his toppling of the Spanish king (he placed his brother Jerome on the throne)[12] gave the conspirators the opportunity they needed to overthrow European rule. Fearing that Napoleon would exercise more power in America than had the weak Spanish government, that he would increase taxes to finance his military ventures, and that he would attempt to export the ideology of the French Revolution (especially that of egalité), many *creoles* organized small councils or committees known as *juntas* that claimed to be the legitimate governing bodies of various regions of Latin America.

And yet, it was by no means clear what path Spain's colonies should take. Many *creoles* viewed the unstable situation as a chance to cast off the monarchy altogether in favor of complete independence. In contrast, other

9. The term *Latin America* was not used until 1856. See Mark A. Burkholder and Lyman L. Johnson, *Colonial Latin America*, 4th ed. (New York: Oxford University Press, 2001), p. 3.

10. The thirteen British colonies that did revolt tried to get Canada to join them, but they were rebuffed. See Justin H. Smith, *Our Struggle for the Fourteenth Colony: Canada and the American Revolution*, 2 vols. (New York and London: G. P. Putnam's Sons, 1907).

11. Richard W. Slatta and Jane Lucas DeGrummond, *Simón Bolívar's Quest for Glory* (College Station: Texas A & M University Press, 2003), p. 48.

12. Napoleon forced King Charles IV to abdicate and then did the same to his son Ferdinand VII. When Napoleon deposed his brother, he restored Ferdinand to the Spanish throne.

powerful forces (the most prominent of which were the *peninsulares*) clung to the Spanish monarchy (which Napoleon restored in 1814) from which they derived their wealth and authority. Thus when fighting erupted between the two sides (one known as Royalists and the other calling themselves Patriots), the wars of independence in Latin America took on the character of civil wars rather than uprisings against a mother country.

One of the principal leaders who emerged in Latin America's wars of independence was Simón Bolívar (1783–1830), called by some "the Liberator." Born to one of the wealthiest families in Venezuela and "one of the most aristocratic in America,"[13] young Simón studied in Europe, was presented at the Spanish court, and in 1802 (at the age of nineteen) married a Spanish noblewoman. When his wife died in Venezuela the next year, Simón returned to Europe. Later he recalled, "The death of my wife put me on the road to politics very early; it made me follow the chariot of Mars instead of . . . the plow of Ceres."[14] He never remarried.

Returning to Venezuela in 1807, Bolívar helped to organize a *junta* in Caracas (he referred to it as a "literary group") that met in his home, and he was a delegate to the first Congress of Venezuela, which on July 4, 1811, voted for independence from Spain. By that time armed conflict had broken out between the Royalists and the Patriots, and Bolívar became the leader of the

Patriot forces. A self-taught military commander, Bolívar directed over five hundred battles, in some of which his forces fell victim to his rashness and impetuosity. In the end, however, his charisma kept his armies together, and on December 9, 1824, at the Battle of Ayacucho, his troops smashed the Royalist army and as a result ended Spain's efforts to reestablish its American empire. Thus Simón Bolívar played a major role in liberating Venezuela, Colombia, Ecuador, Peru, and Upper Peru (later named Bolivia in his honor).

Although he was called "the Liberator," Simón Bolívar certainly was no democrat. Although he often compared himself to George Washington, he believed that the United States's type of government would not work in Latin America, principally because roughly 90 percent of the population was illiterate and had no experience in political participation (he once quipped that he "would rather see his fellow Spanish Americans adopt the Koran . . . than the government of the United States").[15] Therefore, when he could he assumed dictatorial powers. As a result, several of his followers turned against him, and when he died of tuberculosis in 1830 at the age of forty-seven, he was waiting for a ship to carry him to exile in Europe. Soon afterward, however, his reputation was restored and he was honored as a genuine liberator-hero.

Thus each revolution—the American, the French, the Haitian, and the Latin

13. Slatta and DeGrummond, *Simón Bolívar's Quest for Glory*, p. 17.

14. *Ibid.*, p. 20. Mars was the Roman god of war, and Ceres was the Roman goddess of agriculture.

15. For Bolívar's remark about the Qur'an (Koran), see David Bushnell and Neill Macaulay, *The Emergence of Latin America in the Nineteenth Century* (New York: Oxford University Press, 1994), p. 25.

Chapter 6

The Liberator-

Hero and

Western

Revolutions

(1770s–1810s)

American—chose a person who could stand as the symbol of its essence. Your task in this chapter is to analyze how each liberator-hero was portrayed by his contemporaries, through eulogies and portraits, and how each portrayal informs us about the nature of each of the momentous revolutions of the eighteenth and early nineteenth centuries.

THE METHOD

In his provocative book *The Hero in History: A Study in Limitation and Possibility*, historian Sidney Hook observed that the "history of every nation is represented to its youth in terms of the exploits of great individuals—mythical or real. . . . The splendor, the power, the fame of the leader are shared imaginatively. New elements of meaning enter the lives of those who are emotionally impoverished."[16] When those nations are created by revolutions (as were the United States, France, Haiti, and several Latin American nations), the leader is portrayed as the liberator-hero.

What criteria did eighteenth- and early-nineteenth-century revolutionaries use in selecting their liberator-heroes? To begin with, all those chosen were males. Despite the fact that women often played various roles in these revolutions, at the time women generally were not thought of as possessing the necessary characteristics of liberator-heroes.

A healthy proportion of those chosen as liberator-heroes were military leaders (therefore making a direct contri-

bution to the success of the revolution) or men in the political arena. Nothing in the liberator-hero's backgrounds could be in conflict with the nature of the revolution its leaders were trying to communicate. Nor could his personal life be at serious variance with the accepted standards of the time (unless such incidents could easily be covered up). Perhaps most important, the liberator-hero *must be willing to be used* by his contemporaries as symbolic of the revolution's mythology. Such an exalted position is not for the modest, the timid, the unambitious, or the totally candid.

Two especially effective methods of creating a liberator-hero are eulogies of the person and paintings (or statues) of him. Thus the process of creating a liberator-hero usually must begin before the person's death (sitting for paintings) or immediately thereafter (in eulogies that fuse the person's image to the revolution and the national mythology). Moreover, how the liberator-hero is portrayed in eulogies and in contemporary paintings can give us excellent clues as to how revolutionary leaders wanted others to see the essence or meaning of the revolution they had fomented.

Source 1, a eulogy to George Washington, is probably the most widely circulated of the more than four hundred that were delivered and published. It

16. Sidney Hook, *The Hero in History: A Study in Limitation and Possibility* (New York: Humanities Press, 1943), pp. 8, 22.

was commissioned by the Massachusetts legislature and delivered in Boston's Old South Meeting House by Fisher Ames on February 8, 1800.[17] Ames (1758–1808) was an attorney, a former congressman from Massachusetts, and a well-known conservative ally of Washington and Alexander Hamilton. How does Ames portray Washington? When he spoke of Washington conducting "a civil war with mildness, and a revolution with order," Ames was telling his listeners (and, later, his readers) how *he* wanted them to think about the nature of the American Revolution. How did he want people to view that revolution? To Ames, what was the true glory of the American Revolution? As you read the eulogy carefully, think about how Ames was trying to portray Washington as the liberator-hero of the United States.

Jean-Paul Marat was murdered by Charlotte Corday when the French Revolution was in its most radical phase, the Terror of 1793–1794. Source 3 is the eulogy for Marat that was delivered to the National Convention by a Marat ally, F. E. Guiraut. Not much is known about Guiraut except that he was a member of the Paris Jacobin Club and a leader in the Social Contract Section of Paris. His eulogy of Marat seems to have been the most widely circulated tribute, appearing in pamphlet form and in the official bulletin of the Convention. How did Guiraut portray Marat as a liberator-hero? Using that portrayal, what did Guiraut (and, presumably, Marat) *want* the essence of

the French Revolution to be? The name of the newspaper Marat published was *L'Ami du Peuple (The Friend of the People)*. How do Guiraut's word plays on that title give you some important clues?

No formal eulogy of Toussaint Louverture is known to exist, and, since he died in a French prison, it is possible that none ever was delivered. Source 5, however, part of an 1814 manifesto written by Henri Christophe (1767–1820), is quite close to a eulogy. A follower of Toussaint, Christophe was born in the British West Indies (either Grenada or St. Kitts), was taken to the French colony of Saint-Domingue, was sold to a free black who owned a stable, was permitted to purchase his freedom, and became a waiter in a hotel. In 1811, eight years after Toussaint's death, Christophe proclaimed himself Henri I, King of Haiti. His 1814 manifesto was intended to rally Haitians to repulse a threatened French invasion of the island. What lessons did Christophe intend that his readers learn from the life of Toussaint? Toussaint attempted to create a Haiti in which whites, blacks, and mulattos could live in freedom and relative equality. What did Christophe think of Toussaint's goal? Finally, what does Christophe see as the true meaning of the Haitian Revolution?

As noted earlier, at the time of Simón Bolívar's death in 1830, his reputation was at its lowest point and his remains were buried in Colombia. By 1842, however, "the Liberator's" star had begun to rise again, and his body was reinterred in the cathedral in Caracas, Venezuela. In 1876, Bolívar's remains were moved again, this time to a church that had been renamed the

17. The New York Public Library has collected 266 of the 440 Washington eulogies that still exist.

Chapter 6

The Liberator-

Hero and

Western

Revolutions

(1770s–1810s)

National Pantheon. The eulogy delivered on October 28, 1876 (Source 7), was by Dr. Eduardo Calcano, the greatest Venezuelan orator of his day. Finally, Simón Bolívar had been made a liberator-hero.

With a bit of practice, portraits of liberator-heroes can be "read" by historians in order to understand how revolutionary leaders (through the artist) sought to create and shape the image of the liberator-hero and the image of the revolution as well. Examine each portrait carefully, noting how the subject is posed and dressed. Do other objects in the painting help to create and shape the image of the subject? Unlike photographs (especially those that appear in newspapers or magazines), in a portrait nothing is there by chance.

Source 2 is a painting of George Washington by Gilbert Stuart (1755–1828), one of the most noted portraitists of his time. Washington sat for the painting on April 12, 1796, and the work was finished the next year. Measuring almost eight feet by five feet, the painting is filled with clues. First of all, since Washington's role in the American Revolution was primarily a military one, why didn't Stuart choose to paint his subject in uniform and astride a horse (many portraitists of Washington did just that)? Also, examine closely Washington's facial expression. He had just purchased new dentures, which obviously did not fit well, but look beyond that. Look closely at his clothing, his pose, the books on the floor, the table leg, the chair in the background, the sheathed sword in Washington's hand. What clues do each of these provide? What is the overall image that Stuart sought

to convey of Washington? Of the American Revolution?[18]

Source 4 is a painting of Marat by Jacques Louis David (1748–1825), undoubtedly France's best-known Neoclassical painter and an ardent supporter of the French Revolution. Given to oratorical outbursts almost as inflammatory as those of Marat himself, as an elected deputy to the National Convention he urged that the statues of Louis XIV and Louis XV be destroyed and voted for the execution of Louis XVI. David arranged the pageant that accompanied Marat's funeral and presented his portrait of Marat to the National Convention on November 13, 1793. One knowledgeable critic has called it "one of the world's most skillfully executed propaganda pictures."[19]

David could have painted Marat addressing the National Convention, or writing articles for his newspaper, or addressing a crowd of Paris *sansculottes*. And yet he chose to show his hero and political ally at the moment of his gruesome death, complete with bath water tinted with Marat's blood, the bloody wound, the knife on the floor, and the note Charlotte Corday had used to gain entrance to Marat's

18. Washington sat for Stuart to paint the portrait's head only. Various models later posed for Stuart to paint the body. This particular portrait (Stuart actually did three portraits of Washington, plus numerous copies), known as the Lansdowne portrait, was sold to William Bingham to be hung at his country house outside Philadelphia but instead was given to the Marquis of Lansdowne, a British friend of America. In 1800 the U.S. government purchased the painting for $800.

19. David Lloyd Dowd, *Pageant-Master of the Republic: Jacques-Louis David and the French Revolution* (Lincoln: University of Nebraska, 1948), p. 107.

apartment in his hand. Why did he choose to do this? It is important to note that the macabre scene is historically inaccurate, since Marat's mistress and friends quickly carried him to his bed, where he expired. Why did David ignore the truth in his painting? What image of Marat did David seek to communicate? What image of the French Revolution did the thousands who viewed the painting receive? Thousands of cheap reproductions of this painting were distributed throughout France. Why was this done?

Unfortunately, no contemporary portrait of Toussaint Louverture by a Haitian artist is known to exist, and it is possible that one was never done. Source 6 is from the book *An Historical Account of the Black Empire of Hayti,* written in 1802 by Marcus Rainsford, a British officer, and published in London in 1805.[20] Rainsford had met and interviewed Toussaint and obviously admired him. The artist is identified only as J. Barlow, and about him we know nothing. There is no evidence that Barlow ever met Toussaint, and he may have been commissioned in London to illustrate Rainsford's book. But Rainsford almost certainly conferred with Barlow about how Toussaint should be portrayed.

This presents the historian with a very difficult problem, for we cannot be sure that Barlow's portrait of Toussaint would have been similar to portraits by contemporary Haitian artists. How, then, can we use Barlow's portrait to analyze what Haitians thought

of Toussaint as a liberator-hero? And yet, since Rainsford knew Toussaint and admired him, we can suppose that Rainsford instructed Barlow to paint Toussaint Louverture *as Toussaint himself wanted to be portrayed*—as a liberator-hero.

Keeping that problem in mind, examine Barlow's illustration carefully, noting Toussaint's clothing, the fact that his right hand rests on his sword while his left hand holds a copy of Haiti's constitution, and the background matter. What image of Toussaint Louverture did Barlow seek to communicate? What image of the Haitian Revolution?

In contrast to David's portrayal of Marat and Barlow's illustration of Toussaint Louverture, José Gil de Castro's 1830 portrait of Simón Bolívar was done in a series of live sittings by the subject in Lima in 1825. A noted Peruvian artist who is considered to have been one of the most important Latin American painters of the early republican era, José Gil de Castro (1785–1841) served in the Chilean army as a topographer and later designed army uniforms for the Peruvian Patriots during the wars of independence. He completed a number of portraits of the leaders of the independence movements. In 1830 Gil made a copy of his original 1825 painting with a different background, which was not completed until after Bolívar's death. The 1830 painting now hangs in the National Museum of Archeology, Anthropology, and History of Peru in Lima. How did Bolívar want Gil to portray him? Compare and contrast the portrait of Simón Bolívar to those of other liberator-heroes (clothing, posture, etc.).

20. Marcus Rainsford, *An Historical Account of the Black Empire of Hayti* (London: James Cunde, 1805). The portrait is opposite page 241.

Chapter 6
The Liberator-
Hero and
Western
Revolutions
(1770s–1810s)

███████████ THE EVIDENCE ███████████

Source 1 from Fisher Ames, Works of Fisher Ames *(Boston: T. B. Wait and Co., 1809), pp. 115–133.*

1. Fisher Ames's Eulogy for George Washington, Boston, February 8, 1800

Rome did not owe more to Fabius,[21] than America to Washington. Our nation shares with him the singular glory of having conducted a civil war with mildness, and a revolution with order.

The event of that war seemed to crown the felicity and glory both of America and its chief. Until that contest, a great part of the civilized world had been surprisingly ignorant of the force and character, and almost of the existence, of the British colonies. They had not retained what they knew, nor felt curiosity to know the state of thirteen wretched settlements, which vast woods enclosed, and still vaster woods divided from each other. They did not view the colonists so much a people, as a race of fugitives, whom want, and solitude, and intermixture with the savages, had made barbarians.

At this time, while Great Britain wielded a force truly formidable to the most powerful states, suddenly, astonished Europe beheld a feeble people, till then unknown, stand forth, and defy this giant to the combat. It was so unequal, all expected it would be short. Our final success exalted their admiration to its highest point: they allowed to Washington all that is due to transcendent virtue, and to the Americans more than is due to human nature. They considered us a race of Washingtons, and admitted that nature in America was fruitful only in prodigies. . . .

Washington retired to Mount Vernon, and the eyes of the world followed him. He left his countrymen to their simplicity and their passions, and their glory soon departed. . . .

[*Ames then describes the United States's troubles during the period immediately following the War for Independence: economic instability, excessively democratic state governments, the lack of moral discipline or restraint, a weak central government, and the rise of factions. To conservatives such as Ames, it seemed as if the new nation simply would fall apart.*]

At this awful crisis, which all the wise so much dreaded at the time, yet which appears, on a retrospect, so much more dreadful than their fears; some man was wanting who possessed a commanding power over the popular passions, but over whom those passions had no power. That man was Washington.

---

21. Fabius Maximus, hero of the Second Punic War, who adopted the military strategy whereby Rome was able to retain control of Italy in spite of the major successes of Hannibal.

His name, at the head of such a list of worthies as would reflect honour on any country, had its proper weight with all the enlightened, and with almost all the well disposed among the less informed citizens, and blessed be God! the constitution was adopted. Yes, to the eternal honour of America among the nations of the earth, it was adopted, in spite of the obstacles, which, in any other country, and, perhaps, in any other age of *this,* would have been insurmountable; in spite of the doubts and fears, which well-meaning prejudice creates for itself, and which party so artfully inflames into stubbornness; in spite of the vice, which it has subjected to restraint, and which is therefore its immortal and implacable foe; in spite of the oligarchies in some of the states, from whom it snatched dominion; it was adopted, and our country enjoys one more invaluable chance for its union and happiness: invaluable!

No sooner did the new government begin its auspicious course, than order seemed to arise out of confusion. Commerce and industry awoke, and were cheerful at their labours; for credit and confidence awoke with them. Every where was the appearance of prosperity; and the only fear was, that its progress was too rapid to consist with the purity and simplicity of ancient manners. The cares and labours of the president were incessant: his exhortations, example, and authority, were employed to excite zeal and activity for the publick service: able officers were selected, only for their merits; and some of them remarkably distinguished themselves by their successful management of the publick business. Government was administered with such integrity, without mystery, and in so prosperous a course, that it seemed to be wholly employed in acts of beneficence. Though it has made many thousand malcontents, it has never, by its rigour or injustice, made one man wretched.

Such was the state of publick affairs: and did it not seem perfectly to ensure uninterrupted harmony to the citizens? Did they not, in respect to their government and its administration, possess their whole heart's desire? They had seen and suffered long the want of an efficient constitution; they had freely ratified it; they saw Washington, their tired friend, the father of his country, invested with its powers: they knew that he could not exceed or betray them, without forfeiting his own reputation. Consider, for a moment, what a reputation it was: such as no man ever before possessed by so clear a title, and in so high a degree. His fame seemed in its purity to exceed even its brightness: office took honour from his acceptance, but conferred none. Ambition stood awed and darkened by his shadow. For where, through the wide earth, was the man so vain as to dispute precedence with him; or what were the honours that could make the possessor Washington's superior? Refined and complex as the ideas of virtue are, even the gross could discern in his life the infinite superiority of her rewards. Mankind perceived some change in their ideas of greatness: the splendor of power, and even of the name of conqueror, had grown dim in their eyes. They did not know that Washington could augment his fame; but they knew and felt, that the world's wealth, and its empire too, would be a bribe far beneath his acceptance.

Chapter 6

The Liberator-

Hero and

Western

Revolutions

(1770s–1810s)

While the president was thus administering the government in so wise and just a manner, as to engage the great majority of the enlightened and virtuous citizens to co-operate with him for its support, and while he indulged the hope that time and habit were confirming their attachment, the French revolution had reached that point in its progress, when its terrible principles began to agitate all civilized nations. . . .

Who then, on careful reflection, will be surprised, that the French and their partisans instantly conceived the desire, and made the most powerful attempts, to revolutionize the American government? . . . Our liberty depends on our education, our laws, and habits, to which even prejudices yield; on the dispersion of our people on farms, and on the almost equal diffusion of property; it is founded on morals and religion, whose authority reigns in the heart; and on the influence all these produce on publick opinion, before *that* opinion governs rulers. *Here* liberty is restraint; *there* it is violence: *here* it is mild and cheering, like the morning sun of our summer, brightening the hills, and making the vallies green; *there* it is like the sun, when his rays dart pestilence on the sands of Africa. American liberty calms and restrains the licentious passions, like an angel that says to the winds and troubled seas, be still. . . .

It is not impossible, that some will affect to consider the honours paid to this great patriot by the nation, as excessive, idolatrous, and degrading to freemen, who are all equal. I answer, that refusing to virtue its legitimate honours would not prevent their being lavished, in future, on any worthless and ambitious favourite. If this day's example should have its natural effect, it will be salutary. Let such honours be so conferred only when, in future, they shall be so merited: then the publick sentiment will not be misled, nor the principles of a just equality corrupted. . . .

But such a chief magistrate as Washington appears like the pole star in a clear sky, to direct the skilful statesman. His presidency will form an epoch, and be distinguished as the age of Washington. Already it assumes its high place in the political region. Like the milky way, it whitens along its allotted portion of the hemisphere. The latest generations of men will survey, through the telescope of history, the space where so many virtues blend their rays, and delight to separate them into groups and distinct virtues. As the best illustration of them, the living monument, to which the first of patriots would have chosen to consign his fame, it is my earnest prayer to heaven, that our country may subsist, even to that late day, in the plenitude of its liberty and happiness, and mingle its mild glory with Washington's.

2. Gilbert Stuart, *George Washington* (The Lansdowne Portrait),[22] 1797

22. Stuart painted this work for wealthy Philadelphia merchant William Bingham, who then gave it to the Marquis of Lansdowne, an Englishman who favored the American cause. Stuart also painted four copies of this full-length study, one of which Dolley Madison saved from fire in 1814 when the British invaded Washington, D.C., and burned the executive mansion.

Chapter 6

The Liberator-

Hero and

Western

Revolutions

(1770s–1810s)

Source 3 from J. Mavidal and E. Laurent, eds., Archives parlementaires de 1787 à 1860. Recueil complet des débats législatifs et politiques des chambres françaises, *1st series, volume 73 (Paris: Librairie administrative Paul Dupont, 1908), pp. 302–305. Translated by Julius R. Ruff.*

3. F. E. Guiraut, Funeral Oration for Marat, Paris, July 1793

People! It is true that you have lost your friend.[23] A monster vomitted up by tyranny has come to pierce his breast. You have seen his mortal wounds with your own eyes;[24] his body was cold and bloodied, sad remains which for you are the last witnesses of his fidelity.

His funeral, it is true, was one filled with our gratitude! You have carefully placed him in a tomb, you have covered him with garlands and flowers; and you have done more: you bathed him in your tears. Oh Marat, how glorious it is to die in the middle of your brothers! . . .

[*Here Guiraut gives a brief biographical sketch of Marat, emphasizing his education, his hatred of injustice, and his medical degree.*]

Citizens! Follow Marat! Born for liberty, he early experienced acts of despotism caused by ignorance. He could not stand ignorance and, having identified it, would have abolished it in the twinkling of an eye if he could. . . .

. . . For Marat governments were a monstrosity, nothing but a mixture of extortions, crimes, and impudence. He knew governments' politics and he tried to overthrow their monstrous abuses. . . .

Then in 1789 the earthshaking reveille of liberty sounded. The people rose up, stamped its foot on the ground and the throne started to shake. Marat saw it already toppled. "Be watchful," he wrote to his fellow citizens, "the laurels are for you." Intrepid, courageous, he took responsibility for assuring the victory of the Revolution. He advised the people's representatives meeting at Versailles; in Paris he kept the people stirred up, and he was everywhere in the streets and roads fearing that liberty would escape his grasp. Marat was indignant at the deceptive scheme for double representation,[25] and he planned a constitution.

---

23. Note Guiraut's play on words here.

24. Marat's body was on view in the Church of the Cordeliers on July 16, along with the bathtub in which he was murdered and his bloody shirt.

25. **double representation:** In late 1788 Louis XVI conceded a doubling of the number of Third Estate representatives in the Estates General to be elected in February–April 1789. This would have given the commoners a number of representatives roughly equal to those of the clergy and the nobility. What was not conceded was vote by head in place of vote by house. Because the Estates General was, in essence, a three-house legislature that required positive votes by all three estates or houses (the First Estate representing the clergy, the Second Estate the nobility, and the Third Estate the commoners), the maintenance of vote by house meant that the privileged groups could block reform legislation proposed by the commoners of the Third Estate.

He observed events. The people, he concluded, had been deceived, betrayed by its representatives, and he mounted a war to the death against the traitors.

Ignoring all other sentiments than the wish to see his homeland happy, Marat saw all the perils. He feared nothing. He resolved to fight all vices with a daily newspaper whose austere language would remind legislators of their principles, unmask scoundrels and corrupt officials, reveal their plots and sound the alarm bell in moments of danger.

Scarcely had he cast his glance on the Constituent Assembly, than innumerable plots were directed against him. He spoke the truth, his enemies wished to buy his silence. Necker[26] offered him a million in gold, but he refused it. They seized his presses, ordered his arrest, put a price on his head in vain efforts to silence him. His courage sustained him, his paper continued, his energy grew.

Lafayette beseiged his home with 12,000 men but Marat escaped, though his home was pillaged and he was reduced to misery.

In this dreadful situation, he was without domicile and soon without friends. Wandering from one neighborhood on the outskirts of Paris to another, pursued relentlessly, heaped with venom and pain, he was only the more formidable. Everywhere spied on, everywhere he escaped the fury of his enemies' knives. They could not silence him. . . .

When the constitution was proclaimed, Marat sensed that the new order of things could not last a long time. His eye discovered secret plots, and he told the people that the plotters wished to subjugate them and to restore Louis XVI to his former authority. He pursued the deputies of the Legislative Assembly, denouncing their treachery and venality, and found himself charged with a crime and the crowd at his heels. Passion dictated his actions. Didn't he write that "The defense of the people's rights is my supreme law"? Stronger than all the plotters together he defied them, scorned them, revealed conspiracies, and showed the need to exclude priests, nobles, financiers, creatures of the court, and tricksters from all public office. . . .

[*Marat was branded as an enemy of the state and was forced into hiding.*]

On August 10[27] the voice of the people made itself heard and toppled not enormous stones wet with the tears of the oppressed[28] but crowns, *fleurs de lis*[29] and gilded corridors. . . .

Marat was a lone mountain[30] and it was necessary to destroy him at any price. . . .

26. Jacques Necker was a Swiss banker who was made director of finances by Louis XVI in 1777, but who was dismissed when he attempted to reform France's tax structure. During the revolution he played a major role in trying to restructure the nation's finances.

27. On August 10, 1792, Parisian crowds stormed the Tuileries Palace and effectively ended the monarchy founded by the Constitution of 1791.

28. Guiraut refers here to the crowd's capture of the Bastille prison in Paris on July 14, 1789.

29. **fleur de lis**: A three-leaf lily that symbolized the Old Regime monarchy.

30. A clever reference to Marat's political faction, the Montagnard (mountain).

Chapter 6

The Liberator-

Hero and

Western

Revolutions

(1770s–1810s)

Respond, assassins of Marat! You who thrust the knife into his chest, have you, like him, any virtues to offer? Did you ever know this extraordinary mortal? He spent all his life in seclusion and thought but was persecuted by the envious and jealous, pursued by the forces of despotism, abandoned by the timid and weak, hated by those who are evil and corrupt, feared by the ambitious and conspirators, esteemed by the people, and slain by agents of fanaticism. Answer, assassins! Did you know him? . . .

Listen to the last words of this philosopher, citizens:

> People! I was your representative. I defended your rights. I lived in misery, and I died in misery. People! Your confidence was too great and was always your misfortune. Cease to acclaim false idols. Your welfare depends on you. Know your dignity and your strength. Calculate your needs coldly. Faithful observer, no longer allow yourself to be enslaved. Crush intrigue, suppress ambition, scorn evil, esteem talent, honor virtue. . . .
>
> People, do not let yourselves be led astray. Be on guard against those who would deceive you. Never again become the instrument of passion. Do not arm yourselves against your brothers but employ toward them all those means of reconciliation worthy of you. Everywhere arrest the most culpable enemies; they alone deserve to be punished.
>
> People, cherish your liberty! All the social virtues should reign with it. Among you it is in an embryonic state. Be happy and enjoy the charms of philanthropy. Think sometimes of your friend; I make you the trustee of my heart.

Oh Marat, the ever watchful and vigilant sentinel before our gate, we will never again hear: "Here is Marat, the friend of the people!"

Always present in our thought, we will never forget what you have done for us. . . .

4. Jacques Louis David, *Portrait of Marat*, 1793

Chapter 6

The Liberator-

Hero and

Western

Revolutions

(1770s–1810s)

Source 5 from Toussaint L'Ouverture: Biography and Autobiography *(Boston: James Redpath, 1863), pp. 331–336.*

5. Henri Christophe, Manifesto, 1814

At the time when, reduced to our own private resources, cut off from all communication with France, we resisted every allurement; when, inflexible to menaces, deaf to proposals, inaccessible to artifice, we braved misery, famine, and privation of every kind, and finally triumphed over our enemies both within and without.

We were then far from perceiving that twelve years after, as the price of so much perseverance, sacrifice, and blood, France would deprive us in a most barbarous manner of the most precious of our possessions,—liberty.

Under the administration of Governor-General Toussaint L'Ouverture, Hayti arose from her ruins, and everything seemed to promise a happy future. The arrival of General Hédouville[31] completely changed the aspect of affairs, and struck a deadly blow to public tranquillity. We will not enter into the detail of his intrigues with the Haytian General, Rigaud,[32] whom he persuaded to revolt against the legitimate chief. We will only say, that before leaving the island, Hédouville had put everything into confusion, by casting among us the firebrands of discord, and lighting the torch of civil war.

Ever zealous for the reëstablishment of order and of peace, Toussaint L'Ouverture, by a paternal government, restored their original energy to law, morality, religion, education, and industry. Agriculture and commerce were flourishing; he was favorable to white colonists, especially to those who occupied new possessions; and the care and partiality which he felt for them went so far that he was severely censured as being more attached to them than to people of his own color. This negro wail was not without reason; for some months previous to the arrival of the French, he put to death his own nephew, General Moise, for having disregarded his orders relative to the protection of the colonists. This act of the Governor, and the great confidence which he had in the French Government, were the chief causes of the weak resistance which the French met with in Hayti. In reality, his confidence in that Government was so great, that the General had disbanded the greater part of the regular troops, and employed them in the cultivation of the ground.

---

31. Hedouville was the commander of the French forces that Toussaint ultimately defeated in 1797–1798, forcing the French to abandon Haiti until the French invasion of 1802.

32. Rigaud had been second in command to Toussaint but broke with him and led the mulattos in a civil war against Toussaint in 1799–1800. Rigaud's revolt was brutally repressed and approximately 2,000 people were put to death.

Such was the state of affairs whilst the peace of Amiens[33] was being negotiated; it was scarcely concluded, when a powerful armament landed on our coasts a large army, which, attacking us by surprise, when we thought ourselves perfectly secure, plunged us suddenly into an abyss of evils.[34]

Posterity will find a difficulty in believing that, in so enlightened and philosophic an age, such an abominable enterprise could possibly have been conceived. In the midst of a civilized people, a horde of barbarians suddenly set out with the design of exterminating an innocent and peaceable nation, or at least of loading them anew with the chains of national slavery.

It was not enough that they employed violence; they also thought it necessary to use perfidy and villainy,—they were compelled to sow dissension among us. Every means was put in requisition to carry out this abominable scheme. The leaders of all political parties in France, even the sons of the Governor Toussaint, were invited to take part in the expedition. They, as well as ourselves, were deceived by that *chef-d'oeuvre*[35] of perfidy, the proclamation of the First Consul,[36] in which he said to us, 'You are all equal and free before God and the Republic;' such was his declaration, at the same time that his private instructions to General Leclerc[37] were to reëstablish slavery.

The greater part of the population, deceived by these fallacious promises, and for a long time accustomed to consider itself as French, submitted without resistance. The Governor so little expected the appearance of an enemy that he had not even ordered his generals to resist in case of an attack being made; and, when the armament arrived, he himself was on a journey toward the eastern coast. If some few generals did resist, it was owing only to the hostile and menacing manner in which they were summoned to surrender, which compelled them to respect their duty, their honor, and the present circumstances.

After a resistance of some months, the Governor-General yielded to the pressing entreaties and the solemn protestations of Leclerc, 'that he intended to protect the liberties of every one, and that France would never destroy so noble a work.' On this footing, peace was negotiated with France; and the Governor Toussaint, laying aside his power, peaceably retired to the retreat he had prepared for himself.

Scarcely had the French extended their dominion over the whole island and that more by roguery and deceit than by force of arms, than they began to put in execution their horrible system of slavery and destruction.

33. The Peace of Amiens (1802) brought a temporary end to the war between France and Great Britain, thus allowing Napoleon to plan an invasion of Haiti.

34. The French invasion of 1802.

35. *chef-d'oeuvre:* masterpiece.

36. Napoleon Bonaparte.

37. Leclerc was the commander of the 1802 French invasion force.

Chapter 6

The Liberator-

Hero and

Western

Revolutions

(1770s–1810s)

To hasten the accomplishment of their projects, mercenary and Machiavellian writers fabricated fictitious narratives, and attributed to Toussaint designs that he had never entertained. While he was remaining peaceably at home, on the faith of solemn treaties, he was seized, loaded with irons, dragged away with the whole of his family, and transported to France. The whole of Europe knows how he ended his unfortunate career in torture and in prayer, in the dungeon of the Château de Joux.

Such was the recompense reserved for his attachment to France, and for the eminent services he had rendered to the colony.

At the same time, notice was given to arrest all suspected persons throughout the island. All those who had shown brave and enlightened souls, when we claimed for ourselves the rights of men, were the first to be seized. Even the traitors who had most contributed to the success of the French army, by serving as guides to their advanced guard, and by exciting their compatriots to take vengeance, were not spared. At first they desired to sell them into strange colonies; but, as this plan did not succeed, they resolved to transport them to France, where overpowering labor, the galleys, chains, and prisons, were awaiting them.

Then the white colonists, whose numbers have continually increased, seeing their power sufficiently established, discarded the mask of dissimulation, openly declared the reëstablishment of slavery, and acted in accordance with their declaration. They had the impudence to claim as their slaves men who had made themselves eminent by the most brilliant services to their country, in both the civil and military departments. Virtuous and honorable magistrates, warriors covered with wounds, whose blood had been poured out for France and for liberty, were compelled to fall back into the bonds of slavery. . . .

Source 6 from Marcus Rainsford, An Historical Account of the Black Empire of Hayti *(London: James Cundee, 1805), facing p. 241. Photo: Stock Montage, Inc.*

6. J. Barlow, *Portrait of Toussaint Louverture,* ca. 1805

Chapter 6

The Liberator-

Hero and

Western

Revolutions

(1770s–1810s)

Source 7 from Richard W. Slatta and Jane Lucas DeGrummond, Simón Bolívar's Quest for Glory *(College Station: Texas A & M University Press, 2003), pp. 301–302.*

7. Dr. Eduardo Calcano, Oration at the Reinterment of Bolívar, October 28, 1876

Señores:

Like a trembling skiff on the immensity of the ocean, like a migrating bird face to face with the profundities of infinite space that he is forced to traverse, so is the orator of today before the solemn majesty of this most high occasion, with the undeclinable assignment of ascending to inaccessible summits, to Olympic heights that dominate the world, and with my voice broadcast to all people and all generations the colossal glory which is the patrimony of humanity. . . .

Titan[38] [Bolívar] leveled the Andes beneath his stride, and made a seat of Chimborazo[39] on which he conversed with Time and Destiny.

Others dissolved parliaments; he convoked congresses. Others throttled the Republic; he founded republics and gave them as surety his prestige and power. Others beheaded the people; he educated them for liberty. Others divided territories in order to tyrannize and exploit them; he held them together in the powerful unity of democracy and consecrated them, with the kiss of his genius, to be the custodians of civilization with the cult of human rights, the philosophy of justice, the permanent law of progress, the sovereignty of the people, and the ennoblement of man on the throne of personal dignity.

This is the great continental work of Bolívar, that which has elevated his stature to the heavens and transformed him into an object of stupendous admiration for the Ages.

In order to make myself in some degree worthy of the prestigious solemnity that overwhelmed by smallness with its grandeur, I placed myself between two great orators in order that their light might shine on my countenance, and their eloquence lend its vibration to my words.

Thus, after having before my eyes the prophecy of Zea, the great orator of times past, and the virile accent of Guzmán Blanco,[40] the best orator of our times, I pronounce the new apocalypse of Bolívar's future glory.

All that we here witness is not yet the apotheosis[41] of Bolívar. His apotheosis will have effect when more lustroms[42] have passed and the great destinies

---

38. **Titan:** in Greek mythology, a primordial god known for his size and strength.

39. **Chimborazo:** the highest mountain in Ecuador, 20,561 feet.

40. **Guzmán Blanco:** Blanco (1829–1899) was president of Venezuela. He ordered Bolívar's remains to be moved to the Church of the Santisima Trinidad, renamed the National Pantheon.

41. **apotheosis:** an exalted or glorified ideal.

42. **lustrom (lustrum):** a period of five years.

of America have been realized. When ten or more powerful and happy nations seated on the skirt of the Andes from ports of a peaceful Ocean the products needed for the existence of the Old World in exchange for what the Old World has discovered and improved in industry and the arts, for progress and civilization.

When thousands of steamboats plough the immense net of rich rivers from the Orinoco to the Straits of Magellan, and when locomotives cross the vast territory where the sound of labor and the vigor of ideas prevail—then, on top of all this grandeur will be the figure of Bolívar radiating its glory to all horizons of the earth, as the sun radiates its light over the universe.

Chapter 6

The Liberator-

Hero and

Western

Revolutions

(1770s–1810s)

Source 8 from Elizabeth P. Benson, et. al., Retratos: 2,000 Years of Latin American Portraits *(New Haven: Yale University Press, 2004), p. 000.*

8. Jose Gil de Castro's Painting of Simón Bolívar, Lima, 1830

QUESTIONS TO CONSIDER

In this chapter, your task is *not* to find out what each revolutionary leader (Washington, Marat, Toussaint, and Bolívar) was *really* like. Instead, your task is to analyze how each leader's fellow revolutionists or contemporaries created and shaped an *image* of a liberator-hero, and through that image communicated to their contemporaries and to future generations the nature or essence of the revolution.

Fisher Ames's eulogy to George Washington is an excellent case in point. In spite of the fact that Washington's initial prominence came from his military leadership of the Continental Line, Ames spends almost no time on that aspect of Washington's life. Why do you think this is so? As noted earlier, instead of chronicling Washington's military career, Ames concentrates on the years *after* the War for Independence, saying only that Washington and his fellow revolutionists (including Ames himself) "conducted a civil war with mildness, and a revolution with order." What did Ames mean by that statement?

Ames pictured a postwar decade of "awful crisis" and filled with "popular passions." To what was he referring? How did the Constitution solve those problems? Was the acceptance of the presidency by Washington a key factor in overcoming the crisis? How?

Washington was president when the French Revolution broke out in 1789. What opinions does Ames have of that revolution? What dangers does he see in it? On a related note, what does Ames consider the principal threat to the American Revolution? And, from that, what does Fisher Ames see as the true nature of the American Revolution? How can Washington be used to personify or symbolize that true nature?

Of Gilbert Stuart's 1797 portrait of Washington, William Kloss has remarked that no "other portrait conveys the unyielding resolve and severe dignity that made him the embodiment of the young Republic."[43] As you examine the painting, look first at the central figure. What is the expression on Washington's face? What is the significance of the body's pose? of his clothing? The sheathed sword in his left hand?

The table leg is formed to resemble a *fasces*, a band of rods that symbolized authority and justice in the Roman Republic. Does the chair behind Washington contain symbols equal to those of the table leg? What are the titles of the books in the painting, and what is their importance? Is there anything else in the background that Stuart intended to be used as a symbol? Finally, what did Stuart hope that viewers looking at his portrait would see about George Washington? About the American Revolution?

The funeral oration for Jean-Paul Marat is a dramatically different eulogy from Fisher Ames's address. Guiraut begins by referring to Marat as a "martyr." A martyr to what? If Marat was a martyr to the French Revolution, what *particular aspect* of the revolution did he symbolize?

43. William Kloss et al., *Art in the White House: A Nation's Pride* (Washington, D.C.: White House Historical Association, 1992), p. 66.

Chapter 6

The Liberator-

Hero and

Western

Revolutions

(1770s–1810s)

Guiraut intersperses his biographical sketch of his subject with numerous observations and judgments, as if Marat's early life was preparing him for the revolution. How does Guiraut accomplish this? What phases are particularly significant?

As the revolution began, what does Guiraut assert was Marat's warning? What did Marat fear? What message is Guiraut intending to communicate? Why were plots hatched against Marat? What lessons does Guiraut see in those conspiracies? What kind of French Revolution did Marat seek?

The "last words" attributed to Marat were actually those of Guiraut.[44] Through Marat, what does Guiraut see as the true goals of the French Revolution? What are the dangers? Finally, how does Guiraut use the image of Marat to make him into a liberator-hero? What, in Guiraut's view, is the nature of the French Revolution?

As noted above, David's painting of Marat is a magnificent piece of political propaganda. In what ways is it so? Why did David choose to portray Marat in this way, in his grisly death? Why does David have Marat holding the note from Charlotte Corday? What does that say about David's view of the revolution?

At the bottom of the wooden box, David has painted the words *L'An Deux* (the Year Two). Since it was 1793, what is the significance of David's date? Finally, what reaction did David hope

viewers of the painting would have? How could Marat be used as a liberator-hero of the French Revolution?

Henri Christophe, like the preceding two eulogists, is using the career, the accomplishments, and the ideas of Toussaint Louverture to make a point. What is that point? In Christophe's view, what was Toussaint's fatal blunder? (It was *not* his being duped into surrendering.)

Toussaint Louverture tried to build a nation in which whites, blacks, and mulattos would live in peace and mutual trust. What does Henri Christophe think of that goal? How does Christophe use Toussaint as a *negative example* of the liberator-hero? What does that say about Christophe's notion of the true nature of the Haitian Revolution—or what that true nature *should* be?

Unlike Stuart and David, the artist who portrayed Toussaint Louverture probably never met his subject. Yet Marcus Rainsford may well have given Barlow enough details to make this a reasonably accurate portrait—at least according to Rainsford. Examine the artist's representation of Toussaint: his face, his physique, his clothing. What impressions was the artist seeking to convey? What is the significance of the sword and the document (Haiti's constitution, issued by Toussaint in 1801) in his hand? Of the Haitian Revolution?

Dr. Eduardo Calcano's 1876 oration honoring Simón Bolívar is a curious eulogy indeed. For one thing, although many eulogies stretch the truth a bit, this excerpt from Calcano's speech seems to have gone even farther than

---

44. Marat's actual last words were "Help, my dear, help!" Edward S. LeCompte, comp., *Dictionary of Last Words* (New York: Philosophical Library, 1955), p. 144.

that. Based on what you know about Bolívar, how does the oration (especially the excerpt's third paragraph) square with reality? Second, a healthy portion of the address is not about Bolívar at all but rather about how his actions contributed to the *future* of Latin America. How, then, does Dr. Calcano characterize Simón Bolívar as a liberator-hero?

Since Bolívar often compared himself to George Washington, it would be more than a little instructive to compare the two paintings (Sources 2 and 8). Remember that of the four artistic representations in this chapter, these are the only two in which the subjects actually sat for the artists. Thus we must assume that their poses, clothing, and surroundings were approved of by the subjects themselves. How do the two paintings differ? Why do you think this is so? Based on the two paintings, how do you think each subject wanted to be remembered?

Revolutionists face a dual challenge. The first challenge is to win their revolution. The second challenge is to preserve it and to pass it down to future generations. How do the four eulogists and the four artists attempt to do this?

EPILOGUE

As the "revolutionary fever" that "afflicted" Théroigne de Méricourt swept across the Western world in the late eighteenth and early nineteenth centuries, revolutionists sought to justify, legitimate, and explain the true natures of their respective uprisings to their wary contemporaries as well as to generations yet unborn. To do this, they created the images of liberator-heroes, men who could be used as symbols of the revolution and through whose lives the true nature or essence of the revolution could be seen. Some, like Washington and Bolívar, became symbols of revolts that succeeded. Others, like Marat and Toussaint Louverture, became martyrs to revolutions not yet fulfilled. Nevertheless, each one became a liberator-hero, a construction through which the message of the revolution could be communicated.

George Washington became a symbol of a revolution that stopped (according to Fisher Ames) at precisely the right moment—not falling back into monarchy nor veering wildly into democracy. It was a revolution out of which reform and democratization would come gradually, wrenched by only one (albeit bloody) civil war. After his death in 1799, biographers made Washington into a symbol of that revolution. From the wildly creative biography by Mason Locke "Parson" Weems to the magisterial seven-volume work by Douglas Southall Freeman, George Washington continues to reign as the "Father of His Country."

Gilbert Stuart moved to Washington, D.C., soon after the nation's capital was relocated there. He continued to receive enormous fees for painting portraits of the new nation's political

Chapter 6

The Liberator-

Hero and

Western

Revolutions

(1770s–1810s)

and commercial leaders, but died in debt in 1823. When British troops invaded Washington in 1814 (during the War of 1812 between the United States and Great Britain), Dolley Madison, wife of President James Madison, broke the Lansdowne portrait's frame and carried the canvas on its stretcher out of the city to save it from British mutilation. It was returned to the White House in 1817 and hangs there today, in the city that bears its subject's name.

Charlotte Corday went silently to the guillotine, refusing to disclose information on any plot against Jean-Paul Marat. The liberator-hero of the radicals at first was placed in a cave-like tomb on the grounds of the radical Cordeliers Club in Paris. Later Marat's body was moved to the Pantheon, the burial place of France's great figures. But in the conservative Thermidorian Reaction, it was once again moved, to the Sainte-Genevieve Cemetery.

Jacques Louis David survived the French Revolution and became Napoleon Bonaparte's favorite painter (David did several famous paintings of Napoleon), in 1803 was made a knight of the French Legion of Honor, and in 1804 was named First Painter to the Emperor.[45] When Napoleon fell at Waterloo, David went into exile, continued to paint, and died in exile in Belgium in 1825.

The popular revolution Marat, Guiraut, and David hoped for did not come. The French Revolution began to

move into more conservative channels in 1795, capped by the coup d'etat of Napoleon Bonaparte in 1799. Napoleon's fall in 1815 restored the Bourbon monarchy to France, and the nation struggled gradually but perceptibly toward stability throughout the rest of the nineteenth and part of the twentieth centuries. Only after decades would Marat's goal of a democratic republic finally be achieved.

The French invasion of Haiti in 1802 was broken by a yellow fever epidemic that ravaged the French army. In 1804, Jean Jacques Dessalines, a black general, assumed the title of Emperor of Haiti, but was soon assassinated, to be followed by Henri Christophe. Henri I maintained power until 1820, when a paralytic stroke and yet another uprising led to his suicide (October 8, 1820). Since that time, the history of Haiti has been one of grinding poverty, political tyranny, and instability. In 1980 Haiti's illiteracy rate was 85 percent, its infant mortality rate 20 percent, and its per capita income a meager $219 per year. More recently, the United States has intervened in Haiti to install and prop up the government of President Jean Bertrand Aristide. A statue of Toussaint Louverture still stands in Port-au-Prince, a symbol to those who seek to continue the revolutionary struggle. In France, his grave was destroyed between 1876 and 1880 when alterations were made to the prison chapel.

Simón Bolívar's dream of a single Latin American nation-state (to be called Gran Colombia) was never realized. Instead, the wars of independence sapped the continent both demographically and economically, and political

45. David's 1808 portrait of Napoleon in his study has the well-known pose of the subject with his right hand inserted in his vest.

control of the unstable governments often fell to military strongmen (*caudillos*). As for Bolívar himself, as he lay dying he evidently recanted his earlier atheism and on December 10, 1830, made a confession and accepted the last rites of the Roman Catholic Church. In the decades after his death his reputation as a liberator-hero grew, until among some it reached nearly cult status. Some even regularly recite the following Bolivian version of the Apostles' Creed:

> I believe in Liberty, Mother of America, creator of sweet seas upon earth, and in Bolívar, her son, Our Lord, who was born in Venezuela, suffered under Spanish power, was fought against, felt death on Mount Chimborazo, and with the rainbow descended into hell, rose again at the voice of Colombia, touched the Eternal with his hands and is standing next to God! . . .

At his death Bolívar's long-term mistress Manuela Saenz (pronounced "Say anz") was so distraught that she attempted to commit suicide by allowing herself to be bitten by a poisonous snake. She survived, moved to Ecuador, and opened a modest store with a sign outside that read, "Tobacco. English Spoken. Manuela Saenz." Herman Melville stopped at the store while on a whaling expedition, as did the Italian revolutionary Giuseppe Garibaldi. She died in a diphtheria epidemic in 1856.

CHAPTER SEVEN

CONSTITUTIONAL RESPONSES TO

EUROPEAN EXPANSION IN AFRICA

AND THE PACIFIC (1850–1890)

THE PROBLEM

William McNeill, a pioneering scholar of world history, has emphasized that large-scale change in human history tends to be "provoked by encounters with strangers, followed by efforts to borrow (or sometimes to reject, or hold at bay) especially attractive novelties." It could be deeply unsettling to find out that one's own ways of thinking and behaving were only one option among many, but the result was often a dynamic pattern of cultural creativity. As McNeill puts it, these encounters across cultural boundaries have long been "the main drive wheel of social change."[1]

In the past five hundred years, both the tempo and the direction of these encounters were radically altered by the rise of European powers to global predominance. As Europeans expanded their reach around the world, they brought ideas and social practices that seemed very strange to the peoples of the Americas, Africa, Asia and the Pacific, and technologies that made it possible for them to impose their ideas and ideals by force. By the nineteenth century, countries like Britain, France, and the United States were provoking a massive challenge to traditional ways of life all across the globe. The "world revolution of westernization" destabilized and disrupted indigenous societies while challenging their sovereignty.[2] These were not relationships of mutual in-

1. William H. McNeill, "The Changing Shape of World History," *History and Theory,* 34 (May 1995), pp. 14–26; reproduced in Ross E. Dunn, *The New World History: A Teacher's Companion* (Boston: Bedford/St. Martin's, 2000), pp. 147, 150.

2. Theodore H. Von Laue, *The World Revolution of Westernization: The Twentieth Century in Global Perspective* (New York: Oxford University Press, 1987).

teraction, but relationships of external domination.

Most studies of nineteenth-century imperialism have focused on the intentions and actions of European imperialists. In this chapter, however, we will focus on the perceptions and responses of the peoples dismissed by the Europeans as "natives" who were incapable of managing their own affairs in a competitive, modern world. Paradoxically, the strange and threatening new ideas brought by the Europeans could also be modified and used to try to defend the old order. Leaders of indigenous societies in many parts of the world attempted to strengthen themselves against the European on-slaught by adapting European political models, such as written constitutions, to their own circumstances.

Rarely were these indigenous reforms successful in keeping the forces of imperialism at bay. In the two cases on which we will focus in this chapter—the Hawaiians in the Pacific and the Fante in West Africa—constitutional innovation could not prevent incorporation into Western-dominated political systems. But in focusing on the indigenous side of the harsh imperial world of the nineteenth century, we restore voice and agency to peoples who have too often been treated as silent and passive victims of "progress."

BACKGROUND

The rising power of Western Europe in the early modern period posed challenges to societies to which Europeans had previously been completely unknown—American peoples were decimated by disease and coastal West Africans were drawn into the Atlantic slave trade as a result of these encounters—as well as to societies already in commercial, political, and military contact with them, such as the Ottoman Empire.

In all of these cases, and in many others as time went by, the wealth and power of Western Europe acted as a destabilizing force, undermining traditional modes of authority, time-honored religious and ethical systems, and existing systems of production and exchange. What to do in such circumstances? Seeing how strong the Westerners had become, was it best to emulate them and strengthen yourself economically and militarily by following their example? Or was it better to keep them at arm's length, to prevent contamination of your own society by their strange ideas and ways of doing things? Often a combination of both tactics was attempted. Selective borrowing of Western models in military organization, education, religion, economics, and other spheres of life was undertaken in an attempt to preserve the sovereignty and integrity of a society threatened by powerful new forces.

There were a variety of specific ways in which peoples threatened by

Chapter 7
Constitutional
Responses to
European
Expansion
in Africa and
the Pacific
(1850–1890)

the extension of European imperial power could borrow from their adversaries in an effort to hold them at bay. One of the advantages held by the Europeans was their membership in a formal international system, a club that they themselves had formed and to which they held the key to admission. If a society could gain access to that club, if it could be recognized in international law as an independent nation, then perhaps the forces of imperialism could be kept in check. The concept of a formal, written constitution was one idea that could be borrowed from the Westerners that might both strengthen a society internally and lead to international recognition of its sovereignty. One early example of such a constitution is that of the Cherokee nation on the frontier of the expanding United States in the early nineteenth century; another is that of the Japanese later in the same century. (Unlike the Cherokee and most others, the Japanese were successful in defending their sovereignty and autonomy.) The examples in this chapter concern the Hawaiians in the Pacific Islands and the Fante in West Africa.

After their initial contact with the Europeans in the late eighteenth century, the Hawaiians followed a path of political centralization under a new and powerful monarchy. In the early nineteenth century, King Kamehameha the Great unified Hawaii and established a kingdom that would endure until American annexation in the 1890s. Kamehameha was a young man when Captain James Cook of the British Royal Navy sailed into Hawaiian waters. As a prince of the ruling

house of the "big island" of Hawaii, he boarded the *Discovery* and met with the British officers. Though Cook's visit was brief, it changed Hawaiian history forever. Kamehameha took advantage of the new possibilities offered by interaction with the outside world.

Kamehameha had already established himself as king of the island of Hawaii, and was moving to extend his power to the neighboring islands, when another British expedition arrived in 1792. The king secured access to twenty sailing ships of the European type, which were much larger and faster than traditional outriggers, and purchased modern firearms by creating a royal monopoly over the export of sandalwood. Combined with his own political and military abilities, this control of new technologies made it possible for Kamehameha to establish his rule over the entire chain of islands.

Political centralization required a whole new structure of rule to replace the small kingdoms that had previously contended with one another on the islands. Kamehameha appointed a governor for each island, who was responsible for appointing tax collectors and other government officials. He formed a council made up of the chiefs who had demonstrated their abilities and loyalty in his wars of conquest. Just before his death in 1819, Kamehameha added one further constitutional innovation: the office of the *Kuhina Nui*. This official had powers nearly equal to those of the king, and could even veto the king's decisions if he or she had sufficient backing from the chiefs and people. The first *Kuhina Nui* was Kamehameha's favorite wife, Kaahamanu.

Kaahamanu was responsible for the event that, more than any other, signaled the end of the traditional Hawaiian way of life. Before the unification of the islands, public order was kept largely through *kapus,* strict taboos governing the actions and behavior of Hawaiians in every sphere of life. Initiating a social revolution to match Kamehameha's political one, Kaahamanu organized a great feast to which all the leading chiefs were invited. In accordance with a strict *kapu,* men and women sat separately. Following her directive, when the recently installed King Kamehameha II entered, he sat with the women. In an instant the age-old *kapu* system, central to both the traditional religion and traditional political authority, was fatally undermined. Temples associated with the traditional Hawaiian religion were destroyed, and the path was clear for Christian missionary activity.

From the 1820s onward, Europeans and Asians began to arrive in greater numbers. If Kamehameha had recognized the benefits that could come from increasing intercourse with outsiders, now the Hawaiian monarchy had increasingly to deal with the conflicts and dangers that such contacts entailed. By the mid-nineteenth century, the French were busy building an empire in Polynesia, the British Empire was the dominant political force on the globe, and the Russians and Americans were both showing increasing interest in the Pacific as a potential area for political expansion.

Partly in response to such pressure, during the long reign of Kamehameha III (r. 1825–1854) Hawaii became a constitutional monarchy. In 1839 a missionary was enlisted to give the Hawaiian king and his councilors lessons on the American constitution, and a bill of rights and code of laws were drafted in the Hawaiian language. The constitution of 1840 recognized the separation of the executive, legislative, and judicial branches of government, but the king remained the paramount figure in all three.

In 1852 a new constitution was adopted, providing for universal suffrage, stricter separation of powers between the three branches of government, greater restrictions on the power of the king, and an enhanced role for the elected legislature. That constitution was in effect until 1864, when Kamehameha V, the last to rule under that name, ascended to the throne. He refused to take an oath to support the constitution, feeling that it excessively limited royal powers, that the office of *Kuhina Nui* was an anachronistic carryover from an earlier period, and that the Hawaiian people were not yet ready for universal suffrage.

What prompted these constitutional experiments? On the one hand, they were designed to regularize the radically new relationship between political authority and the Hawaiian people that had become necessary. Perhaps more importantly, however, they were directed toward the establishment of a sovereign government that could be recognized under international law during a period when the forces of

Chapter 7

Constitutional

Responses to

European

Expansion

in Africa and

the Pacific

(1850–1890)

imperialism were gathering strength. With the indigenous population in decline and the number of foreign immigrants increasing, the very survival of the Hawaiian people seemed to be at stake.[3] Hawaiian governments sought to play one foreign power off against another in an effort to protect their independence.

By the second half of the nineteenth century, it was clearly the United States that posed the greatest threat. After the entrance of California into the United States in 1850, its ambitions in the Pacific became much greater. The Hawaiian monarchy cultivated a political alliance with England, but pressure from the United States was becoming harder and harder to resist. American interests in Hawaii were both strategic (the islands were an ideal base from which to pursue a more aggressive Pacific policy) and economic (the development of plantation agriculture in such crops as coffee, sugar, and fruit gave Americans another incentive to settle in Hawaii and become involved in its internal affairs).

3. Largely because of diseases introduced during this period, the population of native Hawaiians fell from approximately 300,000 in 1778 to 82,035 in 1850 and 34,436 in 1890. Meanwhile, the population described as "part-Hawaiian" rose from zero in 1778 to 558 in 1850 and 6186 in 1890. Non-Hawaiian residents of the kingdom went from zero in 1778 to 1572 in 1850 and 49,368 in 1890, outnumbering the native population. Two-thirds of the non-Hawaiian population in 1890 consisted of Chinese and Japanese immigrants, most of whom were employed on sugar plantations. Robert C. Schmitt, *Demographic Statistics of Hawaii, 1778–1965* (Honolulu: University of Hawaii Press, 1968), pp. 41, 74.

American interests were increasingly antagonistic to the Hawaiian monarchy, particularly during the reign of the last two independent rulers of the islands, King Kalakaua (r. 1874–1891) and Queen Liliuokalani (r. 1891–1893). The government became indebted to the sugar magnates, and nonnative members of the legislature did not hesitate to point out the administrative and financial shortcomings of the kingdom. As American settlers grew impatient with the monarchy, the United States government was becoming alarmed by German activities in the Pacific. Americans were active in the formation of the Hawaiian League, which forced the king to accept a new constitution in 1887, under which he became a mere figurehead with no active role in government. The king's only alternative was to be forcibly removed from power. When Liliuokalani tried to reassert royal power, she was deposed. In 1893 a republic was declared with American settlers in control; five years later, Hawaii was annexed to the United States. A century of innovation in indigenous political and constitutional development had come to an end.

During this same period, there were numerous societies along the coast of West Africa that had long been in contact with European powers without having been conquered by them. One such was the Fante, found near the coast of what is today the nation of Ghana. The Fante political system was highly diffused, characterized by numerous small chiefdoms and an internal political structure that gave more power to the councils than to the chiefs themselves. This stood in marked contrast to that of their neighbors to the north, the Asante. While the Asante are closely related to the Fante by language and culture, by the eighteenth century they had developed into a highly centralized and aggressively expanding kingdom.[4]

The presence of European traders on the coast, starting in the sixteenth century, gave the Fante a powerful incentive to resist incorporation by the Asante. The goods that the Europeans were interested in procuring came from Asante and other areas to the north: gold at first, and later slaves. The Fante states were in a good position to profit from this trade by acting as intermediaries. As international trade became more important in the seventeenth and eighteenth centuries, a group of Fante merchants emerged who acted as cultural as well as commercial intermediaries on the coast. Often the offspring of European fathers and African mothers, these men were bicultural and bilingual. Since descent in Fante society was matrilineal, these men inherited clan membership from their mothers and were therefore full members of the African community. Since they could also inherit European language and culture, and sometimes property, from their fathers, these men of mixed descent played an important role as cultural intermediaries between the Africans and the British.

4. Note that in the documents "Fante" is sometimes spelled "Fanti," while "Asante" is usually referred to as "Ashanti" or "Ashantee."

In spite of their decentralized and diffuse political system, the Fante needed to create some larger form of cooperation, if for no other reason than to keep the Asante at bay. Military plans were coordinated through meetings of the chiefs, who mustered the Fante *asafo* (military companies). In this way, more than 25,000 soldiers could be deployed. The *asafo* had an independent base of leadership, where prowess rather than royal birth could be rewarded. Men were deeply attached to their *asafo*, and these companies competed with each other for status and reputation. More important than the *asafo* in keeping the Fante independent from Asante, however, was their military and diplomatic alliance with the British. Through their control of Cape Coast Castle, the British dominated the most important military and economic location on the coast.

Britain made a determined effort to stamp out the slave trade after 1808, but trade in other commodities continued to flourish. (Palm oil was particularly important, having become a source of lubrication for machinery in England's early industrial revolution.) The alliance between the British and the Fante held firm, even if its legal basis was ambiguous. In the early nineteenth century, the British government was not anxious to take on the expense of conquest and administration in the tropics. The British directly controlled the immediate environs of Cape Coast Castle, but nothing else. Still, British officials came to play an increasingly important role as judicial arbiters in disputes between the

Chapter 7

Constitutional

Responses to

European

Expansion

in Africa and

the Pacific

(1850–1890)

different Fante chiefdoms. That role seems to have been not only accepted by the Fante, but encouraged by them. Economic and legal connections aside, it was mutual antagonism toward the Asante that really cemented the Anglo-Fante alliance.

In 1844 a treaty between the British and several prominent Fante chiefs formalized the relationship, but there was still significant ambiguity. What support did the British owe the Fante, and vice versa? The issue came to a head in 1863, when the Asante army attacked. The Fante chiefs met at their traditional center of Mankessim to plan a military defense, and the British organized a force to meet the Asante army in the field. The British, however, retreated when disease began to decimate their ranks. The war did not amount to much, except to the Fante chiefs. They saw the British military response as woefully inadequate.

Their worries about the reliability of their British allies were magnified in 1865 when news reached West Africa from London of a parliamentary report that recommended that the British radically reduce their political and military commitments in West Africa. While this policy was never put into effect, it did encourage the Fante to consider that they might henceforth have to organize their own political, judicial, and military affairs without British help.

In addition to the British retreat in 1863 and the parliamentary report of 1865, a third source of disappointment for the Fante was negotiations between the British and the Dutch for an exchange of territories on the West African coast. The problem was that the Dutch were allies of the Asante, and the transfer of some Fante chiefdoms to their jurisdiction was therefore unacceptable. A letter to the *West African Times* captured the Fante mood: "The British government has no right to transfer them like so many bullocks."[5]

In 1868 the Fante chiefs again assembled at Mankessim to plan their strategy. At this meeting, however, there was a greater presence of Western-educated Fante. Many of these men had been educated at Methodist missionary schools on the coast, some were descendants of trading families that had made their fortunes in the eighteenth century, and some had been to England. They were influenced by the writings of James Africanus Horton, an African who had received a medical degree in Britain and who served as a medical officer in the British Army in West Africa. Horton argued forcefully for the development of institutions of self-government among African peoples, and he saw the parliamentary report of 1865 as an indication that the British government agreed. Although he was not present at the Mankessim meeting that led to the formation of a new Fante Confederation, Horton's ideas clearly contributed to that outcome.

The Fante Confederation was a mixture of tradition and innovation. The calling together of a chiefly council at Mankessim at a time of military threat was certainly nothing new, but the

5. Cited in David Kimble, *A Political History of Ghana: The Rise of Gold Coast Nationalism, 1850–1928* (Oxford: Clarendon Press, 1963), p. 226.

role of Western-educated Africans at this meeting was unprecedented. The Constitution of the Fante Confederation, adopted in 1871, was based on a confluence of traditional chiefly authority and the influence of men of Western education.

Unlike the Hawaiian constitution, which was at least for a time put into effect, the Fante constitution was stillborn. The British administrator at Cape Coast Castle, a certain Mr. Salmon, regarded it as a dangerous conspiracy and ordered the arrest of the Western-educated leaders of the movement. One of these was the elected "king-president" of the Fante Confederation, R. J. Ghartey, a man who combined a Western education with royal birth. The Fante leaders were shocked by the British response, since they had acted on the principles encouraging African self-government that had been laid out in the parliamentary report of 1865. But the British official in charge was extremely distrustful of the educated men. Like many Europeans of the day, he dismissed them as a group of "self-interested Mulattos—discontented and unprincipled natives—semi-educated blacks—[and] mischievous half-educated Mulatto adventurers."[6]

The next year, when a more liberal governor arrived, the Fante tried once again to gain British approval for their constitution. By the early 1870s, however, the British had adopted a more proactive imperial policy. Full-scale war erupted between the British and the Asante in 1873. The following year, the Asante capital of Kumasi was captured and ransacked by British troops. At the same time, the British declared a protectorate over the adjacent coastal regions. The Fante, who just ten years earlier had worried that they would be abandoned by their British allies, were now formally incorporated into the British Empire. The "scramble for Africa" between competing European powers was about to begin.

Even more than in the Hawaiian case, the Fante experiment with constitutional government remains nothing more than an indication of what might have been if indigenous societies had been allowed to organize their own responses to intensifying global contact in the nineteenth century. As it was, the forces of imperialism were simply too strong for them to resist.

6. Cited in Lennart Limberg, "The Fanti Confederation, 1868–1872," M.A. Thesis, University of Göteborg, 1974, p. 95.

Chapter 7

Constitutional

Responses to

European

Expansion

in Africa and

the Pacific

(1850–1890)

THE METHOD

The first thing you may notice about the evidence offered in this chapter is that every source represents an indigenous (Hawaiian or African) viewpoint. In the history of imperialism, the point of view of the conqueror is often the only one presented. The evidence selected for this chapter is intended as a corrective to that tendency. As always, you should consider the source of the evidence: who created it, and for what audience.

Your first goal as you evaluate the evidence should be to understand each of the case studies on its own terms. In each case you are given a formal written constitution to analyze. To what extent does this constitution seem to have retained features from the traditional political and social world of the people who promulgated it? To what extent does it show the influence of Western models? How are old and new political elements balanced? How is authority balanced between various branches of government? How "democratic" does the constitution seem? Is there any special mention of the rights of immigrants or other nonnative populations, or of relations with outside powers? What do the other selections tell us about how, why, and by whom the constitution was passed and about its relative success or failure? Once you have understood each case individually, you will be in a position to make comparisons between them. In the meantime, here is some background to help you contextualize each piece of evidence.

Source 1 consists of extracts from the Hawaiian constitution of 1852. In addition to being much more detailed than its 1840 predecessor in spelling out the responsibilities of the different branches of government, the 1852 constitution added a bill of rights and provided for universal suffrage. The roles of the king, of the unique official known as the *Kahina Nui,* and of the legislative and judicial branches of government are all laid out.

This 1852 constitution lasted only until 1864, however. King Kamehameha V refused to swear to abide by it when he came to power and organized a constitutional convention to replace it. When the convention failed to come up with an alternative that he found acceptable, the king imposed a new constitution on his own authority. In Source 2 we find King Kamehameha V addressing the Hawaiian Legislature. In addition to reporting on the state of his kingdom, the king gives his perspective on the constitutional controversy.

Source 3 is taken from the memoirs of Hawaii's last monarch, Queen Liliuokalani. Liliuokalani was overthrown in a revolution led by American settlers, who created a Hawaiian republic. These passages were written in 1897, after she was removed from power but just before the Hawaiian Islands were officially annexed by the United States. One purpose of her autobiography was to influence public opinion in the United States to prevent that annexation.

Before turning to Africa, there is a different type of source to consider. It seems universal that political power is represented by some type of visual imagery. Here is another area in which European influence can be seen, as both Western modes of *representing* royal power and specific Western *symbols* of power came to be adopted by other societies. Just as the Hawaiian constitution blends traditional and Western elements, so the coat of arms of the Hawaiian kingdom, reproduced as Source 4, demonstrates cultural and political syncretism. The coat of arms shown here was adopted in 1845, manufactured in London on the basis of a design by a young chief named Timothy Haalilio. While the form is European, the coat of arms uses a mixture of European and Hawaiian symbols of authority:

In the center . . . is a shield in which the first and fourth quarters contain eight alternating white, red and blue stripes which represent the Hawaiian flag and the eight inhabited islands of the kingdom. The second and third quarters contain a white ball on a staff against a background of royal yellow. Called Puloulou, the ball and staff are ancient symbols of refuge or protection. The triangular flag and crossed spears in the center of the shield also indicate protection as well as tabu. The flag, called Puela, was often raised above the sails on the canoes of Hawaiian chiefs. A crown, ornamented with taro leaves, symbolizes the monarchy and rests atop the shield. The two male supporters dressed in ancient feather cloaks and helmets are purported to be the twin brothers Kameeiamoku and Kamanawa, two chiefs who helped Kamehameha come to power. . . . One brother

holds a spear while the other bears a feathered Kahili, a symbol of royalty. . . . The motto "UA MAU KE EA O KA AINA I KA PONO" means "THE LIFE OF THE LAND IS PERPETUATED BY RIGHTEOUSNESS."[7]

Beginning our consideration of the Fante Confederation, Source 5 is extracted from an 1868 book by James Africanus Horton with the exhaustive title *West African Countries and Peoples, British and Native, with the Requirements Necessary for Establishing that Self Government Recommended by the Committee of the House of Commons, 1865, and a Vindication of the African Race.* Horton's inspirational role in relation to the Fante Confederation has already been explained in the Background section. In this selection, Horton is anxious to convince his British audience that the people for whom he is advocating constitutional government are "civilized" enough to make it work, and to encourage his African readers to take the steps that he believes will lead to effective self-government. He indicates that different types of constitutions are appropriate to different types of African societies, and then proceeds to give specific recommendations for the Fante situation.

Source 6 is another visual source, a Fante *asafo* flag from Ghana. Though the imagery of power is here associated with a military company rather

7. Richard Wisniewski, *The Rise and Fall of the Hawaiian Kingdom: A Pictorial History* (Honolulu: Pacific Basin Enterprises, 1979), frontispiece.

Chapter 7

Constitutional

Responses to

European

Expansion

in Africa and

the Pacific

(1850–1890)

than a king, the same general points made in reference to the Hawaiian coat of arms can be kept in mind here as well: In an attempt to project an image of power, the Fante also combined local and imported elements. Although this particular flag is a twentieth-century design, it follows very much in a tradition that was already well established among the Fante by the mid-nineteenth century. The Fante *asafo*, anxious to promote their reputation for military prowess, borrowed from the Europeans the convention of using flags as a means of expressing power and identity. The basic motif of the flags usually involves the representation of a well-known proverb, in this case:

> "The small boy does not know the lion" (otherwise he would not pull its tail). Besides belittling rivals as foolish "small boys," this flag stresses the importance of education by showing the consequences of ignorance. . . . The lion, a grasslands predator, is not found in the heavily forested ecology of the Fante coast, and its popularity as an emblem of power comes from its frequent use in European heraldry. The lion is nearly always depicted wearing a crown.[8]

The bars of color in the upper left-hand corner are a stylized rendition of the stripes characteristic of European flags. As in the Hawaiian coat of arms, the form itself is European, but the artist who made the flag combined local and European visual references to give the *asafo* company for which it was designed an effective emblem of power.

In much the same way, the Constitution of the Fante Confederation combines African and European elements. In 1871 the Fante Confederation, for reasons discussed in the Background, adopted the constitution extracted here as Source 7. The men who were involved in the Confederation were especially concerned with such issues as assuring Fante unity as a defense against Asante aggression, defining relations with the British authorities at Cape Coast Castle more clearly, balancing the roles played by traditional and Western-educated leaders, and promoting the economic development of their country.

The negative response of the local British officials has already been mentioned. The Fante made one last try to gain British support for their efforts in 1872. Source 8 is from a letter to the British governor of the West African settlements from one of the leaders of the Fante Confederation, J. H. Brew. Brew was a member of an influential African trading family on the coast, a man of considerable education who had traveled to England some years previously. Brew was one of the Fante leaders arrested by a British official named Mr. Salmon when the constitution was first proposed, and here he argues his case with a higher-ranking British official.

8. Peter Alder and Nicholas Barnard, *Asafo! African Flags of the Fante* (London: Thames & Hudson, 1992), p. 72. Among the Fante, it is a stool rather than a crown that is the traditional symbol of kingship.

THE EVIDENCE

Source 1 from http://www.hawaii-nation.org/constitution-1852.html.

1. Kingdom of Hawaii
Constitution of 1852

Granted by His Majesty Kamehameha III., king of the Hawaiian Islands, by and with the advice and consent of the nobles and representatives of the people in legislative council assembled, June 14th, 1852.

DECLARATION OF RIGHTS.

Article 1. God hath created all men free and equal, and endowed them with certain inalienable rights; among which are life and liberty, the right of acquiring, possessing and protecting property, and of pursuing and obtaining safety and happiness.

Article 2. All men are free to worship God according to the dictates of their own consciences; but this sacred privilege hereby secured, shall not be so construed as to justify acts of licentiousness or practices inconsistent with the peace or safety of this Kingdom.

Article 3. All men may freely speak, write and publish their sentiments on all subjects, being responsible for the abuse of that right; and no law shall be passed to restrain or abridge the liberty of speech, or of the press.

Article 4. All men shall have the right, in an orderly and peaceable manner to assemble, without arms, to consult upon the common good; give instructions to their Representatives; and to petition the King or the Legislature for redress of grievances. . . .

Article 12. Slavery shall, under no circumstances whatever, be tolerated in the Hawaiian Islands: whenever a slave shall enter Hawaiian territory he shall be free; no person who imports a slave, or slaves, into the King's dominions shall ever enjoy any civil or political rights in this realm; but involuntary servitude for the punishment of crime is allowable according to law.

Article 13. Every person has the right to be secure from all unreasonable searches and seizures of his person, his houses, his papers, and effects; and no warrants shall issue, but on probable cause, supported by oath or affirmation, and describing the place to be searched, and the person or things to be seized.

[203]

Chapter 7

Constitutional

Responses to

European

Expansion

in Africa and

the Pacific

(1850–1890)

Article 14. The King conducts His Government for the common good; for the protection, safety, prosperity and happiness of His people; and not for the profit, honor, or private interest of any one man, family or class of men among His subjects. Therefore in making laws for the nation, regard shall be had to the protection, interest and welfare of not only the King, the Chiefs, and rulers, but of all people alike.

FORM OF GOVERNMENT.

Article 22. The Government of the Kingdom is that of Constitutional Monarchy, under His Majesty Kamehameha III, His Heirs, and successors. . . .

OF THE EXECUTIVE POWER.
SECTION I. THE KING, HIS PREROGATIVES.

Article 24. The King shall continue to be the supreme Executive Magistrate of this Kingdom under the title of His Majesty.

Article 25. The crown is hereby permanently confirmed to His Majesty Kamehameha III during his life, and to his successor. The successor shall be the person whom the King and the House of Nobles shall appoint and publicly proclaim as such, during the King's life; but should there be no such appointment and proclamation, then the successor shall be chosen by the House of Nobles and the House of Representatives in joint ballot.

Article 26. No person shall ever sit upon the throne who has been convicted of any infamous crime, or who is insane or an idiot. No person shall ever succeed to the crown, unless he be a descendant of the aboriginal stock of Aliis.[9]

Article 27. The King is Commander in Chief of the Army and Navy, and of all other Military forces of the Kingdom by sea and land. . . . But he shall never proclaim war without the consent of His Privy Council. . . .

Article 29. The King, by and with the advice of His Privy Council, convenes both Houses of the Legislature . . . and in case of disagreement between the two Houses, or between His Majesty and them, He adjourns, prorogues, or dissolves them, but not beyond the session of the next year. . . .

Article 33. It is his duty to see that the Treaties and Laws of the land are faithfully observed and executed. . . .

Article 35. The person of the King is inviolable and sacred; . . . to the King belongs the Executive power; all laws that have passed both Houses of the

9. **Aliis:** chiefs.

Legislature, for their validity, shall be signed by His Majesty and the Kuhina Nui; all his other official acts shall be approved by the Privy Council, countersigned by the Kuhina Nui, and by the Minister to whose Department such act may belong.

Article 36. The King is Sovereign of all the Chiefs and of all the People; the Kingdom is His. . . .

Article 39. The King, by and with the approval of His Cabinet and Privy Council, in case of invasion or rebellion, can, place the whole Kingdom, or any part of it under martial law; and he can ever alienate it, if indispensable to free it from the insult and oppression of any foreign power. . . .

Article 42. The King cannot be sued or held to account in any court or tribunal of the Realm.

SECTION II.
OF THE KUHINA NUI.

Article 43. The King appoints some chief of rank and ability to be his Kuhina Nui, . . . and whose title shall be Highness.

Article 44. The Kuhina Nui shall be the King's special Counsellor in the great affairs of the Kingdom. . . . All Acts . . . and other official documents, duly executed by the Kuhina Nui in the name and by the consent of the King, . . . shall be equally binding as if executed by the King himself.

Article 45. All important business for the Kingdom which the King chooses to transact in person, he may do, but not without the approbation of the Kuhina Nui. The King and Kuhina Nui shall have a negative on each other's public acts. . . .

Article 47. Whenever the throne shall become vacant by reason of the King's death, or otherwise, and during the minority of any heir to the throne, the Kuhina Nui, for the time being, shall, during such vacancy or minority, perform all the duties incumbent on the King, and shall have and exercise all the powers, which by this Constitution are vested in the King. . . .

SECTION III. OF THE PRIVY COUNCIL.

Article 49. There shall continue to be a Council of State for advising the King in the Executive part of the Government, and in directing the affairs of the Kingdom, . . . to be called the King's Privy Council of State.

Chapter 7

Constitutional

Responses to

European

Expansion

in Africa and

the Pacific

(1850–1890)

Article 50. The members of the Privy Council are appointed by the King and hold their offices during His Majesty's pleasure. The King's Ministers and the Governors of the Islands, are, ex-officio, members of His Privy Council. . . .

SECTION IV. OF THE KING'S MINISTERS.

Article 51. The Ministers of the King are appointed and commissioned by Him, and hold their offices during His Majesty's pleasure, subject to impeachment.

SECTION V. OF THE GOVERNORS.

Article 55. The King, by and with the advice of His Privy Council, appoints and commissions the Governors of his several Islands; the Governors hold office for the term of four years, subject to impeachment. . . .

OF THE LEGISLATIVE POWER.

Article 60. The Legislative Power of this Kingdom is vested in the King, the House of Nobles, and the House of Representatives; each of whom has a negative on the other.

Article 63. No bill or resolution, although it may have passed the Legislature, shall become a law, or have force as such, until it shall have been presented to the King, through the Kuhina Nui, for the revisal, and if he approve thereof, he shall signify his approbation by signing the same. But if he have any objection to the passing of such bill or resolve, he shall return it with his objections in writing to the House in which it shall have originated, . . . and no such bill shall be brought forward thereafter during the same session. . . .

OF THE HOUSE OF NOBLES.

Article 72. The King appoints the members of the House of Nobles, who hold their seats during life, . . . but their number shall not exceed thirty.

Article 73. No person shall be eligible to a seat in the House of Nobles, who shall not have attained to the age of twenty-one years and resided in the Kingdom for five years.

OF THE HOUSE OF REPRESENTATIVES.

Article 75. The House of Representatives shall be composed of not less than twenty-four nor more than forty members, who shall be elected annually.

Article 77. No person shall be eligible for a Representative of the people . . . unless he be a male subject or denizen of the Kingdom, who shall have arrived at the full age of twenty-five years, who shall know how to read and write, who shall understand accounts, and who shall have resided in the Kingdom for at least one year immediately preceding his election.

Article 78. Every male subject of His Majesty, whether native or naturalized, and every denizen of the Kingdom, who shall have paid his taxes, who shall have attained the full age of twenty years, and who shall have resided in the Kingdom for one year immediately preceding the time of election, shall be entitled to one vote for the representative or representatives, of the district in which he may have resided three months. . . .

Article 79. All bills or resolves for raising the revenue, or calling for any expenditure of the public money, shall originate in the House of Representatives; but the House of Nobles may propose or concur with amendments as on other bills.

OF THE JUDICIARY.

Article 81. The Judicial Power of the Kingdom shall be vested in one Supreme Court, and in such inferior courts as the Legislature may from time to time establish.

Article 83. The Kingdom shall be divided, by law, into a convenient number of circuits, . . . for each of which one or more Circuit Judges, not exceeding three, however, shall be appointed to hold their offices during good behavior, subject to removal upon impeachment. . . .

Article 87. The decisions of the Supreme Court, when made by a majority of the Justices thereof, shall be final and conclusive upon all parties. . . .

Article 89. The King, by and with the advice of His Privy Council, appoints the Justices of the Supreme Court, and all other Judges of Courts of Record; their salaries are fixed by law.

Article 94. The King, after approving this Constitution, shall take the following oath:

> I solemnly Swear, in the presence of Almighty God, to maintain the Constitution of the Kingdom whole and inviolate, and to govern in conformity with that and the laws. . . .

[207]

Chapter 7

Constitutional

Responses to

European

Expansion

in Africa and

the Pacific

(1850–1890)

GENERAL PROVISIONS . . .

Article 99.   No officer of this Government shall hold any office, or receive any pension or salary, from any other government, or power whatever. . . .

MODE OF AMENDING THE CONSTITUTION.

Article 105.   Any amendment or amendments to this Constitution may be proposed in either branch of the Legislature, and if the same shall be agreed to by a majority of the members of each House, such proposed amendment or amendments shall be entered on their journals, with the yeas and nays taken thereon, and referred to the next Legislature; which proposed amendment or amendments shall be published for three months previous to the election of the next House of Representatives; and if, in the next Legislature, such proposed amendment or amendments, shall be agreed to by two-thirds of all the members of each house, and be approved by the King, such amendment or amendments shall become part of the Constitution of this Kingdom.

KAMEHAMEHA.

Keoni Ana

Source 2 from Helen Jennings and William F. Swindler, eds., Chronology and Documentary Handbook of the State of Hawaii *(Dobbs Ferry, N.Y.: Oceana Publications, 1978), pp. 63–66.*

2. King Kamehameha V Addresses the Hawaiian Legislature, 1864

HIS MAJESTY'S SPEECH AT THE OPENING OF THE LEGISLATURE OF 1864.

Nobles and Representatives:

God's hand has been heavy upon Our country since the meeting of the Legislature of 1862. My beloved Brother has been taken from the Throne I now occupy, to wear, as We believe, an immortal crown. . . .

Seeing before Me, as I now do, so many gentlemen of proved loyalty and unquestionable talents, and all interested in the prosperity of Our Common country, I cannot but offer you an earnest welcome as members of the first Legislative Assembly, called together under the provisions of the Constitution which I caused to be proclaimed on the twentieth day of last August.

The debates which were lately had in this place, resulted in much good. The principles upon which the Throne and the political system of this country are based were fully discussed for the first time, and My people have, as a consequence, been confirmed in their belief that a Monarchical Government holds out to them the only guarantee of a permanent independence. In calling a National Convention, I was influenced by a firm conviction of its being necessary that the system under which a people lives should be strictly adapted to its genius and traditions. The Constitution granted by King Kamehameha III, in 1852, had undergone several amendments, and . . . continued, in many important respects, to want the adaptedness to which I refer. The right to the Throne of this country, originally acquired by conquest and birth, belongs hereditarily to the family of Kamehameha I. The Constitution of 1852, by its ninety-fourth article, left the heir to the Throne free to take an oath to support that Constitution or to decline to do so; and its forty-fifth article reserved to the Sovereign the right to conduct personally, in coöperation with the Kuhina Nui, but without the intervention of a Ministry or the approval of the Legislature, such portions of the public business as he might choose to undertake. . . . By the authority inherent in myself, I called the late Convention to remodel the Constitution, and the powers belonging to such a Convention have never been disputed. . . . But the Convention, when assembled, was found to contain elements antagonistic to those very ideas of improvement which I had hoped they would have assisted me in carrying out. On the thirteenth day of August I dissolved that Convention, and . . . by virtue of the same sovereign power which was exercised by King Kamehameha III, in 1852, I caused to be proclaimed a new Constitution, which I believe to be better adapted to the wants of the people. Under this Constitution you are now assembled. The changes made were recommended by the experience of twelve years, and a provision for further changes leaves open a door for any other improvements that the future may suggest. . . .

I do not claim that the existing Constitution is not susceptible of improvement, but I do assert that it was framed with great care, and that even its least important provisions were subjected to long and patient consideration, while . . . it has become imperative upon my successors, at their accession, to take an oath to observe it. . . .

Our relations with other countries were never on a more satisfactory footing than at this moment, and I continue to receive from all quarters the most gratifying expressions of good will and amity, coupled with evidences of strong interest in the perpetuity of my Dynasty and the Independence of my Kingdom. . . .

An important mission has been confided to the Hon. E. H. Allen, Chancellor and Chief Justice of the Kingdom, whom I have accredited my Envoy Extraordinary and Minister Plenipotentiary to the United States. I am satisfied that he will do his utmost to promote our interests, and secure the objects of his mission. . . .

The favorable report and estimates of my Minister of Finance are proper subjects of congratulation. By them you will see that the Finances are in a satisfactory condition, and that there will be no further calls for loans, or for increased taxation, to meet the present exigencies of Government, which will continue to

Chapter 7

Constitutional

Responses to

European

Expansion

in Africa and

the Pacific

(1850–1890)

be conducted with all possible regard to a reasonable economy. Our exports likewise have begun to bear a more satisfactory comparison with our imports.

Justice has continued to be administered during the last two years in an impartial manner to all classes, so that not only our own subjects, but those foreigners who are residents among us, or visit our shores, find the utmost security for life, right and property.

Our Agricultural enterprises have been urged forward with such energy on every Island of the group as to render the importation of laborers necessary. I am of opinion that the Government is the proper agent to carry out such a measure, and that means ought to be placed at its disposal to undertake it promptly. The wants of our agriculture, the dictates of humanity and the preservation of our race demand that the Government should control this operation. An Act to this effect will be submitted to you, together with amendments to the Master and Servant Law. Both deserve and will doubtless have your earnest attention.

The Sanitary condition of the people, and the proper means to improve it, have occupied an important place in the deliberations of my Council. This object, the nearest to my heart, demands your diligent attention, and, I trust, the measures which you may think proper to adopt will counteract the evils which, for years, have conspired against the life of the people. . . .

No subject more justly claims your very serious attention than that of our Public Schools, in the management of which the health and morality of the rising generation should receive as much consideration as the effort to impart knowledge. . . .

The members of the Board of Public Instruction will submit to you the views they respectively entertain upon our present system of education. In a matter of such importance to the country, and on which our whole future advancement rests, I trust you will act with that deliberation and due regard to the interests of the mass of the people, without which no systematic and well devised plan can be started and successfully carried out. . . .

Nobles and Representatives, I rely upon your wisdom and your loyalty to strengthen me in my efforts to advance the good of our Common Country, and, with heartfelt earnestness, I invoke upon your deliberations the blessings of the Almighty. May He, in His infinite goodness, direct you so that all things may be established on a sure foundation, and the interest and happiness of my people be promoted.

Source 3 from Liliuokalani, Hawaii's Story by Hawaii's Queen *(Boston: Lothrop, Lee, and Shepard, 1898), pp. 366–374.*

3. Hawaii's Last Queen on American Annexation

It has been suggested to me that the American general reader is not well informed regarding the social and political conditions which have come about in the [Hawaiian] Islands, and that it would be well here to give some expression to my own observation of them. Space will only permit, however, a mere outline.

It has been said that the Hawaiian people under the rule of the chiefs were most degraded, that under the monarchy their condition greatly improved, but that the native government in any form had at last become intolerable to the more enlightened part of the community. This statement has been substantially repeated recently by certain New England and Hawaiian "statesmen" in speeches made at the Home Market Club in Boston. I shall not examine it in detail; but it may serve as a text for the few remarks I feel called upon to make from my own—and that is to say, the native Hawaiian—standpoint.

I shall not claim that in the days of Captain Cook our people were civilized. I shall not claim anything more for their progress in civilization and Christian morality than has been already attested by missionary writers. Perhaps I may safely claim even less, admitting the criticism of some intelligent visitors who were *not* missionaries,—that the habits and prejudices of New England Puritanism were not well adapted to the genius of a tropical people, nor capable of being thoroughly ingrafted upon them.

But Christianity in substance they have accepted; and I know of no people who have developed a tenderer Christian conscience, or who have shown themselves more ready to obey its behests. Nor has any people known to history shown a greater reverence and love for their Christian teachers, or filled the measure of a grateful return more overflowingly. And where else in the world's history is it written that a savage people, pagan for ages, with fixed hereditary customs and beliefs, have made equal progress in civilization and Christianity in the same space of time? And what people has ever been subjected during such an evolution to such a flood of external demoralizing influences?

Does it make nothing for us that we have always recognized our Christian teachers as worthy of authority in our councils, and repudiated those whose influence or character was vicious or irreligious? That while four-fifths of the population of our Islands was swept out of existence by the vices introduced by foreigners, the ruling class clung to Christian morality, and gave its unvarying support and service to the work of saving and civilizing the masses? Has not this class loyally clung to the brotherly alliance made with the better element of

Chapter 7

Constitutional

Responses to

European

Expansion

in Africa and

the Pacific

(1850–1890)

foreign settlers, giving freely of its authority and its substance, its sons and its daughters, to cement and to prosper it?

But will it also be thought strange that education and knowledge of the world have enabled us to perceive that as a race we have some special mental and physical requirements not shared by the other races which have come among us? That certain habits and modes of living are better for our health and happiness than others? And that a separate nationality, and a particular form of government, as well as special laws, are, at least for the present, best for us? And these things remained to us, until the pitiless and tireless "annexation policy" was effectively backed by the naval power of the United States.

To other usurpations of authority on the part of those whose love for the institutions of their native land we could understand and forgive we had submitted. We had allowed them virtually to give us a constitution, and control the offices of state. Not without protest, indeed; for the usurpation was unrighteous, and cost us much humiliation and distress. But we did not resist it by force. It had not entered into our hearts to believe that these friends and allies from the United States, even with all their foreign affinities, would ever go so far as to absolutely overthrow our form of government, seize our nation by the throat, and pass it over to an alien power.

And while we sought by peaceful political means to maintain the dignity of the throne, and to advance national feeling among the native people, we never sought to rob any citizen, wherever born, of either property, franchise, or social standing.

Perhaps there is a kind of right, depending upon the precedents of all ages, and known as the "Right of Conquest," under which robbers and marauders may establish themselves in possession of whatsoever they are strong enough to ravish from their fellows. I will not pretend to decide how far civilization and Christian enlightenment have outlawed it. But we have known for many years that our Island monarchy has relied upon the protection always extended to us by the policy and the assured friendship of the great American republic.

If we have nourished in our bosom those who have sought our ruin, it has been because they were of the people whom we believed to be our dearest friends and allies. If we did not by force resist their final outrage, it was because we could not do so without striking at the military force of the United States. Whatever constraint the executive of this great country may be under to recognize the present government at Honolulu has been forced upon it by no act of ours, but by the unlawful acts of its own agents. Attempts to repudiate those acts are vain.

The conspirators, having actually gained possession of the machinery of government, and the recognition of foreign ministers, refused to surrender their conquest. So it happens that, overawed by the power of the United States to the extent that they can neither themselves throw off the usurpers, nor obtain assistance from other friendly states, the people of the Islands have no voice in determining their future, but are virtually relegated to the condition of the aborigines of the American continent.

It is not for me to consider this matter from the American point of view; although the pending question of annexation involves nothing less than a departure from the established policy of that country, and an ominous change in its foreign relations. It is enough that I am able to say, and with absolute authority, that the native people of Hawaii are entirely faithful to their own chiefs, and are deeply attached to their own customs and mode of government; that they either do not understand, or bitterly oppose, the scheme of annexation. . . .

Perhaps I may even venture here upon a final word respecting the American advocates of this annexation of Hawaii. . . . Is the American Republic of States to degenerate, and become a colonizer and a land-grabber?

And is this prospect satisfactory to a people who rely upon self-government for their liberties? . . . There is little question but that the United States could become a successful rival of the European nations in the race for conquest, and could create a vast military and naval power, if such is its ambition. But is such an ambition laudable? Is such a departure from its established principles patriotic or politic? . . .

Oh, honest Americans, as Christians hear me for my down-trodden people! Their form of government is as dear to them as yours is precious to you. Quite as warmly as you love your country, so they love theirs. . . . The people to whom your fathers told of the living God, and taught to call "Father," and whom the sons now seek to despoil and destroy, are crying aloud to Him in their time of trouble; and He will keep His promise, and will listen to the voices of His Hawaiian children lamenting for their homes.

It is for them that I would give the last drop of my blood; it is for them that I would spend, nay, am spending, everything belonging to me. Will it be in vain? It is for the American people and their representatives in Congress to answer these questions. As they deal with me and my people, kindly, generously, and justly, so may the Great Ruler of all nations deal with the grand and glorious nation of the United States of America.

4. Coat of Arms of the Hawaiian Monarchy

Source 5 from James Africanus Horton, West African Countries and Peoples *(London: W. J. Johnson, 1868), pp. 3, 96–99, 114–116, 122–123.*

5. An Argument for African Self-Rule, 1868

It will be my province to prove the capability of the African for possessing a real political Government and national independence; and that a more stable and efficient Government might yet be formed in Western Africa, under the supervision of a civilized nation, in conformity with the present Resolution of the Committee of the House of Commons. . . .

The Report of the Parliamentary Committee on the summary of their inquiries states the following: . . .

> The protectorate of tribes about our forts on the Gold Coast assumes an indefinite and unintelligible responsibility on our part, uncompensated by any adequate advantage to the tribes. It is even the opinion of the Colonial Secretary of the Government that it has enervated and disunited the protected chiefs, and that, so far from training the chiefs to a better conduct of their own affairs, it only leads them to lean on the English. . . .
>
> Your committee also deprecate the needless employment of English officers and military on such a shore as costly to this country, not only by actual mortality, but by the numbers invalided in mind and body, and rendered unfit for other active service. . . .
>
> To govern effectually such settlements would require much larger expenditure than has been made, and more thorough occupation, and undertaking of public works of much larger extent than we are ready to recommend, or Parliament would be likely to consent to.

In their recommendations to Parliament, they emphatically state that the protectorate should only be retained while the chiefs may be as speedily as possible made to do without it. Nothing should be done to encourage them to lean on British help, or trust to British administration of their affairs, whether military or judicial. . . .

The Gold Coast under British influence extends over a coast-line of not more than three hundred miles. . . . The inhabitants are the possessors of the lands they now occupy from time immemorial. The natives are almost all alike in habits and customs, in their mode of living, and almost in that of thinking. The effect of British rule is to moderate in a great measure some of their customs; but domestic slavery, the great drawback to material improvement, runs rampant among them. In the interior, the country is open to the attacks of a powerful and hostile neighbour, the King of Ashantee, who lusts after extending his territory to the water side, and has always interfered with the peaceful government of the country. . . .

As a whole, the inhabitants of the Gold Coast are generally of middle size, kind, good-natured, and hospitable; . . . they are not entirely under British rule,

Chapter 7
Constitutional
Responses to
European
Expansion
in Africa and
the Pacific
(1850–1890)

nor are they British subjects; they have their own kings, their own chiefs and caboceers, who exercise indefinite power over them; among those on the sea-coast this power is very limited; the influence of a civilized Government in close proximity to theirs has greatly enlightened the people, and prevented them from receiving any arbitrary treatment from their chiefs. . . .

. . . In the coast towns . . . there is comparatively a great advance in civiliza-tion, although there is vast room for improvement. The principal portion of the inhabitants, who are educated men, are hard-working, pushing, and in many cases thriving; they possess considerable enlightenment of manner. Agriculture forms no part of their occupation, but they are merchants, traders, and agents for English firms. They build and live in large houses, which possess all the air and comforts of civilization; they dress in European costumes, speak English, some can even speak four or five European languages; a great many have re-ceived sound education in England and Scotland; and even some of those who are educated in the old schools of the Coast are not by any means inferior to them; those who have received a middling education, and could read and write letters in English, are called among themselves "scholars."

But the great bulk of the people are still uncivilized. . . .

The next point to be considered is the political union of the various kings in the kingdom of Fantee under one political head. A man should be chosen, either by universal suffrage, or appointed by the Governor, and sanctioned and received by all the kings and chiefs, and crowned as King of Fantee. He should be a man of great sagacity, good common sense, not easily influenced by party spirit, of a kind and generous disposition, a man of good education, and who has done good service to the Coast Government. He should be crowned before all the kings . . . the kings should regard him as their chief; his authority should be recognized and supported by the Governor of the Coast, who should refer to him matters of domestic importance relative to the other native kings, advise him as to the course he should pursue, and see that his decisions be immediately carried out.

He should be assisted by a number of councillors, who, for the time, should swear allegiance to the British Government, until such time as the country is considered fit for delivery over to self-government. They should consist not only of men of education and good, sound common sense, residing in the Coast towns, but also of responsible chiefs, as representatives of the various kings within the kingdom.

. . . Each State should be made to contribute towards the support of the . . . Government; a native volunteer corps should be attached to the Government, officered by natives of intelligence, who should be thoroughly drilled by paid officers and sergeants, supplied from West Indian regiments stationed on the Coast. The English language should be made the diplomatic language with for-eign nations; but Fantee should be made the medium of internal communica-tion, and therefore ought at once to be reduced to writing.

The territory of the kingdom of Ashantee is larger than that of the Protected Territory of the Gold Coast, but we find the reigning king possesses absolute power over the different tribes composing it. True enough, the edifice was constructed on the blood of several nationalities, which gives it greater strength; but the kingdom of Fantee must be erected on a peaceable footing, supported, for a time at least, by a civilized Government, with a prince at the head who is versed in native diplomacy, and well known and respected by the various kings; . . . a prince who would be able, like the potentate of Ashantee, to concentrate a large force at a very short notice, at any given point, when menaced by their powerful neighbours.

. . . The aim, therefore, should be to form a strong, compact native Government, which would command the obedience of all the native kings and chiefs, and which would immediately undertake the quelling of all disturbances in the interior, and command the native force if attacked.

But the present disunited condition of the kings of the Protectorate is woeful in the extreme. If a war should break out with Ashantee, they have got no superior authority to look to, except the Governor, whose instruction is not to give them support in the interior. He will supply them with a few guns and ammunition, but each king will have to take care of his own fireside, with a number of men so small as to be insufficient to withstand a detachment of the Army of Ashantee. The stratagem of the Ashantee generals has always been to fight each king in detail; and having completely mastered one, they proceed to another; and thus always come off in these wars victorious against the various kings. . . . The consequence would be that the people would always feel themselves perfectly insecure, life and property within the Protectorate unsafe, and their condition worse than if they were under the despotic rule of Ashantee.

Let them, therefore, have a ruler in whom they have confidence, and generals experienced in bush fighting; let them be united, offensive and defensive, to one another, under one head, whose authority is paramount; let good, large, open roads be made connecting the kingdoms with one another, which would lead to the easy movement of a large body of men; . . . let him have a good magazine and a large supply of useful rifles, and the people be taught the use of them, and I guarantee that a compact, powerful, and independent Government will be formed, which would defy Ashantee and give confidence to the whole country. . . .

From the foregoing, it is evident that from the unsatisfactory political state of the Western District of the Gold Coast, it cannot, at present, be left to govern itself; that radical reforms are imperatively necessary before this can be done with safety to the population; that no sooner would the British Government be withdrawn, than intestine warfare would spring up, resulting in fearful and barbaric massacre and bloodshed, and every man's hand would be against his neighbour. Before the country should be given up to self-government, a responsible king, of education and experience, must be crowned, assisted, acknowledged and supported by the British authority, both on the Coast and in Downing-street; and a British Consular Agency should be formed, and the Consul appointed be a man who would aid and advise the native Government, and guarantee it against European invasion.

Chapter 7

Constitutional

Responses to

European

Expansion

in Africa and

the Pacific

(1850–1890)

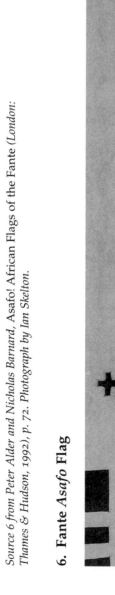

Source 6 from Peter Alder and Nicholas Barnard, Asafo! African Flags of the Fante (London: Thames & Hudson, 1992), p. 72. Photograph by Ian Skelton.

6. Fante *Asafo* Flag

Sources 7 and 8 from John Mensah Sarbah, Fanti National Constitution, *1906, second edition (London: Frank Cass & Co., 1968), pp. 199–209; pp. 188–189.*

7. The Constitution of the Fante Confederation, 1871

To all whom it may concern.

Whereas we, the undersigned kings and chiefs of Fanti, have taken into consideration the deplorable state of our peoples and subjects in the interior of the Gold Coast, and whereas we are of opinion that unity and concord among ourselves would conduce to our mutual well-being, and promote and advance the social and political condition of our peoples and subjects, who are in a state of degradation, without the means of education and of carrying on proper industry, we, the said kings and chiefs, after having duly discussed and considered the subject at meetings held at Mankessim . . . have unanimously resolved and agreed upon the articles hereinafter named.

ARTICLE 1.—That we, the kings and chiefs of Fanti here present, form ourselves into a Committee with the view of effecting unity of purpose and of action between the kings and chiefs of the Fanti territory.

ARTICLE 3.—That this compact body shall be recognized under the title and designation of the "Fanti Confederation."

ARTICLE 4.—That there shall be elected a president, vice-president, secretary, under-secretary, treasurer, and assistant-treasurer.

ARTICLE 5.—That the president be elected from the body of kings, and be proclaimed king-president of the Fanti Confederation.

ARTICLE 6.—That the vice-president, secretary, and under-secretary, treasurer, and assistant-treasurer, who shall constitute the ministry, be men of education and position.

ARTICLE 7.—That it be competent to the Fanti Confederation thus constituted to receive into its body politic any other king or kings, chief or chiefs, who may not now be present.

ARTICLE 8.—That it be the object of the Confederation—

Section 1. To promote friendly intercourse between all the kings and chiefs of Fanti, and to unite them for offensive and defensive purposes against their common enemy.

Section 2. To direct the labours of the Confederation towards the improvement of the country at large.

Section 3. To make good and substantial roads throughout all the interior districts included in the Confederation.

Section 4. To erect school-houses and establish schools for the education of all children within the Confederation, and to obtain the service of efficient schoolmasters.

Chapter 7

Constitutional

Responses to

European

Expansion

in Africa and

the Pacific

(1850–1890)

Section 5. To promote agricultural and industrial pursuits, and to endeavour to introduce such new plants as may hereafter become sources of profitable commerce to the country.

Section 6. To develop and facilitate the working of the mineral and other resources of the country. . . .

ARTICLE 10.—That in order that the business of the Confederation be properly carried on during the course of the year, each king and principal chief shall appoint two representatives, one educated, the other a chief or headman of the district of such king and principal chief, who shall attend the meetings which the secretary may deem necessary to convene for the deliberation of State matters.

ARTICLE 11.—That the representatives of the kings and chiefs assembled in council shall be known under the designation of the "Representative Assembly of the Fanti Confederation," and that this assembly be called together by the secretary as State exigency may require.

ARTICLE 12.—That this representative assembly shall have the power of preparing laws, ordinances, bills, etc., of using proper means for effectually carrying out the resolutions of the Government, of examining any questions laid before it by the ministry and by any of the kings and chiefs, and, in fact, of exercising all the functions of a legislative body. . . .

ARTICLE 15.—That the National Assembly shall appoint an educated man to represent the king-president, and act as vice-president of the Confederation, and that the vice-president shall preside over all meetings convened by the secretary.

ARTICLE 16.—That there shall be in the month of October of each year a gathering of the kings, principal chiefs, and others within the Confederation, when a recapitulation of the business done by the Representative Assembly shall be read, and the programme of the ensuing year discussed.

ARTICLE 17.—That at such meetings the king-president shall preside, and that it be the duty of the king-president to sanction all laws, ordinances, etc., passed by the Representative Assembly, so far as they are compatible with the interests of the country.

ARTICLE 18.—That the king-president shall not have the power to pass any, or originate any, laws, resolutions, ordinances, bills, etc., nor create any office or appointment, excepting by, and under the advice of, the ministry.

ARTICLE 19.—That the representatives of the kings and principal chiefs hold office as members of the Representative Assembly for three years, at the expiration of which it shall be competent for the kings and chiefs to re-elect the same or appoint other representatives. . . .

ARTICLE 21.—That national schools be established at as early a period as possible. . . .

ARTICLE 23.—That schools be also established, and schoolmistresses procured to teach the female sex, and to instruct them in the necessary requisites.

Article 26.—That main roads be made, connecting various provinces or districts with one another and with the sea-coast; that the roads be made after the following standard, viz. fifteen feet broad, with good deep gutters on either side. . . .

Article 29.—That provincial assessors be appointed in each province or district, who shall perform certain judicial functions, and attend to the internal management thereof.

Article 30.—That it shall be the duty of the secretary of the Confederation—

Section 1. To convene meetings of the Representative Assembly, for the purpose of considering State matters, as may appear to the ministry necessary. . . .

Section 4. To inform the king-president of the decision of the Representative Assembly on any resolutions, etc., and to explain to him the nature of whatever resolutions, etc., are passed, as well as to carry to the Representative Assembly his sanction thereof.

Section 5. To promulgate in each province, either through the provincial representatives, or otherwise, whatever resolutions, laws, etc., have been passed, and have received the sanction of the king-president.

Article 31.—That it be the duty of the treasurer—

Section 1. To receive monthly from the secretary all moneys in his possession, keeping accounts thereof, and giving him a receipt for the same.

Section 2. To make no disbursements excepting under instructions, accompanied with approved vouchers from the secretary authorizing the payments. . . .

Article 33.—That in case the cash in hand in the possession of the treasurer should exceed a sum hereafter to be considered, the surplus should be placed in a depôt chest, furnished with three keys, one of which shall be in the possession of the vice-president, another in that of the treasurer, and the third shall be retained by one of the kings. . . .

Article 36.—That it be the duty of the provincial assessors—

Section 1. To hold courts in the districts to which they are appointed, with the assistance of the king or principal chief.

Section 2. To transmit to the secretary a statement of all cases tried during each month, showing the decisions arrived at thereon, according to a form hereafter to be prescribed by the Executive Council. . . .

Section 5. To see that the roads are made according to the approved standard, and that they are kept in proper condition.

Section 6. To see that the national schools are attended by all children between the ages of eight and fourteen, and report thereon to the secretary.

Section 7. To see that summonses, writs, etc., issuing from the British courts on the sea-coast to any of the provincial towns are carried into effect with as little delay as possible, and to aid in the apprehension of criminals.

Article 37.—That in each province or district provincial courts be established, to be presided over by the provincial assessors.

Article 38.—That it be the duty of the Ministry and Executive Council—

Section 1. To advise the king-president in all State matters.

Chapter 7

Constitutional

Responses to

European

Expansion

in Africa and

the Pacific

(1850–1890)

Section 2. To see that all laws, bills, ordinances, resolutions, etc., passed by the Representative Assembly, after receiving the sanction of the king-president, are carried into effect with as little delay as possible.

Section 3. To examine carefully the financial condition of the Confederation.

Section 4. To hear, try, and determine all important appeal cases brought before it by the under-secretary, option being allowed any party or parties dissatisfied with the decision thereof to appeal to the British courts, on application from which the minutes of the proceedings therewith will be forwarded.

Section 5. To hear, presided over by the king-president, and assisted by any king or chief whom it may deem necessary to summon for that purpose, all disputes between any of the kings and chiefs or their peoples.

Section 6. To determine, according to the majority of votes of the people, the succession to the stool[10] of any king or chief.

Section 7. To prepare laws, bills, ordinances, etc., for the consideration of the representative body. . . .

Section 9. To consider all applications of alliances from surrounding tribes, to present them for the consideration of the Representative Assembly, and to frame a reply thereto. . . .

ARTICLE 41.—That all laws, bills, regulations, ordinances, etc., be carried by the majority of votes in the Representative Assembly or Executive Council, in the latter the vice-president possessing a casting vote.

ARTICLE 42.—That it be the duty of the National Assembly, held in October of each year—

Section 1. To elect from the body of kings the president for the ensuing year, and to re-elect, as often as may appear to it fit and proper, the outgoing president.

Section 2. To consider all programmes laid before it by the Executive Council.

Section 3. To place on the stool, in cases of disputed succession thereto, the person elected by the Executive Council, with the concurrence of the municipal inhabitants of the town. . . .

ARTICLE 43.—That the officers of the Confederation shall render assistance as directed by the executive in carrying out the wishes of the British Government.

ARTICLE 44.—That it be competent to the Representative Assembly, for the purpose of carrying on the administration of the Government, to pass laws, etc., for the levying of such taxes as it may seem necessary.

ARTICLE 45.—That all the articles herein above passed be designated "The Constitution of the Fanti Confederation."

ARTICLE 46.—That oaths of allegiance to the Fanti Confederation be taken by the kings and principal chiefs, which shall be held binding on their subjects and peoples as well as by the principal officers of the Confederation and others joining it.

10. The stool is a symbol of chieftainship in this part of West Africa, equivalent to a throne.

8. A Fante Appeal to British Authorities, 1872

Scheme to be submitted to his Excellency Governor J. Pope Hennessey, and to the Home Government, for their approval, as regards the Fanti Confederation. . . .

It will be our duty to attempt to show, in as brief and concise a manner as is consistent with the gravity of the occasion, how the Fanti Confederation came into life; and to do so, we will make our starting-point from the Ashanti invasion of 1863.

We will not here discuss how Her Majesty's Government assumed the protectorate of the Fanti and other tribes on the Gold Coast, nor the moral and legal responsibilities that attached, and, as we say, still attaches, to that Government in consequence thereof; suffice it, however, that Her Majesty's Government did exercise and enjoy certain rights, privileges, etc., and that it was looked up to by all the tribes on the Gold Coast as the protecting and ruling power. Such was the state of affairs when the Ashanti war broke out in 1863.

The disastrous consequences of that war are still evident, and are now matter of history; and that war had this great effect, of causing the natives to perceive for the first time that the British Government on such occasions would let the full brunt fall on them. . . .

. . . This, sir, was the very first idea instilled into the minds of the kings and chiefs of the Protectorate, of the necessity of a Confederacy amongst them, and our people were then taught for the first time to depend entirely on themselves. . . .

We have next the Evidence of the Parliamentary Committee of 1865, which sat on West African affairs, in which it is shown that Her Majesty's Government is not legally possessed of, nor does it claim, a foot of territory outside the gates of its forts, but that it exercised a species of protection and irregular authority which could not and cannot be defined strictly. . . . We now come to the year 1867, a year memorable in the annals of the Gold Coast, as that in which the Fanti Confederation sprang into existence.

In this year (1867) a Convention was entered into between the British Government and that of the Netherlands, for the exchange of territory, by which Convention certain of the tribes . . . who had hitherto lived under British rule, were handed over to the Dutch. These tribes were opposed to such a transfer. . . . The kings and chiefs of Fanti, as soon as they heard of the proposed exchange, convened a meeting at Mankessim, and there entered into a solemn compact to render every assistance to their fellow countrymen should the Dutch attempt to coerce them into "accepting the Dutch flag." The Dutch bombarded Commendah, and as these tribes are the natural allies of the Fantees, they were compelled to take the field on their behalf. The Fantees took a large force to the seat of war, and, together with these other tribes, besieged and blockaded Elmina, the headquarters of the Dutch Possessions on the Coast of Guinea. This was in the early part of 1868. At this time Mr. Ussher had the reins of government, and by active

Chapter 7

Constitutional

Responses to

European

Expansion

in Africa and

the Pacific

(1850–1890)

measures succeeded in inducing the Fantees to raise the blockade and retire. The kings and chiefs of Fanti, and their allies, proceeded direct to Mankessim, and there laid the foundation of the Fanti Confederation. . . .

On the 16th October, 1871, a meeting of all the kings and chiefs of the Fanti Confederation, and the educated natives, was convened for the purpose of maturing a Constitution for the Confederation, and on the 24th November following, the Constitution already laid before Her Majesty's Government was framed and passed by such of the kings and chiefs as were present, or represented, together with some of their educated brethren. This Constitution they instructed and deputed Messrs. Davidson, Amissah, and Brew, to lay before Mr. Salmon,[11] to forward to . . . the Right Honourable the Secretary of State for the Colonies, for the approval of Her Majesty's Government. How Mr. Salmon deported himself, and what steps he took on the presentation of the Constitution and other documents to him, are matter of public notoriety, and will be dealt with by us on a more fitting occasion. Certain of us were imprisoned by him for being concerned, as he alleged, in a "conspiracy," against whom, or for what purpose, the warrants did not specify. In the mean time, during our incarceration, and after our release, Mr. Salmon sent messengers . . . to such of the kings and chiefs as had not been present at the framing and passing of the Constitution, and who had not then signed it, to induce them, by threats, cajolery, and bribery, to repudiate any connection with the movement, and to denounce us as impostors. . . .

We have now to deal with the most important questions, and shall endeavour to discuss them as clearly as possible, and we now lay them before your Excellency for submission to the Home Government, and its approval.

1. In the first place, for the Fanti Confederation to be of real practical use in the amelioration, development, and civilization of the country, it must have the recognition, countenance, and support, and hearty co-operation of Her Majesty's Government, and its friendly aid and advice. We do not for one single moment pretend to be able to carry on a Government in the interior without such recognition and assistance; for without that the interests of both might clash, and a collision . . . could not in any way further our object, and could have but one result, the breaking up of the Confederation, and the checking of all further progress towards the material improvement of the country for some years. . . .

2. That the jurisdiction of the Fanti Confederation shall be recognized and acknowledged to extend, and be exercised in and over all tribes, peoples, provinces, or districts choosing to join it, and that its authority and jurisdiction . . . be clearly and strictly defined in judicial and other matters.

3. That any person or persons, committing any offence or crime within the jurisdiction of the Confederation, and escaping into the sea-coast towns, shall, on representation, be handed over by the [British] local authorities to be tried in

11. **Mr. Salmon:** a British official at Cape Coast Castle.

the courts of the Confederation, if the offence or crime be within their jurisdiction; . . . and, in like manner, any person or persons committing an offence in British jurisdiction, and escaping into that of the Confederation, shall, on representation from the local authorities, be handed over to them for trial. . . .

4. That the courts of the Confederation be recognized as the courts of first instance in matters or disputes between its subjects; option being allowed to parties dissatisfied with the judgments of such courts to appeal to the British courts, as provided for in the 4th section of Article 38 of the Constitution. . . .

7. We now come to the question of questions—the financial. No Government can be administered without a revenue from some source or other, and the Fanti Confederation, if it is to assist in the great work of civilizing and regenerating the interior of the Protectorate, must have the aid of that powerful auxiliary.

On drawing up a rough estimate, and on considering the vast improvements to be made in the country, and the great extent of the Confederation, if recognized by Her Majesty's Government, the vast efforts to be made to open up the country for traffic and other purposes, the want of good and substantial roads, the backwardness of education, and the immense efforts which will have to be made to spread civilization, and diffuse knowledge over the country inland, we find that the Confederation must have a revenue of some £20,000.

It is proposed that one-half of this sum should be placed at the disposal of the Confederation out of the revenue of the Gold Coast,[12] and that the other half be raised by the Confederation itself.

The amount to be raised by the Confederation would be by way of court fees, fines, etc., the Confederation paying the kings and chiefs certain stipends, in lieu of the fees and fines received by them, in consideration of the kings and chiefs foregoing same . . . and it has been rudely estimated that a revenue of some £10,000 would be derived from this source. The Confederation would establish courts of justice in each district, and dispense justice far more impartially, expeditiously, and at less cost, than the present native courts. . . . As regards the sum to be placed at the disposal of the Confederation . . . the [British] Government would by it be relieved of the trouble and expense of governing the interior of the Protectorate, of making the improvements necessary therein, of establishing schools, erecting hospitals, making roads, canals, and other like works, as are really necessary, and yet to be able to check any reckless or useless expenditure, by appointing some one to audit the accounts of the Confederation at stated periods. . . .

Now as regards the Constitution itself, it has been said that we acted therein independently of the Home Government; that we appointed our officers before presenting it to Mr. Salmon, and that it was never submitted by us for the examination and approval of the Secretary of State, but was transmitted for his "information" only. We beg to state that the very act of the presentation of the

12. **out of the revenue of the Gold Coast:** contributed by the British.

Chapter 7

Constitutional

Responses to

European

Expansion

in Africa and

the Pacific

(1850–1890)

Constitution and other documents to Mr. Salmon, to forward to the . . . Secretary of State, was virtually a submission for such examination and approval, and was in itself an acknowledgment of British rule; and as to the Constitution having been acted upon, it was actually necessary that the Home Government should have a real organization to deal with, to which it could plainly state any modifications that might appear desirable, . . . an organization that could deal with, discuss, and deliberate upon any questions that Her Majesty's Government might wish to have solved; in fact, an organization capable of dealing more comprehensively with any matters connected with the Constitution and Confederation than they, the assembled kings and chiefs, could have done. We have now, however, to bring that Constitution to the notice of Her Majesty's Government, and pray its favourable consideration and approval thereof.

. . . If Her Majesty's Government will not furnish it with pecuniary aid . . . , nor, on the other hand, permit it to levy such taxes and duties for the purposes of obtaining a revenue as are necessary, then Her Majesty's Government will have to take over the whole country, and govern it as vigorously and on the same system and principles as it does her other colonies, but not permit us to be governed and ruled in the shameful and neglectful way in which we have been for years past, and give free scope for all legitimate aspirations to raise our benighted country to the same height of civilization as other more favoured nations have attained to.

If in dealing with these questions our language has transgressed against rules, we trust your Excellency will take into consideration the vital importance of our subject-matter, and not impute it to want of respect.

We have to tender your Excellency our sincere thanks for the kind attention you have paid us, and the patient hearing you have given us, and pray your favourable consideration and recommendation of our scheme.

(Signed)   J. H. Brew,

For Self and other Members of the Deputation.

Cape Coast, 16th April, 1872.

QUESTIONS TO CONSIDER

Now that you have acquainted yourself with the two constitutions and the other evidence presented in this chapter, it is possible to begin drawing some connections and comparisons between the nineteenth-century experiences of the Hawaiians and the Fante.

In comparing the constitutions, what different patterns emerge as these societies attempt to merge traditional modes of authority with Western concepts of constitutional government? In each case, what balance of power do you find between older traditions of chiefly power and newer concepts of a limited executive branch of government? What powers are given to the legislatures, and how are their members chosen? Does it seem that the legislature is strong enough to be an effective check on the power of the executive? Does the judicial branch of government have some degree of continuity with traditional practice, or does it seem that the separation of judicial from executive power is something new? Given the structures as defined in the constitutions, how independent is the judiciary likely to be in each case?

To what extent do these constitutions focus on defining the rights of the people as well as the powers of government? What might explain any differences between them in this regard? How well protected are the civil and human rights of the common people? How much voice would they have had in these governments, and how much protection against arbitrary authority could they have expected? Is it possible that under some circumstances some people might prefer to be represented by traditional kings and chiefs rather than by elected representatives? How might that be so?

The Hawaiians and the Fante were both targets of the nineteenth-century European "civilizing mission," in which missionaries played a central role. The goal was not just to bring Christianity to the "heathens" but to instill in them a sense of the superiority of Western social practices. From the evidence in this chapter, how successful was this effort? Do writers such as Liliuokalani and Horton seem to accept or resist the idea of European cultural superiority? What evidence do you see, in both the written and visual sources, of cultural *syncretism*, or the adaptation of foreign ideas to local circumstances? Does this type of syncretism seem to have been limited to a Western-educated elite, or was it found more widely in the societies under consideration? Are there commonalities in the role played by indigenous people (or those of mixed descent) with Western education?

Each of these constitutions was adopted not merely to organize the internal politics of a polity, but also as part of an effort to secure international recognition. What strategies did the proponents of these constitutions use to secure the support of outside powers? What was similar and what was different about the threat from outsiders? Since neither society was ultimately successful in achieving the goal of sovereign independence, how might the writers of these documents have explained that failure?

[227]

Chapter 7

Constitutional

Responses to

European

Expansion

in Africa and

the Pacific

(1850–1890)

EPILOGUE

The stakes were very high in the game of nineteenth-century imperialism. Only a few African and Asian societies managed to retain their independence. The Japanese, with a constitution modeled on the autocratic one of Germany, actually managed to become a player in the game of empire. Ethiopia (in northeastern Africa) and Siam (or Thailand, in Southeast Asia) endured as independent monarchies into the twentieth century. China never lost its formal independence, although by 1900 it was merely a hollow shell, carved up into spheres of influence by European powers. On balance, the experiences of the Hawaiians and of the Fante were representative of the time.

To the extent that indigenous populations were displaced by immigrants or came to be outnumbered by them, the implications were deep and permanent. The Hawaiians have lived to see a time when their language and traditions are no longer scorned, but they have become so thoroughly outnumbered by outsiders that true sovereignty seems unlikely ever to be restored. For peoples like the Fante, however, the European presence turned out to be temporary. Less than a hundred years after they were incorporated into the British Empire, the Fante were citizens of the independent nation of Ghana. As we will later see in Chapter 13, the twentieth century saw the long retreat of European imperial power in Africa and Asia.

The legacies of nineteenth-century empire are enduring, however. The "world revolution of westernization," the European challenge to the culture, beliefs, and political traditions of peoples around the world, continues. But in today's world, cultural influences flow in all directions. William McNeill concludes that encounters with disturbing strangers, long an urban phenomenon, have now become characteristic of the world as a whole: "Multiple and often competing identities, characteristic of cities from ancient times, have begun to open before the astonished and often resentful eye of the human majority.... Today ... ambiguity and uncertainty multiply everywhere."[13]

In the nineteenth century, the Hawaiians and the Fante found themselves in circumstances where they had to try to balance often conflicting ideas and ideals deriving from their own traditions and powerful new ideas brought by strangers. If McNeill is correct, and the "ambiguity and uncertainty" they experienced have now become common to all of us, we may still have something to learn from them.

13. William H. McNeill, "The Changing Shape of World History," *History and Theory,* 34 (May 1995), pp. 14–26.

CHAPTER EIGHT

INDUSTRIALIZING THE NATION:

GERMANY AND JAPAN (1860–1900)

The nation-state by and large has been seen as the main actor or agent of modern history. Beginning in Western Europe, where it originated in early modern times, this unique form of state won nearly worldwide acceptance during the course of Europe's rise to global dominance. In ideal form, such a state represents a distinct "nation" or people whose interests it promotes over those of others. It presupposes a homogeneous population bound together by a common language, culture, and historical tradition and possessed of a collective will. "To achieve this state is the highest moral duty for nation and individual alike," proclaimed one of the nineteenth century's greatest promoters of the ideal, the German historian Heinrich von Treischke, who added that "all private quarrels must be forgotten" in the face

of it.[1] Such unanimity was rare, however, and modern leaders more often found that far from finding a ready-made sense of national identity among their people, they had to cultivate it. The onset of the Industrial Revolution immensely complicated this task, for it created powerful tensions within modernizing societies that strained national unity even as it offered opportunities for mobilizing people behind new national goals.

Leaders in Britain, France, and the United States—the first major countries to industrialize—were able to take the relationship between national unity and economic development for granted because of their early start and their unique political traditions. Already beginning to industrialize by

1. From Heinrich von Treischke, *German History in the Nineteenth Century*, in *Documents of German History*, ed. Louis Snyder (New Brunswick, N.J.: Rutgers University Press, 1958).

Chapter 8

Industrializing

the Nation:

Germany

and Japan

(1860–1900)

the start of the nineteenth century, these countries underwent the process at a relatively slow pace that took generations to complete. Moreover, they benefited from earlier revolutions and reform movements that had modernized their societies and provided them with representative governments founded on the liberal ideals of the European Enlightenment, such as the doctrines of popular sovereignty and individual rights. These changes helped to allay many of the tensions created by industrialization and inspired great optimism about national progress among their leaders. Convinced that an "invisible hand" of providence promoted their improvement, they confidently relinquished the direction of industrialization and subsequent national adjustment mainly to private initiatives.

By the mid-nineteenth century, impressive gains in these states won them the attention and envy of people elsewhere. But because leaders of other countries regarded them as atypical, few sought to adopt their approach. By then the human and material costs of industrializing had grown greater, and the need to speed up economic change while simultaneously introducing social and political modernization posed more of a threat to stability. This chapter thus looks at the way in which Germany and Japan attempted to meet this challenge by finding their own paths to industrial development. As the two dominant states in Europe and East Asia, respectively, throughout most of the twentieth century, they, of course, merit special attention. But more important, Germany and Japan stand out as two of the earliest ex-

amples of states whose governments actively sought to manage industrialization, an approach that increasingly became the norm among developing countries in the twentieth century. As such, they may provide more typical cases of industrialization than Britain or the United States. They may also afford more insight into the ways in which industrialization complicated nation building, for both German and Japanese government efforts to guide economic growth forced frequent and deliberate public debate on the broader impact of industrialization.

Your task here is to assess how industrialization affected efforts to build a sense of national unity in modern Germany and Japan. Industrialization brought profound social changes, creating new groups in the population with new social and political aspirations as well as new economic interests. On the one hand, their competing demands and conflicts could destroy the unity so essential to the nation-state and undermine its stability. On the other, of course, industrialization also posed opportunities for uniting the nation. As a way to increase living standards, strengthen national defense, or enhance a nation's international stature, industrialization promised benefits to all and could be used to mobilize the population behind common goals. Economic achievement, serving as a measure of national success, could give citizens a sense of common pride and accomplishment. In the material that follows, try then to answer this central question: What impact did industrialization have on national unity in modern Germany and Japan?

BACKGROUND

Both Germany and Japan represent a second wave of modernizing nations. Their late start in the second half of the nineteenth century, which came nearly a century after the French Revolution and the beginning of British industrialization, had both advantages and disadvantages. Obviously, they could learn from those who had begun to modernize earlier, both in anticipating their difficulties and in following their models. They could also import technology, experts, and even capital to help them through the initial stages. But they often faced new and unknown problems, for the costs of modernization had become much greater by the century's end.

A major technological shift occurred during the 1860s and 1870s, boosting the cost of development enormously. In the early stage of industrialization, local entrepreneurs and artisans with only modest capital and skill were sufficient to mechanize a small number of pioneer industries with steam power. But the rise of new steel, petrochemical, and electrical industries and the increasing scope of manufacturing in the late nineteenth century demanded large outlays of capital and sophisticated expertise. Huge plants, extensive networks of transport, and armies of skilled workers were now needed, as well as a whole range of new institutions from central banks to public systems of education. Besides such infrastructure, countries that modernized at this time also had to sustain high military expenditures. For it was an age of extreme nationalism in which the Darwinian concept of a "struggle for survival" became a metaphor for international relations. Besides high material costs, the industrialization of this era entailed a great deal of social change, as rural people poured into industrial cities to form new classes of business people and factory workers, creating all kinds of tensions. Fear of riot and rebellion, if not the welfare of the citizenry, forced governments to spend resources on social issues.

Despite such costs, Germany and Japan succeeded in building powerful new nation-states in less than fifty years, half the time it took Britain, France, or the United States. One reason for their quicker development was the active role played by their governments in encouraging and directing change. Fast change, however, imposes severe strains on a population, and the disorienting effect of over-rapid growth under the direction of a powerful state may help to explain the behavior of both countries in the twentieth century. In many ways the pace of change may have outrun the ability of people to adjust, leaving them vulnerable to new forms of mass mobilization and manipulation. Few of the founders of modern Germany and Japan, however, could have foreseen this danger, for disunity and weakness were the dominant problems of their day.

Germany, for example, did not exist as a political entity in the first half of the nineteenth century. Instead of one nation, Germans lived in nearly thirty separate states, each with its own rulers and laws. Although an emerging middle class, inspired by the example of French unity and power,

Chapter 8

Industrializing

the Nation:

Germany

and Japan

(1860–1900)

began to call for a "Greater Germany," the liberal beliefs that they adopted from French and British counterparts made them suspect in the eyes of more traditionally minded Germans. The rulers of the two largest German states, Austria and Prussia, thus took over the cause of nationalism, hoping to win popular support against middle-class challenges to their power. But each envisioned only a "Little Germany" united around a core of its own lands, rather than the Greater Germany of all German-speaking lands favored by liberals. The Austrians had an early advantage in this rivalry. After Napoleon's defeat (1814), they headed a loose German Confederation that offered a potential framework for national unity. But in the end, they were foiled by the Prussians.

The groundwork for Prussian success was laid by Frederick Wilhelm IV, who pushed for military and economic modernization soon after becoming king in 1840. During his reign, the monarchy allowed a limited amount of political reform, tolerating the creation of both a Prussian constitution and a Diet or parliament whose elected lower house came to be dominated by liberals. But decisive moves came later, following the ascension of King Wilhelm II in 1861. As prince regent from 1859 to 1861, he championed German unification by organizing a *Zollverein*, or Customs Union, to create a German free trade area. Then, on his ascension in 1862, Wilhelm appointed a gifted diplomat, Otto von Bismarck, as Prussian chancellor to help him unite Germany politically.

Otto von Bismarck reflected the conservative values of the distinctive Prussian elite, a class of landowning aristocrats known as *Junkers*, of whom he was a member. Originally a feudal nobility with hereditary control of land and serfs, this privileged class supplied the bulk of the civil service and officer corps when the Prussian state began to modernize in the eighteenth century. It thus retained political dominance well into the modern era, eventually gaining control of the upper house of the Diet as well as the state's administrative apparatus. As a class of big landowners who looked abroad for markets in which to sell the produce of their estates, the *Junkers* favored the liberal ideal of free trade. In most other respects, however, *Junkers* held conservative social and political ideas and firmly rejected middle-class attempts to broaden participation in politics. Wilhelm's choice of Bismarck signaled his rejection of liberal, middle-class aspirations and an intention to bolster the traditional alliance of crown and *Junker* conservatism.

For the next thirty years, during which he directed first Prussian and then ultimately German policy, Bismarck posed as the defender of the existing power structure whose chief task was to keep liberals from weakening the monarchy and its traditional supports, the *Junker*-dominated bureaucracy and army. He was helped by the fact that the Prussian constitution severely restricted the authority of the Diet. By its writ, a prime minister was responsible only to the crown, not the Diet or the populace, and needed no parliamentary majority for support. This provision reduced the Prussian Diet to little more than a forum for middle-class and elite opinion, allowing Bismarck to formulate programs in an autocratic manner.

Despite his opposition to liberals, Bismarck did share their interest in German unification, if only to strengthen Prussia. He thus started wars in which Prussia could pose as the protector of German-speaking people and win acceptance of a Little Germany united around and dominated by Prussia. In 1864 he went to war with Denmark to wrest two German duchies from its control. Then in 1866 he risked a more dangerous conflict with Austria to force it to abandon the old German Confederation so that he could replace it with a new North German Confederation under Prussian hegemony. Finally, in 1870, he goaded France, then considered the Germans' greatest enemy, into the Franco-Prussian War to arouse German interest in unification. Prussia's overwhelming defeat of France won Bismarck the acclaim of most nationalistic-minded Germans, including liberals. On the occasion of the French surrender in 1871, Bismarck thus proclaimed the Prussian king, Wilhelm II, *Kaiser,* or emperor, of a new empire embracing all German states save Austria.

The German "empire" heralded in 1871 was far from a cohesive nation-state. As spelled out in a new constitution, it was only a loose union of states still retaining their individual identities and most of their former powers over local administrations, schools, and state enterprises such as railroads and utilities. Sovereignty was vested in a Federal Council, or *Bundesrat,* made up of delegates appointed by the member states. But the imperial monarchy (hereditarily held by the Prussian royal house) quickly emerged as a more significant institution be- cause Bismarck, assuming the role of imperial chancellor, staffed the new government with Prussians loyal to Wilhelm. The constitution also called for an elected parliament, known as the Reichstag, but, subject to the same limitations as the old Prussian Diet, it had little real power. Given the weakness of the legislature—and the emperor's deference to Bismarck—the imperial chancellor dominated the new government, using the threat of lower-class unrest, the "red specter" of revolution, to win liberal and middle-class acceptance of his authoritarian ways.

Bismarck's autocratic rule led him to chart a course for the new Germany that included incongruent elements. On one hand, as a believer in aristocratic rather than democratic rule, he tried to strengthen traditional elites like the *Junkers* and bar emerging social groups from political power. Yet he was wise enough to see that oppression alone could not stave off revolution from below and sought to relieve popular discontent. He thus allowed elections to placate liberals and initiated reforms to improve middle- and lower-class life. Deeply concerned with domestic affairs, he tried to forestall further foreign conflicts by supporting, rather than challenging, the international status quo. Nevertheless, he worked closely with the heads of the armed forces to build a modern army and navy designed to make Germany the most powerful military nation of the day.

Such power required advanced industry. Industrialization, of course, had begun decades earlier in some German states, notably in the Rhine Valley. But the creation of a unified

Chapter 8

Industrializing

the Nation:

Germany

and Japan

(1860–1900)

empire with an integrated market greatly accelerated the process, and in a single generation, from 1871 to 1895, Germany changed from an agrarian to an industrial nation. German industrialization began under the same system of private capitalism that emerged in England, but the imperial government did more than its British or American counterparts to foster industry. Like them, it created a common commercial code, a common currency system—based on the mark—and a new Imperial Bank to regulate the money supply and raise funds through the sale of bonds. But it also built the bulk of modern communication and transportation links at state expense, and it pioneered in setting up a system of secular, state schools from kindergartens to research universities (both German innovations) to allow true mass education.

Germany also departed from Anglo-American practices by abandoning free trade policies in favor of state-guided economic development. Hurt by the prolonged depression of 1873 to 1879, businessmen in key industries called on the government to create protective customs behind which they could complete German industrialization without foreign competition. The government complied by adopting a new tariff policy in 1879. It also assumed an increasingly paternalistic relationship with businesses, offering them frequent aid at the cost of growing state regulation and management of industry. Far from opposing concentrations in industry, therefore, the imperial government promoted it, encouraging the formation of giant interlocking combines called *Kartels,*

through which government leaders could informally influence and guide economic development. Germany thus completed its industrialization under a system of managed capitalism characterized by limited competition and active government involvement in business.

The German government also sought to play an active role in managing the whole of industrial society. Here, too, the depression of 1873–1879 proved decisive, for the labor unrest stirred by sinking wages led to the growth of unions and a socialist movement. Pleading the danger of lower-class revolt in 1878, Bismarck persuaded the Reichstag to outlaw radical socialist parties and their activities, bringing years of police suppression and censorship. In doing so, he skillfully turned liberals and the middle class against the left. But to placate workers and forestall further turmoil, he followed this move with a bold, positive step: the creation of the first comprehensive system of state welfare. He began by introducing compulsory health insurance in 1883, following it the next year with a program for workmen's accident insurance and compensation, and then in 1889 with provisions for old-age coverage and a pension plan. Later, in 1891, the government began to regulate the hours of employment as well as working conditions. Although industrial booms in the late 1880s and 1890s probably did more to raise the wages and living standards of German workers, Bismarck's welfare programs helped Germany reduce the human cost of industrialization better than many other modernizing states.

Unlike Germany, Japan began its modernization as a unified state. The unity of mid-nineteenth-century Japan, however, was loose, for the feudal military regime that ruled the country left most power at the local level. Its head, a military leader called the *Shogun,* nominally ruled in the name of an emperor residing in the ancient city of Kyoto. But the position, hereditarily held in the Tokugawa family, really derived its power from the Shogun's personal lordship over the territorial magnates who controlled local land and people. These vassals, known as *daimyo,* ruled their domains autonomously with the aid of hereditary retainers drawn from the *bushi,* or warrior, class. The shogunate, based in the city of Edo, thus did not have much governing to do other than to keep peace among the daimyo, deal with foreign powers, and respond to problems that threatened the overall security or stability of the system. National unity thus rested upon a delicate balance of regional and central power.

Anxious about this balance from its inception in 1600, the Tokugawa shogunate looked askance at most change, using what powers it had to preserve the status quo—a task made difficult by increasing pressures for economic and social change. A commercial revolution was slowly engulfing the country in a market economy and promoting urbanization, trends that undermined the feudal, agrarian base of the shogunal system. As cities grew in size and prosperity, a new urban class of merchants and manufacturers emerged who ill fit within the hierarchy of feudal, military arrangements but who garnered much of the country's wealth. Rather than adjust to these changes, the shogunate tried to stifle them, relying on rigid class rules, property restrictions, and sumptuary laws to bolster traditional arrangements and secure the rule of the military class. The regime similarly refused to adapt to change in the outside world.

Unsympathetic to foreign trade from the start, the Tokugawa regime became even more wary of international contacts following a rebellion of some of its vassals in the early seventeenth century. Because a few of these insurgents had not only traded with Europeans but embraced Christianity, the shogunate came to view European influence as a source of dangerous ferment. Gradually it broke off relations with outside powers, by 1641 banning all foreign contact except for a limited trade with the Chinese and Dutch on a single island. This policy of *sakoku,* or seclusion, became the bedrock of Tokugawa foreign policy. Though initially accepted by other countries, who largely ignored Japan over the next two centuries, this policy led to a crisis in the mid-nineteenth century when outsiders attempted to "open" the country. Foreign affairs thus became the dominant issue of nineteenth-century Japan, setting the stage for modernization.

The problem arose because of new Western interest in the Pacific and a disparity of power created by the rapid industrial and technological development of the West. While the British and French turned to Qing China following England's victory there in the Opium War of 1839–1842,

Chapter 8

Industrializing

the Nation:

Germany

and Japan

(1860–1900)

the United States, then pursuing a "manifest destiny" in the Pacific after the annexation of California in the 1840s, focused its attention on Japan. In 1853, President Fillmore sent an American naval squadron under Commodore Matthew C. Perry to demand Western-style diplomatic and trade relations. Though aware that the British had started a war with China when refused a similar request, the shogunate temporized. Perry thus had to return for a reply the next year with nearly a quarter of the U.S. Navy to force compliance. Fearful of the military might revealed by Anglo-French victories over Qing China in the Arrow War, the Tokugawa shogunate signed an additional round of treaties with Britain, France, Holland, and Russia, as well as the United States, in 1858. Termed the five-nation "unequal treaties" because they infringed on Japan's sovereignty, these agreements ended Tokugawa isolationism.

Fear of Western power provided an impetus for change. The shogunate, deeply humiliated at succumbing to foreign pressure, tried to strengthen itself by turning first to the Americans and then ultimately to the French for assistance. Many of the elite, however, objected to this receptivity to foreign ways. Some spoke seditiously of turning to the emperor at Kyoto for alternative leadership, touting the slogan *sonno joi*, or "Revere the emperor and expel the barbarian." Anti-shogunal groups found strong support in western Japan, where they built new local governments with westernized forces of their own and began to challenge the Tokugawa regime in the 1860s. But

neither side achieved a decisive victory until 1868. That January, forces from half a dozen rebellious domains seized control of Kyoto and prevailed upon the recently enthroned Emperor Mutsuhito, still a boy of fifteen, to reassert imperial authority and outlaw the Tokugawa regime. With his sanction, rebel forces marched on Edo, where the demoralized Shogun, himself only recently installed, prudently abdicated. Promising a new era of Meiji, or "enlightened rule," under the emperor, the rebels set out to revitalize the nation and regain its lost honor.

This Meiji Restoration of 1868, though nominally a return to tradition, actually proved a revolution that transformed Japan and began its modern age. It brought a new group of leaders, mainly young samurai, to the forefront of national politics. Together with the young emperor Mutsuhito, they formed a cohesive oligarchy at the center of the new regime. For all their original opposition to foreign ways, these pragmatists quickly saw that they could never reverse the humiliating unequal treaties and compete successfully in the new world order without modern military power. And this power, they realized, depended on the latest technology and an industrial base, which in turn required the modernization of society and culture. Guided by an old Chinese adage, *fukoku kyohei*, meaning "enrich the country to strengthen the military," they set out to refashion the basis of national power, even if it meant following foreign models.

First on their agenda was the creation of a stable government in Edo, now renamed Tokyo. By June 1868, Meiji leaders unveiled a brief constitution, inspired by the American example, establishing a Council of State with a Western-style cabinet of ministers. Construction of a centralized system of local administration based on French models followed. In 1871 they induced all daimyo to return their lands and authority to the emperor in return for appointment as prefectural governors with annual stipends. They then introduced a standard land tax to generate steady revenue. Interest in financial security also led them to create a new, decimal monetary system based on the yen and a modern national bank to regulate the supply and circulation of money. Meanwhile, to build an effective new military system, they nationalized all domain forces in 1872, reorganizing them into a Western-style army and navy. The Meiji also developed a modern system of state education based on the latest European examples and a revamped legal system modeled after the Napoleonic Code of France.

Because of the critical importance of new technology and manufacturing to defense, Meiji leaders soon grew interested in industrialization. To foster the process, they set up a postal service and introduced other forms of communication and transportation like telegraph lines and railroads. But initial hopes that traditional merchant firms would complete industrial development proved vain. The high start-up costs, together with lack of familiarity, dissuaded traditional merchants from taking up the challenge. As a result, the state decided to build pilot industries to demonstrate their feasibility. Although it concentrated heavily on strategic industries like steel foundries that supplied materials needed in state shipyards and arsenals, it also set up some nonstrategic enterprises like silk mills to offset the chronic trade imbalances caused by Western imports. Nearly bankrupted by this attempt, the regime sold most off at great discount to a handful of private *zaibatsu*, or "financial groups," largely run by members of the old military elite. Small in number, they gave Japan's industrial sector an oligopolistic character parallel to the Meiji political oligarchy.

Along with efforts to build up national power and wealth, the regime also undertook a program of radical social reform to eradicate surviving vestiges of feudalism. As early as 1869, it outlawed old occupational restrictions, and in 1871 it began a wave of legislation that abolished feudal tenure and the old class structure, effectively ending the legal status of the former military elite. By 1876 the regime felt confident enough to commute annual payments to former daimyo and their retainers into lump sum settlements, undercutting their economic privileges. Even more telling was the government's decision in 1873 to introduce a European system of universal male conscription for military recruitment, a measure that ended the elite's monopoly of military power. In 1877 some more traditional samurai, resentful of such reforms, took up arms against the regime. Suppression of this uprising, known as the Satsuma Rebellion, ended serious

Chapter 8

Industrializing

the Nation:

Germany

and Japan

(1860–1900)

opposition, allowing Meiji leaders to contemplate further changes in national life.

One of the issues that disturbed the rebels, who remained true to the original principles of the restoration, was the growing Meiji adoption of Western ways. Their resentment reflected a dilemma that troubled others, too: In Japan, institutional modernization unleashed a parallel trend of cultural Westernization. People who accepted the former in order to strengthen Japan against Western encroachment often feared that the latter would undermine their efforts. Government adoption of European uniforms, Victorian architecture, and the metric system, for example, troubled the more conservative, as did popular fads, promoted by a Western-style press that provided information on all aspects of foreign life. Even the Meiji leaders themselves had trouble accepting certain Western ways, especially those related to democratic politics.

Nonetheless, the introduction of French and British ideas in the 1870s led a group called the Society of Patriots to launch a "People's Rights" campaign to establish elected assemblies. On the recommendation of prefectural governors, the regime agreed in 1878 to allow local assemblies as advisory bodies. But it continued to reject calls for a national assembly until 1881, when a prominent member broke ranks and petitioned the emperor for a parliament. The next year top officials went to Europe to study Western examples. Impressed by Germany, they set up a Bismarckian-style imperial cabinet under Ito Hirobumi as prime minister in 1885 and went on to promulgate a constitution modeled on German lines in 1889. Declaring the emperor the "sacred and inviolable" source of authority, it empowered him personally to select all top officials and to set policy in consultation with a civil cabinet under a prime minister, and a general staff under a chief of staff. The bicameral Diet, made up of an appointed House of Peers and an elected House of Representatives, had only an advisory role, like its Prussian namesake. Restrictions limited those who could vote for candidates to the one elected branch, the House of Representatives, to only 450,000 males. But this recast balance of political forces brought a decade and a half of stable government in which parties gained a measure of influence.

Foreign affairs helped to promote domestic unity. Unlike modern Germany, which from the time of its birth enjoyed a reputation for military superiority thanks to Prussia's victories, Meiji Japan began as a weak power, vulnerable before even the lesser Western states. Far from content to maintain the status quo in East Asia, therefore, its leaders resolved early on to take aggressive measures to enhance national power and prestige. In pursuit of a dominant role in Korea, they deliberately started two wars, one with Qing China in 1894 and another with the Russian Empire in 1904. Spectacular victories in both instances led to a dramatic reversal in Japan's international position. Suddenly Japan not only exerted colonial control over Korea and an island empire stretching from Taiwan to

Sakhalin off the Siberian coast, but earned Western recognition as a major regional power. By the time the Meiji emperor died in 1912 a powerful new industrial Japan was emerging, belying the idea that modernization was a purely Western phenomenon.

THE METHOD

The question at issue here—how industrialization affected efforts to build a sense of national unity in modern Germany and Japan—certainly involves economic factors, but the problem is not primarily one of economic history. It focuses more on the social and political consequences of industrialization than on its economic ramifications. For this reason, the sources that follow in the Evidence section are not statistical tables and graphs, the usual stock in trade of economic historians. They instead consist of public statements of one sort or another giving different perspectives on the impact of industrialization within Germany and Japan from the final decades of the nineteenth century through the start of the twentieth century. And as you might expect, they occur in two sets, one for Germany and one for Japan.

During this period, rapid industrial growth contributed to the rise of mass society and aroused interest in public opinion in both societies. Political parties in the recently formed parliaments were beginning to challenge the authoritarian ways of the past, and both they and government leaders, who often remained aloof from them, sought ever-increasing popular support for their views. As the Japanese statesman Ito Hirobumi observed in one of the items included here, not only did the populace gain the right "to voice their opinions on the advisability and the faults of their country's administration," but governments found they had "to inform them well so that they will serve well." All of the sources presented here reveal the broadening scope of public debate within mass industrial society—even in such relatively authoritarian states as imperial Germany and Japan—and the growing diversity of opinion within such a society. Those that are graphic in nature especially attest to this trend, for they deliver their message in simple, direct terms accessible to all.

Sources 1 and 2, pictures commissioned by German factory owners to impress the public with their success, vividly depict the changing nature of industrial development during the late nineteenth century. The social and political consequences of these material changes can be gleaned from Source 3, an excerpt from a lecture by the noted German sociologist Max

Chapter 8

Industrializing

the Nation:

Germany

and Japan

(1860–1900)

Weber. As Weber's remarks imply, these consequences unleashed a national debate over how to adjust to new social and political realities. In this debate, the new media often sought to shape opinions through simple, visual statements like Source 4, a German political cartoon from the satirical magazine *Simplicissimus,* or Source 5, one of a series of emotionally intense photographs exposing the nature of working-class life in Berlin. Political leaders, too, often gave in to simplification and overstatement, as you can see in Source 6, the famous Erfurt Programme—or manifesto—of the German Social Democrats, and Source 7, one of Bismarck's parliamentary speeches.

Similar conditions prevailed in Japan. For all the cherry blossoms displayed in Source 8, a traditional Japanese woodblock print, this scene of the 1870s already focuses on the railway, one of the key symbols of modern industrialization. In his celebrated memo to the emperor proposing industrialization (Source 9), one of the key Meiji leaders, Okubo Toshimichi, claimed it was imperative that all Japanese embrace this new direction as a national "duty." For a while most did. As Source 10, a print showing the emperor's open visit to the Tokyo Industrial Fair of 1877, indicates, even the Meiji emperor complied. Over twenty years later, despite the evolution of a Western-style parliamentary system and contending political parties, Japan's first prime minister, Ito Hirobumi, still echoed that demand in his public speeches (Source 11). But by then parliamentary discussions and a mass media

gave voice to other views. Cartoons and prints like Sources 12 and 13 publicized some of the human costs of change. And the exposure of conditions like those revealed in Source 14 through the recollections of some of the victims of industrialization made it clear that certain citizens bore a disproportionately higher share of the cost of change.

In both Germany and Japan, therefore, public debate revealed that industrialization complicated the process of building a modern nation. In theory the populace of a modern nation-state was supposed to be (or to become) a single, homogeneous body. The challenge of building up national industry could, of course, enhance that unity by providing a common purpose. But, as you can see from sources like the one giving voice to the women who crossed Nomugi Pass, many groups of people found themselves set apart from the rest of the population as a result of industrial development and the changes it set in motion. As you read over these sources, therefore, make two lists, indicating ways in which industrialization served to (1) unify or (2) divide the nation. Note any significant groups or categories of people whom the sources mention as either benefactors or victims of industrialization. Pay particular heed to those who became alienated from the rest of the nation, and observe how this affected social and political life. With your list as a guide, you should be able to decide for yourself the impact that industrialization had on the development of national unity in modern Germany and Japan.

THE EVIDENCE

Sources 1 and 2 from Questions on German History (catalog of the Historical Exhibition in the Berlin Reichstag) (Bonn: German Bundestag Press, 1984), illustration 102, p. 167; color plate XVI. Photographs: Source 1: Bildarchiv Preussischer Kulturbesitz/Art Resource, NY; Source 2: Historische Archiv, Fried. Krupp H GmbH, Essen.

1. Hagen Rolling Mill, 1860s

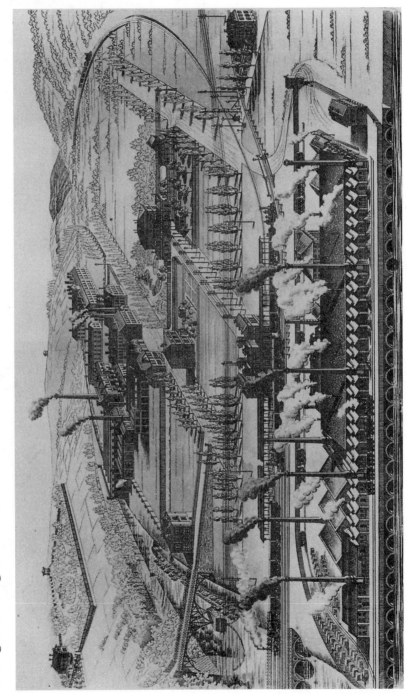

Chapter 8
Industrializing
the Nation:
Germany
and Japan
(1860–1900)

2. Krupp Steel Works, 1912

Source 3 from Nineteenth Century Europe: Liberalism and Its Critics, *trans. Paul Silverman (Chicago and London: University of Chicago Press, 1979), pp. 438–460 ff.*

3. From Max Weber, Inaugural Lecture at Freiberg University, 1895

During the first half of the century, the Polish element in the east appears to have been slowly and continuously pushed back. Since the 1860s, however, as is well known, it has been just as slowly and continuously on the advance. Despite their faulty foundations, linguistic inquiries establish this latter fact for West Prussia in the clearest possible manner. Now a shift of the boundary between two nationalities can come about in two fundamentally distinct ways. One way is for national minorities in a nationally mixed region to have the language and customs of the majority gradually imposed upon them, for them to be "absorbed." This phenomenon can be found in the east. It is statistically demonstrable in the case of German Catholics. The bond of the church is stronger here than that of the nation, memories of the *Kulturkampf* also play a part, and the lack of a German-educated clergy permits them to be lost to the cultural community of the nation. More important, however, and more interesting for us, is the second form in which shifts of nationalities take place—*economic displacement*. This is what we are dealing with here.

One is dealing here with a process of a mass-psychological kind: German agricultural workers can no longer adapt to the *social* living conditions of their home. Reports out of West Prussia from the lords of the estates complain of the "self-assurance" of the workers. The old patriarchical relationship between lord and smallholder, which attached the day laborer directly to the interests of agricultural production as a small cultivator entitled to a portion of the crop, is disappearing. Seasonal work in the beet-growing districts requires seasonal workers and money wages. These workers face a purely proletarian existence, but without the possibility of the sort of vigorous ascent to economic independence that fills the industrial proletariat, crowded together in the cities, with self-confidence. It is those who take the place of the Germans who are better able to accommodate themselves to these living conditions—the Polish migrant workers, bands of nomads recruited by agents in Russia, who cross the border in tens of thousands in the spring and then depart in the autumn.

But, as I have already said, I do not wish to discuss today this practical question of Prussian agrarian policy. I would much prefer to take up the fact that this question has arisen for us at all, that we consider the German element in the east to be something that *ought* to be protected and in defense of which the economic policy of the state *ought* to enter into the lists. It is the fact that our state is constituted as a *national state* that allows us to feel we have the right to make this demand.

Chapter 8

Industrializing

the Nation:

Germany

and Japan

(1860–1900)

In the final analysis, processes of economic development are also *power* struggles; they are *power* interests of the nation, and, where they are placed in question, they are the ultimate and decisive interests in whose service the nation's economic policy has to place itself. The science of economic policy is a *political* science. It is a servant of politics, not of the day-to-day politics of whichever rulers and classes may be in power at the moment, but of the long-term power political interests of the nation. And the *national state* is not a vague something for us that some believe is made all the more majestic the more one shrouds its nature in mystical darkness. It is rather the temporal institution that organizes the nation's power, and in such an institution the ultimate standard of value for us in inquiries regarding economic policy is, as in everything else, *"reason of state."* This does not mean for us, as an odd misunderstanding has led some to believe, "state assistance" instead of "self-help," state regulation of economic life instead of the free play of economic forces. Rather, by means of this term we want to raise the demand that in questions of German economic policy—including, among others, whether and to what degree the state ought to intervene in economic life, and whether and when, on the contrary, the state ought to tear down the barriers standing in the way of the economic powers of the nation and let them loose to develop freely on their own—in individual cases the last and decisive vote ought to belong to the economic and political power interests of our nation and the entity responsible for them, the German national state.

The *attainment of economic power* has, in all times, engendered in a class the notion that it *can expect to assume political leadership.* It is dangerous and, in the long run, incompatible with the interests of the nation when a class that is economically on the decline holds the nation's political power in its hands. But it is still more dangerous when classes that are beginning to *attract* economic power and thus the expectation of gaining political command are not yet politically mature enough to assume the leadership of the state. Both of these things are threatening Germany at the present time and in fact are the key to the present dangers in our situation. Moreover, the upheavals in the social structure of the east connected with the phenomena discussed at the outset also belong within this larger context.

In the Prussian state right up into the present, the dynasty has depended politically on the caste of the Prussian *Junkers.* Admittedly, the dynasty moved against them when creating the Prussian state, but, all the same, it was only with their assistance that its creation was possible. I am well aware that the Junkers' name has an unpleasant sound to South German ears. It may be felt that I am speaking a "Prussian" language if I say a word in their favor. I would not know. In Prussia even today the Junkers have open to them many paths to influence and power as well as many paths to the monarch's ear, which are not accessible to every citizen. They have not always used this power in such a way as to allow them to answer for themselves before history, and I see no reason why a bourgeois scholar ought to have any particular fondness for them. Nonetheless, the strength of their political instincts was one of the most powerful resources that could be applied in the service of the power interests of the state. Now their work is done, and today they lie in the throes of an economic death from which no economic policy of the state could ever retrieve them and lead them back to their old social status. Moreover, the tasks of the present are different from those that could be solved by them. For a quarter of a century the last and greatest of the Junkers [Bismarck] stood at the head of Germany, and, although today some are still unable to see it, the tragic element that, alongside the incomparable greatness, was inherent in his career as a statesman will be discovered by the future in the fact that the work of his hands, the nation to which he gave unity, slowly and irresistibly changed its economic structure under him and became something other than what it was, a people who must demand social forms different from those he was able to provide it and to which his caesarist nature was able to adapt. In the final analysis, this is what brought about the partial failure of his life's work, for this life's work surely ought to have led not only to the outer but also to the inner unification of the nation, and every one of us knows that that has not been achieved. With the means he used it could not be achieved.

I am a member of the bourgeoisie, feel myself to be such, and have been brought up to share in its attitudes and ideals. But it is the calling of precisely our science to say what one would rather not hear—on high, down below, and in our own class too—and when I ask myself whether the German bourgeoisie is at present mature enough to become the nation's political governing class, I cannot *today* answer this question in the affirmative.

The political immaturity of broad sections of the German bourgeoisie is not due to economic causes, nor is it due to "interest politics," something that is often mentioned but that other nations are no less familiar with than we are. The cause lies in this class's unpolitical past, in the fact that a century's worth of political education cannot be made up for in a decade, and in the fact that rule by a great man is not always the best means of political education. The important question for the political future of the German bourgeoisie is whether or not it is now too *late* to make up for this missed political education. No *economic* factor can serve as a substitute for it.

Will other classes become the champions of a politically greater future? The modern proletariat is self-confidently stepping forward as the heir to bourgeois ideals. What can be said of its prospective claim to the political leadership of the nation?

The danger does *not* lie with the *masses*, as those who stare hypnotically into the depths of society believe. The ultimate content of the problem of *social* policy is not a question of the *economic* condition of the *ruled*, but on the contrary a question of the *political* qualifications of the *ruling* classes and those *on the rise*. The goal of our work in the field of social policy is not the spreading of

Chapter 8

Industrializing

the Nation:

Germany

and Japan

(1860–1900)

happiness throughout the world but, rather, the *social unification* of the nation—a condition that modern economic development split apart—so that it will be possible to face the arduous struggles of the future. If a "labor aristocracy" were in fact created that would be the bearer of the political understanding we cannot now see in the workers' movement, then the spear that the arm of the bourgeoisie seems still not strong enough to carry might be transferred to those broader shoulders. But there appears to be a long way to go before that happens.

Source 4: Simplicissimus, *vol. 4 (1899/1900), number 29. Courtesy of the Boston Public Library.*

4. Cartoon, "Through Darkest Germany, a View Inland," 1899

Source 5 from Barbara Franzoi, At the Very Least She Pays the Rent: Women and German Industrialization, 1871–1914 *(Westport, Conn.: Greenwood Press, 1994), figure 10. Photograph: AKG Photo London.*

5. A German Worker's Apartment, 1910

Source 6 from Susanne Miller and Heinrich Potthoff, A History of German Social Democracy From 1848 to the Present, *trans. J. A. Underwood (Hamburg and New York: Berg), Appendix 3.*

6. The Erfurt Social Democratic Party Program, 1890

The economic development of bourgeois society inevitably leads to the destruction of the small enterprise, the basis of which is private ownership by the worker of his means of production. It separates the worker from his means of production and turns him into an unpropertied proletarian, while the means of production become the monopoly of a relatively small number of capitalists and large landowners.

Hand in hand with this monopolisation of the means of production go the displacement of the fragmented small-business sector by gigantic big businesses, the evolution of the tool into the machine, and an enormous growth in the productivity of human labour. All the advantages of this change, however, are monopolised by the capitalists and large landowners. For the proletariat and the sinking middle orders—petty bourgeoisie, peasant farmers—it means a growing increase in the uncertainty of their livelihood and in poverty, pressure, enslavement, degradation, and exploitation.

The number of proletarians becomes ever greater, the army of surplus workers becomes ever more massive, the contrast between exploiters and exploited becomes ever sharper, and the class struggle between bourgeoisie and proletariat, which divides modern society into two hostile camps and is the common feature of all industrialised countries, becomes ever more vehement.

The gap between propertied and unpropertied is further widened by the crises inherent in the nature of the capitalist mode of production, which become more and more expensive and devastating, make the normal condition of society one of generalised insecurity, and prove that the forces of production have got beyond the control of present-day society and that private ownership of the means of production has become incompatible with their being utilised appropriately and developed to the full.

Private ownership of the means of production, once the means of protecting the producer's ownership of his products, has today become a means of expropriating peasant farmers, craft-tradesmen, and retailers and placing the nonworkers—capitalists, large landowners—in possession of the product of the workers. Only the transformation of the capitalist private ownership of the means of production—land, mines, raw materials, tools, machinery, transport—into social ownership and the conversion of commodity production into socialist production, pursued by society for society's benefit, is capable of bringing it about that big business and the constantly increasing yield capacity of social labour cease to be a source of poverty and oppression for the hitherto exploited

Chapter 8

Industrializing

the Nation:

Germany

and Japan

(1860–1900)

classes and become a source of supreme welfare and all-round, harmonious improvement. This social transformation means the emancipation not only of the proletariat but of the whole human race as suffering under present circumstances. It can only be achieved by the working class, however, because all other classes, despite conflicts of interest between them, take their stand on the private ownership of the means of production and have as their common goal the preservation of the foundations of present-day society.

The struggle of the working class against capitalist exploitation is of necessity a political struggle. The working class cannot wage its economic struggles and develop its economic organisation without political rights. It cannot effect the switch of the means of production to common ownership without first acquiring political power.

The task of the Social Democratic Party is to mould that struggle of the working class into a conscious, uniform process and direct it towards its immutable goal.

The interests of the working class in all countries with a capitalist mode of production are the same. With the growth of world trade and production for the world market the position of workers in one country is becoming increasingly dependent on the position of workers in all other countries. The emancipation of the working class is thus a task in which the workers of all civilised countries are equally involved. Recognising this, the Social Democratic Party of Germany feels and declares itself to be one with the class-conscious workers of all other countries.

The Social Democratic Party of Germany is thus fighting not for new class privileges and prerogatives but for the abolition of class rule and of classes themselves and for equal rights and equal obligations for all without distinction of sex and birth. Armed with these opinions it campaigns in present-day society not only against the exploitation and oppression of wage workers but against every kind of exploitation and oppression, be it directed against a class, a party, a sex, or a race.

On the basis of these principles the Social Democratic Party of Germany demands firstly:

1. Universal, equal, direct suffrage with secret balloting for all German citizens of twenty and over without distinction of sex for all elections and votes. A proportional-representation system, and until that is introduced the statutory re-drawing of constituency boundaries after every census. Two-year legislative periods. Elections and votes to be held on a statutory public holiday. Remuneration of elected representatives. The abolition of any restriction of political rights except in the event of legal incapacitation.

2. Direct legislation by the people through the medium of rights of proposal and rejection. Self-determination and self-government of the people at national, state, provincial, and municipal level. The election of public authorities by the people, those authorities to be accountable and liable. An annual grant of supply.

3. Training for universal fitness to fight. A citizen army in place of the regular army. Decisions regarding war and peace to be made by parliament. All international disputes to be settled by arbitration.

4. The repeal of all laws restricting or suppressing the free expression of opinion and the right of association and combination.

5. The repeal of all laws placing women at a disadvantage in terms of public and private law as compared with men.

6. Religion to be declared a private matter. The abolition of all expenditure out of public funds for ecclesiastical and religious purposes. Ecclesiastical and religious communities to be regarded as private associations that order their affairs in complete independence.

7. Secular schooling. Compulsory attendance at public elementary schools. Free education, teaching aids, and food in public elementary schools as well as in more advanced educational institutions for those pupils whose abilities are such that they are considered suitable for higher education.

8. Free justice and legal advice. Jurisdiction by judges elected by the people. Appeal in criminal cases. Compensation for those indicted, arrested, and convicted and subsequently proved innocent. The abolition of the death penalty.

9. Free medical attention including midwifery and medication. Free burial.

10. A graduated income and property tax to defray all public expenditure where this is to be covered by taxation. Compulsory self-assessment. Death duties, graduated according to size of inheritance and degree of kinship. The abolition of all indirect taxes, duties, and other politico-economic measures that sacrifice the interests of the people as a whole to the interests of a privileged minority.

To safeguard the working class the Social Democratic Party of Germany demands firstly:

1. Effective national and international legislation for the protection of labour on the following bases: a) the standard working day to be fixed at a maximum of eight hours; b) paid labour to be prohibited for children under fourteen; c) night work to be prohibited except in those branches of industry that require it by their very nature, whether for technical reasons or for reasons of public welfare; d) a continuous break of at least thirty-six hours in each week for every worker; e) the truck system to be prohibited.

2. The supervision of all industrial and commercial establishments and the study and regulation of labour relations in town and country by national and regional departments of labour and chambers of labour. Effective industrial hygiene.

Chapter 8

Industrializing

the Nation:

Germany

and Japan

(1860–1900)

3. The same legal status for agricultural workers and domestic staff as for industrial workers; the abolition of the special regulations for servants.

4. Guaranteed right of combination.

5. The assumption of all labour insurances by the state with workers playing a decisive part in the administration of it.

Source 7 from Louis L. Snyder, The Blood and Iron Chancellor: A Documentary-Biography of Otto von Bismarck *(Princeton, N.J.: D. Van Nostrand Company, 1967), pp. 280–283.*

7. From Otto von Bismarck, Address to the Reichstag Proposing State Social Insurance, 1881

The field of legislation—justly pronounced by Deputy Richter to be one commanding a vast perspective—opened up by this measure has to do with a question which, in all probability, will not vanish from the order of the day very speedily. For the last fifty years we have been talking about the social question. Since the Socialist Law was passed, I have been repeatedly reminded, in high quarters as well as low, of the promise I then gave that something positive should be done to remove the causes of socialism. Hints of this sort have been imparted to me *toto die;* but I do not believe that our sons, or even our grandsons, will be able finally to solve the question. Indeed, no political questions can ever be mathematically settled, as books are balanced in business; they crop up, have their time, and give way to other questions propounded by history. Organic development wills that it shall be so. I consider it my duty to take up these questions without party feeling or excitement, because I know not who is to do so, if not the imperial government.

Deputy Richter has pointed out the responsibility of the state for what it is now doing. Well, gentlemen, I feel that the state should also be responsible for what it leaves undone. I am not of opinion that *laissez faire, laissez aller,* "pure Manchester policy," "everybody takes care of himself," "the weakest must go to the wall," "to him who hath shall be given, from him who hath not shall be taken even that which he hath," can be practiced in a monarchically, patriarchically governed state. . . .

For my part, I should not have the courage to proceed with this measure if the outlay it involves were to be exclusively borne by industrialists. Were state assistance, in every form now obtaining, to be cut off, I should not venture to assume the responsibility of imposing the bill upon German industry. We may limit the state subvention to a period of three years, or otherwise, as you please; but, without having made any experiment by which we can appraise what is before us, I do not feel justified in saddling our industrialists with the whole cost of these state institutions, or in burdening them more heavily than heretofore with the outlay for injured operatives that has hitherto been defrayed by local poor relief, and will at some future time be disbursed to a greater, completer, and more dignified extent by the insured themselves in partnership with the state. . . .

The invalid workman is saved from starvation by the measure we now advocate. That, however, is not sufficient to make him look forward contentedly to old age. And the bill is animated by a desire to keep alive the sense of human dignity, which I hope the poorest German will preserve, and which prescribes that he should not be forced to accept eleemosynary assistance [charity] (to which he has no right) but should be entitled to something of which nobody can dispose but himself, and of which nobody can deprive him; that doors, hitherto closed to him, should open readily when he knocks, and that better treatment should be accorded to him in his place of refuge by reason of the additional means he brings into it with him.

Whosoever has looked closely into the state of the poor in large towns, or into the arrangements made for paupers in country communes, and has seen for himself how—even in the best-managed villages—a poor wretch is sometimes treated when weakly and crippled, must admit that any healthy operative, contemplating that spectacle, is fully justified in exclaiming: "It is simply horrible that a human being should be treated worse than a dog in his own house!" I say, therefore, our first object in bringing forward this bill is to ensure kindlier treatment to this class of the poor; and next year I will do my best to give Deputy Richter full satisfaction as to the extent of the provision proposed to be made by the state for the better usage of the unemployed. For the present this measure must be regarded as an experiment—an attempt to find out the depth of the financial water into which we ask the country to plunge. . . .

An appropriate title for our enterprise would be "Practical Christianity," but we do not want to feed poor people with figures of speech, but with something solid. Death costs nothing; but unless you will put your hands in your pockets and into the state exchequer, you will not do much good. To saddle our industry with the whole affair—well, I don't know that it could bear the burden. All manufacturers are having hard times. . . .

Source 8 from the Tsuneo Tamba Collection, Yokohama/Laurie Platt Winfrey, Inc.

8. Ando Hiroshíge, Woodblock Print of Tokyo's First Railway Station, 1870s

Source 9 from David John Lu, Sources of Japanese History *(New York: McGraw-Hill Book Company, 1974), vol. 2, pp. 48–49.*

9. From Okubo Toshimichi, Recommendation on Industrialization, 1874

Generally speaking, the strength or weakness of a country is dependent on the wealth or poverty of its people, and the people's wealth or poverty derives from the amount of available products. The diligence of the people is a major factor in determining the amount of products available, but in the final analysis, it can all be traced to the guidance and encouragement given by the government and its officials. . . .

We have come to a point where all the internal conflicts have ceased, and the people can now enjoy peace and can securely engage in their respective callings. This is the most opportune time for the government and its officials to adopt a protective policy which has as its goal the enhancement of people's livelihood. . . .

Anyone who is responsible for a nation or its people must give careful consideration to the matters which can enhance the livelihood of the people, including the benefits to be gained from industrial production and the convenience derived from maritime and land transportation. He must set up a system suitable to the country's natural features and convention, taking into account the characteristics and intelligence of its people. Once that system is established it must be made the pivot of the country's administrative policies. Those industries which are already developed must be preserved, and those which are not in existence must be brought into being.

An example can be found in England which is a very small country. However, she is an island nation and has excellent harbors. She is also richly endowed with mineral resources. Her government and its officials have considered it the greatest fulfillment of their duties when they have made full use of their natural advantages, and have brought about maximum [industrial] development. In this endeavor the Queen [Victoria] and her subjects have put together their ingenuity and created an unprecedented maritime law in order to monopolize the maritime transportation of the world and to enhance her national industries. . . .

In this way her industries have prospered, and there has always been a surplus after providing the necessary commodities to her people. . . .

It is true that time, location, natural features and convention are not the same for each country, and one must not always be dazzled by the accomplishments of England and seek to imitate her blindly. . . .

However, our topography and natural conditions show similarities to those of England. What differs most is the feebleness in the temperament of our people. It is the responsibility of those who are in the administrative positions in the government to guide and importune those who are weak in spirit to work diligently in the industries and to endure them. Your subject respectfully recommends that a clear-cut plan be established to find the natural advantages we enjoy, to measure the amount by which production can be increased, and to determine the priorities under which industries may be encouraged [e.g., subsidized]. It is further recommended that the characteristics of our people and the degree of their intelligence may be taken into account in establishing legislation aimed at encouraging development of industries. Let there not be a person who is derelict in performing his work. Let there not be a fear of anyone unable to have his occupation. If these goals can be attained the people can reach a position of adequate wealth. If the people are adequately wealthy, it follows naturally that the country will become strong and wealthy. . . . If so, it will not be difficult for us to compete effectively against major powers. This has always been your subject's sincere desire. He is even more convinced of the necessity of its implementation today, and is therefore submitting humbly his recommendations for Your Majesty's august decision.

10. **Kawanabe Gyosai, Woodblock Print of Trade Fair of 1877**

Source 11 from Sources of Japanese Tradition, *compiled by Ryusaku Tsunoda, Wm. Theodore de Bary, and Donald Keene (New York: Columbia University Press, 1960), pp. 676–679.*

11. From Ito Hirobumi,
Speech at a Homecoming
Celebration, 1895

Oriental countries—China and Japan included—have the habit of holding foreign countries in contempt and of holding their own country in esteem. But in carrying on relations according to civilized standards of common justice, it is done according to a procedure of mutual equality without contempt for the other and esteem for oneself, or vice versa. . . .

From the standpoint of the sovereign power, that is, the emperor's prerogative to rule the country, the people are one and equal under the constitutional government. They are all direct subjects of the emperor. The so-called "indirect subjects" no longer exist. This means that the Japanese people have been able to raise their status and to achieve for themselves a great honor. They now have the right to share in legislative rights, which come from the emperor's sovereign powers, and to elect and send representatives. Having the right to send representatives they can, indirectly, voice their opinions on the advisability and the faults of their country's administration. Thus, every member of the nation—be he a farmer, craftsman, or merchant—must become familiar beforehand with the merits and demerits of questions of government. Not only on questions of government, but also on matters concerning his own occupation, the citizen must give due thought and become prosperous. When every man becomes wealthy, the village, the county, and the prefecture in turn become wealthy, and the accumulated total of that wealth becomes the wealth of Japan. The expansion of military strength and the promotion of national prestige depend upon the power of the individual members of the country. Therefore, in order to promote the development of military strength and national prestige, it is only proper and necessary to diffuse education so that the people can understand the changes and improvements with respect to their government and their society. In a constitutional government the occasions for secrecy are few—except for laws not yet proclaimed—in contradistinction to a despotic government. The principle of keeping the people uninformed in order to make them obedient has no place here. To inform them well so that they will serve well is the way of constitutional government. . . .

Since government is concerned with the administration of the country as a whole it does not follow that its acts are always favorable to all individuals. The nation's affairs, of their own nature, are not personal and concerned with the individual. They must be carried out according to the nation's aims, the nation's prestige, and the nation's honor. It is for this reason that the people have an obligation to understand the nation's aims. They must regard the nation as their own, meet the military obligation to defend it and to pay for the cost of defending it.

Chapter 8

Industrializing

the Nation:

Germany

and Japan

(1860–1900)

When our enlightened emperor decided to accept the open-door principle as an imperial policy . . . it became a matter of urgent necessity to develop the intellectual faculties of our people and to increase their business activities. This led to the abolition of the feudal system and made it possible for the Japanese people to live in a new political environment and to have diverse freedoms. . . . The first of these freedoms was the freedom of movement, followed by the freedom to pursue an occupation of one's own choosing. Moreover, the freedom to study at any place of one's choosing was given to all. There was also granted freedom of speech in political affairs. Thus, the Japanese today enjoy freedom, each according to his own desires, within the limits of the law. These rights belong to people who live in a civilized government. If these rights are withheld and their enjoyment refused, a people cannot develop. And if the people cannot develop, the nation's wealth and the nation's strength cannot develop. . . . But the fact is that because of the imperial policy of the open-door, we have established a government which is civilized. And as we have advanced to such a position, it has become necessary to establish a fixed definition of the fundamental laws. This, in short, is the reason for the establishment of constitutional government.

A constitutional government makes a clear distinction between the realms of the ruler and the ruled, and thereby defines what the people and the sovereign should do; that is, the rights which the sovereign should exercise and the rights which the people should enjoy, followed by the procedure for the management of the government. According to the Constitution the people have the right to participate in government, but this right is at once an important obligation as well as a right. Government is a prerogative of the emperor. As you will be participating in government—which is the emperor's prerogative—you must regard this right as the responsibility of the people, the honor of the people, and the glory of the people. It is therefore a matter of the greatest importance.

In this connection what all Japanese must bear in mind is Japan's national polity. It is history which defines the national polity; thus the Japanese people have a duty to know their history. . . . The national polity of the various countries differs one from another, but it is the testimony of the history of Japan to this day that the unification of the country was achieved around the Imperial House. So I say that the understanding of the national polity of Japan is the first important duty of our people.

In the next place we must know the aims and the policies of our country. Political parties may have their arguments, and others may have their views about the government, but they must be kept within the bounds of the aims and policies of the government. What then is the aim of the nation? It is the imperial aim decided upon at the time of the [Meiji] Restoration of imperial rule. . . . The aim of our country has been from the very beginning, to attain among the nations of the world the status of a civilized nation and to become a member of the comity of European and American nations which occupy the position of civilized countries.

12. Cartoon from *Tokyo Puck*, "Taxes Rise After the Russo-Japanese War," 1905

Source 13 from the Tsuneo Tamba Collection, Yokohama/Laurie Platt Winfrey, Inc.

13. Ichiyosai Kuniteru, Woodblock Print of an Early Japanese Silk Mill, 19th century

Source 14 from Mikiso Hane, Peasants, Rebels, and Outcastes: The Underside of Modern Japan *(New York: Pantheon, 1982), pp. 178–193 ff.*

14. Oral Records of "Crossing Nomugi Pass" to Work in the Suma Mills, ca. 1900

Where do the cheap workers come from? They all come from the farming communities. . . . People from families that are working their own land, or are engaged in tenant farming but have surplus workers, come to the cities and the industrial centers to become factory workers. . . . Income from the farms provides for the family needs and subsistence of the parents and siblings. The person who takes employment in the factory is an unattached component of the family. All he or she has to do is earn enough to maintain his or her own living. This is why the workers' wages are low. This shows how important a force agriculture is for the development of our nation's commerce and industry.

The money that the factory girls brought back by climbing over Nomugi Pass was often more than a "water-drinking" farmer's income for the entire year. For these families, the girls were an invaluable source of income. The poor peasants of those days had to turn 60 percent of their yield over to the landlord. Thus, the peasants had only broken bits of rice mixed with weeds for food. . . . The poor peasants of this region had a saying: "Shall I hang myself or cross Nomugi Pass?" These were the only alternatives they had. Their only salvation was the girls who went to work in the factories.

Nomugi Pass is where many factory girls fell down into the ravine. When someone slipped and fell down, we would untie our sashes, tie them together to make a rope, and lower it down to the person in the ravine. . . . I can't tell you how many girls died in that ravine. . . . We used to tie ourselves to the girls ahead of us so as not to get left behind. Each step of the way we prayed for our lives.

The wish to make my parents happy with the money I earned with my tears during the year . . . made me cross Nomugi Pass at the end of the year full of joyous expectations. I used to walk 85 miles over the pass in my straw sandals to come home. We didn't have mittens in those days, so we tucked our hands in our sleeves, linked ourselves together with cords, and crossed the pass.

Soon after I went to work in the Yamaichi silk factory in Shinshū [Nagano prefecture], my younger sister Aki came to work there, too. I think she worked for about two years. Then she took to bed because of peritonitis. At that time there were about thirty sick people. Those who clearly had lung trouble were sent

Chapter 8

Industrializing

the Nation:

Germany

and Japan

(1860–1900)

home right away. . . . Everybody feared tuberculosis and no one would come near such patients. My sister Aki was also sent home before long, and she died soon after. She was in her thirteenth year. She had come to the factory determined to become a 100 yen worker and make our mother happy. I can never forget her sad eyes as she left the factory wan and pale. . . . It would be impossible, I felt, for a person as sick as she was to travel over 30 *ri* or more and cross No-mugi Pass. But they would not let her stay in the factory. There was no money to send her to the hospital. There was nothing for her to do but go home.

From morning, while it was still dark, we worked in the lamplit factory till ten at night. After work, we hardly had the strength to stand on our feet. When we worked late into the night, they occasionally gave us a yam. We then had to do our washing, fix our hair, and so on. By then it would be eleven o'clock. There was no heat even in the winter, and so we had to sleep huddled together. Several of the girls ran back to Hida. I was told that girls who went to work before my time had a harder time. We were not paid the first year. In the second year I got 35 yen, and the following year, 50 yen. I felt that it was not a place for a weak-willed person like me. If we didn't do the job right we were scolded, and, if we did better than others, the others resented it. The life of a woman is really awful.

QUESTIONS TO CONSIDER

An important issue to consider as you assess the impact industrialization had on national unity in Germany and Japan is how the process intensified over time with broadening effects. The first two sources demonstrate the changing nature of industry as a result of the technological and organizational innovations of the late nineteenth century. The Hagen rolling mill shown in Source 1 shows a German iron foundry of the 1860s. It clearly belongs to an older phase of small-scale operations. Notice not only its size and rural setting but its location on a river, probably its original form of energy. Who do you think lived in the fenced-in villa on the hill? Small mills of this sort were often family-owned and -run. How would this affect relations with the workers?

Compare this facility to the early twentieth-century Krupp steel mill (Source 2). Obviously bigger, it indicates the greater complexity and urban nature of the massive industrial plants built around the turn of the century. What do these differences suggest about the changing nature of industrial production and its social impact? How would enough workers be found to operate such a mill? Where would they live and what might their lives be like in this setting? Is the lack of an adjoining villa here surprising? How might labor relations be affected by the shift to cities?

Source 3 suggests how urban mills obtained workers. These remarks by one of Germany's most renowned social scientists and liberals, Max Weber, are part of a lecture he gave in 1895. At the time, nationalistic Germans worried about Polish migrants recruited into the eastern portions of the empire by *Junker* landlords to replace German farm workers who were drifting into the cities for factory jobs. Weber uses this issue to show how the "economic dislocation" entailed by development created diversity and divisions in German society, resulting in "*power* struggles." What groups does Weber say economic development has made into rivals? How has the growth of urban industry specifically affected them? An earlier German, Karl Marx, argued that industrialization would precipitate a class war between the bourgeoisie—the middle-class professional and business people who owned and ran the factories—and the proletariat or mill hands who worked in them. Marx believed the latter would win and so dominate modern society. How does Weber think the struggle will end? Why? Who does he say should govern Germany in "the power interests of the nation"? Concern for national unity leads this acknowledged liberal to advocate a powerful state capable of decisive intervention in national life. Why?

State supervision of economic life continued to be debated in German politics during the 1890s. Source 4, a satiric cartoon of 1899, compares such oversight to contemporary efforts of the imperial government to manage recently acquired African colonies. The figures flying over the smoky industries of the Ruhr Valley represent the two chief divisions of the imperial

government, the bureaucracy and the army. Their troubled expressions are explained by the caption "Through Darkest Germany, A View Inland," an allusion to the European conceit that the interior of Africa was a dark land. What makes industrial Germany "dark," too?

Germany's industrial leaders on the whole shared the belief that development required strict control from the top down. Many thus adopted an authoritarian stance in dealing with their own subordinates and workers, equating the management of a firm with the emperor's rule over the nation and workers' obedience with patriotism. In return, some accepted responsibility for the welfare of their employees. German industrial workers of the time thus generally fared better than many others elsewhere, but salaries were often insufficient to support families. You can gain some sense of the material standard of living of German workers from Source 5, a photograph of a typical workman's home in Berlin around the turn of the century. How do their living conditions in tenement rooms like this compare to those of workers today? Notice what the women are doing. Working-class women often had to take in sewing or other handwork to supplement a meager family income. How might that have affected their role in the household—and society?

Low wages, insecurity, and the intrusive authority distressed most German industrial workers. Along with the growing number of unemployed artisans whose labor machine-made goods made obsolete, they agitated for improvement, raising the "social

Chapter 8

Industrializing

the Nation:

Germany

and Japan

(1860–1900)

question" of inequity between classes. Although hampered by the antisocialist law, working-class efforts to unionize and form parties persisted, and by 1890 the largest of the workers' parties, the Social Democrats, took control of the lower house of the Reichstag. Party leaders met the following year to draw up an idealistic program of national reforms.

Source 6 presents excerpts from this Erfurt Program. Notice how it echoes Karl Marx, rejecting not only bourgeois control of industrial wealth but even the nation's claim on its citizens' loyalty. What other group does the manifesto celebrate in place of the nation? Compare this view to Weber's argument that national interests must outweigh class interests. Look at the specific demands for improvement. What problems in the workplace does it single out for reform? What can you infer about working conditions in German industry from the grievances? The program also addresses more universal problems, declaring itself opposed to "every kind of exploitation and oppression." What does it say about sexual discrimination? How did industrialization give this issue new meaning?

The growth of the German socialist movement deeply troubled the imperial government. Bismarck tried to check the threat by a combination of tactics, restricting the party's political activity while reducing the working-class discontent that nourished it. Beginning in the 1880s, he introduced a series of state-run insurance services that by 1911 gave Germany the world's first comprehensive welfare program, a program Bismarck characterized as "state socialism." Source 7, a speech he made to the Reichstag in 1881 when first launching "social insurance," offers his rationale for it. Observe how the chancellor openly rejects socialist demands for reforms that benefit a single class as well as the liberal call for *laissez faire* policies. How does he justify government economic regulation and welfare? Bismarck assumes that the state must transcend narrow interests and protect the weak and poor. Why? What does this tell about actual national unity of the time?

Although industrialization occurred more slowly in Japan than in Germany, changes often proved more disturbing because they provoked radical cultural as well as social adjustment. What in Germany seemed merely "modern" had an alien quality in Japan, where it was also seen as "Western." Woodblock prints made in the late nineteenth century like the one reproduced as Source 8 display this discordance. The scene is a terminal on Japan's first railroad, a line built from Yokahama to Tokyo in the 1870s. Western-style structures contrast sharply with the older Japanese buildings in the background. The mix of traditional and European costumes provides another sign of acculturation. Look carefully at who wears Western clothing. People working in new industries and institutions adopted Western dress first—like the railway workers here, many of whose early customers were Europeans. Notice, too, the telegraph wires. They and the train reflect the revolution in transportation and communication that industrialization unleashed here as well as in Germany.

Unlike Germany's industrialization, which began through piecemeal private ventures launched before the birth of the modern imperial state, Japan's came through the initiative of the new Meiji regime. In Source 9, a government memorial of 1874, the oligarch Okubo Toshimichi gives its reasons. His insistence on government responsibility for national prosperity reflects traditional Confucian belief that the state must benefit the people. But his desire to seek prosperity through modern industry and transportation reveals Western ideas. Why does he single out England as a model for Japan? England's industrial wealth gave it imperial might. How would such might satisfy Okubo's desire "to compete effectively against major powers"—and reverse the humiliating unequal treaties? Given the "feebleness in the temperament" of the Japanese people Okubo notes, how does he think industrialization must be launched?

After modest state pilot projects proved the feasibility of transplanting factories to Japan, Meiji leaders decided to call attention to their efforts by hosting an industrial fair in Tokyo. Such fairs, which began in Europe earlier in the century, had become an acknowledged way of showcasing national development to the world. But Meiji oligarchs were taking a bold step in 1877 when they staged the first industrial fair held outside the West. As Source 10, a print of the fair, shows, traditional architecture and exhibits predominated, for the Japanese still had only modest industrial products to display. But they had already learned how to use the event to celebrate and strengthen national identity in Western terms. Look at the emperor, shown here riding in a foreign carriage and wearing a European military uniform. To depict him so openly and in foreign costume was very alien at the time. Can you spot other Western symbols of power combined with traditional elements to express Japanese national identity? Look at the French-style dragoons, bearing new Japanese *national* flags sporting the image of the rising sun.

Source 11 shows a similar juxtaposition of modern and traditional elements. It comes from a speech given in 1895 by Japan's first Western-style prime minister, Ito Hirobumi. Ito clearly takes pride in Japan's Western-style industrialization, but he views efforts to increase business activities and enhance national wealth first and foremost as ways to further the "imperial aim" for a stronger nation. Likewise, he credits constitutional government and popular freedoms to an imperial quest for national power and prestige rather than to the fulfillment of basic rights and claims that Japan's unique "national polity" make sovereignty "the prerogative of the emperor," not of the people. Compare his view of the state with Bismarck's. Both rejected democracies in favor of strong monarchies on the grounds that monarchies offer the unity and stability necessary for rapid development. Do you find their positions justifiable?

Chapter 8

Industrializing

the Nation:

Germany

and Japan

(1860–1900)

In 1894 new industrial might allowed Japan to defeat China, traditionally the dominant power of East Asia, and then to make a bid for regional mastery by halting Russian expansion into the area in the Russo-Japanese War of 1905. The latter victory electrified nationalists throughout Asia, as well as Japan, for it demonstrated that an industrializing non-Western nation could successfully stand up to the West. But to less nationalistic eyes, the costs of development seemed disproportionately borne. Source 12, a cartoon, depicts all the benefits derived from victory in the Russo-Japanese War: imperial advisers, members of the Diet, local officials, government suppliers, and others in positions of advantage enjoy their rewards. But the only reward presented to the average citizen is a heavy burden labeled "taxes." Look carefully at the dress of the different groups. Who appears Western and who does not? What does the cartoon suggest about the cultural and social associations of modernization in Japan?

Lack of unions and labor movements in Japan until well after the turn of the century left Japanese industrial workers especially vulnerable to exploitation, but women suffered the most. Like textile mills elsewhere, the silk mills that formed the mainstay of Japan's private industry preferred to hire women. Typically recruited as teenagers from rural areas, most lived in company dormitories under strict regulation that allowed little personal freedom, much less opportunities to organize.

A woodblock print (Source 13) shows the Spartan atmosphere of early silk factories. But far worse than the starkness of mill workers' lives was their insecurity. In Source 14, workers recall the harsh lot of rural women who crossed the local mountains through Nomugi Pass to find work in the mills of Okaya near the turn of the century. "Crossing Nomugi Pass" meant more than just traversing a geographic boundary. What was life like for these Japanese working women? What explains their willingness to accept such conditions? Even after the passage of the 1911 Factory Act to reform conditions, Japanese women continued to labor in circumstances that were among the harshest in the industrial world. Moreover, the Meiji regime created no government welfare programs like Germany's regarding such care as the obligation of the family, not the state. But who helped these women in their need?

EPILOGUE

Germany's entry into World War I in 1914 proved disastrous to its industrial growth. Social tensions, intensified by wartime strains, brought a revolution in 1918 that toppled the monarchy and forced acceptance of a humiliating peace. Liberals attempted to construct a democracy out of the ruins of the empire, but the Weimar Republic they created failed to restore Germany's former prosperity and prestige. Nearly bankrupted by war indemnities and the deteriorating postwar international economy, Germany suffered a lack of capital during the 1920s that hindered industrial growth and unleashed damaging inflation. When the Great Depression of the early 1930s brought massive unemployment and new social unrest, the demoralized nation repudiated liberal leadership, turning instead to Adolf Hitler, whose Nazi Party advocated drastic reform under a fascist dictatorship. Hitler's militaristic policies, however, turned a brief industrial recovery into an even greater debacle, for he led Germany to a defeat in World War II marked by total industrial collapse and partition. Not until the 1950s did the divided postwar parts of West and East Germany begin to recover a measure of their former industrial prosperity.

Unlike Germany, Japan profited from World War I. As first European and then American industry turned to war production, Japan found new markets for its own manufactures, particularly in Asia. Having sided with the Allies, Japan was able to seize most of Germany's Asian and Pacific possessions. While the war thus weakened European nations, it left Japan wealthier and stronger than ever. With confidence born of this success, its leaders allowed a shift to true parliamentary rule following the death of the Meiji emperor in 1912. By the 1920s, competing liberal parties began to democratize the country. But social conflict at home and worsening

conditions in the world led critics, especially in the army, to discredit them. When the worldwide Depression intensified social turmoil, army officers began to undermine civilian rule. In the name of preserving domestic harmony and fending off a revival of Western power in Asia, they slowly took control of the government, disbanding the Diet in 1941 and instituting a formal military dictatorship. Hopes of destroying Anglo-American power in Asia led them to ally with Germany in World War II, and like Germany, Japan experienced defeat and economic collapse in 1945. Ruled and rebuilt under American military occupation from 1945 to 1952, Japan, too, was unable to restore its shattered industries until the 1950s.

Despite great initial gains, then, neither nation unequivocally benefited from industrialization. The very development that initially made them so successful may actually have weakened them. Their governments, though claiming to manage economic change in the interest of the nation as a whole, failed to protect many citizens from the effects of that change, leaving them vulnerable and afraid. In the end, that failure left them open to assault from the left and right. Thus modern Germany and Japan may have ultimately foundered upon the kind of power struggles Weber warned would arise from such economic development. Was this the fault of industrialization itself—or their inability to deal effectively with the divisions and tensions it created?

CHAPTER NINE

MODERNITY: FROM PROMISE

TO THREAT (1790–1930)

THE PROBLEM

In his 1921 poem "The Second Coming," the Irish poet William Butler Yeats voiced the dread that many felt as the violence of twentieth-century war and upheaval overtook their lives:

Turning and turning in the widening gyre
The falcon cannot hear the falconer;
Things fall apart; the center cannot hold;
Mere anarchy is loosed upon the world,
The blood-dimmed tide is loosed, and everywhere
The ceremony of innocence is drowned;
The best lack all conviction, while the worst
Are filled with passionate intensity.[1]

1. *The Norton Anthology of Poetry,* 3rd ed. (New York and London: W. W. Norton and Company, 1983), p. 883.

Part of a growing chorus of intellectual discontent, Yeats's lines reflected a widespread fear in the early decades of the twentieth century that the modern world was heading toward some dire catastrophe. This apprehension stood in sharp contrast to the views prevailing in the previous two centuries, at least in the West, where most people welcomed the modern age as the dawn of a better time. With this change in attitude, the characteristic features of this new era, features that had once been associated with improvement and progress, came to be seen as menacing. What had been once exalted as a promise of better life now seemed a threat to many people.

This chapter explores what lay behind this shift in attitudes. It does so by looking at some classic statements about the nature of modern identity, or "modernity," that date from the late eighteenth to the early twentieth century. The earlier pieces reveal a very optimistic view of modern change.

The later ones, in contrast, are more critical and even pessimistic. Your task is to trace the change in opinion that they show and to ask what direction it took. In doing so, think about the following three questions. First, what does each document consider to be the most important or defining features of modernity? Second, which of these features initially seemed to promise improvement, and of what? Third, which proved to have effects other than those predicted? That is, what changes either failed to bring the anticipated benefits or led to unexpected problems?

In analyzing how people of the past understood modernity, you will be playing the role of an intellectual historian who studies how certain views or ideas developed over time and influenced society. In this case, of course, the concept in question was special, for it shaped people's perception of a key historical period. By looking at what people took to be the characteristic traits of modernity, you should gain some insight into what they thought gave the modern era a distinct identity and distinguished it from other times.

The concept of a unique modern character or identity did more than just shape people's perception of a single age. It played an important role in the way modern Western historians "periodized" history, or divided it into meaningful eras for study. Convinced that distinct new trends in their own times marked the end of antiquity, early modern historians began to divide the study of history into two broad periods, ancient and modern, and view it in terms of a development from one to the other. Later historians, finding the centuries between these periods largely intermediate or medial in nature, named these centuries the Middle or Medieval Age. Thus the idea of a unique, modern identity not only influenced the way moderns looked at themselves and their own time, but inspired a broad historical framework that affects the way we view the whole of the past. Clearly, then, the idea of modernity holds a special place in the study of history.

BACKGROUND

Though aspects of modernity can be traced back to Renaissance Europe, it was the Scientific Revolution in the sixteenth and seventeenth centuries that nurtured a distinctly modern outlook. Intellectuals in Western Europe began to question traditional knowledge and the ways it had been acquired. Convinced that they had found a new "mode" of experiencing reality, they began to call themselves "moderns" (i.e., those in the new mode), in contrast to the more traditionally minded, whom they termed "ancients." From the start, then, *modernity* implied a special historical outlook, one assuming a sharp break with the past caused by a unique perspective.

The work of Isaac Newton proved decisive to the new outlook. In his *Mathematical Principles of Natural Philosophy* of 1684, this Englishman provided a new, mathematical model of the universe, portraying it as a materialistic world of mindless bodies coursing in regular motions according to inflexible laws of nature. Even more important, he claimed to have developed this model through a new "scientific method" of interpreting nature based on inductive empiricism, a system of inferring knowledge from evidence that can be seen or touched through the senses. Together his model and his method laid the foundation for modern science. They also inspired a broader intellectual shift, for thinkers outside the natural sciences began to believe that the scientific method could disclose social and ethical truths as well as natural facts. A burst of speculation thus followed the Scientific Revolution, and after another Englishman, John Locke, adapted Newton's method for social analysis in his 1690 *Essay Concerning Human Understanding*, new "social sciences" arose as potential tools for improving humanity.

Europe's educated elite quickly embraced both the new sciences and the scientific method. With them, many concluded, reason could unlock Nature's secrets and enhance life materially while improving social conditions. Many Europeans thus welcomed the start of the eighteenth century with great optimism, convinced that a new "age of reason" was dawning—that, as Immanuel Kant was to put it in 1784, "an age of enlightenment" had begun. Fear of change, which had been nearly universal in other eras, now gave way to welcoming change, for in a constantly improving world,

the future would always be better. From this view came the idea of "progress" based on the belief that humans were advancing in a continuous process of improvement. Where earlier people had looked to the past for inspiration, moderns now began to exalt the future.

The confidence of the age inspired intellectual leaders, known by the French term *philosophes*, to advocate an ambitious program of social and political reform. François Marie de Voltaire (1694–1778), boldly pronounced humans to be inherently good. Crime and poverty, he said, arose from social and economic circumstances that blighted good impulses, not from inborn sin. To do away with evil, society had only to eliminate the underlying causes: sickness, poverty, and injustice. Thus the *philosophes* called for a reform of harsh laws, an end to cruel punishments, more charity for the poor, and more compassion for the lower social strata and less advantaged groups like women and children.

In presuming that people would take responsibility for their own improvement, Enlightenment hopes inspired new interest in the self, which eventually led to a doctrine of individualism. Appreciation of individual uniqueness and worth led logically to the idea that all people deserved respect. From this idea evolved a doctrine of rights asserting that *all* humans had claims—such as to life, liberty, and property—that none could deny. John Locke had pioneered this view in 1690, arguing that because people formed governments to secure civil rights, no government could rescind those rights. The *philosophes* developed the idea further, claiming that all people were endowed by nature with inalienable "human rights" that no one could legitimately violate. This belief in equality of endowment in turn encouraged the idea that wealth and power should be more evenly distributed in society to ensure that all people had the opportunity to realize their birthright. Politically, these ideas promoted interest in democratic governments in which the whole populace would have a say in public decisions, leading to demands for constitutional protection of rights and for elected assemblies.

By the end of the eighteenth century, Enlightenment ideas had crystallized into classical liberalism, a system of thought—and eventually a political movement—dedicated to social betterment through the liberation of individual potential. Deeming individuals the basic unit of society, liberals called for more personal freedom and pressed for constitutional curbs on arbitrary power. Their ideal was a society of autonomous citizens in which the pursuit of rational self-interest brought about the good of all. Adam Smith (1723–1790) adapted these ideas to economic life with a parallel vision of free markets in which the pursuit of individual profit secured the most gain for all. Though at first hopeful that rulers would voluntarily enact their program, liberals grew increasingly frustrated by the indifference and opposition they encountered.

In the last third of the eighteenth century, pent-up popular frustrations exploded, sending tides of revolution across much of the Western world, from Poland to Europe's new Ameri-can colonies. Initial stirrings in Geneva in 1768 and England's North American colonies in 1776 were followed by the French Revolution in 1789, an event that rocked the foundations of the Western world. Under Republican and then Napoleonic leadership, the French armies spread radical ideas across Europe, unleashing decades more of secondary revolutions until these ended with a final round of violence in 1848. Eighty years of revolutionary change and warfare altered Western Europe socially and politically, leaving most of its new leaders committed to Enlightenment ideals and the liberal agenda of making a better world through human emancipation and material improvement.

While political revolution was sweeping across the West, a parallel economic revolution was also taking place. Known as the Industrial Revolution, it entailed the rise of mechanized industries capable of pouring out a vast supply of cheap goods and opening mass markets. Begun in England in the late 1700s with the mechanization of textile making, it soon spread across Western Europe and North America. By the early 1800s, the introduction of steam-driven ships and then of railroads propelled it to a new phase, stimulating growth in coal and steel production while lowering transport costs for all goods. By 1850 England was far enough along in this revolution to gain the title "workshop of the world" and win recognition as the first truly industrial nation. But by then other countries like the United States, France, and Belgium were catching up with it, and basic mechanization was spreading to central and northern Europe. And by the end of the nineteenth century, Japan and Russia were also industrializing.

Industrial growth dramatically altered social patterns. Millions left agriculture for the towns where the new industries were located, bringing rapid urbanization and the rise of huge new cities. These cities provided unprecedented opportunities for advancement, and successful men of business joined traditional commercial and professional groups in an affluent new middle class or *bourgeoisie,* as the French termed it. But most migrants into the cities did not do as well; they joined the industrial working class as mill hands, transport workers, or domestic servants. Wages for such people stayed low and working conditions poor, because their numbers made replacement easy. Women and children especially suffered, for they were paid less and often worked harder than men. The laboring poor, like the unemployed and destitute, often lived in appalling conditions that fostered violence and crime. Yet industrial cities continued to attract newcomers from the countryside because they inspired hope for advancement.

Such cities came to be identified with change. Political revolutions and legal reform had shattered the old corporate, hierarchical nature of Western society, in which people derived their roles, identity, and security from hereditary status in closed groups. In doing so, they eliminated many barriers to geographic and social mobility, freeing people to move in search of better lives. This shift to an open society made the massive migrations into the industrial cities possible in the first place. Then, because people found greater freedom to choose residences, work, and mates in the anonymity of the cities, they seemed less restrictive than the countryside and came to be associated closely with change and modernity. Heightened personal freedom in the new cities also encouraged newly emerging urban groups to press for a greater political say in their societies.

The middle class was the first to succeed. By the early 1830s, as the upper bourgeoisie assumed dominance in a restored French monarchy and the Whig party won control of the British Parliament, a new era of middle-class rule began in Western Europe. Adopting liberalism as their own, middle-class leaders in these countries launched ambitious reforms, inspiring a slow spread of the liberal program across Europe during the mid-nineteenth century. These reforms helped to deflect the rival challenge of working-class groups that arose with the revolutions of 1848 and the cries of radical new thinkers like Karl Marx urging workers to overthrow the existing order. Under pressure from middle-class reformers, rudimentary poor relief and welfare programs were begun and free public schools started. Combined with falling prices made possible by technological advances in the decades after the 1870s, these reforms eased the worst of working-class conditions and afforded workers, too, real hope for a better life. Led by the moderate socialist and labour parties to which they then turned, they also broadened the political franchise; there was universal male suffrage in nearly all industrial states by the early twentieth century.

By then the industrial world was becoming home to "mass society." Expanded manufacturing and agricultural output, improved material conditions, and enhanced public health brought a surge in population that came to be concentrated in the new industrial centers. This trend led in turn to new levels of mass activity in all spheres of modern life. Sprawling plants and towering office buildings replaced small workplaces, requiring the development of mass transit to move large numbers of people between their homes and work. Huge department stores and giant markets crowded out family shops, laying the foundation of a new mass consumerism. Burgeoning popular amusements, from cheap newspapers and dime novels to dance halls and theaters, nurtured the growth of new mass media. And unions and political parties mobilized millions into new mass organizations. But what distinguished mass society more than its numbers was the lack of distinction between its members. The changes that had freed and leveled individuals had also homogenized them into an indistinguishable mass of ordinary or "common men."

Although most concentrated in the industrial nations of the West, these changes had begun to have an effect on the rest of the world by the second half of the nineteenth century. Many industrial nations lacked the domestic resources to sustain their new economies and had to export manufactured goods to obtain needed foodstuffs and raw materials. To increase the supply of such imports, they invested in agricultural and extractive industries abroad, drawing nonindustrial areas into a new integrated and interdependent world economy. This trend increased after the 1880s, when many industrial nations sought to demonstrate their new national power by annexing territories and seizing distant lands as colonies, justifying this on the grounds that they were helping the people of these lands advance. Thus, those outside the industrialized West who failed to embrace "modern civilization" quickly, like the Japanese, soon found it imposed upon them as colonial subjects. Where it was imposed from above, however, modernity conveyed a sense of bondage and despair rather than the emancipation and hope with which it was originally associated.

The devastating wars and economic dislocation of the early twentieth century created an even greater disillusionment with modernity in the West. The Great War—as World War I was then called—proved especially upsetting. During that conflict, which raged from 1914 to 1918, mechanized mass warfare first came of age, and the millions of ordinary citizens drafted to fight were deeply disturbed by the carnage that resulted. At the war's end, many tried to escape in the gaiety of the cabarets and speakeasies associated with the short-lived Jazz Age of the 1920s. But the after tremors of the war, which took the form of revolutions and political reversals in all the advanced industrial countries, made it impossible to regain lost confidence. Once again change seemed uncertain and threatening.

Works as diverse as Oswald Spengler's postwar treatise *The Decline of* the West and T. S. Eliot's 1922 poem "The Waste Land" portrayed modern culture as a decadent final stage of Western civilization. Their authors found its machines and masses emblems of despair, not hope. Out of such views developed a radically new approach to art and literature called *modernism*. Despite its name, this movement rejected modern optimism concerning progress. Its vision of a fragmented and shallow society instead reflected a profound sense of pessimism and a disillusionment with Enlightenment beliefs about human perfectibility. The growing mood of despair also nurtured the rise of radical political movements that promised a return to security through drastic political and economic programs. Many of these, like the Fascists in Europe, the Communists in Russia, and the ultra-nationalists of Japan, openly assailed liberalism and its doctrines of individualism and democracy, denouncing them as sources of decay and collapse.

Yet some found new freedom in the postwar era. Western youth took advantage of the uncertainty of the time to reject long-standing age constraints and launch a revolution in sexuality. Women in the West also benefited from the growing distrust of authority, winning the vote for themselves and beginning a feminist revolution aimed at breaking down old gender barriers. And in colonial lands, new leaders began to challenge imperial rule and talk of national liberation. These groups infused new vitality into the promise of modernity. But their efforts were soon eclipsed by the worldwide economic collapse that ushered in the Great Depression of the 1930s and the subsequent rise of authoritarian movements in key industrial states like Germany and Japan. By the time World War II erupted at the decade's end, life appeared to be growing morally and materially grimmer by the day, making modernity seem more menace than promise.

THE METHOD

The problem posed here requires you to think about both what modernity originally seemed to promise and what went wrong with that promise. So first look through the evidence for statements in praise of specific aspects of modernity, and then review it for negative comments. The initial sources generally view modernity in positive terms, whereas later ones become increasingly harsh. But guard against the simple assumption that they embrace or reject modernity outright. Many who have looked long and carefully at the idea of modernity have remarked on its ambiguity. As one writer notes, modernity is inherently paradoxical:

There is a mode of vital experience—experience of space and time, of the self and others, of life's possibilities and perils—that is shared by men and women all over the world today. I will call this body of experience "modernity." To be modern is to find ourselves in an environment that promises adventure, power, joy, growth, transformation of ourselves and the world—and, at the same time, that threatens to destroy everything we have, everything we know, everything we are.[2]

Rather than just asking whether a given source extols or denounces modernity, see what aspects of modernity it regards as most important and how it reacts to each of these. Jot these down along with some notes about why the source deems each a promise or a threat—or both. See how many of the same features reappear in different sources: They will provide a rough list of what people of the past understood modernity to entail. Then review your notes, paying attention to how each source reacted to these different aspects. Does any pattern emerge? Are some aspects universally deplored and others universally praised? Or are reactions to them mixed?

A number of defining traits, like a scientific outlook, will be easy to find because they will be explicitly cited. But others that are less obvious, may be of equal significance. Notice in the above quotation the reference to a unique modern experience of space and time and of the self and others. Being modern involves accepting certain assumptions about time and history; without knowing them, you cannot fully understand what such modern words as *revolution* and *progress* imply. Modernity also entails spatial connotations. Certain places seem more modern than others, inducing people to see

landscapes and even the world itself as structured in special ways. Pay attention to which locales, globally and regionally, are presumed to be modern and which are not. Modern ideas of self and society similarly entail unspoken assumptions. Note how concern for individualism affects attitudes about personal and community values. In short, look beyond the obvious features of modernity for underlying beliefs and assumptions associated with it.

The Progress of the Human Mind, (Source 1) is an excellent one to begin with for this purpose. Written in 1794 in the midst of the French Revolution by Jean Antoine Nicholas de Condorcet, it reveals the basic beliefs of the Enlightenment. In it, Condorcet presents the idea of history as a process of development and describes what he expects the final stage to be: an age of science and reason, during which humanity frees itself from Nature and folly alike. In doing so, he reveals key Enlightenment assumptions about time, progress, and the world as well as its optimism about the inevitability of attaining human perfection through intellectual and ethical improvement. Contrast this view of progress with that in Source 2, an editorial from the British journal *The Economist*. Inspired by a great world fair held in London in 1851 to celebrate Britain's new industrial status, it shifts the focus of progress to technical and material gains.

Source 3, "Years of the Modern," a poem written by Walt Whitman around 1865, also lauds technology. But it does so on the grounds that machines have freed the "average man"

2. Marshall Berman, *All That Is Solid Melts into Air: The Experience of Modernity* (London: Verso, 1982), p. 53.

to reach hitherto unattainable goals, giving a distinctly American, democratic coloring to the idea of progress. A very different view appears in Source 4, a pamphlet called *Socialism: Utopian and Scientific,* written by Karl Marx's colleague and patron, Friedrich Engels, and first published in 1880. Critiquing modern industrial society from a Marxist perspective, Engels stresses the "crying social abuses" of early industrialization, claiming that, far from benefiting ordinary men, mechanization led to their subjugation and exploitation by the bourgeois class.

The next two sources offer even more caustic views of modernity from the vantage point of other disaffected groups. Source 5, Gandhi's *Hind Swaraj* or *Indian Self-rule,* written in 1909 while he was experimenting with passive resistance against British rule in South Africa, gives a scathing critique of modern civilization from the perspective of those under colonial dominion. But in seeking a better civilization that would revere morality and intellect rather than materialism—while emancipating millions from unjust rule—Gandhi echoes some of the cherished goals of the Enlightenment. *Woman and Labour,* Source 6, looks at modern civilization from a feminist point of view. The author, Olive Schreiner, was a South African novelist of European descent who became active in what she termed the "Woman's Movement," seeking equality between men and women. Deep concerns about the social and psychological costs of modernity led her in this 1911 book to attribute women's plight not to men but rather to the "social disco-ordination" of mod-

ern life, which left both "tortured" amid material plenty.

Source 7, "A Declaration of Beliefs by the *New Youth,*" shows, however, that others outside the West remained enthusiastic about modernity as the new century began. A radical periodical founded in 1915 by students at Beijing University, *New Youth* sought to introduce modern ideas and values into China. Many contributors became leading intellectuals and revolutionaries in the struggle to modernize China, including those who founded the Chinese Communist Party in 1921. But as this 1919 article indicates, its editors espoused a liberal, not Marxist, agenda in their efforts "to cultivate a new spirit for our times, a spirit more conducive to the creation of a new society."

Postwar European intellectuals, by contrast, were losing interest in this agenda. Source 8, stills from a famous early German film, *Metropolis,* illustrates one direction this disillusionment took. Directed by Fritz Lang, who was influenced by German Expressionist art and socialist ideals, this 1927 film projects a sinister view of modern urban life. It depicts a fictional city as a dehumanized world in which a small technocratic elite uses machines to keep the masses subject to their will. An equally negative view colors Source 9, from José Ortega y Gasset's 1930 book, *The Revolt of the Masses.* A liberal intellectual and leader of the Spanish Republican movement, Ortega also decries modern mass, technocratic society. But in his case, it is because he thinks it allows ordinary people to dominate, not because it enslaves them. Deeming popular culture shallow and the values of the "common man" cowardly, he fears that mass, industrial society has abandoned Enlightenment ideals and marks a decline rather than an advance in historical development.

Although European intellectuals may have been despairing over the lost promise of modernity in the postwar era, others outside of Europe still found it—or at least most of it—attractive. Indeed, for the rising generation of Asian and African nationalists, modernization of their peoples had become a largely unquestioned goal. Source 10, excerpts from a book by Jawaharlal Nehru, the future first prime minister

of India, illustrates their continued interest in the modern agenda. At the time he wrote these passages in 1933, Nehru was serving time in a British jail for his efforts to bring about Indian independence, hardly a time of great personal or national success. Yet this work, which he wrote as a series of letters to his daughter to help him fill idle hours in prison, affirms his unshaken belief in the modern idea of human progress toward a better future. For him, as for so many other non-Western leaders, Europe's postwar faltering seems less an obstacle than an opportunity to grasp that future.

THE EVIDENCE

Source 1 from Introduction to Contemporary Civilization in the West *(New York: Columbia University Press, 1946), pp. 1059–1067.*

1. From Jean Antoine Nicholas de Condorcet, *The Progress of the Human Mind*

TENTH EPOQUE: FUTURE PROGRESS OF MANKIND

Will not every nation one day arrive at the state of civilization attained by those people who are most enlightened, most free, most exempt from prejudices, as the French, for instance, and the Anglo-Americans? Will not the slavery of countries subjected to kings, the barbarity of African tribes, and the ignorance of savages gradually vanish? Is there upon the face of the globe a single spot the inhabitants of which are condemned by nature never to enjoy liberty, never to exercise their reason? . . .

In a word, will not men be continually verging towards that state, in which all will possess the requisite knowledge for conducting themselves in the common affairs of the life by their own reason, and of maintaining that reason uncontaminated by prejudices; in which they will understand their rights, and exercise them, according to their opinion and their conscience; in which all will be able, by the development of their faculties, to procure the certain means of providing for their wants; lastly, in which folly and wretchedness will be accidents, happening only now and then, and not the habitual lot of a considerable portion of society?

In fine, may it not be expected that the human race will be meliorated by new discoveries in the sciences and the arts, and, as an unavoidable consequence, in the means of individual and general prosperity; by farther progress in the principles of conduct, and in moral practice; and lastly, by the real improvement of our faculties, moral, intellectual and physical, which may be the result either of the improvement of the instruments which increase the power and direct the exercise of those faculties, or of the improvement of our natural organization itself? . . .

The advantages that must result from the state of improvement, of which I have proved we may almost entertain the certain hope, can have no limit but the absolute perfection of the human species, since, in proportion as different kinds of equality shall be established as to the various means of providing for our wants, as to a more universal instruction, and a more entire liberty, the more real will be this equality, and the nearer will it approach towards embracing everything truly important to the happiness of mankind. . . .

By applying these general reflections to the different sciences, we might exhibit, respecting each, examples of this progressive improvement, which would remove all possibility of doubts as to the certainty of the further improvement that may be expected. . . .

If we pass to the progress of the arts, those arts particularly the theory of which depends on these very same sciences, we shall find that it can have no inferior limits; that their processes are susceptible of the same improvement, the same simplifications, as the scientific methods; that instruments, machines, looms, will add every day to the capabilities and skill of man—will augment at once the excellence and precision of his works, while they will diminish the time and labour necessary for executing them. . . .

In short, does not the well-being, the prosperity, resulting from the progress that will be made by the useful arts, in consequence of their being founded upon a sound theory, resulting, also, from an improved legislation, built upon the truths of the political sciences, naturally dispose men to humanity, to benevolence, and to justice? Do not all the observations, in fine, which we proposed to develop in this work prove, that the moral goodness of man, the necessary consequence of his organization, is, like all his other faculties, susceptible of an indefinite improvement? and that nature has connected, by a chain which cannot be broken, truth, happiness, and virtue?

Among those causes of human improvement that are of most importance to the general welfare, must be included, the total annihilation of the prejudices which have established between the sexes an inequality of rights, fatal even to the party which it favours. In vain might we search for motives by which to justify this principle, in difference of physical organization, of intellect, or of moral sensibility. It had at first no other origin but abuse of strength, and all the attempts which have since been made to support it are idle sophisms.

The people being more enlightened, and having resumed the right of disposing for themselves of their blood and their treasure, will learn by degrees to regard war as the most dreadful of all calamities, the most terrible of all crimes. . . .

The organic perfectibility or deterioration of the classes of the vegetable, or species of the animal kingdom, may be regarded as one of the general laws of nature.

This law extends itself to the human race; and it cannot be doubted that the progress of the sanative art, that the use of more wholesome food and more comfortable habitations, that a mode of life which shall develop the physical powers by exercise, without at the same time impairing them by excess; in fine, that the destruction of the two most active causes of deterioration, penury and wretchedness on the one hand, and enormous wealth on the other, must necessarily tend to prolong the common duration of man's existence, and secure him a more constant health and a more robust constitution. It is manifest that the improvement of the practice of medicine, become more efficacious in consequence of the progress of reason and the social order, must in the end put a period to transmissible or contagious disorders, as well as to those general maladies resulting from climate, ailments, and the nature of certain occupations. Nor would it be difficult to prove that this hope might be extended to almost every other malady, of which it is probable we shall hereafter discover the most remote causes. . . .

Lastly, may we not include in the same circle the intellectual and moral faculties? May not our parents, who transmit to us the advantages or defects of their conformation, and from whom we receive our features and shape, as well as our propensities to certain physical affections, transmit to us also that part of organization upon which intellect, strength of understanding, energy of soul or moral sensibility depend? Is it not probable that education, by improving these qualities, will at the same time have an influence upon, will modify and improve this organization itself? Analogy, an investigation of the human faculties, and even some facts appear to authorise these conjectures, and thereby to enlarge the boundary of our hopes.

Such are the questions with which we shall terminate the last division of our work. And how admirably calculated is this view of the human race, emancipated from its chains, released alike from the dominion of chance, as well as from that of the enemies of its progress, and advancing with a firm and inedviate step in the paths of truth, to console the philosopher lamenting the errors, the flagrant acts of injustice, the crimes with which the earth is still polluted? It is the contemplation of this prospect that rewards him for all his efforts to assist the progress of reason and the establishment of liberty. . . .

Source 2 from The Economist, *Vol. IX, (January 18, 1851), pp. 57–58.*

2. "The First Half of the Nineteenth Century Progress of the Nation, and the Race"

The close of one half-century and the commencement of another offer to us one of those resting places in the march of time which, whenever they occur, at shorter or longer intervals, impressively summon us to the task of retrospect and reflection. "The poorest moment that passes over us is the conflux of two eternities;" we are, it is true, at every moment standing on the narrow isthmus that divides the great ocean of durations ground that, even as we name it, is washed from beneath our feet; but it is only at the termination of the longer epochs by which our life is told off into the past, that we fully feel this truth. At such times it is well to pause for a brief space amid the struggle and the race of life, to consider the rate of our progress and the direction of our course, to measure our distance from the starting-post in relation to the advantages with which we set out and the time we have spent upon the road, and to calculate, as far as may be, the probable rapidity of our future advance in a career to which there is no goal.

Too many of us are disposed to place our Golden Age in the Past: this is especially the tendency of the imaginative, the ignorant, the indolent, and the old. To such it is soothing to turn from the dry and disappointing labours of the present and the hot and dusty pathways of the actual world, and to speculate on that early spring-time of our Race in which Fancy, without toil or hindrance, can construct a Utopia of which History affords us no trace, and which Logic assures us could have had no existence. Another and a larger class are ever prone to seek a refuge from baffled exertions, disappointed hopes, and dissatisfied desires, in a distant Future in which all expectations, reasonable or unreasonable, are to have their fulfilment: But nearly everybody agrees by common consent to undervalue and abuse the present. We confess that we cannot share their disappointment, nor echo their complaints. We look upon the Past with respect and affection as a series of steppingstones, to that high and advanced position which we actually hold and from the Future we hope for the realisation of those dreams, almost of perfectibility, which a comparison of the Past with the present entitles us to indulge in. But we see no reason to be discontented either with our rate of progress or with the actual stage which we have reached; and we think that man must be hard to please who, with due estimate of human powers and human aims, and a full knowledge of the facts which we propose concisely to recall to the recollection of our readers, can come to a different conclusion.

Economists are supposed to be, by nature and occupation, cold, arithmetical, and unenthusiastic. We shall not, we hope, do discredit to this character when we say that we consider it a happiness and a privilege to have had our lot cast in the first fifty years of this century. For not only has that period been rich beyond nearly all others in political events of thrilling interest and mighty moments, but in changes and incidents of moral and social significance it has had no parallel since the Christian era. It has witnessed the most tremendous war and the most enduring peace which we have known for centuries. It has beheld the splendid career and the sad retribution reverses of the greatest conqueror, scourge, and upsetter of old arrangements, since the days of Gengis-Khan, Attila, or Charlemagne. It has witnessed a leap forward in all the elements of material well-being such as neither scientific vision nor poetic fancy ever pictured. It is not too much to say that, in wealth, in the arts of life, in the discoveries of science and their application to the comfort, the health, the safety, and the capabilities of man, in public and private morality, in the diffusion if not in the advancement of knowledge, in the sense of social charity and justice, in religious freedom, and in political wisdom, the period of the last fifty years has carried us forward faster and further than any other half-century in modern times. It stands at the head, *facile princeps,* unrivalled and unapproached, of all epochs of equal duration. Nay, more; it is scarcely too much to say that, in many of the particulars we have enumerated, it has witnessed a more rapid and astonishing progress than all the centuries which have preceded it. In several vital points the difference between the 18th and the 19th century, is greater than between the first and the 18th, as far as civilized Europe is concerned.

As we proceed we shall have occasion to justify this statement in several particulars; but if in the meantime it should seem too startling to any reader, we would ask him to compare Macaulay's celebrated picture of the state of England under the Stuarts with its condition at the close of the last century; and then to compare this last with its condition now; and he will be amazed to find how nearly all those details of its astonishing advance which most bear upon the comforts and welfare of his daily life, are the produce of the last fifty years. The fact is, that the 18th and the last half of the 17th centuries, being a period of nearly incessant war or of perpetual internal strife, were not marked by any decided progress in the arts of civilization, though during the latter portion of the time wealth appears to have increased faster than population, and comfort and plenty to have been, in consequence, more widely diffused. Compare the year 1800 with the year 1650, and we shall find the roads almost as bad everywhere, except near the metropolis; the streets nearly as ill-lighted and not much more safe at night; sanitary matters as much neglected; prisons only less pestilential and ill-arranged; the criminal law as sanguinary, vindictive, and inconsistent; bull and bear-baiting nearly as favourite amusements, and intemperance among the higher classes almost as prevalent; locomotion scarcely more rapid or more pleasant, and the transmission of letters not much less tedious and not at all less costly.

But perhaps the best way of realising to our conceptions the actual progress of the last half-century would be to fancy ourselves suddenly transported back to the year 1800, with all our habits, expectations, requirements and standard of living formed upon the luxuries and appliances collected round us in the year 1850. In the first year of the century we should find ourselves eating bread at 1s 10-½d the quartern loaf, and those who could not afford this price driven to short commons, to entire abstinence, or to some miserable substitute. We should find ourselves grumbling at heavy taxes laid on nearly all the necessaries and luxuries of life—even upon salt; blaspheming at the high prices of coffee, tea, and sugar, which confined these articles, in any adequate abundance, to the rich and the easy classes of society; paying twofold for our linen shirts, threefold for our flannel petticoats, and above fivefold for our cotton handkerchiefs and stockings; receiving our newspapers seldom, poverty-stricken, and some days after date; receiving our Edinburgh letters in London a week after they were written, and paying thirteenpence halfpenny for them when delivered; exchanging the instantaneous telegraph for the slow and costly express by chaise and four; travelling with soreness and fatigue by the "old heavy," at the rate of seven miles an hour, instead of by the Great Western at fifty; and relapsing from the blaze of light which gas now pours along our streets, into a perilous and uncomfortable darkness made visible by a few wretched oil lamps scattered at distant intervals.

But these would by no means comprise the sum total, nor the worst part of the descent into barbarism. We should find our criminal law in a state worthy of Draco; executions taking place by the dozen; the stealing of five shillings punishable and punished as severely as rape or murder; slavery and the slave trade flourishing in their palmiest atrocity. We should find the liberty of the subject at the lowest ebb; freedom of discussion and writing always in fear and frequently in jeopardy; religious rights trampled under foot; Catholics, slaves and not citizens; Dissenters still disabled and despised. Parliament was unreformed; public jobbing flagrant and shameless; gentlemen drank a bottle where they now drink a glass, and measured their capacity by their cups; and the temperance medal was a thing undreamed of. Finally, the *people* in those days were little thought of, where they are now the main topic of discourse and statesmanship; steam-boats were unknown, and a voyage to America occupied eight weeks instead of ten days; and while in 1850, a population of nearly 30,000,000 paid 50,000,000 £ of taxes, in 1801 a population of 15,000,000 paid not less than 63,000,000 £.

Source 3 from Walt Whitman: Complete Poetry and Collected Prose *(New York: Library of America, 1982), pp. 597–598.*

3. Walt Whitman, "Years of the Modern"

Years of the modern! years of the unperform'd!
Your horizon rises, I see it parting away for more august dramas,
I see not America only, not only Liberty's nation but other nations preparing,
I see tremendous entrances and exits, new combinations, the solidarity of races,
I see that force advancing with irresistible power on the world's stage,

(Have the old forces, the old wars, played their parts? are the acts suitable to
  them closed?)
I see Freedom, completely arm'd and victorious and very haughty, with Law
  on one side and Peace on the other,
A stupendous trio all issuing forth against the idea of caste;
What historic denouements are these we so rapidly approach?
I see men marching and countermarching by swift millions,
I see the frontiers and boundaries of the old aristocracies broken,
I see the landmarks of European kings removed,
I see this day the People beginning their landmarks, (all others give way;)
Never were such sharp questions ask'd as this day,
Never was average man, his soul, more energetic, more like a God,
Lo, how he urges and urges, leaving the masses no rest!
His daring foot is on the land and sea everywhere, he colonizes the Pacific,
  the archipelagoes,
With the steamship, the electric telegraph, the newspaper, the wholesale
  engines of war,
With these and the world-spreading factories, he interlinks all geography,
  all lands:
What whispers are these O lands, running ahead of you, passing under the seas?
Are all nations communing? is there going to be but one heart to the globe?
Is humanity forming en-masse? for lo, tyrants tremble, crowns grow dim,
The earth, restive, confronts a new era, perhaps a general divine war,
No one knows what will happen next, such portents fill the days and nights;
Years prophetical! the space ahead as I walk, as I vainly try to pierce it, is full
  of phantoms,
Unborn deeds, things soon to be, project their shapes around me.
This incredible rush and heat, this strange ecstatic fever of dreams O years!
Your dreams O years, how they penetrate through me! (I know not whether I
  sleep or wake;)
The perform'd America and Europe grow dim, retiring in shadow behind me.
The unperform'd, more gigantic than ever, advance, advance upon me.

Source 4 from Friedrich Engels, Socialism: Utopian and Scientific *(New York: International
Publishers, 1982), pp. 40, 51–53, 62–64, 69, 71–72, 75.*

4. From Friedrich Engels,
Socialism: Utopian and Scientific

Whilst in France the hurricane of the revolution swept over the land, in England
a quieter, but not on that account less tremendous, revolution was going on.
Steam and the new toolmaking machinery were transforming manufacture into
modern industry, and thus revolutionising the whole foundation of bourgeois

society. The sluggish march of development of the manufacturing period changed into a veritable storm and stress period of production. With constantly increasing swiftness the splitting-up of society into large capitalists and non-possessing proletarians went on. Between these, instead of the former stable middle class, an unstable mass of artisans and small shopkeepers, the most fluctuating portion of the population, now led a precarious existence.

The new mode of production was, as yet, only at the beginning of its period of ascent; as yet it was the normal, regular method of production—the only one possible under existing conditions. Nevertheless, even then it was producing crying social abuses—the herding together of a homeless population in the worst quarters of the large towns; the loosening of all traditional moral bonds, of patriarchal subordination, of family relations; overwork, especially of women and children, to a frightful extent; complete demoralisation of the working class, suddenly flung into altogether new conditions, from the country into the town, from agriculture into modern industry, from stable conditions of existence into insecure ones that changed from day to day. . . .

. . . The class struggle between proletariat and bourgeoisie came to the front in the history of the most advanced countries in Europe, in proportion to the development, upon the one hand, of modern industry, upon the other, of the newly-acquired political supremacy of the bourgeoisie. Facts more and more strenuously gave the lie to the teachings of bourgeois economy as to the identity of the interests of capital and labour, as to the universal harmony and universal prosperity that would be the consequence of unbridled competition. . . .

. . . The socialism of earlier days certainly criticised the existing capitalistic mode of production and its consequences. But it could not explain them, and, therefore, could not get the mastery of them. It could only simply reject them as bad. The more strongly this earlier socialism denounced the exploitation of the working class, inevitable under capitalism, the less able was it clearly to show in what this exploitation consisted and how it arose. But for this it was necessary 1) to present the capitalistic method of production in its historical connection and its inevitableness during a particular historical period, and therefore, also, to present its inevitable downfall; and 2) to lay bare its essential character, which was still a secret. This was done by the discovery of *surplus value.* . . .

These two great discoveries, the materialistic conception of history and the revelation of the secret of capitalistic production through surplus value, we owe to Marx. With these discoveries socialism became a science. The next thing was to work out all its details and relations.

But the perfecting of machinery is making human labour superfluous. If the introduction and increase of machinery means the displacement of millions of manual, by a few machine workers, improvement in machinery means the displacement of more and more of the machine workers themselves. It means, in the last instance, the production of a number of available wage workers in excess of the average needs of capital, the formation of a complete industrial reserve army, as I called it in 1845, available at the times when industry is working at high pressure, to be cast out upon the street when the inevitable crash comes, a constant dead weight upon the limbs of the working class in its struggle for existence with capital, a regulator for the keeping of wages down to the low level that suits the interests of capital. Thus it comes about, to quote Marx, that machinery becomes the most powerful weapon in the war of capital against the working class; that the instruments of labour constantly tear the means of subsistence out of the hands of the labourer; that the very product of the worker is turned into an instrument for his subjugation. . . . Thus it comes about that overwork of some becomes the preliminary condition for the idleness of others, and that modern industry, which hunts after new consumers over the whole world, forces the consumption of the masses at home down to a starvation minimum, and in doing thus destroys its own home market. . . .

As a matter of fact, since 1825, when the first general crisis broke out, the whole industrial and commercial world, production and exchange among all civilised peoples and their more or less barbaric hangers-on, are thrown out of joint about once every ten years. Commerce is at a standstill, the markets are glutted, products accumulate, as multitudinous as they are unsaleable, hard cash disappears, credit vanishes, factories are closed, the mass of the workers are in want of the means of subsistence, because they have produced too much of the means of subsistence; bankruptcy follows upon bankruptcy, execution upon execution. The stagnation lasts for years; productive forces and products are wasted and destroyed wholesale, until the accumulated mass of commodities finally filter off, more or less depreciated in value, until production and exchange gradually begin to move again. Little by little the pace quickens. It becomes a trot. The industrial trot breaks into a canter, the canter in turn grows into the headlong gallop of a perfect steeplechase of industry, commercial credit and speculation, which finally, after breakneck leaps, ends where it began—in the ditch of a crisis. And so over and over again. . . .

In these crises, the contradiction between socialised production and capitalist appropriation ends in a violent explosion. The circulation of commodities is, for the time being, stopped. Money, the means of circulation, becomes a hindrance to circulation. All the laws of production and circulation of commodities are turned upside down. The economic collision has reached its apogee. *The mode of production is in rebellion against the mode of exchange.* . . .

Whilst the capitalist mode of production more and more completely transforms the great majority of the population into proletarians, it creates the power which, under penalty of its own destruction, is forced to accomplish this revolution. Whilst it forces on more and more the transformation of the vast means of production, already socialized, into state property, it shows itself the way to accomplish this revolution. *The proletariat seizes political power and turns the means of production into state property.* . . .

. . . The socialised appropriation of the means of production does away not only with the present artificial restrictions upon production, but also with the positive waste and devastation of productive forces and products that are at the

[285]

present time the inevitable concomitants of production, and that reach their height in the crises. Further, it sets free for the community at large a mass of means of production and of products by doing away with the senseless extravagance of the ruling classes of today, and their political representatives. The possibility of securing for every member of society, by means of socialised production, an existence not only fully sufficient materially, and becoming day by day more full, but an existence guaranteeing to all the free development and exercise of their physical and mental faculties. . . .

To accomplish this act of universal emancipation is the historical mission of the modern proletariat. To thoroughly comprehend the historical conditions and thus the very nature of this act, to impart to the now oppressed proletarian class a full knowledge of the conditions and of the meaning of the momentous act it is called upon to accomplish, this is the task of the theoretical expression of the proletarian movement, scientific socialism.

Source 5 from Sources of Indian Tradition *(New York: Columbia University Press, 1958), pp. 803–809.*

5. From Mohandis K. Gandhi,
Hind Swaraj

Those who are intoxicated by modern civilization are not likely to write against it. Their care will be to find out facts and arguments in support of it, and this they do unconsciously, believing it to be true. A man whilst he is dreaming, believes in his dream; he is undeceived only when he is awakened from his sleep. A man laboring under the bane of civilization is like a dreaming man. What we usually read are the works of defenders of modern civilization, which undoubtedly claims among its votaries very brilliant and even some very good men. Their writings hypnotize us. And so, one by one, we are drawn into the vortex. . . .

Let us first consider what state of things is described by the word "civilization." Its true test lies in the fact that people living in it make bodily welfare the object of life. We will take some examples. The people of Europe today live in better-built houses than they did a hundred years ago. This is considered an emblem of civilization, and this is also a matter to promote bodily happiness. Formerly, they wore skins, and used spears as their weapons. Now, they wear long trousers, and, for embellishing their bodies, they wear a variety of clothing, and, instead of spears, they carry with them revolvers containing five or more chambers. If people of a certain country, who have hitherto not been in the habit of wearing much clothing, boots, etc., adopt European clothing, they are supposed to have become civilized out of savagery. Formerly, in Europe, people plowed their lands mainly by manual labor. Now, one man can plow a vast tract by means of steam engines and can thus amass great wealth. This is called a sign of civilization. Formerly, only a few men wrote valuable books. Now, anybody writes and prints anything he likes and poisons people's minds. Formerly, men traveled in wagons. Now, they fly through the air in trains at the rate of four hundred and more miles per day. This is considered the height of civilization. It has been stated that, as men progress, they shall be able to travel in airships and reach any part of the world in a few hours. Men will not need the use of their hands and feet. They will press a button, and they will have their clothing by their side. They will press another button, and they will have their newspaper. A third, and a motor-car will be in waiting for them. They will have a variety of delicately dished up food. Everything will be done by machinery. Formerly, when people wanted to fight with one another, they measured between them their bodily strength; now it is possible to take away thousands of lives by one man working behind a gun from a hill. This is civilization. Formerly, men worked in the open air only as much as they liked. Now thousands of workmen meet together and for the sake of maintenance work in factories or mines. Their condition is worse than that of beasts. They are obliged to work, at the risk of their lives, at most dangerous occupations, for the sake of millionaires. Formerly, men were made slaves under physical compulsion. Now they are enslaved by temptation of money and of the luxuries that money can buy. There are now diseases of which people never dreamt before, and an army of doctors is engaged in finding out their cures, and so hospitals have increased. This is a test of civilization. Formerly, special messengers were required and much expense was incurred in order to send letters; today, anyone can abuse his fellow by means of a letter for one penny. True, at the same cost, one can send one's thanks also. Formerly, people had two or three meals consisting of home-made bread and vegetables; now, they require something to eat every two hours so that they have hardly leisure for anything else. What more need I say? All this you can ascertain from several authoritative books. These are all true tests of civilization. And if anyone speaks to the contrary, know that he is ignorant. . . .

This civilization is irreligion, and it has taken such a hold on the people in Europe that those who are in it appear to be half-mad. They lack real physical strength or courage. They keep up their energy by intoxication. They can hardly be happy in solitude. Women, who should be the queens of households, wander in the streets or they slave away in factories. For the sake of a pittance, half a million women in England alone are laboring under trying circumstances in factories or similar institutions. This awful fact is one of the causes of the daily growing suffragette movement. This civilization is such that one has only to be patient and it will be self-destroyed. According to the teaching of Mahomed this would be considered a Satanic Civilization. Hinduism calls it the Black Age. I cannot give you an adequate conception of it. It is eating into the vitals of the English nation. It must be shunned. Parliaments are really emblems of slavery.

If you will sufficiently think over this, you will entertain the same opinion and cease to blame the English. They rather deserve our sympathy. . . .

Civilization is that mode of conduct which points out to man the path of duty. Performance of duty and observance of morality are convertible terms. To observe morality is to attain mastery over our mind and our passions. So doing, we know ourselves. The Gujarati equivalent for civilization means "good conduct."

If this definition be correct, then India, as so many writers have shown, has nothing to learn from anybody else, and this is as it should be. We notice that the mind is a restless bird; the more it gets the more it wants, and still remains unsatisfied. The more we indulge our passions the more unbridled they become. Our ancestors, therefore, set a limit to our indulgences. They saw that happiness was largely a mental condition. A man is not necessarily happy because he is rich, or unhappy because he is poor. The rich are often seen to be unhappy, the poor to be happy. Millions will always remain poor. Observing all this, our ancestors dissuaded us from luxuries and pleasures. We have managed with the same kind of plow as existed thousands of years ago. We have retained the same kind of cottages that we had in former times and our indigenous education remains the same as before. We have had no system of life-corroding competition. Each followed his own occupation or trade and charged a regulation wage. It was not that we did not know how to invent machinery, but our forefathers knew that, if we set our hearts after such things, we would become slaves and lose our moral fibre. They, therefore, after due deliberation decided that we should only do what we could with our hands and feet. They saw that our real happiness and health consisted in a proper use of our hands and feet. They further reasoned that large cities were a snare and a useless encumbrance and that people would not be happy in them, that there would be gangs of thieves and robbers, prostitution, and vice flourishing in them and that poor men would be robbed by rich men. They were, therefore, satisfied with small villages. They saw that kings and their swords were inferior to the sword of ethics, and they, therefore, held the sovereigns of the earth to be inferior to the Rishis and the Fakirs. A nation with a constitution like this is fitter to teach others than to learn from others. This nation had courts, lawyers, and doctors, but they were all within bounds. Everybody knew that these professions were not particularly superior; moreover, these *vakils and vaids*[3] did not rob people; they were considered people's dependents, not their masters. Justice was tolerably fair. The ordinary rule was to avoid courts. There were no touts to lure people into them. This evil, too, was noticeable only in and around capitals. The common people lived independently and followed their agricultural occupation. They enjoyed true Home Rule.

3. Lawyers and doctors.

And where this cursed modern civilization has not reached, India remains as it was before. The inhabitants of that part of India will very properly laugh at your newfangled notions. The English do not rule over them, nor will you ever rule over them. Those in whose name we speak we do not know, nor do they know us. I would certainly advise you and those like you who love the motherland to go into the interior that has not yet been polluted by the railways and to live there for six months; you might then be patriotic and speak of Home Rule. Now you see what I consider to be real civilization.

Source 6 from Olive Schreiner, Woman and Labour *(London: T. Fisher Unwin, 1911), pp. 41–53, 64–67, 252, 258, 264–273.*

6. Olive Schreiner, *Woman and Labour*, 1911

CHAPTER I

[W]e find that wherever that condition which we call modern civilisation prevails, and in proportion as it tends to prevail—wherever steam-power, electricity, or the forces of wind and water, are compelled by man's intellectual activity to act as the motor-powers in the accomplishment of human toil, wherever the delicate adaptions of scientifically constructed machinery are taking the place of the simple manipulation of the human hand—there has arisen, all the world over, a large body of males who find that their ancient fields of labour have slipped or are slipping from them, and who discover that the modern world has no place or need for them. At the gates of our dockyards, in our streets, and in our fields, are to be found everywhere, in proportion as modern civilisation is really dominant. . . .

Yet it is only upon one, and a comparatively small, section of the males of the modern civilised world that these changes in the material conditions of life have told in such fashion as to take all useful occupation from them and render them wholly or partly worthless to society. If the modern man's field of labour has contracted at one end (the physical), at the other (the intellectual) it has immeasurably expanded! If machinery and the command of inanimate motor forces have rendered of comparatively little value the male's mere physical motor-power, the demand upon his intellectual faculties, the call for the expenditure of nervous energy, and the exercise of delicate manipulative skill in the labour of human life, have immeasurably increased.

In a million new directions forms of honoured and remunerative social labour are opening up before the feet of the modern man, which his ancestors never dreamed of; and day by day they yet increase in numbers and importance. The steamship, the hydraulic lift, the patent road-maker, the railway-train, the electric tram-car, the steam driven mill, the Maxim gun and the torpedo boat, once made, may perform their labours with the guidance and assistance of comparatively few hands but a whole army of men of science, engineers, clerks, and highly-trained workmen is necessary for their invention, construction, and maintenance. . . .

In our woman's field of labour, matters have tended to shape themselves wholly otherwise! The changes which have taken place during the last centuries, and which we sum up under the compendious term "modern civilisation," have tended to rob woman, not merely in part but almost wholly, of the more valuable of her ancient domain of productive and social labour; and, where there has not been a determined and conscious resistance on her part, have nowhere spontaneously tended to open out to her new and compensatory fields.

It is this fact which constitutes our modern "Woman's Labour Problem." . . .

Even the minor domestic operations are tending to pass out of the circle of woman's labour. In modern cities our carpets are beaten, our windows cleaned, our floors polished, by machinery, or extra domestic, and often male labour. Change has gone much farther than to the mere taking from us of the preparation of the materials from which the clothing is formed. Already the domestic sewing-machine, which has supplanted almost entirely the ancient needle, begins to become antiquated, and a thousand machines driven in factories by central engines are supplying not only the husband and son, but the woman herself, with almost every article of clothing from vest to jacket; while among the wealthy classes, the male dress designer with his hundred male-milliners and dressmakers is helping finally to explode the ancient myth, that it is woman's exclusive sphere, and a part of her domestic toil, to cut and shape the garments she or her household wear.

Year by year, day by day, there is a silently working but determined tendency for the sphere of woman's domestic labours to contract itself, and the contraction is marked exactly in proportion as that complex condition which we term "modern civilisation" is advanced.

It manifests itself more in England and America than in Italy and Spain, more in great cities than in country places, more among the wealthier classes than the poorer, and is an unfailing indication of advancing modern civilisation. . . .

Further, owing partly to the diminished demand for child-bearing, rising from the extreme difficulty and expense of rearing and education, and to many other complex social causes, to which we shall return later, millions of women in our modern societies are so placed as to be absolutely compelled to go through life not merely childless, but without sex relationship in any form whatever; while another mighty army of women is reduced by the dislocations of our civilisation to accepting sexual relationships which practically negate childbearing, and whose only product is physical and moral disease.

Thus, it has come to pass that vast numbers of us are, by modern social conditions, prohibited from child-bearing at all; and that even those among us who are child-bearers are required, in proportion as the class of race to which we belong stands high in the scale of civilisation, to produce in most cases a limited number of offspring; so that even for these of us, child-bearing and suckling, instead of filling the entire circle of female life from the first appearance of puberty to the end of middle age, becomes an episodal occupation, employing from three or four to ten or twenty of the threescore-and-ten-years which are allotted to human life. . . .

It is this great fact, so often and so completely overlooked, which lies as the propelling force behind that vast and restless "Woman's Movement" which marks our day. It is *this* fact, whether clearly and intellectually grasped, or, as is more often the case, vaguely and painfully *felt*, which awakes in the hearts of the ablest modern European women their passionate, and at times it would seem almost incoherent cry for new forms of labour and new fields for the exercise of their powers. . . .

CHAPTER VI

Our material environment differs in every respect from that of our grandparents, and bears little or no resemblance to that of a few centuries ago. Here and there, even in our civilised societies in remote agricultural districts, the old social conditions may remain partly undisturbed; but throughout the bulk of our societies the substitution of mechanical for hand-labour, the wide diffusion of knowledge through the always increasing cheap printing-press; the rapidly increasing gathering of human creatures into vast cities, where not merely thousands but millions of individuals are collected together under physical and mental conditions of life which invert every social condition of the past; the increasingly rapid means of locomotion; the increasing intercourse between distant races and lands, brought about by rapid means of intercommunication, widening and changing in every direction the human horizon—all these produce a society, so complex and so rapidly altering, that social coordination between all its parts is impossible; and social unrest and the strife of ideals of faiths, of institutions and consequent human suffering is inevitable.

If the ancient guns and agricultural implements which our fathers taught us to use are valueless in the hands of their descendants, if the samplers our mothers worked and the stockings they knitted are become superfluous through the action of the modern loom, yet more are their social institutions, faiths, and manners of life become daily and increasingly unfitted to our use; and friction and suffering inevitable, especially for the most advanced and modified individuals in our societies. This suffering, if we analyse it closely, rises from three causes.

Firstly, it is caused by the fact that mere excessive rapidity of change tends always easily to become painful, by rupturing violently already hardened habits and modes of thought, as a very rapidly growing tree ruptures its bark and exudes its internal juices.

Secondly, it arises from the fact that individuals of the same human society, not adapting themselves at the same rate to the new conditions, or being exposed to them in different degrees, a wide and almost unparalleled dissimilarity has to-day arisen between the different individuals composing our societies; where, side by side with men and women who have rapidly adapted or are so successfully seeking to adapt themselves to the new conditions of knowledge and new conditions of life, that, were they to reappear in future ages in more co-ordinated societies, they might perhaps hardly appear wholly antiquated, are to be found men and women whose social, religious, and moral ideals would not constitute them out of harmony if returned to the primitive camps of the remote forbears of the human race; while between these extreme classes lies that large mass of persons in an intermediate state of development. . . .

Thirdly, the unrest and suffering peculiar to our age is caused by conflict going on within the individual himself. So intensely rapid is the change which is taking place in our environment and knowledge that in the course of a single life a man may pass through half a dozen phases of growth. Born and reared in possession of certain ideas and manners of action, he or she may, before middle life is reached, have had occasion repeatedly to modify, enlarge, and alter, or completely throw aside those traditions. Within the individuality itself of such persons goes on, in an intensified form, that very struggle, conflict and disco-ordination which is going on in society at large between its different members and sections; and agonising moments must arise, when the individual, seeing the necessity for adopting new courses of action, or for accepting new truths, or conforming to new conditions, will yet be tortured by the hold of traditional convictions. . . .

Thus, social disco-ordination, and subjective conflict and suffering, pervade the life of our age, making themselves felt in every division of human life, religious, political, and domestic; and, if they are more noticeable, and make themselves more keenly felt in the region of sex than in any other, even the religious, it is because when we enter the region of sex we touch, as it were, the spinal cord of human existence. Its great nerve centre, where sensation is most acute, and pain and pleasure most keenly felt. It is not sex disco-ordination that is at the root of our social unrest; it is the universal disco-ordination which affects even the world of sex phenomena. . . .

. . . The sexual tragedy of modern life lies, not in the fact that woman as such is tending to differ fundamentally from man as such; but that, in the unassorted confusion of our modern life, it is continually the modified type of man or woman who is thrown into the closest personal relations with the antiquated type of the opposite sex; that between father and daughter, mother and son, brother and sister, husband and wife, may sometimes be found to intervene not merely years, but even centuries of social evolution. . . .

Source 7 from Dun J. Li, The Road to Communism: China Since 1912 *(New York: Van Nostrand Reinhold Company, 1969), vol. II, pp. 40–41.*

7. A Declaration of Beliefs by the *New Youth*

We believe that the world's traditional, conventional concepts in politics, economics, and ethics have in them reactionary and irrational elements. To promote social progress, we have to destroy prejudices camouflaged as "law of Heaven and Earth" or "eternal practice" of all times. We, on our part, have decided not only to discard all these traditional or conventional concepts but also to create new ideas that synthesize old and contemporary philosophies in addition to those of our own. We wish to cultivate a new spirit for our times, a spirit more conducive to the creation of a new society.

The new society we have in mind is characterized by honesty, progress, positivity, liberty, equality, creativity, beauty, goodness, peace, love, mutual assistance, joyful labor, and devotion to the welfare of mankind. In it all the phenomena that can be described as hypocritical, conservative, passive, restrictive, privileged, conventional, ugly, detestable, combative, frictional, inert, gloomy, and oligarchic will be gradually reduced in importance and eventually disappear.

The youths in our new society will of course honor and glorify labor. But the labor they perform should be proportional to their ability and in accordance with their personal interest. Labor should be regarded as something beautiful, free, and enjoyable; being almost sacred, it should not be regarded as merely a means to earn a livelihood.

We believe that man's progress in ethics should be such as to transcend some of his basic animal instincts, whether they be aggressiveness or acquisitiveness. Therefore, we extend our friendship, love, and desire for mutual assistance to all the people in the world. But we will regard as our enemies warlords and financial oligarchs who are reared in the spirit of military aggression and economic acquisitiveness.

We advocate social reform via mass movement. We have decided to cut off our relations with all the political parties or factions, past or present.

Though we do not think that politics can solve every problem, it is nevertheless an important form of public life. We believe in true democracy, a kind of government where political power is in the hands of all the people. If franchise has to be limited, it should be limited on the basis of occupation rather than the amount of property one owns. Government and politics are a necessary, useful instrument not only in the creation of a new era but also in the development of a healthy society. As for political parties, they are, in our judgment, necessary implements in conducting political activities. But we will never join a political party that has in mind only the interest of a few individuals or a particular class while ignoring the welfare of the people as a whole.

We believe that all activities—political, ethical, scientific, aesthetic, religious, and educational—should have as their point of emphasis the actual need of social progress, either of today or in the future.

In order to cultivate a literary ethics necessary to the creation of a new era and a new society, we cannot but abandon the undesirable elements in the conventional literary ethics.

We believe in natural science and pragmatic philosophy. To eliminate superstition and irrational thinking is the prerequisite to social progress.

We regard the respect for women's rights and personal dignity as a necessary ingredient in social progress. We also hope that women should be thoroughly aware that they, too, have responsibilities towards the society in which they live.

Since we take our beliefs very seriously and wish to carry them out, we welcome all constructive criticisms based upon conviction rather than uncritical, meaningless support. However, as long as our critics cannot fully convince us that we are wrong, we shall continue to proclaim our beliefs with audacity and resolution. We have no use for the so-called harmonizing ideas that are as hypocritical and confusing as they are deathly, reactionary, and pretentious. Nor do we wish to embrace skepticism, a negative, fluid, and unproductive concept devoid of convictions and lacking concrete proposals.

Source 8: Museum of Modern Art/Film Stills Archive.

8. Still Shots from Fritz Lang's Film *Metropolis*

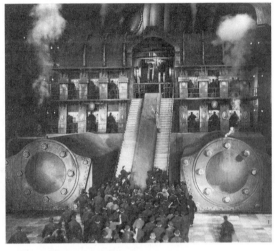

(a) Towering skyscrapers of the upper city

(b) The "Moloch" machine sustaining the city

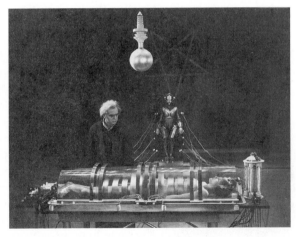

(c) Workers before the master clock

(d) Transferring a human psyche into a robot

Source 9 from José Ortega y Gasset, The Revolt of the Masses (New York: W.W. Norton Co., 1932), pp. 11–13, 17–18, 32–33, 38, 41, 44, 56–57, 89–92, 97, 101–102, 108–109, 120.

9. José Ortega y Gasset, *The Revolt of the Masses*

1

There is one fact which, whether for good or ill, is of utmost importance in the public life of Europe at the present moment. This fact is the accession of the masses to complete social power. As the masses, by definition, neither should nor can direct their own personal existence, and still less rule society in general, this fact means that actually Europe is suffering from the greatest crisis that can afflict peoples, nations, and civilisation. Such a crisis has occurred more than once in history. Its characteristics and its consequences are well known. So also is its name. It is called the rebellion of the masses. . . .

The concept of the multitude is quantitative and visual. Without changing its nature, let us translate it into terms of sociology. We then meet with the notion of the "social mass." Society is always a dynamic unity of two component factors: minorities and masses. The minorities are individuals or groups of individuals which are specially qualified. The mass is the assemblage of persons not specially qualified. By masses, then, is not to be understood, solely or mainly, "the working masses." The mass is the average man. . . .

No one, I believe, will regret that people are to-day enjoying themselves in greater measure and numbers than before, since they have now both the desire and the means of satisfying it. The evil lies in the fact that this decision taken by the masses to assume the activities proper to the minorities is not, and cannot be, manifested solely in the domain of pleasure, but that it is a general feature of our time. Thus—to anticipate what we shall see later—I believe that the political innovations of recent times signify nothing less than the political domination of the masses. The old democracy was tempered by a generous dose of liberalism and of enthusiasm for law. By serving these principles the individual bound himself to maintain a severe discipline over himself. Under the shelter of liberal principles and the rule of law, minorities could live and act. Democracy and law—life in common under the law—were synonymous. To-day we are witnessing the triumphs of a hyperdemocracy in which the mass acts directly, outside the law, imposing its aspirations and its desires by means of material pressure. . . .

The same thing is happening in other orders, particularly in the intellectual. I may be mistaken, but the present day writer, when he takes his pen in hand to treat a subject which he has studied deeply, has to bear in mind that the average reader, who has never concerned himself with this subject, if he reads does so with the view, not of learning something from the writer, but rather, of pronouncing judgment on him when he is not in agreement with the commonplaces that the said reader carries in his head. If the individuals who make up the mass believed themselves specially qualified, it would be a case merely of personal error, not a sociological subversion. *The characteristic of the hour is that the commonplace mind, knowing itself to be commonplace, has the assurance to proclaim the rights of the commonplace and to impose them wherever it will. . . .*

3

. . . The desires so long in conception, which the XlXth Century seems at last to realise, is what it named for itself in a word as "modern culture." The very name is a disturbing one; this time calls itself "modern," that is to say, final, definitive, in whose presence all the rest is mere preterite, humble preparation and aspiration towards this present. Nerveless arrows which miss their mark! . . .[4]

4

The rule of the masses and the raising of the level, the height of the time which this indicates, are in their turn only symptoms of a more complete and more general fact. This fact is almost grotesque and incredible in its stark and simple truth. It is just this, that the world has suddenly grown larger, and with it and in it, life itself. . . .

. . . But what I wanted to make clear just now was the extent to which the life of man has increased in the dimension of potentiality. It can now count on a range of possibilities fabulously greater than ever before. In the intellectual order it now finds more "paths of ideation," more problems, more data, more sciences, more points of view. Whereas the number of occupations in primitive life can almost be counted on the fingers of one hand—shepherd, hunter, warrior, seer—the list of possible avocations today is immeasurably long. Something similar occurs in the matter of pleasures, although (and this is a phenomenon of more importance than it seems) the catalogue of pleasures is not so overflowing as in other aspects of life. Nevertheless, for the man of the middle classes who lives in towns—and towns are representative of modern existence—the possibilities of enjoyment have increased, in the course of the present century, in fantastic proportion. . . .

6

. . . We are, in fact, confronted with a radical innovation in human destiny, implanted by the XlXth Century. A new stage has been mounted for human existence, new both in the physical and the social aspects. Three principles have made possible this new world: liberal democracy, scientific experiment, and industrialism. The two latter may be summed up in one word: technicism. Not one of those principles was invented by the XlXth Century; they proceed

4. The primary meaning of the words "modern," "modernity," with which recent times have baptised themselves, brings out very sharply "the height of time" which I am at present analyzing. "Modern" is what is in fashion, that is to say, the new fashion or modification which has arisen over against the old. The word "modern" then expresses a consciousness of a new life, superior to the old one, and at the same time an imperative call to be at the height of one's time. For the "modern" man not to be "modern" means to fall below the historic level. [Note in original]

from the two previous centuries. The glory of the XlXth Century lies not in their discovery, but in their implantation. No one but recognises that fact. But it is not sufficient to recognise it in the abstract, it is necessary to realise its inevitable consequences.

The XlXth Century was of its essence revolutionary. This aspect is not to be looked for in the scenes of the barricades, which are mere incidents, but in the fact that it placed the average man—the great social mass—in conditions of life radically opposed to those by which he had always been surrounded. It turned his public existence upside down. Revolution is not the uprising against pre-existing order, but the setting up of a new order contradictory to the traditional one. Hence there is no exaggeration in saying that the man who is the product of the XlXth Century is, for the effects of public life, a man apart from all other men. The XVIIIth-Century man differs, of course, from the XVIIth-Century man, and this one in turn from his fellow of the XVIth Century, but they are all related, similar, even identical in essentials when confronted with this new man. For the "common" man of all periods "life" had principally meant limitation, obligation, dependence; in a word, pressure. Say oppression, if you like, provided it be understood not only in the juridical and social sense, but also in the cosmic. For it is this latter which has never been lacking up to a hundred years ago, the date at which starts the practically limitless expansion of scientific technique—physical and administrative. Previously, even for the rich and powerful, the world was a place of poverty, difficulty and danger.

The world which surrounds the new man from his birth does not compel him to limit himself in any fashion, it sets up no veto in opposition to him: on the contrary, it incites his appetite, which in principle can increase indefinitely. Now it turns out—and this is most important—that this world of the XIXth and early XXth Centuries not only has the perfections and completeness which it actually possesses, but furthermore suggests to those who dwell in it the radical assurance that tomorrow it will be still richer, ampler, more perfect, as if it enjoyed a spontaneous, inexhaustible power of increase. . . .

10

. . . The principles on which the civilised world—which has to be maintained—is based, simply do not exist for the average man of to-day. He has no interest in the basic cultural values, no solidarity with them, is not prepared to place himself at their service. How has this come about? For many reasons, but for the moment I am only going to stress one. Civilisation becomes more complex and difficult in proportion as it advances. The problems which it sets before us to-day are of the most intricate. The number of people whose minds are equal to these problems becomes increasingly smaller. The post-war period offers us a striking example of this. The reconstruction of Europe—as we are seeing—is an affair altogether too algebraical, and the ordinary European is showing himself below this high enterprise. . . .

Hence, Bolshevism and Fascism, the two "new" attempts in politics that are being made in Europe and on its borders, are two clear examples of essential retrogression. . . . Typical movements of mass-men, directed, as all such are, by men who are mediocrities, improvised, devoid of a long memory and a "historic conscience," they behave from the start as if they already belonged to the past, as if, though occurring at the present hour, they were really fauna of a past age. . . .

11

. . . The civilisation of the XIXth Century is, then, of such a character that it allows the average man to take his place in a world of superabundance, of which he perceives only the lavishness of the means at his disposal, nothing of the pains involved. He finds himself surrounded by marvellous instruments, healing medicines, watchful governments, comfortable privileges. On the other hand, he is ignorant how difficult it is to invent those medicines and those instruments and to assure their production in the future; he does not realise how unstable is the organisation of the State and is scarcely conscious to himself of any obligations. This lack of balance falsifies his nature, vitiates it in its very roots, causing him to lose contact with the very substance of life, which is made up of absolute danger, is radically problematic. The form most contradictory to human life that can appear among the human species is the "self-satisfied man." Consequently, when he becomes the predominant type, it is time to raise the alarm and to announce that humanity is threatened with degeneration, that is, with relative death. . . .

12

. . . There can be no doubt that it is technicism—in combination with liberal democracy—which has engendered mass-man in the quantitative sense of the expression. But these pages have attempted to show that it is also responsible for the existence of mass-man in the qualitative and pejorative sense of the term.

By mass—as I pointed out at the start—is not to be specially understood the workers; it does not indicate a social class, but a kind of man to be found today in all social classes, who consequently represents our age, in which he is the predominant, ruling power. We are now about to find abundant evidence for this.

Who is it that exercises social power today? Who imposes the forms of his own mind on the period? Without a doubt, the man of the middle class. Which group, within that middle class, is considered the superior, the aristocracy of the present? Without a doubt, the technician: engineer, doctor, financier, teacher, and so on. Who, inside the group of technicians, represents it at its best and purest? Again, without a doubt, the man of science. . . .

And now it turns out that the actual scientific man is the prototype of the mass-man. Not by chance, not through the individual failings of each particular man of science, but because science itself—the root of our civilisation—automatically converts him into mass-man, makes of him a primitive, a modern barbarian. . . .

Source 10 from Jawaharlal Nehru, Glimpses of World History *(New York: The John Day Company, 1942), pp. 685, 688, 690, 951–953.*

10. Excerpts from Jawaharlal Nehru, *Glimpses of World History,* 1933

Now, I am not going into the question here of what our outlook on history should be. My own on the subject has changed greatly in recent years. And just as I have changed my views on this and other matters, so have many others. For the war gave a terrible shaking to everything and everybody. It upset the old world completely, and ever since then our poor old world is trying painfully to stand up again, without much success. It shook the whole system of ideas on which we had grown up and made us begin to doubt the very basis of modern society and civilization. We saw the terrible waste of young lives, the lying, violence, brutality, destruction, and wondered if this was the end of civilization. The Soviet rose in Russia—a new thing, a new social order, and a challenge to the old. Other ideas also floated in the air. It was a period of disintegration, of the breaking up of old beliefs and customs; an age of doubt and questioning which always come in a period of transition and rapid change. . . .

I have told you of three of the outstanding events of the fourteen years after the war: the rise of the Soviet Union; the economic world domination of America and her present crisis; and the European tangle. The fourth outstanding event of this period is the full awakening of eastern countries and their aggressive attempts to gain freedom. The East definitely enters world politics. These eastern nations might be considered in two classes: those that are considered independent, and those that are colonial countries controlled by some imperialist Power. In all these countries of Asia and North Africa nationalism has grown strong, and the desire for freedom insistent and aggressive. In all there have been powerful movements, and in some places even rebellions, against western imperialism. Many of these countries have received direct help and, what was of far greater importance, moral backing at a critical stage of their struggle, from the Soviet Union. . . .

One other outstanding feature of recent years has been the emanciption of women from the many bonds, legal, social, and customary, that held them. The war gave a real push to this in the West. And even in the East, from Turkey to India and China, woman is up and doing and taking a brave part in national and social activities.

Such are the times we live in. Every day brings news of change or important happening, of the friction between nations, of the conflict between capitalism and socialism, and fascism and democracy, of growing poverty and destitution, and over all lies the ever-lengthening shadow of war.

It is a stirring period of history, and it is good to be alive and to take one's share in it, even though the share may consist of solitude in the Dehra Dun Gaol! . . .

The past brings us many gifts; indeed, all that we have to-day of culture, civilization, science, or knowledge of some aspects of the truth, is a gift of the distant or recent past to us. It is right that we acknowledge our obligation to the past. But the past does not exhaust our duty or obligation. We owe a duty to the future also, and perhaps that obligation is even greater than the one we owe to the past. For the past is past and done with, we cannot change it; the future is yet to come, and perhaps we may be able to shape it a little. If the past has given us some part of the truth, the future also hides many aspects of the truth, and invites us to search for them. But often the past is jealous of the future and holds us in a terrible grip, and we have to struggle with it to get free to face and advance towards the future. . . .

The old days were days of faith, blind, unquestioning faith. The wonderful temples and mosques and cathedrals of past centuries could never have been built but for the overpowering faith of the architects and builders and people generally. The very stones that they reverently put one on top of the other, or carved into beautiful designs, tell us of this faith. The old temple spire, the mosque with its slender minarets, the Gothic cathedral—all of them pointing upward with an amazing intensity of devotion, as if offering a prayer in stone or marble to the sky above—thrill us even now, though we may be lacking in that faith of old of which they are the embodiments. But the days of that faith are gone, and gone with them is that magic touch in stone. Thousands of temples and mosques and cathedrals continue to be built, but they lack the spirit that made them live during the Middle Ages. There is little difference between them and the commercial offices which are so representative of our age.

Our age is a different one; it is an age of disillusion; of doubt and uncertainty and questioning. We can no longer accept many of the ancient beliefs and customs; we have no more faith in them, in Asia or in Europe or America. So we search for new ways, new aspects of the truth more in harmony with our environment. And we question each other and debate and quarrel and evolve any number of "isms" and philosophies. As in the days of Socrates, we live in an age of questioning, but that questioning is not confined to a city like Athens; it is world-wide.

Sometimes the injustice, the unhappiness, the brutality of the world oppress us and darken our minds, and we see no way out. With Matthew Arnold, we feel that there is no hope in the world and that all we can do is to be true to one another.

. . . For the world which seems
To lie before us, like a land of dreams,
So various, so beautiful, so new,
Hath really neither joy, nor love, nor light,
Nor certitude, nor peace, nor help for pain;
And we are here, as on a darkling plain
Swept with confused alarms of struggle and flight,
Where ignorant armies clash by night.

[301]

And yet if we take such a dismal view we have not learnt aright the lesson of life or of history. For history teaches us of growth and progress and of the possibility of an infinite advance for man. . . .

I have given you many quotations and extracts from poets and others in this letter. I shall finish up with one more. It is from the Gitanjali; it is a poem, or prayer, by Rabindra Nath Tagore:

Where the mind is without fear and the head is held high;
Where knowledge is free;
Where the world has not been broken up into fragments by narrow domestic
    walls;
Where words come out from the depth of truth;
Where tireless striving stretches its arms towards perfection;
Where the clear stream of reason has not lost its way into the dreary desert
    sand of dead habit;
Where the mind is led forward by thee into ever-widening thought and action
Into that heaven of freedom, my Father, let my country awake.

QUESTIONS TO CONSIDER

Condorcet's *The Progress of the Human Mind* reveals most of the Enlightenment's ideals. Pay particular attention to the title. A key assumption here, as in all modernity, is the belief that humans advance over time "with a firm and indeviate step" toward perfection. Note how this renders history a story of *progress.* Think about the motion implied and the relationship it sets up between past, present, and future. Are all equal? What about people? Why are some more "advanced"? Who are they? Reason and science, Condorcet says, play key roles in progress. Draw up a list of the gains, both material and immaterial, they are said to bring. Which matter most? Finally, note his concern for liberty. What view of self and society does this imply?

The *Economist* editorial recalls Condorcet's work but offers a somewhat different vision of progress. It extolls the present era, which it deems "unrivalled and unapproached." List the advances it celebrates most. How do they compare with those you found before? In this context, note the talk of concrete gains in public health and material well-being—and the claim that the people have become "the main topic of discourse and statesmanship." Whitman, too, stresses this aspect in "Years of the Modern," though as an American he lauds "Liberty's nation" over Europe as the true center of the "unperform'd." For him, machines have created a "new era" in which the "average man" assumes control of advanced societies and "interlinks all geography." But what is his view of the future? Does he welcome the "space ahead," so "full of phantoms," or dread it? Engels, by contrast, sees the immediate impact of industrialization as disastrous to workers. But is it because of the historical process itself or because of those who misdirected it? Given his faith in an ultimate socialist revolution and his optimism about emancipation, is Engels perhaps truer to the beliefs of the Enlightenment than Whitman? What about his view of science?

Gandhi shares no such faith in Western progress. At the time he wrote *Hind Swaraj,* he was encouraging Indians to reaffirm the value of their own tradition in preparation to challenge British rule. Here Gandhi refutes European claims to cultural advancement, deriding modern civilization as "Satanic" and dismissing the modern era as a Black Age. Note that he finds modern life destructive to the colonizers as well as the colonized. Why? What are his grounds for repudiating modernity? He clearly recognizes the benefits Westerners claim to derive from modern life— compare his list of them with those from the other documents. Yet he faults all of them. The modern focus on material welfare and "bodily happiness" bothers him most. Why? What does he rank as a better mark of civilization? Note his special disdain for modern cities and machines and his view that industrial society debases women and enslaves people. Nonetheless, his belief in the importance of human freedom and dignity is not unlike that of Enlightenment writers. Has he accepted at least this part of the modern agenda?

The emancipation of repressed groups, of course, was one of the constant goals of modern reformers. In *Woman and Labour,* Olive Schreiner analyzes the constraints that modernity placed on women. Like many feminists, she advocates equal political rights and economic opportunities for women. But she is unusual in arguing that the "Woman's Movement" is a response to the "social discoordination" of industrial society, with its labor-saving machinery, social unrest, and "strife of ideals." Men and women alike, she warns, suffer from "conflict . . . within the individual." Why? To what aspects of modernity does she attribute this conflict? "A Declaration of Beliefs by the *New Youth*" addresses another group pressing for change: youth. As a call to young Chinese, it shows how modern values and ideas, especially the identification of modernity with youth, were spreading beyond the West at the start of the twentieth century, even as Europeans were starting to doubt them. Compare the list of reforms it seeks for China with those in other documents. The pledge to embrace "positivity" and avoid skepticism hints at growing disillusionment with the modern agenda elsewhere. What may have induced such concern in this 1919 editorial?

The darkening mood of post–World War I Europe clearly colors Fritz Lang's film *Metropolis* and its grim portrayal of the modern city. Lang used the new popular medium to challenge almost all the old assumptions about progress. Science and technology still produce wonders, but not to the benefit of ordinary people. Note the vast scale of the city, with its looming towers and labyrinthine ways. Look how human figures cower before the huge and bewildering machines that control

[303]

their lives. What has become of the promise of a better world through technology—or the hope for a freer, more creative life in modern urban society? The shot of a scientist transferring the psyche of a woman into a robot dramatically portrays the dehumanization of industrial society, which Lang, like Gandhi, deplored. What is the image of science here?

Ortega y Gasset's condemnation of modernity has points in common with Lang's. His view that "technicism" has produced a regimented mass society closely parallels Lang's vision of a technocratic tyranny. And he, too, seems to believe that modern urban life represents a lapse in human development. But whereas Lang laments common people's enslavement to machines and technocracy, Ortega y Gasset worries over their political dominance in "hyperdemocracy." Why? How does his concern contrast with earlier expectations about democracy, egalitarianism, and the value of the "average man"? Like Gandhi, Ortega y Gasset denounces the material abundance of modern society. Why? Compare his view of social fragmentation with Yeats's claim that "things fall apart"? Does he, too, expect a similar catastrophic end of modern civilization?

Contrast these European views with those of Jawaharlal Nehru in Source 10. Far from fearing the rise of the common man, Nehru, who was both an avowed socialist and democrat, welcomed it. In his mind, the collapse of European power brought about by World War I, rather than marking the end of civilization, offered new promise of emancipation and advancement. For him, Europe's decline implied most the end of imperialism and the liberation of millions of Asians and Africans. But what other forms of modern emancipation does he celebrate? And what country does he highlight for its "new social order" and revolutionary inspiration? Despite his constant praise for Gandhi, Nehru did not share Gandhi's deep commitment to religion and disillusionment with materialism. What does he suggest here should replace the "blind, unquestioning faith" of the past as a guide to future advancement? In that context, what do you make of his rejection of Matthew Arnold's poem, "Dover Beach," in favor of the twentieth-century Indian poet Tagore's "Gitanjali"? Which work seems more modern in spirit? And what does this juxtaposition suggest about the intellectual history of modernity?

EPILOGUE

The insecurity of the Great Depression in the 1930s followed by the bloodbath unleashed in World War II confirmed the interwar generation's worst fears that modernity posed a threat rather than a promise to humanity. The specter of death camps and devastated cities, of ruined nations and impoverished populations, undermined belief in rationality and discredited the idea of inevitable advancement. Only in America did a semblance of the old confidence in progress survive into the immediate postwar era. And even there, hopes for a better life focused more on material gains and increased consumption than on the improvement of "the intellectual and moral faculties" that *philosophes* like Condorcet regarded as the highest measures of progress.

The rebuilding of Europe after World War II and the East Asian economic "miracle" of the last quarter of the twentieth century helped these areas catch up with America in prosperity. Combined with the stable order created by the cold war balance of power, affluence in these regions made the second half of the twentieth century less turbulent and insecure than the first. But optimism about humanity's perfectibility did not revive. Material growth, once hailed for its transforming power, seemed a source of problems, from urban sprawl to pollution. Science and technology, formerly viewed as tools for remaking humanity, were now associated with war or environmental degradation. Furthermore, faith in reason and rational efforts to shape a better society were eroded by mounting public cynicism and the rise of contentious interest groups. Instead of a better time, the future increasingly appeared a threshold to one catastrophe or another, whether nuclear war, overpopulation, or global warming. And modern "centers" lost their former luster as decolonization and the rise of the Third World ended Western supremacy while urban blight drove the affluent middle class out of the cities.

The widespread loss of public faith in the values of modernity in the early twentieth century makes some historians see this period as the end of the modern age. They thus locate the start of a new "postmodern" era sometime in the middle decades of the century. But because of its closeness, few are able to define the new period in its own terms. Instead, as the term *postmodern* indicates, they conceive of it in contrast with the prior modern period. The idea of modernity, then, not only affects the way we have periodized and viewed the distant past, it provides the backdrop against which many are presently attempting to delineate a new age. What it meant to be modern and how the meaning of modernity changed in the early twentieth century are thus crucial to any understanding of current approaches to history.

CHAPTER TEN

NATIONALISM, MOTHERHOOD,

AND WOMEN'S RIGHTS IN BRAZIL,

EGYPT, AND JAPAN (1890s–1930s)

The revolutions of the late eighteenth century in the British North American colonies, France, and the French Caribbean colony of Saint Domingue (Haiti) produced strong statements about liberty and equality. "All men are created equal," wrote Thomas Jefferson in the American Declaration of Independence in 1776, with "certain unalienable Rights," including "Life, Liberty, and the Pursuit of Happiness." "Men are born free and remain free and equal in rights," asserted the first article of the French Declaration of the Rights of Man and the Citizen in 1789. "All men are born, live and die free and French," wrote Toussaint L'Ouverture in the Haitian Constitution of 1801. The political structures created through these revolutions slowly put these ideals into practice. The 1791 French Constitution limited voting rights to those men who had some property, but by 1792 all men over age twenty-one

could vote. Voting restrictions based on property ownership were gradually lifted in the United States in the early nineteenth century. Voting in Haiti, according to the provisions of the more liberal of its various nineteenth-century constitutions, was not to be restricted by wealth, family background, status of birth, or social class.

However, to all these revolutionaries, gender remained an unbridgeable chasm. In a letter to a friend, Thomas Jefferson noted: "Were our state a pure democracy . . . there would still be excluded from our deliberations . . . women, who, to prevent deprivation of morals and ambiguity of issue [children born out of wedlock or whose fathers might not be the husbands of their mothers], should not mix promiscuously in gatherings of men."[1] Pierre Gaspard Chaumette, a Parisian official,

1. Letter from Thomas Jefferson to Samuel Kercheval (September 5, 1816), in *The Writings of Thomas Jefferson*, ed. Andrew A. Lipscomb (Washington, D.C.: Thomas Jefferson Memorial Association, 1904), vol. 15, pp. 71–72.

commented in 1792: "Since when is it permitted to give up one's sex? Since when is it decent to see women abandoning the pious cares of their households, the cribs of their children, to come to public places, to harangues in the galleries, at the bar of the Senate? Is it to men that nature has confided domestic cares? Has she given us breasts to feed our children?"[2] The bold proclamations declaring that all men were created free and equal meant exactly what they said—men. To Jefferson, Chaumette, and many other late eighteenth-century thinkers, women's roles as mothers, or even the possibility that they might become mothers, meant that women could not be citizens or part of the political nation in the same way that men could. In the first half of the nineteenth century, political revolutions, such as those in Latin America, and reform movements, such as that in Britain, affirmed this distinction, often specifically including the word *male* in laws and other provisions about the voting franchise.

By the last half of the nineteenth century, however, many women—and a few men—were not so sure that motherhood and political rights were incompatible. Women, including mothers, had been active in the political revolutions of the late eighteenth and early nineteenth centuries, drafting grievances, hosting meetings, serving as spies, signing petitions, carrying weapons and supplies, and caring for the wounded. Some of these women spoke of them-

selves as citizens and as patriots, and they opposed measures limiting political rights to men. In many countries of the world, groups specifically devoted to women's rights began to be established and to communicate with each other in what became an international feminist movement. Debates about the "woman question," as it was known at the time, came to involve a broad range of other issues along with political rights: women's greater access to education and property rights, more equitable marriage and divorce laws, better employment opportunities, reform of laws regarding prostitution and concubinage, and protection for women workers. The women's rights movement was interwoven with other movements of reform and revolution, including socialism, the abolition of slavery, prison reform, workers' rights, anticolonialism, and nationalism.

Some advocates of an expanded role for women argued that political rights and motherhood had nothing to do with one another, that women could very easily vote and still care for their families, or engage in public political discussions without being seduced into adulterous relationships. Others saw motherhood as a key reason *for* women's political rights, often intertwining this with ideas about what would make their nation stronger. Women, they argued, needed the vote to ensure the well-being of their families and children, and they would clean up corrupt politics in the same way that they cleaned up their households.

Women's rights, motherhood, and nationalism were linked by reformers and writers in many countries in the late nineteenth and early twentieth centuries. In areas of the world engaged

2. Pierre Gaspard Chaumette, speech to the Commune of Paris, November 17, 1793. Translated and reprinted in *Women in Revolutionary Paris, 1789–1795*, ed. Darlene Levy, Harriet Applewhite, and Mary Durham Johnson (Urbana: University of Illinois Press, 1979), p. 215.

Chapter 10

Nationalism,

Motherhood, and

Women's Rights

in Brazil, Egypt,

and Japan

(1890s–1930s)

in struggles against Western political and economic domination, these issues were also linked with anticolonialism. Your first task in this chapter is to use the writings of those who argued for an expansion of women's roles in three countries—Brazil, Egypt, and Japan—to analyze ways in which women's rights, motherhood, and nationalism emerged in their arguments. Why, in their opinion, should women be accorded political rights and other opportunities, and how are these rights related to motherhood and the strength of the nation? Second, what similarities and differences do you see among the writers from these three countries, and how might these be connected to their varying cultural contexts and historical circumstances?

BACKGROUND

The movement for women's rights that began in the nineteenth century had different emphases in different parts of the world, and there was often a wide array of plans, proposals, and organizations to address the "woman question" within any one country. There are some common patterns, however. Most of those advocating for an expanded role for women were members of the educated elite, at a time when the vast majority of women and men in their countries were not literate. They often founded women's magazines and newspapers to express their views and to communicate with like-minded men and women throughout the country. The decades between the 1890s and the 1930s saw the drafting of new constitutions in each of these countries, and women's groups were active lobbyists as these constitutions were written. Each of these countries confronted the economic and political power of the West, and women's groups had to balance their aims of enhancing women's rights and strengthening their nation.

Though there were similarities in the women's movement in these three countries, there were also significant differences. In each country (and elsewhere in the world as well), those arguing for an improvement in women's situation and a widening of their roles responded to specific political and economic developments, and they wrote from a particular cultural context. To understand the sources and answer the central questions for this chapter, you will thus need to know something about the relationship between general political changes and the movement for women's rights in each of the three countries you will be comparing.

Brazil, the largest colony in the Portuguese overseas empire, won its independence with relatively little bloodshed in 1821–1823, becoming a constitutional monarchy in which real power was held by wealthy landowners, many of whom were slaveholders. By the 1870s, Brazil was the only noncolonial monarchy in the Western Hemisphere and, other than Spanish-held Cuba, the only state that still allowed slavery. Reformers pushed for the adoption of a republican form of government and for the abolition of slavery. Slavery was abolished in 1888, though many slaves simply remained on the plantations where they had been, now as badly paid wage workers. The monarchy was overthrown in a coup in 1889, and a republican government was established; power remained in the hands of local agrarian landowners, however, especially coffee growers and ranchers who ruled through systems of patronage.

Women in Brazil began to advocate for a wider public role in the nineteenth century. Women's newspapers and journals were founded in several Brazilian cities during the last half of the nineteenth century; some of these simply covered society news and fashion, but others promoted women's education, including higher education. Several women were active as abolitionists in Brazil, and their speaking and writing on the topic of freedom for slaves thrust them into the public political arena. During the 1880s, a few women began to call for the extension of voting rights to women; they took their arguments to the assembly that was drafting a new constitution for Brazil after the overthrow of the monarchy. The Constituent Congress of 1891 heard arguments for and against the broadening of suffrage along many lines, but it ultimately decided that women, along with paupers, illiterates, soldiers, and members of religious orders, should not be allowed to vote. (Because of high poverty levels and few publicly supported schools, these restrictions meant that, through the 1920s, only about 6 percent of the male population had the right to vote.) Women's proper sphere was the private realm of the family, not the public world of politics, argued most representatives to the Congress; women could—indeed should—exert moral influence on society, but from within the household, not through the ballot box.

Despite this setback, women in Brazil continued to organize, founding magazines and forming organizations working for an expanded role for women in the first decades of the twentieth century. The most popular magazine, *Revista Feminina*, founded by Virgilina de Souza Salles and published between 1914 and 1927, had tens of thousands of subscribers at its height, almost all of them women. *Revista Feminina* emphasized domestic concerns and Catholic morality, but since it saw women's duties to their families as extending into the world beyond the home, it also covered world politics, science, and news about women's achievements. Bertha Lutz (1894–1976), a biologist educated in Europe, saw this focus as far too limited, especially after she attended the first Pan American Conference of Women in Baltimore in 1922, where she met many women who were instrumental in the suffrage movement in the United States and elsewhere. With others, Lutz founded the Federacao Brasileira pelo Progresso Feminino (FBPF), a federation of associations that advocated female suffrage along the same lines as male suffrage, which would have limited the right to vote to a small minority of educated women. The middle-class leadership of the FBPF addressed some of the concerns of working-class women, including factory conditions, the length of the workday, and maternity leave, but they

Chapter 10

Nationalism,

Motherhood, and

Women's Rights

in Brazil, Egypt,

and Japan

(1890s–1930s)

rejected discussion of class conflict or social revolution. Other women saw *this* as too limited. They adopted socialist or radical perspectives, setting calls for women's liberation within the context of expanded rights for all workers and the poor, or within the context of personal liberation from the constraints of marriage and motherhood.

At the same time that women's groups were being organized, male nationalist reformers increasingly resented the economic and political domination of the coffee-growing elite; they advocated the modernization of the economy and cultural life, with an eye to making Brazil a more self-sufficient nation. Dissatisfaction grew stronger when coffee exports collapsed with the world economic crash of 1929, and a contested election for president led to a brief rebellion that resulted in Getulio Vargas, the governor of Brazil's southernmost state, assuming power as president. Vargas was an advocate of *corporatism*, a political movement that saw the state as the best mediator between groups with different aims. He promised to use government power to broaden the electorate, give industrial workers better wages, lessen the power of foreign investors, and clean up corrupt local government. Through corporatism, Brazil would become more unified and more prosperous, themes repeated in Mexico and Argentina at the same time. Vargas and other advocates of corporatism used populist and nationalist rhetoric to win wide support, and dissent was characterized as un-Brazilian.

Leaders of the FBPF and other women's organizations convinced Vargas that granting women the right to vote would be both an important symbol of progress and a way to broaden his appeal even further. In 1932, a new Brazilian electoral code enfranchised women under the same conditions as men, making Brazil the second Latin American country (after Ecuador) to extend suffrage to women. Women's right to vote was affirmed in the new constitution of 1934.

At about the same time that Brazil became a Portuguese colony, Ottoman troops conquered North Africa, and Egypt became part of the Ottoman Empire, ruled by Mamluk vassals. Mamluk troops were no match for the French armies of Napoleon, who invaded Egypt in 1798, though French forces eventually withdrew after being defeated by the British fleet. In the disruption after the French withdrawal, power in Egypt was assumed by a young Ottoman army officer, Muhammad Ali, who began a program to modernize the army and enhance Egypt's economic base. His reforms were successful in expanding the production of cotton and other crops, but his attempts to develop Egyptian industry were blocked by opposition from European countries and the importation of cheap European-made manufactured goods. His descendants, known as *khedives*, were even less able to reform Egyptian society or limit European intervention. The construction of the Suez Canal in the 1850s and 1860s gave European powers an even greater financial and strategic interest in Egypt, for the canal allowed for much faster and easier commercial and military links between Europe and its colonial empires in East Africa and Asia. A revolt against the khedives in the 1880s led them to request direct British military assistance, and from that point British officials, advisors, and military officers held actual power, though the Ottoman khedives remained the official rulers.

Intellectuals and reformers in Egypt—and elsewhere in the Muslim world—debated ways to meet the European challenge. Some advocated strict adherence to Islamic tradition, others suggested extensive adoption of Western culture, and others favored blending Western technology with Islamic ways of life. The role of women figured prominently in these debates, as male and female reformers called for an "awakening" of women and their transformation into "new women" who would assist in making Egypt a stronger nation. Toward the end of the nineteenth century, several women's journals and newspapers began publication, some focusing primarily on household management and childcare, but often couching these discussions in terms of raising a "modern" family. Others focused more explicitly on expanding women's roles, calling for female education, an end to child marriage, and the founding of charitable organizations by and for women. A few schools for girls were opened in Cairo, designed to train teachers for all-girls schools.

Just as reformers differed in their views about the relationship between Islam and modernity in general, so they also differed in their views of the role of Islam in expanding women's roles. Some writers avoided any discussion of Islam in their calls for reform, viewing reforms as secular matters. Others suggested changes in Islamic law and customs, including loosening restrictions on women's seclusion and wearing *hijab*, which at that point meant veiling the body and the face. Male reformers advocated unveiling the face as a key symbol of Egypt's awakening, though most female reformers disagreed. They wanted women to have better educations and more experience out in public before they unveiled, for removing their veils would certainly result in harassment and ridicule. Some reformers asserted that Islamic law already provided greater scope for women's activities than many people assumed, and the primary problem was that women did not know the rights that were theirs under Islam. They asserted that many of the restrictions on women were traditional patriarchal practices, not grounded in the Qur'an or other authoritative texts.

In the first decade of the twentieth century, many educated middle-class Egyptians called for an end to British occupation and rule by the khedives. Several nationalist parties were organized, often led by journalists, and harsh British responses to protests and mob actions led to wider support for anti-British agitation. Calls for an expanded role for women emerged as part of nationalist plans for an independent Egypt. Women such as Malak Hifni Nasif, an upper-class teacher known by the pen-name Bahithat Al Badiya (Searcher in the Desert), gave lectures to all-female audiences and wrote articles for nationalist newspapers calling for women's education, right to employment, the right to worship in mosques, and legal rights. In 1913, the British granted Egypt a constitution with voting rights limited to wealthy

Chapter 10

Nationalism,

Motherhood, and

Women's Rights

in Brazil, Egypt,

and Japan

(1890s–1930s)

men, but with the outbreak of World War I the following year the British declared martial law in Egypt and stationed large contingents of troops in the country, primarily to defend the Suez Canal. Food shortages and other problems during the war created mass discontent, and nationalist leaders hoped to put the case for Egyptian independence to the peace conference assembled at Versailles at the end of the war. When the delegation (*wafd* in Arabic) was prohibited from traveling to France, mass demonstrations arose in cities and villages, and the Wafd Party, a more unified and stronger nationalist group, became organized.

The protesters included many upper- and lower-class women, who marched, veiled, in groups separate from those of men. Women demanded that the Wafd Party create a women's section, the Wafdist Women's Central Committee (WWCC), with a clear role in decision making. British attempts to suppress the revolution were met with continued opposition, and in 1922 the British began a gradual withdrawal. A new constitution was written in 1923, which declared all Egyptians "equal before the law," with "civil and political rights . . . and public responsibilities." The constitution appeared to accord rights to women, but an electoral law passed only three weeks later limited voting rights to men. Nationalist support for women waned once independence seemed assured. Women, led by Huda Shaarawi (1879–1947), responded by forming the Egyptian Feminist Union (EFU), which called for access to higher education, reform of laws regarding marriage, divorce, child custody, and prostitution, and

the right to vote. The EFU regarded these demands as fully compatible with Islam, though by the 1930s some educated women in Egypt saw demands for changes in Islamic law as a legacy of Western colonialism. They founded the Muslim Women's Society, which sometimes worked with the EFU but tended to emphasize the complementarity of men and women more than equality.

Japan was never colonized by a European power, but in the last half of the nineteenth century it was subject to various unequal treaties that highlighted its inferior political and economic status vis-à-vis Western countries. Japanese leaders decided to modernize the Japanese economy through industrialization and to enhance Japan's political strength. Several male nationalist reformers argued that the oppression of women made Japan seem backward in Western eyes, and they proposed expanding women's education, opportunities for employment, and legal rights. Such reforms, they argued, would make women "good wives and wise mothers," able to assist their husbands in increasing family productivity and to raise their children—especially their sons—to develop a modern, industrious, "new Japan." "Good wife, wise mother" (*ryosai kenbo*) became a standard government slogan, defining women's appropriate roles in terms of their relationship to a husband and children.

During the 1880s, some reformers in what became known as the "Freedom and People's Rights Movement" went further than this, calling for an expansion of voting rights to a greater share of the male population and perhaps even to women. Kishida Toshiko (1863–1901) traveled around Japan, lecturing to large crowds about the need for equality between men and women and for women's education if women were really to be part of building a strong Japan. But despite the nationalist message of the Freedom and People's Rights Movement, the government suppressed it in the 1890s, forbidding women in particular from organizing or joining political associations or even attending meetings where politics were discussed. In 1898, a new Civil Code made the patriarchal family pattern that predominated among the samurai class standard for all social classes in Japan. Women were completely subordinated to their husbands, unable to make a legal contract or claim their own wages; sons were given complete priority in inheritance. "Good wife, wise mother" defined the limits of women's political and social duties, and it was not to be a springboard for a wider public role.

Although government restrictions prohibited women from speaking, effective censorship of the written or printed word was more difficult. Women active in the socialist movement published a newspaper, *Women of the World*, that included their demands for women's and workers' rights. They highlighted the horrendous conditions faced by workers in Japan's coal mines and textile mills, a majority of whom were women. In 1911, Hiratsuka Raichō (1886–1972), a young middle-class woman, began publishing *Seito* (*Bluestocking*), a literary journal that included women's poetry, fiction, and essays. Many of the articles in *Seito* discussed topics that had political implications, including a debate in its pages and in other journals and newspapers about state protection of motherhood. Eight years later, Hiratsuka, along with Ichikawa Fusae (1893–1981), founded the Association of New Women, an organization devoted to expanding women's political role.[3] This group, and similar associations in other parts of Japan, initially worked for a lifting of the ban on women's right to organize or discuss politics, a ban they challenged by their own existence as political groups. By the end of the 1920s, some within the movement were calling for women's suffrage, particularly as voting rights had been extended to all men with the removal of property qualifications in 1925. During the 1930s, women held a series of All-Japan Women's Suffrage Conferences, organizing in support of bills in the Japanese Diet that would allow women to vote in municipal elections.

These calls for women's greater political voice took place in a Japan that was itself becoming an imperial power. In 1895, Japan conquered Taiwan, making it a colony, and in 1910, Japanese forces conquered Korea, setting the stage for an eventual Japanese occupation of much of East Asia and the western Pacific, and finally leading to World War II. Advocates of women's rights thus had to decide about their relationship to militarism and nationalism. Some, such as the women who organized the Patriotic Women's Association in 1901 to provide aid and comfort to soldiers and their families, proudly asserted

3. In Japan, the family name comes first, followed by the given name; thus Hiratsuka is her family name.

Chapter 10

Nationalism,

Motherhood, and

Women's Rights

in Brazil, Egypt,

and Japan

(1890s–1930s)

that women had an important role in a nation at war. Others were more ambivalent, but by the 1930s many advocated women's willing assumption of various civic duties during a time when large numbers of men were away fighting, such as managing fire brigades or organizing food rationing.

THE METHOD

The types of sources you will be using in this chapter are primarily works intentionally written to be part of a political debate, such as speeches, articles, manifestos, editorials, and letters to the editor. Political debates have been studied by historians for a long time. The earliest works traditionally labeled "history," the stories of various wars involving the ancient Greeks written by Herodotus and Thucydides in the fifth century B.C.E., included descriptions of political debates along with portrayals of battles and heroes. The authors of the sources in this chapter were all intentionally engaged in the debate about women's rights, and they desired to make their points in ways that would be clear to their readers or listeners. This means that they are quite direct in their message, and it should not be difficult for you to follow their basic line of argument as long as you read carefully.

In reading the two central questions for this chapter, you no doubt noted that the first asks you to evaluate the ideas and arguments of the sources as a group. The first step is thus to assemble your information about the three topics being considered: women's rights, motherhood, and the nation. It may be helpful to arrange your notes in a three-column chart, being aware that not every source extensively discusses all three of these topics.

The second question asks you to assess similarities and differences among the sources based on the country from which the author originated and to evaluate possible reasons for these similarities and differences. It is thus a compare-and-contrast question, no doubt a familiar type of question to you, for world history courses, including probably the one you are currently enrolled in, tend to provoke comparative questions. Your answer to the first part of this question should be supported with information drawn directly from the sources, including specific quotes to back up your comparisons. As you turn to the second part of this question, however, you may need to be more speculative. To develop an answer, you will need to use the information in the Background section, paying careful attention to the chronology of political events such as constitutional congresses, revolts, protests, and the founding of organizations, as well as to the discussion of cultural issues such as religion, militarism, and government ideologies. Your textbook may provide additional information. Issues of causation, which is what this question addresses, are often hotly debated by historians, so do not be surprised if there are significant differences of opinion among your classmates in answering this question.

Sources 1 through 3 come from Brazil. Source 1 is an editorial from the women's newspaper, *O Sexo Feminino* (*The Female Sex*) written by its editor, Francisca Senhorina da Motta Diniz, in 1890. *O Sexo Feminino* began publication in 1873 and initially emphasized the importance of women's education. With the overthrow of the monarchy in 1889, the paper became a strong advocate of women's suffrage, even changing its official name to *O Quinze de Novembro do Sexo Feminino* (*The Fifteenth of November of the Female Sex*), using the date of the coup ending the monarchy as a symbol of its goal of full political rights for women. What does Diniz want for women? What abstract principles does she use to support her argument? How does she integrate women's roles as mothers and family members into her line of reasoning? Why does she think an extension of women's rights is especially appropriate for Brazil, as compared to other countries?

Source 2 is a letter to the editor written by Bertha Lutz in December of 1918, in response to an editorial in the Brazilian newspaper *Revista da Semana* about women's gaining the right to vote in Britain. What does she advocate for Brazilian women? How does she think Brazil compares with other nations of the world in terms of the treatment of women? How does she see the progress of women and the progress of Brazil as related? Source 3 comes from several editorials from 1921 and 1922 in *Revista Feminina*, the most popular Brazilian women's magazine of the time. What do the editors see as the reason feminism has emerged? How do they view the relationship between women's rights and the family? Between a wider sphere for women and the health of the nation?

Sources 4 through 6 come from Egypt. Source 4 is an extract from *Tahrir al-mar'a* (*The Liberation of Women*), a book written in 1899 by Qasim Amin (1863–1908), a male well-to-do lawyer and nationalist reformer. Why does Qasim see the liberation of women as important for the future of Egypt as a strong nation? What does he see as the role of Islam in this liberation? How does the situation of women in the West and in Egypt compare, in his opinion? Source 5 comes from the memoirs of Huda Shaarawi, a nationalist and feminist leader, describing protests against the British occupation and women's responses to decisions on the part of male leaders of the nationalist Wafd Party in 1919 and 1920. What does she see as the proper role for women in the nationalist movement? How is this shaped by their relations to family members and to other groups? Source 6 is an editorial from the monthly journal of the Egyptian Feminist Union, *L'Egyptienne*, written by its editor Saiza Nabarawi in 1933, about a decade after the beginning of the British withdrawal and the adoption of the Egyptian constitution. Women had begun to enter the university several years earlier, and a new, more conservative minister of education proposed banning coeducation in the name of morality, which would have closed university education again to women. In her response to this proposal, how does Nabarawi link women's education and the future of Egypt? How are women's rights and Egypt's ability to escape British influence connected?

Chapter 10

Nationalism,

Motherhood, and

Women's Rights

in Brazil, Egypt,

and Japan

(1890s–1930s)

Sources 7 through 10 come from Japan. Source 7 is a speech given by Hiratsuka Raichō at the opening meeting of the association of New Women in 1919. What does she set as the goals for the association? How does she relate these goals to women's responsibilities to their families and communities? In 1920, the Association of New Women lobbied sympathetic members of the Japanese Diet to introduce a bill lifting the ban on women joining or organizing political groups. Source 8 is the preamble to this bill, written by Hiratsuka Raichō and Ichikawa Fusae.

How do they relate an expansion of women's political rights to the good of the country? To women's roles as mothers? Source 9 is a suffrage song written by Yosano Akiko in the 1920s. What reasons does she give for extending votes to women? How would Japan benefit from women's suffrage? Source 10 is the manifesto proclaiming the founding of the League for the Realization of Women's Suffrage in 1924. According to this statement, why should women be accorded political rights? What benefits might result from an extension of suffrage to women?

THE EVIDENCE

Sources 1 and 2 from June Hahner, Emancipating the Female Sex: The Struggle for Women's Rights in Brazil, 1850–1940 *(Durham, N.C.: Duke University Press, 1990), pp. 213–215, 222–224.*

1. Francisca Diniz, "Equality of Rights," *O Sexo Feminino,* 1890

Like a Columbus at the prow of his ship, like an eagle with his eyes fixed on the sun of the future, the nineteenth century proceeds toward a new world, a new paradise, where women shall have their thrones of honor and receive their radiant queens' crowns not from the sacrilegious hands of an Alcibiades[4] but from the sacred hands of Justice and Right, the true sovereigns, who will depose the false kings seated on their thrones of injustice and iniquity brandishing their scepters of despotism. . . . We have faith that this century will triumph through the radiant ideal of justice that surrounds it.

We believe, with the strong faith noble causes inspire, that an ideal state will soon be here, when educated women free from traditional prejudices and superstitions will banish from their education the oppression and false beliefs besetting them and will fully develop their physical, moral, and intellectual attributes.

---

4. **Alcibiades:** an ancient Athenian statesman and general, often considered responsible for the decline of Athens.

Then, linked arm in arm with virtuous, honest, and just men in the garden of spiritual civilization, women will climb the steps of light to have their ephemeral physical beauty crowned with the immortal diadem of true beauty, of science and creativity. In the full light of the new era of redemption we shall battle for the restoration of equal rights and our cause—the Emancipation of Women. . . .

We do not wish to play the role of ornaments in the palaces of the stronger sex. Nor do we wish to continue in the semislavery in which we languish, mutilated in our personalities through laws decreed by men. This is no different from the old days of slave labor when the enslaved could not protest their enslavement.

We are not daunted by such hypocrisy as men's treating us like queens only to give us the scepter of the kitchen, or the procreation machine, etc. We are considered nothing but objects of indispensable necessity! We are cactus flowers and nothing more.

Women's emancipation through education is the bright torch which can dispel the darkness and bring us to the august temple of science and to a proper life in a civilized society.

Moral advancement, which can best lead us to understand our rights and duties, will guide our hearts toward the paradise of goodness and of domestic, social, and human happiness. The union of fine arts with literature, a star in the soul's beautiful sky, will make women men's worthy companions in the struggle for social progress and in the labors of family life.

In short, we want women to be fully aware of their own worth and of what they can achieve with their bodies as well as through their moral beauty and the force of their intellects. We want the lords of the stronger sex to know that although under their laws they can execute us for our political ideas, as they did such ill-fated women as Charlotte Corday[5] and many others, they owe us the justice of equal rights. And that includes the right to vote and to be elected to office.

By right we should not be denied expression in Parliament. We should not continue to be mutilated in our moral and mental personality. The right to vote is an attribute of humanity because it stems from the power of speech. Women are human beings, too.

We Brazilian, Italian, French, and other women of diverse nationalities do not request the vote under the restrictions currently imposed on Englishwomen,[6] but with the full rights of republican citizens. We live in a generous and marvelous country recognized as a world leader in liberal ideas and in the ability to throw off old prejudices.

What we ask is a right never demanded before, and therefore ignored. But it was never deleted from natural law.

5. **Charlotte Corday:** French woman who assassinated the revolutionary leader Jean-Paul Marat, for which she was guillotined.

6. At this point, Englishwomen who owned a certain amount of property could vote in elections for a few low-level local offices.

Chapter 10

Nationalism,

Motherhood, and

Women's Rights

in Brazil, Egypt,

and Japan

(1890s–1930s)

Women must publicly plead their cause, which is the cause of right, justice, and humanity. No one should forget that women as mothers represent the sanctity of infinite love. As daughters they represent angelic tenderness. As wives, immortal fidelity. As sisters, the purest dedication and friendship. Moreover, these qualities the Supreme Creator bestowed on them prove their superiority, not their inferiority, and show that equality of action should be put into practice by those men who proclaim the principle of equality.

We Brazilians, Portuguese, French, English, Italian, German, etc., women, like noble Aspasias,[7] . . . are asking for what is due us and what, by natural right, cannot be denied us.

Our ideas are not utopian but instead great and noble, and they will induce humanity to advance toward justice.

This is our political program.

2. Bertha Lutz, Letter to the Editor, *Revista da Semana*, December 23, 1918

For some time I have been following with the greatest interest your columns in the *Revista da Semana*. The last one, that of December 14, pleased me greatly. Ever since I learned of the new electoral status of women in England, I have been very curious as to whether you would have the courage to write what you did. If you had not, I intended to request that you publish a few lines of mine on the matter. Happily, you did it infinitely better than I would have. I am in complete agreement with your ideas and I congratulate and thank you whole-heartedly.

I am a Brazilian, and during the past seven years I have been studying in Europe. It was with great sorrow that I observed upon my return home the situation you described concerning the lack of veneration and respect for women which one sees here in our capital city. The public treatment of women is painful for them and does little to honor our fellow countrymen. More respect, of course, is accorded a woman among the more cultured sectors; but this is superficial and barely conceals the toleration and indulgence with which she is treated, as though she were a spoiled child. In this regard, despite all the national progress achieved in recent years, we find ourselves lagging far behind the peoples who dominate the world today, and behind the new, regenerated France to which this terrible war[8] gave birth.

Surely the greatest portion of the responsibility for this unfortunate state of affairs falls to men, in whose hands rest legislation, politics, and all public institutions. But we also are a bit to blame. You cited the words of one of our greatest contemporaries, President Wilson, concerning American women: "they have

7. **Aspasias:** consort of Pericles, a ruler of ancient Athens.

8. World War I.

shown that they do not differ at all from us in every kind of practical endeavor in which they engage either on their own behalf or on that of the nation." These words should serve to guide us, for they reveal the secret to which emancipated women owe their equal footing with men. I was in Europe during the war, and I spent the tragic days preceding the victory in England and France. The women's war effort was admirable and heroic. Some were brokenhearted by the death of a son, husband, father, or brother, and each one was full of anxiety and horror, but with great simplicity and courage they all took the soldiers' places and carried out the hardest jobs of the absent menfolk. They brought a lively intelligence and an indomitable energy to those tasks, which until now were considered impossible for women. And this heroic example of sacrifice and will-power secured that which all the social and political arguments had failed to accomplish. Today they harvest the fruit of their dedication. Fortunately for our country and for ourselves, we have not been called upon to provide the same proof. But even so we feel that we are worthy of occupying the same position. But how can we obtain it? We should not resign ourselves to being the only subordinates in a world on which liberty smiles. We must become worthy of that position to which we aspire, and we must prove that we merit it. Clearly, at present almost everything depends on men. But one of the greatest forces for emancipation and progress lies within our power: the education of women and men. We must educate women so that they can be intellectually equal and be self-disciplined. We must educate men so that they become aware that women are not toys created for their amusement, and so that, when observing their wives and sisters or remembering their mothers, they understand and are completely convinced of the dignity of women. For us to achieve this result and to demonstrate our equality, both individual and collective efforts are necessary. Practical demonstrations are infinitely more valuable than anything else; only they are truly convincing. You have provided the best example, demonstrating in your columns that the female spirit can rise to the level of large problems, understand new ideas, and express them with elegance and clarity. . . . All the normal school teachers and other women to whom the nation confides the education of its children prove that there are women of great worth in our country also. Such are the excellent examples which moved me to write this letter and to propose that we channel all these isolated efforts so that together they comprise a definitive proof of our equality. For this purpose I am proposing the establishment of a league of Brazilian women. I am not proposing an association of "suffragettes" who would break windows along the street, but rather of Brazilians who understand that a woman ought not to live parasitically based on her sex, taking advantage of man's animal instincts, that she be useful, educate herself and her children, and become capable of performing those political responsibilities which the future cannot fail to allot her. Thus women shall cease to occupy a social position as humiliating for them as it is harmful to men. They shall cease being one of the heavy links that chain our country to the past, and instead become valuable instruments in the progress of Brazil.

Chapter 10

Nationalism,

Motherhood, and

Women's Rights

in Brazil, Egypt,

and Japan

(1890s–1930s)

Source 3 from Revista Feminina, *vols. 8–9, 1921–1922, trans. Darlene Abreu-Ferreira and Susan Besse.*

3. Editorials from *Revista Feminina*, 1921 and 1922

[*October 1921*]

The growing success of feminism around the world proves that we are dealing with a human evolutionary fact that would be foolish to restrain. The progress of human phenomenon [*sic*] is governed by incontestable laws. . . . That Brazilian feminism exists is an indubitable fact. We need only to visit our departments of science, literature, education, commerce, [and] business, and our offices and industries, to see the Brazilian woman transformed into a useful and productive force after twenty centuries of inaction. . . . Feminism was born with the first cry of hunger that roared from [the woman's] hearth. It was from the maternal breast that feminism sprouted: it is not a fruit of revolution, it is an instinct of survival. The bread earned by the man was not enough. The home endured misery; the children suffered hunger; the mother left to get the crust [of bread] that was lacking. For this two roads would avail her: the easy one, suggestive of deceit and the inviting brilliance of vice: the other, arduous, [a road] of crucifixions, of calvaries, of sweat, of work. She preferred the second. And there she is, courageous, renouncing, stoic, attending to her hearth, maintaining it in equilibrium, earning with her work and her sacrifice the bread for her children. It is this that is called revolution, anarchy, instability! How inverted are all the terms of equation in masculine logic!

[*February 1922*]

Ours is . . . the feminism that preserves religion and family, the feminism that defends our sacred racial traditions, feminism that can only be applauded and lauded by the souls that understand the incontestable laws of progress, and accordingly tread the path in the confidence of their beliefs. Furthermore . . . [we insist] on courageously and fearlessly defending the religion and morals of our grandparents. . . . Now, what we understand feminism to be is simply this: the right to collaborate in the great work of reforming the world, the work of love, of religion, and of piety in the camps of hatred, intolerance, and ambition. . . . We desire to follow the great example of Pope Benedict XV. What we ask for is what he asked for: the reconstruction of morals in religion and traditions. If that is a crime; if that is anarchy; if that is condemnable feminism; if following the currents of progress [in] defending the family, and asking on its behalf for a vote in the political assembly . . . if inviting women to not be disinterested in issues that are linked to the greatest interests of the country . . . if asking for women a little more attention and consideration than is granted to the little pet dogs now lying in the luxurious beds of those who choose to have no children, substituting for the sons who should defend the honor of home, country, and the religion of their elders: well then, yes, complain against our feminism, [the] preserver, moralizer, maintainer of family, and defender of religion and morality.

[*September 1922*]

Feminism among us, presently, is a fact [that] no one can deny. Not this revolutionary feminism that preaches destruction of the family, that disavows the idea of God, that ignores the sentiment of honor and proclaims a liberty that necessarily will be transformed into slavery. [But] pure and Christian feminism, supported in our traditions, claiming for women the rights that are theirs, equalizing them with men, demanding the equality that is indispensable, always seeking the collective happiness and progress of the nation, trying to instruct women so that they will now be able to fulfill their duties with the highest judgment and intelligence. . . . [This was] the great mission of Virgilina de Souza Salles [the founder of *Revista Feminina*]. For a long time we have not heard her wise council, her beneficial teachings, yet we have not forgotten everything that she told us, and by treading the same path we arrive at the conclusion of the great truth she always preached: Without God, Fatherland, Honor, and Family, there is no feminism possible.

Source 4 from Qasim Amin, The Liberation of Women and The New Woman, *trans. Samiha Sidhom Peterson (Cairo: American University in Cairo Press, 2000), pp. 7, 8, 62–64, 70–73.*

4. Qasim Amin, extracts from *The Liberation of Women,* 1899

INTRODUCTION: THE STATUS OF WOMEN IN SOCIETY

[*The author compares efforts toward independence by women in various societies.*]

. . . Women in all these societies have felt that they deserve their independence, and are searching for the means to achieve it. These women believe that they are human beings and that they deserve freedom, and they are therefore striving for freedom and demanding every human right.

Westerners, who like to associate all good things with their religion, believe that the Western woman has advanced because her Christian religion helped her achieve freedom. This belief, however, is inaccurate. Christianity did not set up a system which guarantees the freedom of women; it does not guarantee her rights through either specific or general rules; and it does not prescribe any guiding principles on this topic. In every country where Christianity has been introduced and spread it has left no tangible impact on the normative structure

Chapter 10

Nationalism,

Motherhood, and

Women's Rights

in Brazil, Egypt,

and Japan

(1890s–1930s)

affecting women's status. On the contrary, Christianity has been molded by the traditions and manners of the specific nations in which it was introduced. If there were a religion which could have had power and influence over local traditions, then the Muslim women today should have been at the forefront of free women on earth.

The Islamic legal system, the Shari'a, stipulated the equality of women and men before any other legal system. Islam declared women's freedom and emancipation, and granted women all human rights during a time when women occupied the lowest status in all societies. According to Islamic law, women are considered to possess the same legal capabilities in all civil cases pertaining to buying, donating, trusteeship, and disposal of goods, unhindered by requirements of permission from either their father or their husband. These advantages have not yet been attained by some contemporary Western women, yet they demonstrate that respect for women and for their equality with men were basic to the principles of the liberal Shari'a. In fact, our legal system went so far in its kindness to women that it rid them of the burden of earning a living and freed them from the obligation of participating in household and child-rearing expenses. This is unlike some Western laws, which equate men and women only with regard to their duties, giving preference to men with regard to societal rights. . . .

. . . In summary, nothing in the laws of Islam or in its intentions can account for the low status of Muslim women. The existing situation is contrary to the law, because originally women in Islam were granted an equal place in human society.

What a pity! Unacceptable customs, traditions, and superstitions inherited from the countries in which Islam spread have been allowed to permeate this beautiful religion. Knowledge in these countries had not developed to the point of giving women the status already given them by the Shari'a.

WOMEN AND THE NATION

Every educated Egyptian fortunate enough to recognize and comprehend the conditions and needs of his country knows that Egypt has now entered the most important stage of its history.

Our present era differs from every other era in the history of Egypt. Today, knowledge is widespread, nationalism is evident, safety and order exist in all corners of the country, and circumstances have paved the road for progress. On the other hand, we have never faced as much danger as we do now. Western civilization, speeded by steam and electricity, is advancing and has expanded from its origins to all parts of the earth. Hardly any country, even one as small as the palm of a hand, has been left untouched. Whenever Western civilization enters a country, it seizes the wealth and resources of that country including agriculture, industry, and commerce. In doing so, Western civilization uses every method of achieving its goals, even though some of these methods are harmful to the inhabitants of the regions concerned. . . .

This analysis leads us to conclude that preparing for this battle is the only way by which a country can avoid elimination and destruction. Every country needs to be on the alert, assembling capabilities equal to those of whoever is attacking it, especially those intangible intellectual and education capabilities that are central to every other type of power.

If a nation is as prepared as its competitor in the educational sphere, if it uses comparable methods in raising its children, if it adopts comparable perspectives toward work, and if it arms itself for the struggle with the same armor, it will be able to survive alongside its competitor. In fact it will be able to compete easily, and to succeed in the competition. It will also gain control over its own wealth, and the land will justifiably belong to its inhabitants rather than to strangers. The indigenous people will be better adapted to live in their country, and they will form the majority of its inhabitants. Must not success in this endeavor bring prosperity? . . .

A well-known and undisputed fact is that when men are provided with a proper education, the conditions of the country are positively influenced and its waywardness straightened. However, the proper education of women requires further clarification.

A woman is not a whole creation unless her physical and mental upbringing are completed. Her physical upbringing is important because it provides her with good health and preserves her beauty. She should therefore receive the same physical training and exercise as men, because a weak body can only be inhabited by a weak mind. Many mental and nervous disturbances that women experience are primarily a result of irregularity in the functions of their physical organs. A sound mind with all its manifestations reflects a sound body. . . .

Women's mental development is essential because without it a woman loses her value, as she has done in our present society. Yes, she gives birth, and through that reproductive function she preserves the human species. But this reproductive function is fulfilled by every female in every animal species, and in this there is no difference between a woman and a female cat who frequently produces offspring.

Indeed, we have narrowed the functional role of women to one of child-bearing. In doing so we have not required women to perform any other role. We have imagined them to be unfit for other activities and that men do not need them to contribute to the public and private spheres of life. We have forgotten that an adult man is a product of his mother's influence during childhood. I wish that men would understand the importance of this complete tie between a man and his mother. It is the crux of everything I have written in this book, and I repeat: it is impossible to have successful men unless their mothers can prepare them for success. This is the worthwhile goal that civilization has entrusted to the women of our era. Women carry out these heavy responsibilities in all the civilized countries of the world, bearing children then molding them into adults.

Producing offspring is simply a physical function in which women and other female animals participate. All a woman needs for this activity is a sound physical

Chapter 10

Nationalism,

Motherhood, and

Women's Rights

in Brazil, Egypt,

and Japan

(1890s–1930s)

constitution. The second function, which focuses on the proper upbringing of children, is a mental activity that distinguishes human beings. In order to fulfill this function adequately, a woman requires a broad education, immense experience, and a wide range of knowledge.

Any country concerned with its interests should be concerned with the structure of its families, for the family is the foundation of a country. Consequently, since the mother is the foundation of the family, her intellectual development or underdevelopment becomes the primary factor in determining the development or underdevelopment of the country.

A woman is the yardstick of the family. If she is vulgar, she will be despised by her husband, her relatives, and her children. They will all go their separate ways without a strong bond between them, and their lives will be disorganized and disorderly. Their habits and morals will be corrupt. On the other hand, if the woman is cultured and intellectually able, she can instruct all the members of the family and will be respected by everyone. They will also respect themselves, for they will live in harmony under her banner of love. The family will be united, and will gain strength through its unity. These traits which will characterize the family will also characterize the country. Our behavior on a national level will therefore reflect the way we act within the family. A person cannot act in a particular way in his country without having had such behavior modeled for him at home, nor can he treat his compatriots in a manner different to that in which he treats the members of his family. If an individual exemplifies good character amid his family, he will exemplify good character among his countrymen. On the other hand, if he exemplifies poor character among his family, he will exemplify poor character in the society.

To summarize: the development of a country depends on numerous factors, the most important of which is the development of women. Similarly, the underdevelopment of a country is a product of numerous factors, the most important of which is the inferior position of women. . . .

Everyone familiar with the advances made by women in the West and with their work recognizes that Western women have contributed significantly to the foundation of civilization. Women have contributed shoulder to shoulder with men to every branch of trade and industry, to every branch of knowledge and the arts, to every philanthropic activity, and to every political event. The only difference between men and women is in the realm of political rights. If women are granted all their political rights—as is expected in Europe—equality between the sexes will be achieved. Women have already won a major portion of their political rights: they have been given the right to vote in the municipal councils in America and England, and in the commercial courts in France. Women also sit on some state councils in the United States. Hardly a single capital in Europe or America does not presently have an organization actively concerned with women's rights and with the means by which these rights can be gained. Each passing year reveals a significant impact on the historical record of their work, and ends with a new success. . . .

Source 5 from Huda Shaarawi, Harem Years: The Memoirs of an Egyptian Feminist (1879–1924), *trans. and ed. Margot Badran (New York: The Feminist Press, 1987), pp. 112–114, 118, 122.*

5. Huda Shaarawi, extracts from *Harem Years*, 1940s

We women held our first demonstration on 16 March [1919] to protest the repressive acts and intimidation practised by the British authority. In compliance with the orders of the authority we announced our plans to demonstrate in advance but were refused permission. We began to telephone this news to each other, only to read in *al-Muqattam* that the demonstration had received official sanction. We got on the telephone again, telling as many women as possible that we would proceed according to schedule the following morning. Had we been able to contact more than a limited number of women, virtually all the women of Cairo would have taken part in the demonstration.

On the morning of 16 March, I sent placards to the house of the wife of Ahmad Bey Abu Usbaa, bearing slogans in Arabic and French painted in white on a background of black—the colour of mourning. Some of the slogans read, "Long Live the Supporters of Justice and Freedom," others said "Down with Oppressors and Tyrants" and "Down with Occupation."

We assembled according to plan at the Garden City Park, where we left our carriages. Having agreed upon our route and carefully instructed the young women assigned to carry the flags and placards in front, we set out in columns towards the legation of the United States and intended to proceed from there to the legations of Italy and France. However, when we reached Qasr al-Aini Street, I observed that the young women in front were deviating from the original plan and had begun to head in the direction of *Bait al-Umma* (The House of the Nation), as Saad Zaghlul's[9] house was called. I asked my friend Wagida Khulusi[10] to find out why we were going toward Saad Pasha's house and she returned saying that the women had decided it was a better route. According to our first plan we were to have ended our demonstration there. Reluctantly I went along with this change. No sooner were we approaching Zaghlul's house than British troops surrounded us. They blocked the streets with machine guns, forcing us to stop along with the students who had formed columns on both sides of us.

I was determined the demonstration should resume. When I advanced, a British soldier stepped toward me pointing his gun, but I made my way past him. As one of the women tried to pull me back, I shouted in a loud voice, "Let me die so Egypt shall have an Edith Cavell" (an English nurse shot and killed by the Germans during the First World War, who became an instant martyr).

9. **Saad Zaghlul:** a nationalist leader, the head of the Wafd Party, whom the British had just deported for his political activities.
10. **Wagida Khulusi:** Shaarawi's friend and later also a founding member of the Egyptian Feminist Union.

Chapter 10

Nationalism,

Motherhood, and

Women's Rights

in Brazil, Egypt,

and Japan

(1890s–1930s)

Continuing in the direction of the soldiers, I called upon the women to follow. A pair of arms grabbed me and the voice of Regina Khayyat[11] rang in my ears. "This is madness. Do you want to risk the lives of the students? It will happen if the British raise a hand against you." At the thought of our unarmed sons doing battle against the weaponry of British troops, and of the Egyptian losses sure to occur, I came to my senses and stopped still. We stood still for three hours while the sun blazed down on us. The students meanwhile continued to encourage us, saying that the heat of the day would soon abate. Some of the students departed for the legations of the United States, France, and Italy, announcing that the British had surrounded the women in front of Saad Pasha's house. I did not care if I suffered sunstroke—the blame would fall upon the tyrannical British authority—but we stood up to the heat and suffered no harm. The British also brought out Egyptian soldiers armed with sticks. . . .

The women continued to support the Wafd and at the same time gave encouragement to the people. We consoled relatives of students and others injured by British bullets, visited the wounded, and did what we could to assist the poor and needy among them. In the working class quarters women went to their windows and balconies to applaud their men in displays of national solidarity. Sometimes soldiers fired at the houses, killing and wounding women. Some were hit by bullets that pierced the walls of their houses. The death of Shafiqa bint Muhammad, the first woman killed by a British bullet, caused widespread grief. Egyptians of all classes followed her funeral procession. It became the focus of intense national mourning. Events like these, coming one after the other, did not please the British. They disregarded the solemnity of funeral processions, often scattering the mourners and precipitating bloody confrontations. We women began to compile a list of the dead and wounded. Among the women I remember Shafiqa bint Muhammad, Aisha bint Umar, Fahima Riyad, Hamida bint Khalil, and Najiyya Said Ismail—all from the working classes.

[*In 1920, the male leaders of the Wafd Party developed a proposal for independence, but they did not show it to the women's group. Shaarawi comments in her memoirs.*]

. . . We criticized the delegates from the Wafd for disregarding our rights and our very existence by neglecting to solicit our views.

[*The Wafdist Women's Central Committee then sent a formal letter of protest to the Wafd Party.*]

We are surprised and shocked by the way we have been treated recently, in contrast to previous treatment and certainly contrary to what we expect from you. You supported us when we created our Committee. Your congratulatory telegrams expressed the finest hopes and most noble sentiments. What makes us all the more indignant is that by disregarding us the Wafd has caused foreigners to disparage the renaissance of women. They claim that our participation in the

11. **Regina Khayyat:** another friend and founding member of the Egyptian Feminist Union.

nationalist movement was merely a ploy to dupe civilized nations into believing in the advancement of Egypt and its ability to govern itself. Our women's renaissance is above that as you well know. At this moment when the future of Egypt is about to be decided, it is unjust that the Wafd, which stands for the rights of Egypt and struggles for its liberation, should deny half the nation its role in that liberation.

[The women got a letter of apology.]

Source 6 from L'Egyptienne, *July–August 1933, pp. 8–9. Translated and cited in Margot Badran,* Feminists, Islam and Nation: Gender and the Making of Modern Egypt *(Princeton: Princeton University Press, 1995), pp. 162–163.*

6. Saiza Nabarawi, Editorial in *L'Egyptienne*, 1933

He [the Minister of Education] forgets, no doubt, that the times of seclusion are over and that we live in a postwar era, and that the main task of a minister of public education is to prepare the young, who are entrusted to him, to meet the challenges of the times. Who can deny that in the period of evolution that we have gone through the woman was called upon to play an important role in the intellectual and moral elevation of society? The history of the past twelve years when, by successive stages, the woman was freed from the shackles of the past is testimony to the ceaseless development of her personality. If some people are blinded by outmoded prejudices, obstinately failing to recognize the active part she always takes in all aspects of our national renaissance, it is not the business of the minister of public education to ignore this progress. . . . What a pity for Egypt that in the name of morality (little respected at that) all rights of the individual to knowledge and liberty are suppressed and stifled. The first result of mixed education should have dispelled the fears of the conservatives. It was for naught. . . . [The Minister of Education tries] to revive oriental atavism in addressing the specter of immorality threatening this Muslim country and her ancient traditions, which are not safeguarded by the government. And why this holy crusade? Our world has evolved too much, whether you like it or not, for there to be any question of the harem in the future. . . . It is inevitable that the woman will be side by side with you men. It is not by making her frivolous, ignorant, and self-centered that you prepare her to victoriously take up the battle of life. . . .

[This government policy] admirably serves the imperialist designs of Great Britain. This [colonial] power was always opposed to the development of education in Egypt. Is not ignorance the only way to enslave people and to keep them in a condition in which they are not able to free themselves? . . . It is the

Chapter 10

Nationalism,

Motherhood, and

Women's Rights

in Brazil, Egypt,

and Japan

(1890s–1930s)

same egotistical and personal end that the [government] follows today with this deplorable policy. Thus to solidify the dictatorial regime that is imposed on the country it is necessary to stifle all seeds of liberty. What greater danger is there than the education of the masses who will [then] become conscious of their rights? Far from understanding that they are only responsible to the wishes of the people, who have the task of freeing themselves from foreign tutelage, our ministers confine all their activity to maneuvers to preserve their power for the longest time. . . . Above all it is secondary and higher education for women that is most vigorously combated in the official circles.

Sources 7 and 8 from Hiroko Tomida, Hiratsuka Raichō and Early Japanese Feminism *(Leiden: Brill, 2004), pp. 275–276, 293.*

7. Hiratsuka Raichō, Speech to the Association of New Women, 1919

The time has come for all women to unite in their interest to fulfil their obligations and pursue their rights. Now is the time when women should enrich themselves and broaden their education. Now is also the time when women should make efforts to elevate their social status by their solidarity, and cooperate with men and participate in campaigns to improve society in order to acquire rights as women and mothers. If women do not rise to this opportunity now, there is no doubt that our future society will continue to be a male-dominated one excluding women. We believe that the great majority of misfortunes afflicting mankind and the world result from male-dominated societies. We do not believe that Japanese women will remain ignorant and incapable for ever. There are already quite a few learned and able "new women" in our women's circles. We do not doubt that in addition to these recognised women, there are many more thoughtful and capable women with opinions of their own, who are as yet unknown. Why haven't these women's abilities been united and come into play as a social influence? We wonder whether this is because each woman is in a state of utter isolation, does not have any contact with any other women, and does not make any effort to combine her ability with other women's to work for a common aim. Moreover, there have not been any women's organisations, which help to unite them. In view of these circumstances, we have decided to unite our comrades and found the Association of New Women as an organ for women's collective ability, even though we are fully aware of our limitations. We will dedicate ourselves to promoting women's solidarity, the protection of women, the improvement of women's status in society, the advancement of women's interests, and the acquisition of women's rights. We are determined to achieve all these aims.

8. Hiratsuka Raichō and Ichikawa Fusae, Preamble to Bill Allowing Women to Join Political Groups, 1920

It is a requirement for the people of a constitutional country such as Japan to be politically well-informed. One cannot overlook the significant roles played by mothers and wives who understand politics. They contribute to spreading and broadening of political knowledge among the general public. It is a vital requirement for a *ryōsai kenbo* (a good wife and wise mother) to have an excellent political understanding, to fulfil her duty as her children's educator and bring them up to be good constitutional citizens ... Article 5 of the Peace Police Law prohibits women from joining political organisations, from attending public political meetings and from becoming organisers of political meetings. Continuing to refuse to give women freedom to obtain political knowledge and to engage in political activities is terribly anachronistic. These bans will not bring constitutional government to a successful conclusion in any true sense. Nowadays women are permitted to visit the Diet and listen to debates in sessions of both the House of Peers and the House of Representatives. They are also permitted to engage in political discussions in newspapers and magazines. The legal provisions of Clauses 1 and 2 of Article 5 considerably contradict the above mentioned political rights which women have been enjoying and practising for some time. These provisions should, therefore, be deleted from the law immediately.

Source 9 from Vera Mackie, Feminism in Modern Japan *(Cambridge: Cambridge University Press, 2003), p. 69.*

9. Yosano Akiko, Suffrage Song, 1920s

Women, we are steadfast, honest and upright!
Let us shoulder our duty as human beings,
Be wise mothers and sisters to our people,
And spread women's love throughout our land.

Let us scrub away the age-old corruption
Of a politics run by men and for men,
And transform the wealth built from the sweat of our people
Into a bright and happy future for all.

Our labour, our love and our grace
Over dissension and hatred must prevail;

Chapter 10

Nationalism,

Motherhood, and

Women's Rights

in Brazil, Egypt,

and Japan

(1890s–1930s)

Wherever the power of women is found,
The light of peace will dawn at last!

Source 10 from Barbara Molony, "Women's Rights, Feminism, and Suffragism in Japan," Pacific Historical Review, vol. 69, no. 4 (2000), pp. 656–657.

10. Manifesto of the Founding of the League for the Realization of Women's Suffrage, 1924

1. It is our responsibility to destroy customs that have existed in this country for the past twenty-six hundred years and to construct a new Japan that promotes the natural rights of men and women;

2. As women have been attending public schools with men for half a century since the beginning of the Meiji period and our opportunities in higher education have continued to expand, it is unjust to exclude women from universal suffrage;

3. Political rights are necessary for the protection of nearly four million working women in this country;

4. Women who work in the household must be recognized before the law to realize their full human potential;

5. Without political rights we cannot achieve public recognition at either the national or local level of government;

6. It is both necessary and possible to bring together women of different religions and occupations in a movement for women's suffrage.

QUESTIONS TO CONSIDER

As you look over your notes, some issues will emerge repeatedly, and certain points of comparison will be immediately obvious. One of these is the importance of educating women. Francisca Diniz (Source 1) and Qasim Amin (Source 4) lived halfway around the world from each other, and certainly did not know of each other's existence or read each other's writings. Despite this, what ideas about the impact of educating women did they share? Diniz talks about developing women's "physical, moral, and intellectual attributes." What does Amin say about these three aspects of education? Would Bertha Lutz (Source 2), Saiza Nabarawi (Source 6) and Hiratsuka Raichō (Source 7) agree? What might they add to Amin's discussion?

Francisca Diniz talks about women's rights as a matter of justice, which is a common way to frame issues of human rights. Which other sources bring up the issue of justice in their discussion of expanding women's roles? Diniz also sees her cause as promoting "moral advancement" and the public good, what the editors of *Revista Feminina* (Source 3) refer to as "the collective happiness." How do other authors weave these issues into their arguments? What, for example, does Yosano Akiko (Source 9) portray as the direct result of women becoming involved in politics? What do the other sources predict will be the impact of women's achieving political rights? Yosano uses the word *love* twice in her song; what other emotions and character traits do the authors see as enhancing their arguments?

When Diniz mentions love, she is specifically talking about mothers, who "represent the sanctity of infinite love." Her comments about motherhood are brief and rather vague, but your notes no doubt refer to longer discussions of motherhood in other sources. What does Amin see as the most important role of mothers? How are the health of families and the health of the nation related, in his opinion? Would Hiratsuka Raichō and Ichikawa Fusae (Source 8) agree? What would the editors of *Revista Feminina* (Source 3) add to this? Do the sources seem to be discussing biological motherhood, or are some using motherhood in a more metaphorical way?

Turning to the issue of nationalism, several of the authors present both positive and negative qualities in their own countries. How does Diniz's portrayal of Brazil (Source 1) compare with Amin's portrayal of Egypt (Source 4)? How do they use the positive and negative qualities they identify in their arguments for women's rights? Building a strong nation in each of these three countries meant confronting the power of the West, and many of the sources make explicit comparisons between their own country and Europe. How do Bertha Lutz (Source 2) and Qasim Amin (Source 4) compare the situation of European women with that of women in their own lands? How do they compare the actions of European women with those of women in their own countries? What other lines of comparison do they draw? How does Huda Shaarawi (Source 5) use the West's opinion of Egypt in her argument? What similarities does Saiza Nabarawi (Source 6) see between the Egyptian government and the colonial British authorities? Why do you think she makes this comparison? Explicit comparisons with the West are less evident in the Japanese sources, but can you find implicit comparisons?

As you consider differences as well as similarities, the cultural context and historical development of each country come to play a significant role. How does Brazil's recent prohibition of slavery play in the arguments of Brazilian women for political rights? Why might religion be used by writers from Brazil and Egypt, but not by those from Japan? Why might comparison with the West be most explicit in the Egyptian writers, and least explicit in the Japanese?

You are now ready to use the information you have gathered to answer the central questions in the chapter. In the opinion of those who argued for an expanded role for women in Brazil, Egypt, and Japan, why should women be accorded political rights and other

Chapter 10

Nationalism,

Motherhood, and

Women's Rights

in Brazil, Egypt,

and Japan

(1890s–1930s)

opportunities? How is this reason related to motherhood and the strength of the nation? What similarities and differences do you see among the writers from these three countries, and how might these be connected to their varying cultural contexts and historical circumstances?

EPILOGUE

The extension of political rights to women was a slow process, and one that saw setbacks as well as progress. Just three years after women's suffrage was affirmed in Brazil, Getulio Vargas revoked the constitution, dissolved the Brazilian Congress, and decreed the *Estado Novo* (New State) in which he held authoritarian power. No one voted in the *Estado Novo,* though Vargas remained immensely popular, viewed as a strong father who would stand up against foreign capital and guide his people to a better life. Wages for industrial workers, who were mostly male, increased, allowing at least some of them to support a wife and children. Vargas's role as the father of the country was to be replicated in each home, with wives clearly subordinate to their husbands in the same way that their husbands were subordinate to the benevolent leader. This ideal of a male breadwinner shaped national policy; the few women who had gained relatively high positions in government lost them, and secondary schools were ordered to separate their male and female pupils, though women remained as teachers. Women were to show their support for the nation not through paid work or political actions, but through purchasing locally made consumer products and raising children who would be capable, "modern" workers. Vargas was largely in power, sometimes as dictator and sometimes as elected president, until 1954, after which Brazil went through a long period of military dictatorship. Democracy returned in 1985, with women and men voting once again, though activists and reformers since then have asserted that Brazil cannot be truly politically democratic until it is more socially and economically democratic.

In Egypt, British troops remained for decades after official independence, using the country as a base of Allied operations during World War II. In 1952, a group of army officers under Gamel Abdul Nasser overthrew the ruling king and declared Egypt a republic; his National Democratic Party has been in power ever since. Women were granted the right to vote in 1956, though in 2005 only 4 of the 444 elected members of the National Assembly were women.

In Japan, women hoped their work on the home front during the 1930s might show political leaders that women deserved the vote, but this did not happen; women's primary patriotic duty to the Japanese state remained motherhood, producing more soldiers and workers for the expansionist state. However, groups advocating women's rights reorganized immediately after the Japanese surrender at the end of World War II. Ichikawa Fusae met with the new prime minister in 1945, just one day after he took office, and he agreed to grant women the vote. The postwar Constitution and Civil Code guaranteed equal rights, and most women voted, though only about 3 percent of the Japanese Diet was female during most of the postwar period, a share that has climbed to 7 percent in recent years.

Suffrage was gradually extended to women in most of the countries of the world in the twentieth century. In 2005, Kuwait allowed women to vote for the first time, though Saudi Arabia (which held its first local elections in 2005) continued to limit suffrage to men. Both supporters and opponents of women's suffrage expected women's voting patterns to differ sharply from those of men, but in most elections they did not. After gaining suffrage, many women's groups turned their attention away from women's political status to other types of issues, such as educational, health, and legal reforms or world peace.

By the 1960s, women in many parts of the world were dissatisfied with the pace at which they were achieving political and legal equality beyond the ballot box, and a second-wave women's movement began, often termed the "women's liberation movement." Women's groups pressured for an end to sex discrimination in hiring practices, pay rates, inheritance rights, and the granting of credit; they opened battered-women's shelters, daycare centers, and rape crisis centers, and they pushed for university courses on

women and laws against sexual harassment. The United Nations declared 1975–1985 to be the International Decade for Women, and meetings discussing the status of women around the world were held under UN auspices in Mexico City (1975), Copenhagen (1980), Nairobi (1985), and Beijing (1995). In 1979, the United Nations passed the Convention on the Elimination of All Forms of Discrimination Against Women (CEDAW), which as of 2005 has been ratified by 180 countries, or 90 percent of the members of the United Nations.

Just as had the first movement for women's rights, the reinvigorated feminist movement sparked conservative reactions in many countries, with motherhood and women's roles in the family again a central issue of discussion. Women's rights, argued some, caused an increase in the divorce rate, the number of children born out of wedlock, family violence, and juvenile delinquency. Such arguments were effective in stopping some legal changes; the United States and about twenty other countries did not ratify CEDAW, and in the United States, the Equal Rights Amendment was not ratified by enough states to become law, though Canada passed a similar measure in 1960 and Australia in 1984. Though almost all countries in the world now officially give women and men equal voting rights, other aspects of citizenship, such as becoming a citizen after emigration or passing on citizenship to one's children, have remained easier for men than for women.

CHAPTER ELEVEN

LANDS OF DESIRE: DEPARTMENT

STORES, ADVERTISING, AND

THE NEW CONSUMERISM[1] (1910s–1930s)

The response to the death of American department store magnate John Wanamaker on December 12, 1922, was one normally reserved for important heads of state. In Wanamaker's native Philadelphia, public schools and the stock exchange were closed, the city council suspended its meetings, and thousands filed by the casket to pay their respects as Wanamaker's body lay in state in the Bethany Presbyterian Church. Condolences poured in from around the world and included expressions of sympathy from United States president Warren Harding and the secretary of state, Charles Evans Hughes. Graveside services were attended by inventor Thomas Edison, Chief Justice of the United States William Howard Taft, soup and ketchup king Howard Heinz, politician William Jennings Bryan, and a host of U.S. senators and governors. Indeed, John Wanamaker

was as honored in death as he had been powerful and influential in life.

Wanamaker and men like him throughout the world were products of the Industrial Revolution that swept through much of Europe, the Americas, and Japan in the nineteenth century. Mass production made a host of consumer goods available to the middle and skilled working classes for the first time at reasonable prices. In order to distribute these goods, the institution of the department store was born, the first one opening in Paris in 1852. By 1900, department stores were important in bringing consumer goods to the people in France, England, Germany, Japan, the United States, Canada, Brazil, Mexico, Australia, South Africa, New Zealand, Switzerland, Sweden, Norway, Belgium, and Denmark, and by the early years of the twentieth

1. We are happy to attribute this chapter's title to William Leach, from his excellent book *Land of Desire: Merchants, Power, and the Rise of a New American Culture* (New York: Pantheon Books, 1993), p. 3.

century they could be found in major non-Western cities such as Istanbul and Shanghai. Wherever they were founded, department stores bore remarkable similarities; from country to country they looked the same: a mammoth retail emporium selling a myriad of consumer items reasonably priced and grouped together in "departments."

Department store founders like John Wanamaker, however, could not simply open their establishments and expect masses of customers automatically to flock in. Wage earners had to be convinced that they actually *needed* these goods, that owning a felt fedora or a silk chemise would improve their status and happiness. Led by pioneer John Wanamaker, department store owners spent lavishly on newspaper advertising in order to *create* desire for the consumer goods they sold. As Wanamaker himself was fond of saying, "The time to advertise is all the time," and almost all department store owners did precisely that. So dependent did urban newspapers become on department store advertising that by 1904 one observer did not overstate the case when he remarked that the "newspaper of today is largely the creation of the department store." And, spurred by the spectacular success of department store advertising, other businesses began to advertise their products and services as well, especially the manufacturers of what became "brand name" products.

In this chapter, you will be examining and analyzing a series of department store advertisements from the United States, Brazil, France, Turkey, Canada, Australia, China, and the Union of South Africa. All of these promotions appeared in the first three decades of the twentieth century, which was probably the height of the downtown department store phenomenon. Your task in this chapter is to determine the types of appeals department stores used to convince potential customers that they needed the goods the stores offered. What can these advertisements tell us about middle and skilled working classes' values, fears, aspirations, strivings for identity, and visions of "the good life"? Keep in mind that each advertisement may have more than one appeal. Also be aware that appeals can be overt and obvious or may be quite subtle. What similarities and differences can you find in department store advertisements in different countries? Finally, note that various advertisements may be directed at particular demographic groups—middle-class women, for instance. In all, how did department store advertisements create what historian William Leach calls the "land of desire"?

BACKGROUND

Several interrelated factors were responsible for the rise of mass consumerism in the late nineteenth and early twentieth centuries in Europe, the Americas, Japan, and elsewhere. To begin with, the Industrial Revolution and the evolution of the modern factory system made possible staggering increases in the production of manufactured goods. Traditional methods such as the "putting out system" and

Chapter 11

Lands of Desire:

Department

Stores,

Advertising,

and the New

Consumerism

(1910s–1930s)

the apprenticeship system were fairly quickly replaced by mechanized factories where, until the rise of the trade union movement, men, women, and children worked for slim wages with little hope of advancement or in a piece-work system that paid workers not for their time, but for the amount of goods their machines produced. Beginning in the textile, clothing, shoe, and stick furniture industries, the factory system rapidly spread to most areas of production. Between 1890 and 1900 alone, the production of ready-to-wear clothing doubled; by 1914, factories were turning out almost four times the numbers of cheap glassware, lamps, and tableware as they had in 1890.

Several demographic trends also help to explain mass consumerism's advent. For one thing, Europe and the Americas both experienced rapid population increases between 1750 and 1900. Britain's population alone surged from approximately 8 million people in 1750 to over 40 million in 1900. The number of people in what became Germany in 1871 more than doubled between 1800 and 1900, and France's population growth, while somewhat less dramatic, was also impressive (from over 25 million in 1800 to around 39 million by 1900). Thanks to immigration and high natural increases, the Americas' population increases were even more incredible. At the same time, the birthrate in Europe actually was declining. Population increases, therefore, were largely the result of a higher survival rate, which can be explained primarily by greater food supplies and to a lesser extent by improvements in medicine. Life expectancy in France went from an aver-

age of around twenty-one years in 1660 to approximately thirty-eight years by 1832.

A growing number of these people made their livings in nonagricultural occupations, increasingly in urban factories. Manchester, England, once described by an observer as a "sewer of gold" because of the wealth its factories generated while many lived in horrible conditions, surged from 50,000 people in 1780 to 100,000 in 1801 to 400,000 by 1850. Most of these people had migrated from the countryside as part of a rural-to-urban population shift that took place throughout most of Europe and the Americas during the late eighteenth and nineteenth centuries. In Paris and London in 1850, over one-half of those cities' populations had not been born there. Without these demographic changes, it is questionable whether mass consumerism would have appeared where and when it did.

Finally, in spite of the fact that nineteenth-century writers and thinkers like Charles Dickens, Émile Zola, Karl Marx, Friedrich Engels, and others concentrated their attention on the seamier sides of the Industrial Revolution, for many people the factory system—and the accompanying agricultural and demographic changes—brought better and longer lives.[2] In England, real wages (that is, wages adjusted to take into account the cost of living) actually doubled between 1850 and 1906, and the average per capita consumption of food and goods in Great Britain increased by 75

2. Zola did call the department store the "cathedral of modern commerce."

percent between 1780 and 1851. Other nations in Europe and the Americas could boast of equally impressive gains. Therefore, while the new industrial age meant frightful working and living conditions for many, on the whole the standard of living actually improved during the nineteenth century wherever industrialism had triumphed.

Thus the Industrial Revolution increased the ability to produce goods and, at the same time, increased people's ability to consume them. But how were these products to be distributed (sold), and how would the middle and skilled working classes come to perceive that they actually needed them? Small specialty stores that sold only one type of product (like shoes, for example) and street vendors would be insufficient, and mail-order distribution was far better suited to rural regions than to cities. It was at that point that department stores arose to bridge the chasm between producers and potential consumers.

Most of the nineteenth-century department store barons (including John Wanamaker himself) credited Frenchman Aristide Boucicaut with originating the department store concept. In 1852 in Paris, Boucicaut opened Bon Marché, a huge building that contained several merchandise departments. Markups from the wholesale prices were small, meaning that Bon Marché could sell items from 15 to 20 percent cheaper than single-line specialty shops. All items had fixed, marked prices, something of a revolution in retail trade: Before then, no goods were labeled and prices were negotiated through individual bar-

gaining. Boucicaut opened his doors to everyone and began the practice of free returns and exchanges, equally revolutionary for their time. In 1852 (the year it opened), Bon Marché sold 500,000 francs worth of goods. By 1860 it was selling over 5 million francs annually (20 million by 1870), and by 1990 it had opened a store in Istanbul. The modern department store as a worldwide phenomenon was born. Bon Marché was soon followed by Galeries Lafayette and Le Printemps in Paris; Whiteley's, Harrod's, and Selfridges in London; Wertheim in Berlin; Magasin du Nord in Copenhagen; Steen and Strom in Oslo; Magazine zum Globus in Zurich; Nordiska Kompaniet in Stockholm; Mitsukoshi in Tokyo; Xianshi (Sincere), Yong'an (Wing On), Xinxin (Sun Sun), and Dexin (Sun Co.) in Shanghai; Stuttafords in South Africa; A. T. Stewart in New York; and John Wanamaker's in Philadelphia. Aided by architectural innovations (the escalator, of which there were twenty-seven in New York's Gimbel's when that department store opened in 1927) and by technological improvements (electric lighting in 1878, cash registers in the 1880s, the pneumatic tube by the 1890s), department stores became retailing palaces that (as Wanamaker manager Robert Ogden once observed) "added to the sum of human happiness by increasing the power of money to supply the comforts of life."

To entice customers, department stores spent millions on newspaper advertising. In the United States alone, the total spent on newspaper advertising mushroomed from $40 million in 1880 to over $140 million in

Chapter 11

Lands of Desire:

Department

Stores,

Advertising,

and the New

Consumerism

(1910s–1930s)

1904. John Wanamaker, the bricklayer's son become merchant, opened his first department store in 1877 and is generally credited with being the first to appreciate the value of mass advertising. Wanamaker quickly recognized that mass-circulation newspapers reached tens of thousands of his potential customers every day, and he immediately capitalized on that opportunity. Technological improvements like photoengraving made large "display" advertisements with pictures not only inexpensive but eye-catching. Largely because of his advertising, over 70,000 people swarmed into Wanamaker's Philadelphia department store on its opening day in 1877. As L. Frank Baum (an advertising pioneer who abandoned that field when his enormously popular *The Wonderful Wizard of Oz* was published in 1900) remarked, "Without advertising, the modern merchant sinks into oblivion." Wanamaker and his fellow retail giants recognized the wisdom of Baum's pithy observation. At his death in 1922, Wanamaker's wealth was estimated at well over $25 million.

What appeals did Wanamaker and other department store owners make to their potential middle- and working-class customers? How did their newspaper advertisements create a "land of desire"? What do those advertisements reveal about popular values, fears, aspirations, and visions of "the good life"?

THE METHOD

No historian would suggest that newspaper advertisements of the past (or today's ads, for that matter) simply announce the availability of particular goods for sale. In addition to such announcements, advertisements are created with the intention of making people want to buy those products. Therefore, advertisements contain messages telling consumers why these purchases are desirable. Some of these messages are blatant, whereas others are remarkably subtle—so subtle that readers may not even recognize that a powerful message is being communicated. Yet even though the potential consumers of the past may have been oblivious to their advertising vulnerability, historians can analyze those same advertisements in order to detect those underlying appeals.

Messages communicated in advertisements can be divided into two general categories: *positive* messages and *negative* ones. Positive advertisements show the benefits—direct or indirect, explicit or implicit—that would come from purchasing the advertised product. For example, a *direct* benefit of owning a hat would be to keep rain or excessive sunlight off the head; an *indirect* benefit would be that wearing such a hat would communicate to others that the hat's owner was chic, fashionable, modern, or even affluent. In contrast, negative advertisements demonstrate the disastrous consequences of *not* purchasing the advertised product. And, like positive messages, negative messages can be direct or indirect. Returning to our advertisement for hats, a direct negative consequence would be a wet head (cold, flu, ruined coiffure) or a sunburned head. An indirect negative consequence would be to be thought of as unfashionable, frumpy, or even poor. Most effective advertisements combine positive and negative approaches, thereby evoking strong emotional responses that almost compel consumers to purchase the products being advertised.

By 1900, manufacturers, advertising agencies (an infant industry), and department store owners had developed a number of extremely sophisticated and effective appeals that were used in newspaper and magazine advertisements. As you examine and analyze department store advertisements from the United States, Brazil, France, Canada, Australia, Turkey, China, and South Africa, make a list of the ways in which department stores appealed to potential customers. Keep in mind that each advertisement can contain several types of appeals, or messages. Also remember that neither the very rich nor the very poor did their shopping in department stores. Elite men and women would have been horrified to have been seen in a department store, and the very poor clearly were not welcome. Department stores were primarily for the urban middle and working classes, and all advertising appeals would have been directed at them.[3]

In addition, it might be interesting to compare and contrast advertisements from different nations. Were the appeals to the urban middle and working classes in the United States, Brazil, France, Canada, Australia, Turkey, China, and South Africa similar or different? How would you explain your findings?

Finally, what comparisons can be made between the advertisements of the early twentieth century included here and the advertisements that fill today's newspapers and magazines? If the appeals are similar, how would you explain this consistency? If they are different, does that signify a change in popular values, fears, aspirations, and visions of "the good life"?

The twelve advertisements[4] in the Evidence section of this chapter are fairly representative of department store advertisements during the first three decades of the twentieth century. Source 1 is from the United States: Strawbridge & Clothier of Philadelphia. The majority of all department store advertisements emphasized women's clothing, with children's clothing and toys ranking next in advertising space expended. Why do you think this was so?

Sources 2 and 3 are advertisements from the Mappin Stores, Brazil's largest department store chain (they even sold major appliances, like refrigerators). Source 2 concentrates exclusively on men's clothing, whereas Source 3 reveals the very popular market for women of silks and fabrics—for

---

3. A possible exception might have been department stores in Brazil, where there was a comparatively smaller middle class and where the wealthy did patronize department stores.

4. Although Shanghai's department stores did use advertisements, we have selected evidence from the pictorial magazine *Liangyou buabao (The Young Companion)*, first published in 1926 to appeal to China's young *modeng* ("modern") people by featuring up-to-date products and fashions sold in the city's department stores.

Chapter 11

Lands of Desire:

Department

Stores,

Advertising,

and the New

Consumerism

(1910s–1930s)

those who made their own clothes. Are appeals to men and women different or similar?

Source 4 is from France, from the pioneer Bon Marché, generally believed to have been the world's first department store (*bon marché* can be translated as "good deal"). This advertisement does not contain as much written copy as the advertisements from other nations. Therefore, you will have to interpret from the artwork (as the original viewers of these advertisements had to do) what messages are being communicated. For a clue to the message, look closely at how the figures are drawn.

Source 5 is from the Grande Exposition in Istanbul and appeared in the satirical gazette *Kalem*, founded in 1908. At first one might be shocked by seeing an advertisement for women's corsets appearing in a Muslim country. To be sure, a comparatively bloodless revolution had ousted the notorious Sultan Abd-ul-Hamid II (also Abdul-Hamid or Abdulhamid) and put a temporary end to press censorship. Even so, one would not expect to see such an advertisement in Istanbul in 1911. How would you explain this?

Sources 6 and 7 are from the Hudson's Bay Company of Canada. Chartered as a fur trading company by King Charles II of England on May 2, 1670, it is perhaps the oldest still extant company in the Western Hemisphere. Are the Hudson's Bay Company's appeals different from or similar to the advertisements you have analyzed so far?

Sources 8 and 9 are from Australia, and Source 12 is from Garlick's Department Store in Capetown, South Africa. Garlick's was founded in 1875, and by the 1920s it contained over fifty "departments." What special appeals did these department stores make to customers who clearly felt they were far removed geographically from the latest trends and fashions?

As noted earlier, Sources 10 and 11 are from the Chinese pictorial magazine *Liangyou buabao* (*The Young Companion*), published for the "smart" (we might say "cool") affluent people of Shanghai. How do these "advertisements" combine Western and Chinese cultures?

THE EVIDENCE

Source 1: Philadelphia Inquirer, *December 1, 1922. Courtesy of the Center for Research Libraries.*

1. Strawbridge & Clothier, Philadelphia, 1922

This Great Store is Gloriously Ready to Take Care of School and College Girls To-day

Daughter home from college and little sister with an extra holiday to enjoy, usually, we have discovered, plan this day for the greatest pleasure they can think of —selecting new clothes: A great coat or a darling of a fur neck scarf for that next big sports event; a dance frock to take back to college, or one of the new costume suits to wear on the return trip, or one of the new mannish sweaters—"all the girls are wearing them, mother, indeed they are—they're all the fashion." Oh! They'll all be here to-day, and we are gloriously ready for them.

2. Mappin Stores, Brazil

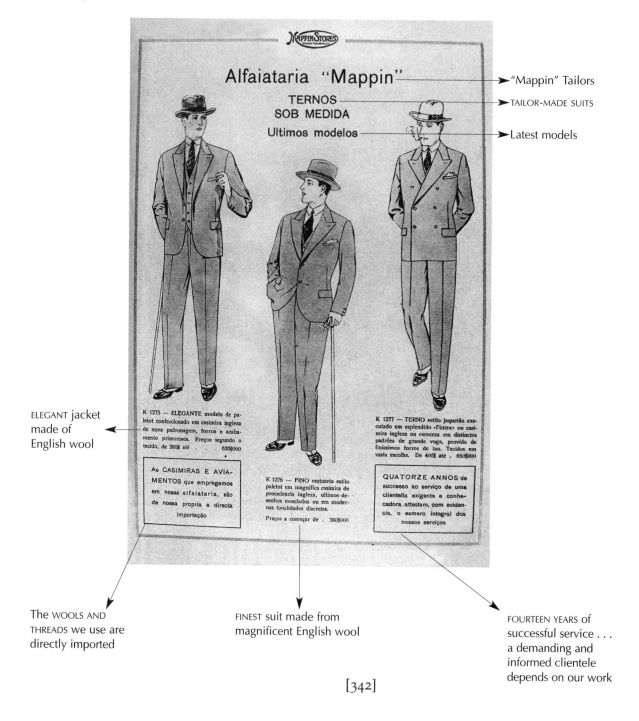

"Mappin" Tailors

TAILOR-MADE SUITS

Latest models

ELEGANT jacket made of English wool

The WOOLS AND THREADS we use are directly imported

FINEST suit made from magnificent English wool

FOURTEEN YEARS of successful service . . . a demanding and informed clientele depends on our work

Source 3: Courtesy of Zuleika Alvim/Grifo.

3. Mappin Stores, Brazil

Silks ◄

The finest products from Lyon, Como and Milan ◄

COTTON from Manchester ►

THREADS ►

HARRIS THREADS for dresses. New colors. ►

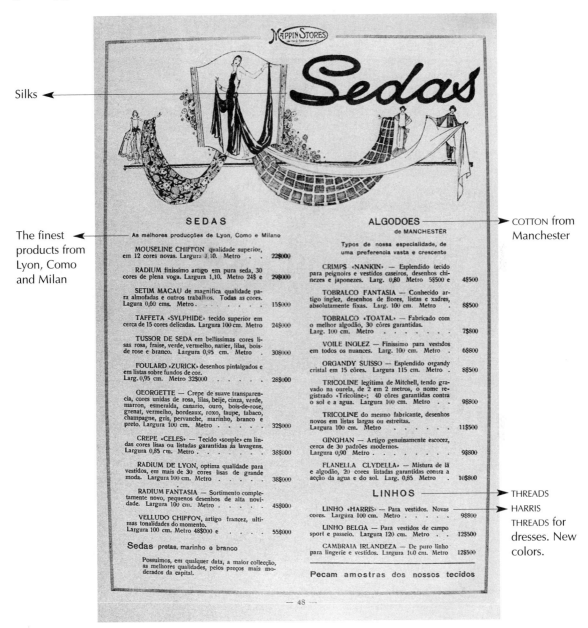

[343]

4. Bon Marché, Paris, 1923

Summer Outfits

Source 5 from Kalem *[Pen], Istanbul, May 18, 1911, in Palmira Brummett,* Image and Imperialism in the Ottoman Revolutionary Press, 1908–1911 *(Albany: State University of New York Press, 2000), p. 231.[5]*

5. Advertisement for corsets, Istanbul, 1911

5. On *Kalem*, see Palmira Brummett, *Image and Imperialism in the Ottoman Revolutionary Press, 1908–1911* (Albany: State University of New York Press, 2000), pp. 30, 43, and *passim.*

Sources 6 and 7: Manitoba Free Press, April 3, 1926; April 19, 1926. Legislative Library of Manitoba. Prints courtesy of Hudson's Bay Company Archives, Provincial Archives of Manitoba.

6. Hudson's Bay Company, Canada, 1926

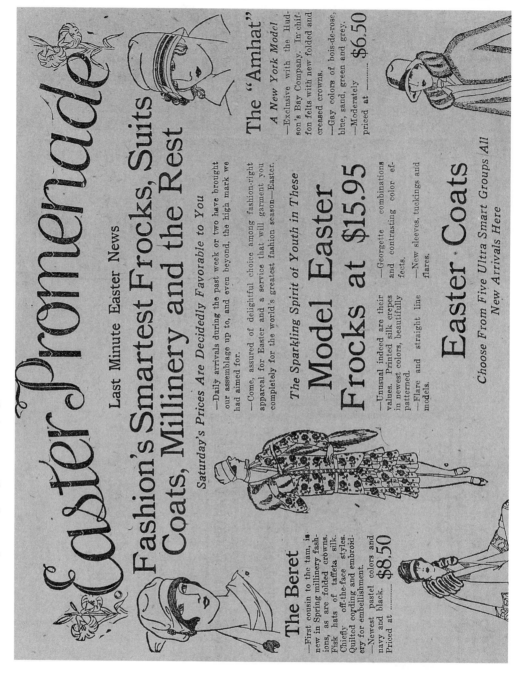

Easter Promenade

Last Minute Easter News

Fashion's Smartest Frocks, Suits Coats, Millinery and the Rest

Saturday's Prices Are Decidedly Favorable to You

—Daily arrivals during the past week or two have brought our assemblage up to, and even beyond, the high mark we had aimed for.

—Come, assured of delightful choice among fashion-right apparel for Easter and a service that will garment you completely for the world's greatest fashion season—Easter.

The Sparkling Spirit of Youth in These

Model Easter Frocks at $15.95

—Unusual indeed are their values. Printed silk crepes in newest colors, beautifully patterned.

—Flare and straight line models.

—Georgette combinations and contrasting color effects.

—New sleeves, tuckings and flares.

Easter Coats

Choose From Five Ultra Smart Groups / All New Arrivals Here

The "Amhat"

A New York Model

—Exclusive with the Hudson's Bay Company. In chiffon felts with new folded and creased crowns.

—Gay colors of bois-de-rose, blue, sand, green and grey.

—Moderately priced at **$6.50**

The Beret

—First cousin to the tam, is new in Spring millinery fashions, as are folded crowns. Fisk hats of taffeta silk. Chiefly off-the-face styles. Quilted cording and embroidery for embellishment. Newest pastel colors and navy and black. Priced at **$8.50**

7. Hudson's Bay Company, Canada, 1926

8. Myer's, Australia, 1929

For the forthcoming *Race and River Carnivals!*

RACE CARNIVAL MODES AT
THE MYER EMPORIUM LTD.!

The Spring Race Toilettes that await your selection at The Myer Emporium. These clever new creations are the most entrancing, the most fascinating fashions imaginable ... you must come in and see for yourself how ravishing the colors, beautiful the new fabrics, which master-couturiers have transformed into the most engaging garments for race and reception occasions!

English, American and Continental Original Models—at Myer's!

Displayed in the Model and Misses' Salons, 2nd and 3rd Floors, Main Store—where the exclusive models from abroad present a collection of indescribable elegance for dinner, dance, daytime and sport occasions.

Hats and Accessories!

The very newest silhouettes in "face-framing" hats of straw, summer felt and fabric to be found on the Fourth Floor. Many are exclusive French and American models featuring lengthened backs, widened sides—in small, medium and large shapes. Shoes, Hose, Gloves, Bags, Sunshades, Scarves, Costume Jewellery and other chic accessories will be found in magnificent assortment —Ground Floor, Main Store.

9. Myer's, Australia, 1922

FREIGHT FREE ——— FROM MYER'S. ——— FREIGHT FREE ——— FROM MYER'S.

A wonderful shipment comes to Myer's !

Daintiest Swiss wovenwear for women!

Unique concessions secured in purchase by Myer Buyer !

JUST OPENED, BY MYER'S! A shipment the Myer buyer journeyed expressly from Melbourne to Switzerland to buy. No looms in the world turn out such perfect woven garments as Swiss looms. The Swiss weaver displays a remarkable aptitude in spinning, weaving, bleaching, and finishing — hence the world-wide reputation for quality that his products have won. For cool comfort, for service and value, the lots listed here would be difficult to surpass. Come, Monday, and see the attractive displays on the 3rd floor!

[The remainder of the text describes the seven items pictured at left, together with their "usual" prices and Myer's "special" prices.]

Chapter 11

Lands of Desire:

Department

Stores,

Advertising,

and the New

Consumerism

(1910s–1930s)

Sources 10 and 11 from Leo Ou-fan Lee, Shanghai Modern: The Flowering of a New Urban Culture in China, 1930–1945 *(Cambridge: Harvard University Press, 1999), following p. 150.*

10. Cigarette Advertisement in *Liangyou buabao*, February 1926[6]

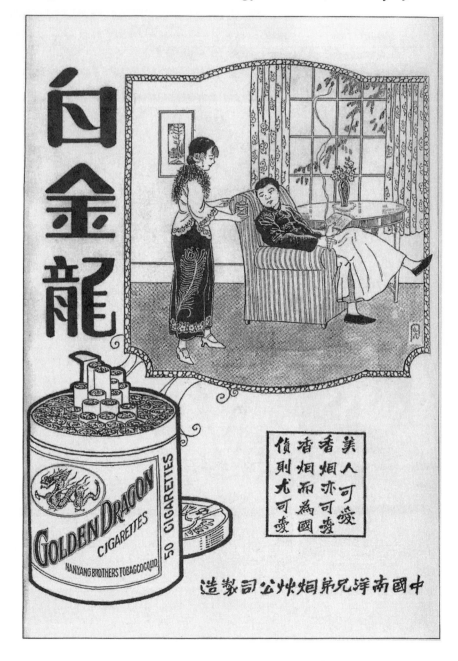

6. The four lines of Chinese read: "Beauty is lovely; cigarettes are also lovely. The cigarette that is a national product is even more lovely."

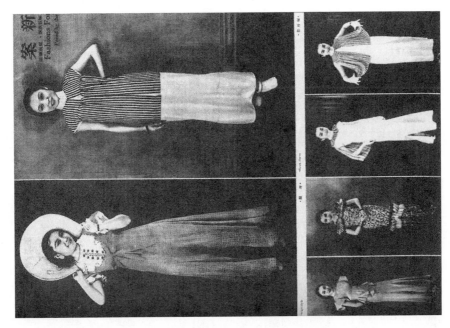

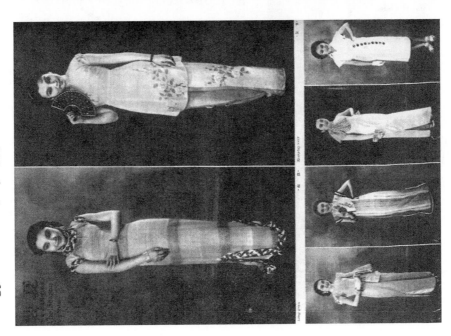

11. Women's Fashions, Both Chinese and "Foreign" Styles, in *Liangyou huabao,* July 1935

Source 12: Capetown (South Africa) Cape Times, *November 4, 1926; Courtesy of the Center for Research Libraries.*

12. Garlick's, South Africa, 1926

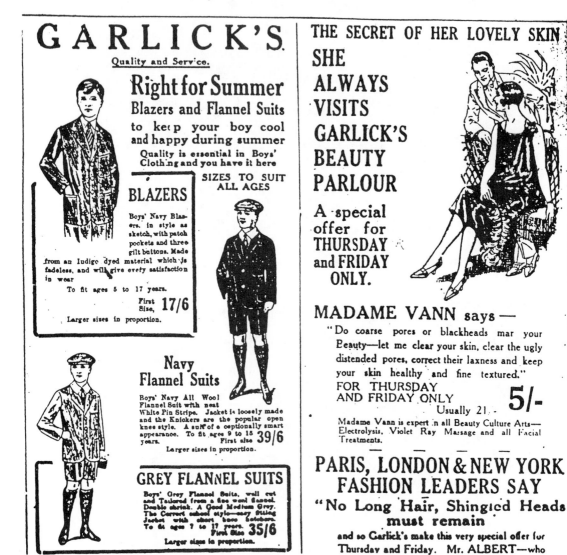

GARLICK'S.

Quality and Service.

Right for Summer

Blazers and Flannel Suits

to keep your boy cool and happy during summer

Quality is essential in Boys' Clothing and you have it here

SIZES TO SUIT ALL AGES

BLAZERS

Boys' Navy Blazers. in style as sketch, with patch pockets and three gilt buttons. Made from an Indigo dyed material which is fadeless, and will give every satisfaction in wear

To fit ages 5 to 17 years.

First Size, **17/6**

Larger sizes in proportion.

Navy Flannel Suits

Boys' Navy All Wool Flannel Suit with neat White Pin Stripe. Jacket is loosely made and the Knickers are the popular open knee style. A suit of exceptionally smart appearance. To fit ages 9 to 15 years. First size **39/6**

Larger sizes in proportion.

GREY FLANNEL SUITS

Boys' Grey Flannel Suits, well cut and Tailored from a fine wool flannel. Double shrunk. A Good Medium Grey. The Correct school style—easy fitting Jacket with short bone buttons. To fit ages 7 to 17 years. First Size **35/6**

Larger sizes in proportion.

THE SECRET OF HER LOVELY SKIN

SHE ALWAYS VISITS GARLICK'S BEAUTY PARLOUR

A special offer for THURSDAY and FRIDAY ONLY.

MADAME VANN says —

"Do coarse pores or blackheads mar your Beauty—let me clear your skin, clear the ugly distended pores, correct their laxness and keep your skin healthy and fine textured."

FOR THURSDAY AND FRIDAY ONLY

Usually 21 - **5/-**

Madame Vann is expert in all Beauty Culture Arts—Electrolysis, Violet Ray Massage and all Facial Treatments.

PARIS, LONDON & NEW YORK FASHION LEADERS SAY

"No Long Hair, Shingled Heads must remain

and so Garlick's make this very special offer for Thursday and Friday. Mr. ALBERT—who

QUESTIONS TO CONSIDER

Your task in this chapter is to analyze department store advertisements of the early twentieth century to determine what types of appeals these advertisements utilized and what those appeals reveal about popular values, fears, aspirations, and visions of "the good life."

As you examine the twelve advertisements presented as evidence, keep in mind that department stores for the most part catered to the middle and skilled working classes, not to the elite or the very poor. In London, most upper-class men and women went to tailoring establishments where their clothes were specially fitted—some had their measurements "on file" at exclusive shops. Similarly, the very poor did not shop in department stores either, mainly because even prices this low were beyond their means. Hence department stores tailored their advertisements to middle- and skilled working-class potential customers. In what ways did they do that?

As you examine each advertisement, you will find it helpful to make notes. First, try to determine the *message* of each advertisement. To what emotions is the advertisement appealing?

As late as the seventeenth century, it was illegal in much of Europe and in some of the English colonies in North America for people to "dress above their station"—that is, to wear clothes normally worn by the elite. People were fined for wearing lace at their wrists and necks! By the nineteenth century, democratic revolutions in Europe and America had done away with such distinctions, and many people in the middle and skilled working classes purposely tried to imitate their "betters" in dress (they "dressed up"). Which advertisements attempt to play upon such yearnings? For example, in the 1920s it was extremely rare for a young woman not from the elite to go to college, and very few college women would have patronized department stores. How, then, can we understand the advertisement from Strawbridge & Clothier (Source 1)?

Middle-class shoppers also were extremely fashion conscious and wanted to purchase only the most up-to-date goods. Indeed, it seems that the farther a department store was from one of the world's centers of fashion, the more advertisements sought to emphasize that these stores carried the latest goods from these fashion meccas. Which advertisements play upon that desire, and how do they do so?

But above all, the middle-class shoppers were interested in value. In addition to the positive messages (be stylish) and the negative messages (don't be ordinary), middle-class shoppers were concerned with price. How did the advertisements emphasize savings?

Many middle-class shoppers deferred buying things for themselves, choosing to help their children leapfrog over humble parents into the upper-middle class. How do these advertisements demonstrate this? How does this fit in with middle-class assumptions of "the good life"?

Chapter 11

Lands of Desire:

Department

Stores,

Advertising,

and the New

Consumerism

(1910s–1930s)

What is remarkable about these advertisements (from the United States, Brazil, France, Turkey, Canada, Australia, China, and South Africa) is not how different they were, but how similar. Indeed, mass consumption in department stores (the "lands of desire") had conquered much of the world. The Industrial Revolution had embraced the world's new middle class.

EPILOGUE

At their peak in the 1920s, urban department stores were important institutions in the industrialized world. To begin with, and as noted above, the department store served as a major way to distribute the goods that industrialism's factories continued to churn out. But in order to perform this function, department stores needed to convince a new generation of consumers, many of whom had been used to making their own clothing, tools, furniture, and toys, that it actually *needed* the goods that department stores offered for sale. This they did by newspaper advertising, using appeals to the middle and working classes to be smart, up-to-date, and stylish, to be generous parents—and all of this at affordable prices and in giant consumer palaces in which they were treated like royalty.

As you can see by the advertisements from these eight countries, mass production and mass consumption through the department store led to a homogenization of dress, furniture, and other goods. Accounting for climate, the middle and working classes in the industrial nations (as well as those in other nations who could afford imported goods) began to dress alike, something they had not done previously when they made most of their own clothes and accessories. Regional variations began to fade as department stores constantly urged the up-and-coming to buy the latest goods from Paris, London, or New York.

The department store was a major factor in the return of middle-class women to the center city, a place they had abandoned in the period from the 1830s to the 1850s as dirty, dangerous, and dominated by males. But department stores, realizing that middle-class women often controlled the homes' purse strings, made every effort to draw middle-class women back downtown. To assist these women with their purchases, department stores offered employment to female salesclerks, albeit at wages considerably lower than those of their male counterparts. By 1907, Germany boasted of approximately 200 department stores, where 80 percent of the clerks were women. In the United States, department stores in 1920 gave employment to 350,000 women salesclerks. Even China, where women's roles were considerably more restricted, saw the introduction of women salesclerks, at first in Xianshi Department Store in the 1920s. A few women rose from salesclerks to buyers, positions considerably elevated in both pay and status. On the other hand, the proliferation of women shoppers also led to an increase in female shoplifters who could operate more boldly amid the new thousands of women shoppers and staff. Thus department stores added employment opportunities—both legal and illegal—for women in industrialized nations.[7]

Although no one could have predicted it, John Wanamaker's death in 1922 came at about the peak of the center-city department store. The Great Depression of the 1930s and World War II (in Europe 1939–1945) severely curtailed consumption, although American journalist James Rorty maintains that the "advanced system of dream-manufacture" survived these periods of cutbacks in the manufacture of civilian consumer goods. At war's end, led by the United States, the industrialized world experienced the profound demographic shift known as *suburbanization,* in which people from the cities and the rural areas took up residence in the rimlands surrounding the urban centers. In the United States, in 1900 a bare 5.8 percent of Americans lived in suburbs. By 1990 that figure had exploded to 46.2 percent, and fourteen of the nation's most populous states had suburban populations over 50 percent.

In the United States and elsewhere, suburbanites often did not return to the city center to shop. By 1978, the United States had over 117 million registered automobiles, which would have created massive congestion and parking problems had shoppers wished to do so. Increasingly suburbanites made their purchases at massive shopping malls, which offered convenience, ample parking, and a variety of retail stores. In the United States, in 1945 only eight shopping malls existed; by 1960, almost 4,000 catered to consumers. Suburbanization proceeded at slower paces in other nations, but the demographic shifts were nonetheless significant. Within a half-century of the department store's peak in the 1920s, the massive downtown palaces of consumer desire were either closed or on the wane. Their own branch establishments in the shopping malls were pale imitations of the center-city retail jewels.

Nevertheless, in its comparatively brief lifetime the department store performed a number of important economic and social functions for the industrialized world. Perhaps most important was its impact on the value systems of the industrialized nations. As middle and skilled working-class people began to shift their self-definition and their definitions of others from who we (they) *are* to what we (they) *own,* a major upheaval in world-views was taking place, both in the industrialized nations and elsewhere.[8] People might continue to tell themselves that money does not buy

7. On women shoplifters in the United States, see Elaine B. Abelson, *When Ladies Go A-Thieving: Middle-Class Shoplifters in the Victorian Department Store* (New York: Oxford University Press, 1989).

8. According to *The New York Times* (Dec. 27, 1991, and Aug. 15, 1992), the Nike Corporation, manufacturers of athletic shoes and sportswear, recorded a 1991 profit of $3 billion, while paying its Indonesian sneaker-makers $1.03 a day.

Chapter 11

Lands of Desire:

Department

Stores,

Advertising,

and the New

Consumerism

(1910s–1930s)

happiness, but judging by their actions, a decreasing number of men and women actually believed it.

In the last decade or so, historians, economists, political leaders, businesspeople, journalists, and average citizens have become concerned about what many people describe as *globalization,* the complex phenomenon in which individuals, companies, nations, and world regions become integrated, driven by the international market economy and the information revolution in which people become interdependent and in which some components of Western culture (Coca-Cola, McDonald's, American films, the English language, and so forth) are undermining traditional cultures—a sort of "cultural imperialism" against which many individuals are increasingly rebelling.[9]

And yet, as this chapter clearly shows, globalization and "cultural imperialism" are hardly new phenomena in world history. What effects did Western-style department stores have on the world's consumers? Were the effects both positive and negative?

9. There are many excellent works on globalization. Two interesting ones are by *New York Times* columnist Thomas L. Friedman: *The Lexus and the Olive Tree: Understanding Globalization* rev. ed. (New York: Anchor Books, 2000) and *The World Is Flat: A Brief History of the Twenty-First Century* (New York: Farrar, Straus and Giroux, 2005). For less positive views, see Barry Smart, *Resisting McDonaldization* (London: Sage, 1999), and Zygmunt Bauman, *Globalization: The Human Consequences* (New York: Columbia University Press, 1998).

CHAPTER TWELVE

THE INDUSTRIAL CRISIS AND THE

CENTRALIZATION OF GOVERNMENT

(1924–1939)

On August 7, 1931, Britain's Chancellor of the Exchequer Philip Snowden wrote an alarming letter to Prime Minister Ramsay MacDonald; in part, it read,

> I have been thinking seriously and constantly about the whole situation these last few days, and the more I think the more I am convinced of the terrible gravity of it.... We cannot allow matters to drift into utter chaos, and we are perilously near that.[1]

The complete letter makes it clear that Snowden was referring to the Great Depression, the economic catastrophe that struck Europe, the Americas, and portions of Africa, Asia, the Middle

East, and Oceania in the late 1920s and 1930s. By 1931 it had become evident that recovery was not in the immediate future. Rather, the situation was growing increasingly grave. Prices of both industrial and agricultural products had collapsed, with world crop prices (which still represented 40 percent of all world trade) only 38.9 percent of what they had been in 1923–1925. Unemployment in the industrialized nations was staggering, creating severe social problems and making millions of men and women potentially easy targets for anyone who promised a return to prosperity. Investments and savings were wiped out as securities markets collapsed around the world and bank failures and bankruptcies mounted. The failure of the Austrian State Bank (Credit Anstalt) in May 1931 dragged other banks, in Germany and in central Europe, down with it, while in the United States the banking system was in a shambles. Bankruptcies of private

1. Snowden to MacDonald, August 7, 1931, quoted in David Marquand, *Ramsay MacDonald* (London: Jonathan Cape, 1977), p. 613.

Chapter 12

The Industrial

Crisis and the

Centralization

of Government

(1924–1939)

businesses reached record proportions in Germany and the United States. In Great Britain, the government was in the process of defaulting on its annual debt payment to the United States. Indeed, Snowden did not exaggerate the bleakness of the economic situation.

The economic collapse caused tremors in the political arena as well. In Great Britain, the Labour Party government was near extinction and would be succeeded at the end of 1931 by a National Coalition government. And in the United States, the Democratic Party made healthy gains in the 1930 off-year elections and appeared poised to chase President Herbert Hoover and the Republicans from the White House in 1932. More ominously, in Germany, the September 1930 elections increased the number of Reichstag seats held by Adolf Hitler's National Socialist (Nazi) Party from 12 to 107. In Japan, parliamentary government found the military to be increasingly out of control. And where there was not political instability, there were other grim repercussions: harsh authoritarian governments in Portugal, Austria, and Spain; the Great Purge in the Soviet Union in 1936–1937; and a rise in militarism in Italy under Benito Mussolini.

Whether unstable or not, all of these governments had to devise methods to respond to the economic catastrophe, the longest and deepest industrial depression the world ever had seen.

Your task in this chapter is twofold. First, you must read and analyze selections from the speeches of five government leaders during the Great Depression: Ramsay MacDonald (prime minister of Great Britain, 1924, 1929–1935), Franklin Roosevelt (president of the United States, 1933–1945), Adolf Hitler (chancellor of Germany, 1933–1945), Hashimoto Kingoro (prominent Japanese army officer, expansionist, and politician), and Josef Stalin (secretary general of the Central Committee of the Communist Party in the Soviet Union, 1922–1953). Then, having analyzed those speeches, you should examine the sets of statistics that follow the speeches to see how the proposals you read about in the speeches were put into effect. How did each of the five major industrialized nations (Great Britain, the United States, Germany, Japan, and the Soviet Union) choose to combat the Great Depression? What were the principal similarities between their approaches? the differences?

BACKGROUND

In order to understand the gravity of the worldwide depression of the 1930s, we should begin by examining the long-term structural changes in the world economy that led to this de-

pression. For most of the nineteenth century, Great Britain had been the world's industrial leader and as such had played a crucial role in the international economy. As the birthplace of the Industrial Revolution in the late 1700s, Britain had taken an early lead in the manufacturing of textiles, clothing, and iron products, all of which were exported to Britain's empire and elsewhere. Profits from manufacturing, shipping, and insurance services had made London a world financial center that directed the extraction and importation of raw materials, the production of finished goods from those raw materials, and the shipment of manufactured products throughout the world.

The gradual spread of the Industrial Revolution not only challenged Great Britain's economic and financial dominance but also resulted in profound dislocations in the international economy. By the end of the nineteenth century, both Germany and the United States equaled Britain's industrial capacity; Japan was offering aggressive rivalry for Asian markets; and France, Italy, Russia, and nations in Latin America were industrializing as well, albeit more slowly. Therefore, nations that once had been primarily importers of industrial products were now beginning to produce these products themselves, thereby decreasing their dependence on the older industrial powers and even generating industrial surpluses that they were able to export into a vastly more competitive world market. Inevitably, this industrial proliferation resulted in intense competition between nations for raw materials, fuel, and (most importantly) markets for manufactured goods. The imperialistic scramble for colonies that gripped the West in the late nineteenth century was a direct product of that competition. Some historians believe that the outbreak of war in Europe in 1914 was another.

At the same time that widespread industrialization was altering the tradi-tional structure of the world economy, the industrial nations were faced with a major agricultural crisis. Worldwide overproduction (in some crops caused by mechanization of farms) drove agricultural prices down until farmers and agricultural workers could no longer afford to buy the manufactured goods pouring off world assembly lines. Those farmers who raised wheat and coffee were especially hard hit, in part because they had mortgaged their farms to buy more land to take advantage of high crop prices in the 1920s. Faced with ruin, millions of farmers abandoned rural regions for the cities, hoping to find jobs in factories. In Japan alone, the urban population went from 12 percent in 1895 to over 45 percent by 1935. And in the United States, the 1920 federal census revealed for the first time over 50 percent of Americans living in cities and towns. But factories, forced to compete with their counterparts throughout the world, could not sell all they were able to produce and therefore could not even hope to employ the horde of rural-to-urban migrants.

Thus, even before the Great War erupted in Europe in 1914, the world economy was undergoing some fundamental structural changes that hinted at some rather frightening consequences. Increased international industrial competition, the collapse of world agricultural prices, and the rural-to-urban migration into already troubled industrial cities all spelled difficulties ahead.

The Great War (World War I, 1914–1918) brought further dislocations and world economic instability. The chief beneficiary of the conflict was the

Chapter 12

The Industrial

Crisis and the

Centralization

of Government

(1924–1939)

United States, already the world's most potent industrial nation before the outbreak of war (by 1913 the United States was producing one-third of the world's manufactured goods). Emerging from the war virtually unscathed, the United States immediately became the world's creditor, with billions of dollars of wartime and postwar reconstruction loans owed by the other participants.[2] Almost overnight, New York replaced London as the world's financial center (by 1930 the U.S. Federal Reserve held over half of the world's stock of gold), and American manufacturing, stimulated by massive production and consumption of automobiles, steel, rubber, and electrical products (radios, vacuum cleaners, refrigerators, and the like) and extensive housing construction, experienced a sustained boom almost unmatched in the history of the Industrial Revolution.

The postwar world was not so pleasant for other nations. After a brief postwar recovery, Great Britain slumped into a sustained recession for most of the 1920s, with never fewer than a million workers unemployed after March 1921. To combat hard times, British leaders were forced to keep wages down in order to keep production costs down (this made British exports cheaper but precipitated the General Strike of 1926) and to raise interest rates (this restored value to the British pound, but choked off borrowing). Once the world's industrial leader, Great Britain in the 1920s was slipping rapidly.

In Germany, the situation was even more distressing. Led by a vengeful France, the victorious nations of World War I demanded that Germany pay huge reparations to compensate for wartime damages it had inflicted. Outraged by German nonpayment, in 1923 French and Belgian forces marched into the Ruhr (Germany's industrial heartland) to force payments or, failing that, to seize anything of value. The Germans responded with passive resistance and printed money to assist the Ruhr's residents. The German currency, already seriously inflated, simply became worthless and the entire economy collapsed, only to be propped up later by continued loans from the United States.[3] By the late 1920s, Germany was borrowing money from the United States in order to make reparation payments to France, Britain, and Belgium, which in turn were repaying their own loans to the United States. These practices were extremely dangerous, since the whole system rested on funding by the United States. Moreover, the cry for reparations left a feeling of extreme bitterness in Germany. Even the French recognized this, as General Ferdinand Foch remarked of the Treaty of Versailles, "This is not a Peace. It is an Armistice for twenty years." Foch's dire prediction was off the mark by only two months.[4]

---

2. Even the majority of wartime and postwar relief deliveries by the United States were not gifts but loans—63 percent, as opposed to 29 percent cash sales and only 8 percent outright gifts.

3. Germany's wholesale price index (1913 = 100) was 245 in 1918, 800 in 1919, 1,400 in 1920, and had reached 126 *trillion* by December 1923.

4. Germany was forced to sign the Treaty of Versailles ending World War I on June 28, 1919; in response to Hitler's invasion of Poland, Britain and France declared war on Germany on September 3, 1939, thus beginning World War II.

Japan had profited immensely from World War I, as it had been able to gain access to markets in Asia that were traditionally controlled by Europe and the United States. Between 1914 and 1919, the Japanese merchant fleet doubled in size, and some corporations experienced such enormous windfalls that they declared dividends of 100 percent of par value on their stock. But at the close of World War I Europe and the United States returned to Asia and shoved the Japanese out of their recently won markets. The Japanese economy collapsed in 1920, and many banks were forced to close. In addition, rapid population growth (from 44 million people in 1900 to 73 million by 1940) meant that for the first time Japan would have to become an importer of food rather than an exporter. Partial recovery came with a drop in the value of the yen in 1924, which made Japanese exports somewhat more attractive. But Japan still faced massive problems: How was the nation to secure access to raw materials for its industries (especially oil to fuel the factories) and markets for its manufactured goods?

Prior to the Great War, tsarist Russia, once a sleeping giant, was beginning to stir and show signs that it was awakening. From 1888 to 1913, Russia's industries grew at the average rate of 5 percent per year, while agricultural income between 1900 and 1913 increased 88.6 percent. National income, foreign investments, urbanization, and the number of rural cooperatives all grew significantly, and a Russian middle class was beginning to emerge. Perhaps most striking, between 1875 and 1913 the literacy of army recruits more than

tripled, to 73 percent. Yet the war, the Bolshevik Revolution, and the resulting civil war of 1918–1921 decimated the Russian economy, until by 1921 gross industrial output was only 31 percent of what it had been in 1913, agricultural production had declined 40 percent, and mass starvation and a series of typhus epidemics drove the once-proud nation to its knees. In response, communist leader Vladimir Lenin relaxed his policies of nationalization of industry, confiscation and redistribution of agricultural land, and an emphasis on centralized planning. By 1924, the year of Lenin's death, the economy was showing some signs of recovery. After a brief power struggle, Josef Stalin emerged as Lenin's successor, the person who would determine in what direction the Soviet Union's economic development would go. "We are fifty or a hundred years behind the advanced countries," Stalin mourned. "We must make good this distance in ten years . . . or we shall go under."[5]

The New York stock market crash of October 1929 was the push that toppled the whole unstable mechanism. American banks and investors, forced to absorb massive losses incurred because they had been speculating in the market, cut off loans to Europe and tried to call back money they already had loaned. In an effort to keep out foreign manufactured goods and thereby protect its own industries, the United States also raised tariffs, setting off a wave of retaliatory increases in

5. Alec Nove, *An Economic History of the USSR* (London: Penguin, 1969), pp. 12, 14, 18–26, 48–55, 67–68, 85–94, 188. Russia became the Union of Soviet Socialist Republics (USSR) in 1923.

Chapter 12

The Industrial

Crisis and the

Centralization

of Government

(1924–1939)

other nations. It was as if each nation was trying to seal itself up, like a water-tight compartment, so as to solve its own economic troubles—an isolationist policy that was both shortsighted and ultimately disastrous.[6]

Great Britain's economy, already paralyzed, sickened even more, with unemployment gradually climbing to 2,725,000 by December 1930. Prime Minister Ramsay MacDonald mourned, "Is the sun of my country sinking?" Dependent on foreign loans, Germany's economy simply fell apart. The government tried to cut the budget, with the result that by the beginning of 1932 one-third of Germany's work force was unemployed and another third was working only part-time. By late 1932, 25 percent of U.S. workers were unemployed and banks were totally closed or only partially operating in forty-seven of the nation's forty-eight states. In Japan, as elsewhere, production and prices both plummeted, while unemployment crept up. For those who had jobs, wages were but 69 percent of what they had been in 1926 (rural cash incomes were only 33 percent), and exports by 1931 had dropped 50 percent. Thus virtually all nations that sought to become participants in the world economic network saw their national economies spiral downward, almost out of control. Worldwide production of manufactured goods (by long-time and newly industrialized nations) outpaced consumers' abilities

6. Over thirty nations had formally protested to U.S. President Herbert Hoover about the tariff, and a thousand economists had urged him not to sign the bill.

to purchase these goods. As surplus items piled up in warehouses, manufacturers were forced to discharge or lay off workers, who then could buy even less than they had before. Farmers and agricultural workers, faced with declining prices, tried to produce even more, which in turn drove farm prices even lower. The world's worst industrial depression had begun.

The worldwide economic collapse had serious political ramifications in virtually every industrial nation. In Britain and the United States, the party in power when the Depression finally struck saw its power dramatically erode. In Great Britain, MacDonald (of the Labour Party) was able to stay on as prime minister, but he was forced to preside over a National Coalition government of Conservatives, Labourites, and Liberals. In the United States, Republican Herbert Hoover was ousted from the presidency by Democrat Franklin Roosevelt, who offered the vague promise of a "new deal" to the American people. In Germany, voters turned to the National Socialists and Adolf Hitler, who preached a message of recovery, national pride, attacks on the struggling Weimar government, and a virulent anti-Semitism. In January 1933, backed by his own party as well as by powerful non-Nazi right-wing politicians and businessmen, Hitler was named chancellor of the German Republic. In Japan, the military increasingly appeared to be the best hope to lead the rapidly industrializing nation out of its economic doldrums as well as to counteract what many Japanese saw as an unhealthy embrace of Western culture (films, clothing, cigarette smoking,

Western alcoholic beverages, Western dancing, and more) by middle-class young people.[7]

This is not to suggest that nonindustrialized nations were able to escape the Great Depression. Low demand for raw materials by the industrial countries virtually destroyed the economies of nations dependent on extracting and exporting those materials. Chile's exports declined over 80 percent between 1928 and 1933, while China's dropped between 75 and 80 percent, and Bolivia's, Cuba's, Malaya's, and Peru's declined by 70–75 percent. Similarly, as the industrial nations raised tariffs on food products (Germany fivefold, France more than twofold),

the economies of Argentina, Brazil, Colombia, and Costa Rica suffered as well, with Argentina showing a decline in exports of 65–70 percent, Brazil of 60–65 percent, and Colombia and Costa Rica of 50–55 percent.[8]

Each nation ultimately devised a plan for rescuing itself. By examining and analyzing the speeches of five prominent leaders of Great Britain, the United States, Germany, Japan, and the Soviet Union, respectively, you will be able to determine how the leaders of each of the major industrialized powers proposed to battle the Great Depression.

7. The 1920s saw the advent in Japan of that nation's version of the "flaming youth" of the West. In the United States, women of this group were nicknamed flappers, and in Japan, such a woman was referred to as a *modan garu*, a Japanese variation of the English words "modern girl"; a male was called a *modan boi*.

8. For declines of exports in forty-nine exporting countries, see Charles P. Kindleberger, *The World in Depression, 1929–1939* (Berkeley: University of California Press, 1973), p. 191. For tariff increases on wheat, see League of Nations, *The Course and Phases of the World Economic Depression* (Geneva: League of Nations, 1932), pp. 324–325. For a good contemporary analysis, see Herbert Feis, *The Changing Pattern of International Economic Affairs* (New York: Harper and Brothers, 1940), pp. 31–32.

THE METHOD

This problem contains two types of evidence: (1) speeches by national leaders of Great Britain, the United States, Germany, Japan, and the Soviet Union concerning how the nation ought to combat the worldwide economic depression of the 1930s, and (2) statistics that will help you see how the proposals you read about in the speeches were put into effect.

Begin by examining and analyzing the five speeches. What does each speaker see as the principal problems

his nation faces? How does each speaker propose that his nation approach those problems? Be careful to read between the lines for more subtle messages. For example, in his speech to the Nazi *Parteitag* (party convention) on September 10, 1936, Hitler brags of the "roaring and hammering of the machines of the German resurrection" in the Krupp factories. What did Krupp manufacture primarily? Make notes as you go along.

Keep in mind that the *purpose* of a speech most often is *not* to present an objective picture of the topic at hand, in this case how to deal with economic

Chapter 12

The Industrial

Crisis and the

Centralization

of Government

(1924–1939)

disaster. Rather, the purpose of a speech is to convince, to exhort, to "sell" a particular idea or program. Thus these speeches are better classified as *propaganda* than as objective analyses of a situation.

Even so, both the speaker's analysis of the problems and the proposed solutions must resonate with his listeners. Otherwise, the speech—and the particular approach—might well be rejected by its audience.

After you have read, examined, and analyzed the five speeches, move on to the sets of statistics that follow them. Many students greet statistics with a mixture (to borrow from writer Hunter S. Thompson) of "fear and loathing." And yet, understanding and being able to work with statistics is as critical to today's men and women as their ability to use computers, operate cellular telephones, or order products over the Internet. Once having learned the skills of analyzing and even generating sets of statistics, many people come to understand how indispensable they are to our knowledge. Indeed, a good number of people have even confessed that they enjoy working with statistics.

As you examine any set of statistics, ask three questions: (1) What variable is being measured in this set? (2) How does this variable change over time? (3) How does this set relate to the other sets and to the economic picture as a whole? Think of each set as a piece of a picture puzzle; by answering question 3 for each set, you will be able to see where that set fits into the overall picture. Whenever you begin to analyze any set of statistics, ask those three questions.

The first statistical set you will confront (Source 6) is an *index*. An index is a statistical measure designed to show changes in a variable (such as industrial production) *over time*. A *base year* is selected and given the value of 100. The index for other years is then expressed as a percentage of the base year level.

Look at the index of industrial production for Germany between 1929 and 1938 (Source 6). How does Germany's industrial production change over time? How can you account for that change? Germany's industrial production did rise significantly (more than doubling between 1933 and 1938) and unemployment (Source 7) did fall, to around 2.0 percent by 1938. How was Germany able to accomplish this impressive feat? Do any of the other statistical sets help you to answer that question?

As you can see, each of the statistical sets is related to all the others. Taking one nation-state at a time, link the sets together like links in a chain. In this way, you will be able to assess the economic problems that each nation faced and to observe how each nation attempted to overcome its economic difficulties. Note that we do not have all the statistical evidence we would like to have—historians rarely do. Let's use Germany again as an example. If you look at the expenditures of the German government from 1924 on (Source 8), you will notice that no statistics are available after 1934; can you guess why? By looking at the government's revenues, however, you can see that from 1924 to 1934 the German government's expenditures almost always exceeded revenues (1933 was the lone exception). Since we do have revenue figures after 1934, and since expenditures in documented years almost always exceeded those revenues, it is reasonable for us to suppose that the German government's expenditures after 1934 were roughly equal to (or greater than) revenues. With this kind of logic, historians can fill in some of the blanks where statistics are missing.

A *tariff* is a tax on *imports* from other nations. Governments may enact tariffs to raise revenues, or they may raise tariff duties so high in order to discourage imports—thus helping native industries. What does Source 9 tell you?

Finally, there are some sets of statistics dealing with military expenditures (Sources 10 to 13). Why are they included in this problem? How (if at all) do they relate to the speeches?

How did each of the five major industrialized nations (Great Britain, the United States, Germany, Japan, and the Soviet Union) choose to combat the Great Depression? What were the principal similarities between their approaches? the differences?

THE EVIDENCE

Source 1 from Parliamentary Debates: House of Commons, *Fifth Series (London: H.M. Stationery Office, 1931), vol. 248 HC, pp. 646–660.*

1. Prime Minister Ramsay MacDonald, February 12, 1931

[*On February 12, 1931, a motion was introduced in the House of Commons calling for the government to "formulate and to present to Parliament an extensive policy" to provide work for the unemployed on public works projects, to be funded by borrowing. The prime minister rose to respond to that motion.*]

There is nothing the country can do with greater wisdom at this moment than to develop its resources, and make them effective as the soil from which our people are going to draw their life-blood, and to find capital for that development.

That is all the truer because the unemployment which we are now facing is not ordinary unemployment. It is not the unemployment we had to face two, three, or four years ago. . . . That was unemployment from day to day, from month to month, from season to season, unemployment of a normally operating capitalist system. The unemployment which we are facing to-day is partly that, undoubtedly. It was that when we came in. But now we are undergoing an industrial revolution. Economic conditions are changing. For instance, in order to face the extraordinarily increased severity of competition which this country has now to meet in the markets of the world, we have to economise our economic and our material power in the shape of machinery and in the shape of

Chapter 12

The Industrial

Crisis and the

Centralization

of Government

(1924–1939)

works. By that economy we cheapen production. But at the same time we are discharging men and women. In order to increase our efficiency, we are reducing employment, at any rate, for the time being.

But, after all, the men and women who live to-day have to face the problem to-day. They cannot be consoled by the fact that perhaps 10 or 12 years after this, owing to the expansion made possible by the cheapening of production, their sons or daughters will be absorbed in the expanded industry. That is not good enough for the men and women who are living to-day. Therefore, on account of the increasing efficiency, and on account of the reconditioning of our industry which is going on, thousands of men and women are being turned out of employment with a very, very small percentage of chance of ever being called upon again to engage in that industry. . . .

These are very important considerations. You are dealing with a body of unemployment which is not merely temporary. Between 2,500,000 and 2,750,000 of people now ranked as unemployed are not people who are out because there has been a breakdown of machinery in some factory, nor because there has been a seasonal change, nor because there has been a fluctuation in fashion, nor because there is a temporary cessation of the free flow of exchange; they are out on account of the reconditioning of the economic world, and, whoever faces the problem of unemployment now, has to face, not only the problem of public works to give temporary relief, but the problem of how to bring back people into contact with the raw material from which they were making their living. . . . The biggest part of the responsibility is not mentioned in this Motion at all, and that is, direct industrial stimulation so that labour may be absorbed not into work provided because of this unemployment, but that labour may be absorbed into normal industry.

We are asked if we can afford money for the relief of the unemployed. I say we can, but I am much more concerned with what, I think, is the more apposite question—Can we afford to have so many unemployed in existence? We cannot. That is the problem we really have to face. As regards public work, we have, first of all, to provide temporary work. Do remember that it is temporary. When the right hon. Gentleman makes an observation about the millions that have been spent on insurance having produced nothing, I disagree with him. If you had not spent a pound of that money, you would have found that you would have had to spend it on something else. If the money had been spent on public works, how many people would have been put to employment? By now these people would have been out of work because the work would have been finished. What struck me most in producing these schemes was how very limited and temporary that kind of work is bound to be. That is the first thing that has to be done. We have to provide it. I am not condemning it at all. I am only trying to impart to the House the kind of problem we are up against when we sit down, not to take part in a Debate in this House, but when we sit down in a committee-room facing the actual details of the problem, and struggling to meet and overcome the whole lot of them.

The second thing that has to be done is, by using neglected resources, the putting of men into permanent ways of earning a living. . . .

[366]

[*MacDonald goes on to remind Parliament of the "lag time" that exists between the appropriation and the actual spending of public funds. He then speaks of programs for slum clearance and new industrial cities and new industries, and of the necessity of the government's maintaining a good credit rating.*]

The problem to be tackled is the provision of public works of a temporary character, the opening up of the land to the people of the country, giving them rights upon the soil and, finally, giving to industry vigilance, activity and adventure to enable it to carry on its production and back up this production by marketing. That is the problem we have to face, and that is the spirit and energy in which the Government are facing it and carrying it through. I appeal for a great national effort to enable us to carry on this work, to increase the programme of public works, to enable us to put more and more men upon them, to put more and more work in hand. I appeal to the country to stop the sort of pessimism to which a great contribution was made by the right hon. Gentleman who opened the Debate yesterday, and which I see is already being used with considerable effect. I appeal to the whole country to see that the prospects of this country are good, that we still have resources, that we still have the command of capital, that we still have the power of production and the energy that has made this country so great and powerful and splendid, and that by mobilising it, and only by mobilising it, to carry out the programme of the Government with energy and resource this problem will solve itself. This problem will be solved, a new source of power and wealth will be created in this nation, and we shall go on facing the world with its new problems even more successfully, on account of the experience of social organisation and the application of Socialist ideas, than has been possible in past generations.

Source 2 from B. D. Zevin, ed., Nothing to Fear: The Selected Addresses of Franklin Delano Roosevelt, 1932–1945 *(Boston: Houghton Mifflin Co., 1946), pp. 132–143.*

2. President Franklin Roosevelt, April 14, 1938[9]

Five years ago we faced a very serious problem of economic and social recovery. For four and a half years that recovery proceeded apace. It is only in the past seven months that it has received a visible setback.

And it is only within the past two months, as we have waited patiently to see whether the forces of business itself would counteract it, that it has become apparent that government itself can no longer safely fail to take aggressive government steps to meet it. . . .

9. The April 14, 1938, address was delivered "live" over the radio, one of President Roosevelt's so-called Fireside Chats. In early 1937, Roosevelt had tried to remove government supports of the economy, but, unable to stand without those supports, the economy began to deteriorate once again. This selection is from the printed release of the speech. Roosevelt deviated slightly from the printed text as he spoke to his radio audience. See Russell D. Buhite and David W. Levy, *FDR's Fireside Chats* (Norman: University of Oklahoma, 1992), pp. 111–123.

Chapter 12

The Industrial

Crisis and the

Centralization

of Government

(1924–1939)

[Here Roosevelt assures listeners that the recession of 1937–1938 is not as serious as that of 1929–1933. Nevertheless, the federal government has learned that it cannot wait for the private sector to provide jobs but rather must act quickly. Roosevelt then asserts that the chief problem both in 1929 and in 1937 was that of underconsumption of manufactured goods and that the purchasing power of the American people must be stimulated to create manufacturing jobs.]

I went on to point out to the Senate and the House of Representatives that all the energies of government and business must be directed to increasing the national income, to putting more people into private jobs, to giving security and a feeling of security to all people in all walks of life. . . .

[Roosevelt quotes what he said to the Congress.]

"I came to the conclusion that the present-day problem calls for action both by the Government and by the people, that we suffer primarily from a failure of consumer demand because of lack of buying power. It is up to us to create an economic upturn.

"How and where can and should the Government help to start an upward spiral?"

I went on to propose three groups of measures and I will summarize the recommendations.

First, I asked for certain appropriations which are intended to keep the Government expenditures for work relief and similar purposes during the coming fiscal year at the same rate of expenditures as at present. That includes additional money for the Works Progress Administration; additional funds for the Farm Security Administration; additional allotments for the National Youth Administration, and more money for the Civilian Conservation Corps, in order that it can maintain the existing number of camps now in operation.

These appropriations, made necessary by increased unemployment, will cost about a billion and a quarter more than the estimates which I sent to the Congress on the third of January.

Second, I told the Congress that the Administration proposes to make additional bank reserves available for the credit needs of the country. About one billion four hundred million dollars of gold now in the Treasury will be used to pay these additional expenses of the Government, and three-quarters of a billion dollars of additional credit will be made available to the banks by reducing the reserves now required by the Federal Reserve Board.

These two steps, taking care of relief needs and adding to bank credits, are in our judgment insufficient by themselves to start the Nation on a sustained upward movement.

Therefore, I came to the third kind of Government action which I consider to be vital. I said to the Congress:

"You and I cannot afford to equip ourselves with two rounds of ammunition where three rounds are necessary. If we stop at relief and credit, we may find ourselves without ammunition before the enemy is routed. If we are fully equipped with the third round of ammunition, we stand to win the battle against adversity."

The third proposal is to make definite additions to the purchasing power of the Nation by providing new work over and above the continuing of the old work.

First, to enable the United States Housing Authority to undertake the immediate construction of about three hundred million dollars of additional slum clearance projects.

Second, to renew a public works program by starting as quickly as possible about one billion dollars worth of needed permanent public improvements in states, counties and cities.

Third, to add one hundred million dollars to the estimate for federal aid [to] highways in excess of the amount I recommended in January.

Fourth, to add thirty-seven million dollars over and above the former estimate of sixty-three million dollars for flood control and reclamation.

Fifth, to add twenty-five million dollars additional for federal buildings in various parts of the country.

In recommending this program I am thinking not only of the immediate economic needs of the people of the Nation, but also of their personal liberties—the most precious possession of all Americans. I am thinking of our democracy and of the recent trend in other parts of the world away from the democratic ideal.

Democracy has disappeared in several other great nations—not because the people of those nations disliked democracy, but because they had grown tired of unemployment and insecurity, of seeing their children hungry while they sat helpless in the face of government confusion and government weakness through lack of leadership in government. Finally, in desperation, they chose to sacrifice liberty in the hope of getting something to eat. We in America know that our own democratic institutions can be preserved and made to work. But in order to preserve them we need to act together, to meet the problems of the Nation boldly, and to prove that the practical operation of democratic government is equal to the task of protecting the security of the people. . . .

History proves that dictatorships do not grow out of strong and successful governments, but out of weak and helpless ones. If by democratic methods people get a government strong enough to protect them from fear and starvation, their democracy succeeds; but if they do not, they grow impatient. Therefore, the only sure bulwark of continuing liberty is a government strong enough to protect the interests of the people, and a people strong enough and well enough informed to maintain its sovereign control over its government.

What I said to the Congress in the close of my message I repeat to you.

"Let us unanimously recognize the fact that the Federal debt, whether it be twenty-five billions or forty billions, can only be paid if the Nation obtains a vastly increased citizen income. I repeat that if this citizen income can be raised to eighty billion dollars a year the national Government and the overwhelming majority of State and local governments will be 'out of the red.' The higher the national income goes the faster shall we be able to reduce the total of Federal and

Chapter 12

The Industrial

Crisis and the

Centralization

of Government

(1924–1939)

state and local debts. Viewed from every angle, today's purchasing power—the citizens' income of today—is not sufficient to drive the economic system at higher speed. Responsibility of Government requires us at this time to supplement the normal processes and in so supplementing them to make sure that the addition is adequate. We must start again on a long steady upward incline in national income.

"... And in that process, which I believe is ready to start, let us avoid the pitfalls of the past—the overproduction, the overspeculation, and indeed all the extremes which we did not succeed in avoiding in 1929. In all of this, Government cannot and should not act alone. Business must help. I am sure business will help.

"We need more than the materials of recovery. We need a united national will. . . ."

Source 3 from Norman H. Baynes, ed., The Speeches of Adolf Hitler, April 1922–August 1939 *(London: Oxford University Press, 1942), vol. 1, pp. 650–654.*

3. Chancellor Adolf Hitler, September 10, 1936[10]

In all spheres of our national life there has been since four years ago an immense advance. The tempo and the scale of the political advance are unique, and above all the inner consolidation of the German nation is unique in history. . . .

On the evening of 30 January 1933 I made known to the German people in a short Proclamation the aims which we had set before us in our battle. I then asked that I might be granted four years: at the end of that time I wished to render account to the German people of the fulfilment or non-fulfilment of that promise.

Our foes were convinced that we should never have an opportunity to ask the nation for such a judgement, for the longest period that they were prepared to allow our Government was barely six to twelve weeks.

And what has National Socialism in these four years made of Germany? Who from amongst our foes would to-day have the effrontery to step forward as our accuser?

What appeared to them then fantastic and incapable of realization in my Proclamation seems to-day the most modest announcement of an achievement which towers above the promises then made. Our opponents thought that we could not carry out the programme of 1933 which now seems to us so small an affair. But what would they have said if I had propounded to them *that* programme which the National Socialist Government has as a matter of fact realized

10. Hitler's speech was intended to answer the question "What has National Socialism made out of Germany in the last four years?"

in not quite four years? How they would have jeered if on the 30th of January 1933 I had declared that within four years Germany would have reduced its six million unemployed to one million!

That the enforced expropriation of the German peasantry would have been brought to an end.

That the receipts from German agriculture would be higher than in any previous year in time of peace.

That the total national income would be raised from 41 milliards annually to over 56 milliards.[11]

That the German middle classes and German artisans would enjoy a new prosperity.

That trade would once more recover.

That German ports would no more resemble ship grave-yards.

That in 1936 on German wharves alone over 640,000 tons of shipping would be under construction.

That countless manufactories would not merely double but treble and quadruple the number of their workmen. And that in less than four years innumerable others would be rebuilt.

That a Krupp factory would vibrate once again with the roaring and the hammering of the machines of the German resurrection and that over all of these undertakings men would recognize as the supreme law of their effort not the unscrupulous profit of the individual but the service of the nation.

That the silent motor-works would not only spring into life but would be enlarged on an unheard of scale.

That the production of motor-cars would rise from 45,000 in the year 1932 to some quarter of a million.

That in four years the deficits of our States and cities would be wiped out.

That the Reich would gain from taxation an annual increase of nearly five milliards.

That the German Imperial Railway would at length recover, and that its trains would be the quickest in the world.

That to the German Reich would be given roads such that since the beginnings of human civilization they have never had their match for size and beauty: and that of the first 7,000 kilometres which were planned already after not quite four years 1,000 kilometres would be in use and over 4,000 kilometres would be in course of construction.

That enormous new settlements with hundreds of thousands of houses would come into being, while in ancient cities of the Reich mighty new buildings would arise which may be said to be the greatest in the world.

That hundreds upon hundreds of gigantic bridges would be thrown over gorges and valleys.

11. **milliard:** one billion (marks, in this case).

[371]

Chapter 12

The Industrial

Crisis and the

Centralization

of Government

(1924–1939)

That German "Kultur" in these and similar new achievements would confirm its eternal value.

That German theatres and concerts of our German music would celebrate their resurrection.

That with all this the German people would take an active share in this revolutionary renewal of the spirit, while not a single Jew would make an appearance in this intellectual leadership of the German people.

If I had prophesied then that in four years the whole German Press would be filled with a new "ethos" and would be in the service of German aims, that for German business life (*Wirtschaft*) the law of a new professional honour would be proclaimed, so that in every sphere the German experiences a renewal of his personality and his action.

If I had at that time foretold that after these four years there would be only one single German people, that no Social Democracy, no Communism, no Centrum, not even a *bourgeois* party would any longer be able to sin against the life of Germany, that no trade union would any longer be able to incite the workers, and no employers' association to ruin the employers, that after these four years no German State would have its separate government, that in Germany there would no longer be any State-parliaments (*Landtage*), that the sixteen flags and the sixteen different traditions which they represented would have ceased to exist and have been brought together as one, and that the whole nation—from the workman to the soldier—would in the future march only in support of a single confession of faith and a single flag.

What would they have said if I had prophesied to them that Germany in these four years would have freed itself from the slave-fetters of Versailles, that the Reich would regain general compulsory military service, that every German, as before the War, would serve two years for the freedom of the country, that a new fleet would be under construction to protect our coasts and our trade, that a mighty new air arm would guarantee the security of our towns, our factories and works, that the Rhineland would be brought under the supremacy of the German nation, and that thereby the sovereignty of the Reich would be restored over the whole of its territory?

What would they have said to my prophecy that the people, at that time so divided, before four years were past would—99 per cent of it—go to the polls and that 99 per cent would say "Yes" in support of the National Socialist policy of reconstruction, of national honour and freedom?

If four years ago I had prophesied this and much else I should have been branded as a madman and the whole world would have laughed at me. But all this is now accomplished fact, and this is the achievement of not quite four years. . . . The National Socialist political leadership of Germany in this short time has wrought a miracle.

Source 4 from Ryusaku Tsunoda, et al., comp., Sources of Japanese Tradition *(New York: Columbia University Press, 1958), vol. 2, pp. 289–291.*

4. Hashimoto Kingoro, Address to Young Men, 1938

We have already said that there are only three ways left to Japan to escape from the pressure of surplus population. We are like a great crowd of people packed into a small and narrow room, and there are only three doors through which we might escape, namely emigration, advance into world markets, and expansion of territory. The first door, emigration, has been barred to us by the anti-Japanese immigration policies of other countries. The second door, advance into world markets, is being pushed shut by tariff barriers and the abrogation of commercial treaties. What should Japan do when two of the three doors have been closed against her?

It is quite natural that Japan should rush upon the last remaining door.

It may sound dangerous when we speak of territorial expansion, but the territorial expansion of which we speak does not in any sense of the word involve the occupation of the possessions of other countries, the planting of the Japanese flag thereon, and the declaration of their annexation to Japan. It is just that since the Powers [United States, Britain, France] have suppressed the circulation of Japanese materials and merchandise abroad, we are looking for some place overseas where Japanese capital, Japanese skills and Japanese labor can have free play, free from the oppression of the white race.

We would be satisfied with just this much. What moral right do the world powers who have themselves closed to us the two doors of emigration and advance into world markets have to criticize Japan's attempt to rush out of the third and last door?

If they do not approve of this, they should open the doors which they have closed against us and permit the free movement overseas of Japanese emigrants and merchandise. . . .

At the time of the Manchurian incident [1931], the entire world joined in criticism of Japan. They said that Japan was an untrustworthy nation. They said that she had recklessly brought cannon and machine guns into Manchuria, which was the territory of another country, flown airplanes over it, and finally occupied it. But the military action taken by Japan was not in the least a selfish one. Moreover, we do not recall ever having taken so much as an inch of territory belonging to another nation. The result of this incident was the establishment of the splendid new nation of Manchuria. The Powers are still discussing whether or not to recognize this new nation, but regardless of whether or not other nations recognize her, the Manchurian empire has already been established, and now, seven years after its creation, the empire is further consolidating its foundations with the aid of its friend, Japan.

Chapter 12

The Industrial

Crisis and the

Centralization

of Government

(1924–1939)

And if it is still protested that our actions in Manchuria were excessively violent, we may wish to ask the white race just which country it was that sent warships and troops to India, South Africa, and Australia and slaughtered innocent natives, bound their hands and feet with iron chains, lashed their backs with iron whips, proclaimed these territories as their own, and still continues to hold them to this very day?

They will invariably reply, these were all lands inhabited by untamed savages. These people did not know how to develop the abundant resources of their land for the benefit of mankind. Therefore it was the wish of God, who created heaven and earth for mankind, for us to develop these undeveloped lands and to promote the happiness of mankind in their stead. God wills it.

This is quite a convenient argument for them. Let us take it at face value. Then there is another question that we must ask them.

Suppose that there is still on this earth land endowed with abundant natural resources that have not been developed at all by the white race. Would it not then be God's will and the will of Providence that Japan go there and develop those resources for the benefit of mankind?

And there still remain many such lands on this earth. . . .

Source 5 from Joseph Stalin, "Report on the Work of the Central Committee to the Seventeenth Congress of the Communist Party of the Soviet Union," January 26, 1934, in Joseph Stalin, Selected Writings (New York: International Publishers, 1942), pp. 313–315, 331, 341, 478. The last five lines are taken from a report to the Eighteenth Congress.

5. Josef Stalin, Report to the Seventeenth Congress, January 26, 1934

[*Stalin begins his report by referring to the economic crisis in all the capitalist countries that, according to him, "is still raging" and has devastated industrial and agricultural economies. He asserts that the crisis is a symptom of the "general crisis of capitalism" that emerged after the "imperialist war" (the Great War), which left a permanent "army of millions of unemployed." The result, he claims, has been a political crisis in all the capitalist countries.*]

I now pass to the question of the internal situation in the U.S.S.R.

From the point of view of the internal situation in the U.S.S.R., the period under review presents a picture of ever increasing progress, both in the sphere of national economy and in the sphere of culture.

This progress has not been merely a simple quantitative accumulation of strength. This progress is remarkable in that it has introduced fundamental changes into the structure of the U.S.S.R., and has radically changed the face of the country.

During this period, the U.S.S.R. has become radically transformed and has cast off the integument of backwardness and medievalism. From an agrarian country it has become an industrial country. From a land of small individual agriculture it has become a land of collective, large-scale, mechanized agriculture. From an ignorant, illiterate and uncultured country it has become—or rather it is becoming—a literate and cultured country, covered by a vast network of higher, intermediate and elementary schools teaching in the languages of the nationalities of the U.S.S.R.

New industries have been created: machine-tool construction, automobile, tractor, chemical, motor construction, aircraft, harvester combines, the construction of powerful turbines and generators, high-grade steel, ferro-alloys, synthetic rubber, nitrates, artificial fiber, etc., etc.

During this period thousands of new, up-to-date industrial enterprises have been built and started. . . .

[*Here Stalin names some of the new industrial giants.*]

More than 200,000 collective farms and 5,000 state farms have been organized, with new distinct centers and industrial centers serving them.

New large towns, with large populations, have sprung up in what were formerly almost vacant spaces. The old towns and industrial centers have grown enormously.

The foundations have been laid for the Urals-Kuznetsk Combine, which unites the coking coal of Kuznetsk with the iron ore of the Urals. Thus, we may consider that the dream of a new metallurgical base in the East has become a reality.

The foundations for a powerful new oil base have been laid in the regions on the Western and Southern slopes of the Ural range—in the Ural Region, Bashkiria and Kazakstan.

It is obvious that the enormous capital invested by the state in all branches of national economy, which in the period under review amounted to over 60,000,000,000 rubles, has not been ill-spent, and is beginning to bear fruit.

As a result of these achievements the national income of the U.S.S.R. has increased from 29,000,000,000 rubles in 1929 to 50,000,000,000 in 1933; whereas there has been an enormous decline in the national income of all capitalist countries without exception during this period.

It goes without saying that all these achievements and all this progress had to lead—and really did lead—to the further consolidation of the internal situation in the U.S.S.R.

How was it possible for these colossal changes to take place in a matter of three or four years on the territory of a vast state with a backward technique and a backward culture? Was it not a miracle? It would have been a miracle had this development proceeded on the basis of capitalism and individual small farming. But it cannot be described as a miracle if we bear in mind that this development took place on the basis of expanding socialist construction.

Chapter 12

The Industrial

Crisis and the

Centralization

of Government

(1924–1939)

It goes without saying that this enormous progress could take place only on the basis of the successful building of socialism; on the basis of the collective work of scores of millions of people; on the basis of the advantage which the socialist system of economy has over the capitalist and individual peasant system.

It is not surprising, therefore, that the colossal progress in the economy and culture of the U.S.S.R. during the period under review has also signified the elimination of the capitalist elements, and the relegation of individual peasant economy to the background. It is a fact that the socialist system of economy in the sphere of industry now represents 99 per cent of the total; and in agriculture, according to area sown to grain crops, it represents 84.5 per cent of the total, whereas individual peasant economy accounts for only 15.5 per cent.

It follows, then, that capitalist economy in the U.S.S.R. has already been eliminated and that the individual-peasant sector in the countryside has been forced back to a secondary position. . . .

[*Stalin then turns to the progress made in the agricultural sector following collectivization.*]

It goes without saying that this historic victory over the exploiters could not but lead to a radical improvement in the material standard of the working people and in their conditions of life generally.

The elimination of the parasitic classes has led to the disappearance of the exploitation of man by man. The labor of the worker and the peasant is freed from exploitation. The incomes which the exploiters used to squeeze out of the labor of the people now remains in the hands of the working people and are used partly for the expansion of production and the enlistment of new detachments of working people in production, and partly for the purpose of directly increasing the incomes of the workers and peasants.

Unemployment, that scourge of the working class, has disappeared. In the bourgeois countries millions of unemployed suffer want and privation owing to lack of work; but in our country there are no longer any workers who have no work and no earnings.

With the disappearance of kulak[12] bondage, poverty in the countryside has disappeared. Every peasant, whether a collective farmer or an individual farmer, now has the opportunity of enjoying a human existence, if only he wants to work conscientiously and not to be an idler, a tramp, and a despoiler of collective farm property.

The abolition of exploitation, the abolition of unemployment in the cities, and the abolition of poverty in the countryside are such historic achievements in the material standard of the working people that they are beyond even the

---

12. **kulak:** Kulaks were well-to-do farmers, whom Stalin vowed to "eliminate . . . as a class." He ordered the seizure of their land and the exile of many of them, some to concentration camps. Millions died. See Robert Conquest, *The Harvest of Sorrow: Soviet Collectivization and the Terror-Famine* (New York: Oxford University Press, 1986).

dreams of the workers and peasants in bourgeois countries, even in the most "democratic" ones. . . .

. . . The Seventeenth Party Conference declared that we are heading for the formation of a classless socialist society. It goes without saying that a classless society cannot come of itself, spontaneously, as it were. It has to be achieved and built by the efforts of all the working people, by strengthening the organs of the dictatorship of the proletariat, by intensifying the class struggle, by abolishing classes, by eliminating the remnants of the capitalist classes, and in battles with enemies both internal and external. . . .

Long live our victorious working class!
Long live our victorious collective farm peasantry!
Long live our socialist intelligentsia!
Long live the great friendship of the nations of our country!
Long live the Communist Party of the Soviet Union![13]

Sources 6 and 7 from League of Nations, Monthly Bulletin of Statistics *(Geneva: League of Nations, 1939), vol. 20, p. 12; pp. 51–52. USSR figures are from Stalin's 1934 and 1939 reports to the Communist Party's Seventeenth and Eighteenth Congresses, in Stalin,* Selected Writings, *(New York: International Publishers, 1942), pp. 301, 436.*

6. Index of Industrial Production, 1929–1938 (1929 = 100)[14]

Year	Germany	Japan	Great Britain	United States	USSR
1929	100.0	100.0	100.0	100.0	100.0
1930	85.9	94.8	92.3	80.7	129.7
1931	67.6	91.6	83.8	68.1	161.9
1932	53.3	97.8	83.5	53.8	184.7
1933	60.7	113.2	88.2	63.9	201.6
1934	79.8	128.7	98.8	66.4	238.3
1935	94.0	141.8	105.8	75.6	293.4
1936	106.3	151.1	115.9	88.1	382.3
1937	117.2	170.8	123.7	92.2	424.0
1938 (May)	127.0	174.8	113.4	72.3	477.0

13. The last five lines are taken from the Eighteenth Congress, March 10, 1939.

14. Many economists and historians question the reliability of the Soviet Union's statistics. Even so, the growth in industrial production was impressive.

Chapter 12
The Industrial
Crisis and the
Centralization
of Government
(1924–1939)

7. Unemployment (Numbers Out of Work and Percentage of Civilian Labor Force), 1930–1938[15]

Year	Germany		Japan	
	Number	*Percentage*	*Number*	*Percentage*
1930	3,075,580	—	369,408	5.3%
1931	4,519,704	23.7%	422,755	6.1
1932	5,575,492	30.1	485,681	6.8
1933	4,804,428	25.8	408,710	5.6
1934	2,718,309	14.5	372,941	5.0
1935	2,151,039	11.6	356,044	4.6
1936	1,592,655	8.1	338,365	4.3
1937	912,312	4.5	295,443	3.7
1938 (June)	429,475	2.0	230,262	2.9

Year	Great Britain		United States*	
	Number	*Percentage*	*Number*	*Percentage*
1930	1,464,347	11.8%	4,340,000	8.7%
1931	2,129,359	16.7	8,020,000	15.9
1932	2,254,857	17.6	12,060,000	23.6
1933	2,110,090	16.4	12,830,000	24.9
1934	1,801,913	13.9	11,340,000	21.7
1935	1,714,844	13.1	10,610,000	20.1
1936	1,497,587	11.2	9,030,000	16.9
1937	1,277,928	9.4	7,700,000	14.3
1938 (Nov.)	1,529,133	10.8	10,390,000	19.0

*United States statistics are from U.S. Department of Commerce, Bureau of the Census, *Historical Statistics of the United States* (Washington: Government Printing Office, 1975), vol. 2, p. 135.

15. Stalin claimed that there was no unemployment in the Soviet Union. See Source 5, p. 376.

Source 8 from B. R. Mitchell, European Historical Statistics, 1750–1970 *(New York: Columbia University Press, 1978), pp. 376–385, and* Historical Statistics of the United States, *vol. 2, p. 1104.*

8. Central Government Revenues and Expenditures in National Currencies, 1924–1940 (in millions)

Year	Germany (mark)			Great Britain (pound)		
	Revenue	Expenditures	Surplus or Deficit	Revenue	Expenditures	Surplus or Deficit
1924	4,650	5,027	−377	799	751	48
1925	4,731	5,683	−952	812	776	36
1926	5,313	6,616	−1,303	806	782	24
1927	6,357	7,168	−811	843	774	69
1928	6,568	8,517	−1,949	836	761	75
1929	6,741	8,187	−1,446	815	782	33
1930	6,634	8,392	−1,758	858	814	44
1931	5,704	6,995	−1,291	851	819	32
1932	4,994	5,965	−971	827	833	−6
1933	6,850	6,270	580	809	770	39
1934	8,220	8,221	1	805	785	20
1935	9,650	Not available	—	845	829	16
1936	11,492	N/A	—	897	889	8
1937	13,964	N/A	—	949	909	40
1938	17,712	N/A	—	1,006	1,006	0
1939	23,575	N/A	—	1,132	1,401	−269

Year	United States (dollar)		
	Revenue	Expenditures	Surplus or Deficit
1924	$3,871,214	$2,907,847	$963,367
1925	3,640,805	2,923,762	717,043
1926	3,795,108	2,929,964	865,144
1927	4,012,794	2,857,429	1,155,365
1928	3,900,329	2,961,245	939,083
1929	3,861,589	3,127,199	734,391
1930	4,057,884	3,320,211	737,673
1931	3,115,557	3,577,434	−461,877
1932	1,923,892	4,659,182	−2,735,290
1933	1,996,844	4,598,496	−2,601,652
1934	3,014,970	6,644,602	−3,629,632
1935	3,705,956	6,497,008	−2,791,052
1936	3,997,059	8,421,608	−4,424,549
1937	4,955,613	7,733,033	−2,777,421
1938	5,588,012	6,764,628	−1,176,617
1939	4,979,066	8,841,224	−3,862,158

Chapter 12

The Industrial

Crisis and the

Centralization

of Government

(1924–1939)

Source 9 from Economic Intelligence Service, World Economic Survey, 1931–1932 *(Geneva: League of Nations, 1932), pp. 319–322.*

9. Tariffs, Import Duties, Taxes Imposed

	Import Duties, Taxes Imposed, Consular Fees (etc.)	
	General Increase (All Items)	*Increases on Individual Items*
June 1930		U.S.A.*
September 1931		Argentina
		Colombia
		Egypt
		Italy
		Latvia
		Poland
October 1931	India	Argentina
	South Africa	Australia
		Canada
		Czechoslovakia
		Denmark
		Egypt
		Lithuania
		Poland
		Roumania
November 1931	Netherlands	Belgium
		United Kingdom
		Bulgaria
		France
		Persia
December 1931	Brazil	United Kingdom
		Colombia
		Czechoslovakia
		Estonia
		France
		Lithuania
		Switzerland
January 1932	Norway	Austria
		Colombia
		Germany
		Hungary
		Irish Free State
		Italy
		Poland
		Salvador
		Switzerland
February 1932	Australia	Belgium
	Finland	Estonia
	Persia	Germany

(continues on next page)

	Portugal Siam	Italy Lithuania Mexico South Africa Sweden Switzerland Venezuela
March 1932	Belgium United Kingdom Poland South Africa Venezuela	Bolivia Brazil Egypt Estonia France Guatemala India Irish Free State Mexico Netherlands Roumania Salvador Spain
April 1932	France U.S.A.	Belgium United Kingdom Canada China Egypt Irish Free State Italy Mexico Netherlands Spain Sweden Uruguay
May 1932	Czechoslovakia Egypt	Belgium United Kingdom Chile Greece Irish Free State Italy Mexico Sweden
June 1932	Japan Estonia Lithuania	United Kingdom Denmark Egypt Germany Italy Norway Roumania
July 1932		United Kingdom Irish Free State U.S.A.

*For the United States tariff (the Hawley-Smoot Act), see F. W. Taussig, *The Tariff History of the United States*, 8th ed. (New York: G.P. Putnam's Sons, 1931), p. 518.

Chapter 12

The Industrial

Crisis and the

Centralization

of Government

(1924–1939)

Source 10 from Paul Kennedy, The Rise and Fall of the Great Powers: Economic Change and Military Conflict from 1500 to 2000 *(New York: Random House, 1987), p. 296.*

10. Defense Expenditures of Great Britain, the United States, Germany, and Japan, 1930–1938 (in millions of current dollars)

Year	Great Britain	United States	Germany	Japan
1930	512	699	162	218
1933	333	570	452	183
1934	540	803	709	292
1935	646	806	1,607	300
1936	892	932	2,332	313
1937	1,245	1,032	3,298	940
1938	1,863	1,131	7,415	1,740

Source 11 from David Chandler, ed., The Oxford History of the British Army *(Oxford: Oxford University Press, 1994), p. 256; Robin Higham,* Armed Forces in Peacetime: Britain, 1918–1940 *(Hamden, Conn.: Archon Books, 1962), p. 95; Peter Dennis,* Decision by Default: Peacetime Conscription and British Defense, 1919–1939 *(Durham, N.C.: Duke University Press, 1972), p. 27; U.S. Bureau of the Census,* Historical Statistics of the United States, Colonial Times to 1957 *(Washington, D.C.: Government Printing Office, 1960), p. 736; Matthew Cooper,* The German Army, 1933–1945: Its Political and Military Failure *(New York: Stein and Day, 1978), pp. 50, 130–131.*

11. Sizes of Armies, Great Britain, United States, Germany

Year	Great Britain	United States	Germany
1920	370,000*	204,292	100,000**
1921	285,300	230,725	
1922	235,000	148,763	
1923		133,243	
1924		142,673	
1925		137,048	
1926		134,938	
1927		134,829	
1928		136,084	
1929		139,118	
1930		139,378	

(continues on next page)

*Does not include the British army in India or in the Territories.

**The Treaty of Versailles limited the size of the German army to 100,000, although there is evidence that even before Hitler became chancellor Germany was evading that limit.

Year	Great Britain	United States	Germany
1931		140,516	
1932		134,957	
1933	206,000	136,547	100,000
1934	195,845	138,464	240,000
1935	196,137	139,486	450,000
1936	192,325	167,816	
1937	190,830	179,968	
1938		185,488	
1939		189,839	730,000 (1 June)
			3,706,104 (1 Sept)

Source 12 from Paul Kennedy, Rise and Fall of the Great Powers: Economic Change and Military Conflict from 1500 to 2000 *(New York: Random House, 1987), p. 300.*

12. Armed Services Spending as a Percentage of Total Government Expenditures, Japan, 1931–1938

1931–1932	31%
1936–1937	47%
1937–1938	70%

Source 13 from Alec Nove, An Economic History of the U.S.S.R., *3rd ed. (New York: Penguin, 1993), pp. 227–228.*

13. Total Budget, USSR, and Percentage Spent on Defense, 1933–1940

Year	Total Budget (millions of rubles)	% Defense Spending
1933	42,080	3.4
1934	55,444	9.1
1935	73,571	11.1
1936	92,480	16.1
1937	106,238	16.5
1938	124,038	18.7
1939	153,299	25.6
1940	174,350	32.6

Chapter 12
The Industrial
Crisis and the
Centralization
of Government
(1924–1939)

QUESTIONS TO CONSIDER

Ramsay MacDonald's speech in Parliament is a defense of his approach toward combating unemployment in Great Britain. MacDonald begins by explaining what he believes were the causes of the Great Depression in Britain. What factors does he cite? Note that the prime minister does not see the economic downturn as temporary in Britain. Therefore, his remedy is twofold, the first part consisting of temporary work for the unemployed, but the second involving a permanent restructuring of the British economy. How does MacDonald propose to accomplish phase two? What should government's role be? What should government's role *not* be?

Franklin Roosevelt's Fireside Chat details his strategies and principles for mobilizing the federal government to deal with the sudden economic downturn of 1937–1938. Like MacDonald, Roosevelt also begins with his own analysis of the causes of the Depression, although this time in the United States. How does Roosevelt's analysis differ from MacDonald's? Roosevelt believed that the 1937–1938 downturn was a repeat of what had occurred in 1929–1932. Contrast Roosevelt's suggested solutions with those of MacDonald. How is the role of the central government different? How does each leader approach the notion of "deficit spending" (in which expenditures exceed revenues, the difference to be made up by borrowing, principally through government bonds)? Roosevelt concludes his radio address by insisting that "business must help." What would MacDonald's reaction be to such a statement?

On the surface, Adolf Hitler's speech at the opening of the Nazi Party's 1936 convention is a simple listing of what Germany has accomplished since he became chancellor in January 1933. Faintly visible beneath the gloating, however, is an obscure outline of Hitler's plan to end the Depression in Germany (see the Epilogue section for a brief explanation of that plan).

Hitler begins by boasting of Germany's significant reduction in unemployment since the Nazi rise to power (from 6 million to 1 million). Do the statistics (Source 6) confirm his claim (by September 1936 the 1 million figure probably was an accurate one)? The main question is, how were the National Socialists able to bring this about? Hitler gives broad hints when he refers to the Krupp industries, the "silent motor-works," the revival of vehicle production, compulsory military service, the requirement of two years of service "for the freedom of the country" (see Epilogue for an explanation), the production of ships and airplanes, and the freedom "from the slave-fetters of Versailles." He also mentions the Rhineland being "brought under the supremacy of the German nation," a reference to the military occupation of that region in 1936 by Germany's revived half-million-man army. The other world powers did nothing, thereby encouraging Hitler's later aggressions. Finally, look at Hitler's comment regarding labor unions ("that no trade union would any longer be able to incite the workers"). What does Hitler really mean by that (see Epilogue)?

Hashimoto's address is as clear as Hitler's is vague. To Hashimoto, Japan's central problem is overpopulation, and he envisions only three possible resolutions. What were those three potential options? Why, in Hashimoto's opinion, were two of the three not possible? How would territorial expansion, in his view, solve Japan's economic problems? What would that expansion bring to Japan economically? Finally, how many of Japan's economic obstacles does Hashimoto attribute to anti-Japanese attitudes (racism?) on the part of other nations? Explain.

Stalin's 1934 report to the Seventeenth Congress of the Communist Party of the USSR is a remarkable document, both for what it says and for what it does not say. Despite the fact that a good number of economists and historians are suspicious of statistics circulated by the Soviet government, there is no doubt that industrial and agricultural gains during the 1930s were impressive. How did Stalin explain those significant gains, even as the economies of other industrial nations were experiencing severe difficulties? From your reading and discussions, what did Stalin *omit* from his generally glowing report?

Once you have analyzed the speeches to discern how each national leader proposed to deal with the Great Depression, it would be appropriate to compare and contrast the approaches urged upon Great Britain, the United States, Germany, Japan, and the Soviet Union. How were these approaches different? In what ways were they similar? For example, how would each nation deal with unemployment? Were Germany and Japan similar in their approaches? Was the United States similar to or different from Germany and Japan, and in what ways? What about Great Britain? In what ways was the Soviet Union's approach to its economic troubles similar to or different from those of other nations? How did each nation propose to involve government in ending the Depression?

After you have analyzed, compared, and contrasted the five speeches, examine the sets of statistics (Sources 6 through 13). Some of the dimensions of this decline, the deepest in world history, are revealed in Source 6, the indexes of industrial production for Germany, Japan, Great Britain, the United States, and the Soviet Union—five major industrialized nations that were affected at somewhat different times. Note that Japan and Great Britain did not experience the collapse of production in the 1930s in the same manner as Germany and the United States. How would you explain this? As for the USSR, its most severe economic difficulties took place during and immediately following its civil war. Even so, how was the Soviet Union able to make significant gains in industry at the same time that almost all other industrialized nations were almost floundering? Also, both Germany and the United States "hit bottom" in the same year, 1932, and then began slowly to recover. Can any of the other statistical evidence help you to understand why this was so? At the same time, how can the changing unemployment figures (Source 7) be explained by other statistical sets? How can Source 8 prove helpful (recall the speeches, especially those of MacDonald and Roosevelt)?

As noted above, tariffs can be used both to raise revenue for the government (as a tax on imports) and to assist native industries by raising tariff schedules so high as to discourage

Chapter 12

The Industrial

Crisis and the

Centralization

of Government

(1924–1939)

imports from elsewhere. How does Source 9 clarify governments' policies to combat their nations' economic troubles? Most economists—both then and now—criticized such a policy as shortsighted and detrimental. What is your opinion of these economists' assertion?

Sources 10 through 13 concentrate on military expenditures. How are these statistics related to individual governmental policies to combat the Depres-sion? What is your opinion of these policies?

Now put the speeches and the statistics together. How did each of the five major industrial nations choose to combat the Great Depression? What were the principal similarities between their approaches? the differences? Finally, on a larger scale, how would you *evaluate* these policies? What were their immediate effects? their long-range effects?

EPILOGUE

In some ways, the Great Depression of the 1930s was one of the eventual results of the Industrial Revolution. As industrialization expanded into nations and regions that previously had been consumers of the manufactures of others, international markets diminished and the scramble for the remaining markets became fierce. In order to secure raw materials and guarantee markets, in the late nineteenth century almost all Western nations engaged in an almost frantic imperialism. And during the Great Depression of the 1930s, some nations kept a certain level of manufacturing going by forcing products on their respective empires. Finally, in order to keep exported manufactures as inexpensive as possible (to make them more competitive in world markets), industrial wages had to be kept low, thus making it difficult for domestic workers to increase their own consumption of manufactured goods. In some ways, then, the Industrial Revo-lution was undermined by its own snowballing success.

As noted earlier, the Depression shook the industrialized nations' political foundations as profoundly as it did their economic ones. Japan suffered a wave of political assassinations and attempted coups (at least two of which were masterminded by Hashimoto) until the military finally emerged as the controlling force in that nation's politics, a position in part strengthened by the military's uneasy alliance with Japan's giant corporations (*zaibatsu*).[16] In Germany, the National Socialists had garnered 14.5 million votes in the 1932 election, in part a response to Hitler's promise of economic recovery. When prominent industrialists and army officers fell into step, German president Hindenburg was persuaded to name Hitler

16. A *zaibatsu* resembles an American holding company, manufacturing several types of products and providing many services as well. In the 1920s, Mitsui was Japan's largest zaibatsu, having assets representing approximately 15 percent of all Japanese business firms.

Germany's chancellor, on January 30, 1933. Within a year, the Nazi leader had turned Germany into a totalitarian state.

Political reactions in Great Britain and the United States were less extreme. In Britain, MacDonald was forced to accept a coalition government but was able to retain his post as prime minister. In the United States, in spite of some dire warnings that capitalism was near death, in 1932 voters elected moderate Democrat Franklin Roosevelt, and government changed hands peacefully in March 1933. As for the Soviet Union, Stalin consolidated his power in the 1930s by eliminating opposition to him in a series of purges.

As you might expect after reading the speeches in this chapter, each of the major industrial powers sought to loosen the grip of the Depression in its own way; any international or cooperative efforts were abandoned following the collapse of the World Economic Conference of sixty-six nations in 1933. In some ways, Great Britain was the most fortunate. High interest rates and the economic slump of the 1920s had created pent-up demand for manufactured products. When Britain abandoned the gold standard[17] in 1931, prices fell and a natural "boomlet" was created. Unemployment remained high, however, and was not eradicated until Britain entered World

War II in September 1939. But Britain did not need the massive infusions of government money into the economy that was necessary in other industrialized nations (see Source 8). This was indeed fortunate because the British government could ill afford the deficit financing that Germany and the United States utilized.

Germany's approach to the Depression was considerably more severe. Hitler instituted the compulsory National Labor Service to staff public works projects, tried to drive women out of the work force (to make room for unemployed males), smashed labor unions, and increased government revenues for investment in fresh industrial production. Ominously, much of that industrial production was military goods, a policy that eventually would drive that nation into war (that, along with Hitler's megalomania).

As President Franklin Roosevelt's New Deal gradually took shape, its general philosophy seems to have been to stimulate domestic consumption in a variety of ways. Consumer demand, New Dealers reasoned, would bring people back to work to fill that demand. Hence the federal government engaged in deficit financing to put money in the hands of farmers (Agricultural Adjustment Act), the unemployed (Works Progress Administration), the elderly (Social Security), unemployed youth (Civilian Conservation Corps), and other groups. Yet unemployment in the United States remained high (over 10 million in 1938, 19 percent of the civilian labor force) until the nation's entrance into World War II in 1941.

17. **gold standard:** an international system in which each nation's currency was equal in value to and exchangeable for a specified amount of gold. The system provided monetary stability. Great Britain abandoned the gold standard in order to let the value of the pound fall, thereby instigating an inflationary trend.

Chapter 12

The Industrial

Crisis and the

Centralization

of Government

(1924–1939)

After 1931, recovery in Japan was comparatively rapid. Unemployment dropped steadily and real wages increased. This was partly the result of military expansion into Manchuria, but even more, Japan was able to orchestrate an enviable economic marriage of Western industrial technology and low Asian wages, a union that made Japan's manufactured goods more competitive in Asian markets.

The price that the Russian people paid for the nation's industrial progress was fierce. To gain needed capital for industrial expansion, Stalin ordered agricultural crops to be requisitioned or seized so they could be sold overseas. The result was the terrible famine of 1933 in which millions starved. Pilfering and hoarding were severely punished. In the cities, industrial workers lived in frightful conditions, as housing construction and consumer goods were ignored in order to achieve impressive industrial gains. Those who questioned Stalin's policies or disobeyed them were executed or shipped to *gulags* (forced labor camps). Although many Westerners who visited the Soviet Union were impressed by what they saw (American journalist Lincoln Steffens exclaimed, "I have seen the future and it works"), in reality the picture was considerably more somber.

Taken as a whole, the industrial world's varied responses to the Great Depression raises a number of questions. To begin with, we are almost compelled to question whether *any* actions of a central government can *cure* the ills of a depression. Doubtless governments may *alleviate* the worst effects of an economic collapse, but whether they can engineer national economic recovery is more debatable. In Great Britain, a natural economic upturn did more to move that nation toward recovery than all the government's nostrums. In the United States, it appears that the New Deal, although it gave Americans a tremendous psychological lift, had rather anemic results when it came to stimulating permanent recovery, perhaps because (as some economists claim) the extent of government intervention in the United States was too limited to stimulate total restoration. Neither nation experienced full employment until the war. And, of course, it was precisely that military buildup that allowed Germany and Japan to experience comparatively rapid turnarounds. Did it, therefore, take the horrific slaughter of World War II to bring the Depression to an end? What in fact had been the roles of governments and their policies and programs to battle the economic crisis? Were they effective, apart from the war?

Finally, the national responses to the Great Depression show that the refusal of nations to work together can have disastrous consequences, as the almost endless spiral of tariff wars (Source 9) ultimately showed. Speaking of the relationship between the crisis in Britain and the world situation, British government official Sir John Anderson wrote in 1930, "You cannot drain a bog while the surrounding country is still under water." In the nineteenth century, Britain had provided a kind of world leadership that benefited other nations as well as itself. When the world's economic center of gravity shifted to the United States about the time of World War I, that nation lacked the vision and experience to exercise a similar style of world leadership. Instead, the United States started the round of tariff increases in 1930, refused to participate in the World Economic Conference of 1933 (and actually was a major contributor to the summit's collapse), and followed a path toward recovery that (if it worked) would benefit no one but itself. And yet the United States was hardly alone in pursuing self-serving policies. Indeed, it is likely that the wisdom of King Solomon himself could not have persuaded the industrialized nations to work together.

Overworked and sick, Ramsay MacDonald resigned as prime minister in 1935 and died soon after, in 1937. Franklin Roosevelt won unprecedented third and fourth presidential elections (in 1940 and 1944), but did not live to see Allied victories over Germany and Japan in World War II. He died on April 12, 1945.

Adolf Hitler, driven by his own dark dreams and hatreds, committed suicide in his fortified bunker underneath a decimated Berlin just eighteen days after Roosevelt's death. Hashimoto Kingoro survived the war. Tried as a war criminal by the Americans, he was sentenced to life imprisonment but was released in 1955. He died in 1957.

Josef Stalin ruled the Soviet Union with an iron hand until his death in 1953. Gradually, however, it became evident that total centralized planning enforced by the brutal methods of Communist Party leaders and the secret police (KGB) were increasingly ineffective. In 1953, Party General Secretary Nikita Khrushchev (1894–1971) denounced Stalin's despotic methods and in 1961 had the dictator's body removed from the Lenin Mausoleum. Meanwhile, the industrial and agricultural gains made in the 1930s were not sustained and the USSR was forced to import wheat to avoid massive famines. At the same time, the Communist Party bureaucracy was becoming increasingly large and inefficient, people began to seek more economic and social freedoms, and some of the republics were showing unmistakable signs of nationalism. In response to these difficulties, Mikhail Gorbachev (1931–) introduced policies of political and cultural openness (*glasnost*) and economic reforms (*perestroika*). Some people embraced these changes, while others feared them. By late 1991, the situation had grown so dire that the USSR formally was dissolved. The largest of the now-independent republics, Russia, tried to steer a middle path between communism and capitalism and between democracy and despotism. Stalin's Soviet Union simply had disappeared.

CHAPTER THIRTEEN

TOTAL WAR: THE COST

OF UNLIMITED CONFLICT (1914–1945)

Appalled by the terrible slaughter that occurred during the Battle of the Somme in World War I, one of the British soldiers who survived, Edmund Blunden, asked himself if anyone could claim victory in such warfare. In the end, he decided, "[B]oth sides had seen, in a sad scrawl of broken earth and murdered men, the answer to the question. . . . Neither race had won, nor could win, the War. The War had won, and would go on winning."[1] Like countless others to come, Blunden discovered that in twentieth-century mass warfare, winners and losers alike paid a high price.

War, of course, has always been destructive. But until the late eighteenth century, practical constraints limited

1. Quoted in Paul Fussell, *The Great War and Modern Memory* (New York: Oxford University Press, 1975), p. 13.

its scale and the devastation it caused. The emergence of modern society, which allowed nations to overcome so many traditional limitations, freed them from most of the old constraints on warfare as well. Beginning with the French Revolution, the scope and violence of warfare increased steadily, reaching new levels of potential destructiveness in the nineteenth century. But because Europe, then the most developed part of the world economically and technologically, remained free of major wars toward the century's end, many people concluded that modern warfare between "advanced" countries would be like the Franco-Prussian War of 1870: quick and without great loss of life or property. When World War I erupted in 1914, people were unprepared for what was to follow—over four exhausting years of carnage in the very heart of the "advanced" world. Destructive as that conflict proved, it was soon eclipsed by the greater violence that exploded a generation later in World War II. By the close of that war in 1945, Europe and the rest of the world had to face the fact that modern nations had unleashed a new kind of unlimited and extremely destructive warfare that had the potential to destroy all of humanity.

As their names imply, World Wars I and II raged across the entire globe. Yet it was in their intensity more than in their geographic extension that they stood out from earlier conflicts. They overwhelmed all aspects of life in the countries involved. Truly "nations in arms," the combatants struggled not just for material gain or even victory itself, but ultimately for national survival. They sought every advantage that modern technology and industry could give them to wage unrestrained warfare. To sustain such warfare, they had not only to draft huge numbers of their citizenry into arms but organize most of the rest for war-related work. They had to intervene in their economies, diverting production from peacetime goods to the manufacture of an unending supply of armaments and military equipment. And they had to curtail many ordinary pursuits and freedoms, imposing general rationing, enforcing widespread censorship, and often suspending normal laws and civil liberties. This nearly complete disruption of civilian life as much as the fury of modern combat earned this type of conflict a new name: total war.

This chapter takes a look at the nature of such warfare. It asks you to consider what made total war so all-encompassing and, perhaps more importantly, what the consequences were. The focus here, however, is not just on the immediate cost to the losers— or the winners—for the impact of total war cannot be measured solely by the number of the dead and the defeated. Total war deeply affected the living and the victors, too, and in ways far beyond their immediate losses. The economic, social, psychological, and moral effect these wars had on those who survived them must be taken into account, along with the legacy they left to all who came after them later in the twentieth century. In asking you to consider the consequences of total war, then, this chapter asks you to think about the broader impact this new form of combat had on the modern world.

BACKGROUND

Prussian General Carl von Clausewitz, the great European authority on modern combat, warned in his classic work, *On War*, that warfare should always be seen as a means to a higher end and never allowed to become an end in itself. Clausewitz considered war "an extension of policy," a calculated use of violence to compel others to political objectives. Combat, he felt, should be a limited affair that in its ideal form approached what he called "absolute war": the elimination of all the "friction" or obstacles of warfare in order to allow the delivery of a single swift stroke that renders enemy forces powerless and willing to accept terms. How to achieve such a sudden, telling blow thereafter became the goal of most modern Western military planners.

The great social and economic changes of late eighteenth- and nineteenth-century Europe, however, confounded the efforts to attain this ideal. First, the French Revolution and Napoleonic Wars encouraged the use of citizen armies. Though individually less capable than professionals, patriotic citizen soldiers made effective fighters when deployed in large numbers and equipped with weapons that compensated for their inexperience. Industrialization provided a way to supply such weapons at low cost, and also provided new forms of transport and communication that allowed large armies to be moved and managed in battle. By the mid-nineteenth century, therefore, a new kind of mass warfare had emerged whose scale and complexity defied efforts to gain sudden, telling victories. Success depended increasingly on the efficient mobilization of huge citizen armies and their deployment in battle. It also required constant replenishment of the equipment and weaponry that such troops needed in order to maintain their fighting strength. Production, transportation, and supply thus began to eclipse tactical brilliance as factors determining victory. The changing nature of combat could already be seen in the American Civil War of the 1860s, but most Europeans dismissed this conflict as a distant affair between unprofessional forces, and few paid it much mind. Further

evidence of change appeared in the Franco-Prussian War of the early 1870s, but the speed with which this conflict ended again kept most observers from noticing it.

The lack of any big wars in Europe in the last decades of the nineteenth century further obscured the transformation of warfare. So when World War I broke out in August 1914, most Europeans thought that the conflict would be a short-lived one, decided by a few battles in which the valor of fighting men would win the day. Many naively assumed that the troops would be back home by Christmas. But during the more than four years that the war raged, people slowly awoke to the fact that the limited combat of the past had given way to a new kind of unrestrained war. Ultimately, as the scope and intensity of the war mounted beyond anything previously known, they paid it an off-handed compliment, naming it "the Great War" to distinguish it from all earlier conflicts. And it was this Great War that first revealed to the combatants what made war total.

Their first insight came with the discovery that an all-out conflict would not be brief. At the start, Germany planned for a quick war and tried to attain it by mounting a rapid, massive invasion of France through neutral Belgium, hoping then to turn its attention to helping its ally, Austria-Hungary, defeat Russia in the east. But when French and British troops halted the German offensive in northern France, the contending forces dug into fixed positions in a long line of trenches running from Switzerland to the English Channel. This became the infamous western front. After two years of inconclusive fighting, both sides attempted massive breakouts in 1916, leading to the battles of Verdun and the Somme, in which first the Germans and then the British went on the offensive. In these battles, great masses of men charged and counter-charged across "no man's land" between opposing trench systems; because of the destructiveness of new weaponry, the losses were incredible. But despite casualties in the hundreds of thousands over a few days—with a high point of 60,000 in one day at the Somme—neither side could win a significant victory.

Gradually generals and other national leaders realized that the technological advances in warfare had favored defense over offense. Improved rifles, grenades, machine guns, and explosive artillery shells, along with abundant barbed wire and mines, made frontal assault ruinous in casualties. Efforts at outflanking positions also failed, because railroads and trucks allowed defenders to rush reserve forces forward in sufficient numbers to launch huge counteroffensives. Governments thus enlisted scientists and engineers to come up with new weapons and devices that would improve offensive capability. All sides experimented with battlefield innovations from gas warfare to tanks, submarines, and airplanes. Science was thus mobilized as never before to turn out ever more deadly weapons in the interest of narrow national goals, ignoring the larger human costs. The result was the development on both sides of what came to be called the "killing machine," a form of warfare

designed to wear out and exhaust the enemy through mass slaughter.

Although they gave neither side a decisive edge, these innovations constantly increased the material and economic cost of the war, demanding ever greater sacrifices from civilians and overstraining industrial production. As the conflict lengthened into a grim war of mass attrition, the strength and will of civilians and the resilience of the combatants' political and economic systems became as important to victory as their military forces. By 1917 the German decision to use unrestricted submarine warfare to blockade Britain threatened the British with mass starvation, a possibility already haunting Germany as a result of an Allied naval blockade. Struggling to keep up flagging morale under worsening conditions at home as well as on the battlefields, all the belligerents increasingly used modern mass media to disseminate propaganda and make patriotic appeals. But beginning in Russia in 1917, and then in most of the Central Powers in 1918, overstrained populations revolted, toppling governments and leaving their armies stranded in the field. Peace came not from defeat in battle but from failures on the home front, failures prompted by the collapse of political and economic institutions under the stress of prolonged wartime conditions. Such defeat entailed not just the frustration of war aims, but almost total national breakdown.

World War I thus revealed the deadly nature of total war, in which whole nations rather than just their armies were locked in conflict. In 1935, General Eric von Leudendorf, who had served on the German general staff during the Great War, analyzed the new form of combat in a book called *Total War*. Such warfare, he noted, could no longer be confined to battlefields. Because of the ease and speed of modern transportation, it would spread everywhere, erasing the distinction between the front lines and other areas. Belligerents would thus have to mobilize their entire civilian populations to wage war. This effort, in turn, would require constant propaganda campaigns and government control over media to sustain national morale. In short, total war demanded total national readjustment. And to make this occur smoothly, plans for mobilization and a wartime economy must be made well in advance to ensure their swift implementation once war erupted. Finally, he warned, leadership in a total war must be vested in a single authority, preferably a military one, to prevent dissent and confusion from weakening the all-out national effort.

Analyses of this sort suggested that disrupting an enemy's home front would be as effective as defeating its armies. Strategists thus began to consider ways to strike behind enemy lines, either to demoralize populations or to destroy crucial support systems, ignoring traditional distinctions between combatants and noncombatants in war. Small-scale experiments in World War I of attacking enemy cities with long-range guns and bomb-laden Zeppelins had not been very effective. But younger military planners felt confident that newer weapons would make this tactic more feasible and spoke of the need to or-

ganize "civilian defense" to protect populations from it. In a struggle for all-out victory, they warned, countries could not expect any quarter— nor could they give any in turn. The alternative to total triumph would be total annihilation.

Many postwar leaders, particularly in liberal, democratic states like Britain and France, recoiled from such ideas, fearing that their people would refuse to enter another bloodbath like World War I, and so sought other options. French military leaders responded by fortifying the entire Franco-German frontier to create an impregnable front line. Built at great expense, this Maginot line, as it was called, was supposed to make another invasion of France too costly to contemplate. More forward-looking military men, however, realized that such a defensive solution invited a return to deadly fixed fronts. So they looked for new offensive strategies based on highly technical weapons that would allow small, professional forces to strike deeply into enemy territory without the static battlefields and high attrition associated with World War I.

British planners, taking advantage of their country's island nature and its large navy, which protected it from immediate attack, grew interested in a new offensive form of air power called strategic bombing. Fleets of airplanes, they said, could be used to strike directly at the enemy's critical home front and either destroy its inhabitants outright or cripple their ability to support a war. They thus lobbied for a force of long-range planes that could bomb the continental cities of their most likely enemies. For a while in the

1920s and early 1930s, Britain's efforts in this direction made its Royal Air Force the world's first significant form of air power. But the primitive nature of planes through the 1930s and the lack of experienced pilots made this a risky approach to national defense, especially for landlocked nations with potential enemies all around their borders.

Continental European innovators thus took another tack, focusing on mechanized, mobile forces that could rapidly penetrate an enemy's front lines and strike at its home territory. Charles de Gaulle, later head of the Free French forces in World War II, advocated this approach. In his 1934 book *Army of the Future,* he argued for a "completely motorized" professional army that would move on "caterpillar wheels."[2] But France had already committed its defense to the Maginot line and ignored his ideas. It was thus left to German generals to develop similar ideas into what came to be called *blitzkrieg,* or "lightning war." *Blitzkrieg* was a form of combat using a relatively small and highly mechanized army designed to fight a short, limited war. Instead of a mass infantry of conscript riflemen, it relied on a well-trained force of professional soldiers organized around tanks and other motorized units and provided with air cover by squadrons of accompanying airplanes. Ready at all times, such an army could be launched instantly into the heart of an enemy nation before that nation had time to

mobilize and deploy a more traditional mass army of citizen soldiers. German strategists initially favored this approach because postwar agreements severely limited the size of Germany's army. But once they were convinced of its merits, they held to it even after Hitler came to power in 1933 and began a major military buildup. Germany's rearmament thus focused on building a mechanized army with the most up-to-date equipment then known. Hitler's air minister, Hermann Goering, also used this opportunity to press for advanced airplanes, and by 1935 his *Luftwaffe* or air force approached Britain's Royal Air Force in both design and numbers.

The world got its first glimpse of this new weaponry when Germany intervened in the Spanish civil war. During the fighting there in 1937, the German Condor Legion staged the world's first major air raid against civilians, dropping incendiary and high-explosive bombs on the small Spanish town of Guernica. The act brought a loud outcry from across the world against the killing of civilians (and occasioned Pablo Picasso's famous painting in protest). But the effectiveness of the tactic convinced the Germans to add more bombers to their air force and increase its size.

The ability of air power to disrupt and demoralize enemy defenses was further shown in Germany's invasion of Poland in 1939 and then in its "lightning war" against France in the spring of 1940. German air strikes against cities and strategic centers behind the lines terrorized civilians and confused defense measures, creating a mood of helplessness that hastened

2. Charles de Gaulle, *The Army of the Future* (New York and Philadelphia: J. B. Lippincott Co., 1941), p. 100.

surrender. In the fall of 1940, however, when the German military machine turned its might against Britain, it faced a nation with air power of its own. Before Germany could risk an invasion across the English Channel, it had to destroy the Royal Air Force. Determined RAF resistance in the air and effective "civilian defense" on the ground to help people survive air raids allowed the British eventually to win the Battle of Britain. In the process, they became even more appreciative of air power. Once they had achieved mastery in the air, they realized, they could use bombers to attack the industrial base on which Germany's highly mechanized army depended for resupply. When the United States joined the war on Britain's side at the end of 1941 following the Japanese attack on Pearl Harbor, British leaders accordingly called for fleets of English and American bombers to strike directly at German cities.

American military men were already familiar with the idea of strategic bombing, because U.S. Army General William "Billy" Mitchell had been one of its earliest proponents in the interwar period. A veteran of World War I, Mitchell tried to convince his countrymen that airplanes could form a first line of defense for North America, especially if they were based on specially designed ships stationed at sea. Such a force, he argued, could also be sent to strike directly at a distant enemy's homeland. Technological problems and economic constraints kept the U.S. Army from taking his ideas seriously during the interwar period. But with the outbreak of war in Europe and the rapid advance of aircraft it inspired,

American war planners began to reevaluate them.

One of the attractive features of strategic bombing was that it allowed the Americans and British to strike back at Germany at a time when they felt unable to launch a land assault against its heavily fortified European base. It also provided a way to aid the beleaguered Russian forces. Drawn into the war in mid-1941 by a German surprise attack, the Soviet Union was initially unable to halt the advance of German forces. Appealing to Britain and the United States, with whom it soon allied, it asked them to attack Germany in the west to relieve German pressure on Soviet forces. Unwilling to commit to an all-out invasion of Europe, the combined chiefs of staff coordinating the British and American forces instead announced their decision in February of 1943 to begin what they called the Combined Bomber Offensive to destroy Germany's ability to remain in the war by demolishing its industrial base and terrorizing its people.

Inasmuch as Germany had pioneered air attacks against nonmilitary targets, the offensive was not a new idea. But the scale and intensity of these air raids dramatically changed the nature of modern warfare. Fleets of hundreds of aircraft, many specially designed for the task like the American B-29 bomber, attacked German cities around the clock. Attempts at precision bombing, or hitting select targets, proved too costly and soon gave way to "saturation bombing," or indiscriminate attacks on urban areas. Occasionally bombers equipped with special incendiary bombs even attempted to set large sections of cities aflame. These attacks brought the war directly to German civilians and destroyed much of German industry. Allied land offensives from Russia, Africa, and then France were ultimately required in order to defeat the German military forces, but the Anglo-American air offensive contributed greatly to their defeat. A postwar U.S. government survey concluded that "Allied air power was decisive in the war in Western Europe," noting:

> It brought the economy which sustained the enemy's armed forces to virtual collapse, although the full effects of this collapse had not reached the enemy's front lines when they were overrun by Allied forces. It brought home to the German people the full impact of modern war with all its horror and suffering. Its imprint on the German nation will be lasting.[3]

Strategic bombing proved so effective in Europe that the United States

3. *The United States Strategic Bombing Survey, Summary Report (European War)*, Sept. 30, 1945 (Washington, D.C.: U.S. Government Printing Office, 1945), pp. 15–16.

used it in the Pacific theater, too, once American forces pushed past the outer Japanese defenses to secure bases within air range of Japan itself. Japan began to experience this new form of warfare late in 1944. By March of the next year, air raids against Tokyo and other Japanese cities had escalated into massive attacks that unleashed thousands of tons of incendiary bombs, burning large portions of these cities to the ground. When Japanese resistance continued despite this destruction, U.S. leaders decided to introduce the world's first atomic bombs into the air campaign. Originally developed to deter a German nuclear threat, the atomic bomb proved the ultimate weapon for total war. For as the two dropped on Hiroshima and Nagasaki in August 1945 showed, a single atom bomb could obliterate an entire city. Armed with such weapons, nations could now truly annihilate one another. Realizing that fact, the Japanese government offered unconditional surrender, even though most of its armies in Asia remained undefeated and no invasion of its home territories had yet begun. Again, defeat on the home front made resistance on the battlefield futile.

THE METHOD

Each of the sources in the Evidence section deals with one or more aspects of total war. Try first to determine which characteristic features of this warfare each source reveals. Then look within the source for hints or suggestions about the likely consequences of these features. You may find it helpful to make a written list of both as you proceed, not only to provide a reminder later of what you found, but also to obtain a broad overview from which to attempt some final generalizations about the nature and cost of total war.

The first source, excerpted from Carl von Clausewitz's 1832 classic study

On War, offers a definition of limited war against which to contrast the concept of total war. A veteran of the Napoleonic Wars, Clausewitz was a career officer in the Prussian army whose views on strategy dominated nineteenth-century military thought and continued to exert an influence throughout the twentieth century. By World War I, however, the shift in modern war that he feared had reached a new level, as Source 2, a passage from the memoirs of David Lloyd George, illustrates. A liberal reformer with pacifist leanings who became British prime minister in the midst of the war, Lloyd George was appalled by the mounting casualties of 1916. Not only did enlistment fail to keep pace with them, but they threatened the stability and structure of society, as he hints here.

The war consumed unprecedented quantities of funds, too, and hard-pressed governments appealed to their people for wartime loans to finance soaring budgets. France, known for its artists, benefited from their help in launching poster campaigns in 1915 to bring this appeal to the masses. Soon other governments followed suit, using propaganda posters like those depicted here as Source 3 to raise funds, solicit enlistment, and boost morale. Source 4 helps to explain why such measures were needed in order to sustain popular support for the war. Taken from the final dispatch written by the head of the British Expeditionary Forces on the western front, Field Marshal Sir Douglas Haig, at the war's end, it outlines the overall scope and nature of the conflict. Often called "the butcher of the Somme" because of his willingness to expend so many forces in that battle, Haig here details the enormous needs of an army fighting a modern mass war of attrition.

The next two documents represent assessments of the conflict's postwar impact. Source 5 comes from an essay called "The Crisis of the Spirit" written in 1919 by Paul Valéry, one of France's most outstanding poets. His focus is not just on France but on the entire European world, for in his view the war had fatally damaged Europe's "spirit" to the detriment of its intellectual and cultural standing. Veterans had special problems after the war, for its carnage left most of them deeply disillusioned with all ideals and authority. Source 6, excerpts from a popular novel of 1929 called *All Quiet on the Western Front*, indicates why. Based on the experiences of its German author, Erich Maria Remarque, it portrays the numbing effect of the war on the soldiers and how it made survivors view themselves as a "lost generation," without hopes or dreams. Their demoralization helps to explain why the world was soon plunged into the even more costly Second World War.

This apathy encouraged authoritarian leaders to seize power in Italy, Germany, and Japan, and then to risk limited conflicts against disillusioned neighbors that were unwilling to engage in more fighting. Japan led in this effort to change the balance of power, invading China as early as 1931. By 1937, as Japan launched an all-out offensive against China, it began to introduce tactics to demoralize the civilian populace in what would become an all-too-familiar pattern of new warfare as conflict flared around the world. The aerial bombardment of Shanghai and other eastern Chinese cities gave the world a foretaste of this warfare; like the German bombing of the small Basque town of Guernica in the Spanish Civil War in May of 1937, it marked the start of a new callousness in waging war against noncombatants. But even this onslaught on civilians was soon overshadowed by Japanese actions following the seizure of China's capital, Nanking, in December of 1937. Known as the "Rape of Nanking," the Japanese army's systematic plundering and butchery of thousands of innocent victims heralded the start of a new age of atrocities. Source 7 is a *New York Times* article from 1937 on this massacre.

Leaders of other countries often had difficulty arousing their citizens to oppose such aggression until directly attacked. Thus Source 8, President Roosevelt's first address to Congress in January 1942, shows him trying to rally the American people for what he warns will be another "all-out" war to counter the aggression of the Axis nations. Source 9, a government poster and popular song featuring a fictitious "Rosie the Riveter," illustrates one consequence of the massive mobilization of the home front that followed: the effort to engage women in the national war effort. The escalating nature of the conflict can also be seen in Source 10, the transcript of a radio broadcast delivered to the German public in October 1942 by Hermann Goering, Hitler's second in command, who was then trying to mobilize his nation's economy more fully to match the growing demands of the war. Any Axis hope for limiting the scale and intensity of the war was dashed at the Casablanca Conference between Roosevelt and British Prime Minister Winston Churchill in January 1943. For as Source 11, a subsequent radio announcement by Roosevelt, reveals, he and Churchill there decided that they would accept nothing less than a total victory over their enemies.

It was also at Casablanca that the two Allied leaders agreed to mount the full-scale Combined Bombing Offensive against German cities. Source 12, an official U.S. government survey, made in 1946, of the damage inflicted upon Japan by the American strategic bombing offensive there, provides a detailed description of the devastation this new form of total war inflicted upon enemy home fronts. Like a similar survey conducted on Germany, it reveals that massive air strikes nearly leveled entire cities. Its final remarks about the atomic bomb, however, reveal how this new weapon introduced near the war's end approached the "untrammeled, absolute manifestation of violence" that Clausewitz warned might come of unrestrained warfare. What this weapon meant in human terms can be seen in Source 13, a recollection of the Hiroshima atomic blast by a Japanese schoolboy, Iwao Nakamura, taken from a collection of Japanese children's accounts compiled in 1951. It poignantly illustrates the ultimate consequences of total war between modern nations.

███████████████   THE EVIDENCE   ███████████████

Source 1 from Carl von Clausewitz, On War *(Princeton, N.J.: Princeton University Press, 1976),*
pp. 86, 588–593.

1. Carl von Clausewitz, *On War,* 1832

When whole communities go to war—whole peoples, and especially *civilized*
peoples—the reason always lies in some political situation, and the occasion is
always due to some political object. War, therefore, is an act of policy. Were it a
complete, untrammeled, absolute manifestation of violence (as the pure concept would require), war would of its own independent will usurp the place of
policy the moment policy had brought it into being; it would then drive policy
out of office and rule by the laws of its own nature. . . .

. . . The end of the seventeenth century, the age of Louis XIV, may be regarded
as that point in history when the standing army in the shape familiar to the
eighteenth century reached maturity. . . .

The conduct of war thus became a true game, in which the cards were dealt
by time and by accident. In its effect it was a somewhat stronger form of diplomacy, a more forceful method of negotiation, in which battles and sieges were
the principal notes exchanged. Even the most ambitious ruler had no greater
aims than to gain a number of advantages that could be exploited at the peace
conference. . . .

This was the state of affairs at the outbreak of the French Revolution. . . . Suddenly war again became the business of the people—a people of thirty millions,
all of whom considered themselves to be citizens. We need not study in detail
the circumstances that accompanied this tremendous development; we need
only note the effects that are pertinent to our discussion. The people became a
participant in war; instead of governments and armies as heretofore, the full
weight of the nation was thrown into the balance. The resources and efforts now
available for use surpassed all conventional limits; nothing now impeded the
vigor with which war could be waged, and consequently the opponents of
France faced the utmost peril. . . .

Since Bonaparte, then, war, first among the French and subsequently among
their enemies, again became the concern of the people as a whole, took on
an entirely different character, or rather closely approached its true character,
its absolute perfection. There seemed no end to the resources mobilized; all limits disappeared in the vigor and enthusiasm shown by governments and their
subjects. Various factors powerfully increased that vigor: the vastness of available resources, the ample field of opportunity, and the depth of feeling generally aroused. The sole aim of war was to overthrow the opponent. Not until

he was prostrate was it considered possible to pause and try to reconcile the opposing interests.

War, untrammeled by any conventional restraints, had broken loose in all its elemental fury. This was due to the peoples' new share in these great affairs of state; and their participation, in turn, resulted partly from the impact that the Revolution had on the internal conditions of every state and partly from the danger that France posed to everyone.

Will this always be the case in the future? From now on will every war in Europe be waged with the full resources of the state, and therefore have to be fought only over major issues that affect the people? Or shall we again see a gradual separation taking place between government and people? Such questions are difficult to answer, and we are the last to dare to do so. But the reader will agree with us when we say that once barriers—which in a sense consist only in man's ignorance of what is possible—are torn down, they are not so easily set up again. At least when major interests are at stake, mutual hostility will express itself in the same manner as it has in our own day.

Source 2 from David Lloyd George, War Memoirs of David Lloyd George, 1915–1916 *(Boston: Little, Brown, 1933), pp. 9–10.*

2. Lloyd George on the Battle of the Somme, July 1, 1916

So, much to the secret satisfaction of General Joffre, we turned our backs on Salonika and our faces once more to the Somme. It ranks with Verdun as one of the two bloodiest battles ever fought on this earth up to that date. The casualties on both sides were well over a million. It was not responsible for the failure of the German effort to capture Verdun. It was only an element in slackening up a German offensive which had already slowed down and was by now a practical and almost an acknowledged failure. The French Commander-in-Chief said in May that the Germans had already been beaten at Verdun. Had the battle continued to rage around the remaining forts which held up the German Army we could have helped to reinforce the hard-pressed French Army either by sending troops to the battle area or by taking over another sector of the French Front. The Somme campaign certainly did not save Russia. That great country was being rapidly driven by the German guns towards the maelstrom of anarchy. You could even then hear the roar of the waters. That is, we might have heard it had it not been for the thunders of the Somme. These deafened our ears and obscured our vision so that we could not perceive the approaching catastrophe in Russia and therefore did not take measures to avert it. One-third of the Somme guns and ammunition transferred in time to the banks of another river, the

Dnieper, would have won a great victory for Russia and deferred the Revolution until after the war.

It is claimed that the Battle of the Somme destroyed the old German Army by killing off its best officers and men. It killed off far more of our best and of the French best. The Battle of the Somme was fought by the volunteer armies raised in 1914 and 1915. These contained the choicest and best of our young manhood. The officers came mainly from our public schools and universities. Over 400,000 of our men fell in this bullheaded fight and the slaughter amongst our young officers was appalling. The "Official History of the War," writing of the first attack, says:

> For the disastrous loss of the finest manhood of the United Kingdom and Ireland there was only a small gain of ground to show. . . .

Summing up the effect on the British Army of the whole battle it says:

> Munitions and the technique of their use improved, but never again was the spirit or the quality of the officers and men so high, nor the general state of the training, leading and, above all, discipline of the new British armies in France so good. The losses sustained were not only heavy but irreplaceable.

Source 3: Photo (a): Hoover Institution Archives; Photo (b): The Imperial War Museum, London.

3. French and British World War I Posters

(a) French Loan Poster

"We'll get them!
Second National Defense Loan
Subscribe"

(b) British Recruiting Poster

Source 4 from Field Marshal Sir Douglas Haig, "Features of the War," U.S. War Department Document No. 952 (Washington, D.C.: U.S. Government Printing Office, 1919). Obtained from The World War I Document Archive, *http://www. lib.byu.edu/~rdh/wwi/1918p/haigdesp.html.*

4. Field Marshal Sir Douglas Haig, "Features of the War," Fourth Supplement to *The London Gazette*, Tuesday, April 8, 1919

(10) If the operations of the past four and a half years are regarded as a single continuous campaign, there can be recognized in them the same general features and the same necessary stages which between forces of approximately equal strength have marked all the conclusive battles of history. There is in the first instance the preliminary stage of the campaign in which the opposing forces seek to deploy and maneuver for position, endeavoring while doing so to gain some early advantage which might be pushed home to quick decision. This phase came to an end in the present war with the creation of continuous trench lines from the Swiss frontier to the sea.

Battle having been joined, there follows the period of real struggle in which the main forces of the two belligerent armies are pitted against each other in close and costly combat. Each commander seeks to wear down the power of resistance of his opponent and to pin him to his position, while preserving or accumulating in his own hands a powerful reserve force with which he can maneuver, and when signs of the enemy becoming morally and physically weakened are observed, deliver the decisive attack. . . .

In former battles this stage of the conflict has rarely lasted more than a few days, and has often been completed in a few hours. When armies of millions are engaged, with the resources of great Empires behind them, it will inevitably be long. It will include violent crises of fighting which, when viewed separately and apart from the general perspective, will appear individually as great indecisive battles. To this stage belong the great engagements of 1916 and 1917 which wore down the strength of the German armies.

Finally, whether from the superior fighting ability and leadership of one of the belligerents, as the result of greater resources or tenacity, or by reason of higher morale, or from a combination of all these causes, the time will come when the other side will begin to weaken and the climax of the battle is reached. . . . In this World War the great sortie of the beleaguered German armies commenced on March 21, 1918, and lasted for four months, yet it represents a corresponding stage in a single colossal battle. . . .

(12) Obviously the greater the length of a war the higher is likely to be the number of casualties incurred in it on either side. The same causes, therefore,

which served to protract the recent struggle are largely responsible for the extent of our casualties. There can be no question that to our general unpreparedness must be attributed the loss of many thousands of brave men whose sacrifice we deeply deplore, while we regard their splendid gallantry and self-devotion with unstinted admiration and gratitude.

 . . . The total British casualties in all theaters of war, killed, wounded, missing, and prisoners, including native troops, are approximately three millions (3,076,388). Of this total some two and a half millions (2,568,834) were incurred on the western front. The total French losses, killed, missing, and prisoners, but exclusive of wounded, have been given officially as approximately 1,831,000. If an estimate for wounded is added, the total can scarcely be less than 4,800,000, and of this total it is fair to assume that over four millions were incurred on the western front. The published figures for Italy, killed and wounded only, exclusive of prisoners, amount to 1,400,060, of which practically the whole were incurred in the western theater of war.

Figures have also been published for Germany and Austria. The total German casualties, killed, wounded, missing, and prisoners, are given at approximately six and a half millions (6,485,000), of which the vastly greater proportion must have been incurred on the western front, where the bulk of the German forces were concentrated and the hardest fighting took place. In view of the fact, however, that the number of German prisoners is definitely known to be considerably understated, these figures must be accepted with reserve. The losses of Austria-Hungary in killed, missing, and prisoners are given as approximately two and three-quarter millions (2,772,000). An estimate of wounded would give a total of over four and a half millions. . . .

During the second half of the war, and that part embracing the critical and costly period of the wearing out battle, the losses previously suffered by our Allies laid upon the British Armies in France an increasing share in the burden of attack. From the opening of the Somme Battle in 1916 to the termination of hostilities the British armies were subjected to a strain of the utmost severity which never ceased, and consequently had little or no opportunity for the rest and training they so greatly needed.

In addition to these particular considerations, certain general factors peculiar to modern war made for the inflation of losses. The great strength of modern field defenses and the power and precision of modern weapons, the multiplication of machine guns, trench mortars, and artillery of all natures, the employment of gas, and the rapid development of the aeroplane as a formidable agent of destruction against both men and material, all combined to increase the price to be paid for victory.

If only for these reasons, no comparisons can usefully be made between the relative losses incurred in this war and any previous war. There is, however, the further consideration that the issues involved in this stupendous struggle were far greater than those concerned in any other war in recent history. Our existence as an Empire and civilization itself, as it is understood by the free western nations, were at stake. Men fought as they have never fought before in masses. . . .

(16) A remarkable feature of the present war has been the number and variety of mechanical contrivances to which it has given birth or has brought to a higher state of perfection.

Besides the great increase in mobility made possible by the development of motor transport, heavy artillery, trench mortars, machine guns, aeroplanes, tanks, gas, and barbed wire have in their several spheres of action played very prominent parts in operations, and as a whole have given a greater driving power to war. The belligerent possessing a preponderance of such mechanical contrivances has found himself in a very favorable position as compared with his less well provided opponent. The general superiority of the Allies in this direction during the concluding stages of the recent struggle undoubtedly contributed powerfully to their success. In this respect the army owes a great debt to science and to the distinguished scientific men who placed their learning, and skill at the disposal of their country. . . .

(19) The immense expansion of the army, from 6 to over 60 infantry divisions, combined with the constant multiplication of auxiliary arms, called inevitably for a large increase in the size and scope of the services concerned in the supply and maintenance of our fighting forces.

As the army grew and became more complicated the total feeding strength of our forces in France rose until it approached a total of 2,700,000 men. The vastness of the figures involved in providing for their needs will be realized from the following examples. For the maintenance of a single division for one day, nearly 200 tons dead weight of supplies and stores are needed, representing a shipping tonnage of nearly 450 tons. In an army of 2,700,000 men, the addition of 1 ounce to each man's daily ration, involves the carrying of an extra 75 tons of goods. . . .

(20) . . . No survey of the features of the war would be complete without some reference to the part played by women serving with the British Armies in France. . . . Women in the British Red Cross Society and other organizations have driven ambulances throughout the war, undeterred by discomfort and hardship. Women have ministered to the comfort of the troops in huts and canteens. Finally, Queen Mary's Auxiliary Army Corps, recruited on a wider basis, responded with enthusiasm to the call for drafts, and by the aid they gave to our declining man power contributed materially to the success of our arms.

Source 5 from "La crise de l'ésprit," in Paul Valéry Oeuvres *(Paris: Librairie Gaillimard, 1957), vol. 1, pp. 990–991, 1000–1001. Translated by Franklin M. Doeringer.*

5. Paul Valéry, "The Crisis of the Spirit," 1919

The military crisis is perhaps over. The economic crisis is visible in all of its force; but the intellectual crisis, more subtle, and by nature more deceptive in appearances (because it takes place in the very realm of deception)—this crisis renders its full extent or stage difficult to grasp.

No one can say what will be dead or alive tomorrow in literature, in philosophy, or in aesthetics. No one knows yet which ideas and modes of expression will be inscribed in the list of things lost, or what novelties will be proclaimed. . . .

. . . The facts, however, are clear and unrelenting. Millions of young writers and young artists are dead. There is the lost illusion of European culture and proof of the powerlessness of knowledge to save anything whatsoever; there is science, fatally stricken in its moral ambitions, and seemingly dishonored by the cruelty of its applications; there is idealism, enduring with difficulty, profoundly maimed, and liable to its dreams; deluded realism, beaten down, overwhelmed with crimes and mistakes; covetousness and renunciation equally scorned; beliefs confounded between camps: cross against cross, crescent against crescent; there are skeptics who themselves, unhinged by events so sudden, so violent, and so moving, toy with our thinking like a cat with a mouse—skeptics who shed their doubts, rediscover them, and shed them again, but no longer know how to make use of the workings of the spirit.

The boat has been so forcibly rocked that even the most securely hung lamps have in the end been overturned. . . .

The storm has just ended, and yet we are as disquieted, as anxious, as if the storm were still to break upon us. Nearly all things human remain in terrible uncertainty. We look at what has vanished—we are almost destroyed by what is destroyed; we do not know what will come forth: still we can reasonably fear it. We hope in vagueness; we dread with precision. Our fears are infinitely more precise than our hopes; we admit that the best of life is behind us, that fullness is behind us, but disarray and doubt are in us and with us. There is no thinking mind, however wise or educated we imagine it, that can flatter itself with control over this affliction, or escape from this impression of darkness, or measure the likely duration of this troubled period in the vital exchanges of humanity.

We are a very unfortunate generation to whom it has fallen to see the moment of its passage through life coincide with the arrival of great and frightful events whose reverberations will fill all of our lives.

We can say that all the essential things of this world have been affected by the war, or more exactly, by the circumstances of the war. The erosion ate away something deeper than the renewable parts of the being. You know what the trouble is in the general economy, the politics of states, and even in the lives of individuals: the constraint, the hesitation, the universal apprehension. *But among all these wounded things is the spirit.* The spirit in truth is cruelly stricken. The heart of man laments over the spirit and sadly judges itself. It doubts itself profoundly.

Source 6 from Erich Maria Remarque, All Quiet on the Western Front, *trans. I. W. Wheen (Boston: Little, Brown, 1930), pp. 104–105, 111, 113, 133, 266, 279–280, 283, 289–290.*

6. Erich Maria Remarque, *All Quiet on the Western Front,* 1929

All day the sky is hung with observation balloons. There is a rumour that the enemy are going to put tanks over and use low flying planes for the attack. But that interests us less than what we hear of the new flame throwers.

We wake up in the middle of the night. The earth booms. Heavy fire is falling on us. We crouch into corners. We distinguish shells of every caliber. . . .

Every man is aware of the heavy shells tearing down the parapet, rooting up the embankment and demolishing the upper layers of concrete. When a shell lands in the trench, we note how the hollow, furious blast is like a blow from the paw of a raging beast of prey. Already by morning a few of the recruits are green and vomiting. They are too inexperienced. . . .

Suddenly the nearer explosions cease. The shelling continues but it has lifted and falls behind us, our trench is free. We seize the hand grenades, pitch them out in front of the dug-out and jump after them. The bombardment has stopped and a heavy barrage now falls behind us. The attack has come. . . .

We have become wild beasts. We do not fight, we defend ourselves against annihilation. It is not against men that we fling our bombs, what do we know of men in this moment when Death with hands and helmets is hunting us down— now, for the first time in three days we can see his face, now, for the first time in three days we can oppose him; we feel a mad anger. No longer do we lie helpless, waiting on the scaffold, we can destroy and kill, to save ourselves, to save ourselves and be revenged.

We crouch behind every corner, behind every barrier of barbed wire, and hurl heaps of explosives at the feet of the advancing enemy before we run. The blast of the hand-grenades impinges powerfully on our arms and legs; crouching like cats we run on, overwhelmed by this wave that bears us along, that fills us with ferocity, turning us into thugs, into murderers, into God only knows what devils; this wave that multiplies our strength with fear and madness and greed of life, seeking and fighting for nothing but our deliverance. If your own father came over with them you would not hesitate to fling a bomb into him. . . .

Bombardment, barrage, curtain-fire, mines, gas, tanks, machine-guns, hand-grenades—words, words, but they hold the horror of the world.

Our faces are encrusted, our thoughts are devastated, we are weary to death; when the attack comes we shall have to strike many of the men with our fists to waken them and make them come with us—our eyes are burnt, our hands are torn, our knees bleed, our elbows are raw. . . .

How long has it been? Weeks—months—years? Only days. We see time pass in the colourless faces of the dying, we cram food into us, we run, we throw, we shoot, we kill, we lie about, we are feeble and spent, and nothing supports us but the knowledge that there are still feebler, still more spent, still more helpless ones there who, with staring eyes, look upon us as gods that escape death many times. . . .

I am young, I am twenty years old; yet I know nothing of life but despair, death, fear, and fatuous superficiality cast over an abyss of sorrow. I see how peoples are set against one another, and in silence, unknowingly, foolishly, obediently, innocently slay one another. I see that the keenest brains of the world invent weapons and words to make it yet more refined and enduring. And all men of my age, here and over there, throughout the whole world, see these things; all my generation is experiencing these things with me. What would our fathers do if we suddenly stood up and came before them and proffered our account? What do they expect of us if a time ever comes when the war is over? Through the years our business has been killing;—it was our first calling in life. Our knowledge of life is limited to death. What will happen afterwards? And what shall come of us? . . .

From a mockery the tanks have become a terrible weapon. Armoured they come rolling on in long lines, and more than anything else embody for us the horror of war.

We do not see the guns that bombard us; the attacking lines of the enemy infantry are men like ourselves; but these tanks are machines, their caterpillars run on as endless as the war, they are annihilation, they roll without feeling into the craters, and climb up again without stopping, a fleet of roaring, smoke-belching armour-clads, invulnerable steel beasts squashing the dead and the wounded—we shrivel up in our thin skin before them against their colossal weight, our arms are sticks of straw, and our hand grenades matches.

Shells, gas clouds, and flotillas of tanks—shattering, starvation, death.

Dysentery, influenza, typhus—murder, burning, death.

Trenches, hospitals, the common grave—there are no other possibilities. . . .

Had we returned home in 1916, out of the suffering and the strength of our experiences we might have unleashed a storm. Now if we go back we will be weary, broken, burnt out, rootless, and without hope. We will not be able to find our way any more.

Source 7 from F. Tilman Durdin, "All Captives Slain," New York Times, December 18, 1937, pp. 1, 10.

7. Report on Rape of Nanking,
New York Times, 1937

**BUTCHERY MARKED
CAPTURE OF NANKING
ALL CAPTIVES SLAIN
CIVILIANS ALSO KILLED AS
THE JAPANESE SPREAD
TERROR IN NANKING**

Aboard the U.S.S. Oahu at Shanghai, Dec. 17 [1937]. Through wholesale atrocities and vandalism at Nanking the Japanese Army has thrown away a rare opportunity to gain the respect and confidence of the Chinese inhabitants and of foreign opinion there.

The collapse of Chinese authority and the break-up of the Chinese army left many Chinese in Nanking ready to respond to order and organization which seemed in prospect with the entry of the Japanese troops. A tremendous sense of relief over the outlook for a cessation of the fearful bombardment and the elimination of the threat of serious disorders by the Chinese troops pervaded the Chinese populous when the Japanese took over control within the walls.

It was felt that Japanese rule might be severe, at least until war conditions were over. Two days of Japanese occupation changed the whole outlook. Wholesale looting, the violation of women, the murder of civilians, the eviction of Chinese from their homes, mass execution of war prisoners and the impressing of able-bodied men turned Nanking into a city of terror.

Many Civilians Slain

The killing of civilians was widespread. Foreigners who traveled widely through the city Wednesday found civilian dead on every street. Some of the victims were aged men, women and children. Policemen and firemen were special objects of attack. Many victims were bayoneted and some of the wounds were barbarously cruel.

Any person who ran because of fear or excitement was likely to be killed on the spot as was anyone caught by roving patrols in streets or alleys after dark. Many slayings were witnessed by foreigners.

The Japanese looting amounted almost to plundering of the entire city. Nearly every building was entered by Japanese soldiers, often under the eyes of their officers, and the men took whatever they wanted. The Japanese soldiers often impressed Chinese to carry their loot. . . .

Many Chinese men reported to foreigners the abduction and rape of wives and daughters. These Chinese appealed for aid, which the foreigners were apparently powerless to give.

The mass executions of war prisoners added to the horrors the Japanese brought to Nanking. After killing the Chinese soldiers who threw down their arms and surrendered, the Japanese combed the city for men in civilian garb who were suspected of being former soldiers.

In one building in the refugee zone 400 men were seized. They were marched off, tied in batches of fifty, between lines of riflemen and machine gunners, to the execution ground.

Just before boarding the ship for Shanghai the writer watched the execution of 200 men on the Bund [the center of the International Settlement]. The killings took ten minutes. The men were lined against a wall and shot. Then a number of Japanese, armed with pistols, trod nonchalantly around the crumpled bodies, pumping bullets into any that were still kicking. The army men performing the gruesome job had invited navy men from the warships anchored off the Bund to view the scene. A large group of military spectators apparently greatly enjoyed the spectacle. . . .

The Japanese appear to want the horrors to remain as long as possible, to impress on the Chinese the terrible results of resisting Japan.

Source 8 from President Roosevelt's 1942 Annual Message to Congress. Obtained from http://www.ibiblio.org/pha/policy/1942/420106a.html.

8. President Franklin D. Roosevelt, Annual Message to Congress, January 6, 1942

Exactly one year ago today I said to this Congress: "When the dictators are ready to make war upon us, they will not wait for an act of war on our part . . . They—not we—will choose the time and the place and the method of their attack."

We now know their choice of the time: a peaceful Sunday morning—December 7, 1941.

We know their choice of the place: an American outpost in the Pacific.

We know their choice of the method: the method of Hitler himself. . . .

With Hitler's formation of the Berlin-Rome-Tokyo alliance, all of these plans of conquest became a single plan. Under this, in addition to her own schemes of conquest, Japan's role was to cut off our supply of weapons of war to Britain, Russia, and China—weapons which increasingly were speeding the day of Hitler's doom. The act of Japan at Pearl Harbor was intended to stun us—to terrify us to such an extent that we would divert our industrial and military strength to the Pacific area or even to our own continental defense.

The plan failed in its purpose. We have not been stunned. We have not been terrified or confused. This reassembling of the Seventy-seventh Congress is proof of that; for the mood of quiet, grim resolution which here prevails bodes ill for those who conspired and collaborated to murder world peace. . . .

Plans have been laid here and in the other capitals for coordinated and cooperative action by all the United Nations—military action and economic action. Already we have established unified command of land, sea, and air forces in the southwestern Pacific theater of war. There will be a continuation of conferences and consultations among military staffs, so that the plans and operations of each will fit into a general strategy designed to crush the enemy. . . .

But modern methods of warfare make it a task not only of shooting and fighting, but an even more urgent one of working and producing. . . .

The superiority of the United Nations in munitions and ships must be overwhelming—so overwhelming that the Axis nations can never hope to catch up with it. In order to attain this overwhelming superiority the United Nations must build planes and tanks and guns and ships to the utmost limit of our national capacity. We have the ability and capacity to produce arms not only for our own forces but also for the armies, navies, and air forces fighting on our side. . . .

This production of ours in the United States must be raised far above its present levels, even though it will mean the dislocation of the lives and occupations of millions of our own people. We must raise our sights all along the production-line. Let no man say It cannot be done. It must be done—and we have undertaken to do it.

I have just sent a letter of directive to the appropriate departments and agencies of our Government, ordering that immediate steps be taken:

1. To increase our production rate of airplanes so rapidly that in this year, 1942, we shall produce 60,000 planes, 10,000 more than the goal set a year and a half ago. This includes 45,000 combat planes—bombers, dive bombers, pursuit planes. The rate of increase will be continued, so that next year, 1943, we shall produce 125,000 planes, including 100,000 combat planes.

2. To increase our production rate of tanks so rapidly that in this year, 1942, we shall produce 45,000 tanks; and to continue that increase so that next year, 1943, we shall produce 75,000 tanks.

3. To increase our production rate of anti-aircraft guns so rapidly that in this year, 1942, we shall produce 20,000 of them; and to continue that increase, so that next year, 1943, we shall produce 35,000 anti-aircraft guns.

4. To increase our production rate of merchant ships so rapidly that in this year, 1942, we shall build 8,000,000 deadweight tons as compared with a 1941 production of 1,100,000. We shall continue that increase so that next year, 1943, we shall build 10,000,000 tons. . . .

Our task is hard—our task is unprecedented—and the time is short. We must strain every existing armament-producing facility to the utmost. We must convert every available plant and tool to war production. That goes all the way from the greatest plants to the smallest—from the huge automobile industry to the village machine shop.

Production for war is based on men and women—the human hands and brains which collectively we call labor. Our workers stand ready to work long hours; to turn out more in a day's work; to keep the wheels turning and the fires burning 24 hours a day and 7 days a week. They realize well that on the speed and efficiency of their work depend the lives of their sons and their brothers on the fighting fronts.

Production for war is based on metals and raw materials—steel, copper, rubber, aluminum, zinc, tin. Greater and greater quantities of them will have to be diverted to war purposes. Civilian use of them will have to be cut further and still further—and, in many cases, completely eliminated.

War costs money. So far, we have hardly even begun to pay for it. We have devoted only 15% of our national income to our national defense. As will appear in my budget message tomorrow, our war program for the coming fiscal year will cost 56 billion dollars, or, in other words, more than one-half of the estimated annual national income. This means taxes and bonds, and bonds and taxes. It means cutting luxuries and other non-essentials. In a word, it means an "all-out" war by individual effort and family effort in a united country. . . .

We must, on the other hand, guard against defeatism. That has been one of the chief weapons of Hitler's propaganda machine—used time and again with deadly results. It will not be used successfully on the American people. . . .

When our enemies challenged our country to stand up and fight, they challenged each and every one of us. And each and every one of us has accepted the challenge—for himself and for the Nation. . . .

That is the conflict that day and night now pervades our lives. No compromise can end that conflict. There never has been—there never can be—successful compromise between good and evil. Only total victory can reward the champions of tolerance and decency and freedom and faith.

9. Rosie the Riveter, American Propaganda Icon

"Rosie the Riveter"
by Redd Evans and John Jacob Loeb

All the day long,
Whether rain or shine,
She's a part of the assembly line.
She's making history,
Working for victory,
Rosie the Riveter.
Keeps a sharp lookout for sabotage,
Sitting up there on the fuselage.
That little girl will do more than a male will do.
Rosie's got a boyfriend, Charlie.
Charlie, he's a Marine.
Rosie is protecting Charlie,
Working overtime on the riveting machine.
When they gave her a production "E,"
She was as proud as she could be.
There's something true about,
Red, white, and blue about,
Rosie the Riveter.

Source 10 from transcript of Hermann Goering's radio address, The New York Times, *October 5, 1942.*

10. Reichsmarschal Hermann Goering, German Radio Broadcast, October 4, 1942

National comrades, men and women! Germans on the land! We are at the beginning of the fourth year of the war, and today we celebrate the German harvest thanksgiving. Today we cannot celebrate the nation's festivals in the scope and manner to which we were formerly accustomed.

Today great masses of the German country folk cannot appear before the Fuehrer through their deputations, to bring him a harvest wreath and fruits of the last harvest, because we are in a war, in the most difficult war of the German people, and in this war there is only one thing: work, work, fighting and work, and again fighting and work.

The last three harvest years, in particular the first two of them, were by no means favorable. Quite unexpectedly, three terribly hard and severe winters broke upon us and destroyed much of the labor that had previously been put into the ground.

But, nevertheless, it was possible, first of all, to guarantee nourishment of the people absolutely; for at that time, when I spoke in this same hall on taking over the responsibility of carrying out the Four-Year Plan, many a compatriot will still be able to remember how, right at that time, I laid very strong emphasis on the concept and the term "enemy blockade." . . .

Now that the future is clearer, the meat ration is to be increased by another fifty grammes in the raid-threatened areas. . . .

By no means let us forget that when it is a question of raw materials for armament, there are two raw materials which are just as fundamental for feeding our people as for their subsistence as a whole. And these raw materials are coal and iron, and both raw materials we ourselves possess in sufficient quantities, and we have also—thank God—won enormous additional quantities by conquest.

Bear in mind, therefore, that since we do not have a sufficient surplus of this valuable material, coal, we should not waste it unnecessarily. And every one who turns on a single light or other electrical appliance unnecessarily, or who leaves it on longer than necessary, is committing a sin. Any one who uses too much gas should remember that this gas comes from coal, and that a worker has to slave for it by the sweat of his brow hundreds of meters underground. Any one who uses too much power, should also consider that fact.

But, my dear German comrades, one thing more I should like to say here quite plainly. When a national community is being created, and when an entire nation, as a totality and a single entity, must win a victory and must secure its freedom, then the individual, too, must be ready to submit to more or less stringent limitations on his personal freedom.

This limitation of personal freedom is necessary even in peacetimes. In democracy, to be sure, there is always one thing only—freedom of the individual. That is what we National Socialists call license. If every one may do as he likes, if no one has to have any consideration for his neighbors or his relatives, and even gets ahead by doing so, then you can imagine how such a community gets along. . . .

I should like now to broach a topic that indeed concerns me very especially as the Commander in Chief of the air force and Reich Air Minister. It is about the heavy enemy air attacks on German cities. Here, too, my dear fellow countrymen, there must often be a very great restriction of personal freedom.

I am far from belittling these attacks or anything like that. I know how it is. I am an expert. I know what it means when a hundred or two hundred planes drop their bomb load. I know that many innocent people must die, in this way, absolutely to no purpose.

[415]

The Fuehrer told our enemies in his Reichstag speech some time ago that one should at least stop attacking absolutely harmless people where there is no war industry. And today they cannot get out of it by saying that they just accidentally missed, they were aiming at industrial plants, because we are in possession of their original orders.

Mr. British Air General instructed his fliers that war industry was not the important thing to destroy, but residential sections . . . terrorizing the German population, dropping bombs on children and women. That is the main thing for these gentlemen, even though a few decent fliers have protested against being assigned again and again to this slaughter.

So I know how hard all this is and how terrible and how senseless this destruction of cultural values. If that fool would reflect on the virtues of German culture, and that German culture exists not only for Germans—it has made endless contributions to Europe and the world—that simple respect for it should keep the wretches from destroying German seats of culture. . . .

You may be sure—I am now speaking to our fellow countrymen of those regions that are subject to the threat of air raids—that everything humanely possible is being done in my efforts to alleviate the situation and to prevent such attacks, first of all by active counter defense. . . .

I shall see to it myself that steadily increasing and additional camps shall be prepared that will take care of the victims of the air raids. I have purchased supplies in all countries to which I had access, on a tremendously large scale. . . .

And, my dear fellow-citizens, everything is in our favor when we consider the situation. Just how are our enemies going to be able to carry out their continued assertions and declarations that they are going to win this war?

They have some hope or other in the astronomical figures of American production. Now, I would be the last person to underestimate American production. In certain fields the Americans have made colossal achievements in technique and in production.

We know they have done a stupendous amount with the auto. They have also won special merit with the radio and the razor blade. In these three fields they have undoubtedly wrought ever colossally, but these things are, nevertheless, something else yet than what one needs for war. . . .

And even in America nothing gets done faster than with us, but slower rather, and even in America raw materials are necessary, workers are necessary. You can't at the same time build up an army of several million, and on the other hand triple the number of workers. That doesn't work in America, either.

Source 11 from The Public Papers of F. D. Roosevelt, *vol. 12, p. 71. This version obtained from* World War II Resources, Words of Peace. Words of War, *http://www.ibiblio.org/pha/policy/1943/ 430212a.html.*

11. President Roosevelt's Radio Address on Casablanca Conference, February 12, 1943

The decisions reached and the actual plans made at Casablanca were not confined to any one theater of war or to any one continent or ocean or sea. Before this year is out, it will be made known to the world—in actions rather than words—that the Casablanca Conference produced plenty of news; and it will be bad news for the Germans and Italians and the Japanese. . . .

In an attempt to ward off the inevitable disaster, the Axis propagandists are trying all of their old tricks in order to divide the United Nations. They seek to create the idea that if we win this war, Russia, England, China, and the United States are going to get into a cat-and-dog fight.

This is their final effort to turn one nation against another, in the vain hope that they may settle with one or two at a time—that any of us may be so gullible and so forgetful as to be duped into making "deals" at the expense of our Allies.

To these panicky attempts to escape the consequences of their crimes we say—all the United Nations say—that the only terms on which we shall deal with an Axis government or any Axis factions are the terms proclaimed at Casablanca: "Unconditional Surrender." In our uncompromising policy we mean no harm to the common people of the Axis nations. But we do mean to impose punishment and retribution in full upon their guilty, barbaric leaders. . . .

In the years of the American and French revolutions the fundamental principle guiding our democracies was established. The cornerstone of our whole democratic edifice was the principle that from the people and the people alone flows the authority of government.

It is one of our war aims, as expressed in the Atlantic Charter, that the conquered populations of today be again the masters of their destiny. There must be no doubt anywhere that it is the unalterable purpose of the United Nations to restore to conquered peoples their sacred rights.

Source 12 from United States Strategic Bombing Survey (Pacific War) (Washington, D.C.:
U.S. Government Printing Office, 1946), pp. 15–17, 21–22, 29–30.

12. United States Strategic Bomb Survey (Pacific War), 1946

Basic United States strategy contemplated that the final decision in the Japanese
war would be obtained by an invasion of the Japanese home islands. The long-
range bombing offensive from the Marianas was initiated in November 1944,
with that in mind as the primary objective. As in Europe prior to D-day, the
principal measure of success set for strategic air action was the extent to which
it would weaken enemy capability and will to resist our amphibious forces at
the time of landings. This led, originally, to somewhat greater emphasis on the
selection of targets such as aircraft factories, arsenals, electronics plants, oil re-
fineries, and finished military goods, destruction of which could be expected to
weaken the capabilities of the Japanese armed forces to resist at the Kyushu
beachheads in November 1945, than on the disruption of the more basic elements of Japan's social, economic, and political fabric. . . .

On 9 March 1945, a basic revision in the method of B-29 attack was instituted.
It was decided to bomb the four principal Japanese cities at night from altitudes
averaging 7,000 feet. Japanese weakness in night fighters and antiaircraft made
this program feasible. Incendiaries were used instead of high explosive bombs
and the lower altitude permitted a substantial increase in bomb load per plane.
One thousand six hundred and sixty-seven tons of bombs were dropped on
Tokyo in the first attack. The chosen areas were saturated. Fifteen square miles
of Tokyo's most densely populated area were burned to the ground. The weight
and intensity of this attack caught the Japanese by surprise. No subsequent
urban area attack was equally destructive. Two days later, an attack of similar
magnitude on Nagoya destroyed 2 square miles. In a period of 10 days starting
9 March, a total of 1,595 sorties delivered 9,373 tons of bombs against Tokyo,
Nagoya, Osake, and Kobe destroying 31 square miles of those cities at a cost of
22 airplanes. The generally destructive effect of incendiary attacks against
Japanese cities had been demonstrated. . . .

A striking aspect of the air attack was the pervasiveness with which its
impact on morale blanketed Japan. Roughly one quarter of all people in cities
fled or were evacuated, and these evacuees, who themselves were of singularly
low morale, helped spread discouragement and disaffection for the war
throughout the islands. This mass migration from the cities included an estimated 8,500,000 persons throughout the Japanese islands, whose people had always thought themselves remote from attack. United States planes crisscrossed
the skies with no effective Japanese air or antiaircraft opposition. That this was
an indication of impending defeat became as obvious to the rural as to the
urban population. . . .

The interrelation of military, economic and morale factors was complex. To a certain extent each reacted on the other. In the final analysis the Japanese military machine had lost its purpose when it could no longer protect the Japanese people from destruction by air attack. General Takashima when asked by the Survey as to his reaction to the Imperial Rescript, stated that surrender had become unavoidable; the Army, even should it repel invasion, could no longer protect the Japanese people from extermination. . . .

On 6 August and 9 August 1945, the first two atomic bombs to be used for military purposes were dropped on Hiroshima and Nagasaki respectively. One hundred thousand people were killed, 6 square miles or over 50 percent of the built-up areas of the two cities were destroyed. The first and crucial question about the atomic bomb thus was answered practically and conclusively; atomic energy had been mastered for military purposes and the overwhelming scale of its possibilities had been demonstrated. . . .

Does the existence of atomic bombs invalidate all conclusions relative to air power based on pre-atomic experience? It is the Survey's opinion that many of the pre-existing yardsticks are revolutionized, but that certain of the more basic principles and relationships remain. The atomic bomb, in its present state of development, raises the destructive power of a single bomber by a factor of somewhere between 50 and 250 times, depending upon the nature and size of the target. The capacity to destroy, given control of the air and an adequate supply of atomic bombs, is beyond question. Unless both of these conditions are met, however, any attempt to produce war-decisive results through atomic bombing may encounter problems similar to those encountered in conventional bombing.

The problem of control of the air, primarily of our own air, and should we be attacked, of the enemy's air as well becomes of even greater significance. The most intense effort must be devoted to perfecting defensive air control both by day and night, through the improvement of early warning and fighter control apparatus, anti-aircraft ordnance and defensive fighters, not only from the standpoint of technological improvement and volume, but also of disposition and tactics. It would be rash, however, to predict an increase in the effectiveness of defensive control sufficient to insure that not a single enemy plane or guided missile will be able to penetrate. It therefore behooves us to accept the possibility that at least a small number of enemy planes or guided missiles may be able to evade all our defenses and to attack any objective within range. . . .

If we are not to be overwhelmed out of hand, in the event we are nevertheless attacked, we must reduce materially our vulnerability to such attack. The experience of both the Pacific and European wars emphasizes the extent to which civilian and other forms of passive defense can reduce a country's vulnerability to air attack. Civilian injuries and fatalities can be reduced, by presently known techniques, to one-twentieth or less of the casualties which would be suffered were these techniques not employed. This does not involve moving everything underground, but does involve a progressive evacuation, dispersal, warning, air-raid shelter, and postraid emergency assistance program, the foundations for which can only be laid in peacetime. The analysis of the effects of the atomic bombs at Hiroshima and Nagasaki indicates that the above statement is just as true and much more terrifyingly significant in an age of atomic bombs than it was in an age of conventional weapons. Similarly, economic vulnerability can be enormously decreased by a well worked out program of stockpiles, dispersal and special construction of particularly significant segments of industry. Such a program in the economic field can also be worked out satisfactorily only in peacetime.

In the strictly military field the impact of atomic weapons and guided missiles on strategy and tactics can only be developed by specialists. It is the Survey's opinion, however, that mature study by such specialists will support the conclusion that dispersal of military forces, and therefore space and distance in which to effect such dispersal will be significant considerations; that heavy bombers similar to those used in this war will not be able to operate effectively and on a sustained basis much beyond the range of protective fighters, and that newer types of offensive weapons and new tactics must be developed to do so; that forward air bases will have to be defended or more advanced bases acquired step by step in actual combat; and that the basic principles of war, when applied to include the field of the new weapons, will be found to remain. If such be the case, atomic weapons will not have eliminated the need for ground troops, for vessels, for air weapons, or for the full coordination among them, the supporting services and the civilian effort, but will have changed the context in which they are employed to such a degree that radically changed equipment, training and tactics will be required.

Source 13 from Arata Osada, Children of Hiroshima *(London: Taylor and Francis, 1981), pp. 265–269.*

13. Iwao Nakamura,
Recollections of August 6, 1945

In an instant it became dark as night, Hiroshima on that day. Flames shooting up from wrecked houses as if to illuminate this darkness. Amidst this, children aimlessly wandering about, groaning with pain, their burned faces twitching and bloated like balloons. An old man, skin flaking off like the skin of a potato, trying to get away on weak, unsteady legs, praying as he went. A man frantically calling out the names of his wife and children, both hands to his forehead from which blood trickled down. Just the memory of it makes my blood run cold. This is the real face of war. To those who knew nothing of the pitiful tragedies of Hiroshima's people, the scene would seem like a world of monsters, like Hades itself. A devil called war swept away the precious lives of several hundred thousand citizens of Hiroshima. . . .

It was after eight on August 6 and the midsummer sun was beginning to scorch down on Hiroshima. An all-clear signal had sounded and with relief we sat down for breakfast a little later than usual. Usually by this time, my father had left the house for the office and I would be at the hospital for treatment. I was just starting on my second bowl of rice. At that moment, a bluish-white ray of light like a magnesium flare hit me in the face, a terrific roar tore at my eardrums and it became so dark I could not see anything. I stood up, dropping my rice bowl and chopsticks. I do not know what happened next or how long I was unconscious. When I came to . . . I looked around in the dim light and glimpsed the hazy figures of my parents looking for me. I hurried over to them. Their hair was disheveled and their faces pale. When they saw me, they sighed with relief, "Oh you're safe, you're safe." . . .

Nothing was left of the Hiroshima of a few minutes ago. The houses and buildings had been destroyed and the streets transformed into a black desert, with only the flames from burning buildings giving a lurid illumination to the dark sky over Hiroshima. Flames were already shooting out of the wreckage of the house next door. . . . It must have been by the mercy of God that we were able to rescue my brothers from under the wreckage before the flames reached them. They were not hurt, either. The five of us left our burning home and hurried toward Koi. Around us was a sea of flames. The street was filled with flames and smoke from the burning wreckage of houses and burning power poles which had toppled down blocked our way time after time, almost sending us into the depths of despair. It seems that everyone in the area had already made their escape, for we saw no one but sometimes we heard moans, a sound like a wild beast. I began to shudder as I thought that everyone on earth had perished, leaving only the five of us here in an eerie world of the dead. As we passed Nakajima Primary School area and approached Sumiyoshi Bridge, I saw a damaged water tank in which a number of people had their heads down, drinking. I was so thirsty and attracted by the sight of people that I left my parents' side without thinking, and approached the tank. But when I got near and was able to see into the tank, I gave an involuntary cry and backed away. What I saw reflected in the blood-stained water were the faces of monsters. They had leaned over the side of the tank and died in that position. From the burned shreds of their sailor uniforms, I knew they were schoolgirls, but they had no hair left and their burned faces were crimson with blood; they no longer appeared human. After we came out on the main road and crossed Sumiyoshi Bridge, we finally came across some living human beings—but maybe it would be more correct to say that we met some people from Hell. They were naked and their skin, burned and bloody, was like red rust and their bodies were bloated up like balloons. Nevertheless, since we had not seen any living person on the way, we felt better seeing them and soon joined this group in our attempt to escape from Hiroshima. The houses on both sides of this street, which was several dozen yards wide, were in flames so that we could only move along a strip in the center about three or four yards wide. This narrow passage was covered with seriously burned and injured people, unable to walk, and with dead bodies, leaving hardly any space for us to get through. At places, we were forced to step over them callously, but we apologized in our hearts as we did this. Among them were old people pleading for water, tiny children seeking help, students unconsciously calling for their parents, brothers, and sisters, and there was a mother prostrate on the ground, moaning with pain but with one arm still tightly embracing her dead baby. But how could we help them when we ourselves did not know our own fate?

When we reached the Kori First Aid Station, we learned that we were among the last to escape from the Sumiyoshi Bridge area. After my father had received some medical treatment, we hurried over Koi Hill to our relatives at Tomo Village in Asa County. When we were crossing the hill late that evening, we could see Hiroshima lying far below, now a mere smoldering desert. After offering a silent prayer for the victims, we descended the hill toward Tomo.

QUESTIONS TO CONSIDER

The important thing to remark in the first selection is Clausewitz's view that war must be limited in order to avoid its "tendency to extreme." Notice how he credits seventeenth- and eighteenth-century European rulers with success in this task. In their hands, he claims, war served to gain advantages in negotiations, making it a "somewhat stronger form of diplomacy." What does he say limited the scope and devastation of these rulers' wars? The dramatic change in war, according to Clausewitz, came with the French Revolution, which revealed "all its elemental fury." What did he think brought about this change? Note his remarks about the role of "the people" in war and how a popular war affects the nature of conflict and of peacemaking. Keep his views in mind as you look over later sources. Could total war be a consequence of increasing democratization?

In Source 2, Lloyd George addresses the most obvious cost of unrestrained combat: high casualties. How does he assess British losses in the Battle of the Somme, both in size and in significance? What advantages did he think the deaths of so many gained the nation? Observe his general attitude toward what he calls "this bullheaded fight." Is it what you would expect of a prime minister recalling a great battle? His claim that "the losses sustained were . . . irreplaceable" hints at more than just concern over the number of battlefield deaths. What social implications does he seem to find in them—and perhaps even more in the losses that Britain's ally Russia was suffering on the eastern front? As Lloyd George points out, the original British Expeditionary Army was a volunteer force. Recruitment required intensive enlistment drives. These campaigns, and the loan appeals made by the French government, prompted the use of new propaganda tools like Source 3, public posters. At whom were these posters aimed? What view of warfare do they project? How does this view compare with the tone of Lloyd George's comments?

Source 4, Field Marshal Haig's final dispatch as commander of the British Expeditionary Force, offers a broad assessment of the first total war. As Haig explains, by 1916 and 1917 the war had lapsed into a series of "indecisive battles" waged only to "wear down" the enemy through attrition. What did he find so unique about this war, leading him to think that Britain's "existence as an empire and civilization itself . . . were at stake?" Think about the "factors peculiar to modern war" that he lists, as well as his comments on the "mechanical contrivances" introduced in the war and the complications occasioned by the size of the armies. His remark about the way women bolstered "our declining man power" merits attention, too. Women gained the vote in England and other democratic nations right after the war. How might total war have hastened this change?

Sources 5 and 6 show aspects of the conflict's effect on postwar Europe. Valéry's essay alludes to the financial crisis then threatening European nations faced with vast war debts and reparation payments. But something else bothers him more. What is it? Note his talk of darkness and overturned lamps. Consider these metaphors in the context of the European Enlightenment. Valéry speaks of the failure of knowledge, science, and idealism. But what is the "spirit" that he says has been so "cruelly stricken?" Think about the war's effect on European claims to worldwide intellectual and cultural leadership. Valéry speaks on behalf of intellectuals, but Remarque's novel voices the alienation and despair that ordinary people felt in the war's aftermath. Notice the young protagonist's claim that the war made him and his fellows "wild beasts." What does he say led them to this extreme? And what does he say they have lost? His lament that they are "weary, broken, burnt out, rootless, and without hope" is chilling. What do these works suggest about the war's psychological and intellectual impact on Europeans—and their future actions in the world?

The devastation experienced in Europe during the First World War gave an indication of what total war entailed. But as terrible as the loss of life was in that conflict, it was still overwhelmingly limited to military personnel. That situation would soon change as the collapse of international security arrangements in the 1930s brought the world into the even greater conflict known as World War II. For in this subsequent round of global struggle, all combatants abandoned the long-standing rules of modern warfare, which prohibited assaults on unarmed civilians. Indeed, as Source 7 on the Rape of Nanking shows, in World War II civilians became a major target. For in a total war of nations, as opposed to a limited war of armies, entire populations were to be terrorized with the possibility of annihilation to force them into abandoning the fight. In this early example at Nanking, methods were generally primitive. What tactics does the report stress, and against whom were they used? Notice, however, mention of the "fearful bombardment" that preceded the city's capture. As the war intensified, bombing would prove a far more effective method for the mass execution and demoralization of civilians.

Although at its start, the war affected Americans far less, it led them to retreat into isolationism. The United States thus refrained from helping its former allies sustain the collapsing world order in the 1930s or coming to their aid when Germany attacked them. But once aroused by Japan's surprise attack on Pearl Harbor late in 1941, it quickly resolved on an all-out fight. Source 8, President Roosevelt's 1942 Annual Message to Congress, shows this determination. Notice how he links "modern methods of warfare" with "working and producing" as well as "shooting and fighting" and calls for all-out economic mobilization, conceding that "it will mean the dislocation of the lives and occupations of millions." How much diversion of national labor and income does he say the war will require? Pay attention to his final call for "total victory." Do either the means he proposes for fighting the war or this end suggest concern with limiting the war? Source 9, the poster and song dealing with Rosie the Riveter, represents one effect of this all-out effort: To compensate for the fifteen million people, mostly men, who were drafted into the armed forces, six million American women were drawn into war work. According to these materials, what were they asked to do? How might such work have affected conventional ideas about gender roles and women's rights?

Source 10, Hermann Goering's address to the German people, reveals how the American entry into the war

and its escalation into a total conflict began to affect Germany. Despite having control over most of Europe and eastern Russia, Germany was beginning to suffer from scarcities by late 1942. What seems to have been most lacking? Observe how Goering reminds the Germans that in the face of such hardships, they must set aside personal interests and fight as "an entire nation, as a totality." What does he say they must be prepared to give up, and why? His comments on "enemy air attacks" are also worth noting. How does he characterize them? What does he claim they will destroy along with "harmless people?" Do his remarks suggest that the air raids were having a significant effect? What about his reaction to the American threat to wage an all-out economic war against the Axis? Source 11, part of a radio address by President Roosevelt on his return from Casablanca, first revealed the Allied demand for "unconditional surrender," a term derived from the Union terms for ending the American Civil War. What did "unconditional" imply in this older context? How might it have affected enemy fighting in World War II? Notice in this regard the call for "punishment and retribution."

The Allied refusal to negotiate terms of surrender may have prolonged Japanese resistance despite the vast loss of civilian lives to American bomb raids. Source 12, the bomb survey, assesses the impact of those raids. What specific areas did they target, and why? How effective do they seem to have been—and in what ways? The survey acknowledges that atomic bombs were a significant new weapon. Note its shift from reporting their effect on Japan to discussing how they may have changed the nature of warfare in general. What does it conclude? Specifically, how does it react to the fact that nuclear warfare focuses on the destruction of cities and civilians rather than armies? Source 13, the account of the Hiroshima blast, gives a personal view of what this fact means. Compare the way the two documents assess the significance of nuclear weapons. Were they merely a means of making total war truly total or an unjustifiable new weapon?

EPILOGUE

Atomic bombs may have provided the United States with the ultimate weapon for waging total war in 1945, when it had a monopoly of such weapons, but the further development and spread of nuclear arms in the postwar era soon made them problematic. When the rivalry between the Soviet Union and the United States, the two principal victors of World War II, erupted into the Cold War in the late 1940s, further conflict seemed likely. But after the Soviet Union perfected an atomic bomb in 1949 and began to build a nuclear arsenal of its own, neither side could hope to benefit from a future total war. Even a limited exchange of these highly destructive weapons, particularly after both nations developed hydrogen bombs in the 1950s, could mean mutual annihilation. The spread of these weapons to other powers in the ensuing decade further complicated the problem. So, too, did the development of new delivery systems based upon rockets rather than manned bombers. Because of the speed with which such missiles could move and the ability of their nuclear warheads to obliterate most of a nation's cities in a first strike, they ruled out long wars of attrition. All-out nuclear war would probably end in a few hours, leaving both sides totally destroyed—thus raising total war to an absolute but absurd level.

After nearly two decades of a vain arms race and a close brush with a full-scale nuclear war between the Soviet Union and the United States at the time of the Cuban missile crisis in 1962, both sides sought ways to reduce the danger of a nuclear war. Unable to negotiate an effective ban on nuclear weapons or reduce their number, they eventually settled for a rough parity of enough destructive power to annihilate each other. Termed MAD or mutually assured destruction, this policy helped to reduce tensions between the United States and the Soviet Union. In essence, it marked their recognition that total war was no longer a rational option for enemies armed with nuclear weapons. If they were to fight each other, they could only do so in limited wars or through nonnuclear client states. Ironically, then, weapons of total destruction may have rendered total war between major powers obsolete in the late twentieth century.

CHAPTER FOURTEEN

CRUCIBLE OF CONFLICT:

THE SUEZ CRISIS (1956)

Looking across the vast sweep of world history, the power and glory of empires and emperors seem fleeting and ephemeral. The poem "Ozymandias," written by Percy Bysshe Shelley, tells of an imposing yet decrepit monument to a dead king:

And on the pedestal these words
    appear:
"My name is Ozymandias, king of
    kings:
Look on my works, ye Mighty, and
    despair!"
Nothing beside remains. Round the
    decay
Of that colossal wreck, boundless and
    bare
The lone and level sands stretch far
    away.

The irony is that when Shelley wrote these lines in the early nineteenth century, his native England was poised to become the greatest empire of modern times. The British would soon be ruling over African and Asian deserts such as those where rulers like Ozymandias had once held sway.

By the late nineteenth century, it could truthfully be said that "the sun never sets on the British empire." By the end of the twentieth century, however, almost nothing was left of that empire except monuments to its now faded glory in cities like Calcutta, Hong Kong, Nairobi, and Alexandria. The reversion of Hong Kong to China in 1997 represented the setting of Britain's imperial sun. As the British flag was lowered and the Chinese flag raised, as "God Save the Queen" gave way to the Chinese national anthem, a process that had begun with the independence of India some fifty years earlier was drawing to a close.

How do we account for imperial decline? One historian, looking at such once impressive empires as those of the Spanish, the Austrians, the French, the Russians, and the British, has identified a common theme in their fall from power:

> The relative strengths of the leading nations in world affairs never remain constant, principally because of the uneven rate of growth among different societies and of the technological and organizational breakthroughs which bring a greater advantage to one society than to another. . . . [W]ealth is usually necessary to underpin military power, and military power is usually needed to acquire and protect wealth. If, however, too large a proportion of the state's resources is diverted from wealth creation and allocated instead to military purposes, then that is likely to lead to a weakening of national power over the longer term. In the same way, if a state overextends itself strategically—by, say, the conquest of extensive territories or the waging of costly wars—it runs the risk that the potential benefits from external expansion may be outweighed by the expense of it all—a dilemma which becomes acute if the nation concerned has entered a period of relative economic decline.[1]

In this view, military and strategic commitments that are appropriately made by an imperial power during a time of growth can become dysfunctional when they are retained during a period of relative economic decline.

This broad assessment has great relevance to the case of Great Britain in the twentieth century. Through the

1. Paul Kennedy, *The Rise and Fall of the Great Powers: Economic Change and Military Conflict from 1500–2000* (New York: Vintage Books, 1987), pp. xv–xvi.

shocks of two world wars and a great depression, Britain retained control of its vast overseas territories. But the economic power that had allowed Britain to gain that empire was no longer sufficient to sustain it, at least not without severely compromising Britain's economy and international standing. The problem came to a head in a series of events known as the Suez crisis of 1956. After the Egyptian government nationalized the Suez Canal, the British colluded with the French and Israelis to manufacture a war that would give the British a pretext to intervene and reestablish control over that strategic waterway. The Suez crisis was a contest of power between the British and Egyptian leaders, Sir Anthony Eden and Gamal Abdel Nasser, that epitomized a larger crisis for the British Empire. In the end, Eden resigned in disgrace and Nasser became firmly established as an Arab hero.

The Suez crisis offers an important context in which to explore issues of late twentieth-century history broader than this particular Anglo-Egyptian conflict. Two fundamental rifts marked the global community in the 1950s. The first lay across the east/west axis, that is, it followed the lines of the cold war conflict between the United States and the Soviet Union, each with its allies and client states. The second involved conflict between north and south, between long-dominant colonial powers like Britain and the societies of Asia and Africa that were struggling toward national independence and a more nearly equal position in global affairs. These two vectors of conflict have often been confused, but to understand the Suez crisis and the world in which it took place, we must keep both firmly in mind.

What was at stake in the Suez crisis? What inspired Eden and Nasser to behave as they did before, during, and after the crisis? How were their actions interpreted by various other actors across the east/west and north/south divides? Why did the United States not give stronger backing to its British ally? How did the Soviet Union relate to the crisis? What does this story tell us about issues of anti-colonial nationalism and the end of empire during the era of the cold war? These and other questions will emerge from the documents in this chapter.

BACKGROUND

The troubled relationship between Britain and Egypt that culminated in the Suez crisis had its origin in the early nineteenth century. Napoleon's invasion of Egypt in 1798 was part of an ongoing series of conflicts between the British and French empires. While Britain had no territorial claims in North Africa, Napoleon's adventure was a threat to its control of Mediterranean trade and its growing interests in India. Napoleon's decision to attack Britain indirectly through an invasion of Egypt led to a British counter-invasion that successfully chased the French from the Nile.

The British forces then retreated. However, the European invaders had disrupted the political status quo in Egypt by undercutting the power of the local representatives of the Ottoman Empire. Order was soon restored by a dynamic leader named Muhammad Ali (r. 1808–1848), who was successful in building a strong, centralized Egyptian state. He realized that Egyptian autonomy required significant political, military, and economic reorganization. He established

new schools, built up a powerful army, and sponsored infrastructural improvements, especially in irrigation, to strengthen the Egyptian economy.

The British were worried about Muhammad Ali's rise to power because he posed a threat to the Ottoman Empire, whose continued existence was considered necessary to maintain the balance of power in the region. They intervened to prevent his rule from spreading beyond Egypt. At the same time, the British began to benefit from an expansion of Egyptian cotton production. By the 1840s, Egyptian cotton was a mainstay of the British textile industry. For the time being, Britain could benefit from its economic relationship with Egypt without having to bear the heavy costs of occupation and colonial rule.

The relationship between Egypt and the Europeans became less equal, however, as time went on. Increasing government debt led Muhammad Ali's successors to support the building of the Suez Canal. Completed in 1869, the canal was designed by a French engineer, financed by European capital, and built with Egyptian labor. The Egyptian government saw the canal as a means of improving its financial situation, but in fact it only deepened Egypt's dependence on European creditors. By 1875 Egypt had to sell its 44 percent stake in the canal company to the British government in order to help pay off its debt. Western creditors were so concerned about the ability of the Egyptian government to pay its debts that they imposed Anglo-French control over Egyptian finances. Britain now had both a military and a financial stake in the Suez Canal.

The Egyptians' sense that their country was being taken over by Europeans led to a nationalist backlash. In 1882 a revolt within the ranks of the Egyptian army was put down by a British invasion. What was originally intended as a temporary military action to restore order led to the stationing of British forces in Egypt from 1882 to 1954. The British did not feel that it was safe to leave Egypt to its own devices lest it come under the sway of another power. If nothing else, the Suez Canal was now vital to Britain's communication with India, the "jewel in the crown" of the British Empire. Opposition to the British occupation never died away; modern Egyptian nationalism had been born.

Britain was anxious to find a formula that would allow it to control Egyptian affairs without formally adding Egypt to its colonial possessions. Though Egypt was still nominally a part of the Ottoman Empire and was ruled by an Egyptian king (the *Khedive*), British advisers were "temporarily" imposed on the country and became the de facto rulers of the Nile, maintaining "a formidable and ambitious structure of colonial rule" in which "the Egyptian financial system was directed by British financial advisers; Egyptian irrigation schemes were managed by British engineers; judicial advisers devised reforms of the legal system; Egyptian schools were inspected by British inspectors; the Egyptian army was commanded by a British Sirdar."[2] Needless to say, the Suez Canal was guarded by troops under British command.

As impressive as this governmental structure was, British rule in Egypt was never really secure. British governors preferred to deal with Egyptian royalty and the traditional elites, largely ignoring the Western-educated Egyptians, who were beginning to form nationalist political parties and to influence public opinion. Dealing with the forces of Egyptian nationalism became even more difficult during World War I, when the Ottoman Empire, which still claimed Egypt as a province, allied itself with Germany. Many Egyptians sympathized with the Ottoman Turks, and by extension their German allies, on the basis of the old adage "the enemy of my enemy is my friend."

From 1914 to 1918 the Middle East was a theater of war, and issues of military security were paramount. Britain declared a formal protectorate over Egypt, insulting those Egyptians who were seeking to lessen rather than deepen their dependence on Britain. Many sources of friction and confusion in the later history of North Africa and the Middle East can be traced back to the First World War. At

2. P. J. Marshall, ed., *Cambridge Illustrated History of the British Empire* (Cambridge: Cambridge University Press, 1996), p. 74.

the same time as the British were allying themselves with an Arab army to overthrow the Ottoman Turks, they were also promising support to the Zionists, who sought a "national home" for the Jewish people in Palestine. Meanwhile, they were making secret plans with the French to divide former Ottoman provinces (such as Palestine, Syria, Lebanon, and Iraq) between themselves after the war. Intense conflict would result from these incompatible promises.

The effect of World War I on the British Empire as a whole was contradictory. On the one hand, Britain not only successfully defended itself but also accumulated substantial new territories. With the approval of the new League of Nations, former Ottoman provinces like Palestine, Jordan, and Iraq fell under British authority, as did some former German colonies in Africa. At the same time, the cost of the war effort was enormous. The British were forced to sell off many of their global investments. Britain was expanding its empire while at the same time suffering relative economic decline compared to emerging economic powers like the United States. But the two great powers of the twentieth century, the United States and the Soviet Union, largely withdrew from global affairs in the 1920s, giving the British (and the French) a false sense of imperial "normalcy."

One of the promises the British had made during the war was to revisit the question of self-government for Egypt once the emergency was over. But on whose terms would that question be reopened? Egyptian nationalists wanted to put their own case before

world leaders at the Paris Peace Conference, but British officials refused to allow them to attend. Public disturbances were the result. In 1922 a new constitution was imposed on Egypt that granted "independence" but kept foreign and military affairs in British hands; the Suez Canal was still guarded by British troops. Tension was rife. Some Egyptian nationalists opposed the British from within the parliament, while those with less patience resorted to violence and terrorism.

The Anglo-Egyptian Treaty of 1936 restored most of Egypt's sovereign rights, but the British were still allowed to keep troops in the canal zone, and the more militant Egyptian nationalists felt that their leaders had once again sold them out to Western powers. The coming of the Second World War revealed the inadequacies of the 1936 treaty. As the war moved into North Africa and Italian forces in Libya threatened Egypt, the British were faced with Egyptian opposition to the deployment of their forces outside the canal zone. They occupied Cairo, and the Egyptian government was forced to acquiesce. The British military effort in North Africa was successful, but the means employed to achieve that success reinforced Arab perceptions of the British as unreformed imperialists.

Once again the victorious British had significant contradictions to deal with after their victory in a world war. On the one hand, Britain remained one of the dominant great powers, had successfully mobilized its empire in the struggle, and was one of five countries with a permanent seat (and veto power) in the new United Nations Security

Council. On the other hand, the cost of the war had been catastrophic. The British pound, which had been the principal currency of the world economy for over a century, was weakened by massive debt to the United States. The problem of maintaining strategic and military commitments that were too great for the country's economic strength became difficult to ignore.

It did not take long for the world to learn that Britain could no longer sustain its traditional imperial role. Unable or unwilling to resolve the conflict between Zionists and Arab nationalists, Britain walked away from Palestine. The new nation of Israel came into being, and warfare born of competing Jewish and Arab nationalisms began. India, Britain's most important colony, became independent and joined the family of nations in 1947. While the British were more optimistic about the future of their role in Africa, here too nationalist leaders like Kwame Nkrumah in the Gold Coast were finding audiences receptive to their calls for self-government.

The eastern Mediterranean was another area where the British had long been dominant, but in the late 1940s Britain was unable to hold the balance of power between Greece and Turkey. The United States intervened, and with the Truman Doctrine in 1948 announced that it intended to be the dominant force in the struggle to contain communism. Britain's world role now required compromise with American governments as well as with colonial nationalists.

The cold war gave Britain some room for maneuver. While the United States was anxious to secure access to global markets that had been tilted toward European colonialists, the communist threat was enough to keep it from rocking the boat. The new power of the Soviet Union and the rise of communism in China gave the British an excuse to keep their imperial project alive: It was all too easy to brand anyone in Africa or Asia who opposed them as a "communist." Britain retained its policy of seeking out moderate nationalists who were willing to compromise in a way that protected Britain's economic and strategic interests.

King Farouk of Egypt was one Arab leader who was willing to play by those rules, but in doing so he lost the respect and support of his own people. On July 23, 1952, he was overthrown by a group of Egyptian Army officers led by Colonel Gamal Abdel Nasser. Nasser's ambition was not only to bring true sovereignty to his own country, but to unite the Arab peoples more widely to protect their interests against both Western powers and Israel. At the Bandung Conference in 1955, Nasser joined such other leaders as Jawaharlal Nehru of India and Sukarno of Indonesia in declaring that their newly independent nations would retain their freedom of action in international affairs. As "nonaligned nations," they would not be forced to choose between the power blocs sponsored by the United States and the Soviet Union. Nasser positioned himself as a pan-Arab leader working toward the greater unity of the Arab peoples in an effort to give them a greater voice in world affairs.

None of this was very appealing to the Western powers. For the next four years, Nasser pursued policies that challenged Britain's hegemony in the region. First, he worked to eliminate the single most embarrassing remnant of the old colonial relationship: the presence of British troops in his country. The Evacuation Treaty of 1954 led to the final withdrawal of British troops from the Suez Canal. Second, he refused to consider the entrance of Egypt into a British-sponsored security arrangement known as the Baghdad Pact. Nasser regarded the Baghdad Pact, which was signed in 1955 by Britain, Turkey, Iraq, and Pakistan, as part of Britain's effort to continue its old game of working through compliant Muslim elites to further its own imperial aims. The United States was also reluctant to join the Baghdad Pact, being cautious about taking on more responsibilities in that volatile part of the world.

Having broken his country's military relationship with Britain, and refusing to play by the rules of the Baghdad Pact, Nasser needed a new source of arms for his military. The United States considered negotiating an arms deal with Egypt, but sensitivity over the U.S. relationship with Israel made that politically impossible. Acting on the principle he had affirmed at Bandung, Nasser turned to the Soviet bloc for help. An arms deal was struck with communist Czechoslovakia in 1955, much to the chagrin of the Western powers.

Another contentious issue was the proposal to build a great dam on the Nile at Aswan. The United States and Britain frustrated Nasser by keeping him waiting and finally refusing his request for financial and technical as-sistance. By refusing to supply arms or finance the dam, the Western powers lost whatever leverage they had retained in Nasser's Egypt. On July 26, 1956, Nasser surprised the world by announcing the nationalization of the Suez Canal.

The British prime minister, Sir Anthony Eden, saw Nasser's move as an intolerable threat. The British government was now desperate to return its troops to Suez, which they had left just two years earlier, and the removal of Nasser was a subject of conversation at the highest levels of government. But how could Britain justify the introduction of troops into a sovereign state? Publicly, the British government joined the United States and the United Nations in calling for an international conference to defuse the crisis. But while these meetings were being held in London, the British government was pursuing a very different strategy.

In the summer and fall of 1956, Eden, increasingly obsessed with Nasser and the Suez problem, entered into a series of secret talks with representatives from France and Israel. The French were the ones who actually proposed the scheme. Israel would invade Egypt across the Sinai desert. France and Britain would then send troops to the canal to "protect" it. The illusion was to be created that the European powers were disinterested parties who were merely doing their best to separate the Egyptian and Israeli forces while keeping the canal open to international traffic. The United States government was not consulted as this secret plan was devised.

On October 29, 1956, the Israeli army entered the Sinai. Britain and France issued an ultimatum to both Egypt and Israel, demanding that they retreat ten miles from the canal pending an Anglo-French "police action." French and British troops landed in Egypt a few days later under the pretext of separating the two Middle Eastern adversaries. Nasser responded by shutting down the canal to deprive the invasion force of oil and ordering ships to be sunk in order to block canal traffic. He became an instant hero for standing up to the great powers, not only among Egyptians and Arabs, but throughout the colonial and recently colonial world. The Baghdad Pact collapsed, as British allies like Turkey and Iraq, embarrassed by their association with Eden's government, supported the Egyptian cause. Most importantly, the government of the United States reacted with shock and dismay.

Why did the Eisenhower administration not support its old war allies against radical Arab nationalism? After all, the United States had a very recent history of covert action against governments that it saw as falling into the communist camp. In 1953 the Central Intelligence Agency had secretly orchestrated a campaign against the nationalist prime minister of Iran and helped restore the dictatorial powers of the shah. In 1954 the democratically

elected government of Guatemala was overthrown by a military dictator backed by the CIA. That did not mean, however, that the American government felt it could safely turn a blind eye to covert actions organized without its input or support. The United States did not want to be too closely associated with a decaying European colonialism. Moreover, the Suez invasion came at a very bad time in cold war relations. The Soviet Union had invaded Hungary in the fall of 1956, and President Eisenhower could not credibly criticize the Russians for invading Hungary and at the same time support the British and French in what might be seen as a similar endeavor. Eisenhower and his secretary of state, John Foster Dulles, supported a Security Council resolution condemning the invasion and began laying the groundwork for United Nations troops to replace the invaders at the canal.

The British were forced to retreat from Suez, having gained nothing and having lost significantly in terms of international prestige. Eden's political career was over. The canal remained in Egyptian hands, and Nasser became a world figure, completing the Aswan Dam with Russian help. The sources of tension between Israel and the Arab world remained unresolved.

THE METHOD

In analyzing the following documents, you will need to keep in mind the perceptions and interests of the various players in the Suez drama as it

unfolded in 1956. As always, it is important to consider the origins of the documents and their intended audience. Some of the sources in this chapter were meant to be kept private; others were intended for public audiences. Some were created at the time;

others were the product of later reflection. Keep these distinctions in mind as you read.

What led the Egyptian president, Colonel Nasser, to nationalize the canal? What prompted the British prime minister, Sir Anthony Eden, to organize an armed response in collaboration with the French and Israelis? To what extent, and using what arguments, did Eden attempt to bring the United States on board with his plan? What explains the unwillingness of the United States under President Dwight D. Eisenhower to support armed intervention, and its decision to seek a resolution through the United Nations? How did the affair relate to the two basic global conflicts of the time: the cold war and anticolonial nationalism? How did the world respond to the Anglo-French invasion of the canal zone in November 1956? What were the consequences of the Suez crisis for the roles of Egypt, Britain, and the United States in the Middle East?

To help answer these questions, you may find it useful, in your notes, to keep track of the actions of the various players in the drama, and of the motivations that inspired them to act as they did. As you read the sources, you will want to refer back to the following section, which gives additional context for each of the documents.

Source 1 is an evaluation by the British foreign secretary, Sir Anthony Eden (who later became prime minister), of the relationship between his country's economy and its military in the early 1950s, with special reference to relations with the United States.

Out of this thinking came the British effort to create the Baghdad Pact—which was weakened by the refusal of the governments of Egypt and the United States to join—and the 1954 agreement to withdraw British forces from the Suez Canal.

On July 23, 1952, King Farouk was forced to abdicate and the rise of Gamal Abdel Nasser began. Source 2 is an extract from Nasser's *The Philosophy of the Revolution*. In this book he attempted to justify and explain the military intervention in Egyptian politics by placing it in the larger context of Egyptian and Arab nationalism.

Source 3 deals with the military balance of power between Egypt and Israel. In 1950, the United States, Britain, and France had agreed not to contribute to an arms race in the Middle East by favoring one country or the other in its arms sales. Frustrated by his inability to secure American arms, and following his policy of "nonalignment," in 1955 Nasser struck a deal to purchase arms from Soviet-allied Czechoslovakia. This document registers the Israeli government's response and gives a general impression of Israeli attitudes toward Egypt at the time.

In the summer of 1956 Nasser received the news that no American support for the Aswan Dam project could be expected. Nasser then stunned the world by announcing the nationalization of the Suez Canal. All of the previous tensions in the region were now focused on Suez. Source 4 is an extract from Nasser's speech of July 26, 1956. Sources 5 and 6 are visual ones, the first a photograph taken a week later, the second a cartoon from an English publication. (The man with the fishing pole is the Soviet foreign minister.) It is useful to compare the similarities and differences in the portrayal of Nasser in these two representations.

Source 7 is part of a record of a British Cabinet discussion of the nationalization issue. As the British considered the consequences of Nasser's action and appropriate lines of response, the United States worked through the United Nations to convene a conference in London to resolve the dispute. Though an agreement was reached, Egypt's lack of participation made it unclear whether such diplomacy would be enough. Knowing that Britain was considering military options, President Eisenhower wrote the telegram reproduced as Source 8 to Prime Minister Eden, and received the reply included as Source 9.

Meanwhile, Israel had its own concerns. Source 10 is an extract from the memoirs of Moshe Dayan, the Israeli minister of defense at the time. In the wake of the Czech arms sales to Egypt, Dayan describes the process by which France, Britain, and Israel came together to develop a common plan, as shown in Source 11, a record of the Sèvres Protocol signed at a secret meeting. Eden was alarmed that a record was kept of this accord, and had the British copy destroyed. This version of the document was reconstructed and translated from the French and Israeli versions.

Less than a week after the Sèvres Protocol was signed, Israeli troops invaded Egypt across the Sinai Peninsula. The next group of sources records world reactions to the Israeli occupation, the Anglo-French ultimatum, and the subsequent invasion of the Suez Canal area by British and French forces. Source 12 is a draft resolution submitted to the United Nations Security Council by the United States. It was vetoed by France and Britain, but the next day in an emergency meeting the General Assembly of the United Nations, where no nation holds a veto, voted overwhelmingly in support of a similar resolution. Source 13 is from a statement by the Indian prime minister, Jawaharlal Nehru, who had cooperated with British authorities to secure Indian independence and retained ties to Great Britain through the Commonwealth. On the other hand, Nehru had cooperated with Nasser in defining the principles of the Non-Aligned Movement at the Bandung Conference just a year earlier. Source 14 records the response of the Soviet government.

Within a week of the Israeli invasion, the British government, isolated in the international community, considered means of extricating itself from the situation. However, it was only when the financial implications of the Suez invasion became clear, as mentioned in Source 15, that Eden and his cabinet moved toward withdrawal of British troops from Egypt. Soon after, the Anglo-French forces were replaced by the United Nations, and the Suez Canal was restored to order. Source 16, an exchange between the American secretary of state and a member of the Senate, deals with the implications of the Suez crisis for American foreign policy. Three days after this statement by Secretary of

State Dulles, the "Eisenhower Doctrine" was announced, committing the United States for the first time to significant military and economic responsibilities in the Middle East.

The remaining documents all concern the outcome of the Suez crisis. In Source 17, Eden, soon to resign as head of the British government, informs his colleagues of the lessons he had learned. In Source 18, President Nasser of Egypt, in an interview on a televised British news show from 1966, reflects back on the events that had occurred a decade earlier, drawing very different conclusions from those reached by Eden.

Finally, Source 19 is a British cartoon from 1962. By that time the Kennedy administration in the United States was playing a much more proactive role in the politics of the Middle East, Southeast Asia, and Africa, regions where the French and the British had long been dominant. Harold Macmillan is shown as a partially submerged "Britannia," surrounded by sea creatures representing Mao Zedong of China, Charles de Gaulle of France, Fidel Castro of Cuba, and Nikita Khrushchev of the Soviet Union. In the speedboat above is the American secretary of defense, offering precious little help.

THE EVIDENCE

Source 1 from Anthony Gorst and Lewis Johnman, The Suez Crisis *(London: Routledge, 1997), pp. 28–30.*

1. Sir Anthony Eden, British Foreign Secretary, Discusses British Obligations, June 18, 1952

The essence of a sound foreign policy is to ensure that a country's strength is equal to its obligations. If this is not the case, then either the obligations must be reduced to the level at which resources are available to maintain them, or a greater share of the country's resources must be devoted to their support. It is becoming clear that rigorous maintenance of the presently-accepted policies of Her Majesty's Government at home and abroad is placing a burden on the country's economy which it is beyond the resources of the country to meet. A position has already been reached where there is no reserve and therefore no margin for unforeseen additional obligations.

The first task must be to determine how far the external obligations of the country can be reduced or shared with others, or transferred to other shoulders, without impairing too seriously the world position of the United Kingdom and sacrificing the vital advantages which flow from it. But if, after careful review, it is shown that the total effort required is still beyond the capacity of existing national resources, a choice of the utmost difficulty lies before the British people, for they must either give up, for a time, some of the advantages which a high standard of living confers upon them or, by relaxing their grip in the outside world, see their country sink to the level of a second-class Power, with injury to their essential interests and way of life of which they can have little conception. . . .

If, on a longer view, it must be assumed that the maintenance of the present scale of overseas commitments will permanently overstrain our economy, clearly we ought to recognise that the United Kingdom is over-committed, and reduce the commitment. The only practical way of removing this permanent strain would be for the United Kingdom to shed or share the load of one or two major obligations, e.g., the defence of the Middle East, for which we at present bear the responsibility alone. . . .

The success of this policy will depend on a number of factors, some favourable, some unfavourable. The United States is the only single country in the free world capable of assuming new and world-wide obligations; being heavily committed to the East–West struggle they would not readily leave a power-vacuum in any part of the globe but would be disposed, however reluctantly, to fill it themselves if it was clear that the United Kingdom could no longer hold the position (as they did, for example, in Greece). On the other hand, the history of the Middle East Command negotiations and the unwillingness of the United States Chiefs of Staff to commit forces to it illustrates the American reluctance to enter into new commitments in peacetime. . . . Moreover, distrust of the British and fear of becoming an instrument to prop up a declining British Empire are still strong. . . . As regards the United Kingdom part, a policy of this kind will only be successful with the United States in so far as we are able to demonstrate that we are making the maximum possible effort ourselves, and the more gradually and inconspicuously we can transfer the real burdens from our own to American shoulders, the less damage we shall do to our own position and influence in the world. . . .

[It is] clearly beyond the resources of the United Kingdom to continue to assume the responsibility alone, for the security of the Middle East. Our aim should be to make the whole of this area and in particular the Canal Zone an international responsibility. Hence every step should be taken to speed up the establishment of an Allied Middle East Defence Organisation. It should, however, be recognised that the setting up of such a defence organisation will not result in any immediate alleviation of the burden for the United Kingdom. The United States have refused to enter into any precise commitments in the Middle East or to allocate forces and it should be the constant object of Her Majesty's Government to persuade them to do so. In addition, every possibility should be explored of committing the United States militarily, e.g., to the building of bases, the provision of material, the sharing and reconstruction of airfields. . . . The dilemma is that until we can come to an agreement with Egypt no effective international defence organisation for the Middle East can be established; and so long as there is no settlement with Egypt and no international defence organisation we are obliged to hold the fort alone.

Source 2 from Gamal Abdel Nasser, The Philosophy of the Revolution *(Buffalo, N.Y.: Economica Books, 1959), pp. 43, 49–52, 58–60, 62–66.*

2. From Gamal Abdel Nasser, *The Philosophy of the Revolution,* 1959

What is it we want to do? And which is the way to it?

There is no doubt we all dream of Egypt free and strong. No Egyptian would ever differ with another about that. As for the way to liberation and strength, that is the most intricate problem in our lives. . . .

Fate has so willed that we should be on the crossroads of the world. Often have we been the road which invaders took and a prey to adventurers. . . .

European society passed through the stages of its evolution in an orderly manner. It crossed the bridge between the Renaissance at the end of the Middle Ages and the Nineteenth Century step by step. The stages of this evolution systematically succeeded one another.

In our case everything was sudden. European countries eyed us covetously and regarded us as a crossroad to their colonies in the East and the South.

Torrents of ideas and opinions burst upon us which we were, at that stage of our evolution, incapable of assimilating. Our spirits were still in the Thirteenth Century though the symptoms of the Nineteenth and Twentieth Centuries infiltrated in their various aspects. Our minds were trying to catch up the advancing caravan of humanity. . . .

We live in a society that has not yet crystallized. It is still boiling over and restless. . . .

. . . Any nation, exposed to the same conditions as our country, could be easily lost. It could be swept away by the torrents that fell upon it. But it stood firm in the violent earthquake.

. . . As I consider one normal Egyptian family out of the thousands that live in the capital, I find the following: the father, for example, is a turbanned "fellah" from the heart of the country; the mother a lady descended from Turkish stock; the sons of the family are at a school adopting the English system; the daughters the French. All this lies between the Thirteenth century and the outward appearances of the Twentieth. . . .

Such are, then, the roots from which sprang our conditions of today. Such are the sources from which our crisis flows. If I add to these social origins the circumstances for which we expelled Farouk and for which we wish to liberate our country from every foreign soldier; if we add all these together, we shall discover the wide sphere in which we labour and which is exposed, from every side, to the winds, to the violent storm that raged in its corners, to flashing lightning and roaring thunder. . . .

We should first of all agree upon one thing before we proceed further and that is to define the boundaries of place as far as we are concerned. . . . If I were told that our place is limited by the political boundaries of our country I also do not agree. . . .

We cannot look stupidly at a map of the world not realizing our place therein and the role determined to us by that place. Neither can we ignore that there is an Arab circle surrounding us and that this circle is as much a part of us as we are a part of it, that our history has been mixed with it and that its interests are linked with ours. These are actual facts and not mere words.

Can we ignore that there is a continent of Africa in which fate has placed us and which is destined today to witness a terrible struggle on its future? This struggle will affect us whether we want or not.

Can we ignore that there is a Muslim world with which we are tied by bonds which are not only forged by religious faith but also tightened by the facts of history? . . .

There is no doubt that the Arab circle is the most important and the most closely connected with us. Its history merges with ours. We have suffered the same hardships, lived the same crises and when we fell prostrate under the spikes of the horses of conquerors they lay with us. . . .

. . . As far as I am concerned I remember that the first elements of Arab consciousness began to filter into my mind as a student in secondary schools, wherefrom I went out with my fellow schoolboys on strike on December 2nd of every year as a protest against the Balfour Declaration whereby England gave the Jews a national home usurped unjustly from its legal owners. . . .

And when the Palestine crisis loomed on the horizon I was firmly convinced that the fighting in Palestine was not fighting on foreign territory. Nor was it inspired by sentiment. It was a duty imposed by self-defense.

I do not want now to discuss the details of the Palestine War. This is a subject that needs several many-sided discussions. But one strange lesson of the Palestine War I care to mention: The Arab nations entered the Palestine War with the same degree of enthusiasm. . . . They came out of the war with the same bitterness and frustration. Every one of them was thus exposed, in its own country, to the same factors and was governed by the same forces, that caused their defeat and made them bow their heads low with shame and humiliation. . . .

. . . This was how I felt when, in my wanderings I came upon the children of refugees who were caught in the tentacles of the siege after their homes had been demolished and their property lost. I particularly remember a young girl of the same age as my daughter. I saw her rushing out, amidst danger and stray bullets and, bitten by the pangs of hunger and cold, looking for a crust of bread or a rag of cloth. I always said to myself, "This may happen to my daughter." I believe that what was happening in Palestine could happen, and may still happen today, in any part of this region, as long as it resigns itself to the factors and the forces which dominate now.

After the seige and the battles in Palestine I came home with the whole region in my mind one complete whole. . . . An event may happen in Cairo today; it is repeated in Damascus, Beirut, Amman or any other place tomorrow. This was naturally in conformity with the picture that experience has left within me: One region, the same factors and circumstances, even the same forces opposing them all. It was clear that imperialism was the most prominent of these forces; even Israel itself was but one of the outcomes of imperialism. If it had not fallen under British mandate, Zionism could not have found the necessary support to realize the idea of a national home in Palestine. That idea would have remained a foolish vision, practically hopeless.

Source 3 from Harry Browne, Flashpoints: Suez and Sinai *(London: Longman, 1971), pp. 22–23.*

3. Statement on Foreign Affairs by Moshe Sharett, Israel Premier and Foreign Minister, October 18, 1955

EGYPT–CZECHOSLOVAK ARMS DEAL

And now, honoured members of the Knesset, I come to the very serious event which occurred some three weeks ago and which has cast a deep shadow on the entire scene of the State's foreign and defence affairs. I refer to the agreement between the ruler of Egypt and the Czechoslovak Government—which from a political and military standpoint implies the linking up between Egypt and the entire Soviet Bloc—for the supply of heavy and modern arms to Egypt, by all accounts in very considerable quantities.

This departure is liable to bring about a revolutionary and ominous change in Israel's security situation.

Both parties attempted to describe the arrangement as a purely commercial deal—perfectly simple and legitimate. Both parties went on to explain that the arms were merely intended to satisfy the defence needs of a free and sovereign state. Neither of the parties ignored Israel or pretended that the arms were not destined to be used against her.

Both sought to justify this great addition to Egyptian arms with the argument that they were to enable a handicapped Egypt to attain to Israel's level of armament.

EGYPT'S 'DEDICATION TO PEACE'

Here is his [Nasser's] pledge of dedication to peace as made in a statement to an Egyptian paper:

'It is utterly inconceivable that Egypt should ever consider peace with Israel or even think of recognising it'

And in another statement:

'The problem of Palestine will not be solved and there will be no peace between us and the Jews so long as even the slightest right of the Arabs of that country is controlled by the enemy. A man can forget everything except blood, vengeance and honour' . . .

Yet another clarion call from the same bugle:

'We cannot but be in a state of war with Israel. This impels us to mobilise all Arab resources for its final liquidation. We ask that our production should be military production and meet our war needs. We want all our newspapers and radio stations to proclaim the total mobilisation of forces for the liberation of Palestine.'

WIDENING GAP . . .

The supply of arms by Czechoslovakia to Egypt is dangerous because it flows to an Egypt which is hostile to us. The same applies to the American arms which are at present being supplied to Iraq or to arms of any power which may at any future time be supplied to Syria. These countries are hostile towards us and their arms are liable to be used against us. It is our position that arms must not be given or sold to states which do not seek peace—states whose declared and real policies are war.

Thus it is our stand that there is a duty and an obligation to sell or grant arms to that state which offers peace—but which is compelled to defend itself as against neighbours who deny it peace and conspire aggression against it.

Source 4 from Harry Browne, Flashpoints: Suez and Sinai *(London: Longman, 1971), pp. 34–35.*

4. Gamal Abdel Nasser Announces the Nationalization of the Suez Canal, July 26, 1956

Now, O citizens, . . . now that our rights in the Suez Canal have reverted to us after 100 years, we are building the real foundations of sovereignty and the real edifice of grandeur and dignity. The Suez Canal was a state within a state; it was an Egyptian limited company which depended on foreign plots and on imperialism and the supporters of imperialism. The Suez Canal was built for Egypt and for Egypt's interests but it was a source of exploitation and extortion.

... The Suez Canal was one of the facades of oppression, extortion and humiliation. Today, O citizens the Suez Canal has been nationalised and this decree has in fact been published in the Official Gazette and has become law. Today, O citizens we declare that our property has been returned to us. The rights about which we were silent have been restored to us. Today, citizens, with the annual income of the Suez Canal amounting to £35,000,000—that is, 100,000,000 dollars a year, and 500,000,000 dollars in five years—we shall not look for the 70,000,000 dollars of American aid.

Today we greet the fifth year of the revolution and in the same way as Farouk left on 26 July 1952, the old Suez Canal Company also leaves on the same day.... We shall march forward as one people who have vowed to work and to proceed on a holy march of industrialising and construction—nay, as one people who are solidly united in opposition to treachery and aggression and to imperialism and the supporters and antics of imperialism.

At this moment as I talk to you some of your Egyptian brethren are proceeding to administer the canal company and to run its affairs. They are taking over the canal company at this very moment—the Egyptian canal company, not the foreign canal company. They have started to take over the canal company and its property and to control shipping in the canal—the canal which is situated in Egyptian territory, which goes through Egyptian territory which is part of Egypt and which is owned by Egypt. They are now carrying out this task so that we can make up for the past and build new edifices of grandeur and dignity. May the Almighty grant you success, and may the peace and blessing of God be upon you.

Source 5: Hulton-Deutsch collection/Corbis.

5. Gamal Abdel Nasser, Egypt, August 1, 1956

Source 6: Courtesy of the Centre for the Study of Cartoons and Caricature, University of Kent, Canterbury.

6. English Cartoon, "The Colossus of Suez," 1956

THE COLOSSUS OF SUEZ

Source 7 from Anthony Gorst and Lewis Johnman, The Suez Crisis *(London: Routledge, 1997), pp. 56–60.*

7. The British Cabinet Reacts to the Nationalization of the Suez Canal, July 27, 1956

The Cabinet considered the situation created by the decision of the Egyptian Government to nationalise the Suez Canal Company.

The Prime Minister said that, with some of his senior colleagues, he had seen the French Ambassador and the United States Chargé d'Affaires on the previous evening and had informed them of the facts as we knew them. He had told them that Her Majesty's Government would take a most serious view of this situation and that any failure on the part of the Western Powers to take the necessary steps to regain control over the Canal would have disastrous consequences for the economic life of the Western Powers and for their standing and influence in the Middle East. . . . Our first aim must be to reach a common understanding on the matter with the French, as our partners in the Canal enterprise, and with the United States Government. . . . The Cabinet were given the following information of the importance of the Suez Canal to trade and the flow of supplies and of Egypt's financial position:—

1. Oil—Of a total of some 70 million tons of oil which passed annually from the Persian Gulf through the Suez Canal, 60 million tons were destined for Western Europe and represented two-thirds of Western European oil supplies. . . . If the Egyptian Government decided to interfere with the passage of oil through the Canal, it would be necessary for Western Europe to turn to the Western hemisphere for supplies; as much as 10 million tons might be involved, and it would be necessary to ask the Americans to divert to Western Europe the supplies they now receive from the Persian Gulf. We ourselves had supplies sufficient to last for about six weeks. In order to conserve these it would be necessary at an early date to introduce some arrangement for the restriction of deliveries to industry and to garages.

2. Trade—Interference with the traffic passing through the Suez Canal would not seriously affect the flow of imports other than oil into this country, but it would seriously hamper the export trade, particularly to India. Our exports costs would also rise as freight charges would go up. . . .

The Cabinet next considered the legal position and the basis on which we could sustain and justify to international opinion, a refusal to accept the decision of the Egyptian Prime Minister, Colonel Nasser, to nationalise the Canal.

The Cabinet agreed that we should be on weak ground in basing our resistance on the narrow argument that Colonel Nasser had acted illegally. The Suez Canal Company was registered as an Egyptian Company under Egyptian law; and Colonel Nasser had indicated that he intended to compensate the shareholders at ruling market prices. From a narrow legal point of view his action amounted to no more than a decision to buy out the shareholders. Our case must be presented on wider international grounds: our argument must be that the canal was an important international asset and facility and that Egypt could not be allowed to exploit it for a purely internal purpose. The Egyptians had not the technical ability to manage it effectively; and their recent behaviour gave no confidence that they would recognise their international obligations in respect of it. . . .

The Cabinet agreed that for these reasons every effort must be made to restore effective international control over the Canal. It was evident that the Egyptians would not yield to economic pressures alone. They must be subjected to the maximum political pressure which could be exerted by the maritime and trading nations whose interests were most directly affected. And, in the last resort, this political pressure must be backed by the threat—and, if need be, the use—of force.

The Cabinet then considered the factors to be taken into account in preparing a plan of military operations against Egypt. . . .

The Prime Minister said that against this background the Cabinet must decide what our policy must be. He fully agreed that the question was not a legal issue but must be treated as a matter of the widest international importance. It must now be our aim to place the Suez Canal under the control of the Powers interested in international shipping and trade by means of a new international Commission on which Egypt would be given suitable representation. . . . The fundamental question before the Cabinet . . . was whether they were prepared in the last resort to pursue their objective by the threat or even the use of force, and whether they were ready, in default of assistance from the United States and France, to take military action alone.

The Cabinet agreed that our essential interests in this area must, if necessary, be safeguarded by military action and that the necessary preparations to this end must be made. Failure to hold the Suez Canal would lead inevitably to the loss one by one of all our interests and assets in the Middle East and, even if we had to act alone, we could not stop short of using force to protect our position if all other means of protecting it proved unavailing.

Source 8 from Anthony Gorst and Lewis Johnman, The Suez Crisis *(London: Routledge, 1997), pp. 76–77.*

8. U.S. President Dwight D. Eisenhower Cautions Sir Anthony Eden on the Use of Force, September 3, 1956

As to the use of force or the threat of force at this juncture, I continue to feel as I expressed myself in the letter Foster carried to you some weeks ago. Even now military preparations and civilian evacuation exposed to public view seem to be solidifying support for Nasser which has been shaky in many important quarters. I regard it as indispensable that if we are to proceed solidly together to the solution of this problem, public opinion in our several countries must be overwhelming in its support. I must tell you frankly that American public opinion flatly rejects the thought of using force, particularly when it does not seem that every possible peaceful means of protecting interests has been exhausted without result. Moreover, I gravely doubt we could here secure Congressional authority even for the lesser support measures for which you might have to look to us.

I really do not see how a successful result could be achieved by forcible means. The use of force would, it seems to me, vastly increase the area of jeopardy. I do not see how the economy of Western Europe can long survive the burden of prolonged military operations, as well as the denial of Near East oil. Also the peoples of the Near East and of North Africa and, to some extent of all of Asia and all of Africa, would be consolidated against the West to a degree which, I fear, could not be overcome in a generation and, perhaps, not even in a century particularly having in mind the capacity of the Russians to make mischief. Before such action were undertaken, all our peoples should unitedly understand that there were no other means available to protect our vital rights and interests.

Source 9 from Sir Anthony Eden, Full Circle *(London: Cassell, 1960). Reprinted in Harry Browne,* Flashpoints: Suez and Sinai *(London: Longman, 1971), pp. 42–44.*

9. Sir Anthony Eden, British Prime Minister, Replies to President Dwight D. Eisenhower, September 6, 1956

Thank you for your message and writing thus frankly.

There is no doubt as to where we are agreed and have been agreed from the very beginning, namely that we should do everything we can to get a peaceful settlement. . . .

We are both agreed that we must give the Suez Committee every chance to fulfil their mission. This is our firm resolve. If the committee and subsequent negotiations succeed in getting Nasser's agreement to the London proposals of the eighteen powers, there will be no call for force. But if the committee fails, we must have some immediate alternative which will show that Nasser is not going to get his way. . . .

You suggest that this is where we diverge. If that is so I think that the divergence springs from a difference in our assessment of Nasser's plans and intentions. May I set out our view of the position.

In the nineteen-thirties Hitler established his position by a series of carefully planned movements. These began with the occupation of the Rhineland and were followed by successive acts of aggression against Austria, Czechoslovakia, Poland and the West. His actions were tolerated and excused by the majority of the population of Western Europe. It was argued either that Hitler had committed no act of aggression against anyone, or that he was entitled to do what he liked in his own territory, or that it was impossible to prove that he had any ulterior designs, or that the Covenant of the League of Nations did not entitle us to use force and that it would be wiser to wait until he did commit an act of aggression.

In more recent years Russia has attempted similar tactics. The blockade of Berlin was to have been the opening move in a campaign designed at least to deprive the Western powers of their whole position in Germany. On this occasion we fortunately reacted at once with the result that the Russian design was never unfolded. But I am sure that you would agree that it would be wrong to infer from this circumstance that no Russian design existed.

Similarly the seizure of the Suez Canal is, we are convinced, the opening gambit in a planned campaign designed by Nasser to expel all Western influence and interests from Arab countries. He believes that if he can get away with this, and if he can successfully defy eighteen nations, his prestige in Arabia will be so great that he will be able to mount revolutions of young officers in Saudi Arabia, Jordan, Syria and Iraq. (We know that he is already preparing a revolution in Iraq, which is the most stable and progressive.) These new Governments will in effect be Egyptian satellites if not Russian ones. They will have to place their united oil resources under the control of a united Arabia led by Egypt and under Russian influence. When that moment comes Nasser can deny oil to Western Europe and we here shall all be at his mercy. . . .

In short we are convinced that if Nasser is allowed to defy the eighteen nations it will be a matter of months before revolution breaks out in the oil-bearing countries and the West is wholly deprived of Middle Eastern oil. In this brief we are fortified by the advice of friendly leaders in the Middle East. . . .

. . . I can assure you that we are conscious of the burdens and perils attending military intervention. But if our assessment is correct, and if the only alternative is to allow Nasser's plans quietly to develop until this country and all Western Europe are held to ransom by Egypt acting at Russia's behest it seems to us that our duty is plain. We have many times led Europe in the fight for freedom. It would be an ignoble end to our long history if we accepted to perish by degrees.

Source 10 from Moshe Dayan, Story of My Life: An Autobiography *(New York: William Morrow, 1976), pp. 183–184.*

10. From the Memoirs of Moshe Dayan, Israeli Minister of Defense, 1976

Soviet political backing . . . had given Egypt formidable military might and her president, Gamal Abdel Nasser, a tremendous feeling of confidence. On July 26, 1956, he stunned the world with the announcement, made before a cheering crowd of tens of thousands in Cairo's Independence Square, that he had nationalized the Suez Canal. It was undoubtedly the most significant political event of the year, with far-reaching international consequences. One of them was an immediate decision by France and Britain to consult on the steps to be taken, and the French foreign minister arranged to leave for London the next day to meet Prime Minister Anthony Eden. I heard about this move from our representatives in Paris, who informed us that they had been approached by our friends in the French Defense Ministry. They said that Christian Pineau, their foreign minister, would be accompanied by military experts, suggesting that military action against Nasser was not ruled out. What the French wanted from us was up-to-the-minute information on the strength and locations of the Egyptian formations—land, sea and air—so that their delegation to London could be well briefed.

...I met with Ben-Gurion and proposed that in the situation created by Nasser's Suez action, and before Egypt attacked us, we should launch one of three operations: capture the Sinai Peninsula up to the Canal and establish international control of the waterway; capture Sharm el-Sheikh and lift the blockade of the Aqaba Gulf; take over the Gaza Strip. ...

That opportunity was being busily developed in London and Paris in the weeks that followed. After the first meeting of the French delegation with Eden in London, the governments of Britain and France resolved to launch a joint military operation to seize and hold the Suez Canal Zone, cancel the nationalization order, and restore their rights in the Canal Authority. It was also their aim to topple Nasser. The General Staffs of both countries began planning a large-scale operation. Reserves were to be mobilized, forces were to be concentrated in Malta and Cyprus, and ships were to be assembled for a huge amphibious operation, almost on a World War Two scale, to follow up an initial paratroop drop in the Canal area. ...

France was the driving force behind the policy of action. Britain's Prime Minister Eden also favored military measures, but he faced serious opposition inside his own country. And the United States, even though she had been the object of gross vilification in Nasser's nationalization speech, was firmly opposed to the projected operation by her European allies against Egypt. There was to be doubt and wavering right up to the last moment—and vestiges of this mood were to linger even after the twelfth hour had struck.

Source 11 from Keith Kyle, Suez *(New York: St. Martin's Press, 1991), pp. 565–566.*

11. Sèvres Protocol, October 22–24, 1956

PROTOCOL

The results of the conversations which took place at Sèvres from 22–24 October 1956 between the representatives of the Governments of the United Kingdom, the State of Israel and of France are the following:

1. The Israeli forces launch in the evening of 29 October 1956 a large scale attack on the Egyptian forces with the aim of reaching the Canal zone the following day.

2. On being apprised of these events, the British and French Governments during the day of 30 October 1956 respectively and simultaneously make two appeals to the Egyptian Government and the Israeli Government on the following lines:

   A. *To the Egyptian Government*
      (a) halt all acts of war.
      (b) withdraw all its troops ten miles from the Canal.
      (c) accept temporary occupation of key positions on the Canal by the Anglo-French forces to guarantee freedom of passage through the Canal by vessels of all nations until a final settlement.

   B. *To the Israeli Government*
      (a) halt all acts of war.
      (b) withdraw all its troops ten miles to the east of the Canal.

In addition, the Israeli Government will be notified that the French and British Governments have demanded of the Egyptian Government to accept temporary occupation of key positions along the Canal by Anglo-French forces.

It is agreed that if one of the Governments refused, or did not give its consent, within twelve hours the Anglo-French forces would intervene with the means necessary to ensure that their demands are accepted.

   C. The representatives of the three Governments agree that the Israeli Government will not be required to meet the conditions in the appeal addressed to it, in the event that the Egyptian Government does not accept those in the appeal addressed to it for their part.

3. In the event that the Egyptian Government should fail to agree within the stipulated time to the conditions of the appeal addressed to it, the Anglo-French forces will launch military operations against the Egyptian forces in the early hours of the morning of 31 October.

4. The Israeli Government will send forces to occupy the western shore of the Gulf of Akaba and the group of islands Tirane and Sanafir to ensure freedom of navigation in the Gulf of Akaba.

5. Israel undertakes not to attack Jordan during the period of operations against Egypt.

   But in the event that during the same period Jordan should attack Israel, the British Government undertakes not to come to the aid of Jordan.

6. The arrangements of the present protocol must remain strictly secret.

7. They will enter into force after the agreement of the three Governments.

(signed)

DAVID BEN-GURION   PATRICK DEAN   CHRISTIAN PINEAU

Source 12 from Harry Browne, Flashpoints: Suez and Sinai *(London: Longman, 1971), p. 75.*

12. Draft Resolution from the United States to the UN Security Council, October 30, 1956[3]

Noting that the armed forces of Israel have penetrated deeply into Egyptian territory in violation of the General Armistice Agreement between Egypt and Israel. Expressing its grave concern at this violation of the Armistice Agreement,

1. Calls upon Israel immediately to withdraw its armed forces behind the established armistice lines:

2. Calls upon all Members:
    (a) to refrain from the use of force or threat of force in the area in any manner inconsistent with the purposes of the United Nations;
    (b) To assist the United Nations in ensuring the integrity of the armistice agreements;
    (c) To refrain from giving any military, economic or financial assistance to Israel so long as it has not complied with this resolution;

3. Requests the Secretary-General to keep the Security Council informed on compliance with this resolution and to make whatever recommendations he deems appropriate for the maintenance of international peace and security in the area by the implementation of this and prior resolutions.

Source 13 from The Hindu, 2 November 1956. *Reprinted in J. Eayrs,* The Commonwealth and Suez *(London: Oxford University Press, 1964), pp. 249–251.*

13. Statement by Jawaharlal Nehru, Indian Prime Minister, November 1, 1956

After fairly considerable experience in foreign affairs, I cannot think of a grosser case of naked aggression than what England and France are attempting to do, backed by the armed forces of the two great powers. I deeply regret to say so, because we have been friendly with both the countries and in particular our relationship with the U.K. has been close and friendly ever since we attained

---

3. A similar resolution was submitted by the Soviet Union. In both cases it was vetoed by Britain and by France.

independence. I realize also that the U.K. has made many liberal gestures to other countries and has been a force for peace, I think, for the past few years. Because of this my sorrow and distress are all the greater at this amazing adventure that England and France have entered into. . . .

In the middle of the 20th century we are going back to the predatory method of the 18th and 19th centuries. But there is a difference now. There are self-respecting independent nations in Asia and Africa which are not going to tolerate this kind of incursion by the colonial powers. Therefore I need not say that in this matter our sympathies are entirely with Egypt.

Source 14 from Harry Browne, Flashpoints: Suez and Sinai *(London: Longman, 1971), pp. 68–69.*

14. Soviet Response to the Aggression Against Egypt, October 31, 1956

Egypt has fallen victim to aggression. Her territory has been invaded by Israeli forces and she faces the danger of a landing by British and French forces. . . .

The action of the Israeli government constitutes armed aggression and an open breach of the United Nations Charter. The facts indicate that the invasion by the Israeli forces has clearly been calculated to be used as an excuse for the Western powers, primarily Britain and France, to bring their troops into the territory of the Arab states, notably, into the Suez Canal zone. . . . The government of Israel, operating as a tool of imperialist circles bent on restoring the regime of colonial oppression in the East, has challenged all the Arab peoples, all the peoples of the East fighting against colonialism. The course which the extremist ruling circles of Israel have taken is a criminal one and dangerous, above all to the state of Israel itself and to its future. . . .

The government of the Soviet Union resolutely condemns the act of aggression against Egypt by the governments of Britain, France and Israel. The freedom-loving peoples of the world fervently sympathise with the Egyptian people waging a just struggle in defence of their national independence. . . .

The Soviet government holds that all responsibility for the dangerous consequences of these aggressive actions against Egypt will rest entirely with the governments which have taken the line of disturbing peace and security, the line of aggression.

Source 15 from Anthony Gorst and Lewis Johnman, The Suez Crisis *(London: Routledge, 1997), pp. 142–143.*

15. Discussion by the British Cabinet, November 28, 1956

The Chancellor of the Exchequer said that it would be necessary to announce early in the following week the losses of gold and dollars which we had sustained during November. This statement would reveal a very serious drain on the reserves and would be a considerable shock both to public opinion in this country and to international confidence in sterling. It was therefore important that we should be able to announce at the same time that we were taking action to reinforce the reserves both by recourse to the International Monetary Fund and in other ways. For this purpose the good will of the United States Government was necessary; and it was evident that this good will could not be obtained without an immediate and unconditional undertaking to withdraw the Anglo-French force from Port Said. He therefore favoured a prompt announcement of our intention to withdraw this force, justifying this action on the ground that we had now achieved the purpose for which we had originally launched the Anglo-French military operation against Egypt and that we were content to leave the United Nations, backed by the United States, the responsibility, which the General Assembly could now be deemed to have accepted for settling the problems of the Middle East.

Source 16 from Anthony Gorst and Lewis Johnman, The Suez Crisis *(London: Routledge, 1997), pp. 156–157.*

16. Exchange Between U.S. Secretary of State John Foster Dulles and U.S. Senator Richard Russell, January 2, 1957

SECRETARY DULLES: The fact is that it is more and more developing to be the fact that the British and the French are not going to be able to carry even the share of the so-called free world defense which they had been trying to carry up to the present time.

Their own difficulties are weakening them. The French position is very considerably weakened by the hostilities in North Africa. The British position has been greatly weakened by the effort which they made in the recent attack on Egypt.

Now, partly that created, partly it disclosed, the vulnerability of the British economic and financial position. But it brought the British to a realisation of the fact that they have got to cut their costs more.

They have been cutting these, and this present task of their Secretary of Defense Sandys reflects what they regard as the imperative necessity of getting a sounder economy by cutting out a good many of their military burdens, and particularly their overseas commitments.

SENATOR RUSSELL: Well, I was not dealing with that in this series of questions. But as they do reduce theirs, the total strength of the free world is decreased, unless we fill whatever position they abandon, militarily and economically, is it not?

SECRETARY DULLES: Broadly speaking, that is so, yes.

Source 17 from Anthony Gorst and Lewis Johnman, The Suez Crisis *(London: Routledge, 1997), pp. 151–152.*

17. Letter from British Prime Minister Eden to Senior Cabinet Ministers, December 28, 1956

We have to try and assess the lessons of Suez. The first is that if we are to play an independent part in the world, even on a more modest scale than we have done heretofore, we must ensure our financial and economic independence. Since we have no raw materials but coal, this means that we must excel in technical knowledge. . . .

In the strategic sphere we have to do some re-thinking about our areas of influence and the military bases on which they must rest. Some of the latter seem of doubtful value in the light of our Suez experience. . . .

The conclusion of all this is surely that we must review our world position and our domestic capacity more searchingly in the light of the Suez experience which has not so much changed our fortunes as revealed realities.

Source 18 from Peter Calvocoressi, Suez: Ten Years After *(London: British Broadcasting Corporation, 1967), pp. 55–58.*

18. President Gamal Abdel Nasser of Egypt Discusses Suez, 1966

CALVOCORESSI [NARRATOR]: Here to end the programme are President Nasser's own general conclusions on the impact of Suez:

NASSER: I was accused of many, many things. But all my object was, was to have complete independence in the Arab countries. Some people said Nasser wants to have an empire for himself. It is not a question of a person. As I said before . . . all that we do and all that we work for now is to have independent countries and united Arab countries; but united Arab countries do not mean an empire for somebody; it means to have a strong Arab nation. . . .

CHILDERS: Do you think the Suez could happen again?

NASSER: Yes, yes.

CHILDERS: Do you really think there could be another British or French attack on Egypt?

NASSER: You know, we insist about our independence, but we feel now that they do not like that. I want to add—the United States, they do not like what we say about our independence. They do not like what we feel about the Arab countries. They do not like our insistence to be completely independent. Of course there is also the supplies of arms to Israel. The United States gave Israel two hundred tanks through Germany; then two hundred tanks through the United States; then aeroplanes, helicopters, through Germany. So Israel now is full of arms, and still the policy of Israel is to force a settlement.

CHILDERS: You think that there might again still be an Israeli attack into Sinai?

NASSER: Yes, of course; because there is an Israeli threat continuously not only against Sinai—against Syria, against Jordan, against Lebanon. . . .

CHILDERS: Looking back then overall, what do you think was the outcome of Suez, the effect of Suez, first on Egypt?

NASSER: We were able after Suez to nationalize all the foreign assets in our country and by that Suez regained back the wealth of the Egyptian people to be used for the interests of the Egyptian people. Then, of course, on the other hand it was clear for the Egyptian people that they could defend their country and secure the independence of their country. So we mobilized ourselves for development and raising the standards of living of the people.

CHILDERS: Now, what do you think the effect of Suez was on the Arab nation, the Arab world as a whole?

NASSER: Well, of course, Suez helped the Arab nation, the Arab world, to regain confidence; and it proved to the Arab nation that Arabs are one nation because the reaction was not here in Egypt alone.

CHILDERS: Looking at international history throughout the world, if you were asked by an historian to say what the meaning of Suez was to world history in this mid-twentieth century, what would you say it was?

NASSER: Well, the meaning of Suez is that there is an end to the methods of the nineteenth century: that it was impossible to use the methods of the nineteenth century in the twentieth century. On the other hand, Suez gave confidence to many countries. I think Suez helped many of the African countries to be sure of themselves and insist about their independence.

Source 19: Courtesy of the Centre for the Study of Cartoons and Caricature, University of Kent, Canterbury.

19. British Cartoon, 1962

QUESTIONS TO CONSIDER

Now that you have analyzed the documents and placed them in their historical context, it is time to focus on some more specific questions. Many conflicting perspectives are represented in the documents, so it will be important to consider the various ways in which the different participants might have answered these questions at the time.

The most basic questions, perhaps, are these: Why did Britain, France, and Israel decide to launch a military invasion of Egypt? Why did they receive so little support for that action in the wider global community?

In a more general vein, what do the events preceding and following the military action in Egypt in October and November 1956 tell us about the north/south axis of global conflict—that is, about the relationship between colonial powers and their colonies and former colonies? How did Nasser present Egypt's relationship with Britain and Israel? How similar was Nasser's analysis to that of Jawaharlal Nehru of India? How did the British explain or justify their actions in light of their history of colonial empire in the Middle East?

In another context, how do these documents inform our understanding of the east/west axis of conflict—the cold war? The Soviet Union actually played a relatively small role in the crisis, as it was preoccupied with troubles in its own Eastern European sphere of influence at the time. Nevertheless, various actors in this drama invoked the Soviets as having an actual or potential role. How did the British present the

Soviet threat? How did the Americans respond? How did the Soviet Union itself portray its relationships with the Arabs and Israelis? Why did the artist who created Source 6 draw in the Soviet foreign minister as he did? At several points, world leaders wondered if the Suez crisis might lead to World War III. From these documents, can you explain why that did *not* happen?

While the various countries involved had different opinions about Egypt at the time, everyone seemed to agree that Gamal Abdel Nasser was the key figure. In his writings and speeches, what sort of image of himself did Nasser seek to promote? How was he seen by other Arabs? by the Israelis? by the British, French, and Americans? From the understanding you have gained of Nasser's role in Egyptian and Middle Eastern politics, how closely did these varying images correspond to reality? Comparing Sources 5 and 6, what similarities and differences do you find in the representations of Nasser? Which is more sympathetic to him, and why?

The other key figure was the British prime minister, Sir Anthony Eden. What was the source of Eden's personal antipathy toward Nasser? Did he allow his personal obsession with the Egyptian leader to influence his political decisions? How truthful was Eden with the British public and with the American government? Why did he undertake this adventure without firm backing from the United States? Are the "lessons" he says he learned from Suez appropriate or sufficient?

Another set of questions has to do with those issues of imperial decline introduced at the beginning of this chapter. Why did the British reintroduce troops into Egypt in 1956, just two years after they had agreed to remove them permanently? More generally, what factors worked against the British in their drive to maintain a dominant role in the Middle East? Were other policies considered that might have been more successful? Does it seem that the Suez crisis was a symptom or a cause of British imperial decline? What does Source 19 tell us about Britain's self-image six years after Suez?

Finally, we might consider that many of these documents refer to his-tory itself as an explanation or justification for the actions of various participants in the drama. How did Nasser relate Egyptian history to his own actions as president? How did the British and French leaders apply the "lessons of history" to their own actions? What were the American and Israeli perspectives on the ways in which the Suez crisis fit into the history of the Middle East and of the world? Are there aspects of the Suez crisis that still help us to understand the Middle Eastern and world situations today?

EPILOGUE

That final question leads us to ponder the outcomes of the Suez crisis. For Nasser and for Egypt, it represented, at least in the short term, a great victory. Nasser was acclaimed as a hero in the Arab and Muslim worlds, and throughout much of Africa and Asia, for having stood up to the arrogance of an old colonial power. With Soviet help, the Aswan Dam was built, symbolizing Egypt's modernization. But Nasser's dreams of pan-Arabism, of uniting the Arabs in a single political system, came to little. The balance of power between Israel and Egypt turned against Egypt in the Six Day War of 1967. The Sinai was once again invaded by Israel, this time to be occupied for over a decade. In 1979, Nasser's successor, Anwar Sadat, made peace with Israel in meetings coordinated by the United States. But some Egyptians, nostalgic for Nasser's forthright nationalism, opposed the Camp David accords, and Sadat was subsequently assassinated. Egypt today walks a fine line: As a "moderate" Arab nation, it is willing to work with the United States, but at the same time it retains Nasser's commitment to the liberation of the Palestinian people.

Great Britain has still not entirely resolved the question that the Suez crisis brought so clearly to its attention: how to maintain a role in global affairs. Four possibilities presented themselves. First, Britain could go it alone. That possibility was never a viable one after World War II, as Suez so clearly indicated. Second, Britain could seek influence in global affairs through association with the United States. The breach in Anglo-American relations caused by the Suez crisis was very brief, and the foundations of the "special relationship" between the two nations still stood. But it could no longer be an association of equals. Even when Ronald Reagan and Margaret Thatcher created a solid personal and political alliance in the 1980s, there was never any question but that American priorities came first. Third, the British could use the Commonwealth as a means of maintaining their power and prestige in former colonies and possessions even after the Union Jack was replaced by the flags of independent states. This policy was pursued with some vigor in the 1960s, but the Commonwealth proved to be more a cultural organization than a body with real political clout. Fourth, the British could seek a closer association with Europe. But as the Germans and the French laid the foundations of what would become the European Union, the British remained aloof. Ambivalence about the European option is still characteristic of Britain today.

None of these options has proved particularly successful. But there are many people in Great Britain who are not all that concerned. Unlike those of Anthony Eden's generation, many British citizens, including some who trace their own families back to Asia, Africa, or the Middle East, take the decline of the British Empire as a simple fact of life.

For the United States, the Suez crisis marked the beginning of its role as the principal power broker in the Middle East. This was just one example of the international commitments that the United States made in the 1950s and 1960s to fill the power vacuum left by the departing Europeans. Vietnam, where the United States succeeded the French as the dominant Western power, is another example. An adequate understanding of the world role of the United States in recent times, including the Persian Gulf War of 1991, as well as the American-led invasion of Iraq in 2003, also requires close attention to the history of Suez.

CHAPTER FIFTEEN

RELIGIOUS FUNDAMENTALISM IN THE

MODERN WORLD: FAITH, IDENTITY,

AND CONTEMPORARY POLITICS

(1970s–PRESENT)

THE PROBLEM

On August 28–31, 2000, over 1,000 of the world's most prominent religious and spiritual leaders representing over ninety nations and more than fifteen faith traditions gathered at the United Nations for the Millennium World Peace Summit of Religious and Spiritual Leaders. The idea for such a conference originated in a conversation between UN Secretary-General Kofi Annan and United States media tycoon Ted Turner, who, along with grants from the Ford, Rockefeller, and Carnegie Foundations, financed the conference. A virtual "who's who" of world religious figures,[1] the summit gathering ultimately approved a set of resolutions, two of which were

To manage and resolve nonviolently the conflicts generated by religious and ethnic differences, and to condemn all violence committed in the name of religion. . . .

To appeal to all religious communities . . . to respect the right of freedom of religion, to seek reconciliation, and to engage in mutual forgiveness and healing.[2]

And yet, even as the Millennium Peace Summit was discussed, planned, and convened, people throughout the world were witnessing not a *waning* of religious-based hostilities but instead a disturbing *increase* in them, leading to even greater levels of violence. In large part responsible for this trend was the almost simultaneous emergence within every major religious tradition of "a militant piety popularly known as 'fundamentalism.'"[3] And while by no

1. The most prominent absentee was Tibet's Dalai Lama, who was not invited for fear of angering the People's Republic of China. The decision caused quite a stir. See *New York Times*, August 7, 2000.

2. For the resolutions, see www.milleniumpeace summit.org.

3. Karen Armstrong, *The Battle for God* (New York: Knopf, 2000), p. ix.

means all Christians, Jews, Muslims, and Hindus who might be called fundamentalists embraced acts of violence and terrorism, the small minority of individuals in those faiths who did so represented what former U.S. secretary of state Warren Christopher described as early as 1996 as "one of the most important security challenges we face in the wake of the Cold War."[4]

How can we explain the almost simultaneous emergence of militant fundamentalism in Christianity, Judaism, Islam, and Hinduism in the latter decades of the twentieth century? What beliefs do militant fundamentalists in each of these faiths embrace? What ideas and beliefs do they have in common? What compels those among them

to advocate violence? Your task in this chapter is to examine and analyze the Background section and the Evidence to answer these questions.

Of all the trends that emerged in the latter part of the twentieth and early years of the twenty-first centuries (the end of the cold war, economic and cultural globalization, concerns over the environment, migration, the potential depletion of natural resources, and so forth), which ones will shape our future and the lives of future generations of the world's citizens? At this point we cannot know for sure. Many scholars and world leaders, however, believe that the rise of militant religious fundamentalism might be one of the world's most important immediate challenges.

BACKGROUND

Throughout history, organized religion has provided its adherents with four important social benefits. To begin with, religion gives people *a sense of identity*, a way to define a group and give it unity. In ancient Greek and Roman times, many cities had their own gods and goddesses, giving those who venerated these deities a sense of unity. Second, religion offers its believers an interpretive framework for understanding the world's past, present, and future. Third, organized religion contains rules and standards that are supposed to guide the thoughts and actions of believers. Finally, through

a temple, mosque, church, or educational institution, religion provides the methods for passing its beliefs, rules, and institutions from one generation to the next. In all, then, organized religions throughout the world have offered believers identity, security, codes and rules, and ways to transmit these things to future generations.[5]

Beginning in the West in the eighteenth century, however, the Enlightenment and the emergence of the modern nation-state challenged religion for the minds and loyalties of men and women. For its part, the Enlightenment offered the West an alternative way to understand the world, nature, and history, a way based on rational thought, the scientific method, and an emphasis on

4. For Christopher's comments, see Mark Juergensmeyer, *Terror in the Mind of God: The Global Rise of Religious Violence* (Berkeley: University of California Press, 2000), p. 6.

5. For the four social functions served by religion, see Jonathan Fox, *Ethnoreligious Conflict in the Late Twentieth Century* (Lanham, Md.: Lexington Books, 2002), p. 29.

Chapter 15

Religious

Fundamentalism

in the Modern

World: Faith,

Identity, and

Contemporary

Politics

(1970s–Present)

the individual's power to question, analyze, experiment, and invent.

As for the nation-state, its advocates hoped that loyalty to the state would supplant devotion to religion, ethnic group, race, class, or locality. In order to bring this about, nationalists consciously created what might be called a *civil religion,* complete with national holidays ("holy days"), heroes (saints), monuments, national anthems, commemorative coins and stamps, and rituals. As M. T. d'Azeglio commented on the founding of the Italian nation, "We have made Italy: *now* we must make *Italians."*[6]

Taken together, in the West the Enlightenment and modern nationalism sought to take upon themselves the functions traditionally performed by religion. Nationalists attempted to shift people's identity and loyalty from the church to the state and to establish institutions of public education to replace church schools. At the same time, state laws were intended to take precedence over religious rules and standards. And for its part, the Enlightenment emphasized rational thought and the discovery of scientific "laws" as preferable to divine revelations when it came to understanding and explaining natural phenomena as well as the behavior of living things. Great scientific discoveries and technological inventions and improvements seemed to tip the balance in favor of modern thinking and institutions, and religion itself appeared to retreat from

the public sphere into private enclaves of churches and homes. Indeed, many people took it for granted that *secularism* (the emphasis of the temporal over the spiritual) was a powerful and irreversible trend and that religion itself would play a diminishing role in the lives of Western people.[7]

Nineteenth-century imperialism brought these ideas to the non-West, where they were embraced by those who sought to construct modern nation-states in the non-West as well as to bring modern technology and institutions to their lands. Great Britain was especially active in bringing Western technology, institutions, and thought to its colonies, which in the late nineteenth century accounted for approximately 20 percent of the world's total population. In their own eyes, as well as in the eyes of the Westernized elites in Britain's possessions, the British were bringing gifts of inestimable value to large portions of the Middle East, East Asia, and Africa: railroads and telegraphs, medical improvements, modern bureaucracies, educational institutions, and Christianity, to name but a few. In the eyes of European imperialists, it was the "white man's burden" to bring modern "civilization" and thought to peoples who had lived so long in darkness. Native religions such as Islam and Hinduism

6. On the "invention" of civil religion, see Eric Hobsbawm and Terence Ranger, eds., *The Invention of Tradition* (Cambridge: Cambridge University Press, 1983), pp. 1, 263–267. For d'Azeglio, see *ibid.,* p. 267 (*italics ours*).

7. Marshall Berman, *All That Is Solid Melts into Air: The Experience of Modernity* (New York: Simon and Schuster, 1982), pp. 16–30; Armstrong, *The Battle for God,* p. x. The word *secular* is from the Latin *saeculum,* which means "worldly." Originally *secularization* referred to the process of leaving a religious cloister or monastery. See Jose Casanova, *Public Religions in the Modern World* (Chicago: University of Chicago Press, 1994), p. 13.

were used to prop up and give legitimacy to the new nation-states and their Westernized or dependent rulers.

And yet, in spite of the predictions of many that over time modern thought and institutions would *replace* religions and that, like Karl Marx's state, religions ultimately would wither away, neither phenomenon actually occurred. Instead, even in the West an unresolved tension between modern and traditional religious thought remained and occasionally came to the surface. In the United States in the early twentieth century, a group of conservative theologians published a series of essays that collectively became known as *The Fundamentals.* Approximately 3 million copies of the twelve volumes were distributed. *The Fundamentals* defended biblical *inerrancy* (that everything in the Christian Bible was factually correct) and attacked what the essays called the evils of secularism and modern thought. Much of the criticism focused on Charles Darwin's theory of evolution, leading directly to the 1925 Scopes Trial in Dayton, Tennessee. From this series of essays the term *fundamentalist* was born, a term that ultimately was used to identify those of all religious faiths who defended traditionalism and opposed modern thought, institutions, and imperialism.[8]

In spite of the fact that "fundamentalist" movements had surfaced sporadically in both the West and the non-West in the years following World War II, few people paid much attention to them until the 1990s, when a wave of violence threatened the authority and stability of many societies and governments. In what seems to have been nearly helpless horror, the world witnessed the destruction of a mosque in Ayodhya, India; almost two hundred anti-Christian attacks in India; the bombing of a Jerusalem shopping mall; the destruction of the federal building in Oklahoma City in the United States; attacks on U.S. Embassies in Africa; and ultimately the destruction of the World Trade Center in New York on September 11, 2001. Many people came to agree with British scholar, writer, and journalist Malise Ruthven when he commented that militant religion seemed to have replaced Marxism-Leninism, National Socialism, and other systems as "the principal challenge to a world order based on the hegemonic power of the liberal capitalist West."[9]

Roused by what they generally referred to as religious-based "terrorism,"[10] scholars, journalists, and political leaders began to look for the roots of what appeared to be almost simultaneous outbreaks of militant fundamentalism. In the United States, many credited the movement of Christian fundamentalism from the rural areas

---

8. On *The Fundamentals*, see Casanova, *Public Religions*, pp. 142–144; John L. Esposito et al., *World Religions Today* (New York: Oxford University Press, 2002), p. 42. On Scopes, science, and religion, see Edward Larson, *Summer of the Gods: The Scopes Trial and America's Continuing Debate over Science and Religion* (New York: Basic Books, 1997). The term *fundamentalist* has no corresponding word in either Arabic or Hebrew. Arabs often refer to fundamentalists as *usuli* (roots), whereas Jews use the term *yamina dati* (the "religious right").

9. Malise Ruthven, *Fundamentalism: The Search for Meaning* (Oxford: Oxford University Press, 2004), p. 5.

10. **terrorism:** from the Latin word *terrere* ("to cause to tremble"). The word was first used in 1795, during the French Revolution.

Chapter 15
Religious
Fundamentalism
in the Modern
World: Faith,
Identity, and
Contemporary
Politics
(1970s–Present)

and small towns to the mushrooming suburbs and midsized cities to Pat Robertson and Jerry Falwell. Although neither man advocated violence, both Robertson and Falwell maintained that the United States had lost its way in the thickets of secularism and moral relativism, supported what they insisted were the Christian foundations of the early nation, urged their followers to make their strength felt in the political arena, and assaulted what they considered to be the sins of abortion, pornography, the elimination of prayer in the public schools, and the antireligious mainstream media. Through the Christian Broadcasting Network that Robertson founded in 1960 and the Moral Majority of the Rev. Jerry Falwall (1979–1989), both wielded considerable influence.

To the right of Robertson and Falwell, however, was a very small number of Christian zealots who *did* advocate violence. Antiabortion leader Randall Terry, the founder of Operation Rescue, was reputed to call for attacks on abortion clinics, and he once explained, "I want you to let a wave of hatred work over you. Yes, hatred is good. . . . We have a biblical duty, we are called by God, to conquer this country." In addition to Terry, author William Pierce, who once warned of a "Jewish takeover of the Christian churches," wrote *The Turner Diaries* (1978), in which a person destroyed a federal building with a truckload of ammonium nitrate fertilizer. It was known that Oklahoma City bomber Timothy McVeigh was influenced by the book. Running the gamut from peace loving to violent,

American fundamentalism played an increasing role in the nation's social and political debates.[11]

The roots of Islamic fundamentalism can be found in the Middle East in the years following World War I. After that conflict and the final collapse of the tottering Ottoman Empire, Western nations had carved the Middle East into largely artificial nation-states and then installed pro-Western rulers or dynasties to govern them. Political parties for the most part were constructed on Western models, and Islam itself was relegated to supporting Western economic and political interests. Yet beneath the surface, Muslims spoke of a golden age in which Arab caliphs had ruled the Muslim world from Iraq to Spain and during which Islamic cultural achievements far exceeded those of the West. Westerners in the twentieth century, it was believed, were the new crusaders who exploited Muslim lands for their rich natural resources.

Many Muslims were particularly shamed by the creation of Israel and its support by the new crusaders. But they were even more outraged by anticolonial revolutionists like Gamal Abdel Nasser of Egypt who, instead of leading Muslims back to a supposed "golden age," embraced Western technology and political institutions. Underground networks of militant Islamic

11. On Robertson, see www.PatRobertson.com. On Falwell, see Casanova, *Public Religions*, pp. 147, 153; Robert William Fogel, *The Fourth Great Awakening and the Future of Egalitarianism* (Chicago: University of Chicago Press, 2000), pp. 25–26. On Terry, see Benjamin R. Barber, *Jihad vs. McWorld* (New York: Random House, 1995), p. 213; www.randallterry.com. On Pierce, see Juergensmeyer, *Terror in the Mind of God*, pp. 31, 219.

cells called for a *jihad* (struggle) against both imperialism and economic and cultural globalization as well as against modern leaders such as Nasser, Shah Reza Pahlavi of Iran, Feisel of Iraq, the pro-Russian government in Afghanistan, and others.

The intellectual father of militant Islamic fundamentalism was Sayyid Qutb (1906–1966). An Egyptian, Qutb believed in a universal law of confrontation between the forces of Islam and those of all other systems, a struggle between belief and unbelief. Especially hated were the Western imports of secularism, capitalism, nationalism, and democracy, together with Middle East rulers like Nasser who "have themselves forfeited the right to be called 'Muslims' as they have joined the ranks of the enemy by adopting his laws and way of life." As for most Muslims, Qutb preached that they unwittingly had renounced their own faith and had slipped into a state of ignorance (*jahiliyya*). As Qutb became increasingly critical of Nasser (whom he once referred to as "secular and soul-less"), the Egyptian ruler finally tired of Sayyid Qutb's increasingly bellicose writings and had him executed in 1966. Even so, Sayyid Qutb's ideas lived on, through younger converts such as Osama bin Laden and others. And while only a minuscule fraction of Muslims were drawn to militant Muslim fundamentalism and violence, those who joined such movements in Afghanistan, Iran, Iraq, Saudi Arabia, Syria, the Palestinian territories seized by Israel in the 1967 war, Jordan, and elsewhere threatened to destabilize the Middle East and drag both the non-West and the West into successive levels of mass violence.[12]

Although some scholars trace the roots of Jewish fundamentalism to the origins of the Zionist movement in the late nineteenth century, a majority of the students of Israeli history assert that modern Zionism (or Jewish fundamentalism) was born during the 1967 six-day war between Israel and the surrounding Arab states. In that conflict, Israeli forces seized the Golan Heights, the West Bank (of the Jordan River), the Gaza Strip, and the Sinai Peninsula.[13] At that time, a small group of religious zealots (developed and nurtured throughout most of the twentieth century by Palestine's chief rabbi, Abraham Yitzhak Kook (d. 1935), and his son rabbi Tzvi Yehuda Kook (d. 1981), called for a return to traditional Judaism and a new form of *religious* Zionism. To these devout individuals, the Jews were still the chosen, covenanted people to whom God had promised (through Abraham) "the land where you are now an alien, all the land of Canaan, for perpetual holding.'"[14]

To this group of Jewish fundamentalists, the coming of the promised Messiah was imminent. In order for the Messiah to appear, however, Jews must return to the land promised to them

12. On Sayyid Qutb, see Youssef M. Choueiri, *Islamic Fundamentalism*, rev. ed. (London: Pinter, 1997), pp. 91–92; Bruce Lincoln, *Holy Terrors: Thinking About Religion After September 11* (Chicago: University of Chicago Press, 2003), p. 3.

13. The Sinai Peninsula was returned to Egypt in 1982.

14. Genesis 17:8, in Michael Coogan, ed., *The New Oxford Annotated Bible*, 3rd ed. (Oxford: Oxford University Press, 2001), p. 34.

Chapter 15

Religious

Fundamentalism

in the Modern

World: Faith,

Identity, and

Contemporary

Politics

(1970s–Present)

by God (*aliya,* the "in-gathering"), for, in their view the Jewish people and the land of Israel were one and indivisible. Furthermore, they believed that the Jews' exile had been not only a physical dispersal but a *spiritual* exile as well. Those Jews who had embraced modern secular thought and Western lifestyles must discard those things and return to the true way. Only then could the golden age of kings Solomon and David be restored.

Few people took this movement seriously—until it began to grow. In part responsible for this growth was a reaction against secularism and modernity. If Israel was not a *Jewish* state, an increasing number of people wondered, then what was it? Equally important, many scholars believe, was the growing fear among Israeli citizens that, in order to resolve the Muslim-Jewish conflict, Israel would have to make concessions that might well endanger the nation's security.

Most responsible for the movement's growth, however, was the establishment in 1974 of *Gush Emunim,* a group of Jewish settlers who began occupying the lands seized by Israel in the 1967 war. These lands, the pressure group and settlement organization insisted, had been promised to the Jews by God. Those Jews who had negotiated with Arabs over these lands were "traitors" to Judaism and the Jewish people. Bargaining with Muslims was unthinkable, *Gush Emunim* maintained, and the only possible resolution was for Jews to occupy the disputed lands—and hold them. By the late 1980s there were approximately 100,000 Israelis living in settlements in the West Bank, and those who were

reported to be Jewish fundamentalists constituted between 20 and 25 percent of Israel's total population, a potentially powerful political group.[15]

It is not difficult to see how such thoughts, words, and actions could lead to violence. While one must be reminded that most Jewish fundamentalists, like fundamentalists of other faiths, opposed violence, the heated atmosphere, to say nothing of Arab violence and terrorist acts against Israelis, made violence not only possible but very nearly inevitable. In February 1994, during the celebration of the Muslim holy days of Ramadan, Baruch Goldstein, an Israeli citizen who had been born in the United States, entered a mosque in Hebron and killed twenty-nine Muslim worshipers before turning the gun on himself. According to Middle East scholar David Hirst, not a few rabbis praised Goldstein's act, and polls showed a disturbingly high percentage of Israelis who approved of the killings. Then in November 1995, an Israeli extremist assassinated Prime Minister Yitzhak Rabin for having negotiated a United States–brokered peace with the Palestinian Liberation Organization (PLO). Together with Muslim violence against Israelis, Jewish extremists, almost surely fueled by Jewish fundamentalism, threatened to

15. On *Gush Emunim,* see Israel Shahak and Norton Mezvinski, *Jewish Fundamentalism in Israel,* 2nd ed. (London: Pluto Press, 2004): David Newman, ed., *The Impact of Gush Emunim: Politics and Settlement in the West Bank* (London: Croom Helm, 1985); Niels C. Nielsen, Jr., *Fundamentalism; Mythos; and World Religions* (Albany: State University of New York Press, 1993), pp. 70–82; David Hirst, *The Gun and the Olive Branch: The Roots of Violence in the Middle East* (London: Faber and Faber, 1984), especially pp. 377–384.

throw the entire Middle East into terrorism and mass violence.[16]

Perhaps in no other country is the tension between traditional and modern as dramatic as it is in India. The computer and communications revolutions allowed Western corporate giants such as General Electric, Microsoft, IBM, Dell, Hewlett-Packard, and Texas Instruments to establish large regional offices and manufacturing facilities in cities such as Bangalore, thereby "outsourcing" jobs from the West to India, where salaries and labor costs were lower. Indeed, several American publishing companies actually produce many of their books, including English dictionaries, in India. In addition, modern communications allowed Western companies to employ Indians to take telephone orders and offer assistance to customers. By 2004, there were roughly 245,000 Indians answering telephone inquiries from all over the world. Not surprisingly, Indian men and women employed in these new positions generally were fluent in English and began to adopt Western dress, diet (including pizza, a particular favorite), music, customs, and so forth. Indeed, a growing number of Indians, mostly young adults, were becoming almost indistinguishable from their counterparts in the United States, Western Europe, and the larger cities of Latin America, the Middle East, and East Asia.[17]

As with other regions where modernization had taken place, reaction was swift and strong. Hindu resistance to rule by outsiders (first by Moghuls and then by the British) had existed for centuries, until India's independence in 1947. Immediately following independence, violence against Muslims had taken hundreds of thousands of Hindu and Muslim lives, including that of Mohandas Gandhi, who had hoped for a secular state in which all religious traditions could live peacefully but instead was shot to death by a Hindu extremist.

To Hindu fundamentalists, the adoption, particularly by young people, of the communications revolution, economic globalization, and Western culture (especially Christianity, which made up 7.5 percent of India's population) was merely another form of imperialism and therefore must be vigorously resisted. Employing a mixture of Indian anti-imperialism with calls for a revival of traditional Hindu culture (*Hindutva*, or "Hindu-ness") and the establishment of India as a Hindu state (*Hindu rashtra*), this newer form of Hindu fundamentalism began to attract followers, especially in the cities. To increase sympathizers and enthusiasm, the *Rashtriya Srayamsevak Sangh* (RSS, the National Union of Volunteers) was established in 1925, with its political expression the *Bhavatiya Janata Party* (BJP). In 1984 the BJP won only 2 seats in the Indian parliament. By 1996 it had 186 seats and two years later won enough seats to form a government.[18]

---

16. For Hirst's claims, see David Hirst, "Pursuing the Millennium: Jewish Fundamentalism in Israel," *The Nation,* February 16, 2004.

17. For India's participation in economic and cultural globalization, see Thomas L. Friedman, *The World Is Flat: A Brief History of the Twenty-First Century* (New York: Farrar, Straus and Giroux, 2005), especially pp. 3–32, 106–107.

18. Sumit Sarkar, *Beyond Nationalist Frames: Postmodernism, Hindu Fundamentalism, History* (Bloomington: Indiana University Press, 2002); Esposito, *World Religions Today,* pp. 274–278.

Chapter 15

Religious

Fundamentalism

in the Modern

World: Faith,

Identity, and

Contemporary

Politics

(1970s–Present)

The principal intellectual father of modern-day Hindu fundamentalism was Madhav Sadashiv Golwalkar (1906–1973), who headed the RSS for thirty-three years. Golwalkar (whose nickname was "Guruji," or "the Guru") preached a mixture of aggressive Hindu nationalism and a return to traditional Hindu religion and Indian culture. He condemned the "educated class" who (in his words) "became in truth the slaves of the English" and charged these apostates with "corroding our national life." Hindu "racial purity" was critically important to Golwalkar, and Hindus should not share power with Muslims, Christians, or any other false teachers. Those of other faiths who chose to remain in India must subordinate themselves to traditional Hindu culture.[19]

Not surprisingly, the increasingly strident rhetoric led to outbreaks of violence. In December 1992 thousands of militant Hindu fundamentalists converged on Asyodhya (which many Hindus believe is the site of the birth-place of Rama, the human incarnation of the god Vishnu) and destroyed a mosque that had been constructed on the site in 1528. In December 1998 some Christian churches were burned, adding to the 184 reports of anti-Christian violence in 1998–1999, the most reported of which was the killing of Australian missionary Graham Staines and his two sons (ages 11 and 6) by a mob on January 23, 1999.[20]

Having surveyed the origins, worldviews, ideologies, and programs of Christian, Islamic, Jewish, and Hindu religious fundamentalism, we now can see that, while they are different from one another in certain ways, in other ways they bear some interesting and even remarkable similarities. As you examine and analyze the Evidence in this chapter, you will be able to deepen your understanding of those differences and similarities as well as discover others. Be sure to make lists of the differences and similarities as you go along.

19. On Golwalkar, see www.dalitstan.org/journal/recthist/rastra/gov.

20. Asian Pacific Human Rights Network, "The Staines Killings," http://www.hrdc.net/sahrdc, and Sarkar, *Beyond Nationalist Frames,* pp. 215–234.

THE METHOD

In previous chapters of this book, you have learned to use a wide variety of historical evidence to "solve" several problems. And yet, whether that evidence is statistics, cartoons, newspaper advertisements, art and music, letters and diaries, government documents, photographs, journalists' and eyewitnesses' accounts, and so forth, you also have learned some basic rules on how to examine and analyze primary sources:

1. Approach all historical evidence with skepticism. Who created that piece of evidence? What biases might that person or persons have

had? Remember that *all evidence* contains biases, even when it *appears* to be objective.

2. Was the person or persons who created the evidence in a good position to know about or observe what he/she/they said? If there is another piece of evidence that directly contradicts the piece you are examining, which is closer to the truth? Can you find any *other* pieces of evidence that corroborate one or the other piece of evidence?

3. Remember that you *may not* "prove" a hypothesis (statement of opinion that answers a question) with another hypothesis. Sometimes a person may disguise a statement of opinion to make it *appear* to be a factual piece of evidence. For example, what is wrong with this historical process? Hypothesis: the United States should withdraw all its troops from foreign soil. "Evidence": the United States is an imperialist power. Can you see why you may not "prove" a hypothesis by using another hypothesis?

4. Do not add or delete parts of a piece of evidence because it does not "prove" your hypothesis. The worst accusation that can be leveled at a historian is that he/she saw some evidence that was contrary to his/her own hypothesis and so ignored it.

These rules are especially important when historians deal with especially sensitive subjects, such as religion. Evidence must be approached dispassionately and sensitively, for, as you can see from this chapter, many people's

basic world-views and ethical codes come directly from their religious faith traditions.

Finally, keep in mind that twentieth-century religious fundamentalists of all faith traditions are not a monolithic group, but instead can be divided into four general categories:

1. Those who practice religious fundamentalism but who maintain a separation between their religion and their nonreligious activities (work, socialization, etc.)

2. Those who practice religious fundamentalism and attempt to adapt their work and lifestyles to their religious teachings, including participating peacefully in society and politics (voting, etc.), and who advocate narrowing or even closing the gap between church and state

3. Those who practice religious fundamentalism, attempt to adapt their lifestyles, participate in the public arena, advocate closing the gap between church and state, and *sympathize with* (although they do not participate in) acts of violence and terrorism

4. Those religious fundamentalists who commit acts of violence and terrorism to further their beliefs

As you read the Background section and Evidence in this chapter, keep in mind the central questions you must answer:

1. How can the almost simultaneous emergence of militant religious fundamentalism in Christianity,

Chapter 15
Religious
Fundamentalism
in the Modern
World: Faith,
Identity, and
Contemporary
Politics
(1970s–Present)

Islam, Judaism, and Hinduism be explained?

2. What beliefs and ideas do fundamentalists in each of these faith traditions embrace?

3. What ideas and beliefs do fundamentalists in the various faith traditions have in common?

4. What compels those among them to advocate violence?

Take detailed notes or construct a chart, returning first to the Background section and then going ahead to the Evidence.

THE EVIDENCE

CHRISTIANITY

Source 1 from Pat Robertson, Bring it On: Tough Questions. Candid Answers *(Nashville: W Publishing Group, 2003), pp. 262–264.*

1. Pat Robertson, "God's Protection Lifted from America," 2003

The first English settlers to America landed on April 26, 1607, near the mouth of the Chesapeake Bay at what is now known as Cape Henry. Three days later, on April 29, 1607, the travel-weary settlers carried ashore a rough-hewn, seven-foot cross they had brought along with them across the Atlantic. They plunged that cross into the sandy shore and claimed the land for the Lord. Almost without exception, the founders of America were devout Christian men and women. Many of them felt they were planting a "new Israel," a nation that would exalt the name of the Lord. Similarly, the Massachusetts colony was settled as a city set on a hill, a bright-shining witness of God to the nations.

All of our nation's early institutions presupposed the existence of God. In early elections, pastors instructed their congregations concerning the political issues of the day and urged the people to vote according to biblical principles and mandates. People had a consensus concerning right and wrong, based on the Bible. In some states in the middle or late 1800s, citizens could not vote unless they were members of a Christian church.

All that changed, however, after World War I, when an even more deadly assault was launched against our nation by left-wing, radical groups who no longer wanted the United States to be one nation under God. By the 1920s, liberals had taken the mainline Protestant denominations and seminaries.

By 1930, humanism and cultural relativism were beginning their assault on the Christian values in our universities and our public schools. During the 1920s and 1930s, Marxist Communism began to take hold among a number of intellectuals and the cultural elite in academia, in the media, and in the world of art and entertainment. By World War II, our joint war effort with Russia against Nazi Germany brought a number of procommunists into the sphere of government.

After World War II, with most Americans preoccupied with rebuilding their personal lives, the assault on Christianity took on a new intensity. The strategy of the ACLU and the law school liberals was to accomplish in the courts what could never happen in the popular democratic processes. In 1948, the Supreme Court defied the Constitution and ruled that its decisions were "the supreme law of the land." In 1962, prayer was ruled out of schools. In 1963, Bible reading was struck down. In 1973, the Supreme Court made up a law to strike down all state laws opposed to abortion.

In 1972 and 1973, the radical feminists and the homosexuals assaulted state laws forbidding divorce except for adultery and cruelty. The snowball gained greater momentum as values clarification, amoral sex education, and situational ethics hit classrooms that had been stripped of their religious anchors.

Whether by accident [or] satanic design, the 1960s and 1970s saw our faltering nation sucked into a horrible war, which it lost, a president and two prominent leaders assassinated, an elected leader resigned to avoid impeachment, many of our youth in rebellion, and, under the leadership of charlatans like Timothy Leary, the drug culture destroying the lives of millions of young people.

By 2001, the Supreme Court had ruled God and His commandments out of our schools. Across the land, symbols of our Christian heritage were taken down for fear of lawsuits. Divorce is rampant, teenage pregnancy is rampant, there have been an estimated forty million abortions, and pornography seems pervasive. The American people profess to a belief in the fundamental teachings of Christianity, but in their lives and practice deny them.

The Bible says that without a revelation of God the people are unrestrained and run amuck. Certainly, this describes American society over the past fifty years. As the moral structure of our nation has been dismantled, we see increasingly blatant violations of common sense, right and wrong, and values based on the moral law of God. In the government, the church, the workplace, schools, and in our homes, every person is left to do what is right or wrong in his or her own eyes. Coupled with ever more shocking corruption within the U.S., our nation exported our immorality through business, music, movies, and literature to other countries around the world.

It is logical to assume that any nation that has willingly slaughtered more than forty million innocent unborn babies, as we have done in the United States, would be subject to the wrath of God. Indeed, any nation that has embraced sodomy, adultery, fornication, and all manner of debauchery, as we in America have done should live in terror not from Islamic fanatics, but terror at what

Chapter 15

Religious

Fundamentalism

in the Modern

World: Faith,

Identity, and

Contemporary

Politics

(1970s–Present)

Almighty God will do when His patience is exhausted. At minimum, God is no longer bound to protect such a nation from its enemies. What right have we in America to expect God's blessing, much less to demand it?

Source 2 from New York Times, *September 15, 2001.*

2. After the Attacks:
Finding Fault

Did God allow the terrorist attacks?

The Rev. Jerry Falwell and Pat Robertson set off a minor explosion of their own when they asserted on television on Thursday that an angry God had allowed the terrorists to succeed in their deadly mission because the United States had become a nation of abortion, homosexuality, secular schools and courts, and the American Civil Liberties Union.

Liberal groups and commentators denounced their remarks yesterday, as did President Bush, who has long enjoyed the political support of the two evangelists.

"The president believes that terrorists are responsible for these acts," said a White House spokesman, Ken Lisaius. "He does not share those views, and believes that those remarks are inappropriate."

Yet Mr. Falwell's and Mr. Robertson's remarks were based in theology familiar and adopted by many conservative evangelical Christians, who believe the Bible teaches that God withdraws protection from nations that violate his will.

Several conservative theologians and evangelists said in interviews yesterday that they agreed with the basic notion but rejected the idea that mere humans can ever know which particular sins lead to which particular tragedies.

The Rev. R. Albert Mohler Jr., president of the Southern Baptist Theological Seminary in Louisville, Ky., and a friend of Mr. Falwell's, said, "There is no doubt that America has accommodated itself to so many sins that we should always fear God's judgment and expect that in due time that judgment will come. But we ought to be very careful about pointing to any circumstance or any specific tragedy and say that this thing has happened because this is God's direct punishment."

Mr. Falwell, chancellor of Liberty University in Lynchburg, Va., and senior pastor of Thomas Road Baptist Church there, was in Washington yesterday in a service at the National Cathedral at Mr. Bush's invitation, a spokesman for Mr. Falwell said.

Mr. Falwell released a statement yesterday on the controversy, saying, "Despite in the impression some may have from the news reports today, I hold no one other than the terrorists and the people and nations who have enabled and harbored them responsible for Tuesday's attacks on this nation."

"I sincerely regret that comments I made during a long theological discussion on a Christian television program yesterday were taken out of context and reported and that my thoughts—reduced to sound bites—have detracted from the spirit of this day of mourning."

What Mr. Falwell said on Thursday on "The 700 Club," while chatting with the program's host, Mr. Robertson, was this:

"What we saw on Tuesday, as terrible as it is, could be miniscule if, in fact, God continues to lift the curtain and allow the enemies of America to give us probably what we deserve."

Mr. Robertson responded, "Jerry, that's my feeling. I think we've just seen the antechamber to terror. We haven't even begun to see what they can do to the major population."

A few moments later Mr. Falwell said, "The abortionists have got to bear some burden for this because God will not be mocked. And when we destroy 40 million little innocent babies, we make God mad. I really believe that the pagans, and the abortionists, and the feminists, and the gays and the lesbians who are actively trying to make that an alternative lifestyle, the A.C.L.U., People for the American Way, all of them who have tried to secularize America, I point the finger in their face and say, 'You helped this happen.'"

To which Mr. Robertson said, "Well, I totally concur, and the problem is that we have adopted that agenda at the highest levels of our government."

Mr. Robertson also issued a press release on Thursday saying that in a country rampant with materialism, Internet pornography and lack of prayer, "God almighty is lifting his protection from us."

James Robison, a well-known evangelist in Euless, Tex., and host of the Christian television program "Life Today," concurred, but emphasized a different catalog of what he saw as sins: arrogance in relationships with Third World and foreign countries, plundering other countries for resources while supporting their despots and indifference to others' poverty and pain.

"Any time you get away from God, you do become vulnerable," Mr. Robison said. "If it is a parent who stays out all night, the children become vulnerable and are left to fend for themselves. Bad judgment always leaves the door open to perpetrators of pain."

Mr. Robison is one pastor called on for advice and prayer by the president. Mr. Robison said that in August, he spent morning praying with Mr. Bush at the president's Texas ranch, and counseled that "love can break the conspiracy of terrorism."

Among evangelicals, the terrorist attacks have unleashed renewed calls for repentance, prayer and spiritual revival. A nationwide prayer vigil planned for Saturday is to be broadcast by satellite into 1,500 churches. Next week will bring newspaper advertisements by evangelical groups calling for the nation to unite in prayer.

Chapter 15
Religious
Fundamentalism
in the Modern
World: Faith,
Identity, and
Contemporary
Politics
(1970s–Present)

Source 3 from Randall Terry interview, www.forerunner.com/forerunner/XO471_Randall_Terry_Interv.html.

3. Interview with Randall Terry, founder of Operation Rescue,[21] September 1988

Q: What is the philosophy behind Operation Rescue?

TERRY: The foundation of Operation Rescue is a call to people and the Church to repent. The Church has sinned before God by allowing children to be ripped apart and mothers to be exploited. We have sat idly by and have done virtually nothing.

Q: Why are those being arrested in Atlanta withholding their names? Why are they identifying themselves as "Baby John Doe" or "Baby Jane Doe"?

TERRY: We are withholding our names because the unborn children we represent have no names and no voice. We are identifying with them. We are making a statement to the system by identifying with their suffering. We want their plight to be known to the American people.

Q: Were there any rescues held prior to the conception of Operation Rescue in 1986?

TERRY: There were no large rescues before that. I realized that we were losing the war. The pro-life movement is losing. Unless the Church repents and rises up to do rescues, which is the fruit of repentance, we will never win.

Q: What motivated you to start Operation Rescue?

TERRY: In the spring and summer of 1986, during prayer and introspection, I began looking at American history and realized that we were losing the war. I began to get a sense of what God wanted to do.

Q: How long have you been involved in pro-life activism?

TERRY: About four and a half years. The Lord got a hold of my heart and showed me that I had a responsibility to do something to protect the mothers and children from the holocaust. I wasn't influenced by any books or films. But at a prayer meeting God spoke to me, and all I knew was that I was supposed to do something. . . .

Q: How do all the arrests affect your family?

TERRY: I look at it as a time of sacrifice. I have enemies and lawsuits and I try to keep my family out of it. I would rather not say anymore.

Q: How do you justify violating the law in your fight against abortion?

TERRY: Easily. When God's law and man's law conflict, Scripture clearly teaches that man is not to obey that law. Some examples are when the three Hebrew children were thrown into the fire, when the apostles were jailed for preaching

---

21. **Operation Rescue:** a group that opposed abortion and demonstrated outside of offices of physicians that performed abortions. Some believe Operation Rescue encouraged attacks on these doctors.

the Gospel, and when the stone was rolled away from the Lord's tomb. That was in defiance of a manmade law. God never gave the government a blank check to do what it wants to do. It is a heresy to teach Christians to obey a law which runs counter to His law.

ISLAM

Source 4 from Sayed Kotb (Sayyid Qutb), Social Justice in Islam, *trans. John B. Hardie (Washington, D.C.: American Council of Learned Societies, 1953), pp. 2, 7–8, 13–15; originally published in Arabic in Cairo, 1945.*

4. Sayyid Qutb, "Religion and Society in . . . Islam"

At this moment we profess Islam as a state religion; we claim in all sincerity to be true Muslims—if indeed we do not claim to be the guardians and missionaries of Islam. Yet we have divorced our faith from our practical life, condemning it to remain in ideal isolation, with no jurisdiction over life, no connection with its affairs, and no remedy for its problems. For, as the popular saying goes, "Religion concerns only a man and his God." But as for ordinary relationships, the bonds of society and the problems of life, political or economic theory—religion has nothing to do with these things, nor they with it; such is the view of those who are not actively hostile to religion. As for the others, their reaction is: Make no mention of religion here; it is nothing but an opiate employed by plutocrats and despots to drug the working classes and to paralyze the unfortunate masses.

How have we arrived at this strange view of the nature and the history of Islam? We have imported it, as we import everything, from across the deserts and beyond the seas. For certainly the fable of a divorce between faith and life did not grow up in the Muslim East, nor does Islam know of it; and the myth that religion is but a drug to the senses was not born of this faith at any time, nor does the nature of the faith even sanction it. We merely repeat these things parrot-wise, and accept them at second-hand like monkeys; we never think of looking for their origin and their sources, nor of learning their beginning or their results. Let us see first, then, whence and how these strange opinions came about. . . .

. . . The conditions of our history, and the nature and circumstances of Islam have nothing in common with any of these things. Islam grew up in an independent country owing allegiance to no empire and to no king, in a form of society never again achieved. It had to embody this society in itself, had to order, encourage, and promote it. It had to order and regulate this society, adopting from the beginning its principles and its spirit along with its methods of life and work. It had to join together the world and the faith by its exhortations and laws. So Islam chose to unite earth and Heaven in one spiritual organization, and one which recognized no difference between worldly zeal and religious coercion.

[475]

Chapter 15

Religious

Fundamentalism

in the Modern

World: Faith,

Identity, and

Contemporary

Politics

(1970s–Present)

Essentially Islam never infringes that unity even when its outward forms and customs change.

Such was the birth of Islam and such its task; so it was not liable to be isolated in human idealism far removed from practical worldly life; nor was it compelled to narrow the circle of its action out of fear for an Empire or a monarch. For the center of its being and the field of its action is human life in its entirety, spiritual and material, religious and worldly. Such a religion cannot continue to exist in isolation from society, nor can its adherents be true Muslims unless they practice their faith in their social, legal and economic relationships. And a society cannot be Islamic if it expels the civil and religious laws of Islam from its codes and customs, so that nothing of Islam is left except rites and ceremonials. . . .

We have, then, not a single reason to make any separation between Islam and society, either from the point of view of the essential nature of Islam, or from that of its historical course; such reasons as there are attach only to European Christianity. And yet the world has grown away from religion; to it the world has left only the education of the conscience and the perfecting of piety, while to the temporal and secular laws has been committed the ordering of society and the organizing of human life. . . .

The conclusion from this is that we should not put away the social aspect of our faith on the shelf; we should not go to French legislation to derive our laws, or to Communist ideals to derive our social order, without first examining what can be supplied from our Islamic legislation which was the foundation of our first form of society. But there is a wide ignorance of the nature of our faith; there is a spiritual and intellectual laziness which is opposed to a return to our former resources; there is a ridiculous servility to the European fashion of divorcing religion from life—a separation necessitated by the nature of their religion, but not by the nature of Islam. For with them there still exists that gulf between religion on the one hand and learning and the State on the other, the product of historical reasons which have no parallel in the history of Islam.

Source 5 from Frank Logevall, Terrorism and 9/11: A Reader *(Boston: Houghton Mifflin, 2002), pp. 61, 63–65, 67.*

5. *Frontline* interview with Osama bin Laden, May 1998

Q: . . . What is the meaning of your call for Muslims to take arms against America in particular, and what is the message that you wish to send to the West in general?

A: The call to wage war against America was made because America has spearheaded the crusade against the Islamic nation, sending tens of thousands of its troops to the land of the two Holy Mosques over and above its meddling in its affairs and its politics, and its support of the oppressive, corrupt and tyrannical regime that is in control. These are the reasons behind the singling out of America as a target. And not exempt of responsibility are those Western regimes whose presence in the region offers support to the American troops there. We know at least one reason behind the symbolic participation of the Western forces and that is to support the Jewish and Zionist plans for expansion of what is called the Great Israel. Surely, their presence is not out of concern over their interests in the region. . . . Their presence has no meaning save one and that is to offer support to the Jews in Palestine who are in need of their Christian brothers to achieve full control over the Arab Peninsula which they intend to make an important part of the so called Greater Israel. . . .

Q: We heard your message to the American government and later your message to the European governments who participated in the occupation of the Gulf. Is it possible for you to address the people of these countries?

A: As we have already said, our call is the call of Islam that was revealed to Mohammed. It is a call to all mankind. We have been entrusted with good cause to follow in the footsteps of the Messenger and to communicate his message to all nations. It is an invitation that we extend to all the nations to embrace Islam, the religion that calls for justice, mercy and fraternity among all nations, not differentiating between black and white or between red and yellow except with respect to their devotedness. All people who worship Allah, not each other, are equal before Him. We are entrusted to spread this message and to extend that call to all the people. We, nonetheless, fight against their governments and all those who approve of the injustice they practice against us. We fight the governments that are bent on attacking our religion and on stealing our wealth and on hurting our feelings. And as I have mentioned before, we fight them, and those who are part of their rule are judged in the same manner. . . .

The Western regimes and the government of the United States of America bear the blame for what might happen. If their people do not wish to be harmed inside their very own countries, they should seek to elect governments that are truly representative of them and that can protect their interests. . . .

The enmity between us and the Jews goes far back in time and is deep rooted. There is no question that war between the two of us is inevitable. For this reason it is not in the interest of Western governments to expose the interests of their people to all kinds of retaliation for almost nothing. It is hoped that people of those countries will initiate a positive move and force their governments not to act on behalf of other states and other sects. This is what we have to say and we pray to Allah to preserve the nation of Islam and to help them drive their enemies out of their land.

Q: American politicians have painted a distorted picture of Islam, of Muslims and of Islamic fighters. We would like you to give us the true picture that clarifies your viewpoint. . . .

A: The leaders in America and in other countries as well have fallen victim to Jewish Zionist blackmail. They have mobilized their people against Islam and against Muslims. These are portrayed in such a manner as to drive people to

Chapter 15

Religious

Fundamentalism

in the Modern

World: Faith,

Identity, and

Contemporary

Politics

(1970s–Present)

rally against them. The truth is that the whole Muslim world is the victim of international terrorism, engineered by America at the United Nations. We are a nation whose sacred symbols have been looted and whose wealth and resources have been plundered. It is normal for us to react against the forces that invade our land and occupy it. . . .

Q: Mr. bin Laden, you have issued a fatwah[22] calling on Muslims to kill Americans where they can, when they can. Is that directed at all Americans, just the American military, just the Americans in Saudi Arabia?

A: Allah has ordered us to glorify the truth and to defend Muslim land, especially the Arab peninsula . . . against the unbelievers. After World War II, the Americans grew more unfair and more oppressive towards people in general and Muslims in particular. . . . The Americans started it and retaliation and punishment should be carried out following the principle of reciprocity, especially when women and children are involved. Through history, America has not been known to differentiate between the military and the civilians or between men and women or adults and children. Those who threw atomic bombs and used the weapons of mass destruction against Nagasaki and Hiroshima were the Americans. Can the bombs differentiate between military and women and infants and children? America has no religion that can deter her from exterminating whole peoples. Your position against Muslims in Palestine is despicable and disgraceful. America has no shame. . . . We believe that the worst thieves in the world today and the worst terrorists are the Americans. Nothing could stop you except perhaps retaliation in kind. We do not have to differentiate between military or civilian. As far as we are concerned, they are all targets, and this is what the fatwah says. . . . The fatwah is general (comprehensive) and it includes all those who participate in, or help the Jewish occupiers in killing Muslims.

JUDAISM

Source 6 from Israel Shahak and Norton Mezvinsky, Jewish Fundamentalism in Israel, *2nd ed. (London: Pluto Press, 2004), p. xi.*

6. From Rabbi Eliezer Waldman,[23] article in *Jewish Press* (New York), June 21, 2002

The unique attachment of the Children of Israel to the Land of Israel cannot be compared to the ties of any nation to its land. Our attachment originates in the Divine Plan of the Creation of Heaven and Earth. Our hand is destined to bring life to the Jewish people, and the Jewish people are destined to bring life to the

22. **fatwah:** a legal opinion or interpretation issued by a legal expert.
23. Waldman is a prominent *Gush Emunim* leader.

Land. Just as the Jewish nation, when in Exile, is described as "dry bones in a graveyard" (Ezekiel 37:11:12), in the same manner the Land of Israel, without the Jewish people is decreed to G-d to be "a desolate land" (Leviticus 26:32). These divine decrees are the reality of the rebirth of state of Israel, being nurtured by the faith, courage and from the hills of Judea and Samaria. This light is meant to pierce the darkness of the countries surrounding the Land of Israel with a Divine blessing of progress and human values.

Let us say clearly and strongly: we are not occupying foreign territories in Judea and Samaria. This is our ancient home. And thank G-d that we have brought it back to life. Unfortunately, some of our ancient towns in YESHA are still illegally occupied by foreigners, interfering with the Divine process of redemption of Israel.

Our responsibility to Jewish faith and redemption commands us to speak up in a strong and clear voice. The Divine Process of uniting our people and our Land must not be clouded and weakened by seeming logical concepts of "security" and "diplomacy." They only distort the truth and weaken the justice of our cause, which is engraved in our exclusive national rights to our land. We are a people of faith. This is the essence of our eternal identity and the secret of our continued existence under all conditions.

When hiding our identity, we were humiliated and trodden upon. The redemption process, bringing us back home to our land, has also brought [*us*] back to our true self, which can no longer be hidden. We have [*been*] brought back to the world stage, putting us back into a position of responsibility from which we will never shirk again. Only this clear courageous and consistent expression of our position will eventually impress both friend and foe to respect the eternal reality of the Jewish people and the Land of Israel.

Source 7 from Eliezer Waldman, "The Divine Zionist Roadmap," www.freeman.org/m_online/ jun03/waldman.htm.

7. From Eliezer Waldman, "The Divine Zionist Roadmap," 2003

[*After the Six Day War of 1967, Jews began to establish settlements in the territories occupied by Israel. There was considerable criticism of Israel by several nations, including the United States, claiming that these Jewish settlements would undermine any "roadmap for peace."*]

We have our own biblical roadmap that has been guiding the Jewish people from its very inception by the divine plan revealed to our father Abraham. The Almighty calls upon Abraham (Genesis 12:1) and tells him "Get thee out of your country . . . unto a land that I will show you." These words created the roadmap along which the Almighty led the People of Israel. "For all the land which

Chapter 15

Religious

Fundamentalism

in the Modern

World: Faith,

Identity, and

Contemporary

Politics

(1970s–Present)

you see, I will give you and to your children forever" (Genesis 13:15). These words of G-d bound together the eternal destiny of the people of Israel with the Land of Israel.

Many years later, the visionary words of the prophet Ezekiel aptly describe the Zionist awakening and ingathering of the exiles of our generation. "I will sanctify my great name . . . I will take you from among the nations . . . and will bring you to your land" (Ezekiel 36:23, 24). The prophet continues, "When I purify you from all your sins, I will resettle the cities and rebuild the ruins" (Ezekiel 36:33). The authentic roadmap is one that sanctifies the Almighty's name and purifies the Jewish people in this process of returning to the Land of Israel, resettling its towns, and rebuilding its ruins. Each of these steps is another milestone on the Jewish roadmap to redemption. All of us traveling on this road of redemption, are witness to the spiritual elevation experienced in the last thirty six years of courageous Jewish life in Yesha.

I would like to direct some very serious words of advice to our friend President Bush. We just read in this week's Portion of the Bible: "I will make the land desolate and your enemies who live there shall be barren" (Leviticus 26:32). Our sages explain that there is a blessing within this curse. G-d is telling the Jewish people that when they will be in exile, the land of Israel will remain desolate, it will not bear its fruit for anyone else. No foreigners will ever succeed in bringing life to the soil of Israel. Our enemies can only bring terror and destruction to the land as they have done all these years. Only the Jewish People can bring the land back to life as has been proven by 55 years of Jewish independence in Israel.

Mr. Bush, this is a G-dly decree which actually happened. During 2000 years of Jewish exile, the land remained desolate until G-d brought us back home to Israel within the last century. At first, the road was paved to only small parts of our homeland. The establishment of Jewish independence broadened the roadmap to include larger parts of Eretz Yisrael.[24] Finally, the Six Day War brought us back to the hills of Judea and Samaria where, with the help of the Almighty, we will continue to flourish and thrive. This is the essence of the Zionist roadmap.

In contrast, a roadmap which endangers our very existence by planting a terrorist state within our borders cannot be acceptable to the Jewish People. Mr. Bush, your roadmap does not only reward Palestinian terror, but is an offense to the divine roadmap presented to our father Abraham and implemented by his children in our generation. True, the road to redemption is paved with Jewish blood and pain, but there is no other road open to us. We will not be detoured by the hatred and cruelty of our enemies nor by the foolish promises and dangerously booby trapped road plans of our "friends."

One last word to our Prime Minister, Mr. Sharon: There is always a possibility of returning to the main road of Zionist faith and courage. This is the only way

24. **Eretz Yisrael:** Land of Israel.

for you to ensure your position of honor in Jewish history so richly deserved by someone whose life has been one of devotion to defending and building the State of Israel.

Source 8 from Shlomo Avineri, The Making of Modern Zionism: The Intellectual Origins of the Jewish State *(New York: Basic Books, 1981), pp. 222–223.*

8. Shlomo Avineri, "Zionism as a Permanent Revolution," 1981

The emergence of Israel as such a normative center for Jews all over the world, nonetheless, is not an immutable given, whose position is assured by its very existence. Far from it. The historical conditions that gave rise to Israel made it into what it has become for world Jewry: the failure of Emancipation, the breakdown of the dream of universal socialism as a solution to the Jewish problem, the Holocaust, the mass immigration to Israel (The Ingathering of the Exiles in the evocative language of Zionism), the stubborn Israeli resistance to its surrounding enemies and its successful feats of arms. All these dramatic and traumatic events have by their own weight transformed the Israeli experience into something directly shared by Jewish people all over the world. When it appeared that the Jews might be exterminated from the face of the earth, when both liberalism and socialism appeared powerless to solve the problems of Jewish existence and identity, the emergence of a Jewish state, under such conditions, became an almost wonderous image of Jewish survival, of *netzah Yisrael.*[25]

Yet once this novelty wears off—and some of it is already wearing off—such an almost automatic identification of world Jewry with Israel may be gradually eroded. When Jewish life was being threatened by extermination, when the Jewish state was in danger of being destroyed, the preservation of the very *existence* of Israel naturally became the highest priority. In the long run, however, it will be the *content* of Jewish life in Israel that will determine whether Israel will continue to be viewed by world Jewry as its normative center or become just one more aspect, among many others, of Jewish life, commanding no special standing and no special allegiance. If the content and quality of life of Israel will not make Jews all over the world proud to continue this identification, then this unusual bond will be severed. And, dialectically, it can continue to exist only if Diaspora[26] Jewry is able to discover in Israel such qualities as it lacks in itself.

This is certainly one of the more perplexing dilemmas governing the relationship between world Jewry and Israel: Israel can continue to be the normative focus of identity for Jews abroad only if it is different from Jewish life in the

---

25. **netzah Yisrael:** the eternity of Israel.

26. **Diaspora:** the dispersal of the Jews from their geographical homeland, beginning in the sixth century B.C.E.

Chapter 15

Religious

Fundamentalism

in the Modern

World: Faith,

Identity, and

Contemporary

Politics

(1970s–Present)

Diaspora. If Israel becomes only a mirror-image of Diaspora life, if it becomes, for example, just another Western consumer society, then it will lose its unique identification for world Jewry. If an American or French Jew discovers in Israel only those qualities which he already possesses (and cherishes) in his own society, then he will not be able to raise Israel to that normative pedestal with which he would identify.

HINDUISM

Source 9 from A. G. Noorani, The RSS and the BJP: A Division of Labour, *at www. sabrang.com/gujarat/rssbible.*

9. M. S. Golwalkar, Selections from *We, or Our Nationhood Defined*, 1938

Ever since that evil day, when Moslems first landed in Hindusthan, right up to the present moment, the Hindu Nation has been gallantly fighting on to shake off the despoilers. . . . The Race Spirit has been awakening. . . .

The idea was spread that for the first time the people were going to live a National life, the Nation in the land naturally was composed of all those who happened to reside therein and that all these people were to unite on a common "National" platform and win back "freedom" by "Constitutional means." Wrong notions of democracy strengthened the view and we began to class ourselves with our old invaders and foes under the outlandish name—Indian—and tried to win them over to join hands with us in our struggle. The result of this poison is too well known. We have allowed ourselves to be duped into believing our foes to be our friends and with our hands are undermining true Nationality. . . .

[In other places,] where religion does not form a distinguishing factor, culture together with the other necessary constituents of the Nation idea become the important point in the making up of individual Nationality. On the other hand in Hindusthan Religion is an all-absorbing entity. Based as it is on the unshakable foundations of a sound philosophy of life (as indeed Religion ought to be), it has become eternally woven into the life of the Race, and forms, as it were, its very Soul. With us, every action in life, individual, social or political, is a command of Religion. We make war or peace, engage in arts and crafts, amass wealth and give it away, indeed we are born and we die—all in accord with religious injunctions. Naturally, therefore, we are what our great Religion has made us. Our Race-spirit is a child of our Religion and so with us. Culture is but a product of our all-comprehensive Religion, a part of its body and not distinguishable from it. . . .

All those not belonging to the national, i.e. Hindu race, Religion, Culture and Language, naturally fall out of the pale of real "National" life. We repeat: in

Hindusthan, the land of the Hindus, lives and should live the Hindu Nation—satisfying all the five essential requirements of the scientific nation concept of the modern world. Consequently only those movements are truly "National" as aim at re-building, revitalizing and emancipating from its present stupor, the Hindu Nation. Those only are nationalist patriots, who, with the aspiration to glorify the Hindu race and Nation next to their heart, are prompted into activity and strive to achieve that goal. All others are either traitors and enemies to the National cause, or, to take a charitable view, idiots. . . .

The foreign races in Hindusthan must either adopt the Hindu culture and language, must learn to respect and hold in reverence Hindu religion, must entertain no idea but those of the glorification of the Hindu race and culture, i.e., of the Hindu nation and must loose their separate existence to merge in the Hindu race, or may stay in the country, wholly subordinated to the Hindu Nation, claiming nothing, deserving no privileges, far less any preferential treatment—not even citizen's rights. There is, at least, should be, no other course for them to adopt. We are an old nation; let us deal, as old nations ought to and do deal, with the foreign races, who have chosen to live in our country. . . .

To keep up the purity of the Race and its culture, Germany shocked the world by her (sic) purging the country of the Semitic Races—the Jews. Race pride at its highest has been manifested here. Germany has also shown how well nigh impossible it is for Races and cultures, having differences going to the root, to be assimilated into one united whole, a good lesson for us in Hindusthan to learn and profit by. . . .

This "educated" class of Hindus became in truth slaves of the English, as the late Dr. S. V. Ketkar has aptly described them. They had cut their traces, lost their footing in the National past, and become deculturized, denationalized people. But they also formed the bulk of the "Congress" and found no difficulty in eagerly gulping down the extra-ordinary absurdity, that their country was not theirs, but belonged to strangers and enemies of their Race equally with them. . . .

Some wise men of today tell us that no man is born as Hindu or Muslim or Christian but as a simple human being. This may be true about others. But for a Hindu, he gets the first samskar[27] when he is still in the mother's womb, and the last when his body is consigned to the flames. There are sixteen samskars for the Hindu which make him what he is. In fact, we are Hindus even before we emerge from the womb of our mother. We are therefore born as Hindus. About the others, they are born to this world as simple unnamed human beings and later on, either circumcised or baptized, they become Muslims or Christians. . . .

Most of the tragedies and evils that have overtaken our country during the last few decades and are even today corroding our national life are its direct outcome. . . . In their phantom chase of achieving new unity and new nationality, our leaders raised the slogan of "Hindu-Muslim unity." . . . The first thing

---

27. **samskar:** a step in the life cycle, such as birth, childhood, and so forth.

Chapter 15

Religious

Fundamentalism

in the Modern

World: Faith,

Identity, and

Contemporary

Politics

(1970s–Present)

they preached was that our nationality could not be called Hindu, that even our land could not be called by its traditional name Hindusthan, as that would have offended the Muslim. The name "India" given by the British was accepted. Taking that name, the "new nation" was called the "Indian Nation." And the Hindu was asked to rename himself as "Indian."

QUESTIONS TO CONSIDER

Although the Background section of this chapter will help immensely in answering the first central question (dealing with the almost simultaneous emergence of militant fundamentalism in the four principal religions under consideration), some of the Evidence can offer some helpful clues as well. For example, how does Pat Robertson (Source 1) explain the rise of Christian fundamentalism in the twentieth century? What was this movement reacting *against*? Would Jerry Falwell and Randall Terry (Sources 2 and 3) agree or disagree with Robertson? How do Sayyid Qutb and Osama bin Laden (Sources 4 and 5) explain the appearance of a corresponding phenomenon in Islam? Are the Islamic explanations similar to or different from those of Robertson, Falwell, and Terry? With regard to Judaism, how do Eliezer Waldman and Shlomo Avineri (Sources 6–8) account for Jewish fundamentalism? How do the causes they introduce differ (if at all) from the explanations offered by Christian and Muslim fundamentalists for their respective movements? Finally, do you see M. S. Golwalkar's interpretation (Source 9) as generally similar to or different from the previous interpretations? What are the differences? similarities?

Questions 2 and 3 require you to identify the basic beliefs and ideas of each of the spokespeople for Christian, Muslim, Jewish, and Hindu fundamentalism and *then* note the points that the fundamentalists from the four faith traditions have in common. Actually, by answering question 1, you already have begun to do so. The following questions might help you:

1. Do fundamentalists in all four faith traditions look backward to some ideal past time or "golden age"?

2. What were the principal features of that supposed "golden age?" What were the distinctions (if any) between the secular and religious spheres?

3. What forces *destroyed* that ideal time? What were the results?

4. How can that ideal time be recaptured (if at all)? What methods must be employed to do so?

Answering those questions will help you identify and explain any commonalities between militant fundamentalism in Christianity, Islam, Judaism, and Hinduism. It also may be useful in answering question 4 (on what compels a minority of fundamentalists in each faith tradition to advocate, support, and/or participate in acts of violence and terrorism).

In a world growing ever smaller and with diverse peoples coming into ever closer contact with one another (through massive intercontinental migration, the Internet, the increasing use of English as the preferred language of business and technology, the almost universal adoption of the Gregorian calendar as the "modern" way in which to measure time,[28] and the spread of a nearly worldwide popular culture), a growing number of men and women in both the West and the non-West are beginning to express what appears to be an almost universal desire to reestablish their own identity, to retain—or return to—many features of their own traditional culture, to know about their own history and uniqueness. In such an atmosphere, religious fundamentalism could serve a number of purposes, not the least of which would be to satisfy those impulses and yearnings for uniqueness and identity.

Thus it is ironic that, while fundamentalists in Christianity, Islam, Judaism, and Hinduism seek to assist their adherents in establishing or reestablishing their own pride and identity, their ideas and approaches have so much in common. As you already have determined, fundamentalists in each of these faith traditions harken back to an almost surely mythical "golden age" when that particular reli-

gious faith was at the core of a person's being, when there was no separation between the secular and the sacred, when sacred texts were taken literally, and when the true believers dominated all nonbelievers.

In addition, all point to a *conspiracy* and an insistence that they, as the heirs of the true believers, are under attack from enemies both from without and within (imperialists, unbelievers), that they are being persecuted by these evil forces, and that they are the genuine upholders of that faith or ethnic group's identity and human dignity. Therefore, there must be a struggle, complete with heroes, martyrs, and the uses of warlike terms and metaphors ("Army of the Faithful," "Soldiers of the Cross"). The struggle will be long, thus requiring a new way of measuring time.[29] But the victory will be assured.

Because all these diverse fundamentalists look upon the distant past as a "golden age," an age in which the leadership of the four principal faith traditions primarily—and sometimes exclusively—were male, the status of women in most of these fundamentalist movements is less than that of full equality with males. In their defense, many fundamentalist men and women assert that in their traditional societies women are *more* valued, not less.

Finally, as we enter the twenty-first century, it is clear that fundamentalism in all the major faith traditions is growing. Thus, to borrow a term from

28. The Gregorian calendar, named for Pope Gregory XIII of the Roman Catholic Church who sponsored it, was introduced in 1582 and was gradually adopted throughout most of the world as a standard method for measuring time.

29. As one example, Dr. Abdul Aziz Rantisi of the Palestinian organization Hamas has remarked, "Palestine was occupied before, for two hundred years. We can wait again—at least that long." Juergensmeyer, *Terror in the Mind of God,* p. 217.

Chapter 15

Religious

Fundamentalism

in the Modern

World: Faith,

Identity, and

Contemporary

Politics

(1970s–Present)

the religious people, those Enlightenment thinkers who believed that in time reason would replace religions were "preaching a false prophesy."[30]

And yet, in spite of those on both extremes of the secularism vs. religion

30. In a 2005 poll taken in the United States, 33 percent of all respondents described themselves as "evangelical Protestants." See *Newsweek*, August 29/September 5, 2005.

controversy, the vast majority of those men and women who have been touched by modernization appear to mix their faith and their reasoning together and do not seem to see any insurmountable problem or sin in doing so. Most hope—and pray—for a cessation of conflict, violence, insecurity, and want. In the end, those yearnings may overcome all others.

TEXT CREDITS

Chapter 8   Page 243: From "Nineteenth Century Europe: Liberalism and Its Critics," translated by Paul Silverman, 1979, pp. 438–460. Reprinted with permission of The University of Chicago Press. **Page 249:** From Suzanne Miller and Heinrich Potthoff, *A History of German Social Democracy From 1848 to the Present,* translated by J. A. Underwood, as Appendix 3. Reprinted by permission of Berg Publishers. **Page 252:** From Louis L. Snyder, *The Blood and Iron Chancellor: A Documentary-Biography of Otto von Bismarck,* as item 73, pp. 280–283. Reprinted by permission of Wadsworth Publishing Co. **Page 254:** From David J. Lu, *Japan: A Documentary History* (N.Y. Armonk: M. E. Sharpe, 1996) pp. 321–322. Reprinted by permission of the author. **Page 257:** From *Sources of Japanese Tradition* by William Theodore de Bary. Copyright © 1960 by Columbia University Press. Reprinted with permission of the publisher. **Page 261:** From Mikiso Hane, *Peasants, Rebels, and Outcasts: The Underside of Modern Japan,* Pantheon, 1982, pp. 178–193 ff. Reprinted with permission of Rose Hane.

Chapter 9   Page 277: Excerpted from Introduction to *Contemporary Civilization in the West* (New York: Columbia University Press, 1946), pp. 1059–1067. Reprinted by permission of Columbia University Press. **Page 283:** From Fredrick Engels, *Socialism: Utopian and Scientific* (New York: International Publishers, 1982), pp. 40, 51–53, 62–64, 69, 71–72, 75. Reprinted by permission of International Publishers. **Page 286:** Excerpted from *Sources of Indian Tradition* (New York: Columbia University Press, 1958), pp. 803–809. Reprinted by permission of Columbia University Press. **Page 296:** From *The Revolt of the Masses* by José Ortega y Gasset. Copyright © 1932 by W. W. Norton & Company, Inc., renewed © 1960 by Teresa Carey. Used by permission of W. W. Norton & Company, Inc. **Page 300:** From Jawaharlal Nehru, *Glimpses of World History,* The John Day Company, 1942, pp. 685, 688, 690, 951–953. Reprinted with permission of Jawaharlal Nehru Memorial Fund, New Delhi.

Chapter 10   Page 320: Translated from *Revista Feminina* by Darlene Abreu-Ferreira and reprinted with permission.

Chapter 12   Page 370: From Norman H. Baynes (ed.), *The Speeches of Adolf Hitler, April 1922–August 1939,* vol. I. Copyright © 1942. Published by Oxford University Press for the Royal Institute of International Affairs, London. Reprinted by permission of the Royal Institute of International Affairs. **Page 373:** From *Sources of Japanese Tradition* by William Theodore de Bary. Copyright © 1960 by Columbia University Press. Reprinted with permission of the publisher. **Page 374:** From Joseph Stalin, "Report on the Work of the Central Committee to the Seventeenth Congress of the Communist Party of the Soviet Union," January 26, 1934 in Joseph Stalin, *Selected Writings,* International Publishers, 1942, pp. 313–315, 331, 341, 478.

Chapter 13   Page 400: From Paret, Peter; *On War.* Copyright © 1976 by Princeton University Press, 2004 renewed by PUP. Reprinted by permission of Princeton University Press. **Page 401:** Excerpted from Lloyd George, *War Memoirs of David Lloyd George, 1915–1916* (Boston: Little, Brown, 1933), pp. 9–10. Reprinted by permission of AMS Press, New York. **Page 407:** From Valery, Paul; *The Collected Works of Paul Vallery.* Copyright © 1971 Princeton University Press, 1999 renewed PUP. Reprinted by permission of Princeton University Press. **Page 408:** Excerpt from *All Quiet on the Western Front,* by Erich Maria Remarque. "Im Westen Nichts Neues," copyright © 1928 by Ullstein A.G. Copyright renewed © 1956 by Erich Maria Remarque. "All Quiet on the Western Front," copyright 1929, 1930 by Little Brown and Company. Copyright renewed © 1957 by Erich Maria Remarque. All rights reserved. **Page 410:** From F. Tilman Durdin "All Captives Slain," the *New York Times,* December 18, 1937, pp. 1, 10. Copyright © 1937 by the New York Times Co. Reprinted with permission. **Page 414:** *Rosie the Riveter,* words and music by Redd Evans and John Jacob Loeb. Copyright © 1942 (renewed) by Music Sales Corporation (ASCAP) and Fred Ahlert Music Corporation. International Copyright secured. All rights reserved. Reprinted by permission. **Page 414:** From transcript of Hermann Goering's radio address, the *New York Times,* October 5, 1942. Copyright © 1942 by the New York Times Co. Reprinted with permission. **Page 420:** Arata Osada, *Children of Hiroshima* (London: Taylor and Francis, 1981), pp. 173–177; originally published in 1980 by Publishing Committee for "Children of Hiroshima."

Chapter 14   Page 448: From *Moshe Dayan: Story of My Life* by Moshe Dayan, pp. 183–184. Copyright © 1976 by Moshe Dayan. Reprinted by permission of HarperCollins Publishers, Inc. **Page 449:** From Keith Kyle, *Suez*, St. Martin's Press, 1991, pp. 565–566.

Chapter 15   Page 470: Reprinted with permission from *Bring It On: Tough Questions, Candid Answers*, by Pat Robertson, 2003, W. Publishing, a division of Thomas Nelson, Inc. Nashville, Tennessee. All rights reserved. **Page 472:** After the Attacks: Finding Fault; Falwell's Finger-Pointing Inappropriate, Bush Says, by Laurie Goodstein, *New York Times*, September 15, 2001, page A15. Copyright © 2001 by The New York Times Co. Reprinted with permission. **Page 474:** From Randall Terry Interview, www.forerunner.com. Reprinted with permission. **Page 475:** From Sayed Kotb [Sayyid Qutb], *Social Justice in Islam*, trans. John B. Hardie, ACLS Near Eastern Translation Program, American Council of Lerned Societies, 1953 [orig. pub. in Arabic in Cairo 1945], pp. 2, 7–8, 13–15. Reprinted with permission. **Page 476:** From Frank Logevall, *Terrorism and 9/11: A Reader*, Houghton Mifflin, 2002, pp. 61, 63–65, 67. Originally a *Frontline* interview with Osama Bin Laden, May 1998. **Page 478:** From an article in *The Jewish Press*, June 21, 2002, by Rabbi Eliezer Waldman. **Page 479:** Reprinted with permission of the Freeman Center for Strategic Studies, www.freeman.org. **Page 481:** From *Making of Modern Zionism* by Schlomo Avineri. Copyright © 1981 by Basic Books, Inc. Reprinted by permission of Basic Books, a member of Perseus Books, L.L.C. **Page 482:** From A.G. Noorani, *The RSS and the BJP: A Division of Labour*, at www.sabrang.com/gujarat/rssbible. Reprinted with permission of LeftWord Books, New Delhi.